YOU
AND YOUR
RIGHTS

YOU AND YOUR RIGHTS

A practical guide for all Canadians

Published by the Canadian Automobile Association, in conjunction with The Reader's Digest Association (Canada) Ltd.

Acknowledgments

The editors wish to pay tribute to the work of the late Hugh Durnford, who was Managing Editor of Reader's Digest Books during most of the period when this book was being planned and written. They also acknowledge the efforts of the large number of qualified individuals and organizations who have rendered material assistance in the preparation of the book. Among these persons may be mentioned:

Vasco d'Avillez
Julia Ann Backholm
Maura Beam
Jean Butler
A. D. Cameron
Bruno Cavion
Linda Chisholm
Len Coates
Larry Collins
Kenneth J. M. Coull
Evelyn Crandell
Yvonne Crittenden
Dorothy Davies
Nathan Dreskin
Michel Duchesneay
David Dunbar
Gail Guttentag
G. M. B. Hannon
Marie-Eve Hart
Roger J. Harvey

Donna Haynes
Gerald Heifetz
Elizabeth Helleur
Douglas J. Higgins
Abby Hoffman
Iain D. Hughes
R. W. Johnston
J. W. P. Laurin
Rebecca Leano
Peter V. MacDonald
Ross L. McDougall
P. C. McGuire
Gilles Menard
Yvonne Miles
Paul Minvielle
Helen J. Morningstar
Alice Murray
George W. Nightingale
L. Richard O'Hagan
Larry Ouellette

Colin Pickering
Alan Phillips
Enn Raudsepp
Ernest Renouf
S. P. Reston
W. F. Rombaugh
R. M. Ryan
Udo Salewsky
Michael Schelew
Mary Simonds
Harry D. Smith
Kerry J. Soden
Rosemary Speirs
John S. Stock
Noel Stockton
Jerry Tutunjian
Anthony Warren
Douglas I. Williamson
E. Evelyn Williamson
John Wintermeyer

TEXT PREPARATION: Lonsdale Requirement Limited
TEXT: Leslie F. Hannon
EDITORS: Peter Madely, Philomena Rutherford
ART DIRECTOR AND DESIGNER: Val Mitrofanow
ASSISTANT EDITORS: Sandy Campbell and Natalie King, Ian Walker
COPY STYLING: Margot Weinreich
TEXT RESEARCH: Risë Segall (chief), Caroline Miller, Allan Reznik
ART RESEARCH: Rachel Irwin (picture editor), Michelle Turbide
PROJECT COORDINATOR: Susan Wong
COPY PREPARATION: Gilles Humbert (chief), Joseph Marchetti
INDEX: Carolyn McConnell
PRODUCTION: Holger Lorenzen

Contents

To the reader—a caveat

This book addresses itself to the creation and application of the constitutional, legal and customary rights of the individual in Canada in everyday life.

Where references are made in these pages to the present law or regulations, they mean the law or regulations of 1979. And while care has been taken to ensure that such references are up to date, the reader is reminded that the law is dynamic: it is in a process of continual revision and change. He is reminded, too, that this book is a layman's guide. It cannot be a substitute for professional counsel.

The reader seeking a broader or deeper knowledge of how Canadian statutory or common law affects the lives of the average person is referred to the companion volume, *You and the Law*, published by The Reader's Digest Association (Canada) Ltd., Montreal.

—The Editors

Introduction

It's a modern paradox that the more we try to legislate improvements in the quality of life, to make society more humanitarian and just, the more complicated life becomes. As governments at every level—federal, provincial, regional and municipal—strive to protect the law-abiding from the criminal, and from commercial exploitation, discrimination, abuse, need, and just plain bad luck, a veritable avalanche of laws, regulations, restrictions, official forms and licenses descends to cover the scene.

The average citizen finds it hard to make his way through the drifts of paper. Faced by big government, big business, big unions, he begins to feel frustrated and manipulated. There's a pervading sense of having lost control in matters that affect our personal rights and interests. A distrust of all bureaucracy is a characteristic of our time.

Yet, you are assured ceaselessly that you have rights that must be respected. You hear this at school and college, from newspapers, radio and television, from books written by scholars and experts, from unions, social workers, consumer agencies and even from the neighbors. You grasp that these rights, on paper, seem to apply to just about every conceivable activity, job, profession or situation, in your home, in your neighborhood and in the wide world. But putting them into effect is something else.

You and Your Rights sets out to explain your rights and recourses in simple, day-to-day terms. Obviously, given the vast complexity of our legal system, the multitude of specific situations that crop up cannot be covered completely in this or any other single volume. But *representative* problems, and potential solutions, are presented in straightforward, down-to-earth language which avoids the legal and technical jargon that so often irritates and fails to inform the lay reader.

What are your rights when a neighbor's tree falls on your property, damaging your gate and crushing flower beds? What happens if there is water damage in your apartment while you are away? What recourse do you have when your car is repaired and the bill far exceeds the estimate? How can you protest most effectively if you feel that you are unfairly denied unemployment insurance benefits? What can you do if your child is injured in a schoolyard and you believe there was inadequate supervision?

You and Your Rights is designed to aid you in every major walk of life—as parent and spouse, as citizen, as worker, as consumer, as patient, as student, as motorist, as dependent or beneficiary—indeed, in every capacity in which you might find yourself at odds with authority or with other people.

This book is, therefore, very broad in its scope and scheme. It attempts to explore various conditions and circumstances that may reasonably be construed as "rights" rather than adhere to a rigid definition of the word. Few concepts, in fact, are more difficult to pin down than that of a "right." But for our purposes, these meanings from *Webster's New World Dictionary* are the ones that fit: that which a person has a just claim to; power, privilege, etc., that belongs to a person by law, nature, or tradition.

Essentially, a right is the claim to justice that society accords each of us. The ramifications of this are great: at one extreme is the important issue of civil liberties, the right to be free and to be treated with dignity; at the other extreme is the right to expect fairness in our day-to-day, over-the-counter dealings. It is understood in our society that no man should be deprived of freedom without benefit of a trial; it is equally understood that when we purchase something—whether it be a button or a bulldozer, a can opener or a convertible—the item should work "reasonably" well and last a "reasonable" length of time. That is why we deal in these pages not just with problems that raise fundamental questions of human rights, but also with homelier matters such as warranties and insurance.

Canadians are fortunate in being citizens of one of

Landmark legislation

Here are excerpts from the Bill of Rights, which in 1689 became part of that body of statute law and common law that is the British "constitution." With this bill, the Englishman's right to free speech was enshrined in law, as was Parliament's fiscal and legislative supremacy over the king. Note that *only* "the subjects which are Protestants" had the right to bear arms for their personal protection.

And thereupon the said lords spiritual and temporal and commons pursuant to their respective letters and elections being now assembled in a full and free representative of this nation, taking into their most serious consideration the best means for attaining the ends aforesaid, do in the first place (as their ancestors in like case have usually done) for the vindicating and asserting their ancient rights and liberties, declare:

That the pretended power of suspending of laws or the execution of laws by regal authority without consent of parliament is illegal.

That the pretended power of dispensing with laws or the execution of laws by regal authority as it hath been assumed and exercised of late is illegal.

That the commission for erecting the late court of commissioners for ecclesiastical causes and all other commissions and courts of like nature are illegal and pernicious.

That the levying of money for or to the use of the crown by pretence of prerogative without grant of parliament for a longer time or in other manner than the same is or shall be granted is illegal.

That it is the right of the subjects to petition the king and all commitments and prosecutions for such petitioning are illegal.

That the raising or keeping a standing army within the kingdom in time of peace unless it be with consent of parliament is against law.

That the subjects which are Protestants may have arms for their defence suitable to their conditions and as allowed by law.

That election of members of parliament ought to be free.

That the freedom of speech and debates or proceedings in parliament ought not to be impeached or questioned in any court or place out of parliament.

That excessive bail ought not to be required nor excessive fines imposed nor cruel and unusual punishments inflicted.

That jurors ought to be duly impanelled and returned and jurors which pass upon men in trials for high treason ought to be freeholders.

That all grants and promises of fines and forfeitures of particular persons before conviction are illegal and void.

And that for redress of all grievances and for the amending, strengthening and preserving of the laws parliaments ought to be held frequently.

the most dynamic democracies in the world, of a country where the individual is respected. As a citizen of this country, you are entitled to certain fundamental rights and freedoms—of conscience, of religion, of opinion, of expression and of peaceful assembly.

You have a right to life and personal inviolability, to the safeguard of reputation and to respect for private life, home and property. You have a right to enter a public place, to rent accommodation, to become a party to a contract, to obtain work, promotion and pay without discrimination on grounds of sex, race, color, civil status, religious or political views, language, ethnic or national origin, or social position. If, for any reason, you are ever accused, detained or arrested, you have an undiminished right to be treated with humanity and respect. Furthermore, you have a right to be informed without delay of reasons why you have been deprived of your freedom, and to be given a fair and public hearing by an independent and impartial tribunal. You also have a right to the preservation of your own cultural interests, to fair and reasonable conditions of work, to the dignity of equitable treatment in all situations. An additional right—the right of special protection—goes to children, senior citizens, the handicapped, the retarded and the mentally ill.

Although there is a tendency among some of us to take many of these rights for granted, it should not be forgotten that they are the result of centuries of struggle, dating back to the origins of society. Indeed, the instinctive awareness of personal rights predates man-made statutes. The notion that we have rights finds classical expression in Socrates' dialogue with Thrasymachus the Sophist, wherein Socrates demolishes the argument that justice is the interest of the stronger; and in Aristotle's *Politics*, in which the great philosopher, postulating three forms of government—monarchy, aristocracy and commonwealth (democracy)—says all three may be good or bad depending on whether or not the rights and interests of the citizens are respected. But while *Politics* has influenced men's thinking for 23 centuries, the doctrine of the divine right of kings persisted in some form until modern times, supporting autocracy, or even despotism, with a theological underlay.

If we explore our Canadian heritage specifically, the earliest solid landmark we see is the Magna Carta, which King John of England signed in 1215 at the demand of his nobles. It granted special liberties to "all free men of the realm," focusing on items ranging from the levying of taxes to the marriage of ladies in the king's wardship. The most significant clause—certainly by today's standards—is the one that states that no free man can be arrested, imprisoned, exiled or executed except by the lawful "judgment of his peers or by the law of the land." Admittedly, this clause was of limited scope at the time, for not every man was a "freeman" in the eyes of the law. "It was a very short step," wrote George Macaulay Trevelyan in his *History of England,* "but it was the first, and it is the first step that counts."

The essence of this document is that it was an acknowledgment of the king's submission to law—a forerunner of the concept of justice for all. Down through the centuries, the Magna Carta inspired the writing of legal treatises that were eventually read by scholars, lawmakers and statesmen throughout the world. In time, it helped to shape the constitutional frameworks of Canada and the United States. By then, of course, all Englishmen had become "freemen" as a result of three centuries of legal and social evolution. Capstone of this evolution was the 1689 Bill of Rights, which is one of the great instruments of the British "constitution," and therefore of ours. This statute declared that the king's subjects had certain inviolable rights, such as the right of free speech, the right to petition the king, and the right to challenge a selection of jurors. Some of these rights had already been claimed by some Englishmen, but now they were enshrined in the law. The Bill of Rights established the fiscal and legislative supremacy of Parliament. It eliminated divine right as a working principle of government among the English-speaking peoples.

For perhaps another century, it was possible else-

Mankind's conscience

This charter of fundamental freedoms and human rights was approved on Dec. 10, 1948, by the General Assembly of the three-year-old United Nations. More than three decades later, with despots still walking roughshod over many peoples, it is evident that the organization hasn't been able wholly to achieve its noble goals of international peace, harmony and friendship. Nevertheless, this declaration still serves as a bench mark of the collective conscience of mankind.

UNIVERSAL DECLARATION OF HUMAN RIGHTS

PREAMBLE

Whereas recognition of the inherent dignity and of the equal and inalienable rights of all members of the human family is the foundation of freedom, justice and peace in the world,

Whereas disregard and contempt for human rights have resulted in barbarous acts which have outraged the conscience of mankind, and the advent of a world in which human beings shall enjoy freedom of speech and belief and freedom from fear and want has been proclaimed as the highest aspiration of the common people,

Whereas it is essential, if man is not to be compelled to have recourse, as a last resort, to rebellion against tyranny and oppression, that human rights should be protected by the rule of law,

Whereas it is essential to promote the development of friendly relations between nations,

Whereas the peoples of the United Nations have in the Charter reaffirmed their faith in fundamental human rights, in the dignity and worth of the human person and in the equal rights of men and women and have determined to promote social progress and better standards of life in larger freedom,

Whereas Member States have pledged themselves to achieve, in co-operation with the United Nations, the promotion of universal respect for and observance of human rights and fundamental freedoms,

Whereas a common understanding of these rights and freedoms is of the greatest importance for the full realization of this pledge,

Now, therefore,

The General Assembly

Proclaims this Universal Declaration of Human Rights as a common standard of achievement for all peoples and all nations, to the end that every individual and every organ of society, keeping this Declaration constantly in mind, shall strive by teaching and education to promote respect for these rights and freedoms and by progressive measures, national and international, to secure their universal and effective recognition and observance, both among the peoples of Member States themselves and among the peoples of territories under their jurisdiction.

ARTICLE 1

All human beings are born free and equal in dignity and rights. They are endowed with reason and conscience and should act towards one another in a spirit of brotherhood.

ARTICLE 2

Everyone is entitled to all the rights and freedoms set forth in this Declaration, without distinction of any kind, such as race, colour, sex, language, religion, political or other opinion, national or social origin, property, birth or other status.

Furthermore, no distinction shall be made on the basis of the political, jurisdictional or international status of the country or territory to which a person belongs, whether it be independent, trust, non-self-governing or under any other limitation of sovereignty.

ARTICLE 3

Everyone has the right to life, liberty and the security of person.

ARTICLE 4

No one shall be held in slavery or servitude; slavery and the slave trade shall be prohibited in all their forms.

ARTICLE 5

No one shall be subjected to torture or to cruel, inhuman or degrading treatment or punishment.

ARTICLE 6

Everyone has the right to recognition everywhere as a person before the law.

ARTICLE 7

All are equal before the law and are entitled without any discrimination to equal protection of the law. All are entitled to equal protection against any discrimination in violation of this Declaration and against any incitement to such discrimination.

ARTICLE 8

Everyone has the right to an effective remedy by the competent national tribunals for acts violating the fundamental rights granted him by the constitution or by law.

ARTICLE 9

No one shall be subjected to arbitrary arrest, detention or exile.

ARTICLE 10

Everyone is entitled in full equality to a fair and public hearing by an independent and impartial tribunal, in the determination of his rights and obligations and of any criminal charge against him.

ARTICLE 11

1. Everyone charged with a penal offence has the right to be presumed innocent until proved guilty according to law in a public trial at which he has had all the guarantees necessary for his defence.

2. No one shall be held guilty of any penal offence on account of any act or omission which did not constitute a penal offence, under national or international law, at the time when it was committed. Nor shall a heavier penalty be imposed than the one that was applicable at the time the penal offence was committed.

ARTICLE 12

No one shall be subjected to arbitrary interference with his privacy, family, home or correspondence, nor to attacks upon his honour and reputation. Everyone has the right to the protection of the law against such interference or attacks.

ARTICLE 13

1. Everyone has the right to freedom of movement and residence within the borders of each State.

2. Everyone has the right to leave any country, including his own, and to return to his country.

ARTICLE 14

1. Everyone has the right to seek and to enjoy in other countries asylum from persecution.

2. This right may not be invoked in the case of prosecutions genuinely arising from non-political crimes or from acts contrary to the purposes and principles of the United Nations.

ARTICLE 15

1. Everyone has the right to a nationality.

2. No one shall be arbitrarily deprived of his nationality nor denied the right to change his nationality.

ARTICLE 16

1. Men and women of full age, without any limitation due to race, nationality or religion, have the right to marry and to found a family. They are entitled to equal rights as to marriage, during marriage and at its dissolution.

2. Marriage shall be entered into only with the free and full consent of the intending spouses.

3. The family is the natural and fundamental group unit of society and is entitled to protection by society and the State.

ARTICLE 17

1. Everyone has the right to own property alone as well as in association with others.

2. No one shall be arbitrarily deprived of his property.

ARTICLE 18

Everyone has the right to freedom of thought, conscience and religion; this right includes freedom to change his religion or belief, and freedom, either alone or in community with others and in public or private, to manifest his religion or belief in teaching, practice, worship and observance.

ARTICLE 19

Everyone has the right to freedom of opinion and expression; this right includes freedom to hold opinions without interference and to seek, receive and impart information and ideas through any media and regardless of frontiers.

ARTICLE 20

1. Everyone has the right to freedom of peaceful assembly and association.

2. No one may be compelled to belong to an association.

ARTICLE 21

1. Everyone has the right to take part in the government of his country, directly or through freely chosen representatives.

2. Everyone has the right of equal access to public service in his country.

3. The will of the people shall be the basis of the authority of government; this will shall be expressed in periodic and genuine elections which shall be by universal and equal suffrage and shall be held by secret vote or by equivalent free voting procedures.

ARTICLE 22

Everyone, as a member of society, has the right to social security and is entitled to realization, through national effort and international cooperation and in accordance with the organization and resources of each State, of the economic, social and cultural rights indispensable for his dignity and the free development of his personality.

ARTICLE 23

1. Everyone has the right to work, to free choice of employment, to just and favourable conditions of work and to protection against unemployment.

2. Everyone, without any discrimination, has the right to equal pay for equal work.

3. Everyone who works has the right to just and favourable remuneration ensuring for himself and his family an existence worthy of human dignity, and supplemented, if necessary, by other means of social protection.

4. Everyone has the right to form and to join trade unions for the protection of his interests.

ARTICLE 24

Everyone has the right to rest and leisure, including reasonable limitation of working hours and periodic holidays with pay.

ARTICLE 25

1. Everyone has the right to a standard of living adequate for the health and well-being of himself and of his family, including food, clothing, housing and medical care and necessary social services, and the right to security in the event of unemployment, sickness, disability, widowhood, old age or other lack of livelihood in circumstances beyond his control.

2. Motherhood and childhood are entitled to special care and assistance. All children, whether born in or out of wedlock, shall enjoy the same social protection.

ARTICLE 26

1. Everyone has the right to education. Education shall be free, at least in the elementary and fundamental stages. Elementary education shall be compulsory. Technical and professional education shall be made generally available and higher education shall be equally accessible to all on the basis of merit.

2. Education shall be directed to the full development of the human personality and to the strengthening of respect for human rights and fundamental freedoms. It shall promote understanding, tolerance and friendship among all nations, racial or religious groups, and shall further the activities of the United Nations for the maintenance of peace.

3. Parents have a prior right to choose the kind of education that shall be given to their children.

ARTICLE 27

1. Everyone has the right freely to participate in the cultural life of the community, to enjoy the arts and to share in scientific advancement and its benefits.

2. Everyone has the right to the protection of the moral and material interests resulting from any scientific, literary or artistic production of which he is the author.

ARTICLE 28

Everyone is entitled to a social and international order in which the rights and freedoms set forth in this Declaration can be fully realized.

ARTICLE 29

1. Everyone has duties to the community in which alone the free and full development of his personality is possible.

2. In the exercise of his rights and freedoms, everyone shall be subject only to such limitations as are determined by law solely for the purpose of securing due recognition and respect for the rights and freedoms of others and of meeting the just requirements of morality, public order and the general welfare in a democratic society.

3. These rights and freedoms may in no case be exercised contrary to the purposes and principles of the United Nations.

ARTICLE 30

Nothing in this Declaration may be interpreted as implying for any State, group or person any right to engage in any activity or to perform any act aimed at the destruction of any of the rights and freedoms set forth herein.

Hundred and eighty-third plenary meeting.
10 December 1948.

where in Europe to regard the English as heretical in this matter. Then the French Revolution swept away the *ancien régime*, and while it brought no end to autocracy, kingly or otherwise, it destroyed once and for all the belief that anyone was commissioned by God to wield absolute power. Its Declaration of the Rights of Man and Citizen—fashioned on the U.S. Declaration of Independence of 1776—enunciated "inalienable rights" to "liberty, property, security and resistance to oppression," to freedom of speech and of the press. By its assertion of the equality of men, and its assault on class and privilege, this document has profoundly influenced modern thinking about man's place in society. So powerful, indeed, have the concepts of liberty, equality and fraternity become that, nowadays, almost every nation professes dedication to them. The United Nations Declaration of Human Rights, enacted in 1948, affirms that all people are entitled to the liberties that we, in this country, have always taken to be part of our birthright.

This is not, however, an age of smugness on the subject of rights in Canada, good as our record may be in comparison with that of so many other countries. On the contrary, there is a heightened awareness of problems of discrimination and exploitation.

In 1960, Parliament enacted the Canadian Bill of Rights, enumerating the basic rights and freedoms held to exist in our country. Specific laws, federal and provincial, have removed a variety of obstacles, especially those based on prejudice, to the exercise of human rights in particular areas, or created instruments to assist us all in the fuller affirmation of our rights. This is the age of the ombudsman, of the human rights commissioner, of jobs that must be open to men and women alike, of equal pay for equal work. Let us make the most of it. There is no reason today for any Canadian citizen to be unaware of his rights, or to lack assistance in exercising them.

The Editors.
Montreal, March 1980

1 | YOUR RIGHTS AS A CITIZEN

1 Civil rights

The preamble to Canada's Human Rights Act (1977) is cautious. "Every individual should," it says, "have an equal opportunity to make for himself or herself the life that he or she is able and wishes to have, consistent with his or her duties and obligations as a member of society, without being hindered in or prevented from doing so by discriminatory practices."

It is no accident that the authors of this milestone legislation, which supplements earlier provincial acts, used the words "should have"—rather than "must have." Laws alone won't change human nature, as any civil-rights activist will tell you. Prejudice, bigotry, discrimination and hatred are international, their roots are deep and often obscure. The United Nations Declaration on Human Rights (1948) has not noticeably reduced them and neither has the Canadian Bill of Rights (1960) created a Shangri-La in the frozen north. But in seeking Utopia, man's reach should always exceed his grasp. The decades since World War II have brought tremendous change to our nation and a matching surge in efforts to entrench and expand the rights and freedoms of the individual—in legislation and through education. Those efforts, and their results, are the theme of this book.

While it is virtually impossible to define "civil rights" other than to say that they are an amalgam of individual freedoms, civil liberties, constitutional rights and personal dignity, there is a broad consensus that the main struggle lies between the giant power of the state and man's fierce will to live the life he chooses. Alan Borovoy of the Canadian Civil Liberties Association puts it this way: "The only meaningful question concerns what restrictions are appropriate in a democracy where the object is to promote the greatest possible freedom of the individual."

For no personal liberty is without limit. A venerable legal cliché warns that your freedom to wave your fists ends where the other man's nose begins. The rights of any one class or group must be dovetailed harmoniously with the rights of all other classes and groups. That our society is not "fair" to all is obvious. But it stands with the best that man has devised since putting aside the law of the jungle.

And the winds of change are still blowing briskly. In 1793, the first Legislative Assembly of Upper Canada prohibited the importation of slaves and ruled that the children of slaves already there be liberated when they reached their 25th birthday. Two centuries later, the country is concerned about rather more complex freedoms. Women are often denied equality of opportunity. Innocent people suffer when policemen or firemen or others in essential public services go on strike. Some Canadians have no chance to educate their children in their mother tongue unless they can afford private school. However, there are still "democratic" countries where men are forbidden to wear long hair and women to wear long trousers, where the church doors are nailed shut by official decree, and where the newspapers may publish only the news considered suitable by the authorities. By these measures, Canada has come a long way.

DUE PROCESS OF LAW

You have been in custody in another province for almost three months awaiting trial. Your case is called but the Crown offers no evidence and the charge is withdrawn.

There's no law in Canada that guarantees an early trial, and the Crown—that is, the state—may decide to "drop the charges" at any time. When this happens, it's usually because the prosecution can't prove its case. However, the Crown is not admitting that your arrest was unfounded. If you are innocent, and there were no reasonable grounds for your detention, you could charge the police with false arrest (*see* Chapter 2, "You and the police") and possibly seek compensation for being wrongly held in jail. Only an experienced lawyer could properly weigh your chances.

The Canadian Bill of Rights merely confirms the right not to be deprived of liberty "except by due process of law." The bill declares "arbitrary detention or imprisonment" to be wrong and restates the ancient right of *habeas corpus* under which the accused must be brought forward and the legality of imprisonment examined in open court. (*See* "Four powerful writs" in Chapter 4.)

The Criminal Code provides that when an accused person is still in custody 30 days after the date of his first court appearance on a summary offense, or 90 days in the case of an indictable offense, the Crown must seek a judicial ruling on whether continued detention is justified. In effect, this is a practical nationwide application of the safeguard of *habeas corpus*. Quite separate from this is the right of an individual held without apparent cause to ask a higher court to rule on his detention. If the court finds no legal basis for the confinement, the person must be released.

Bail, or "judicial interim release" as this process of conditional freedom is now called, comes into consideration immediately after an arrest. (*See* "Arrest" in Chapter 2 and "Bail" in Chapter 4.) Your right to this release cannot be denied without just cause. The Bill of Rights doesn't say exactly what is to be considered "just cause," but the 1972 amendments to the bail provisions of the Criminal Code make it almost certain that you will be granted "judicial release" in the great majority of situations. (In fact, the onus is on the prosecutor to convince the judge that bail should *not* be allowed.) The important considerations are the seriousness of the charge and the likelihood that you will show up for the trial. If your place of residence is in a distant province, or abroad, bail might be opposed for that reason alone.

When arrested, you have the right to know the precise charge. If necessary, your lawyer, or a Legal Aid lawyer or the Public Defender, will insist that you be told.

PROPERTY RIGHTS

Your family farm is being expropriated to make way for an airport. You are not willing to sell.

That a man's home is his castle is not absolutely true. We enjoy our freehold land rights only at the pleasure of the Crown. (*See* Chapter 12, "When you buy.") Property rights are limited by laws such as zoning and building regulations, fire-safety measures, and bylaws against noise and pollution. And beyond all these, there is government's power to require us to sell our property for some public purpose. Expropriation is one of the most arbitrary of the laws we live under, and hundreds of agencies have the right to seize property in the public interest.

It doesn't really matter whether the government wants your land for an airport, a jail, a park or a road. Or whether it wants all or part of it. It can take what it wants, on the basis of "fair" compensation. If the highways department decides to build a road across a corner of your property, it may do so, and it won't ask your permission first. However, you do have the right to advance notice of any expropriation, its purpose and the proposed compensation. You can refuse the offer and negotiate with, or even sue, the responsible government agency for more generous compensation. But your chances of stopping the expropriation are almost nil.

EQUALITY BEFORE THE LAW

The police are slow to respond to calls from your neighborhood, which doesn't happen to be the most expensive in town.

The Bill of Rights guarantees "equality before the law and the protection of the law." Similar lofty phrases are enshrined in every constitution and declaration of human rights. But that is the written law. Alongside is the everyday reality of man's injustice to man, especially to the man who cannot afford the best advice. An English judge once put it succinctly: "The courts are open to everybody—just like the Ritz Hotel."

Although the provincial Legal Aid systems have done much to balance the scales, it is the wealthy man or woman who can afford to hire the most talented or seasoned lawyer. It would be reassuring to think that judges cannot be swayed by polished and sophisticated argument—but, after all, they are human! The more experienced the lawyer, the greater his skill in bringing out the evidence that favors his client and demolishes the opposition. Senior lawyers do take some Legal Aid cases— and will accept the occasional interesting brief without charge—but the "public defender" systems are staffed overwhelmingly by recent graduates or unimaginative plodders. (*See* Chapter 4, "You, the defendant.")

It should be easier to ensure equal treatment from the police, for they are sworn to keep the peace and pursue the lawbreaker in city ghetto and suburb alike. If you are convinced that your neighborhood is being neglected, or poorly served by law-enforcement officers (or, conversely, that it is being over-zealously patrolled), you have the right to lodge a complaint with your municipal or provincial authorities. Write to the chairman of your local police commission, or your alderman.

Hostile reception. "The police at all times should maintain a relationship with the public that gives reality to the historic tradition that the police *are* the public and that the public are the police." So said Sir Robert Peel, who as Britain's Home Secretary reorganized the London police service in the 19th century. The traditions of this service were imported with the immigrant waves to Canada.

But the police officer is a human being first, subject to the same fears and frailties as everyone else. It is often far from simple to make inquiries, let alone an arrest, in those neighborhoods where an inborn suspicion of the police almost guarantees a hostile reception. If

your neighborhood has a record of violence and the duty patrolman does not respond swiftly to calls, he may be waiting for backup personnel. Certain taverns, for example, are notorious on the police blotter as the origin of a disproportionate number of calls.

Complaints against the police come most often from the "visible minorities" in the low-rent areas of cities most available to recent immigrants. Virtually every Human Rights Commission in Canada has recorded complaints of police harassment from Indians, blacks or Asians. (*See* Chapter 6, "Discrimination.") The frequency of these complaints and occasional admissions by police officers suggest that racism—overt or not—is not entirely unknown among the peacekeepers.

Police and the young. Crime in heavily populated neighborhoods is often centered around the juvenile delinquent. Yet Canadian courts, traditionally gentle with tender youth, have been slow to adjust to serious juvenile crime. And police are wary of physical contact with juveniles. A knife in the hand of a teenager is as lethal as one wielded by a 30-year-old and far more likely to produce a scuffle leading to accusations of police brutality. The average juvenile arrest is unlikely to lead to a conviction; if it does, the judge is unlikely to impose imprisonment. The cop on the beat faces the same cocky, or embittered, youngster on the street next week.

WORK AND RELIGION

The personnel manager tears up your application form when you refuse to answer any questions about your religious affiliation.

Such an action is discriminatory and illegal unless church membership is related directly to the job. For example, a church-affiliated charity is entitled to know the religious affiliation of applicants for the job of treasurer.

Everyone has the right to practice his own religion and the atheist can freely proclaim his nonbelief. However, the law of the land takes precedence if there is any conflict. For example, the adult Jehovah's Witnesses' right to refuse blood transfusions is respected but the law rejects the principle when a child is involved. British Columbia's Doukhobors (a Russian Christian sect) are in periodic trouble for arson and nude parades advocated by church leaders.

When their extremist Sons of Freedom, claiming that public schooling interfered with their religious freedom, kept their children at home, the Supreme Court of Canada ruled: "The claim that religious sects may make rules for the conduct of any part of human activity, and that these rules thereby become for all the world a part of the sect's religion, cannot be so." Religious beliefs do not relieve you of responsibility to obey the law.

It's okay to ask. It's not unusual for job application forms to contain some reference to religious beliefs, but you don't have to answer if you don't want to. Unless the church or an affiliated body is the prospective employer, you can't legally be refused consideration for a job solely on the grounds of religion. Some employers try to discover a prospective employee's religion in order to avoid problems connected with religious observance. For ex-

---

People or Planes

When the federal government announced in 1972 that it would expropriate some 7,300 hectares of Pickering Township northeast of Toronto for an international airport, 100 property owners banded together to fight the plan. They called themselves People or Planes.

The area included some long-established family farms and the homes of bankers, engineers, journalists, judges, lawyers and teachers. Together with conservationists from distant points, these residents launched what was certainly one of the most vigorous anti-expropriation campaigns ever staged in Canada. They lodged protests and appeals, got 10,000 signatures on a petition, made a movie and published a book, financing their $100,000 crusade with hayrides, square dances, horseshoe-pitching contests and bake sales.

Caught in this uncomfortable glare of publicity, the government mounted its own campaign. When P.O.P. said the project would interfere with birds nesting in the area, Ottawa spent $253,000 on an exhaustive study to disprove the claim.

The federal Department of Transport must hold a public hearing before building an airport. P.O.P. leaders turned up in force, with top-drawer legal advisers, and made their pitch at the Pickering hearing. But they were not permitted to cross-examine the experts favoring the plan. The federal government merely "received" the report of the hearing and confirmed the expropriations.

P.O.P. redoubled its efforts, holding a rally in Toronto's St. Lawrence Center where the airport plan was duly shouted down. A newspaper poll indicated that 56 percent of Toronto residents were against it.

In 1974, the federal government appointed Judge Hugh Gibson of the Federal Court to head the Airport Inquiry Commission. But the commission would accept only written briefs and examine only evidence that had not been presented at the original public hearing. In vain, P.O.P. tried to contest the whole concept of the new airport and to promote a free-swinging open forum.

The inquiry dragged on for six months, at great public expense, then found in favor of the airport development. The government announced it would go ahead with a scaled-down version. The land remained expropriated, the owners became tenants, and when the planners are ready, the bulldozers will begin to carve out the runways and the jets will scream into Pickering.

The moral: fighting expropriation is a no-win situation. Concentrate on getting the best possible price for your property.

ample, some members of the Jewish faith, Seventh-Day Adventists, Seventh-Day Baptists and members of the Worldwide Church of God decline to work on Saturday.

Some occupations have requirements that conflict with religious beliefs. For example, police and security guards are usually required to wear uniforms, including hats, and to be cleanshaven. Ishar Singh, a member of the Sikh faith, could not comply with the dress requirements of a Toronto security firm because Sikhs wear beards and turbans as a mark of devotion. So, he was not considered for a security guard's post. He took his case to the Ontario Human Rights Commission and a board of inquiry found the company guilty of discrimination.

The inquiry chairman, law professor Peter Cumming, ruled that an employer must adapt operations to accommodate the sincere expression of an employee's religious beliefs. If it fails to do this, and is unable to show that "undue hardship" would result, the employer is contravening the Human Rights Code.

RIGHT TO DISSENT

You are strongly opposed to a multimillion-dollar arts center, but its proponents won't permit you to address their meetings.

You have as much right to speak out *against* the project as its promoters have to agitate *for* it. But don't expect them to help you!

You cannot be refused admittance to a public meeting, provided your behavior is within reasonable bounds and the hall is not yet filled. Some heckling is usually tolerated and can be very effective, especially if it's witty. If questions or comments are invited from the audience, you should get your chance to make a brief statement. But the chairman is not bound to permit you to address the meeting.

Why not picket the meeting hall carrying an informational message? This is a highly visible protest and others may be encouraged to join you. You'll likely get some publicity in your local paper, and thus reach thousands of concerned taxpayers.

You could even organize your own public meeting. If your point of view attracts a sizable number of supporters, the financing agency for the arts center may reconsider the expenditure. Of course you may be fighting an entrenched establishment which won't hesitate to label you a "redneck" or a "yahoo." But don't give up! Remember David and Goliath.

Curbs on the tongue. Your freedom of speech, like every other civil right, is not absolute. It is conditioned by the rights of every other individual. The principle of free speech does not permit the shouting of "Fire!" in a public place when there is no danger. Even the Bill of Rights, which exists through an act of Parliament, can be abrogated by that same Parliament on a simple majority vote. Unlike the United States, Canada does not have a written constitution, as such, where individual liberties are named and placed beyond the reach of evanescent politicians.

It's an offense to incite other persons to hatred against any identifiable group. To defame another person's character ("That John Doe is a damn liar!") is to risk a suit. You can detest the Prime Minister as much as you like but don't go about suggesting that he and his cabinet should be shot; that's the serious offense of sedition. The free speech of your local merchant is curbed to the extent that he can't say that he's running a sale unless the price reductions he is offering are genuine. (*See* Chapter 20, "Advertising.")

ASSEMBLY AND ASSOCIATION

You are outraged by the behavior of a local motorcycle gang and you want the police to close the group's clubhouse.

Ask yourself why the police haven't acted already. They know about the gang and are under no illusions about their behavior and attitudes. But dislike and outrage are not sufficient grounds for police action. They must have reasonable cause to believe that an offense has been or will be committed.

The same Bill of Rights that protects your

freedoms also protects those of the swaggering "bikers." The fact that, from time to time, motorcycle gangsters have been convicted of crimes, or that they tend to intimidate many citizens merely by their presence, provides no license to curtail their right of peaceable assembly.

Your obvious course is to lay a complaint with the police. But don't waste your time unless you can provide evidence, backed up with the testimony of reputable witnesses, of unlawful actions by the club members. Allegations of excessive noise, obscene or insulting remarks, even littering, could trigger police action. Keep a low profile. A large portion of the gangs' intimidation power stems from their threat of vengeance on "squealers." Police do not advise that, in these circumstances, you exercise your right to make a citizen's arrest. (*See* Chapter 2, "You and the police.")

Disturbance and riot. In law there is no essential difference between a motorcycle club meeting and a gathering of philatelists, bird watchers or trapeze artists. If any of them "disturb the peace," they can expect the police to intervene. Even bird watchers sometimes lose their tempers.

Disturbing the peace is generally treated as a relatively minor (summary) offense but it can bring up to six months' imprisonment, plus a fine of $500. A "disturbance," in legal definition, can be caused by one or more persons in or near a public place, swearing, singing, screaming, shouting, fighting, using insulting or obscene language, or impeding or molesting other persons. Even if the actions were only *likely* to disturb the public, a conviction will probably follow. Three or more persons who persist in disturbing the peace tumultuously ("violently") may be charged with the more serious offense of unlawful assembly. This can escalate to the very serious charge of riot.

Just about everybody has heard of the expression "reading the Riot Act." What it means is this: when more than 12 persons are unlawfully assembling, a sheriff or a justice of the peace or the mayor will order them to disperse. If they don't, he can read out a few sentences from the Criminal Code informing

the mob that the Crown requests them to leave the scene and behave peaceably. If they don't obey, they'll be liable, upon conviction, to life imprisonment.

It may well be a long time since anyone has been sent to jail for life for rioting, but no government in our history has seen fit to weaken the penalty. Canada is not about to encourage mobs running wild.

The local police are the front-line soldiers when there's violence in the streets. When necessary they will be backed up by provincial police forces, the Royal Canadian Mounted Police, and even the military.

Subject only to municipal bylaws, we have the right to gather in twos or in thousands to discuss any idea, plan or "common enterprise." It matters not whether we are protesting the construction of a nuclear-power plant or applauding the construction of a community center.

As long as there's no threat to the peace, or to private property, or any dissemination of hate propaganda, there'll be no intrusion by the authorities. In fact, the police will protect your right to peaceful protest. Without dissension, and the opportunity to express it, democracy would soon wither and die.

RIGHT TO ORGANIZE

Your efforts to form a union local at your small plant are frustrated by the boss.

Freedom of assembly and association is guaranteed in the Bill of Rights and federal and provincial labor codes grant workers the right to form or join trade unions. Once certified, these unions have the right to represent their members in all further negotiations with the employer.

If the boss blocks or intimidates you in your efforts to unionize your plant, he is acting illegally and can be brought to book. (*See* Chapter 26, "Labor relations.") He may not discriminate against you either, if your organizing drive fails.

No dark threats. Your employer has the right to address the staff during paid working time and try to convince the employees that they are better off without a union. He is free to improve wages, hours or working conditions at any time prior to the union's application to be certified. But if he uses any threats, however subtly phrased, to anybody attempting to organize the plant, he's breaking the law. Union officials would likely press charges before the provincial or federal Labor Relations Board. The findings of tribunals appointed by the boards have the force of law.

FREEDOM OF THE PRESS

An editorial in your local paper describes your union as a communist front.

It's not a new problem; in Cicero's day, noble Romans often complained about items in the *Acta Diurna* (the "Day's Happenings")—a whitewashed board that hung in the city square. But it's a persistent one. Freedom of

How Mackenzie King stopped the presses

The secret life of Prime Minister William Lyon Mackenzie King, who sought advice from the spirit world, while leading the country for 23 years, was revealed to the public only after his death in 1950. Nearly 30 years later, Canadians also learned that, as a deputy minister, he had used the courts to prevent publication of a book about his maternal grandfather, William Lyon Mackenzie, instigator of the 1837 uprising in Upper Canada. King was brought up to idolize the rebel ancestor who had died in 1864, 13 years before the grandson's birth; and the grandson felt marked by destiny to wear Mackenzie's mantle.

The victim was William Dawson LeSueur, a well-known writer on literature and politics. LeSueur began writing Mackenzie's biography in 1906 and was soon convinced that the view of the famous rebel as a father of Canadian nationhood was false. He referred to the 1837 action as an "*opéra bouffe* rebellion," noting that Mackenzie "fled incontinently at the first shot, leaving his lieutenants to expiate on the gallows the crime which was chiefly his own." He suggested Mackenzie had actually delayed reform in Upper Canada.

First, King appealed to LeSueur's publisher to dump the writer. When that failed, he tried to persuade the author to abandon the work, but LeSueur refused. King wrote in his diary that the new book would be "a campaign document for the Tories" and stepped up the pres-

sure. The publisher, George Morang, finally wilted and the project was shelved.

But King wanted the manuscript suppressed forever. LeSueur had to go to the Supreme Court of Canada to get it back. Through relatives, King then charged that the author had gained access fraudulently to the Mackenzie family papers and an injunction against publication was sought. King attended the trial daily and watched the family lawyers depict LeSueur as a reactionary bent on rewriting the accepted version of Canadian history. Sometimes King, now a rising star in the Liberal hierarchy, appeared as a witness. The court ruled against LeSueur and he had to forfeit his manuscript. When an appeal failed, the determined LeSueur set about writing a second version of the biography for another publisher—this time without any direct use of papers still privately held by the Mackenzie clan. In 1915, just when that book was about to appear, his new publisher, Robert Glasgow, canceled it.

The handwritten Morang manuscript was not destroyed, however. It was filed, eventually, with other Mackenzie documents in the Public Archives of Ontario. There it lay, a brown paper parcel tied with string, until in the 1970s it attracted the attention of a young historian, Brian McKillop. And in 1979, LeSueur's book was finally published by Macmillan of Canada, under the title, *William Lyon Mackenzie: A Reinterpretation*.

the press is confirmed in the Bill of Rights and, generally speaking, our laws permit the press to publish anything.

No censor sits in the newspaper office with scissors at the ready. We expect our publishers and journalists to exercise a self-regulating responsibility. If they don't, they can expect to appear in either the civil or criminal courts. And police and customs officers can seize and confiscate any publication, script, film or electronic tape that they believe may be unlawful.

Legally, freedom of the press is just an extension of freedom of speech. But the press has a shadowy extra right—a "qualified privilege" of "fair comment." A newspaper can publish an inaccurate opinion or assessment of a public figure or organization, without fear of penalty, as long as that opinion was honestly held at the time and was presented without deliberate intent to cause harm. A retraction or apology is usually published if the newspaper finds it has made a serious error.

Union not defamed. Even if you are convinced your union was smeared in an editorial, your legal recourse is virtually nil. A large group or organization cannot sue for libel; only an identified person can be defamed. If the union secretary was named as a communist—and if he was not a member or associate of that political party—he'd have an outside chance with a civil suit for damages. But the Communist Party, though suspect in many minds, is legal in Canada and he would have to prove that his ability to make his living had been damaged and that his character had been injured in the minds of reasonable, levelheaded people.

Few newspaper readers accept journalistic opinions—especially editorials—as Holy Writ. A patently unfair attack will most likely win public sympathy and support for the victim.

Trying to put the brakes on. The British Columbia Supreme Court jolted the entire national press in 1979 by finding the *Victoria Times*, editor Barbara McLintock and cartoonist Bob Bierman guilty of libel for a cartoon showing a provincial cabinet minister pulling the wings off a fly. Not long before the Supreme Court of Canada had ordered the *Saskatoon Star-Phoenix* to pay $25,000 dam-

ages to Saskatoon alderman Morris Cherneskey because of a Letter to the Editor written by two law students at the University of Saskatchewan. The letter, published in 1973, criticized Mr. Cherneskey for opposing a proposed Indian alcohol rehabilitation center. The court ruled that the newspaper did not have the defense of free comment because it did not agree with the letter-writers' views.

But while everyone agrees that the freedom of the press is not absolute, legislators always run into trouble when they try to write specific curbs into the law. In blocking one evil—say, hate propaganda or hard-core pornography—they fear tampering with the essential flow of free expression. Beneath an antidiscrimination section in the Ontario Human Rights Code is a notation: "Nothing in this section shall be deemed to interfere with the free expression of opinion on any subject."

Expressing a dissenting view in the Cherneskey judgment, Mr. Justice Robert George Brian Dickson stated: "It is not only the right, but also the duty of the press, in pursuit of its legitimate objectives, to act as a sounding board for the free flow of new and different ideas."

SLANDER

Half the neighborhood hears a litany of obscenities hurled at you by the untutored loudmouth next door. You want to sue him.

He probably damaged himself more than he did you. Ignore him, unless you can prove that his tirade actually injured your reputation or your ability to earn your living. Name-calling or vulgar abuse will not necessarily qualify as defamation anyway; the author may have hurt your pride, but such abuse usually does not impair your reputation in the eyes of reasonable people.

Defamation is a tort (a civil wrong), not a crime, unless it is malicious in the legal sense and could lead to a breach of the peace. If the defamatory remarks are spoken and conveyed to, or overheard by, a third person, they are regarded as slander. If they are published in any permanent form, the offense is libel.

If you told people that your lawyer was incompetent and dishonest, you could find yourself in serious trouble. The lawyer's reputation is his bread and butter and to broadcast such an accusation might harm him financially. If you feel compelled to make such an accusation, you had better make sure that you can prove it to be true.

Libel or slander can be committed carelessly as well as intentionally. The law will recognize that things said "in the heat of passion" are not of the same quality as remarks uttered after due reflection. It really boils down to whether the defamed person can prove he has suffered in some material way.

CITIZENSHIP RIGHTS

You become a Canadian citizen just before a federal election but are denied a vote because your name isn't on the voters' list.

If you live in a rural area and were missed in the enumeration of voters, which is carried out before all elections, have someone who has been enumerated accompany you to the polling station to vouch for your eligibility. Urban dwellers who are not on the voters' list don't get to vote.

If you miss the enumeration, you should get in touch with the local returning officer. If you, or someone acting on your behalf, are unable to visit his office to fill out the necessary forms, the returning officer will have two revising officers visit your home and the information required will be obtained under oath from you or a member of your household.

Check your status. Until June 26, 1975, any British subject could vote in a Canadian federal election. Now you have to be a Canadian citizen. If you are seeking citizenship, and your documentation is in order, your application should be processed in about three months. The nearest Court of Canadian Citizenship will be listed in the telephone book under "Government of Canada," or you can write to the Registrar of Canadian Citizenship, Department of the Secretary of State, Ottawa, Ontario, K1A 0M5.

It's still possible to reside in Canada indefinitely as a landed immigrant without taking out citizenship papers. You will be protected by the laws of Canada in the same way as anybody else. But full rights are preserved for those who are citizens, either by birth or by naturalization. About 6 percent of the population are landed immigrants but not citizens.

How to get citizenship. Let's say you have landed immigrant status and want to become a citizen. First, apply to the Registrar of Canadian Citizenship. If you are not already a British subject, you will be required to swear allegiance to Queen Elizabeth II. The person who is already a British subject has previously accepted allegiance to the Queen and therefore does not have to swear fealty again.

Each prospective adult citizen must make personal application on a form provided at your local courthouse, or at any of the 13 Courts of Canadian Citizenship. Parents may apply for children under 18 years of age. Besides hearing about their rights and privileges, new citizens are advised that they can be conscripted into the armed forces in time of war, can be called for jury duty, and must go to the aid of the police or fire rangers if called upon to do so.

Getting into Canada. All prospective immigrants—whether they seek entry to work or study—must make all arrangements before leaving home. The law states that no visitor to Canada can change his status while inside Canada. It must be acknowledged, however, that the federal authorities do make exceptions to this rule, especially when the aspiring immigrant has the backing of a highly vocal pressure group. The would-be immigrant should never pay anything to anybody to "grease the wheels." All the help required is available free at any Canadian consulate.

Immigration officers may not discriminate on the grounds of color, race or religion, although entry is not as easy today as it was until the mid-1970s. Possession of portable capital can certainly smooth the path. If you are an "entrepreneur" (an active businessman or businesswoman) with the equivalent of about $150,000, your chances of acceptance are very good. Canada is actively seeking those who can inject money and progressive business ideas into the country. Of course, ownership of capital is not specifically mentioned in the regulations! A report to Parliament by the Department of Immigration stated that 1,056 entrepreneurs entered Canada in 1977, bringing in a total of $207 million. When the director of the department's recruitment branch was asked how the government ensures that the entrepreneurs' projects are carried through, he stated: "We don't give the visas until they have transferred the money!"

THE OMBUDSMAN

You believe you've had a raw deal from a government department and you can't get any action on your complaint.

With a federal government, 10 provincial governments, two territorial councils, several hundred Crown corporations and agencies, and at least a dozen major municipal governments with staff numbering in the thousands, Canada has constructed a huge official bureaucracy that often seems impenetrable and unresponsive to the individual citizen. His legitimate complaint so easily gets pigeonholed and he

can't find his way through the maze of "official channels" in the paperwork empire. He becomes angry and frustrated by what Shakespeare's Hamlet called "the insolence of office." Worse, he becomes cynical about the integrity of all those who work "for the government." If you find yourself in this fix, having tried all the routine avenues in vain, there's still a last recourse: the ombudsman. In 1967, Alberta appointed Canada's first ombudsman (a Swedish word meaning "representative") and all provinces except Prince Edward Island have since followed suit. Appointed by the legislature but independent of it, the ombudsman, upon written complaint from a citizen, will investigate administrative acts, decisions or omissions by the provincial bureaucracy. In Quebec the title of the appointee is Le Protecteur du Citoyen.

After a preliminary investigation of your complaint, the ombudsman's investigative staff can enter government premises, open relevant files, summon witnesses and demand that they give evidence under oath.

The ombudsman is not a judge. He has no enforcement powers, but should his recommendation be ignored he can report directly to the premier and thus bring pressure to bear. Each year, the ombudsman's annual report is

Your S.I.N. will find you out

The Social Insurance Number (S.I.N.) puts a dog tag on each of us and makes life a lot simpler for the record keepers. The centralized use of the numbers in government computers helps control fraud in unemployment insurance and other social security systems. S.I.N. is a "prime identifier" for 48 federal services. In the private sector, it is used for identification and credit checks in department stores, banks, libraries and hospitals.

When S.I.N.'s were introduced in 1964, the intent was that they be used only to register people for two programs—social insurance and the Canada (or Quebec) Pension Plan. But to-

day, the Metric Commission won't mail out cheques for converting tools to metric unless you supply your S.I.N. The magic number must be produced at the registration of a birth in Prince Edward Island, to register entrants to a Winnipeg ballet school and to enrol peewee players for intercity hockey in Belleville, Ont.

When the three branches of the armed forces were fused in 1967, the traditional service numbers were replaced by social insurance numbers. Servicemen's mail has sometimes been returned marked "incomplete address," when the envelope didn't show the addressee's S.I.N.

tabled in the legislature and becomes available for public debate.

As a rule, the provincial ombudsman must confine his investigations to administrative decisions. He can't stray into policy or judicial decisions. And all actions by the federal government or its agencies are outside his jurisdiction, as are those of municipal governments, which rules out anything relating to the local police. Nor can he accept complaints against individuals or private companies.

Don't lose heart at these hurdles. Ombudsman staff will quickly advise you whether or not they can help. A written complaint is required. If your case is taken up, you have the right to be informed about the outcome. If the ombudsman cannot act on your behalf, he may be able to recommend other doors you can knock on. For example, complaints about discrimination often reach the ombudsman's desk when they should be directed to the provincial Human Rights Commission.

Champion of the underdog. Once the ombudsman gets his teeth into a legitimate complaint, he's hard to shake loose. Nova Scotia's Harry Smith (who, contrary to the rule in most other provinces, can investigate municipal decisions) persuaded a school board to reroute a bus to pick up a five-year-old girl, who lived some two kilometres off the bus route without bus service.

In Quebec, Louis Marceau won $10,000 in traveling expenses for a government engineer who had been severely injured in a traffic accident seven years earlier. The engineer's speech and memory had been impaired and the expense vouchers had been lost. The provincial treasurer eventually paid up, at compound interest.

Manitoba's George Maltby, a former chief of police, dug into a complicated situation concerning the estate of an 80-year-old woman in a mental hospital. The woman's daughter had not been told that she could apply for permission to look after her mother's affairs. The Public Trustee had rented the mother's house for $60 a month and spent a large sum from the estate for repairs. Much of the furniture in the house had disappeared. After a long dispute, the Public Trustee paid $13,093 in compensation.

VICTIMS OF CRIME

You may be permanently disabled as a result of a bank robber's getaway car crashing into yours.

Any innocent person injured during the commission of a crime can apply for compensation either to the Criminal Injuries Compensation Board, if your province now has one, or to the Department of Justice. If you were helping the police to catch an escaping criminal—whether asked to or not—your appeal is likely to receive sympathetic consideration. Any bystander hurt because of a crime has a strong case, too.

You can also attempt to recover compensation from the criminal. In May 1978, the Supreme Court of Canada ruled that courts could order convicted persons to compensate victims for loss or damage to their property or person. The ruling was made in the case of a Winnipeg woman convicted of converting her employers' money orders and merchandise to her own use. She was sentenced to two years in jail and ordered to compensate her employers for their loss. The Supreme Court added that such compensation should not be used as a substitute for a civil suit for damages. (In most cases, seeking financial compensation from the criminal is like trying to get blood from a stone.)

Staking your claim. An inquiry at your local courthouse or police station will provide the address of your provincial board. (The titles differ across the country.) It is necessary to prove only that a crime was committed and that you were injured as a totally innocent party.

The Ontario Criminal Injuries Compensation Board reported awards totaling $1,611,836 in 1978. The average was $2,328. To protect the victims' privacy, their names and addresses are not included in the report.

A farmer was sitting quietly in his home when an armed neighbor burst in and wounded him in the right hand, causing permanent mutilation and a 50 percent loss of use. The assailant was sentenced to 12 months in jail and the board awarded the victim $7,999 for his pain and suffering.

A visitor to Canada became mixed up in a

fight at a Sikh temple. He was stabbed and hit on the head with a blunt instrument. Although 13 persons were arrested, the Crown did not proceed with criminal charges. The victim got $3,000 in public funds.

Policemen injured in the line of duty can claim compensation. A constable hit on the head with a beer bottle was awarded $6,224.05; another, wounded in a police station shoot-out, received $11,866.55; a third, shot in the hip, has difficulty walking. His assailant got three years and he got $1,500.

IN THE MINORITY

With a B.A. and a good record on the job, you still don't get promoted. You think it's because your skin is black.

All of Canada's 11 human rights codes—10 provincial, one federal—forbid discrimination on account of color, race or religion. While it's reassuring to see those proud phrases in black and white, they don't confirm that discrimination has vanished from the marketplace. We live on earth, not in heaven.

If you have a reasonable suspicion that your promotion is blocked solely because of the color of your skin, get in touch with your provincial Human Rights Commission or ombudsman's office. (*See* Chapter 6, "Discrimination.") You don't need *proof*; the commission's investigator will look into the situation. Further action will depend on the findings. You needn't fear any backlash because of your complaint. Any action of that kind would be itself regarded as discrimination.

The ideal is that all hiring and promotion should be based solely on merit. But there can be many factors in an individual case that may not be apparent to the aggrieved worker. We all tend to overrate our own value in the marketplace—that's called ambition.

Don't be surprised if the boss's son leapfrogs the competition—that's called nepotism. He'll probably own the business one day and must be groomed for responsibility. If you owned the plant, you'd probably follow the same course. Promotion usually involves assuming responsibility, or directing the work of others. That can call for communications skills, patience, a warm personality—factors not necessarily related to normal work performance.

Hidden prejudice. None of the provinces attempt to lay down specific, detailed anti-discrimination regulations about promotions, working conditions and other intracompany matters. The variations are simply too numerous. But the commissions are trying to push their legislatures to ban several practices which, while not illegal in themselves, permit concealed discrimination to flourish. As things stand, if a householder contracts for home-repair service with an appliance company but rejects the serviceman who arrives to do the job on the grounds of color or race, the employee can't file a complaint unless he is penalized or fired by his company over the incident.

Acts of discrimination are at times so covert that even the victim may not be aware of being shafted. Personnel policies may demand certain entry-level qualifications unnecessarily restrictive, or not really closely related to the job at stake. These provide a screen for sorting out applicants on grounds that would otherwise be illegal.

Educational qualification is a common hurdle that can't be legislated away. It would require a new civil-service army to set and enforce educational standards for every job in the country. Native Indians are frequent sufferers. The fault there appears to lie with the social system that has failed to provide access or incentive to normal educational development. The hurdle can best be jumped by taking advantage of the virtually limitless educational enrichment offered everywhere in Canada at high-school night classes, community colleges and through correspondence courses.

PERSONAL FILES

You fear that the federal government may have inaccurate information on file about you.

Through the 1970s the public grew increasingly aware of the tremendous amount of detail on private lives being accumulated by the bureaucracy's computers. The Canadian Human Rights Act, proclaimed on March 1, 1978, guarantees your right to find out whether a federal government department or agency holds information about you, and you have the right to challenge the accuracy of the information.

Before personal information provided to a federal department or agency for a specific purpose can be used for another purpose, the person who provided it must consent to such other use, or the use must be authorized by law. You can demand to know what use has been made of information provided since the act came into force.

You can find out exactly where the information is stored by studying an index available at your post office. There's an application form

A clean slate

The recipient of this pardon—his name has been blanked out—paid his debt to society, then convinced the authorities he had turned his back on crime. Now that his slate is wiped clean, he can truthfully say he doesn't have a criminal record.

Legalese is responsible for the clumsy wording of the opening paragraph.

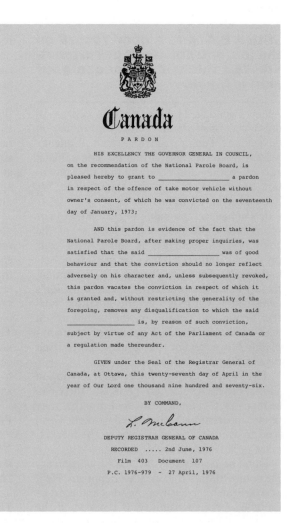

Canada

PARDON

HIS EXCELLENCY THE GOVERNOR GENERAL IN COUNCIL, on the recommendation of the National Parole Board, is pleased hereby to grant to _____ a pardon in respect of the offence of take motor vehicle without owner's consent, of which he was convicted on the seventeenth day of January, 1973;

AND this pardon is evidence of the fact that the National Parole Board, after making proper inquiries, was satisfied that the said _____ was of good behaviour and that the conviction should no longer reflect adversely on his character and, unless subsequently revoked, this pardon vacates the conviction in respect of which it is granted and, without restricting the generality of the foregoing, removes any disqualification to which the said _____ is, by reason of such conviction, subject by virtue of any Act of the Parliament of Canada or a regulation made thereunder.

GIVEN under the Seal of the Registrar General of Canada, at Ottawa, this twenty-seventh day of April in the year of Our Lord one thousand nine hundred and seventy-six.

BY COMMAND,

L. McCann

DEPUTY REGISTRAR GENERAL OF CANADA

RECORDED ..... 2nd June, 1976

Film 403 Document 107

P.C. 1976-979 - 27 April, 1976

you may use to list the files you wish to search and there is no charge.

If you want to challenge the accuracy of the information, write to the department or agency concerned. If you get a refusal or runaround, complain to the Privacy Commissioner, Canadian Human Rights Commission, Ottawa, Ontario, K1A 1E1.

Some files still shut. But you won't be shown everything. Exemptions to the right of access to personal files are listed in the act. You won't get to see anything relating to federal-provincial or international relations, national defense or security, investigation of offenses under federal law, the administration or enforcement of any act of Parliament, cabinet secrets, legal opinions and information about other persons.

How much does Big Brother know about you? Well, the index lists 27 federal departments and 62 agencies (including the RCMP) that could be compiling a taped dossier. They have tax files, drug-user files compiled over the last 15 years, appeals for pensions, employment records and penitentiary files.

The degree of secrecy in government is usually up to the civil servant who originates the document or receives it from outside consultants.* Almost everything is classified "for internal use only"—which sometimes blocks even the Member of Parliament who seeks access. In the higher echelons of the bureaucracy, papers are generally labeled "confidential." Material for the cabinet's eyes is always stamped "secret."

Many laws in Canada demand such secrecy. For example, income tax regulations deny the public access to another person's financial information. Patent laws and trade acts prevent disclosure of the confidences of private business. The Official Secrets Act, under which the government can legally conceal all its skeletons, is a main bone of contention. This act makes it a crime to *receive* government secrets, not merely to *disclose* them.

---

*At the time of writing, a bill was before Parliament to establish the opposite principle. Under the new Freedom of Information Act, the government would be obligated to release all documents not covered by exemptions as defined in the act. The exemptions were similar to those listed in the Human Rights Act.

2 You and the police

A visitor from outer space, exposed to newspapers and television documentaries, might well ask whether Canadians live under the iron heel of a police force intent on eavesdropping, beating up the citizenry, faking evidence, and violating civil rights.

The last decade appears to have been one long open season on the police forces of Canada. Public inquiries probed allegations of breaking and entering, illegal seizure of property, electronic bugging and wiretapping, surreptitious opening of mail, and brutality (even torture) by police.

The Canadian Civil Liberties Association petitioned the government to prosecute members of the Royal Canadian Mounted Police, once regarded as incorruptible. Newspapers reported antipolice allegations under bold headlines.

The truth, however, is that Canada is a notably peaceful and tolerant state. We do not live in fear of a knock on the door at midnight. The peace officer's powers of interrogation, search and arrest are limited by law. He can arrest without a warrant only under specific circumstances, such as finding someone committing an offense, or about to commit one. He cannot, on a whim, stop a pedestrian on the street and demand identification, but he can ask a driver to produce license, registration and insurance card. He has the power to search your person or vehicle when he has "reasonable grounds" for doing so, but he cannot search your home without your permission unless he has a warrant, or unless he has reasonable grounds to believe a crime is being committed or has just been committed there. The average man and his family respect the law, which is written by their elected representatives and enforced by their employee, the policeman.

But, there are a few rotten apples in every barrel and there are a few corrupt cops. "No police force is perfect," says Chief Harold Adamson of the Metropolitan Toronto Police, the largest urban force in Canada. "We monitor all complaints against the police. If we find a corrupt officer, we fire him."

ANSWERING QUESTIONS

A policeman stops you on the street and questions you for no apparent reason.

A policeman has the right, as has any citizen, to approach you and ask questions. However, unless he provides legal grounds for his queries, the law doesn't require you to identify yourself or to supply any other information.

The situation is different if you are the driver of a vehicle. Provincial laws require that you produce your driver's license, vehicle registration and insurance card. Passengers are in the same category as pedestrians; police cannot question them without providing a legal reason, unless one happens to be the owner of the vehicle.

Generally speaking, police don't stop and question citizens arbitrarily. Usually, they have a justifiable (and legal) reason, and most citizens don't mind cooperating when they understand the officer's interest.

A late-night stroll. A police officer may be entitled to know who you are and what business you have in a particular area, if, say, you are walking late at night in a business district.

To the officer, you are an unknown person in an area where normal activity has ceased. It may be a high-crime district. He knows that break-and-enter teams often have lookouts wandering about. In those circumstances, your silence might be considered "reasonable and probable grounds to believe an indictable offense is, has been or is about to be committed," and you could be arrested.

SELF-INCRIMINATION

You talked freely with detectives investigating a theft at your place of work. No one said you were under suspicion but now you have been arrested.

No person can be compelled to incriminate himself, that is, to give information that will assist in his conviction. This common law principle is one of the "Judges' Rules," established in 1912 by judges of the King's Bench in England at the request of the British police. Though lacking the force of law, these rules are followed by the Canadian courts. The "caution" or warning read to a suspect at the time of arrest has been in formal use since the 1912 ruling. The caution, however, refers only to questions about the offense as charged; merely identifying oneself is not usually regarded as self-incriminating.

In the course of an investigation, the police may talk to hundreds of persons. They are not required to "caution" everyone they question. It is only when the investigating officer makes up his mind to charge a person with an offense that he should warn that person against self-incrimination.

Withholding such a warning, when it is apparent a person should be cautioned, can cause the evidence gained to be thrown out of court.

In any case where self-incrimination appears to be at issue, the court holds an inquiry, called a *voir dire*. At this trial within a trial, the judge hears testimony, usually a confession, then decides on the admissibility of the evidence.

ARREST

You are asked by an officer to accompany him to the station for questioning.

It's only a request, not an order, and the decision is up to you. If the officer decides that your attendance at the station is essential, he will arrest you. This is done by stating formally that you are under arrest, by laying a hand on your arm (any touch will suffice) and by informing you of the reason for the arrest. If a warrant has been issued, you will receive a copy. If you submit to the arrest, the physical touching is not essential.

Any attempt to force you into a police car and take you to the station without a formal arrest might provide grounds for a charge of assault against the officer concerned and for a civil suit for damages.

All about arrests. The powers of arrest differ with the gravity of the offense. For relatively minor or summary offenses, the police can arrest you if you are committing a crime or leaving the scene, or by producing a warrant issued by a justice of the peace. Summary offenses include common assault, causing a disturbance, soliciting for prostitution, many traffic and liquor charges. These are tried in the lower courts.

In more serious matters—known as indictable offenses—you can be taken into custody if the officer *believes* you have committed the offense or that you are about to do so. Indictable offenses include breaking and entering, theft or fraud of more than $200 and most sexual charges.

Some offenses can be treated as either summary or indictable, at the option of the Crown. These include most narcotic charges, and assault or obstruction of the police. The accused also has some options—if he is charged with an indictable offense which is not in the exclusive jurisdiction of a lower or higher court.

He can elect trial by provincial judge, or by a higher court judge, or higher court judge and jury. If he elects trial in higher court, the magistrate will conduct a preliminary hearing to decide whether the Crown has sufficient evidence to warrant a trial.

The magistrate could dismiss the charge and set the accused free. At any rate, the court appearance provides an opportunity to hear the Crown's evidence. If the accused elects to be tried by a magistrate, he goes directly to trial without preliminary hearing. If found guilty, the maximum penalty will be as stated in the law under which the charge was laid;

the maximum penalties for conviction on a summary offense ($500 or six months, or both) do not apply in such cases. (*See* Chapter 4, "You, the defendant.")

Nowadays, an arrest seldom involves handcuffs and a frog-march to the local police station. For the majority of minor violations, the peace officer issues a "notice of appearance," requiring the person named to attend court at a given time and date. When the arresting officer is satisfied that the identity of the suspect is known, that the evidence of the offense is secure, and that the offense will not be continued or repeated, he will issue a "notice of appearance." By accepting the notice, you agree to appear at court on the stated date.

Let's say that you are arrested in downtown Vancouver on a charge of theft of goods valued at under $200. You give an address in the suburbs and you appear to be sober, rational and reasonably cooperative. The constable will almost certainly take your word that you will appear as directed.

If, however, you are visiting from another province, the officer would think twice about your promise to appear. He would probably, in a peaceful situation, release you on your promise to pay $500 if you don't turn up at the court. You are not required to produce the money or sign a cheque. If you don't honor your promise, you owe $500 and a warrant will be issued for your arrest.

'I give you my word, officer'

If you are arrested and taken to the police station, the officer in charge of the shift has the power to release you. One way he can do it is by having you sign a "Promise to Appear." (If you don't show up at the promised time—for a court hearing, or for fingerprinting and photographing—a warrant can be issued for your arrest.) The officer can also release you unconditionally, with intention of compelling appearance by way of summons; on your own recognizance, without surety or deposit; or, in the case of nonresidents, on cash bail not exceeding $500.

Only if the constable believes that the conditions for your immediate release are not met—let's say you threaten to harm the person who called the police—will he take you into custody. If the charge was impaired driving, he would probably hold you because of the danger that you might continue to drive.

When a notice of appearance is issued, the policeman files his charge—it's called an "information." This is studied by a justice of the peace, who confirms—or cancels—the notice of appearance.

Identification parade. The notice of appearance, or any other alternative to detainment in custody, may require you to present yourself at police headquarters at a stated time and date for identification. This is likely if the charge concerns an indictable offense—one that could carry a sentence of two years' imprisonment, or more.

Identification basically consists of a suspect being photographed and fingerprinted.

If you fail to show up when ordered to do so, a warrant will be issued for your arrest. This time you can expect to see the inside of a cell.

Getting out on bail. If you are arrested and taken into custody, you have a right to be released on bail unless your offense is indeed grave. The police must show cause why you should not be released on your own "recognizance," that is, your promise to appear when called and to behave yourself in the interim. (*See* "Bail" in Chapter 4.)

When bail is granted, a cash deposit or a surety is usually not demanded unless the suspect resides more than 100 kilometres away, or in another province.

If you are taken into custody, the arresting officer has to convince a justice of the peace that you should be held in the public interest. The J.P. also has to record his reasons for detaining you.

For murder, or a few other grave offenses, the accused can be released only on the order of a Superior Court judge.

Crimes committed abroad. Arrests are made in Canada on behalf of foreign countries with which we have extradition treaties. A Canadian court then decides whether the accused will be returned to his country of origin, and the accused can argue his right to stay.

At one hearing, a man pleaded that if he were extradited to his homeland, he would be torn apart by camels. He was not sent back.

No one can be tried in Canada for committing an offense outside the country, with one exception. Crimes committed in Canadian-registered aircraft or ships, even half the world away, will be prosecuted in Canada.

A crime is "committed" in the territory where the last event that completes the act occurs. For instance, if a man in Saskatchewan fires his rifle at and wounds someone in Montana, the crime is regarded as committed in Montana. But if the Montana postal or telephone services were used to obtain something by false pretenses from someone in Saskatchewan, the actual "obtaining"—the crime—would occur in Canada. Prosecutions, however, could occur in both Canada and the United States.

You can be arrested and prosecuted for having something that you know was obtained abroad in circumstances that would constitute an offense if they had occurred in Canada. In such instances, "possession" is the offense.

Conspiracy—plotting to commit crime—also provides knotty problems of jurisdiction. However, it is widely accepted that the crime of conspiracy is regarded as having happened in the same place as the planned crime. For example, if a plot to rob a bank in Quebec was hatched in New Brunswick, charges of bank robbery and of conspiracy would be laid in Quebec.

FALSE ARREST

In the supermarket, you dropped a package of ball point pens in your pocket and forgot about them at the checkout. You were detained outside by a store employee. You want to sue for false arrest.

Any person may arrest another who is committing a criminal offense. If, on the other hand, you have been wrongfully arrested or detained, you can sue your accoster for false imprisonment, and perhaps for malicious prosecution.

If a policeman arrests you, he will be protected from civil action if he had reason to believe you had committed a crime, and it may be irrelevant whether you are subsequently acquitted. Should you make a citizen's arrest, be sure you have the right person, lest you be sued for wrongful arrest.

When you were detained, you had the pens in your pocket. You face a tough task convincing anyone you did not intend to steal them, but it is not impossible. We can all be forgetful. If you are acquitted of a criminal charge, you may decide to sue. Your action might succeed but your damages are not likely to be large because the defendant's action was reasonable and not malicious.

Damages will depend on how long you were detained, how much publicity the matter received and how much your reputation was injured.

Turkey on the knee. If you think that store detectives are overzealous, consider the woman who was found walking out of a supermarket with a frozen turkey clasped between her knees, under her skirt.

In any big supermarket, a store detective is always on the lookout for shoplifters. He, or she, will be dressed like an ordinary shopper, and will know all the tricks. A woman seen pocketing a pound of butter in one store hotly denied she had done so. The detective took her to his well-heated office, where the butter began to melt and run down her leg.

UNIFORMS AND IDENTIFICATION

A young man in jeans and sweat shirt tells you that he is a police officer and that you are under arrest.

There is no requirement in law that a peace officer wear any kind of uniform. It's a matter of regulation within a force.

Many convictions, especially for narcotic offenses, follow the infiltration of criminal groups by undercover police officers.

However, at the point of an arrest, you have the right to demand proof of a police officer's identification. He must produce his official badge or his force's identification card bearing his photograph.

ASSISTING THE POLICE

A young policeman, struggling with a group of toughs, orders you to help.

Although it is seldom exercised, a police officer has the right to require an onlooker to assist him in making an arrest or in "preserving the peace." In fact, it is an obligation of every citizen to "preserve the peace."

In practical terms, this is a cloudy area of the law. There is no suggestion that the citizen should take the law into his own hands. But anyone who witnesses a breach of the peace is justified in preventing its continuance or renewal, and in detaining anyone involved for delivery to a peace officer.

The law protects citizens who respond to a police call for help. It is an offense to assault any person assisting a peace officer. Damages for any injury received could be sought from the assailant, or from the provincial agencies which compensate the victims of crime. (*See* Section 10, "Effective complaining.")

CITIZEN'S ARREST

There are cries of "Stop thief!" and you see a man running from a store.

Every citizen has the right of arrest in these circumstances, but whether you exercise that right is a matter of conscience. What if the escaper is armed? Even if his hands are empty, he could have a gun or another weapon in his pocket.

Police suggest a sensible approach: note automobile license number and direction of travel, the suspect's physical description, name used, accent, distinguishing marks, method of operation and give such information to the police.

Arrest by the private citizen can be a complex matter. Lest vigilantes get loose in the streets, lawmakers hedge the power of citizen's arrest with tightly worded clauses.

A private person may arrest anyone whom he finds *committing* an indictable offense, or who he reasonably believes committed a criminal offense and is escaping from persons with authority to arrest him, such as the storekeeper who is shouting "Stop thief!" However, the ordinary person does *not* have the right to arrest anyone who has (previously) committed an offense, *unless that person is under hot pursuit*, that is, actually being chased.

If you are the owner, or legal possessor, of property and you find someone committing an offense against that property, you may make a legal arrest. The same right extends to your agent. This item legalizes the action of a store detective or security guard.

Catalogue of crimes. The private citizen has no right to arrest someone committing a summary, or minor offense. And spur-of-the-moment distinctions between summary and indictable offenses may defeat the average person. Indictable offenses include treason, murder, breaking and entering, escaping from jail, theft, fraud and false pretenses involving more than $200, serious assaults and sexual offenses, and most charges relating to weapons and narcotics.

If you attempt to arrest the escaping thief, take care that you use no more force than is necessary to subdue him. If you are changing

John Wilson Murray—the great detective

At age 35, Scottish-born John Wilson Murray was appointed Detective to the provincial government of Ontario. His beat covered 263,488 square kilometres. It was the fall of 1874.

When he retired 30 years later, Murray had become one of the world's first scientific detectives and one of the best-known men in Canada.

Thirteen years before Conan Doyle published his first Sherlock Holmes story, Murray was using analysis and deduction as his main weapons against the criminal. He slowly cross-checked every alibi and his unflurried patience was a byword as he tracked down an amazing number of murderers, counterfeiters, swindlers and armed robbers.

Convinced that criminal tendencies were inherited and therefore that rehabilitation was next to impossible, Murray watched with satisfaction as many of his quarries dropped from the gallows.

Tall, wide-shouldered and with clear blue eyes above a generous, sandy mustache, Murray was something of an actor. His voice could switch from a gentle, persuasive tone to a frightening boom that prompted many a confession. Several times he ran younger suspects down in foot races, relying on stamina rather than speed.

Murray's most famous case ended with the hanging of Englishman Reginald Birchall in Woodstock on the cold gray morning of Nov. 14, 1890. The case revealed Murray at his brilliant best.

Birchall, son of a well-known cleric, advertised in English papers for well-to-do young men as investing partners in make-believe Ontario farms near Niagara Falls and Woodstock. He exchanged references and drew up contracts offering 5 percent interest on the money over the first year.

The body of one of the first takers, Frederick Benwell, was found in Blenheim Swamp near Woodstock. Murray took up the trail and arrested Birchall.

While awaiting execution, Birchall, who never admitted to the murder, wrote his captor: "I found you always a gentleman, and I have no hard feelings against you." Murray couldn't spare time to visit Birchall in jail, but he did take a morning off to watch him hang.

a tire in the supermarket parking lot, think twice before you clout him with the jack handle.

Should you make a citizen's arrest, remember that you have no powers of search, seizure or interrogation, and that you must hand your prisoner over to a peace officer as soon as possible.

In Kitchener, Ont., a man sought in the stabbing death of a woman was arrested by a teen-age boy at a shopping center. The boy had three men hold the suspect while he called the police. He had seen the man running from the town house when the woman was killed during a robbery.

POLICE BRUTALITY

You are outraged when you see two burly policemen using force on a thin, longhaired youth outside a tavern.

Everyone authorized or required to enforce the law is permitted to use such force as is reasonably necessary. Therefore, if a suspect resists arrest, the police may take such steps as are necessary to subdue him and take him into custody.

Uniformed police are highly visible and arrests involving force often attract the attention—and sometimes the ire—of observers. Realizing such difficulties must arise, the lawmakers made resisting arrest of oneself or others an offense. To obstruct the police, or anyone assisting them, is also an offense.

It can happen that a police officer will arrest the wrong person. Provided he acts in good faith, using no more force than is necessary, he is protected against civil and criminal liability.

If you are innocent of any wrongdoing, or even if the exact legal requirements of the arrest are not followed, you should make your protest politely and "go along quietly." You have the right to call a lawyer or other adviser from the police station.

Accusations of police brutality are investigated by senior police officers who report to the civilian police commission, and, of course,

the courts are open to any citizen who wishes to "press charges." (*See* Section 10, "Effective complaining.")

SEARCH OF A PERSON

As a woman, you believe you can't be forced to submit to a search at the police station.

Not so. Police have the right to search both the person and the effects of anybody in custody for an alleged offense. The search of a female is done by a policewoman.

SEARCH WARRANTS

Some policemen knock on your door and demand entry to search for suspected stolen goods.

A man's home is his castle and the law will protect your sovereignty . . . up to a point.

The core of the matter of entry to your home is your invitation. The majority of citizens do invite the police into their homes and try to be helpful. But to some people the law means trouble, or they would rather avoid involvement.

Thus, the law arms the police with all manner of rights to pursue their duty. The most common power is the search warrant, obtainable under several federal statutes, including the Criminal Code, Narcotic Control Act, and the Food and Drugs Act. With such a warrant, the police can even break your door down. (*See* "Search warrants" in Chapter 15.)

To get a warrant, a police officer must convince a justice of the peace that circumstances justify a warrant.

If the police demand entry, ask to see the warrant; they probably have a carbon copy. It will specify the purpose and scope of the search. If you don't ask to see it, they become invitees.

The warrant can be for a house, apartment or car—in fact, any "place" at the given address. Unless it states otherwise, it must be executed by day (between sunrise and sunset).

Search without warrant. Your right to bar your dwelling to the police vanishes if they invoke any one of half a dozen laws. Most of these involve customs, liquor, weapons or drug charges. In pursuit of a lawbreaker, police could charge into the House of Commons and, in fact, have done just that.

Under the Narcotic Control Act, the police can search for drugs, without a warrant, any "place" that is not a residence. An RCMP officer may search your home if he possesses a writ of assistance. This blanket search document, issued by the Federal Court of Canada to members of the RCMP only, remains valid for two years.

Peace officers, conducting a lawful search, can break open any window, door, lock, floor, wall, ceiling, compartment, plumbing fixture, container or any other thing.

Looking for liquor. Liquor laws vary from province to province, but all allow some right to search. Everywhere, police have the power to search a vehicle without a warrant and they can conduct body searches as well. They can search any "place" (except a dwelling) without a warrant.

Searches for stolen property are common and are usually conducted under warrant. The overwhelming motive for all types of theft is money and the thief is seldom in a position to sell his loot on the open market. Therefore, he must either store it till the heat dies down or

Open up! It's the police!

Except under special circumstances (such as when a crime is actually being committed), police must have a search warrant to enter your home or private property. When police knock (or hammer) at your door, ask to see the warrant. It has been sworn out before a magistrate by a peace officer who has "reasonable grounds" (not necessarily certain proof) that he'll find somebody or something that will assist in the solving of a crime.

sell it to a dealer in stolen goods—a "fence." The punishment for possession is therefore on the same level as for the theft itself.

If stolen goods are found on your property, you'll have some tall explaining to do. "Looking after them for someone else" will be a poor excuse, especially if the goods are under floorboards or in a hole in the garden.

Everyone commits an offense who has any property or thing that he knows was obtained in Canada from the commission of an indictable offense. The same applies to goods obtained from abroad in circumstances that would have been criminal in Canada. It also is an offense to have *control* or possession over stolen goods, or to help conceal or dispose of them.

The maximum penalty for possession is 10 years' imprisonment.

A CRIMINAL RECORD

Your son has been in trouble a few times for stealing and the police are always calling to question him.

Anyone convicted of any offense under the Criminal Code, the Narcotic Control Act or the Food and Drugs Act will have a criminal record. Your past history is always available to the police unless you have been granted a pardon.

You can, however, plead guilty to a crime and even be found guilty, without sustaining a conviction. It happens if you are discharged, absolutely or conditionally, as unlikely to offend again, or because there were mitigating circumstances, such as intolerable provocation at the time of the offense.

With an absolute discharge, you walk away unpunished. The conditional discharge involves a probationary period during which you have to fulfill certain conditions. But whether the discharge is absolute or conditional, you can't truthfully say that you don't have a criminal record until you obtain a pardon.

A record for, say, shoplifting may influence a justice of the peace if you are seeking bail

after arrest for a subsequent offense. It undoubtedly will be considered by a judge before passing sentence on later charges. The Crown prosecutor is not permitted to mention your record during the trial unless you take the stand yourself.

To a landed immigrant, a criminal record can be a serious obstacle to Canadian citizenship. It won't prevent a citizen from getting a Canadian passport, although it could hinder entry into some foreign countries. It won't help on any job application and it could rule out certain positions because it makes you ineligible for bonding.

Obtaining a pardon. Two years after sentence has been served for a summary offense—whether it involved a jail term, probation or fine—you can apply to the National Parole Board in Ottawa for a pardon. If you were convicted of an indictable offense, you can apply five years after sentence has been served. In the case of a conditional or absolute discharge, you wait only one year before applying for a pardon if the offense was summary; three years if it was indictable.

THE BREATHALYZER

You're not convinced that the breathalyzer test is fair or accurate, and when you refuse to take one you are arrested.

The breathalyzer test can be demanded of anyone who has "care and control" of a vehicle and who occupies the seat normally used by the driver—even if the engine is switched off, or the ignition key is not in your possession. Suspicion that a driver has been drinking is enough to make a breath test mandatory.

If roadside equipment is not available, a suspect must accompany the police to the station where the full-scale test will be made.

If the machine reveals a level above 80 mg of alcohol in 100 ml of blood, you are considered impaired. The penalty for a first impaired driving offense is a fine of from $50 to $2,000, or imprisonment for up to six months, or both. For a second conviction, it's jail for not less than 14 days and perhaps for a year. Subsequent convictions bring a minimum of three months' imprisonment and a maximum of two years. The penalties for refusing the test are the same as those imposed for failing it.

Bucking the breathalyzer. Almost every phase of the breathalyzer law is being tested by drivers caught in its chemical coils.

An accused Newfoundland driver was acquitted when he claimed the protection of the Canadian Bill of Rights. He admitted having two drinks after work, but he demanded to call a lawyer before giving the required breath sample. There was no telephone available and the police, knowing they must take the sample within a prescribed time, gave him the choice of providing the sample or being charged with refusal. The outcome was a court ruling that he had the right to counsel and that the police acted contrary to the Bill of Rights.

A British Columbia driver, involved in a collision, showed a high alcohol level but claimed that he had drunk two bottles of beer between the accident and the taking of the breath sample. The police could not refute the post-accident drinking and the man was acquitted.

In an Ontario appeal, the accused was acquitted because his two adverse breathalyzer tests were taken at an interval of exactly 15 minutes—2:50 a.m. and 3:05 a.m.—not 15 minutes apart. The court held that in computing the time interval, the first and last minute named in the test period should not be included.

Notwithstanding the cases quoted, when the breathalyzer needle swings over .08, chances are you've had it.

Apart from breathalyzer evidence, you can be convicted of driving while your ability is impaired (by alcohol or drugs) if there is evi-

The dabs—your unwritten signature

If you are arrested and charged with an indictable offense, you will be finger-printed and photographed. It has nothing to do with guilt or innocence. It's strictly a matter of identification, sanctioned by the law. A convicted criminal's "record" is tied to him by photograph, fingerprints and a number.

Stories about criminals who elude identification through fingertip skin grafts, or acid baths, are mostly hokum. The identification of your unique "dabs" is incredibly accurate.

If the charge against you is dropped, or if you are acquitted, you can insist that your photograph and fingerprints be destroyed. By law, a "criminal record" does not exist unless there has been a conviction, but, once taken, your finger-prints and photo could find their way into the files of the RCMP Identification Branch in Ottawa, regardless of the final disposition of the charge.

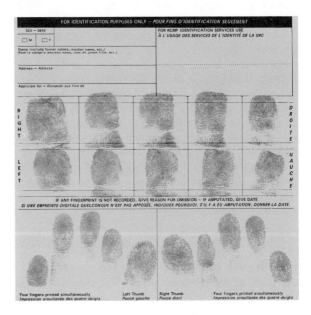

dence you drove erratically, staggered upon getting out of your car or that your speech was slurred.

On the decision of the constable on the spot, your driving license can be lifted for 24 hours.

PRIVATE POLICE

You were threatened with arrest unless you got off some property near the rail yards. The officer didn't look like a regular policeman.

Numerous private police forces exist in Canada and within their jurisdiction they can exercise all the duties of municipal police. The railway companies, the National Harbours Board and several universities, for example, maintain their own forces, sworn in as peace officers.

All police officers, private or regular, must carry official identification, and if you have any doubt about an officer's identity or authority, you should not hesitate to question either.

The uniformed security guards you often see about the city or at the airport are not peace officers. In the main, they act as agents of their employers, utilizing the powers of arrest contained in the Criminal Code and Petty Trespass Act. They have no power to do such things as control traffic on the public highway. A small number are sworn in as special constables to issue parking tickets.

Private detectives have no more power or authority than ordinary citizens, unless employed as agents to protect their employer's person or property.

GUN CONTROL

You have a World War I souvenir pistol at home; you wonder if that's legal.

In 1978, federal gun-control laws were tightened in the hope of reducing firearm deaths and preventing the easy availability of guns to criminals. Citizens, however, still have the right to possess firearms for lawful purposes. (*See* "Intruders" in Chapter 15.)

Since Jan. 1, 1979, a firearms acquisition certificate has been required for the purchase of any kind of gun, including sporting rifles and shotguns. (You aren't required to register or acquire a certificate if you owned a rifle or shotgun prior to that date.) Application forms for this certificate (and others required in connection with owning, carrying and conveying restricted weapons) are available from gun dealers or the local police.

Applicants for the basic acquisition certificate, who must be over 16, are checked out by police, who can refuse a permit for such things as an applicant's history of violent behavior, or conviction for a gun offense. The certificate costs $10, is valid for five years and allows the holder to purchase any number of guns.

Under the new legislation, courts have authority to prohibit the ownership of guns by "dangerous persons." Mandatory prison sentences are imposed for violations. Police can, in "threatening situations," search anywhere for weapons, without a warrant.

Your grandfather's pistol could be classed as a restricted weapon. (To be rated as an antique collector's item, it must have been manufactured before 1898 and must be incapable of discharging rimfire or centerfire ammunition.)

To possess such a restricted weapon, you need a registration certificate from your local police station. It's free but you won't get it easily. First you must be 18 or older and have the basic firearms acquisition certificate mentioned above. You must convince the police you need a gun to protect life where other protection is inadequate, or for your lawful occupation, or for target practice with an approved gun club, or to form part of a bona fide gun collection.

To transport a restricted weapon from one place to another, you need a special permit—even when you change your residence.

Fully automatic weapons, such as machine guns, and rifles or shotguns with sawed-off barrels, are prohibited. Exceptions are those which have been rendered inoperable in collections already registered with the RCMP.

3 You, the plaintiff

If you have been wronged, or if someone has caused injury to you or damage to your property, you have the right to seek compensation under the law. The many-layered system of the courts may seem impenetrable and unwelcoming, but in reality you can find your way about quite easily. It's your system—you pay for it with your taxes—and lawyers are readily available to guide and counsel you.

As the plaintiff, you bring a civil action against another party, the defendant, to get compensation for injury or damage you have suffered. If you prove your case, the wrongdoer will be forced to pay up. Don't expect to make money out of a suit. The financial punishment known as punitive or exemplary damages is rarely imposed.

Civil wrongs—they are known as "torts"—come in infinite variety. The most common actions arise from contracts, accidents, financial dealings, defamation of character, defective products or services, false arrest, neighborhood disputes and marital problems.

Small claims courts, sometimes called division courts, exist in six of the provinces, where you can argue your own case for compensation, up to certain limits. (In the Atlantic provinces such cases are heard in the regular courts.) But, except for relatively small, straightforward cases, your first move as a prospective plaintiff should be to consult a lawyer. Even lawyers hire other lawyers, recognizing that perspective is easily lost in the emotion of personal involvement.

If you hesitate to sue because of fears about legal costs you should broach that subject at your first meeting with your lawyer. He won't be embarrassed. Your provincial law society publishes a schedule of suggested fees, or will advise you privately. These are not binding on the lawyer members but will give you an idea of the basic cost. If you cannot afford a lawyer, get in touch with your nearest Legal Aid office or consumer-advice bureau. (*See* Section 10, "Effective complaining.")

The question of the legal and court costs of civil action always looms large. Devotees of detective novels and television crime drama may suggest that you find a lawyer who will agree to charge you only a percentage of the damages you collect. This is the "contingency fee" often used in the United States. In setting the fee, your Canadian lawyer will not work for a portion of the damages, although he can take into account the amount you recover, or he can agree not to charge a fee unless you recover damages.

Time is often crucial. You can lose your right to sue by not filing certain papers within a prescribed time limit. Deadlines for initiating legal actions vary widely—from seven days to more than two years. Your lawyer is responsible for seeing that your suit is properly presented, that all documents are prepared and served, that the evidence is gathered and evaluated. Shop around before purchasing legal services. It is said that any lawyer can win a good case, but just "any" lawyer may not be good enough to win your case.

You can help your lawyer, and yourself, by thinking about your proof from the earliest moment. Careful notes, photographs (of an accident), names and addresses of witnesses (if any), receipts for all expenditures, medical prescriptions and records—all of these can document your case. Memories are unreliable, and it may be many months before your case is heard.

Your lawyer's most valuable advice might be not to sue at all. The court is not the place for wounded pride, or revenge. Litigation is expensive, and even if you win you can't count on the court ordering the loser to pay your legal costs. You could wind up with a net loss. Consider this true story:

A little girl was standing beside a soft-drink

cooler when it exploded. She received minor burns. The total damages claimed amounted to $3,000. The law required that she (through her family) prove that the soft-drink company was negligent. An engineering firm, which specializes in tracing these things to the source for the purpose of litigation, said it would charge $2,500 for its investigation and report. Since the parents couldn't count on the court awarding this "cost," plus a lawyer's fee, they reluctantly decided against suing.

Similarly, wealthy persons or companies will not contest suits if the cost of winning is likely to exceed the amount claimed. Hence, the out-of-court settlement. If there is an important principle at stake, however, beware.

Suppose, for example, that your fuel tank exploded when your car was struck from behind by another vehicle, and you received severe burns. You sue for $10,000, pretty small change to a car manufacturer, yet the firm mounts an awesome defense. Unless you are financed by some consumer group or government agency, you might not be able to afford to do battle. The company will not readily permit any court anywhere to find against it in such a suit, which could open the floodgates to thousands of claims.

SHARED RESPONSIBILITY

You are suing for damages for your child, injured in a traffic accident. You are partly to blame for his injuries.

Let's say your 6-year-old son was in the front seat of your car and was not wearing a seat belt. You were driving on a through street and the defendant turned onto that street from a side street posted with a stop sign, so you are sure the accident was his fault. Yet you fear you may lose the case because you were traveling over the speed limit and had not ensured that the boy was wearing his seat belt. Besides, the defendant was charged in traffic court with failing to stop at a stop sign and found not guilty. He argued that he had stopped and then turned because he thought he had time to do so safely.

This mix of fact and event is not unusual in a suit for damages. In untangling the situation, your lawyer would point out:

■ The other driver's acquittal of failing to stop at a stop sign is not a bar to your child's claim. Having stopped, a driver must also yield the right of way to pedestrians and through traffic before proceeding through the intersection.

■ Your negligence does not necessarily prevent your child from recovering damages from the other driver. If the defendant was negligent to any degree, and if his negligence caused or contributed to your son's injury, he could be judged liable in some degree, even though you are found liable as well.

■ In the given circumstances, it is probably in the child's best interests to sue you, as well as the driver of the other car. Where seat belts are mandatory, you have a duty to see that a child under the age of 16 is fastened in. You were also speeding. A judge would assess the liability of each driver. He might decide that the defendant must pay 50 percent of the child's damages and you must pay the other half. (In Quebec, which has a no-fault insurance plan, injured persons claim through the automobile insurance board, not the courts.)

Your child (under age 18) cannot sue in his own name but must do so in the name of a "next friend" or, in Quebec, a tutor. Anyone 18 or older and mentally competent can be the "next friend." Ordinarily, your lawyer will suggest that you as the parent be the next friend. However, if your son brings a claim against you, someone else will be called to stand in for him since you would be considered to have an "adverse interest." (See Chapter 11, "Children in trouble.")

IMPARTIALITY

You believe that the judge hearing your case is a friend of the defendant and you fear you might not get a fair trial.

All judges in the higher courts are appointed by the governor general, acting for the federal cabinet; provincial court judges (or magistrates) are appointed by the lieutenant-governor of the province concerned, on the advice of the provincial cabinet. Appointments are to retirement age. In cases of misconduct, there are provisions for canceling a judge's appointment if he can't be persuaded to resign.

A judge who has any relationship with plaintiff or defendant must excuse himself from hearing the case. Notwithstanding this, if you have reasonable grounds for doubting his impartiality, your lawyer can petition to have your case heard by another judge.

The court system, step by step

Each of Canada's 10 provinces maintains a separate judicial system. Only the Supreme Court of Canada and the Federal Court (which handles suits against the government) lie outside provincial control. The federal government does, however, appoint and pay all judges except those on the lowest tier of the chart below.

The chart illustrates the ascending importance of our courts, whose names vary widely from province to province. The heavy line shows the route of appeal, ending at "the court of last resort."

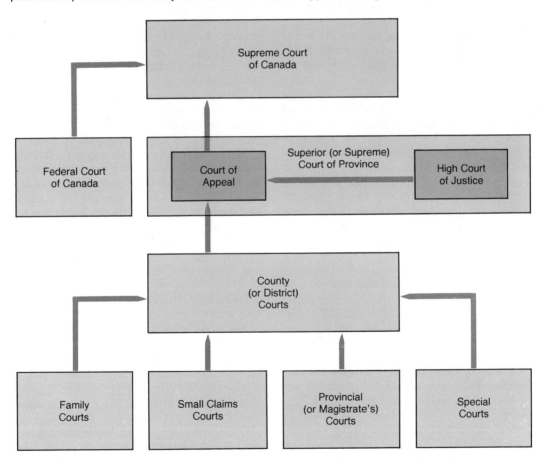

A century-old ruling by the New Brunswick Court of Appeal lays down the basic principle: "The slightest interest of a judge, pecuniary or otherwise, should stay his hand and prevent him from taking any part whatever in the decision of a cause unless there should be absolute necessity for his doing so, or some legislation expressly requiring he should act. . . . The honor, dignity and independence of the Bench demand that the remotest suspicion of bias on the part of the judge should be most scrupulously guarded against and most tenaciously avoided."

CHANGING LAWYERS

You suspect that your lawyer is handling your case improperly.

No doubt about it: some lawyers are better than others. If you feel that your case is not being presented effectively, you would be smart to change lawyers.

You can walk into your lawyer's office and demand your file, or go to another lawyer and ask him if he will take the case. If he agrees, he will obtain your file. A client's file belongs to the client and must be released once the lawyer's fee has been paid.

You're not likely to succeed if you seek a second lawyer's "opinion." Legal problems are different from medical problems, and most lawyers regard second opinions as tantamount to second-guessing a colleague.

A lawyer who is approached to take over a case from another lawyer will be very cautious. The problem might not be with the other lawyer, but with you, or with your case: You may have been told that you can expect $5,000 in damages for an injury, but you keep insisting on more; you simply may have refused to accept that you have a poor case.

If it's a question of delay, your lawyer may be doing all he can. There are dozens of things that can slow the wheels of justice. But your lawyer should be willing to explain the delays to you. In a sense, you are his patient and you have the right to know what the trouble is and what he proposes to do about it. After all, it's your money.

If you have difficulty finding a satisfactory replacement for your lawyer, you can get guidance from policemen, court officials and others who are familiar with the legal practitioners in your area. They will know which lawyers have experience in cases like yours. The law societies in British Columbia, Alberta, Manitoba, Ontario and Quebec provide referral services to people seeking counsel. Lawyers in some areas are winning the right to advertise.

The lawyer who handled your house purchase or prepared your will may not be a good choice to handle your suit, unless he also does lots of court work. Many lawyers never appear before a judge.

Do not rule out a lawyer simply because you think he will demand a stiff fee. Top lawyers will sometimes take on a case for a modest fee if they think it interesting or challenging, and there is probably as much social conscience among lawyers as there is in any profession.

Certain cases are not popular with lawyers. Claims against doctors can be hard to prove, claims against policemen are equally difficult, and can make a lawyer unpopular.

If you have a complaint against a lawyer, take it to the law society in your city or county. It is a self-governing profession but all law societies have a vested interest in maintaining standards of ethics and competence. They can discipline and even disbar members.

There is a public official in every large center who will settle disputes about overcharging. He is called the taxing officer or syndic.

STATUTE OF LIMITATIONS

You are told that you didn't act quickly enough and your suit cannot be heard.

All cases in the civil courts—that is, all cases except those involving criminal charges—must be started within a definite period. Your right to sue must be exercised within a prescribed time, because it is not fair to keep the threat of a suit hanging over a person's head indefinitely. Also memories dim with the passing of time, and documents get mislaid or destroyed if there's no apparent need for them to be kept.

If you feel you have been wronged and you want to seek a remedy in the courts, consult a lawyer as soon as possible. There may be plenty of time to lodge your suit, but the earliest briefing gives the lawyer the best chance of protecting your rights. This is particularly important if you are suing a public body, such as the police or a hospital.

A woman who was unable to file notice of a street accident within the required seven days—because she was unconscious in hospital—had her statement of claim rejected.

Another woman, injured when she tripped over broken pavement, did notify the city of the accident within seven days, but she lost any chance of recovering damages because she was not aware that her formal statement of claim had to be filed within 90 days of the incident.

The city's claims investigator had advised that she file "at the earliest possible date," but did not inform her specifically of the 90-day cutoff. When she presented her claim 10 months after the event, she was told it was too late to be considered. Efforts by her provincial legislature member to have the time limit waived revealed that the city's legal depart-

How to brief a lawyer

The word "brief" goes back to our legal inheritance from England. There, two kinds of lawyers are involved in a case. The first, the solicitor, deals with the plaintiff in the preliminary stages. He advises the client on the law, gathers the evidence, chooses the right court and takes care of the paperwork. But he almost never appears in court. This is the domain of the barrister.

Traditionally, the solicitor would prepare a summary of the case and take this to the Inns of Court in a folder, usually a leather-bound satchel (hence our "briefcase"). He would chalk a fee, agreed to by the client, on the outside. The barristers of the Inns would look over the "briefs" and decide which cases they were prepared to argue in the courts.

In Canada, a qualified lawyer may carry out all functions, although only a minority perform both roles. You should choose a lawyer experienced in your type of suit.

Everything a lawyer does for you will be charged for. A base charge of $100 an hour for the experienced lawyer is not unusual. The federal Combines Investigation Act does not permit pricing agreements among lawyers; the fee schedules drawn up by provincial law societies are suggested minimums.

You should take your lawyer fully into your confidence; professional ethics bind him to silence, and he must not attempt to profit financially from any information you disclose to him, without your permission. As an officer of the court, he is bound to serve not only his client, but the ends of justice. If he thinks you do not have a winning case, he must tell you so. He will do his best to get an out-of-court settlement. At least 90 percent of lawsuits never come to trial.

When you call at your lawyer's office, you should have all documents and other evidence with you. If you have to return another day, there will be another charge. Be brief and to the point, unless you want to pay a lawyer to listen to your opinions about politics and the cost of living.

The lawyer is under no obligation to accept your case. But once he does agree to represent you—probably after accepting a retainer fee—he is bound to do his utmost, within the law, to win for you.

He can withdraw from a case only under certain conditions laid down by the Bar Association, such as your refusal to advance enough money to get the case to court, or his conclusion that your case is fraudulent.

ment did not consider it had any duty to inform a claimant of the time limitation.

Tomorrow is too late. The statute of limitations (each province has one) lays down generous periods for suits concerning breach of contract, debt and negligence. In Ontario, for example, if you wish to sue a private individual or company for compensation for injuries received in an automobile accident, you must issue your writ within two years of the day of the accident. If you exceed the limitation period—even by one day—you are barred forever. The limitation relates to the day that you commence your suit, not to the date of the trial. In all jurisdictions there is some document that you must file in court to begin your action. In most provinces, a writ of summons or statement of claim must be presented to the clerk of the court in which you wish to sue.

Limitation periods run from a week to more than two years. Usually you have only six months to begin a suit against the Crown or the police; suits against doctors must usually be started within a year. Short limitation periods can trap the unwary. But once an action is begun, no court will allow it to be lost by reason of technical slips or omissions.

TAKING THE WITNESS STAND

The defendant's attorney confuses you during your testimony and you feel the truth has not come out at all.

Most citizens will never be called to the witness stand; yet, conditioned by dramatizations of courtroom battles, most get damp palms at the prospect of being cross-examined.

It is seldom like that in real life. Your lawyer has ample opportunity to help you set the record straight, and the presiding judge will make sure you are not browbeaten or tricked.

As the plaintiff—the injured party bringing the suit—the onus is on you to prove your case. You don't have to prove it absolutely—civil matters are less demanding of proof than criminal matters. It is sufficient to convince the judge or jury that, on the balance of prob-

abilities, your action should be maintained against the defendant. In a criminal case, however, the plaintiff—the Crown—must remove any reasonable doubt in the minds of the judge or jury as to the accused's guilt.

Examination of witnesses begins when your lawyer calls a witness and examines him "in chief"; the defendant's counsel is then permitted to cross-examine, and finally your lawyer may ask the witness to qualify or clarify his answers. Then the process is reversed, with the defense calling its witnesses.

The side calling a witness cannot attempt to discredit his testimony, because it has implied to the court that the witness is honest and reliable. Nor can words be put in the witness's mouth by leading questions. No such restrictions are put on the cross-examining counsel who can lead a witness, contradict him, and ask him questions aimed at raising doubts about his bias, reliability and honesty.

However, suppose a friend of the defendant has knowledge that would greatly strengthen your case. The defendant's lawyer will not call him as a witness, for the obvious reason that his testimony would hurt rather than help the defendant's case. If you call him as a witness, he is unlikely to be forthcoming with evidence that would be detrimental to his friend, and your lawyer will not be able to bring out such evidence without cross-examination. Under these circumstances, and subject to the applicable provincial act on civil evidence or procedure, you have the right to call the witness and to have the court declare him "hostile," so that your lawyer may cross-examine him.

The "adversary system." Witnesses often suspect that the other party's lawyer is trying to confuse them or to show that they are lying. Sometimes he is, but most often he is trying to establish that you do not know what you are talking about.

Most of us haven't the powers of observation, memory and analysis we think we have, and few of us admit to any prejudices. If our evidence is challenged and we look bad, we tend to overlook our shortcomings and blame our poor showing on clever but unscrupulous lawyers. A witness can testify only about things he knows "of his own knowledge," not about what others have told him—that's called "hearsay."

In the end, the witness does tell his story, whether or not he realizes it. Some witnesses leave the court feeling that they have been manipulated or put down. Others leave with a sense of triumph. The disgruntled witness may, in fact, have done a good job, while the triumphant witness may be totally ignorant of the fact that he has been quietly discredited.

Some witnesses fall into the trap of feeling obliged to make a good showing on the stand, often at the expense of accuracy, and sometimes of truth. Reluctant to say "I don't know" or to admit a slip, they may exaggerate or even lie.

A famous barrister once wrote: "No one can frequent our courts of justice for any length of time without finding himself aghast at the daily spectacle presented by seemingly honest and intelligent men and women who array themselves upon opposite sides of a case and testify under oath to what appear to be absolutely contradictory statements of fact."

How to sue for your money

A legal right is not much comfort without a corresponding legal remedy. You have the right to payment for work done, services or goods supplied, or compensation ("damages") for injury or loss suffered through the action of another. If you can't collect any small sum due to you (the maximum varies across the country), your remedy may lie in the Small Claims Court.

You don't need a lawyer to file your claim or to conduct your suit. You do need invoices, receipts or other evidence to prove your case. The court officials will assist you in filling out the required simple forms—such as this statement of claim.

Newsome and Gilbert Limited
STATEMENT OF CLAIM

IN THE FIRST SMALL CLAIMS COURT OF THE COUNTY OF HASTINGS

BETWEEN:

RICHARD A. ROE   Plaintiff or
_____   Primary Creditor
                            AND

SAMUEL SNOW   Defendant or
_____   Primary Debtor
                            AND

_____   Garnishee

The above named Plaintiff or Primary Creditor claims from the above Defendant or Primary Debtor the sum of five hundred and thirty dollars and no cents

($ 530.00   ) as per details below.

The plaintiff performed repairs to the roof of the defendant's home at 100 Maple Street, Stirling, Ontario, on March 1 and 2, 1979, at the request of the defendant. The plaintiff supplied roofing materials at a cost of $350 and 12 hours of labor at the agreed hourly rate of $15.

The Plaintiff or Primary Creditor further claims from the Defendant or Primary Debtor the costs of the within action.

Dated at Belleville, Ontario
this   first   day of   September
               A.D. 19 79

SMALL CLAIMS COURT

You want to collect a $300 debt, but you're not quite sure how to proceed.

The judicial system is not just for the "big guy." You enjoy an undoubted right to recover money or goods owing to you, no matter how small the value, and six provinces have set up a simple legal machine to help you do so. It is usually known as the Small Claims Court, but the names vary across the land. (In the four Atlantic provinces, special provisions are made to handle small claims in regular courts.)

A recent survey of Ontario's small claims courts (sometimes called division courts) revealed that most suits were by corporations or debt-collection agencies. Only 3 percent were lodged by individuals. In contrast, Quebec bars lawyers and corporations from its small claims courts, where all claims have to be lodged by individuals.

These courts resolve money claims (up to $2,000 in P.E.I.) and also disputes over the recovery of goods, the quality of work done or services performed, arrears of rent and acts of negligence (including vehicle accident claims). They will not hear actions for libel or slander, seduction, breach of promise, recovery of land, or conflicts over pensions or wills. They will not issue injunctions. These actions are heard at higher levels.

Fees (ranging from 50 cents to $30) are paid when you lodge your claim, but if you win, they are added to the costs to be paid by the other party.

Getting a judgment is one thing, collecting the money due is another. If the debt is not paid within the time prescribed, the plaintiff can ask for certain actions against the debtor. These include garnishing of up to 30 percent of wages, and the seizure and sale of assets. The debtor would probably be brought before the court to explain the nonpayment. In Canada there is no imprisonment for debt.

No lawyer required. Informality is the keynote of a Small Claims Court. The judge, however, is still addressed as "Your Honor" and will demand reasonable decorum.

Lawyers are generally reluctant to represent individuals in Small Claims Court because their fees will usually exceed the amount in dispute. The judge and court staff will help you present your case, but not to the point of appearing to be unfair to the other party. No one can be both advocate and judge in the same case.

However sympathetic the court may be toward the unsophisticated claimant, the basic rules apply. You must first lodge two statements of claim, stating the last-known name and address of the defendant, and setting out clearly both the amount owed and exactly why it is owed.

The defendant is then given 10 days to file a "dispute," stating whatever reasons there are for nonpayment. If this rejoinder is not forthcoming, the plaintiff will be granted a default judgment without the necessity of a trial.

If the claim is disputed, the trial proceeds. Testimony can include witnesses, documents and photographs. Even though the judge may admit evidence in a form frowned upon in higher courts, it still must serve as reasonable proof of your claim.

If, as the defendant, you feel the plaintiff also owes you money as often happens in minor traffic accidents when both vehicles suffer some damage—file a counterclaim with your dispute. This, in effect, makes you a plaintiff also. The judge will decide the matter—perhaps by reducing the original plaintiff's claim by the amount of your counterclaim.

What if you alone are named in the summons but you believe another person is wholly or partly responsible? In that case, you have to enter a third-party claim with the clerk of the court. Once again, you have changed from the defendant to the plaintiff. The third party will be served a summons and a copy of your claim against him. The judge will sort out the whole issue at the one trial.

4 You, the defendant

Criminal charges for serious (indictable) offenses can be laid under any of the 773 sections of the Canadian Criminal Code (which applies equally in all parts of the country) or under several other federal statutes. Charges for less serious (summary) criminal offenses can be laid under provincial laws and municipal bylaws, which, of course, vary from place to place. You acquire a "criminal record" if you're convicted under the Criminal Code, the Narcotic Control Act, or the Food and Drugs Act, regardless of whether the offense was indictable or summary. The record is tied to you by your name and a number—and your photograph and fingerprints, if you were charged with an indictable offense.

Some five million offenses, excluding several million parking violations, were recorded in the last census year. Even allowing for the numerous cases where the defendants face more than one charge, this means that a disturbingly high percentage of Canadians get into worse trouble than illegal parking. The list of indictable offenses includes treason, murder, breaking and entering, escaping from jail, assault with intent to commit bodily harm, serious sexual offenses, most charges relating to weapons and narcotics, theft, fraud and false pretenses involving more than $200.

Many offenses under the Criminal Code can be either indictable or summary at the option of the Crown prosecutor. Things were simpler when all crimes were divided into the old common law classifications of treason, felony or misdemeanor. (These are still used in the United States and other countries abroad.) The Canadian summary offense is close kin to the misdemeanor.

Summary offenses are heard in Magistrate's or Provincial Court. (See "The court system, step by step" in Chapter 3.) Maximum penalties are a $500 fine and six months' imprisonment. The most serious indictable offenses (murder and rape) must be tried in the highest courts (Supreme, Superior, Queen's Bench, High Court, depending on province), and penalties can range up to life imprisonment. Almost all these cases are heard by judge and jury—except in Alberta, where the accused can waive the right to a jury.

Some of the less serious indictable offenses are tried in the lower courts, but again Alberta is an exception: there, all indictable offenses are heard in Supreme Court.

If an offense does not fall within the exclusive jurisdiction of either level of court, the accused may "elect" to be heard by the magistrate or provincial judge without jury, or by a High Court judge, with or without jury. If the accused elects High Court, there is a preliminary hearing to determine whether there is enough evidence to warrant a trial.

Your liberty or your pocketbook, or both, are at stake whenever you are charged with an offense. It's advisable to have a lawyer to defend you. Legal Aid is available without charge for those who pass the means test.

About 80 percent of all those charged with crimes plead guilty. In some instances, a lawyer succeeds in getting a charge reduced before trial and advises his client to plead guilty to the lesser charge. This is called plea bargaining and there's no corruption involved. It won't happen as a favor. Justice will still be served. It may suit the Crown to reduce the charge if the case against you is watertight on the lesser charge but a bit shaky on the greater. Maybe the court is facing a huge backlog of cases and you've already suffered during the wait for trial. A remorseful accused who helps the police with his own case or with others may be rewarded with a reduction of the charge against him.

If you plead guilty, the judge will ask the Crown prosecutor to outline the facts of the case. If the judge is not satisfied that your guilty plea is warranted, he can set aside your plea and order a trial.

If the prosecutor presents new evidence, making the offense appear more serious, you have a right to challenge. You can demand he bring his witnesses and evidence to court so you can cross-examine. You can also intervene if the prosecutor leaves out facts that would be in your favor.

THE SUMMONS

You receive a summons to appear in court on a charge which you think was trumped up by a hostile neighbor.

Your rights are not diminished just because a criminal charge is laid against you. In fact, our judicial system is weighted in favor of the accused, who must get the benefit of any reasonable doubt. A judge will enter a not-guilty plea on behalf of any accused whom he thinks confused or badly advised.

But you must obey the order to appear in court; if you fail to do so, the judge will issue a warrant for your arrest. The onus will then be on you to show why you should be released from custody.

Provided you can satisfy the court that you will appear and that you will not break any law in the meantime, you might be released on your own recognizance, or on bail. Otherwise, you will be jailed ("remanded in custody") until your trial. You may now face the extra charge of "failing to appear" which could be a more serious offense than the one you chose to ignore. Acquittal of the original charge will not be a defense for failing to appear.

If the Crown prosecutor agrees that the charge against you is without grounds, the case will be dropped. If the trial proceeds and the charge is found to be without substance, it will be dismissed. You might then consider suing your difficult neighbor if malicious prosecution seems apparent.

The civil summons. A few months ago you were involved in an automobile accident. You have just been notified that the other driver is suing you for damages. You think the accident was not your fault so you decide to ignore the summons. You will not be arrested, or forced by any other means to appear. But your failure to appear will be taken as an indication that you do not wish to defend the action, and the plaintiff may get a judgment against you.

The plaintiff can take further proceedings to collect the amount owing under the judgment, plus interest. He can get an order compelling you to attend at the courthouse and be examined under oath about your income and assets. He may get permission to garnishee your wages, or seize your bank account or goods—even your house.

If you receive a summons from the Small Claims Court and a statement of claim naming you as defendant, you have the right to dispute the whole or part of the claim, to file a counterclaim or to settle the debt out of court (but plus the court costs).

If you owe only part of the sum claimed, pay the lesser amount into the court within 10 days and file a dispute over the remainder.

Perhaps you admit the debt but are strapped for ready cash. In that case, offer installment payments to be paid directly or to the clerk of the court. There may be a public referee in your judicial district who will help you work out this kind of arrangement.

If you feel the plaintiff or a third party also owes you money, file a counterclaim with your defense. This makes you a plaintiff also. (*See* "Small Claims Court" in Chapter 3.)

PUBLICITY

You are charged with a crime that you did not commit. Proving your innocence will require disclosures that could embarrass your family or perhaps cost you your job.

You must decide whether the consequences of pleading guilty outweigh the effects of proving your innocence.

Consult a capable criminal lawyer and make a clean breast of all the circumstances relating to the charge, no matter how incrimi-

Private enterprise at the Bar

Legal Aid plans exist in all provinces to ensure that no one charged with a criminal offense goes undefended because of poverty. Counsel may be provided in some civil suits as well. Applicants who meet income qualifications will be represented by a Legal Aid lawyer, or by their choice of any lawyer participating in the plan, depending on the province.

Quebec has more than 300 salaried public defenders. Quebec applicants may choose between a public defender or a private lawyer who will be reimbursed by the government.

Other provincial governments, beset with complaints about the quality of counsel under present Legal Aid plans, are evaluating the Quebec public defender system. Law reform activists claim the present plans are ignored by the most qualified and experienced lawyers, who are reluctant to accept the modest fees.

The "duty-counsel"—a lawyer paid by Legal Aid—is present at most provincial courts to advise defendants. He may see as many as 40 "clients" in a day, most of whom plead guilty. About 80 percent of all criminal cases are already partly or wholly paid for by Legal Aid.

"Public defender" has a noble ring, but critical lawyers point out that such appointees are really civil servants who extend state control over the justice system: judges, court officials, prosecutors and police are already paid by the state.

If the public defender idea does spread nationwide, who would apply for the jobs? In the main, say the law societies, exactly the less-experienced lawyers who handle most of the Legal Aid work now. The glamorous stars of the criminal courts are hardly likely to give up their six-figure incomes.

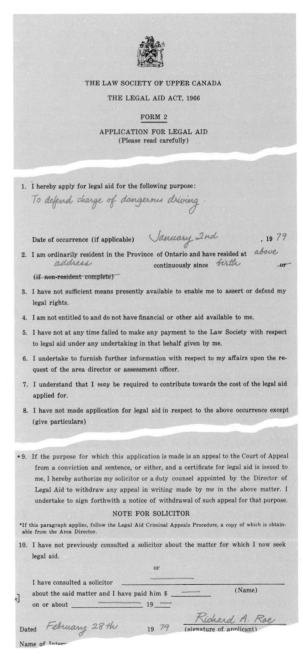

THE LAW SOCIETY OF UPPER CANADA

THE LEGAL AID ACT, 1966

FORM 2

APPLICATION FOR LEGAL AID
(Please read carefully)

1. I hereby apply for legal aid for the following purpose:

   To defend charge of dangerous driving.

   Date of occurrence (if applicable) *January 2nd*, 19 *79*

2. I am ordinarily resident in the Province of Ontario and have resided at *above address* continuously since *birth* ~~or~~
   (if non-resident complete)

3. I have not sufficient means presently available to enable me to assert or defend my legal rights.

4. I am not entitled to and do not have financial or other aid available to me.

5. I have not at any time failed to make any payment to the Law Society with respect to legal aid under any undertaking in that behalf given by me.

6. I undertake to furnish further information with respect to my affairs upon the request of the area director or assessment officer.

7. I understand that I *may* be required to contribute towards the cost of the legal aid applied for.

8. I have not made application for legal aid in respect to the above occurrence except (give particulars)

*9. If the purpose for which this application is made is an appeal to the Court of Appeal from a conviction and sentence, or either, and a certificate for legal aid is issued to me, I hereby authorize my solicitor or a duty counsel appointed by the Director of Legal Aid to withdraw any appeal in writing made by me in the above matter. I undertake to sign forthwith a notice of withdrawal of such appeal for that purpose.

NOTE FOR SOLICITOR

*If this paragraph applies, follow the Legal Aid Criminal Appeals Procedure, a copy of which is obtainable from the Area Director.

10. I have not previously consulted a solicitor about the matter for which I now seek legal aid.

or

I have consulted a solicitor _____

about the said matter and I have paid him $ _____ (Name)

on or about _____ 19 ____

Dated *February 28th* 19 *79*   *Richard A. Roe*
                              (signature of applicant)

Name of Inter

nating or embarrassing they may seem. If he is convinced of your innocence, he will attempt to persuade the Crown prosecutor to withdraw the charge.

Don't expect the prosecutor to do you a favor—even to save your marriage or job. However, if he is reliably informed that you may be innocent, he might ask the police to investigate further before proceeding with the charge.

If the Crown refuses to withdraw the charge, you must face a trial—or plead guilty.

Criminal courts must be open to the public. The only exceptions are courts convened under the Official Secrets Act.

A judge has some discretion about hearing evidence in camera, especially in a morals case, but no court can compel anyone to refrain from publishing its proceedings. During the preliminary hearing, called the *enquête préliminaire* in Quebec, evidence may not be published if the accused requests this.

Don't ask a reporter or editor to withhold your name from court proceedings. If you do, you risk additional publicity about your attempt to pressure the press. And never, never offer a bribe—that will guarantee you a headline.

TESTIFYING

You fear that if you testify with complete frankness in your own defense, you run the risk of additional charges.

As the accused in a criminal trial you cannot be compelled to give evidence, but if you do testify you will have to answer all the questions put to you by the Crown prosecutor.

Any witness in a criminal trial can seek the qualified protection of the Canada Evidence Act. He must answer, but the testimony cannot be used against him. However, he can be charged with perjury if the "protected" evidence is false. Refusal to answer a question on the direction of a judge can be contempt of court ("obstructing justice"), a serious offense which can bring immediate imprisonment.

Tampering with witnesses. Attempts to obstruct justice by dissuading, threatening or bribing a witness (or anyone else concerned with the trial), or altering evidence, are dealt with severely.

It is equally a crime for any witness or juror to seek or accept a bribe, and no one can be paid a fee or commission for providing bail for an accused.

Protection of witnesses. The most common form of evidence offered in the courts is the testimony of witnesses. This kind of "proof" is so important to the dispensing of justice that only the Queen is exempt from the *subpoena*. This Latin term describes the writs of summons issued by a court demanding the appearance of the person addressed to give testimony ("subpoena ad testificandum"), or to produce documentary or other evidence ("subpoena duces tecum").

If you fear that you or your family might be in danger because of evidence you may be ordered to give in court, talk to a lawyer or to the police. There is a process for protecting key witnesses.

Certain relationships are regarded as privileged and can justify a refusal to testify. The most common is the confidential relationship between client and lawyer.

Confidentiality of communication between a person and a priest, minister or other religious adviser is guaranteed only in Quebec and Newfoundland. The Crown is never eager, however, to compel such testimony.

Journalists have begun demanding the right not to reveal their sources. Courts refuse to grant this and holdouts have been jailed for contempt of court.

MURDER OR MANSLAUGHTER

You get into a fight at a disco and a man dies. You had no intention of injuring anyone but you are charged with murder.

Since 1976, Canada has recognized two kinds of murder: first-degree (premeditated) murder carries a mandatory sentence of 25 years' imprisonment; second-degree (unpremeditated) murder, a mandatory 10-year sentence. A mandatory term is the minimum a judge can impose for the specific offense. Such sentences, however, can be reduced by decisions of the National Parole Board. Capital punishment (by hanging) was abolished in 1976.

A death caused in the heat of passion, without any intention to kill, may be classified as manslaughter. The Crown prosecutor will decide. The punishment can range from a suspended sentence to life imprisonment.

The disco death described contains the basic ingredients for a charge of second-degree murder or manslaughter. The law of homicide is complex, and simplifications are dangerous. Assault with intent to cause bodily harm that the attacker should know could result in death is murder. But if the aggressor didn't mean to kill or didn't know that his act could cause death, the deed is probably manslaughter.

Fighting off the ice. In a 1977 Ontario case, a young man was charged with manslaughter after he killed another youth with a kick. Accused and victim, players in a minor league hockey game, had been ejected for fighting. Outside the arena, the accused challenged his opponent to fight but was refused. He then kicked his victim in the stomach. The blow was fatal.

The accused was black and it was alleged he had been subjected to racial taunts during the game. This did not alter the facts and he was convicted of manslaughter.

In Saskatchewan in 1976, the accused in a manslaughter case testified that the victim invited him to "come outside." He maintained that he did not know why. Once outside, the victim verbally abused him and attempted to hit him.

The accused then struck his attacker, who went down and later died. The accused offered two defenses to the charge: first, that he was acting in self-defense; and, second, since the two had agreed to fight, his act was not criminally negligent. He had not caused death by an unlawful act. The court agreed.

Death of a burglar. A householder intercepted a burglar, whom he repeatedly struck on the head with a rifle butt. The housebreaker died of his injuries and the householder was charged with murder. The Crown claimed that while the accused did not intend the death of his victim, he did intend to cause him bodily harm likely to cause death, and that he was reckless whether death ensued or not.

The householder was convicted of murder but he appealed and was granted a new trial. The appeal court judges ruled that jurors must be instructed that not only must they be satisfied beyond reasonable doubt that the accused intended to cause bodily harm, but also that he knew that the bodily harm was likely to cause death. The prosecution must prove there was "criminal intent." The fact that the accused did intend to cause bodily harm is not enough for a murder conviction. A jury must be satisfied that the accused knew that the injury was likely to cause death.

Each case of homicide really turns on its own facts and the best advice is, stay out of fights. As Oscar Wilde said: "Conscience and cowardice are really the same things."

COURT INTERPRETERS

Even though your mother tongue is Italian, you can speak a fair amount of English. You are accused of shoplifting and the judge refuses your request for an interpreter.

If you are on trial and you don't understand what's going on, you are entitled to have an interpreter. Normally, this is arranged in advance by your lawyer. Your choice is not narrowed to either English or French. Canada is a country of 46 recognized ethnic origins. The right to have an interpreter is quite distinct from any right to have the proceedings conducted in English or French, Canada's "official languages."

Every accused has the right to answer any charge in court and this implies that he or she fully understands all that is being said.

Since Confederation, an accused in Quebec Provincial Court has had the choice of being tried in English or French. New Brunswick, the only province officially bilingual (since 1969), has offered the choice of trial language since 1972 and Ontario did the same in 1979. Federal courts have always been bilingual.

Under the Official Languages Act (1970), all federal court decisions, and certain orders and regulations, are to be made or issued in both official languages. In the National Capital Region (Ottawa and Hull), and in federally designated bilingual districts, government services are to be available in both languages.

Under the Canadian Bill of Rights, no one can be deprived "of the right to the assistance of an interpreter in any proceedings in which he is a party or a witness before a court, commission, board or other tribunal if he does not understand or speak the language in which such proceedings are conducted."

According to the Bill, "every law of Canada, unless there is express alleviation by Parliament, shall be construed and applied so as not to deprive a person of the right to the assistance of an interpreter in any proceedings" in which he is a party.

If the judge refuses. If the judge at your trial is satisfied that you speak English adequately, he may deny you an interpreter. If you disagree with this decision, you might obtain a prerogative writ. This order, issued through a provincial High Court judge, is a command to do or cease doing something. In this instance it could be an order prohibiting the trial judge in a lower court from proceed-

ing with your case until the interpreter question is thrashed out.

If your case is being heard in the High Court (Supreme, Superior or Queen's Bench), you will not be able to obtain a prerogative writ. Your only remedy will be by way of an appeal at the end of your trial.

BAIL

You are arrested on an assault charge and refused bail.

After being arrested and charged, you have the right to be freed "on bail" (it's now called "judicial interim release") within 24 hours, unless the police can convince the sitting justice of the peace (J.P.) or magistrate that you should be kept in the cells. The onus is not on you to show why you should be released.

Only people charged with an indictable offense can be fingerprinted and photographed by police.

The two main arguments for imprisonment pending trial are that you may simply take off or that you are too dangerous to be at large. If you foolishly threatened to "get" a prosecution witness or if you are likely to commit another crime while at large, you may well be refused bail.

Bail requires that you, or someone who

Four powerful writs

The prerogative writ is a citizen's first defense against arbitrary or unfair action by the "powers that be." The four most common prerogative writs are:

Habeas corpus. A command that you must be brought before a judge forthwith so that the lawfulness of your custody will be considered. If you are being held unlawfully, you will be released.

Prohibition. This commands someone not to proceed further with a particular matter—per-

haps a trial in a provincial court, or before any kind of tribunal.

Certiorari. This order will quash a finding or order made by a lower court or tribunal.

Mandamus. This is in the form of a command directed to any servant of the Queen to do something—it could be just about anything. A writ of mandamus can force a judge to do something he is supposed, by law, to do, such as hear certain evidence that he may be refusing to hear, or permit you to have an interpreter.

trusts you, put up a sum of money set by the court guaranteeing your good behavior while awaiting trial and your attendance in court on the trial date. If you fail to show up, or get into further trouble in the meantime, you or your bondsman will forfeit the money.

The court rarely requires cash bail. The police officer in charge can grant bail of up to $500. He, too, does not necessarily demand that you produce the cash.

If you are arrested and refused bail, you may ask for a review by a higher court. These hearings are usually conducted quickly.

Suspects in minor cases are seldom taken to the police station today. The arresting officer issues a summons on the spot ordering you to appear in court on a given date.

ASSAULT BY OTHER PRISONERS

While you are a prisoner in the city lockup you are homosexually assaulted by older prisoners.

The stark fact that you are in jail does not impair your right to the protection of the law. Even though homosexual acts between consenting adults in private are not illegal, any such act by force is classed as indecent assault, punishable by up to 10 years' imprisonment.

The victim should demand an immediate medical examination and an interview with a lawyer, who will probably lay an "information" before a justice of the peace or magistrate naming the person or persons responsible. A police investigation should follow.

If you have been injured, you can bring a civil suit for damages against either the prisoners who attacked you or the prison itself or both. The common law requires jailers to take reasonable care of their prisoners. If prison officials were not properly supervising inmates, they may have breached their duty of care toward you. (*See* "Statute of limitations" in Chapter 3.)

As a victim of crime you may be entitled to compensation under the provincial plans which exist everywhere except in Nova Scotia and Prince Edward Island. (*See* "Victims of crime" in Chapter 1.)

BEFORE AND AFTER A TRIAL

Your community and the local press have been in an uproar about your case and you've received anonymous threats. You don't think you'll get a fair trial.

Counsel for the accused, or the Crown prosecutor, may request the judge to move the trial to another place, when there is concern about finding an impartial jury.

The courts are usually reluctant to grant such changes, because the accused can challenge and reject prospective jurors whom he thinks may be prejudiced against him. To win a change of venue, you must establish a probability of prejudice to such a degree that your right of challenge will not give you sufficient protection.

Although most accused are tried in the county or district where the offense was committed, the law permits a criminal case to be heard by any court in the land empowered to deal with crimes of that type.

How the jury is chosen. Except for members of certain groups, all adults between voting age and age 70 are liable to be called for jury duty—one of the highest duties in the democratic state. A juror gets a modest daily fee ($6 to $25) plus expenses.

Names are chosen from voters' lists or assessment rolls. When a court sitting includes jury trials, a large number of prospective jurors are called and they must appear for selection. In nine provinces, a criminal jury consists of 12 members; Alberta and the Territories require only six.

As the court sitting commences, the persons summoned for jury duty come in and sit in the courtroom. The clerk of the court then draws names by lot and the prospective jurors come forward. The defendant may now challenge those selected, either peremptorily or for cause. A peremptory challenge is simply saying, without offering any reason, that you do not want a person as a juror.

The number of peremptory challenges allowed varies. A person accused of first-degree murder is entitled to challenge 20 jurors peremptorily. For offenses that carry a sentence of imprisonment for more than five years, the accused is entitled to 12 peremptory challenges. For other offenses, the number is four.

An accused may also challenge any number of jury candidates for cause. You must make a specific allegation—bias, mental illness, drunkenness or a physical infirmity such as deafness—against the individual.

If you challenge for cause, a hearing must take place. It will be presided over by two of the jurors already chosen or, if two have not yet been chosen, from persons selected from the jury panel.

The prosecution has certain challenge rights also, including the one of "standing aside" up to 48 jurors. Whole groups—women, for example—may be stood aside.

New trials and appeals. If, after the jury is chosen, you learn that one member may be hostile, it's too late. If the jury finds you guilty, sentence will be passed upon you. If it

When your debt to society is paid

A crime occurs and the offender is convicted and punished. But even after the debt is paid, the record of that conviction limits one's career and travel opportunities. The Criminal Records Act provides a way for the rehabilitated offender to clean the slate and start afresh.

Anyone convicted of a federal offense—all crimes are "federal"—can apply to the National Parole Board in Ottawa for a pardon. For a provincial violation, contact the attorney-general of your province. Investigation will take some eight months.

Eligibility depends on the length of time since your sentence was served. For a minor offense (summary conviction), the waiting time is two years. For the more serious (indictable) offenses, it's five years.

If you are not sure where you stand, send in the application form at right anyway. Inquiries will be conducted discreetly—people contacted are not told the purpose of the inquiry. If there's anyone who might hold a grudge against you, be sure to note that in your application.

cannot agree on a verdict, it's a "hung jury." There will be a new trial and you will have to go through the entire process again.

If you're found guilty, your lawyer can appeal to a higher court, but only on points of law or a combination of points of law and fact, not because you have new evidence. Your case will not be retried in the appeal, which is an examination by more senior jurists of the legal correctness of your trial. The Crown prosecutor can also appeal the result on a question of law alone. Either side can appeal the sentence as too harsh or too light.

Stage by stage, at ever-increasing cost, appeals (on questions of law) against convictions for indictable offenses can continue to the apex of our judicial system, the Supreme Court of Canada, sitting in Ottawa.

OBSTRUCTION

There was a near-riot at a protest rally. You were only watching on the sidelines but the police arrested you along with a dozen others.

The primary duty of law enforcement officers is to preserve the public peace. Everyone has seen outnumbered policemen struggling with militant strikers, students, demonstrators, un-ruly sports fans, rock concert mobs, even normally stolid farmers seeking higher produce prices. When fists and sticks are swinging, mistakes are easily made.

But your accusers are going to have to offer evidence that you committed an offense. You cannot be found guilty by association.

If all you did was watch, or even cheer, you can't be convicted. On the other hand, if, by standing there, you were blocking a policeman who was attempting to carry out his lawful duty, you may well be found guilty of obstruction.

Better go along quietly. In some cases, police are permitted to make arrests on reasonable grounds of suspicion; they don't have to be right—that's for the courts to decide. (*See* "Arrest" in Chapter 2.)

Never resist arrest, even if a mistake is being made. The police can use any force that may be necessary to subdue you and you'll almost certainly face a more serious charge than obstruction.

Protest and the right of free assembly are precious elements of the democratic society, and as long as public order is maintained, police have a duty to make sure everyone is able to exercise these rights. Which is why they sometimes find themselves protecting neo-Nazis and others from outraged citizens who try to curtail their rights.

5 The question of morals

The law governing morals in Canada is a labyrinth of contradictions and confusion. And for almost two decades, criminal conduct in this sphere has been increasingly measured against "contemporary community standards." But against the shifting social mores in modern Canada, "community standards" are not always easily determined.

Reformers press constantly for ever-wider liberalization of the Criminal Code. There is continuing debate on whether or not prostitution, homosexuality and the use of marijuana and other narcotics should be legalized, and on what is and is not obscene.

The Law Reform Commission of Canada recommends that incest between consenting adults be no longer a crime, and that the maximum penalty for rape be reduced from life imprisonment to 10 years.

Many people believe that the state has no more business in publishing or movie houses than it has in the bedrooms of the nation. They would permit hard-core pornography in our magazines and explicit sex and violence in our films. Opponents urge stricter government censorship, some even demanding that W. O. Mitchell's *Who Has Seen the Wind* be banned from schools because someone in the book says "goddam." Yet the nation's highest literary honor, the Governor General's Award, has been presented to Marian Engel for *Bear*, a novel in which a librarian enjoys repeated sexual acts with the title character.

There is an ongoing battle to legalize the use of cannabis (marijuana or "pot"), an offense for which thousands of young Canadians hold criminal records.

The smuggling of cannabis into the country, and its undercover sale, is a huge and very profitable business that shows no sign of slackening. In 1979, for example, the Ontario Ministry of Education found that more than 33 percent of 9,000 high-school students surveyed had used or were using marijuana or hashish; in Grade 12, it was 41 percent. In British Columbia that year, some 10,000 heroin users committed a wide range of crimes to buy drugs worth about $250 million.

Meanwhile, varying public attitudes on everything from nudity to abortion, and a general disagreement on an acceptable moral code, affect morality law enforcement. The police are reluctant to lay charges which the courts consistently dismiss.

POSSESSION OF DRUGS

Your teen-age son is caught with a small quantity of marijuana in his pocket.

The possession of any amount of a prohibited drug is a crime. If the police find even a single joint (marijuana cigarette), they have no alternative but to charge your son.

The Narcotic Control Act and the Food and Drugs Act control the use and distribution of drugs. Both laws impose heavy penalties on traffickers (importers, manufacturers and distributors) of proscribed or restricted drugs. The maximum is life imprisonment.

Drugs proscribed by the Narcotic Control Act include heroin, cocaine, marijuana and hashish. The Food and Drugs Act restricts methamphetamine (speed), lysergic acid diethylamide (LSD) and barbiturates such as Nembutal and Seconal. Possession of a controlled drug is not an offense if the drug was prescribed by your physician for your use. Cocaine, heroin, morphine, LSD and speed are described as "hard" drugs, whereas marijuana and hashish are commonly regarded as "soft" (less detrimental).

The use of LSD and speed has declined since the 1960s while marijuana and cocaine are increasingly popular. The tranquilizers

Valium and Librium are the largest-selling drugs in Canada. Most tranquilizers are obtained by prescription so their black market trade is small.

Confusion in the courts. The teen-ager convicted on a first-offense charge of simple possession of marijuana could be fined $1,000, jailed for six months, or both. For a second offense, the maximum penalties are doubled.

But such penalties are unlikely, and would cause a public outcry if imposed. In a typical Magistrate's Court today, the accused would be discharged without suffering a material penalty.

If the youth had no previous record and was living at home and attending school or college, he would probably get an absolute discharge. If he (or she) was living alone, a conditional discharge would be granted. Conditions might include six months' probation, during which the offender would have to report periodically to a probation officer.

On a second conviction, a small fine (say $50) might be imposed.

If a discharge is granted, the charge is recorded but no conviction is registered. If the offender stays out of trouble for 12 months, he can apply to have the charge wiped from the files.

Possession of a "hard" drug would be dealt with much more firmly. The maximum penalty is seven years' imprisonment. However, a first-time offender would likely get off with a $100 fine if only a small quantity of the drug was involved.

Proving possession. To get a conviction for possession, the police must prove who actually had possession of the drugs. Suppose your son is one of several youths in a neighbor's house when the police find marijuana on the kitchen table. If nobody admits ownership, the only person against whom there would be a reasonable chance of conviction is the person who owns or occupies the house and, as such, has control over what goes on inside his house. But the prosecution would have to prove that the person or persons charged knew that the drug was marijuana, had some measure of control over it, and consented to its being there.

TRAFFICKING IN DRUGS

You suspect that your neighbor's layabout son is selling drugs.

Any person convicted of trafficking in drugs or of possession for the purpose of trafficking will be fined and probably sent to jail. The penalty will depend on his previous record and on the nature and quantity of the drug he was caught with.

If you have evidence or a strong suspicion that the youth is dealing in drugs, you could urge your neighbor to dissuade his son from further trafficking. If the youth is dealing in "hard" drugs, you may feel obliged to report him to the police.

When a person is charged with possession for the purpose of trafficking, the prosecution must prove that the accused was in possession of the drug. The accused can try to prove that his possession was only for his own use. But without evidence to the contrary, a large quantity will be proof that he intended to traffic.

There is also the offense of actually trafficking in a narcotic. To traffic means to manufacture, sell, give, administer, transport, send, deliver or distribute, or to offer to do any of these things. Thus, even giving away a joint can amount to trafficking.

Softening the blow. The maximum penalty for trafficking is life imprisonment. Crown prosecutors seldom press this charge, preferring the lesser one of "possession for the purpose of trafficking." This offense carries no mandatory minimum sentence and usually draws from one to three years.

In deciding which charge to press, prosecutors consult with the police and consider the value of the seized drugs as well as the "cooperation" of the accused (the provision of information about the drug traffic). Spill the beans and be spared the rod.

Drugs for the doctor. Both the Narcotic Control Act and the Food and Drugs Act permit doctors and pharmacists to have drugs in their possession and to administer them to patients. But the Narcotic Control Act prohibits even the medical use of some drugs, particularly heroin. This highly addictive derivative of morphine is a product of the opium poppy.

Heroin addicts are sometimes treated with methadone but this can produce a dependence essentially as severe.

SUICIDE AND EUTHANASIA

A friend has been charged with helping a crippled neighbor to commit suicide. She purchased a drug that he requested.

Although it is no longer illegal to attempt suicide, it is still a crime to counsel a person to commit suicide, or to aid anyone to do so.

If your friend knew that the suffering neighbor intended to use the drug—perhaps a bottle of sleeping pills—to commit suicide, yet got it for him, or lent him her own prescribed supply, she would probably be guilty of the offense and could be sentenced to 14 years in prison. Being motivated by pity or kindness is not accepted as a defense.

In Canadian law, euthanasia (mercy killing) is "culpable homicide," that is, murder. Even a written request or consent from the sufferer has no validity.

MINORS AND FOUND-INS

Your 17-year-old son was caught in a police raid. He and some friends were drinking, smoking marijuana and watching pornographic films.

Neither your son nor anyone else can be prosecuted for watching dirty movies at a private party. Unless he was caught with marijuana in his possession, he cannot be prosecuted on that score either.

In 1976, the RCMP raided a motel where a large number of teen-agers were having a "pot" party and arrested everyone found there. A judicial inquiry into the incident ruled that the police had acted unlawfully in arresting the youths solely on the grounds that they were found where the offenses were being committed.

But drinking is something else. Your son could be arrested for under-age drinking—or for being in a public, licensed drinking establishment, such as a tavern or pub, where alcoholic beverages were being consumed. The age limit for drinking is either 18 or 19 years, depending on the province.

Beauty in the buff

Since the Italian Renaissance of the 15th century, artists have been painting nudes. With the development of photography, it became common for women to pose unclothed for the camera too. In every city, and most small towns, are movie houses where complete or partial nudity is a stock feature of the adult film fare.

Without doubt, many of these pictures have artistic merit, but most are made purely for sexual titillation. Be that as it may, no court today would hold a picture of a naked woman to be obscene. And if your 17-year-old daughter posed in the buff for a photographer, neither she nor he would be charged.

If the girl performed indecent acts for the camera, both she and the photographer could be charged under the obscenity laws. But judging from the magazines and films generally available today, the acts would have to be extraordinarily indecent.

If the girl was a juvenile within the meaning of the Juvenile Delinquents Act, both she and the photographer would be charged under that act. If the model was, say, a 14-year-old boy or girl, the photographer would certainly be charged with corrupting the child's morals. He could also be charged with making obscene pictures. "Kiddy-porn" is almost universally conceded to be obscene.

A person can be arrested as a found-in for offenses relating to gambling, prostitution and liquor, but not to drugs.

'OBSCENE' LITERATURE

You feel that police should close down the local bookstore where obscene books and lurid magazines proliferate.

The Criminal Code defines obscene matter as any publication which has as a dominant characteristic the undue exploitation of sex, or of sex and one or more of the following: crime, horror, cruelty and violence. Because of this definition, each case must be judged independently. What is held to be obscene in one book might not be ruled obscene in another.

Decisions on what constitutes undue exploitation, or what offends contemporary community standards of modesty or decency, are up to the individual court, a task one judge called "treacherously subjective."

A conviction for openly selling pornographic material can bring a hefty fine. The seller can also go to jail—although such a penalty is rare.

The police are unlikely to prosecute anyone for selling pictures of nude men or women or for selling books describing sexual acts. But pictures of men or women which might be appropriate in a professional gynecological journal have been ruled obscene in general publications. Books or pictures depicting sexual acts involving children and animals, or acts of gross indecency between adults, are frequently ruled obscene.

Sex education. A book genuinely devoted to sex education would not be judged obscene, notwithstanding that it depicted various acts of sexual gratification.

The Macmillan Company of Canada, publisher of one such book, *Show Me*, was prosecuted for publishing obscene literature. *Show Me*'s large illustrations showed nude children engaged in sexual fondling and adults engaged in intercourse.

Macmillan was acquitted, the court ruling that the book was acceptable according to community standards. The court also held that the fact that acts of gross indecency were depicted did not, by itself, render the book obscene.

This judicial decision seemed to throw the gate wide open. Nevertheless, the police usually act upon a complaint by a responsible citizen. The fate of any charge will, of course, rest with the courts.

Private collections. The laws against obscene literature are directed at the manufacturer and distributor, not at the consumer. Simply being in possession of obscene books and films is not an offense; neither is putting on a private showing for friends.

If the presentation was advertised in any way, or if an entrance fee (or any material consideration) was charged, then the host would be liable to a criminal charge of "distributing."

PROSTITUTION

You suspect that the dating service you joined is a cover for a prostitution ring.

If you feel you were duped, you can write it off to experience or you can complain to the police and provide evidence which is otherwise difficult to obtain. For prostitution itself is not a criminal offense. It's the sell that's the crime, not the sale.

Offering one's body for sexual intercourse in return for payment, or the paid performance by male or female of any act for sexual gratification of others, constitutes prostitution. The person who masturbates another for a price is considered by the courts to be engaging in prostitution. The law specifically forbids soliciting in a public place for the purpose of prostitution.

The roving male. In some city districts, respectable women are harassed by men on the sidewalk or are propositioned from cars.

For many years, it was believed that only the person who received the payment could be convicted of soliciting for the purpose of prostitution. But the Ontario Court of Appeal has ruled that anyone—male or female, payer or payee—who sought to engage in sexual intercourse could be convicted of soliciting.

The landmark case involved what is called "curb-crawling." The accused man saw a girl walking along the sidewalk and, believing her to be a prostitute, pulled his car to the curb and propositioned her. The target, a policewoman in disguise, kept walking but the man persisted. The policewoman then entered his car and arrested him on a charge of soliciting.

The man was acquitted but, when the Crown appealed, the acquittal was set aside and a conviction entered. The court ruled that a male who offers payment to a female in return for sexual favors is soliciting for the purpose of prostitution, if his offer is made in a persistent manner in a public place.

The undercover girls. Civil-rights activists were quick to cry "entrapment." We all use sidewalks. What if one of us innocently stopped to talk to a prostitute? They don't wear placards or badges. A policeman could jump to conclusions and arrest us.

These fears are probably unjustified. A charge of soliciting must be proved by the prosecution in the same way as any other criminal charge. If the constable did not know why you stopped to talk to the woman, and if both you and she testified you were merely asking for directions, an acquittal would result.

The bawdy house. It's a criminal offense to keep a common bawdy house, defined in the Criminal Code as "a place that is kept or occupied, or resorted to by one or more persons for the purpose of prostitution or the practice of acts of indecency." "Keeping" applies to anyone who operates such a place, works in it or is found in it.

The woman next door, or down the hall in your apartment building, may entertain men at all hours but can you or the police obtain enough evidence to satisfy a judge beyond a reasonable doubt that she's running a bawdy house? The fact that many men come and go is not enough evidence. The police might send in a plainclothes policeman who could arrest the woman as soon as the deal was struck. His evidence, together with yours, would probably secure a conviction.

However, one act of prostitution does not turn a house into a common bawdy house. The police might pay more than one call to prove the place was continuously or habitually used as a place for prostitution.

Some people argue that prostitution is a crime without a victim, and should be made legal. Both the seller and the buyer are presumably satisfied with the deal. But the majority of Canadians regard sex for sale as immoral and degrading to both parties.

Prostitution preys on youth. Many victims are first hooked on drugs by a pimp and then forced into prostitution to obtain their "fixes." It is unlikely that legalization would change the manner in which they are recruited.

HOMOSEXUALITY

Your teen-age son tells you that he is a homosexual. You are worried about his prospects.

Until the late 1960s, homosexual persons kept their inclinations to themselves as much as possible. There were no gay activist organizations, and only a few discreet meeting places in big cities such as Montreal, Toronto and Vancouver. Discovery probably meant the loss of a job, and social disaster as well. Any homosexual act was an offense that could result in a 14-year prison term.

In 1969 the Criminal Code was amended to make homosexual acts between two consenting adults *in private* no longer a crime. Suddenly it was possible for homosexuals to "come out of the closet" and admit or even proclaim their sexual preferences. Many men and women, including some public officials, have done so.

You can suggest counseling for your son. He may be confused as a result of some now-regretted homosexual experimentation. On the other hand, he may spurn your advice: studies, including one by sex therapists Dr. William Masters and Dr. Virginia Johnson, show that few genuine homosexuals would prefer to be "straight."

Only Quebec, of all the provinces, protects the civil rights of homosexuals in employment and housing. A recommendation by the Ontario Human Rights Commission that discrimination on the basis of sexual orientation be prohibited was not acted upon. In Saskatchewan, the Court of Queen's Bench ruled that the Saskatchewan Human Rights Commission could not inquire into alleged discrimination against a homosexual teacher, declaring that the province's Fair Employment Practices Act deals with discrimination on the basis of sex (male or female) but not of sexual orientation.

An admitted homosexual who chose to work as a truck driver or a stevedore could probably expect some abuse from his macho workmates; life might be easier for him as a writer or artist, where he would be judged more by what he created than by how he lived. Also, living openly as a homosexual is more difficult in a small town or city than in a large, cosmopolitan city.

Homosexuality constitutes an immediate ground for divorce, and any marriage between persons of the same sex is automatically void. Homosexual acts in public are still criminal offenses; they are classed as gross indecency.

INDECENT ACTS

Your host at a party laughs at your prudishness when you complain about other guests openly conducting indecent acts.

Since an indecent act committed in a private place is an offense if there is intent to insult or offend any person, you can "lay an information" with the police. The better course probably is to leave the party and to be more selective about which invitations you accept in the future.

The police would be reluctant to charge the people involved, and the judge reluctant to convict them. The participants would almost certainly say that they intended no offense. They might also argue successfully that the acts which offended you were not indecent by community standards.

The outcome of such a case could turn on the judge's views on indecency. The fact that it was a private party would be an important element. The law, in this instance, is concerned with acts done in public, or in private but visible from a public place.

Heavy petting in public. If you were strolling by the lake with your wife and came across a car in which a young, half-naked couple were engaged in sexual acts, you could complain to the police. If they chose to proceed, the charge would probably be gross indecency. Committing an act of gross indecency with another person is an indictable offense, punishable with imprisonment for five years.

The Criminal Code does not define gross indecency. According to one judge, it is "a very marked departure from the decent conduct expected of the average Canadian in the circumstances that you find existed." But there's no settled agreement anymore on what constitutes "indecent conduct." The law has shifted at least to the extent that sexual activities between male and female adults, both of whom are willing participants, are highly unlikely to be prosecuted as gross indecency.

Suppose that the young couple in the car were engaged in oral sex, that is, in *fellatio* and *cunnilingus.* These acts in themselves are no longer considered to be grossly indecent, but much depends on when and where they are performed, who is present, and whether or not one of the participants is forced to commit the act. If you discovered three or more men or women performing those acts on each other, convictions would probably result. Three's not only a crowd, but a crime.

The age of the participants is another important matter. In the law pertaining to gross indecency, "adult" means a person 21 years of age or more. All other laws in Canada set the age of majority at either 18 or 19.

If two homosexuals engage in sexual acts in private and one or both are under 21, they could be prosecuted for gross indecency.

The law and privacy. Clearly, your bedroom is a private place and, equally clearly, a city park is a public place. But what about all the places in between?

A public place is one to which the public has access as a right (such as a park or sidewalk), or by express or implied invitation (such as a theater, beverage room, hotel corridor, or a public washroom). The Supreme Court of Canada recently ruled that the interior of an automobile is a private place.

EXHIBITIONISM

Your daughter is shocked when a man exposes himself to her as she walks through the park.

The Criminal Code provides that everyone who willfully does an indecent act in a public place in the presence of one or more persons or *in any place* with intent thereby to insult or offend any person is guilty of an offense. The code does not explain an "indecent act" but judges have defined it as conduct that would be considered morally objectionable by people generally. The problem is to discover what people in general consider offensive.

Exhibitionism ("flashing") is a bizarre attempt by a male to attract female attention. His pleasure or satisfaction lies in the reaction of shock, fear or disgust he provokes. There is practically no danger of further action. Most exhibitionists actually fear women. Many are prudish and feel sexually inadequate.

The victim should try to form a clear picture of the offender and note his car license plate number. The less reaction she shows, the better.

Any occurrence should be reported to the police. The offense is classified as disorderly conduct. The court may decide that psychological help is needed.

What is an exhibition? If a man was urinating in an alley or behind a bush, and was trying to be reasonably inconspicuous, it is unlikely he would be found guilty of an indecent act. It could not be said that he did it willfully.

None of the following fall within the clinical definition of exhibitionism: "streaking"; exposing the buttocks; nude bathing; males exposing to other males; the uncovering of the male genitals as a prelude to sexual activity between a consenting male and female. Females exposing themselves are excluded. (*See* "Peeping Toms" in Chapter 15.)

NUDITY

You and your wife want to sunbathe nude in your garden but you wonder whether it's illegal.

Sunbathing in the nude, even on your own private property, can be a criminal offense in certain circumstances. The laws dealing with *obscene* or *indecent* conduct are in a very confused state, but Section 169 of the Criminal Code states:

"Everyone who willfully does an indecent act in any place, with intent thereby to insult or offend any person, is guilty of an offence punishable on summary conviction."

Section 170 continues:

"Everyone who, without lawful excuse, (a) is nude in a public place, or (b) is nude and exposed to public view while on private property, whether or not the property is his [or her] own, is guilty of an offence punishable on summary conviction."

The code explains that a person is "nude" who is so clad as to offend against public decency or order. No charges of nudity can be laid without the consent of the attorney general of the province. (It's one of the rare instances where, in effect, a person rather than the letter of the law determines whether or not a crime has been committed. Rather than seek the necessary consent, the police are inclined to prosecute for committing an indecent act.) To further confuse the issue, the code indicates that the law is not aimed at the casual act of sunbathing in the raw.

Cases that have reached the courts have been decided on their own facts. If a man appears nude on his lawn each day at the time that girls pass his house on their way to a nearby school, he may be open to a conviction for an indecent act. But a man who "streaked" through a football stadium was acquitted: the court ruled he did it as a joke, and there was no moral turpitude.

If your son was collecting for his paper route and one woman answered the door wearing little or nothing, you could complain to the police. But it's unlikely they would accuse or arrest the woman. If the nudity was repeated several times, however, she could hardly say it was accidental, and she might be charged with committing an indecent act. It does not differ in law from the act of a man exposing himself to young girls. Both offenders probably need medical help rather than punishment.

Skinny dipping. If nude swimming is in a public place, the offense of nudity has been technically committed. The same will hold true if the spot is on private property but the swimmers are exposed to public view. However, the police will be reluctant to intervene—

especially if the spot is secluded—unless the carefree swimmers are otherwise annoying or disturbing people.

Anyone who swims nude at a public family beach will be lucky to escape with a nudity charge. He may also get his nose bloodied by an outraged father.

At the nudist camp. Sun worshiping has been around as long as people and the sun. If it is on private property and the participants are not exposed to public view, there is no offense—even if there are several participants. There is no intent to insult or offend anyone.

Security and the single girl

In not-so-distant days, unmarried women mostly lived at home, or "boarded" with "respectable" families. Today, millions of working women live alone in apartments, townhouses and condominiums, fending for themselves in a supposedly unisex world.

Criminals, however, continue to regard women as the weaker or gentler sex. To the malefactor, the woman alone is a prime, preferred target. The thief sees less risk of resistance or trouble than from a man, while equal-pay laws have raised the loot potential. The rapist knows there's little chance of being disturbed in a one-girl pad. The con man looks for sympathy or lack of hard-edge business knowledge.

To basic advice about installing wide-angle door peepholes and solid deadbolt locks, police add the following "Dont's" for all women living alone:

Don't reveal your feminine status unnecessarily. Use only your initials with surname on the mailbox or in the phone book.

Don't remain alone in an apartment laundry room or parking garage.

Don't admit anyone who is unknown to you unless proper credentials are presented. If doubtful, check by phone with his stated home base.

Don't enter your home (or call out) if the door has been tampered with. A thief may still be inside. Go to a neighbor and call the police.

Don't walk home through empty parks, vacant lots or unlit areas.

Don't overburden yourself with packages and a bulky purse.

Don't go home if you think you are being followed. Go into the nearest lighted home, gas station or store and call the police.

Don't talk to a stranger in a dark parking lot. Jump into your car, lock the doors, flash your lights and sound the horn.

Don't stop to offer help to an apparently stranded motorist. Halt at the next phone booth and call for assistance.

Don't sit alone at the back of a bus or subway car. Sit near other women, or near the driver.

Don't sit in a dark corner at the movies. Take an aisle seat.

Don't hitchhike, under any circumstances.

Don't carry large sums of cash. If someone grabs for your purse, don't resist. Take note of his appearance and call the police.

Don't investigate strange noises outside the house at night. Check the locks and phone the police.

Even if you are proud of your liberated status, relax a little and allow that chauvinistic male friend to walk you home when it's dark.

Nudist camps or colonies generally take great care to avoid prosecution and to discourage voyeurs.

RAPE

You are flagged down one evening by a crying girl who says she has been raped.

Your actions in this emergency could be crucial in apprehending the rapist and in restoring the girl's morale. Treat her as the innocent victim of a vicious crime. Record the time and her exact words. Call the police so that a search can begin.

Take the victim to the nearest hospital or doctor's residence. Don't permit her to wash or tidy herself. Her appearance may prove she was attacked: her person may yield evidence such as a piece of her assailant's hair or traces of semen.

There is a risk she is lying. To avoid false charges, the law has developed the "doctrine of recent complaint." A rape victim is expected to complain as soon after the event as she reasonably can. A prolonged, unexplained delay weakens her story. However, a court has accepted evidence from one young girl who failed to confide in her mother for several weeks after the rape for fear of reprisal from her assailant.

A complaint of rape must be spontaneous and not elicited by leading, suggestive or intimidating questions. The offense is punishable by life imprisonment. Nevertheless, most men who are charged are eventually acquitted.

It's tragically unfair that the trial can be more of an ordeal for the victim than for her assailant, and no doubt many rapists have counted on that.

Recent changes in the law have gone at least part of the way to protecting a woman's privacy. Tight restrictions have been placed on the right of the defense counsel to pry into the previous intimate affairs of the victim. A man can now be convicted solely on the evidence of the complainant, without the necessity of independent, corroborating evidence.

Rape is defined as sexual intercourse by a man with a woman who is not his wife, without her consent, or with consent obtained by threats, impersonation (pretending to be her husband while she is asleep or drunk), or by "false and fraudulent representations." The man who obtains consent by telling a woman it will clear up her acne may be convicted of rape.

The law does not consider that a woman can rape a man, but a woman who assists a man to rape another woman could be convicted. The least penetration of a woman's labia, without consent, is enough for rape. If there is an attempt but no penetration, the man can still be convicted of attempted rape or indecent assault.

About half of all reported rapes are committed by men who are total strangers to their victims. Most of the remainder are committed by men known only on a casual basis. Rapes committed by men who have broken into apartments or houses are relatively rare.

Many rapes occur when women invite a casual male acquaintance into their homes, or accept an invitation to enter his. Maybe there's something to be said for a handshake at the door or a fleeting good-night kiss.

A husband cannot be convicted of raping his wife, even when they are separated. A man who forced his wife to engage in sexual intercourse could be convicted of common assault, or assault causing bodily harm if he causes her injury.

ABORTION

You and your spouse can barely support your four children. Now an unexpected pregnancy threatens to push you over the economic brink. You feel that an abortion is the answer.

Abortion is legal in Canada within closely defined conditions, but it isn't always easy to get and it poses a moral dilemma. Those who favor abortion on demand argue that childbirth is a personal matter best left to a woman and her doctor, taking into account the woman's physical and mental health, her economic status, the possibility of defects in the fetus, and perhaps whether the pregnancy resulted from rape or incest. They argue that medically sound abortion has always been available to the rich, while poor women faced the prospect of clandestine back-room operations or those they performed on themselves with hatpins, pencils or bent coat hangers. Both types of operation are illegal, and both carry grave risks to health and even life.

In recent years, as abortion has become more widely accepted, powerful counterarguments have been reaffirmed by "pro-life" groups. They insist that life begins at the moment of conception, and that abortion is therefore murder. The Roman Catholic Church proclaimed in 1869 that the soul enters the embryo at the moment of conception. Anti-abortionists point out that all human organs are functioning 56 days after conception, and that *any* abortion involves medical risks including infection, hemorrhaging and sterility.

The law does not recognize the existence of a child until it is born, and therefore does not regard abortion as murder. In 1969, the Criminal Code was amended to permit abortion if continuation of a pregnancy was likely to endanger the life or health of a woman. ("Health" includes mental health; this can be—and is—interpreted in a wide variety of ways.)

To be legal, the operation can only be performed in a properly accredited hospital and any such hospital can refuse to carry out any abortions at all.

If a hospital is willing to perform abortions, it must form a therapeutic abortion committee of no fewer than three doctors appointed by the hospital board. Each abortion requires permission from the committee. These committees are permitted to set their own rules. Early abortions are safer: most hospitals refuse to perform the operation after the twelfth week of pregnancy.

Under the letter of the law, a woman who gets an abortion without the sanction of a hospital committee is guilty of a crime and can be imprisoned. The same applies to the doctor who performs the operation. The Canadian Medical Association is on record as favoring the repeal of abortion legislation, leaving the matter up to each woman and her doctor.

6 Discrimination

No one is immune to discrimination. In someone's estimation, you may be too young or too old to hold a particular job. Your color or ethnic background, your sex or sexual preference, or your religious beliefs may be held against you, as may certain physical handicaps.

Until very recent times such questions were generally swept under the rug. Blacks and other "visible minorities" were refused entry to many public places and Jews were openly banned from certain beaches, hotels and restaurants.

In 1940, the Supreme Court of Canada, hearing the appeal of a black who had been refused service in a tavern, ruled that "any merchant is free to deal as he may choose with any individual member of the public." During World War II, thousands of Japanese Canadians were interned and humiliated. Postwar immigrants were scorned as "DPs" (displaced persons) and had to scramble for the most menial jobs.

In the 1960s and 1970s, there were outbreaks of violence against West Indians and East Asians. Discrimination was common against homosexuals and women.

Gradually, however, change occurred. Since Ontario enacted its Racial Discrimination Act in 1944, province after province has formulated a human rights code or similar legislation. The Canadian Bill of Rights was enacted in 1960. A federal Human Rights Commission has existed since 1977, and provincial commissions exist across Canada.

Preventing discrimination against any person in Canada, citizen or not, on the basis of race, creed, color, sex, marital status, physical handicaps, nationality, ancestry or place of origin is the goal of these commissions. Their doors are open to any complaint.

The commissions prefer to overcome by persuasion rather than by legal action, but they have extraordinary powers to enforce their rulings.

The Ontario Human Rights Code, for example, permits a commission board of inquiry to "order any party who has contravened this Act to do any act or thing that, in the opinion of the board, constitutes full compliance with such provision, and to rectify any injury caused to any person or to make compensation therefor." The term "any act or thing" sets almost no limits.

The federal commission warns that any person who fails to comply with the imposed terms of a settlement of a complaint, or who obstructs an investigator or a tribunal, is subject to a criminal charge. The maximum fine for an individual is $5,000; for an employer or a trade union, it is $50,000.

Unlike the Canadian Bill of Rights, the Canadian Human Rights Act does not apply to matters which fall within the terms of the Indian Act. Thus the Human Rights Commission cannot go to bat for Indian women who by marrying white men lose their treaty rights but can intervene if an Indian suffers discrimination in housing or employment because of his ethnic background.

All provinces make it unlawful to retaliate against a complainant. In one case where retaliation against an employee was proved, his boss was ordered to pay $2,000.

Most human rights commissions play an educational and public relations role as well as enforcing the law. The Manitoba commission, for example, has published a teachers' handbook about potential discrimination in textbooks and in teaching techniques. The commission also conducts random surveys of application forms, checking for job qualifications which may be discriminatory. Other forms are also examined. Of 48 pension and fringe-benefit packages examined in 1977, 23 contained illegal provisions, as did nearly all of 204 job-application forms. Most employers revised their forms to conform to the Human Rights Code.

EMPLOYMENT

At your plant three blacks in a row have been laid off, but no whites.

If you have "reasonable grounds" to believe that the layoffs were because of color, contact your Human Rights Commission. Having "reasonable grounds" doesn't mean you have to be absolutely certain; it's sufficient to have an honest belief, or even a strong suspicion.

Your complaint should be in writing—and signed. Anonymous accusations are usually ignored. Most provinces also require you to complete an official complaint form.

The human rights investigator has wide powers when tracking down a complaint. He will usually examine the employer's record, and speak to other workers and to officers of the union if there is one. Layoffs might have been necessary for legitimate reasons, but if the investigation reveals that color was in any way a consideration in selecting those to be laid off, the employer has broken the law.

An investigator's suggested terms of settlement often include pay from the time of the incident until the victim finds other employment. The employer must also satisfy the commission that he has changed his ways.

If the employer disputes the finding, the issue will be submitted to the commission members. They might ask the appropriate provincial government department to appoint a board of inquiry, whose ruling has the force of law. The decision can be appealed to the provincial Supreme Court.

Harassment on the job. If your fellow workers are giving you a hard time because of your color or race, or if your boss continually insults you because of your background, complain to the provincial Human Rights Commission. The law states that there must be no discrimination in "terms and conditions" of employment.

Recently, a large Toronto hospital was found to have all white supervisors although a large proportion of the workers were blacks or Asians. A black woman who had applied for a supervisory position and wasn't even granted an interview complained to the Ontario Human Rights Commission. Although she didn't get the job she was awarded almost $2,000 for "injured feelings."

HOUSING

Your offer to buy a condominium at the asking price was not accepted. You think your color was a deciding factor.

Barring some overt words or act before witnesses, it may be difficult to prove discrimination, but if you believe that the real estate agent is in cahoots with the seller, bring your suspicions to the attention of his supervisor or head office.

If the sale is private, file a complaint with your Human Rights Commission, which has at least the authority to speak to the seller, and can attempt to change his attitude.

Recourse to the courts is unlikely to succeed because they are reluctant to enforce a sale of property unless there is a clear contract. Even if there is, a judge would prefer to award damages for breach of contract rather than to order that a sale go through.

Renting and race. Discrimination on the grounds of color, race, ancestry or religion in the renting of accommodation is against the law everywhere in Canada. In Manitoba, an Indian who wanted to rent a furnished apartment was told: "You Indians drink too much. Get out of here." He complained to the Human Rights Commission. The investigation showed that the landlady had recently evicted an Indian tenant because of excessive drinking and rowdy parties. She had rejected the new applicant without any attempt to establish his personal qualifications as a tenant.

At the insistence of the commission, the owner wrote a letter of apology to the applicant, paid him $90 as compensation for insult and inconvenience, and promised to comply with the law in all future rental transactions.

Commissions at work

This chart shows the steps taken by the Manitoba Human Rights Commission, from preliminary investigation of a complaint to rejection or settlement. A similar procedure is followed in the other provinces.

Rights commissions have definite legal powers but are not courts of law. Note that there are three avenues of legal appeal against decisions of the Manitoba commission.

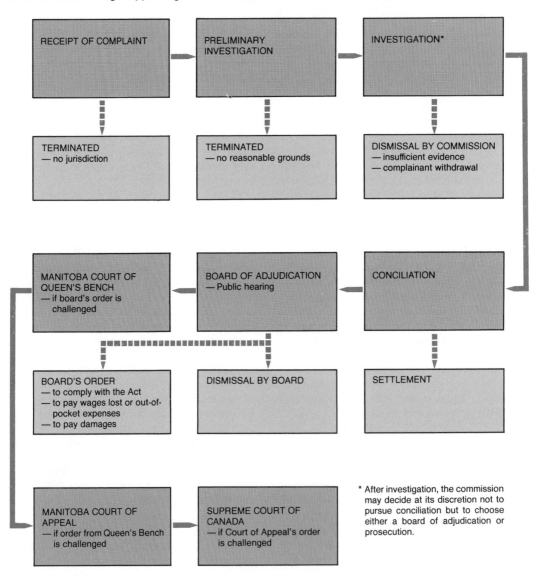

RECEIPT OF COMPLAINT

PRELIMINARY INVESTIGATION

INVESTIGATION*

TERMINATED
— no jurisdiction

TERMINATED
— no reasonable grounds

DISMISSAL BY COMMISSION
— insufficient evidence
— complainant withdrawal

MANITOBA COURT OF QUEEN'S BENCH
— if board's order is challenged

BOARD OF ADJUDICATION
— Public hearing

CONCILIATION

BOARD'S ORDER
— to comply with the Act
— to pay wages lost or out-of-pocket expenses
— to pay damages

DISMISSAL BY BOARD

SETTLEMENT

MANITOBA COURT OF APPEAL
— if order from Queen's Bench is challenged

SUPREME COURT OF CANADA
— if Court of Appeal's order is challenged

* After investigation, the commission may decide at its discretion not to pursue conciliation but to choose either a board of adjudication or prosecution.

Living common law. Manitoba also forbids landlords to refuse to rent on grounds of age or marital status. In a recent case, a 17-year-old girl and her 20-year-old boyfriend were refused a one-bedroom apartment. The agent did not check the couple's references or ability to pay the rent, and said he would not rent to any 18-year-old or to a male and female who were not married.

With intervention by the Human Rights Commission, the young lovers got the apartment, and the agent agreed to assess future applications without regard to age or marital status.

In other cases, landlords have been ordered not to refuse to rent to "welfare cases" on the grounds of lack of income security.

The vanishing vacancy. A black couple who looked at an apartment in Sudbury, Ont., were told by the vacating tenants that they were the first to apply. But when the couple drove to the landlord's home to sign the lease, he said the apartment had already been rented.

The couple complained to the Ontario Human Rights Commission. An investigation confirmed that the apartment had been available when they applied. The previous tenants confirmed discrimination by reporting that the landlord had called them after the incident and ordered them not to show the apartment to blacks.

After a conciliation hearing, the landlord promised to follow the Human Rights Code, and paid $100 to the complainants for their expenses in finding another place to live.

AGE

You have 30 years' experience as a waiter but are turned down for an advertised job. The swinging young boss indicates you are too old for his disco crowd.

If you feel you were denied employment because of your age, get in touch with the Human Rights Commission.

In all provinces except Quebec and Saskatchewan, it is unlawful to discriminate in hiring on the basis of age—although the regulations vary. In Alberta and British Columbia, workers between the ages of 45 and 65 are specifically protected, while in Nova Scotia and Ontario, protection begins at 40. Prince Edward Island grants protection to 18-year-olds, while Newfoundland covers persons between the ages of 19 and 65. Manitoba and New Brunswick have no minimum or maximum limits. At 65, when you begin to receive old-age security payments, you are officially a "retiree," although even this barrier is now under attack.

Most provincial human rights codes allow exemptions if the employer can prove that age is a *bona fide* requirement of the position. This means that the boss must show that his business would be seriously disrupted or that it couldn't be carried on by an older (or younger) worker.

A person's sex may be another *bona fide* requirement of the position. In British Columbia, a firm which provided airport security guards needed one to conduct body searches on female passengers. A board of inquiry agreed that being female was a valid requirement, and the company was permitted to discriminate against male applicants.

When is a firefighter too old? In Ontario, one board decided that a fireman should not be forced to retire at 60 if he could still do his work efficiently. At about the same time, also in Ontario, another board ruled that compulsory retirement for a fireman was not against the Human Rights Code—which seems to leave that issue up in the air.

CHILDREN WHO ARE 'DIFFERENT'

You made a "mixed marriage" and now your children return home from school crying about bullying.

This is a frequent problem, affecting not only "visible minority" groups but all children who vary, even slightly, from the "norm." It has its roots, psychologists say, in the common fear of the unknown. The most important thing is to make sure your child knows he is loved, and is secure and happy with his identity and self-worth. (*See* Chapter 9, "You, the parent.")

If there are a number of children from mixed marriages in your local school, you could suggest that the staff discuss the special problems of minority-group pupils. Teachers are usually allowed paid time off—called "professional development days"—to upgrade their skills and to keep abreast of social change.

The Human Rights Commission of your province will arrange for lectures on race relations for students and teachers and will provide films and literature to help dissolve negative stereotypes.

LANGUAGE OF EDUCATION

You are moving to Quebec and are worried that your children will have to attend French-language schools.

Public education is within the jurisdiction of the provinces—and they are jealous of that right. (*See* Chapter 10, "Education.")

At the time of writing, Quebec permits children who are entering the province *temporarily* from another province to continue their education in English for a period of three years, renewable for a further three years, if one of the parents was educated in English. If

Fighting back

Your Human Rights Commission will insist that you complete an official form for any complaint about discrimination. Assistance will be forthcoming, when necessary, in filling in the details.

This form, which is typical, is provided to complainants in Manitoba. When mailed or delivered by hand, it sets the wheels turning. If the incident falls within the terms of the legislation, an investigation follows.

THE MANITOBA HUMAN RIGHTS ACT
(S.M. 1974 c. 65 — Cap. H 175)

Case No. *A 30-451*

To: The Manitoba Human Rights Commission
in respect to the complaint of . . *RICHARD ROE*
against *XYZ NOVELTIES CO. LTD.*

PLEASE PRINT

I, *RICHARD ROE*
living at *10 MAPLE, WINNIPEG.* Telephone . . . .
complain against *XYZ NOVELTIES CO. LTD.*
whose address is *20 ELM STREET*
. . . . . . *WINNIPEG, MANITOBA* . . . .
who allegedly violated The Human Rights Act on or about *1.9.79.*
(Date)
through *SAMUAL SNOW, PERSONNEL OFFICER*
(Name and Position of Person committing alleged violations)

because of: ➡

Check Appropriate Box(es)

☑ Race
☐ Nationality
☐ Religion
☑ Colour
☐ Sex
☐ Age
☐ Marital Status
☐ Family Status
☑ Ethnic or National Origin
☐ Source of Income
☐ Political Belief
☐ Physical Handicap
☐ Without Reasonable Cause

The particulars are as follows:

When I was interviewed for the position of clerk with XYZ Novelties Co. Ltd., I was told by Mr. Samual Snow, the personnel officer, that he had had trouble with blacks before and he was not going to hire any more. He told me not to bother filling in an application form. I am a black man from Jamaica and believe I am qualified for the job.

Dated at *Winnipeg*
(City of Town)
on *October 1st* 19 *79*
(Month) (Day) (Year)

Richard Roe
(Signature of Complainant)

THIS COMPLAINT IS TO BE MAILED OR DELIVERED TO:

MANITOBA HUMAN RIGHTS COMMISSION
200 - 323 Portage Avenue,
Winnipeg, Manitoba R3B 2C1

OR

Room 21, Provincial Building,
P.O. Box 2550,
The Pas, Manitoba R9A 1M4

Form MHRC-CHRO-2 AG-am-4

a family moves *permanently* into the province, the law requires the children to attend French schools.

The cultural advantage to children of becoming bilingual—it's relatively easy for the young—should not be overlooked. And bilingualism is a definite plus in the job market.

A Quebec family moving to an English-speaking province will probably find it more difficult to continue the children's education in French.

PHYSICAL HANDICAPS

You have to use a wheelchair and you are unable to shop in the supermarket because you can't get through the turnstiles.

Canada lags behind other countries in legislating for the handicapped, even though it is estimated that one of every seven Canadians has some physical handicap. However, many hospitals, government buildings and other institutions are adding ramps and handrails, and lowering drinking fountains and elevator-control buttons.

Through recent amendments to human rights legislation, British Columbia, Manitoba, New Brunswick, Nova Scotia, Prince Edward Island, and the federal government have made it unlawful to discriminate in employment against a physically handicapped person. The handicap must not, of course, prevent the person from doing the job.

But in half of the provinces—including the two most populous—the person with a physical handicap must still largely fend for himself, in employment and in the streets.

RELIGION

You have stopped practicing any religion, but you and your children are still subjected to religious rules or customs.

A sign of intellectual and emotional maturity is the ability to tolerate other peoples' points of view—even if you disagree. That's the essential core of democracy. But you cannot be forced to take part in any religious ceremony and cannot be punished if you don't.

Certain customs, such as morning prayers or saying grace at meals, or even singing "God Save the Queen," are often just a traditional way of beginning or ending group activities. You don't have to be a believer to understand the motive behind these expressions.

All human rights codes protect the freedom to worship—you can even pay homage to Satan. The Supreme Court of Ontario ruled in 1978 that a Satanist who refused to swear on the Bible could still give testimony at a trial.

"Moral depravity," said the judge starchily, "does not render a witness incompetent to testify, nor does a disposition to lie." Such a witness can make an affirmation (a promise to tell the truth) as provided for under the Canada Evidence Act.

Even in the workplace, minority religious customs are protected. A Sikh worker was fired from his job at an air-conditioning plant because he insisted on wearing his *kirpan* (a ceremonial dagger) to work. Daggers are classed as offensive weapons under the Criminal Code.

Nine months later, following the intervention of the Human Rights Commission, he was reinstated and paid more than $2,000 in back pay. He still packs his kirpan—under his shirt.

A CRIMINAL RECORD

You were doing well at your new job until your employer learned that you had a conviction for theft. You have been let go.

A criminal conviction for which the offender has not been pardoned is legitimate grounds for dismissal anywhere in Canada.

However, discrimination because of a pardoned conviction is prohibited in businesses under federal jurisdiction—such as the banks, Air Canada, Bell Canada or the Canadian Broadcasting Corporation—and in British Columbia *unless* the charge relates to your occupation. If your pardoned conviction was for

THE LAW DECIDES: A POLICYHOLDER'S RIGHT

Two laws in conflict

Background

In 1976, shortly after Robert Heerspink of Sidney, B.C., was charged with possessing and trafficking in marijuana, the Insurance Corporation of British Columbia canceled his fire insurance policy and refunded the unspent portion of the premium. Mr. Heerspink, convinced that the termination was directly related to the criminal charge (of which he had not been convicted), complained to the Human Rights Commission. Since the B.C. Human Rights Code forbids discrimination in the provision of services to the public "without reasonable cause," a board of inquiry was appointed. When hearings began in March 1977, the Insurance Corporation pointed out that British Columbia's insurance legislation permits the cancellation at will of an insurance contract. Mr. Heerspink's policy contained such a clause.

The company lawyer said the Insurance Act gave the corporation the right to discriminate, and the Human Rights Code could not override that act. Even if there was discrimination against Mr. Heerspink because of the charge, there was nothing in the Human Rights Code making such discrimination unlawful, said the lawyer.

Clearly, the human rights law conflicted with the Insurance Act. Inquiry chairman Leon Getz halted the hearings to determine which law had precedence. Finally, he ruled that British Columbia law had received "a new and guiding principle of fundamental and far-reaching importance" from the Human Rights Code. If the code were to achieve its purpose of preventing discrimination, it must be interpreted in a "fair, large and liberal manner." He found that insurance matters were subject to the Human Rights Code and ordered the hearings resumed.

The insurance company appealed his ruling to the Supreme Court of British Columbia, lost, and promptly appealed to the province's highest court, the Court of Appeal. On Oct. 5, 1978, three judges ruled that the board of inquiry had authority to hear the complaints.

Judgment

In January 1979, the board of inquiry ruled that the Insurance Corporation of British Columbia did discriminate against Mr. Heerspink and ordered the company to cease such discrimination against its policyholders.

theft and you work in the stockroom, your B.C. boss may dismiss you on these grounds.

Except in British Columbia and for positions under federal jurisdiction, job applications can ask about the existence of a criminal record and the employer can refuse to hire you on the basis of your answer. Failure to answer truthfully could be grounds for later dismissal.

If you have been convicted of a crime and been punished, you can apply for a pardon. If it is granted, you can state, quite legitimately, that you have no criminal record. (*See* "When your debt to society is paid" in Chapter 4, and "A criminal record" in Chapter 2.)

SEXISM

A local bar refuses to serve any woman who is not accompanied by a man.

The barriers are coming down, but discrimination on the grounds of sex still exists. If you have been refused service in the bar because you are alone and a woman, complain to the Human Rights Commission; you are practically assured of getting your beer or cocktail. (Whether you will be made welcome is another matter.)

You could also complain to your provincial liquor board, sending a copy of your letter to the management of the bar. Taverns and bars operate under provincial regulation and are very sensitive to any threat to their licenses.

Harassment on the job. The picture of the portly boss chasing the pretty secretary around the desk is common enough in cartoons, but it has a real and ugly underside: some bosses do demand sexual favors from women employees. The law is on the woman's side, but it is often hesitant to venture into non-violent man-woman relationships without substantial evidence.

In one case brought before the Saskatchewan Human Rights Commission, a secretary soon learned that her boss expected sexual favors. She quit immediately and suffered financial loss while she looked for another job.

An investigation confirmed sexual harassment. The employer apologized to the woman, compensated her for the financial loss, and assured the commission that he wouldn't pull that trick again.

In Ontario, a cocktail-lounge waitress was fired after she complained that two male bartenders were sexually harassing the female staff. The proprietor had to pay her $250 (part-time wages for four weeks) and issue a memorandum to all staff forbidding "personal indignities and horseplay."

In the unisex world. A 19-year-old London, Ont., man who applied for a position installing home draperies was told flatly that the job was open only to women. He filed a complaint of sex discrimination with the Human Rights Commission.

The employer argued that he sold his draperies almost exclusively to women and that he did not think it right to send a man into his customers' homes. He said that only women had the right "touch" when it came to pleating, fixing hemlines, or adjusting drapes.

A board of inquiry said that the idea that men are not satisfactory in jobs requiring care, taste and delicacy is old-fashioned and divorced from reality. It ordered the employer to abide by the Human Rights Code, to advise the commission of any further job openings, to allow an official to check the premises periodically and to pay the complainant $100 for "cavalier treatment."

2 | YOUR RIGHTS IN THE FAMILY

7 Engagement and marriage

Family law is being revised across Canada. Ontario led the way in 1978 and British Columbia, Alberta, Saskatchewan, Manitoba and Prince Edward Island followed suit within a year. Similar legislative changes are likely in the remaining provinces and Territories.

Not all the new laws or amendments are identical nor have all been fully proclaimed, but the main thrust of the legislation is everywhere the same. The old order of family relationships that built and sustained our society until the mid-20th century has cracked. Indeed, some of the legislative proposals might lead one to believe that the family as we know it is doomed. For example, the Law Reform Commission of Canada has asked the federal government to permit wives to charge their husbands with "sexual aggression" or "interference"—for even a touch without consent—and to legalize incest between consenting adults. Apart from media reaction to these recommendations, there was hardly a ripple from the public. On the incest issue, the commission heard from some 300 opponents and eight supporters. Four persons wrote in support of the "sexual aggression" recommendation and two persons objected.

The preamble to Ontario's ground-breaking Family Law Reform Act declares its laudable intent of encouraging and strengthening "the role of the family in society," but the legislative reformers' concepts of that time-tested unit often are quite different from the traditional view.

The new acts do not speak simply of "marriage"—the chosen words are "obligations between married persons and in other family relationships." Don't look for the hallowed labels of "husband" and "wife." They're to be "spouses."

Creating new legal status for informal relationships leads inevitably to basic change in just about every facet of the traditional male-female associations. The legal trend appears to be that marriage is a legal partnership, with the contract terms stated in black and white, witnessed and sealed.

Courtship, engagement, marriage, separation, divorce, illegitimacy, parental authority, children's rights—all of these seem to be going into the melting pot. Decisions from the Bench swing this way and that as the courts try to translate the sometimes radical reforms of politicians and social scientists into everyday rules for the citizenry.

But is the family really finished? Many people believe that marriage is something more than a "business deal" whose terms are defined only in positive law, as opposed to natural law or the law of God. An American sociologist, Prof. Reuben Hill, sums up the situation: "We had communes and multiple marriage in the 1870s, the free-love and trial-marriage movement of the 1920s. It would be hard to keep up with the forms that have been advocated and tried . . . There just is no solid research to support the notion that meaningful trends toward new marital arrangements exist."

DATING DILEMMA

You have been dating a girl for three years and her parents demand that you announce your engagement or quit seeing her.

The parents are confusing their "rights" with their legitimate concern about their daughter's future. It's not uncommon for the "over fifties" to believe that a young woman's security is best safeguarded by marriage to a suitable young man. Even if the parents like you, they probably feel that you are jeopardizing their daughter's future by not declaring your intentions.

They can make life difficult for you but they can't force a formal engagement. They can't even make you stop seeing her—the law protects your right to free association with anyone you choose—although they can forbid your entry to their house if she's living at home. But there are lots of places to meet besides the parlor.

However, if you are hesitating on the brink of marriage after three years' courtship, perhaps you should seek "outside" advice, formally or informally. A trusted friend or relative could be helpful, or your provincial Association of Marriage and Family Counselors (the names vary across the country) or your family doctor will refer you to qualified counselors in your area.

Age requirements. If either of you isn't of the minimum age prescribed for marrying, the parents can refuse consent to the union and probably make it stick. In 1979, the provincial limitations were:

British Columbia. Anyone under 19 required parental consent unless a court order permitting the marriage had been obtained.

Alberta. Between 16 and 18, both required the consent of parents or guardians. Marriage under 14 years was not permitted unless the female was pregnant or the mother of a child.

Saskatchewan. The minimum age without parental consent was 18.

Manitoba. Persons under 16 needed permission from the Family Court. Between 16 and 18, they had to have parental consent.

Ontario. No marriage was permitted under 14 years, except with pregnancy. Consent from both parents was required for persons under 18, although exceptions were made in cases of one parent or separated families.

Quebec. The minimum legal age was 14 for boys and 12 for girls. Without permission from parents, no marriage was possible before age 18.

New Brunswick. Under 18, you needed permission from your father; if he was dead, the consent of the guardian would suffice.

Nova Scotia. There was no legal minimum but those under 19 required parental consent. Under 16, you needed the approval of the Family Court.

Prince Edward Island. You could marry at 16 with parental consent, or under 16 if you were the mother of a child or if you were pregnant.

Newfoundland. If under 16, and pregnant, a doctor's certificate and permission of a magistrate were required. You had to be 19 before you could dispense with the approval of parents.

When parents object. If parents refuse to give their blessing to an offspring's marriage, the young couple might ask their clergyman to discuss the matter with the parents. The courts may come to the rescue of young love, also. If you apply to the court, a judge will decide if parental consent is necessary in your case.

In 1973, a Manitoba court granted a 16-year-old girl permission to marry a 27-year-old man against her parents' wishes. Said the judge: "Parents cannot choose a mate for their sons or daughters. The decision has to be made by the individual. The life style which they have chosen may not be my life style. That is not the important thing. It is their life style." The judge believed the marriage was being blocked by the "blind hatred" of the girl's parents for the intended husband and he thought the union had "a reasonable chance of succeeding."

In a Saskatchewan case, a 17-year-old girl and her 21-year-old fiancé, with whom she had been living for nine months, applied for an order to wed without her parents' consent. The judge granted the application. Both young people, he felt, "understood the meaning and responsibilities attached to marriage," and had "the means to carry out its economic and social responsibilities."

BREACH OF PROMISE

Your fiancé changes his mind and leaves the province a few days before the marriage date.

You can sue him for breach of promise of marriage in any province except Ontario, where this right was abolished in 1978. If you've been jilted elsewhere, you can seek damages for any financial loss—perhaps even for emotional harm. But in these days of equality of the sexes, the charge will be difficult to prove. Also, because your fiancé has skipped to another province, you'll have to get a judge's order permitting service of the documents *ex juris* (outside the province). This won't do you much good unless you know exactly where he is.

Mistake no defense. If you say "yes" when he pops the question, this proposal and its acceptance can constitute a legal contract. But it needs a "consideration" to make it binding. "Consideration" in the legal sense means "something of value." If a promise is given in exchange for a promise, you've got "consideration"—your promise to marry him in exchange for his promise to marry you is enough. But, an engagement ring on the fourth finger of your left hand is more substantial evidence.

If the case goes to court, your fiancé will find that it's no defense to say he made a mistake. He may well find that, as one judge put it, he must "pay something for indulging in a tardy change of mind and obstructing the plaintiff's matrimonial outlook."

Sometimes a planned marriage is conditional. For example, a girl might promise to marry on the condition that her boyfriend "absolutely refrain from using intoxicating liquors" and then break off the engagement when he proved that he loved the bottle more than her. If he had changed his mind about marriage before he fell off the wagon, however, the girl might collect damages.

Let's say that a man asks his "intended" if she's a virgin and she says yes. Should he discover otherwise, he might claim that his proposal was conditional on that fact. If he hadn't asked the question, however, she would not be legally bound to tell him.

Voluntary servitude. The engagement contract must be entered in complete free will. A promise to marry made under threat of violence, or while a person's mind is deranged, or seriously impaired by drugs or liquor, can be broken. Marriages contracted in such circumstances can be annulled by a court.

An Alberta man won an annulment after he convinced the court that he had been tricked into taking narcotics before going through a marriage ceremony. Afterward he lived with the woman for 28 days in a condition of helplessness. The judge ruled that the marriage was void *ab initio* (from the start) because the man's ability to consent had been impaired by the drugs. The courts have also annulled marriages in a case where a man threatened to shoot a woman unless she married him and in another where a sailor, arrested at the insistence of a woman who falsely alleged that he had made her pregnant, went through a form of marriage with her.

A mistake as to the identity of one of the parties will invalidate the marriage—but only if it results in the mistaken party failing to marry the person he or she intended to marry. In one case, a woman married a man in the mistaken belief that he was really a well-known boxer. The marriage was ruled *valid* because she had married the individual she meant to marry.

Another kind of mistake can arise over the nature of the ceremony. A woman who spoke no English went through a ceremony mistakenly believing it was only a betrothal, customary in her native country. The marriage was held to be invalid.

If a woman became engaged to a man whom she wrongly assumed to be wealthy, the ensuing marriage would not be invalid.

The cost of a broken heart. Judges are often stumped when trying to put a price on the emotions. They have far less trouble with material damages—the cost of a trousseau, wedding invitations, or setting up a future home. One embittered lover who sued for breach of promise thought he should be compensated, not only for the time he had wasted courting the girl, but for the cost of the stamps for his love letters, too. He didn't get a cent.

Although more boys are born in Canada than girls (about 105 to 100), after one year the balance starts to swing the other way. More males than females die in infancy. By marriageable age (say, 25), the male shortage is already apparent. Maybe that's why "breach of promise" stays in most of the law books.

License issued or banns read

Couples planning to be married must either acquire a marriage license or have the banns published in the church, or the local courthouse, for 21 days preceding the wedding. These Ontario forms are typical of those used in all provinces. The marriage must not take place sooner than three days after license issue or five days after publication of banns, nor later than three months in either case. Anyone found guilty of violating this provision of the Marriage Act is liable to a fine of up to $500. Banns are generally not published when either of the parties has been married previously and the marriage has been dissolved or annulled.

FORM 8
The Marriage Act, 1977
PROOF OF PUBLICATION OF BANNS

No: 7890

On the 27TH day of JANUARY, 19 80

I DULY PUBLISHED the banns of marriage between

RICHARD ALBERT ROE

of the CITY of ANYWHERE, ONTARIO

and SALLY DOE

of the CITY of ANYWHERE, ONTARIO

in THE UNITED Church in

the CITY of ANYWHERE, ONTARIO

I FURTHER CERTIFY that I verily believe the said

RICHARD ALBERT ROE

(and) SALLY DOE

ARE in the habit of attending worship at the said Church.
(is or are)

DATED this 27TH day of JANUARY, 19 80

Rev. Vincent Campbell
(Signature)

123 GLEN MANOR ROAD
(Address)

ANYWHERE, ONTARIO

PROVINCE OF ONTARIO

I do hereby authorize and grant this licence for the solemnization of marriage between

RICHARD ALBERT ROE
(name in full)

of 123 MAIN STREET, ANYWHERE, ONT.,
(address)

and SALLY DOE
(name in full)

of 321 MAPLE BLVD., ANYWHERE, ONT.
(address)

Provided always that, by reason of affinity, consanguinity, prior marriage, or other lawful cause there is no legal impediment in this behalf; but if otherwise, this licence is null and void to all intents and purposes whatsoever.

Dated at the City of Toronto in the Province of Ontario this first day of August 1978.

Deputy Registrar General
Registraire général adjoint

Issued this 8TH day of FEBRUARY 19 80
Délivrée le jour de

issuer of marriage licences at TORONTO, ONTARIO
chargé de délivrer les licences de mariage à

J'a...
ma...

domicilié à
(adresse)

avec
(nom en toutes lettres)

domiciliée à
(adresse)

A condition qu'aucun empêchement légal dû à une raison d'affinité ou de consanguinité, à un mariage antérieur ou à toute autre cause légale ne s'y oppose, auquel cas cette licence est nulle et de nul effet virtuellement et en fait.

Fait en la Ville de Toronto, dans la Province de l'Ontario, le premier jour d'août 1978.

THE CANCELED WEDDING

Your wedding is called off and you don't know what to do with the shower and wedding gifts.

They should all be returned promptly with a brief explanatory note. Anything given solely in contemplation of marriage is deemed "conditional"—that is, subject to the overriding condition that if the marriage fails to take place, the gift is to be returned.

In a cancellation by mutual agreement, this would also apply to gifts the couple exchanged, including the engagement ring. If, however, the man breaks his promise of marriage, he will not be entitled to the return of personal gifts, including the ring, given during the engagement and in contemplation of marriage. The woman will not be entitled to keep furnishings bought with his money for the home they had planned to set up. If the woman breaks the engagement, without legal justification, then she has to return the ring and other personal gifts made "in contemplation."

The revised Ontario Marriage Act provides that where one person makes a gift to another in contemplation of marriage to that person and the marriage doesn't take place, "the question of whether or not the failure or abandonment was caused by or was the fault of the donor shall *not* be considered in determining the right of the donor to recover the gift."

It doesn't sound very romantic but a couple might be wise to enter into a premarriage contract. This could spell out who owns what, and what must be returned to the other party if the wedding is canceled. The same contract could also establish separate ownership if the wedding does take place.

'CONDITIONAL GIFT'

You bought a new house for your fiancée. She jilts you but claims the house is still hers.

Your property rights don't change just because the property in question is real estate. If you can prove the gift or the purchase was "conditional" on the wedding, or on "cohabitation," you'd have a good chance of winning in court.

In a British Columbia case, a man had the title to a property registered jointly to himself and his betrothed. He claimed he did this on the condition that she would live with him in the house and marry him. When she didn't, the judge ruled that the gift was conditional, and that the man was entitled to sole ownership of the property.

But in a fairly similar case in New Brunswick, a judge came to the opposite conclusion. He ruled that a cottage presented as a gift to a woman could not be taken back by the man who gave it to her during the year they were engaged. It was an "absolute" gift. The woman owned the land on which the man built the cottage for her. When she broke off the engagement the man removed the cottage to land of his own. The judge said that when the man built the cottage he hadn't anticipated a breakup and so could not be taken to have attached any strings to the gift. The woman was awarded $10,000, the value of the cottage.

ILLEGITIMACY

You don't want to get married, but you are pregnant and you want the baby. Must it be stigmatized as illegitimate?

It could depend on the province in which you live. In our inheritance of English common law, so concerned with rights to property and a class-graded society, the child born outside marriage was rated a bastard and had virtually no rights at all. In 1978, Ontario ruled that personal rights are to be determined quite apart from the fact of whether or not the parents were married. Elsewhere in Canada, you should check with a lawyer in this field. It can be a very tricky subject, rarely cut and dried.

Throughout British and Canadian history, the illegitimate child has been given a very rough time. He was *filius nullius*, a "child of no one." Whenever there was a reference to a child in a statute or a legal document, such as a will, it was deemed to mean only a legitimate child—unless the reference specifically stated otherwise. Children born outside marriage usually had no inheritance rights, even if they had always lived with their parents as a family.

Ifs, ands and buts. Many laws have been passed in Canada improving the legal position of the illegitimate child, *without* proclaiming him to be legitimate. Up to 1979, only Ontario had taken the bull firmly by the horns. Some provinces have given the illegitimate child the right to succeed to the estate of mother or father or, through the mother, to the estate of more remote kin. Some have also permitted the illegitimate child to bring an application against the estate of the mother or father if not adequately provided for.

In British Columbia, an illegitimate child may obtain judgment for a share of the father's estate if the father had maintained him. Saskatchewan law gives the same right if the court is satisfied that the father has publicly or otherwise acknowledged that he was the father, or if at the time of the birth the father was living with the mother as her husband and "seemed to have accepted the child as his own." In Alberta, an illegitimate child has a valid claim against his father's estate *if* his mother is not alive, no brothers or sisters survive and parenthood has been established by court proceedings, or by an acknowledgment by the father.

But in some provinces, as yet, the right of an illegitimate child to sue either the father's or mother's estate doesn't exist.

RIGHTS OF CLERGY

The clergyman refuses to officiate at your wedding unless you attend premarital courses at his church. You wonder if he can really impose such conditions.

He certainly can. He not only has the right to perform marriages, but also the right to decide not to do so. Many churches and individual clergymen impose conditions. Many congregations are disturbed when couples who have no intention of becoming members ask to be married in their church. A 1979 meeting of the 50 United Churches of the Winnipeg Presbytery debated whether the church should close its doors to such weddings. "We don't want to write people off because they never come to church," said the Rev. John Freeman, "but there's much more to marriage than just a legalization."

Many churches place restrictions on those they will marry. Couples must take counseling and some kind of commitment is required. This is particularly true among Canada's largest denomination, the Roman Catholics. A priest will not marry a divorced person if the former partner is still alive, unless the first marriage was declared void.

Kathryn Cook, a well-known Toronto Unitarian chaplain, has performed marriages at golf clubs, on yachts, in open parks; once she officiated when the bridegroom had a parrot perched on his shoulder. But she, too, refuses to tie the knot in certain circumstances. She doesn't agree with teen-age marriages, nor believe that pregnancy alone is a valid reason to marry.

The marriage lines. Under the British North America Act each province may pass laws relating to "The Solemnization of Marriage in the Province." The laws do vary from province to province, but they're pretty similar at base.

To get married anywhere in Canada, you must either obtain a marriage license from your municipal clerk or have banns published. Banns are an official announcement read—or posted—for several (usually 21 days) in the church or courthouse where the ceremony is to take place or in a designated area in the community where the couple lives; their publication gives anyone the chance to object to the marriage. Banns do not suffice in Alberta, Nova Scotia and Prince Edward Island, nor in other provinces except Quebec, which does not issue licenses, if you are divorced. And you won't get a marriage license in Alberta, Manitoba or Prince Edward Island until you produce a medical certificate saying you don't have venereal disease. All provinces and both Territories authorize the solemnization of marriage by clergymen and by civil marriage officers—judges, justices of the peace, court clerks or specially appointed marriage commissioners.

The provincial laws all agree on certain basic points: one of the persons to be married must be male and the other female (homosexual "marriages" have no legal standing); both must be present at the time of the ceremony; the marriage must be witnessed by at least two other persons; the parties must affirm that they are legally qualified to be married and they must be declared to be married.

Good faith, good marriage. It occasionally happens that a marriage is solemnized by a clergyman who for technical or other reasons is not properly registered under the provincial Marriage Act. Is that marriage invalid? Very unlikely. A marriage solemnized "in good faith" and "in intended compliance" with the law is deemed to be valid, even if the person conducting the ceremony lacked civil authority, and despite any irregularity in the publication of banns or the issue of the license.

Saskatchewan's marriage law states, "No marriage shall be invalid by reason only that the person performing the ceremony is not then registered under this act." The courts usually rule that unless the statute provides otherwise—by plain language or clear inference—the marriage will be valid. The official may be fined but the marriage stands.

In a famous Ontario case—Alspector versus Alspector—a Jewish couple was married by a cantor whom the couple presumed knew the provincial law. The ceremony complied with the requirements of their faith but a marriage license had not been obtained. In 1957, after the husband's death, one of his relatives contested the validity of the marriage. The trial judge ruled that it was valid, and the Court of Appeal later agreed. Both courts held that a marriage solemnized "in good faith and intended to be in compliance with" the act was valid "notwithstanding the entire absence" of a license.

The vows that matter. Many couples today shun words that used to be central to wedding ceremonies—words like "until death do us part," and "obey." Some think it's more realistic to substitute something like "as long as we both shall love" or "as long as we shall share life together." Many women object to the promise to "obey," which implies a "master-servant" relationship. Instead there are declarations of mutual respect, love and sharing. Most church marriage ceremonies have a prescribed wording. Several provincial marriage statutes spell out the essential words in the civil ceremony: "I call upon all persons present to witness that I, John Doe, do take thee, Sally Snow, to be my lawful wedded wife." But no matter how expressed, the words that matter are those by which the participants take each other as husband and wife. The vows seal the contract.

MARRIAGE LICENSES

You both want to marry before you leave on a cruise, but city hall says you must wait five days before your marriage license may be used.

Each province has a minimum "cooling-off" period between the time the license is issued or the banns are posted and the time the vows are said. It runs from 24 hours in Manitoba to 20 days in Quebec. Almost all provinces will issue a special permit in "urgent" or "exceptional" circumstances. Usually, what is considered urgent or exceptional is undefined in legal terms, however. (In Ontario, it's the Minister of Consumer and Commercial Relations who decides!) The special circumstances permitting an instant marriage in British Columbia include "imminent danger of death" of either of the parties; and avoiding "illegitimacy of offspring."

You'll have to pay for your marriage license—from $5 in Manitoba to $40 ($65 on weekends) for a Quebec civil marriage. If you happen to be an Indian living on a reserve in Ontario, it's free. You must reside in a province for a stated period before you can be legally married there. The time span varies, but it's generally two weeks. If you are marrying for the second time, you must get a license and file certified proof that your first marriage ended in divorce or annulment or death.

IMPEDIMENTS OF KINDRED

You want to marry your brother's stepdaughter, but he says that the family relationship will be an impediment.

If it's okay with her, it's okay with the law. Such a union is not prohibited by the marriage laws relating to relationships. These rules— handed down from the Scriptures—absolutely prohibit marriage between certain related persons.

Some are barred from marrying because they're too closely related by blood (consanguinity) and others because they're too closely related by marriage (affinity). It does not matter whether the relationships are legitimate or illegitimate, or by the "whole" or "half" blood. (*Whole blood* means relationship

---

The 'orrible threat of the 'yphen

North Americans often chuckle at the boxcar family titles from Britain.

There's Sir Ranulph Twisleton-Wykeham-Fiennes, Bt., who set out in 1979 to cross the polar regions by snowmobile for the glory of the "empyah." And Walter John Montagu-Douglas-Scott, the 10th Duke of Queensbury, and the 8th of Buccleuch. Don't overlook Henry Edward Hugh Pelham-Clinton-Hope, the 72-year-old Duke of Newcastle-Under-Lyme, or Gilbert James Heathcote-Drummond-Willoughby, the Rt. Hon. the Earl of Ancaster—who also happens to be the 26th Baron Willoughby de Eresby.

But multiple names and double-hyphenation may be coming to Canada. Some women insist on using their own family names (their father's names) after marriage, or on linking husband's and wife's family names—with or without a hyphen. The Ontario Law Reform Commission has recommended that the Marriage Act be amended to allow a husband to take his wife's name, a wife her husband's, and the children either name or a hyphenated combination.

The *Toronto Star* then commented: If John Jones marries Jean Smith, should they be known as Mr. and Mrs. John Jones (the accepted formality), Mr. and Mrs. Jean Smith, Mr. and Mrs. John Jones-Smith (or Smith-Jones), Mr. and Mrs. John-Jean Jones-Smith (or Jean-John Smith-Jones), or plain John Jones and Jean Smith who happen to be married? A tongue-in-cheek correspondent in the letters-to-the-editor section of the Toronto *Globe and Mail* found the prospect even more dismaying.

He wrote:

Dear Sir—,

My problem is that I was born in England where hyphenated surnames are not uncommon. My father was John Burrows-Hyde and my mother was Jane Cholmondley-Featherstonehaugh. That made me Joseph Burrows-Hyde-Cholmondley-Featherstonehaugh when I was born.

But in 1964 my parents were divorced and my custody was awarded to my mother who later married James Scarborough-Yoicks. Since I was still a minor at that time and my stepfather wished to adopt me legally, my name thus became Joseph Burrows-Hyde-Cholmondley-Featherstonehaugh-Scarborough-Yoicks. I am now engaged to be married to a girl named Jean Gormley-Nash-Fallingbroke-Czyczyczynski, whose parents were also divorced.

Do you think it would be all right if we named the child she is expecting Jack?

Or should we stick to plain Burrows-Hyde - Cholmondley - Featherstonehaugh-Scarborough - Yoicks - Gormley - Nash - Fallingbroke-Czyczyczynski?

Yours, etc.

through both parents; *half blood* through one parent only.)

The various provincial marriage acts list the ancient taboos: generally a man may not marry his grandmother, grandfather's wife, wife's grandmother; his aunt, uncle's wife (unless the uncle is dead), wife's aunt; his mother; his daughter, wife's daughter, son's wife; his sister; his granddaughter; his grandson's wife, wife's granddaughter; his niece, nephew's wife, wife's niece (unless the wife is dead), or his brother's wife (unless the brother is dead).

A woman may not marry her grandfather, grandmother's husband, husband's grandfather; her uncle, aunt's husband (unless the aunt is dead), husband's uncle; her father, stepfather, husband's father; her son, husband's son, daughter's husband; her brother; her grandson, granddaughter's husband, husband's grandson; her nephew, niece's husband, husband's nephew (unless the husband is dead) or husband's brother (unless the husband is dead).

The Marriage Act of Canada has been amended to validate marriages with a deceased wife's sister or niece, or with a deceased husband's brother or nephew.

Most provinces have laws requiring persons planning marriage to swear that there's no affinity or consanguinity which would bar or hinder their nuptials. Statutes prohibit the marriage of mentally incapacitated persons, and those incapacitated because of liquor or drugs. The Criminal Code says a person commits incest who has sexual intercourse with another person *knowing* that this person is by blood relationship his or her parent, child, brother, sister, grandparent or grandchild. Brother and sister include half-brother and half-sister. If you should marry within any of the prohibited degrees of consanguinity or affinity, your marriage must be ruled void (without legal existence).

The brother's wife. In 1952, the Supreme Court of British Columbia ruled that a woman's divorce "did not destroy the affinity" to her in-laws and so her marriage to her former husband's brother was void. In another case, 15 years later, the B.C. Court of Appeal set a new precedent, ruling that the old prohibition did not include the brother's divorced wife, since she was now not the brother's wife but his former wife.

YOUR MAIDEN NAME

You want to retain your own family name after you are married. Your fiancé fears that you will not be able to get a passport.

You're not obliged by law to take your husband's surname when you marry. The custom developed in Western countries largely because of the doctrine of "unity of legal personality," but also to simplify record-keeping.

Formerly, the law regarded husband and wife as one person and that person was the husband. Most provinces have abolished this concept and have proclaimed that men and women have independent legal personalities. But even before this reform, a married woman could keep her maiden name—or resurrect it after many years—simply by declaring publicly that she wanted to do so. Common law has always upheld the right of people to give themselves whatever name they like as long as it's not done to defraud or deceive. A name is a symbol of identity. What gives it validity is its use.

With a few exceptions, your husband's name need not play any part in your legal identity. A woman can change her name on social insurance records, bank accounts, driver's license and credit cards without much difficulty. With credit cards, it's a lot easier for wives who have an income of their own. In Quebec, a woman's birth name remains her name throughout life, even after marriage. She might use her married name for social purposes, as the majority do, but if she sues someone, or buys real estate, she does so under her maiden name.

If you are going to use your husband's name when you marry, your passport in your maiden name will no longer be valid. You'll have to apply for a new one that gives your husband's name. But if you are keeping your original name, you can obtain a passport in that name provided you can produce evidence at renewal time—a driver's license, credit or social insurance cards—to show that you are publicly known by that name. If you are returning to your single name after a divorce, you can get a new passport by producing your decree absolute. (*See* Chapter 8, "Separation and divorce.")

Changing your driver's license to the name of your choice can be a bit trickier. If you want to revert to your maiden name, you will likely have to produce a birth or marriage certificate to confirm what your name used to be.

You can get an informal name change on your social insurance card by completing a form showing the information on your present card and the name you wish to be known by. If you are making the name change because of marriage or divorce, you have to produce your birth and marriage certificates and/or divorce decree.

After divorce. If you're divorced, reverting to the name you had before marriage requires a bit of planning. In British Columbia, New Brunswick and Ontario you may return to your previous name, whether it's your maiden name or the name of a former husband, when you get your final divorce decree—as long as the decree contains no objection to this. In Saskatchewan, a simple application form is involved. In the Yukon and Northwest Territories, a married woman may resume use of her maiden name at any time without further ado. In some other provinces, to switch back legally to the name you had before marriage, you have to go through the rigmarole—and considerable expense—of the Change of Name Act.

Alberta, Newfoundland and Ontario won't allow women to use the Change of Name Act to revert to their maiden names. In Manitoba and Nova Scotia the maiden name can be retrieved under the act only if the husband consents. In Prince Edward Island, however, you simply draw up a "deed poll," a sworn declaration outlining the intended name change and the reasons for it, along with proof of identity. In Ontario, a married woman finds it difficult to revert legally to her maiden name under any circumstances. First, her husband and children must change to the same name at the same time, though an exception may be made when couples have lived apart for at least five years. She must publish her notice of application once in the Ontario *Gazette* and for three consecutive weeks in a local newspaper, and must convince a court that there is no unsatisfied judgment against her and that she hasn't gone bankrupt. There is a similar procedure in New Brunswick, where a court appearance is also required.

DEBTS INCURRED BY SPOUSE

Right after the wedding, you are dunned by three stores to pay debts previously incurred by your wife. Do you have to pay?

In times past, the answer was yes. Today it is probably no. But it depends on the circumstances. It may make a difference if you now own property that belonged to your wife before the marriage.

Once, when a man took a wife he also took over any debts she had incurred, whether he knew about them or not. This was fair because on marriage the husband acquired any property that his wife owned outright. Gradually, however, the law permitted a married woman to make contracts on her own behalf, and these could protect her as to "separate property," before and after marriage. Correspondingly, husbands were freed from the responsibility of paying debts run up by their wives before the wedding.

All provinces now give the married woman the same rights as a single woman to enter into contracts and her husband's liability for her premarriage contracts and debts in such circumstances is, in most places, totally abolished.

In Newfoundland, New Brunswick, Ontario, Manitoba, Saskatchewan, Alberta and the Territories, a wife can be sued, or can sue, as if unmarried. She is now liable on all her contracts, whether made before or after marriage (except those made for "necessaries" or as agent for her husband). Because her liability is personal, she can be adjudged bankrupt and have debt judgments enforced against her.

THE LAW DECIDES: A WOMAN'S RIGHT

'Identical' isn't 'Equal'

Background

In 1974, there were about 35 women among the some 700 employees at the Lornex Mining Corporation copper mine in the Highland Valley near Ashcroft, B.C. The company provided housing for families and bunkhouses for single men, but no accommodation for single women. As a result, all single women employed at the Highland Valley site had to commute from Kamloops, 55 miles away.

On Aug. 14, 1974, the B.C. Human Rights Commission ordered Lornex to make its camp accommodation available to female employees "on the same terms and conditions as to male employees." The company then announced that its bunkhouses would be available to women staff.

Jean Tharp, a laboratory technologist, and another woman, applied for accommodation and found that each of the 14 bunkhouses had common washing and toilet facilities in the center and 10 double rooms on the perimeter. The common facilities consisted of a washer and dryer, a laundry tub, three sinks, two shower stalls with a common toweling area, three partially enclosed toilets and one urinal.

The second woman promptly withdrew her application but Miss Tharp moved into a bunkhouse on Sept. 17, 1974. Her room was satisfactory but the lack of privacy made use of the toilets intolerable and she had to travel to Kamloops to shower.

The Human Rights Commission intervened, but management protested it was doing exactly what it was ordered to do: making camp accommodation available to female employees on the same terms and conditions as to male employees. It repeated this argument to the board of inquiry, denying discrimination on the grounds that Miss Tharp was offered precisely the same accommodation as every other employee at the campsite.

Judgment

Identical treatment does not necessarily mean equal treatment, the inquiry chairman, Rod Germaine, ruled; neither does it indicate an absence of discrimination. By placing Miss Tharp in a demeaning and insulting position, the Lornex Mining Corporation attempted to discourage female occupancy of the camp, Mr. Germaine said.

The company viewed its own conduct as a clever means of complying with the letter but not with the spirit of the commission's 1974 order, said the chairman. This showed wanton disregard for the provisions of the Human Rights Code and he ordered Lornex:

▓ to refrain from such violations in the future;

▓ to pay $513 damages to Miss Tharp.

Saskatchewan and Nova Scotia don't go this far. In those provinces, the husband is still liable on his wife's premarriage contracts to the extent of all property he may have acquired through her. British Columbia, Nova Scotia and Prince Edward Island have kept the phrase "separate property" and so, in those provinces, a married woman became liable for any contracts, incurred before and during the marriage, that were related to her separate property.

In Quebec, debts incurred by either spouse before marriage are the responsibility of that individual, unless they have entered into a marriage contract stipulating that they will be jointly liable for their debts contracted before marriage.

The husband's agent. Traditionally, the law has held that where a wife lives with her husband there is "presumption" that she has his authority to pledge his credit for household necessaries suitable to their "station in life." This concept, which may also apply where the couple is not married but living together, is "rebuttable." In other words, it may be upset by evidence that the man has revoked the woman's authority to run up bills in his name, or that the spouse has extravagantly overstepped reasonable spending, or that she had been provided with an adequate allowance to pay cash. If the husband can "rebut," the wife will be personally liable. However, the husband won't have much chance of dodging the bill if he has paid all the bills without complaint in the past.

If husband and wife have ceased living together (cohabiting), and if the husband has stopped making support payments, the wife may have the right to pledge his credit if she has no other income. In British Columbia and Alberta, the husband is liable for necessaries supplied to his legally separated wife when financial support has been ordered but not paid. In Ontario and Prince Edward Island, both spouses may pledge the other's credit for necessaries, except where the credit grantor is notified that the authority has been withdrawn.

In most provinces, a wife who is living apart from her husband for "just cause"—such as desertion—may bill him for necessaries or borrow money on his credit to meet her basic needs. This "agent on necessity" cannot be revoked by the husband, but the wife loses it if she commits adultery or if it's shown she had enough money of her own.

"Necessaries" are just that—not luxuries. By and large, they would include adequate clothing, food, lodging and medical services.

ANNULMENT

Your new spouse thinks that sex is distasteful. You wonder if your marriage can be annulled.

A marriage is "consummated" as soon as the parties have full sexual intercourse, after the marriage. Failure to consummate could provide grounds for annulment if it's caused by an "incurable inability" on the part of one or both spouses to have sexual intercourse. And impotence or frigidity need not arise from physical causes only. In one case, when a wife revealed an "invincible repugnance" to the sex act—stemming from her belief that marriage was an entirely spiritual union—her husband succeeded in having the marriage annulled.

Bars to annulment. If the impotence sets in after the marriage, however, annulment is ruled out. If your marriage is unconsummated because of some sort of mental block or hang-up, an annulment won't be granted unless the condition is proven to be permanent. The spouses must, in good faith, try to solve the problem. If medical treatment or counseling would correct impotency or frigidity, the courts won't grant an annulment.

Refusal is guaranteed also if it is shown that the petitioner for an annulment knew before marriage of the impotence of the spouse. A court might rule that a young woman who married an old man should have realized he was probably impotent. "Unreasonable delay" might be a bar. Except in Quebec, where you can't apply for an annulment after three years from the marriage date, there's no set time for applying for an annulment based on impotence. Judges, however, might differ on how much time is "reasonable."

CHILDREN

Before the wedding you both believed you wanted a family, but now your husband says no.

Presumably, he hasn't said he doesn't want sex. It's the responsibility of children that he doesn't want. If there has been sexual intercourse, refusal to cooperate in having children is not, directly, grounds for anything in the eyes of the law. Of course, unless matters are resolved between yourselves, it's a sure recipe for eventual marriage breakdown. (*See* Chapter 8, "Separation and divorce.") Husbands and wives owe each other by right "exclusive consortium"—a very awkward and unromantic term for their promise to live with each other, consummate the marriage and grant each other reasonable sexual love, services and companionship.

In most provinces, an outsider can be sued for damages if he does anything to diminish or take away this consortium. This particular right to sue has been abolished in Ontario and British Columbia, but that relates only to third parties and has nothing to do with the right of each spouse to expect the love, services and companionship of the other.

THE MATRIMONIAL HOME

Despite your strong objections, your husband is pressing ahead with plans to list the family farm for sale.

He can list it, but he won't be able to sell it without dealing fairly with you. If you own the farm jointly, your signature on the deed of sale is essential. If you refuse to sign, your husband could ask a court to order the farm sold and the net proceeds shared evenly between you. He might succeed, depending on which province you live in and whether you want to continue to make your home on the farm.

In Saskatchewan, a wife has the right to stay on as long as the property "is in her use or enjoyment or that of her children and is neces-

sary for the support of any of them." In Alberta and Manitoba, and conditionally in British Columbia, a wife can prevent a husband from disposing of the matrimonial home (the homestead) during his lifetime, even if it is registered in his name only. If the husband dies, the wife has the right to stay on until her death. To protect her rights, a B.C. wife has to register on the title to the property a short document stating that the homestead is subject to the provisions of the Wives' Protection Act. Any transfer of the homestead without the written consent of the wife (or a judge's order dispensing with the consent) is invalid in the West. In fact, any Alberta husband who attempts to do this is in line for criminal prosecution and his wife can sue him for damages.

The matrimonial home. Some family law reform proponents want to wipe out separate ownership of the family residence, giving both husband and wife control over the home and an equal right to possession, no matter which partner actually owns the home.

In provinces where reforms are already in effect, the matrimonial home may not be sold, or mortgaged, unless both spouses consent in writing. If the property was sold regardless, a judge could set the transaction aside. In the event of separation or divorce, the court can evict one party and let the other remain in the home, or order that the home be sold and the proceeds be divided between the spouses.

Courts have been recognizing the contributions of married women toward the acquisition and building up of property registered in their husbands' names. Housework and child-rearing are now scoring big points in matrimonial-property disputes.

In a landmark decision in 1978, the Supreme Court of Canada awarded Helen Marie Rathwell a half-interest in the family farm in Saskatchewan—a claim that a lower court had rejected. For 23 years, Mrs. Rathwell "did the chores when her husband was busy on the land; she looked after the garden and canned the produce; she milked cows and sold the cream; she drove machinery, baled hay, provided meals and transportation for hired help and kept the books and records of the farming operation." She also "raised and educated four children." What she failed to do was see to it that her name was on the deed as joint owner of the farm.

THE COMMON-LAW SPOUSE

Your boyfriend wants to move in with you but doesn't want to get married. You do.

Living together; cohabiting; married but not churched; common-law relationship. There have been many labels over the years for the unconventional long-term alliance of man and woman, including the censorious "living in sin." In recent times our lawmakers and judges have been granting some legal recognition to the status of those who choose to take the plunge unofficially, and to their children.

Historically, a common-law marriage was one that lacked only formal solemnization according to the written statute. Everything else was there; agreement and capacity to marry, consummation, cohabitation, a permanent or lasting relationship, an open display of the marriage and public recognition of it.

Sometimes one of these elements is missing: capacity to marry. For example, if either of the parties is still married to someone else the law regards the new union as "meretricious"; the partners are regarded as living "in concubinage." The courts tend to step warily with couples who don't have a *real* common-law marriage going.

Ontario and Prince Edward Island permit cohabiting couples, who are not married and not common-law mates, to make legally binding contracts relating to support and ownership and division of property, though not of the matrimonial home; although there's a home, there's no matrimony. The parties also have the right to "direct the education and moral training of their children." However, they cannot write their own rules regarding the right to custody of or access to the children. Reformers want similar cohabitation agreements legalized across the country.

Time the essence. Alberta, Saskatchewan and Quebec excepted, all provinces recognize the common-law relationship after a couple has lived together for a certain time. The length of that time and the conditions under which needy spouses are eligible for support payments for themselves or children vary from province to province. In British Columbia, the relationship has common-law status after a cohabitation of two years. In Newfoundland and Manitoba, it's one year— but only if a child has been born to the couple. In Ontario, in similar circumstances, it's also a year; otherwise it's five years. In Nova Scotia, it's one year—but only if desertion is proved.

Some provinces have made unwed partners partially eligible for welfare benefits. (*See* Chapter 27, "Salary and benefits," and Chapter 45, "When in need.") A British Columbia statute has been amended to provide for inheritance by a common-law wife, a meretricious spouse and an illegitimate child, if the deceased hasn't left a will.

ALIENATION OF AFFECTION

Your wife was persuaded to leave home for a religious commune. You think you're entitled to damages.

The action for alienation of affection, or more properly, enticement, has been abolished in most provinces, and allowed to wither away in some of the others. The outdated offense of enticement was based on the notion that the wife was the husband's property. In most provinces today, there is nothing a husband or wife can do in law to prevent or punish unfaithfulness. What you can do is sue for divorce. (*See* Chapter 8, "Separation and divorce.")

If you caught your wife in bed with another man and beat him up and threw your wife out, you might find yourself in more trouble than your faithless wife and her beau. You could be charged with assault—although the fact that you have been offended would certainly mitigate the punishment. You might even end up paying your wife support and going to jail for assaulting the Lothario. The wife who finds her husband with his paramour is subject to the same benefits and burdens of the law.

8 Separation and divorce

Has "marriage-on-the-rocks" become the cocktail of our times? According to Statistics Canada, the divorce rate in 1978 was 243 per 100,000 population for a total of 57,155 divorces. In 1975 there were 50,611 divorces, and a decade earlier the yearly total was about 11,000.

British Columbia leads easily with 310 divorces for each 100,000 population. This is double New Brunswick's rate. In Ontario there were 27,041 marriages and 10,624 divorces in the first six months of 1979, a 12 percent increase in divorces over the same period in 1978.

Sociologists believe that the Canadian family scene is in a state of flux. The move to the "no-fault" concept in the 1968 federal Divorce Act—requiring only three years' separation as evidence of marriage breakdown—and the 1978 provincial laws, permitting a more or less equal division of family assets upon divorce, reflect changing social values. The Canada and Quebec Pension Plans have been amended to provide that the pensionable earnings credited to both spouses during a marriage can be divided equally upon divorce or annulment.

Federal law provides grounds for divorce under two headings: matrimonial offenses and marriage breakdown. The first category includes adultery, bigamy, physical or mental cruelty, sodomy, bestiality or rape, and commission of a homosexual act.

Marriage breakdown includes the sentencing of either spouse to a long prison term, gross addiction to alcohol or a narcotic with no reasonable hope of cure, disappearance of the partner for at least three years, refusal or inability to consummate the marriage for at least a year, and living separate and apart for at least three years.

But marriage and the family are still strong and thriving, according to a University of Sas-katchewan study. Prof. S. P. Wakil says neither the national marriage rate nor the number of children born has declined to any marked degree, despite experiments with "alternative life styles." He points out that most nonmarital unions eventually result in conventional marriage and that divorced persons frequently remarry quickly.

Reform of family law seems far from over. Federal and provincial governments agree in principle that all family law should be under provincial jurisdiction. But if each province begins making its own laws on separation and divorce, some fear that a Reno-type situation could result. Ten different divorce laws would be a distinct possibility, because our provincial lawmakers rarely see exactly eye to eye on any issue. The result could be that one province might refuse to recognize a divorce decree granted 10 miles away across the nearest border.

Whatever the reason behind the split, it's always the children of the marriage who suffer most from divorce, according to Dr. Bonnie Robson, a Toronto child psychologist, who interviewed a large number of 11- to 18-year-old children from divorced families: "While it cannot always be observed by parents or friends, the pain is vividly clear." Dr. Robson has also found that all the youngsters opposed the rigid visiting rights handed down by the courts when custody of children is given to one parent.

Studies at the Kitchener-Waterloo (Ont.) Child and Family Centre indicate that children aged 3½ to 4¾, too young to understand what has happened and unable to express their need for comforting and reassurance, may suffer most. Children between 7 and 11 had recurring fears that they would be abandoned by the remaining parent, and some children feel a responsibility to try to reunite the family. An English survey reveals that the children of divorced parents have higher mortality rates, more illness and an earlier school-leaving age than children whose parents stay together.

LEGAL SEPARATION

You and your spouse parted amicably and no documents were signed. Now you've met someone else and you're worried the separation may not be legal.

There are two kinds of legal separation: a mutual agreement worked out by the parties themselves, and a judicial separation issued by a court. Both spell out the rights and obligations of the spouses, but neither separation conveys the right to remarry.

Either spouse can sue for a judicial separation, except in Ontario where only mutual agreements are used. A separation agreement settles such things as maintenance, custody and access to any children of the marriage. The judicial separation is useful when the "right of cohabitation" is ended because of a marital offense such as adultery, physical or mental cruelty or desertion, but the offending party refuses to enter into a separation agreement.

The peaceful path. If the parting was amicable there's no point in either of you going to the stress and expense of court proceedings. Even if there was adultery or cruelty, your friendly farewell probably constitutes "condonation"—that is, forgiveness—which erases the right to sue on such grounds. Your best bet then is to get a lawyer and arrange a mutual separation, negotiating property, maintenance, custody of children, and anything else that should be resolved. After three years of living apart, both of you will be eligible to petition for divorce on the grounds of marriage breakdown; if these matters aren't already straightened out, they will have to be settled at the divorce hearing.

It is not necessary for a husband and wife to have a legal separation before seeking a divorce, but it's still wise to work out an agreement in advance. A divorce petition can then proceed as an undefended case, with the separation agreement approved by the court when the decree is granted.

It's quicker and cheaper to settle such matters as maintenance, custody and access to children beforehand than to fight them out in court. Also, a separation agreement can cover far more territory than a court order usually can, including such things as payment of debts, responsibility for carrying insurance, ownership of car or boat, club memberships, use of charge accounts. A separation agreement can be varied by the court, usually with respect to custody, access or maintenance payments. If reconciliation occurs, a separation agreement is terminated—but only if the parties resume "cohabitation." In this context, that means sexual relations on a regular basis. The courts have ruled that "mere casual acts of intercourse are not conclusive evidence of the resumption of cohabitation." Nor are they always enough to break the three-year separation required to bring a divorce petition based on marriage breakdown.

Letter and spirit. A husband's obligation for maintenance could actually continue after his ex-wife's remarriage, unless the separation agreement makes it clear that this is not the case. If the husband dies, his estate may have to continue maintenance payments.

A separation agreement may seem simple but it is a complex contract which you may have to live with for many years. Only a skilled lawyer should handle the job.

If you have separated from your spouse by mutual consent, or if your spouse has left you without your consent, the judge will almost certainly take the three-year separation as proof in itself of marriage breakdown. If a husband has left his wife, he can bring a petition based on desertion—his own—after five years. A wife has the same right.

A number of Canadian judges have ruled, after careful examination of the facts, that the husband and wife were living "separate and apart" even though they continued to live under the same roof. But absence of a sexual relationship is not enough by itself; there must be "a complete removal from every aspect of the marriage relationship." In cases where this evidence has been successfully used, there was no sexual, social or other domestic relationship between the spouses. The wife did not sleep with the husband, didn't go anywhere with him, didn't cook or keep house for him. The couple merely shared a residence because of financial necessity.

Generally, you won't be granted a judicial separation unless there has been adultery, cruelty or desertion over a period of at least two years. Saskatchewan, Alberta and the Northwest Territories have the additional grounds of sodomy and bestiality. Adultery and cruelty are the only grounds in New Brunswick, Prince Edward Island and Newfoundland.

When a judicial separation is granted on the grounds of adultery, Alberta law permits a court to dispose of the adulterer's property for the benefit of the innocent spouse and children. Saskatchewan and the Northwest Territories allow a judge to exercise this power in respect to a guilty wife's property, no matter on what grounds the separation is based.

Quebec has elaborate laws related to "separation from bed and board." The grounds are adultery, outrage, ill-usage and grievous insult, and refusal of a husband to take his wife into his home and "furnish her with the necessaries of life, according to his rank, means and condition." While some of these conditions are obscure in today's terms, their meaning pretty well boils down to making life unbearable for the other spouse. Every separation agreement in the province must be pronounced by the court.

SUPPORT PAYMENTS

Under your separation contract, your husband has agreed to support you, but he stops sending the cheques after you land a good job.

You can sue your husband for breach of contract. If you get a judgment against him and he still refuses to pay, you can garnishee his wages or have the sheriff seize and sell some of his assets. Your husband will probably ask the court to relieve him of some or all of his financial obligations under the agreement.

Your lawyer might be able to convince your husband to resume payments if you offered to reduce the amount somewhat because of your earnings. That would be less expensive—and easier on the nerves—than clashing in court.

No additional claims can be made as long as spouses continue to live up to the terms of a separation agreement, subject to any variation imposed by a court. But once the contract is breached, either party is free to propose additional terms and conditions.

Reluctant to interfere. Canadian courts usually interpret the terms of separation agreements as "severable," meaning that the entire agreement doesn't stand or fall as a unit. Because your husband has broken the contract by not paying maintenance as agreed, you have the right to claim it in court. But even if the court reduces the amount payable to you, it's unlikely that support payments for your children would be reduced. Courts are reluctant to interfere with financial arrangements in a separation agreement—except for provisions concerning child support—unless the agreement was brought about through "fraud, duress or undue influence," or is an "unconscionable bargain." The party asking for a change in payments must show "clear and compelling reasons" for change. If your husband is in a financial bind, a court might grant his request for temporary relief, no matter what your separation agreement says.

The Divorce Act, which applies everywhere in Canada, says a court may order a wife to support her husband and children. According to the matrimonial laws of British Columbia, Manitoba, Ontario, Quebec, Prince Edward Island and Newfoundland, there is an "equality of obligation" on the part of spouses for each other's support, depending on the spouses' respective needs and means.

All Canada honors the Reciprocal Enforcement of Maintenance Acts. If your husband moves to another province and falls behind in his support payments, you can obtain a maintenance order from a court in your home province. A certified copy is sent to the appropriate province, registered in the proper court and becomes enforceable as an order of that court.

Sample marriage contract

THIS INDENTURE made the 22nd day of May, 1979

BETWEEN: Richard Albert Roe of the City of Toronto, in the Municipality of Metropolitan Toronto

OF THE FIRST PART

—and—   Sally Doe of the City of Toronto, in the Municipality of Metropolitan Toronto

OF THE SECOND PART

WHEREAS the parties hereto are engaged to be married and the marriage is intended to be solemnized on the 3rd day of August, 1979;

AND WHEREAS the parties hereto are desirous of making the provisions hereinafter set out in order to set forth their present intentions with regard to certain matters;

NOW THIS INDENTURE WITNESSETH that in consideration of the premises and other good and valuable consideration, the parties hereto agree as follows:

1. The parties hereto covenant and agree that each of them shall be and continue completely independent of the other as regards the enjoyment and disposal of all property owned by either of them at the commencement of the marriage or received by either of them by gift, bequest, or inheritance during the marriage.

This separation of property shall apply during the marriage, in the event of a marital breakdown, or in the event of the death of either party, notwithstanding the provisions of The Family Law Reform Act, 1978.

2. The parties hereto agree that all property acquired by either of them during the marriage, whether for personal, business or commercial purposes, shall be shared equally by the parties in the event of a marital breakdown, or on the death of either party. Provided, however, that any proportion of the property referred to in paragraph 2 hereof shall be excluded from this paragraph to the extent and in the proportion that the property was acquired by the use of or any proceeds of any separate property referred to in paragraph 1 hereof.

IN WITNESS WHEREOF, the parties hereto have hereunto set their hands and seals on the date first above mentioned.

SIGNED, SEALED
AND DELIVERED
In the presence of:

_____

RICHARD ALBERT ROE

_____
Witness

_____

SALLY DOE

INTERRUPTED SEPARATIONS

Your daughter and her husband are separated but occasionally spend weekends together. Surely this damages her grounds for divorce?

Three years' separation constitutes marriage breakdown and grounds for divorce. The Divorce Act says that a period of separation is not interrupted or ended "by reason only that there has been a resumption of cohabitation by the spouses during a single period of not more than 90 days, with reconciliation as its primary purpose."

But courts have disagreed on the meaning of "a single period of not more than 90 days." In a Manitoba case, where the parties had tried to reconcile on several occasions, none of which exceeded 90 days, a divorce decree was granted. In Saskatchewan, there was an unsuccessful attempt to reconcile, lasting less than 90 days, and in addition the spouses had had sexual relations on four or five occasions but never for the purpose of reconciliation. The judge, holding that the acts of intercourse interrupted the period of separation, dismissed the divorce petition. He was overruled, however, by the Court of Appeal which viewed the acts of intercourse merely as "liaisons." An Ontario judge has ruled that couples get only one single period of up to 90 days to attempt reconciliation.

Act of forgiveness. Sometimes, a matrimonial offense—perhaps, adultery—is considered to be *condoned* (forgiven) if the marriage relationship is resumed with full knowledge of the offense. Condonation was an absolute bar to divorce before 1968. Now, if a matrimonial offense occurs, the spouses can stay together, or get back together, for up to 90 days in an attempt to work things out, without losing the grounds for divorce provided by the offense.

The Divorce Act formally encourages reconciliation. "Except where the circumstances of the case are of such a nature that it would clearly not be appropriate to do so," the lawyer in a divorce action has the duty to discuss the possibility of reconciliation, to draw attention to the provisions of the act about reconciliation and to inform the client of marriage counseling or guidance services.

Before he hears any evidence, the judge is required to ask the partners if there's a possibility of reconciliation. The trial proceeds if one or both of them say there isn't, but if both are willing to try, the case must be adjourned. If, after 14 days, the parties are not reconciled, either may apply to the court to resume the proceedings.

LEGALITY OF MARRIAGE

You have just discovered that when your wife was a teen-ager she married and was deserted by a man who is still living.

If they were never divorced, she's married to him—not you. Your marriage is void *ab initio* (from the beginning). You don't need any legal document to clean your slate because your marriage never existed, but a "declaratory" statement can be issued to regularize your status. The records of the false marriage ceremony—yours—will be corrected. Your partner could be charged with bigamy.

A marriage can be void because: (a) it's bigamous; (b) the parties are within forbidden degrees of blood relationship; (c) one of the parties lacks the mental capacity; (d) one of the parties is not of age; (e) formalities prescribed by law have not been observed; or (f) because of a mistake by one party as to the nature of the marriage ceremony or the identity of the other party.

Annulment is different and distinct from divorce. (*See* Chapter 7, "Engagement and marriage.") A divorce decree dissolves an existing marriage because of something that has arisen since the marriage. A nullity decree declares that a marriage did not exist, because of a state of affairs existing at the time of the ceremony but discovered later.

A decree of nullity of a *void* marriage may be applied for by either of the partners, or any third person—such as a relative or the executor of the estate of either party having an interest. The decree may be applied for during the lifetime or after the death of either or both of the partners. Only the partners may apply for a decree of nullity of a *voidable* marriage. The decree must be issued while both partners are alive. Otherwise, the marriage is valid for all purposes and can't be questioned after the death of either of the parties.

A party to a void or voidable marriage may have the right to financial support or division of property, just as if he or she had been validly married. The Ontario Family Law Reform Act, 1978, defines "spouse" to include either a man or a woman (a) who is married by a form of marriage that is *voidable* and hasn't been voided by a decree of nullity, or (b) who has, in good faith, cohabited in a *void* marriage.

FOREIGN DIVORCE DECREES

Your spouse suggests you try for a "quickie" divorce in Mexico. You wonder if this will be legal in Canada.

Swift and easy divorces in foreign countries have become much rarer since the 1968 Divorce Act that made divorce a great deal simpler to get at home. But some couples in a hurry will have one partner establish residence for a few weeks in another country and file a petition for divorce there. The recognition of foreign divorce decrees in Canada is a tricky subject, abounding with rules and legal nuances—all of which spell big trouble. Your lawyer will almost certainly want to consult with one of the few specialists in the field. Inquiries abroad may also be necessary.

Sometimes a foreign divorce does not conform to our laws and is therefore invalid. In this case, later marriages by either spouse will be invalid—raising the possibility of criminal prosecution for bigamy.

Canadian courts are guided by the following general rule: if the parties were domiciled in the foreign country when proceedings began there, the decree of the foreign court will be recognized as valid, unless it was "contrary to principles of natural justice," or based on fraud.

Foreign decrees have been held to offend against notions of "natural" or "substantial" justice—and acceptance has been refused—where the domicile or permanent place of dwelling on which jurisdiction was based is so minimal that the foreign jurisdiction must be deemed to be, as one judge put it, "purveying divorce to foreigners who wish to buy it."

Foreign decrees granted on grounds that are, by Canadian standards, totally unacceptable, won't be recognized. A foreign divorce must be what Canadian courts regard as a genuine divorce—not a "judicial farce." A decree obtained by fraud—for example, by deliberately misleading a foreign judge—doesn't stand a chance.

THE FRIENDLY DIVORCE

You both agree to a divorce and want it to be simply a farewell between friends.

When spouses decide to part as friends and remain friends, the best route is to live "separate and apart" for three years and then file for divorce on grounds of marriage breakdown. This is really all there is to it. No one has to take any blame. As long as all property and support questions have been settled, it's about as automatic as the law ever gets. If your spouse has committed a matrimonial offense—say, adultery—and won't challenge your use of the offense as grounds, you can proceed with your divorce petition right away. You'll probably be granted a decree within months. However, you'll need an experienced lawyer if your spouse insists you prove the offense. A court may hold that a marital indiscretion does not amount to "adultery."

PROOF OF ADULTERY

You are convinced your husband is having an affair with his secretary and you want to divorce him.

One act of adultery can be enough to constitute grounds for divorce if it is proved in the proper manner. But suspicion, gossip, hearsay, embarrassment, hurt feelings—these things have no standing or weight in the courtroom. If you allege that your husband and his secretary are more than business associates, he doesn't have to prove he's innocent of adultery; you have to prove he's guilty. It's an important difference.

Many people think that adultery must be proved by direct observation. Not so. Courts will usually be satisfied with evidence from which adultery can be inferred—the "familiarity" of the individuals, and the opportunity to commit the offense. That's why evidence that the respondents spent a night together in a motel room will often be accepted as inferential proof of adultery.

Courts are not enthusiastic about evidence of adultery presented by private detectives, although it can't be brushed aside. The "private eye" has all the fundamental rights of the citizen acting within the law. If his evidence passes judicial scrutiny, it's as good as anyone else's, but judges usually prefer testimony from such neutral sources as motel operators, bellboys or chambermaids.

Admission without guilt. The majority of divorces are undefended, simply because both parties want the marriage ended. The defended divorce case rarely has anything to do with keeping the marriage intact. The fight at that point is usually about money, property or children.

Generally, most divorces based on adultery require cooperation of the parties. This is made easy because the law protects a person against self-incrimination where adultery is alleged, unless that person has already given evidence in the same proceedings in disproof of adultery. The effect is to make it difficult to compel an unwilling party to provide admissions needed to prove adultery. So when a petitioner brings divorce proceedings based on adultery against a reluctant respondent, he or she had better have independent evidence to present.

The Divorce Act forces the judge to refuse a divorce decree based solely on the consent, admissions or default of the parties. Unlike all other civil cases, it is impossible to settle a divorce petition "out of court." You can't get a divorce without a trial.

ALCOHOL AND DRUGS

Your husband is an alcoholic and your life is awful, but he won't agree to a divorce.

Alcoholism is valid grounds for divorce—by either spouse—if the judge finds the situation intolerable. The relevant section of the Divorce Act has some pretty woolly language. You must prove that you're living "separate and apart" and that for at least three years your spouse has been "grossly addicted" to alcohol or a narcotic. There must be "no reasonable expectation" of rehabilitation "within a reasonably foreseeable period."

Something more than excessive or habitual drinking must be proved. It's preferable that medical or clinical evidence be presented to show a psychological or physical dependency on liquor or drugs. The onus is on the petitioner to prove that there's no reasonable expectation of rehabilitation; it's not up to the respondent to prove he can kick the habit.

In most cases where drinking is the problem, especially where the respondent refuses to seek help, the petitioner has a better chance if he or she seeks divorce on the grounds of cruelty. Habitual drinking and related conduct are likely to "render intolerable the continued cohabitation of the spouses." *Cruelty* is not, of course, restricted to physical acts alone.

VIOLENCE

Each time that your husband has a bad day at work, you wind up with a black eye.

Your husband can be charged with common assault, or even with assault causing bodily harm—a serious offense, punishable by up to five years in the penitentiary. "Bodily harm" must be of such a nature as to interfere with the victim's health or comfort. A black eye could qualify, as it includes the possibility of damage to vision.

The days when the wife was the husband's "chattel" are long past. A man has no more right to hit his wife than he has to strike any other person. The fact that victim and assailant are husband and wife is of no relevance to the court. Provocation—such as insults or taunts—is not a legal defense for assault, although the bench may weigh the extent of the provocation in fixing the penalty.

In Quebec, you can sue your spouse for damages to your personal property or physical person. In all other provinces, a married woman can bring a civil suit against her husband for damage to her personal property, but not to her physical person and a husband cannot sue his wife for any tort (civil wrong) at all. Of course, physical or mental cruelty is grounds for divorce. If you are planning to divorce your husband for cruelty, you must have proof that his behavior is destroying your health or sanity, and that you can't live with him any longer. His conduct must be of "a grave and weighty" nature. What has been described as the "rough and tumble" of marriage does not add up to *cruelty*.

Saskatchewan and Alberta courts are inclined to restrict the definition of cruelty to conduct that is dangerous to life, limb or health, or is "so grossly insulting as to be intolerable." Quebec courts recognize more subtle forms such as "outrage, ill-usage or grievous insult."

Courts have made it quite clear that the cruelty ground does not provide a shortcut to easy divorce for the adolescent, the incompatible, the disappointed or the unhappy. Some conduct clearly constitutes cruelty: a series of beatings until the wife can take no more; a single savage, premeditated attack; harassment and abuse; degradation that drives the spouse to seek psychiatric help. But cruelty sufficient for divorce has been found in less-than-obvious situations: the practice of *coitus interruptus* damaging the wife's health; the husband's willful refusal to recognize the wife's right to his society; transvestism causing continual stress to the wife; the husband's sexual interest in children; the adoption by the husband of an unorthodox life style and use of drugs; the husband ignoring the wife, neglecting her medical needs and making unreasonable sexual demands; the husband's

domineering, tyrannizing or abusive conduct. Some judges have ruled that persistent refusal of intercourse amounts to cruelty.

The fact that a respondent was insane at the time of committing the cruelty does not prevent the granting of a divorce. Cruelty doesn't have to be intentional; a divorce can be granted where the conduct that makes cohabitation intolerable is caused by delusions.

Maltreatment of children may constitute cruelty. Where it takes the form of beatings, the onus is on the complaining spouse to prove that the treatment was unreasonable and unjustifiable. A parent is entitled to inflict "reasonable chastisement" on his or her children. As always, the conduct must be so bad that it makes continued cohabitation intolerable.

CUSTODY AND ACCESS

Your wife was awarded custody of the children and is remarrying and moving to a distant city. You fear you won't see the children again.

When marriage breaks up, the courts will not worry over much about your happiness or convenience. The guiding principle in custody cases is the welfare and happiness of the children. Each case is decided on its own merits and any order is open to review, but the parent who is awarded custody is usually entitled to move with the children away from the place where custody was granted. Courts hold that when a parent who has unrestricted custody takes a child to "a distant place," the other parent must be prepared to travel to where the child is living or to pay traveling expenses of the child, if he or she wants to exercise visiting rights.

A parent is not allowed to deny access rights because of arrears in child-maintenance payments; nor is he or she allowed to withhold such payments because the other parent is blocking access. A judge may suspend maintenance payments if the "custodial" parent frustrates a court order for access. The offending parent can also be punished for contempt of court.

Sample separation contract

THIS SEPARATION AGREEMENT made in duplicate this 10th day of June, 1979

BETWEEN: Sally Roe of the City of Toronto, in the Municipality of Metropolitan Toronto
(hereinafter called the "Wife")
OF THE FIRST PART

—and— Richard Albert Roe of the City of Toronto, in the Municipality of Metropolitan Toronto
(hereinafter called the "Husband")
OF THE SECOND PART

WHEREAS the Husband and Wife were lawfully married to each other on the 10th day of August, 1958;

AND WHEREAS there are no children born of the marriage save and except Lesley Roe, born October 9, 1961; Robert Roe, born April 12, 1964, and Alice Roe, born March 17, 1967, all of whom are collectively called the "children" throughout and each of whom is individually called the "child" throughout;

AND WHEREAS irreconcilable differences have arisen between the Husband and Wife by reason whereof it became impossible for them to live together as Husband and Wife;

AND WHEREAS the Husband and the Wife have been living separate and apart since February 14, 1979;

AND WHEREAS the parties hereto have agreed to settle and determine all issues between them at the present time;

NOW THEREFORE THIS AGREEMENT WITNESSETH that in consideration of the premises and of the mutual covenants of the said parties, they have covenanted each with the other and agreed as follows:

1. The Husband and Wife intend to and will continue to live separate and apart from each other for the rest of their lives.

2. Neither the Husband nor Wife nor any person on his or her behalf will at any future times directly or indirectly molest, annoy, disturb or interfere with the other, in his or her person, business or manner of life, nor at any time require or by any means, either by taking judicial proceedings or otherwise, endeavor to compel the resumption of cohabitation between the Husband and Wife or to endorse any restitution of conjugal rights and will not for that purpose use any force or restraint to the person or persons for receiving, protecting or entertaining him or her, but that the Husband and Wife may in all things live as if they were not married.

3. (1) The Wife shall have custody of the children. The Husband shall have access to the children at all reasonable times. The Wife acknowledges that it is essential for the welfare of the children that they have as full a communication and contact with their father as is reasonably possible commensurate with the best interests of the children.

(2) The children shall be free to visit their father at any time they wish and shall be free to communicate with their father by letter and telephone as often as they wish.

(3) The Husband shall have the right to have the children visit with him outside of the residence of the Wife, as often as is reasonably convenient to the Husband, the Wife and the children.

(4) The Husband and Wife shall confer with each other on all plans and arrangements relating to access to the children, and generally on all important matters relating to the children's health, welfare, education and upbringing, with a view to arriving at an harmonious policy calculated to promote the children's best interests.

4. (1) The Husband warrants that he is maintaining in force for the benefit of the Wife and children a plan issued by the Ontario Health Insurance Plan.

(2) The Husband covenants that he will maintain for the Wife and children aforesaid cover-

age for hospitalization under the Ontario Hospital Insurance Plan coverage together with coverage against medical bills, at least to a standard which is equivalent to the coverage presently in existence, or in the alternative, will make payment of all such hospital or medical bills for the Wife or children. In addition, the Husband shall make payment of all necessary and proper dental or orthodontic bills incurred for the children during the period in which they are entitled to payments hereunder.

(3) If the Husband fails to maintain this plan of insurance, he is responsible for all hospital and medical expenses incurred by or on behalf of the Wife or the children as long as he is required to provide for the support of the Wife and children under paragraphs 14 and 15 of this agreement.

5. The Husband and Wife each acknowledge that:

(a) all their personal property has been divided between them to their mutual satisfaction;

(b) each is entitled to the personal property now in his or her possession free from any claim by the other; and

(c) each may dispose of the personal property now possessed by him or her as if he or she were unmarried.

6. (1) Neither the Husband nor the Wife shall contract in the name of the other nor in any way bind the other for any debts or obligations.

(2) If debts or obligations are incurred by the Husband or the Wife on behalf of the other before or after the date of this agreement, he or she shall indemnify the other from all (a) claims; (b) costs; (c) expenses; (d) damages; and (e) actions, arising from those debts or obligations.

7. The Husband and Wife release each other from all claims and rights that he or she may have had, or afterwards may acquire,

(a) in the estate of the other upon the other

dying intestate, whether by way of statutory allowance or right under the laws of any jurisdiction and in particular The Succession Law Reform Act in force from time to time in the Province of Ontario;

(b) upon the death of the other, under the laws of any jurisdiction and in particular The Succession Law Reform in force from time to time in the Province of Ontario; and

(c) to act as executor or administrator of the other's will or estate.

8. (1) The Husband and Wife each accept the terms of this agreement in satisfaction of all claims and causes of action each now has except for claims and causes of action

(a) arising under this agreement; or

(b) for a decree of divorce,

including but not limited to claims and causes of action for custody, child-maintenance, alimony, maintenance, interim alimony, possession of or title to property, and any other claims arising out of or during the marriage of the Husband and the Wife.

(2) Nothing in this agreement constitutes a bar to any action or proceeding of either the Husband or the Wife to enforce any of the terms of this agreement.

9. If either the Husband or the Wife obtains a decree of divorce, all the terms of this agreement shall survive and continue in force.

10. The Husband and Wife shall at any time and from time to time execute and deliver to the other any document or documents that the other reasonably requires to give effect to the terms of this agreement.

11. The Husband and Wife each acknowledge that each,

(a) has had independent legal advice; (b) understands their respective rights and obligations under this agreement; and (c) is signing this separation agreement voluntarily.

12. The Husband shall reimburse the Wife for legal fees and disbursements in the amount of $600.00 incurred by her in engaging the services

of Messrs. Brown & Brown, Barristers and Solicitors, for the negotiation and preparation of this agreement.

13. (1) On the 1st day of July 1979 and on the first day of each month following, during the joint lives of the Husband and Wife, the Husband shall pay to the Wife the sum of $500.00 for her own support until she remarries or lives openly with another man as if they were husband and wife.

(2) In addition to the Wife's maintenance payments contributed by the Husband under this paragraph 13, the Wife shall contribute to her own maintenance. The Wife acknowledges that it is her desire and intention to maintain gainful employment and to become self-supporting and independent of the Husband. The Wife's maintenance payments which the Husband is obliged to pay under this paragraph 13 define the full extent of the Husband's obligation to support the Wife.

(3) The Wife's maintenance payments shall be subject to the right of the Husband to apply for a variation under paragraph 15 herein and to deduct a sum equal to the amount by which the Wife's gross income from employment exceeds $200.00 per month.

(4) On or before the last day in each calendar month the Wife shall furnish to the Husband satisfactory evidence of her gross income from all sources of employment for the immediately preceding calendar month, and a deduction (if any) in accordance with paragraph 13(3) shall be made from the support owing in the calendar month next following the month in which such evidence of employment income was or ought to have been given.

(5) On or before the last day in April in each year the Wife shall furnish to the Husband a copy of any income tax return filed by her for the immediately preceding calendar year, and an adjustment shall then be made, if necessary, to comply with the terms of paragraph 13(3) to compensate the Husband for any overpayment of the Wife's maintenance payments during that year.

14. (1) On the 1st day of July, 1979 and on the first day of each month following the Husband or the estate of the Husband shall pay to the Wife as maintenance payments for each child (the "child maintenance payments") the sum of Two Hundred Dollars ($600.00 for 3 children) until one or more of the following arises:

(a) the child becomes 16 years old and ceases to be in full-time attendance at an educational institution;

(b) the child ceases to reside with the Wife, other than for the purposes of attending a post-secondary institution on a full-time basis;

(c) the child becomes 18 years old or as long as the child is a child within the meaning of the Divorce Act (Canada);

(d) the child marries; or

(e) the child dies.

(2) In addition to the child maintenance payments contributed by the Husband or his estate under this paragraph 14 the Wife shall contribute to the maintenance of the above children. The child maintenance payments which the Husband or his estate is obliged to pay under this paragraph 14 define the full extent of the Husband's or the Husband's estate's child maintenance obligations. These payments shall be supplemented by the contribution of the Wife to the maintenance of the children and all reasonable living expenses, schooling fees, tuition and reasonable allowances for the children shall be payable from the aggregate child maintenance contributions of both parties and not from the contributions of either the Husband or the Wife.

15. (1) The Husband and the Wife agree that all paragraphs hereof are to be final except for variation by reason of a material change in circumstances that affects:

(a) the welfare of any child;

(b) the needs of any child during the period

of maintenance referred to in paragraph 14 hereof;

(c) the financial needs and obligations of either the Husband or the Wife;

(d) the financial resources of either the Husband or the Wife.

(2) Obligations arising out of the remarriage of the Husband or the Wife or both are to be taken into account in determining whether there has been a material change in circumstances.

(3) The party seeking the variation referred to herein shall give to the other party notice of the variation sought and the Husband and Wife may thereupon confer either personally with each other or with their respective solicitors to determine the terms, if any, of the variation.

16. (1) The Husband and Wife acknowledge that they hold as joint tenants the matrimonial house and lot municipally known as 123 Glen Manor Avenue, in the City of Toronto, in the Municipality of Metropolitan Toronto, in the Province of Ontario.

(2) The Wife shall be entitled to remain in and enjoy exclusive use and possession of the land and premises known as 123 Glen Manor Avenue, Toronto, Ontario, subject to the following terms:

(a) The Wife covenants and agrees to pay all sums which shall fall due or become payable for principal and interest under the existing mortgage registered against the said premises, or any other encumbrances thereon.

(b) The Wife covenants and agrees to pay municipal taxes, insurance for fire and supplemental perils, repairs and maintenance and other carrying charges including charges for fuel, heating, hydro and water with respect to the said premises.

(c) The Husband and the Wife covenant and agree that the matrimonial home shall not be sold until such time as the youngest of the children reaches the age of 18 years or shall no longer reside with the Wife, whichever is sooner.

(d) Upon the occurrence of the circumstances noted in clause (c), the matrimonial home shall be sold and the Husband and Wife shall share equally in the net proceeds of such sale.

17. Nothing in this agreement constitutes a condonation by either Husband or Wife of any conduct or circumstances, which, but for this agreement would entitle the Husband or Wife to a decree of divorce.

IN WITNESS WHEREOF the Husband and the Wife have hereunto set their hands and seals.

SIGNED, SEALED
AND DELIVERED
In the presence of:

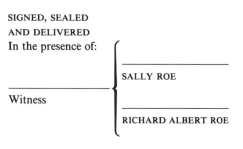

_____
Witness

_____
SALLY ROE

_____
RICHARD ALBERT ROE

The lady vanishes. If the wife simply vanished, taking the children with her, and the other parent was stymied in his efforts to exercise his access rights, he can probably win court support for a search. The Family Law Reform Acts of Ontario and Prince Edward Island, quickly being copied elsewhere, provide that "the court may order any person or public agency to provide such particulars of the address as are contained in the records in its custody, and the person or agency shall provide such particulars as it is able to provide." This will bring most hide-and-seek parents out of the woodwork.

If you learn that your ex-wife or her new husband are neglecting or mistreating the children or harming their morals, you should quickly present evidence of these matters to a judge. He won't feel bound by a custody order that was made at a different time in a different situation. You may win a reversal of the original custody order or have your access rights strengthened.

DIVIDING ASSETS

Your husband inherited a large sum during the marriage. He says that won't be part of the divorce settlement.

Your husband may not have the sole right to make that decision, for there's been a revolution in matrimonial-property legislation. By 1979, all provinces except New Brunswick and Newfoundland had legislation calling for equal division of "family assets" when a marriage breaks down or is dissolved. But there can be complications. Formerly every province except Quebec had statutes and precedents dealing with family property, built around the idea that husband and wife were "separate as to property." Neither spouse was, as a result of marriage, specifically entitled to anything the other brought into the marriage or acquired during the marriage. Each owned what he or she bought or received as a gift or legacy.

The "separation of property" was actually introduced as a move toward the emancipation of women who, until then, had generally surrendered their property to their husbands upon marriage. After World War II, this doctrine was attacked as not taking into account the contributions of wives to the acquiring and increasing of family property.

Family assets. At the core of the new statutes is the concept of "family assets"—generally speaking, the matrimonial home and any property owned by one or both spouses and ordinarily used by them or their children while residing together. Family assets could include the family car, cottage, boat, furniture, furnishings, household bank account, savings or investments. Just about anything. If spouses separate permanently, are divorced, or the marriage is annulled, the main thrust of the reform is that each is entitled to an equal share of the family assets, regardless of whose name they are registered in. But there are exceptions.

The court may order an unequal division of family assets if an equal division would be unfair, having regard to any agreement between the parties, the length of the marriage or separation, the date when the property was acquired, the extent to which the property was a gift to one of the spouses from a third party, or an inheritance, or "any other circumstance" the court thinks should result in the division being unequal.

Ontario and Prince Edward Island now provide that the judge should take into account the fact that one of the spouses received certain property or money by way of gift or inheritance, without stating flatly that this ends the matter in that spouse's favor. Alberta, Saskatchewan and Nova Scotia exempt gifts and inheritances outright from the category of family assets, at least to the extent of their value at the time of the marriage or the time of acquisition, whichever is later. British Columbia and Manitoba include gifts and inheritances.

As one response to the new laws, more and more people are now drawing up marriage contracts in which they state specifically who owns what and who will get what if the marriage should break down. In effect, they are writing their own rule book in the expectation their agreement will override the law of their province.

Quebec reformed its matrimonial-property law back in 1970, creating a "partnership of acquests," roughly similar to the other provinces' family-asset sharing. It grants full right to switch later to one of the other plans of distribution, either "community of property" or "judicial separation of property." Under a "partnership of acquests," husband and wife are separate as to property while the marriage lasts. They may deal with their own separate property as they see fit, except that there are some restrictions on gifts of property to third parties during the marriage. When the marriage ends, by death or divorce, part of the property of either is subject to sale and division of the proceeds. Property exempted from partition includes what either party had before marriage or received during marriage by gift or inheritance.

PROTECTING ASSETS

Your husband threatens to abandon his lucrative one-man consulting business if you demand a 50-50 split in the divorce settlement.

You can't force him to keep his business going but an interim court order can prevent sale, dissipation or waste of property pending a hearing. This applies to all assets, not only family property. You have a real interest in seeing that his business continues to produce income. If the judge finds that a spouse has "unreasonably impoverished" the family assets, or that the result of equal division would be unfair, he may order other property to be shared even though it may not be a family asset. The modern wife-homemaker can confidently argue she should have some share of her husband's business assets because of her contribution in staying home and looking after the house and children, leaving him free to build up the business. An Ontario judge awarded $774,000 to the estranged wife of a millionaire architect, noting that the wife had borne the main responsibility for household management and child care which had left her husband "physically, intellectually and mentally free to concentrate on earning money and acquiring and managing his nonfamily assets."

Right down the middle. The California divorce courts are not quibbling about establishing the wife's financial rights on the basis of her contribution to "household management and child care." It's a split right down the middle. Canadian husbands should note that provincial courts in Canada are following American precedents more and more as "the British connection" fades into the past.

In exercising its power to divide family assets, the court may order transfer of property ownership for a fixed term, physical division of assets, sale and share of the proceeds, payment of money, placing property in trust for a child, and posting of security to ensure that the order is properly carried out.

UNJUST ENRICHMENT

You put everything in your wife's name for business and tax reasons. Now she maintains everything will belong to her after the divorce.

Many a husband has been stung in the past by such arrangements, but the new laws cut both ways. A husband in this situation is in a much better legal position today.

Courts used to take the position that the man was presumed to have made a gift in favor of his wife and he faced an uphill battle in proving that he hadn't meant to. This presumption is still hard to overcome. The courts say a man can't use his own evasive tactics as a reason for recapturing a property interest he had parted with. But this presumption has been abolished in Prince Edward Island, Ontario and Alberta—subject to specific exceptions concerning real estate taken in the joint names of spouses and concerning spouses' bank accounts. No matter who provides the money, if one spouse buys property in the name of the other, it will be presumed that the person in whose name the property is bought holds it in trust for the buyer. If joint title is taken in the name of both spouses, it will be presumed that joint ownership was intended. The same goes for joint accounts in banks or other financial institutions.

You should be able to win back half of what you put in your wife's name, at least of the property classed as "family assets." There's a chance that you'd also regain business assets you put in her name. You would have to convince a court that your wife, in effect, holds them in trust for you and that she would be "unjustly enriched" if allowed to keep them.

In Manitoba you'll have fewer problems. The Marital Property Act says that on marriage breakdown there's to be equal sharing of family and commercial assets. You'd almost surely get back half of the assets you transferred to your wife, whether they are family or nonfamily assets. If either spouse seeks more than an equal sharing of assets, he or she will have a tough time in the courtroom.

DOUBLE JEOPARDY

Your former wife heard about your promotion and she demands an increase in her maintenance. She's living with a man who makes more than you do.

The law is blind to your wife's new romantic arrangements and, at this stage, her new lover has no legal financial responsibilities toward her. But you do have room to maneuver. Maintenance awards may be reduced or even canceled if you can prove there's been marked improvement in your ex-wife's economic situation. The same is true of alimony—that is, support payments received by one spouse from the other while they are separated but still married.

The conditions for the granting of alimony and maintenance are essentially the same everywhere in Canada. A husband and father must provide for his family as far as he is capable of doing so. Maintenance payments are almost always ordered as part of a divorce and the law permits that an order "may be varied from time to time or rescinded by the

court that made the order if it thinks fit and just to do so, having regard to the conduct of the parties since the making of the order or any change in the condition, means or other circumstances of either of them."

Your former wife has to show need on her part and ability to pay on yours. If she makes no secret of the fact that she's living with someone else, you may be able to have maintenance payments lowered because of her "conduct" and her improved standard of living. When she does remarry, she will acquire the usual legal rights against the new husband. Her "condition" and "means" are improved and you have a good chance of having the maintenance order in her favor reduced or canceled, but remarriage doesn't automatically wipe out a maintenance order unless the original order specifically says so. A lot depends on the relative means of past and present husbands. It can get more tangled. If your ex-wife does not marry the other man, or splits up with him, she may be more in need than ever and you could be liable to pay her more.

DESERTION

When you didn't agree to a separation, your husband stomped out of the house and didn't return. He's been gone for months.

Desertion is a matrimonial offense—easy to say, but hard to define in its multitude of forms. Basically, it consists of either partner leaving the other without a good enough reason and without the other's consent. Being deserted for three years constitutes marriage breakdown and you can petition for divorce.

It may seem a bit bizarre but the courts could decide that *you* did the deserting, even though you stayed in the matrimonial home. You can be guilty of "constructive desertion" if, in effect, your conduct drove your husband out of the house. You can still sue for divorce, but you must wait five years.

Let's say your husband was asking for a separation because he could no longer stand what he termed your misconduct—infidelity, drinking or whatever—and you told him you had no intention of reforming. He could argue, with a fair prospect of success, that he had to leave an intolerable situation. This makes *you* the deserter. On the other hand, if you left the house because of an intolerable situation caused by him, *he* would be the deserter. You could then petition for divorce after three years.

If you've been deserted, you can petition for divorce, alleging marriage breakdown, and ask for a property settlement, custody, support for you and your children, plus court costs.

The disappearing act. If your husband has simply disappeared, how can he be served with the divorce papers? The court may allow you to effect service by advertising in a newspaper or by mailing the divorce petition to someone who is likely to bring it to your husband's attention.

Most provinces now have a marriage prop-

After the moonlight and roses

Divorce is never a laughing matter for those involved. Yet the cartoonist provokes mirth, when his creations display absurdly fey attitudes toward marriage breakup—attitudes that are incongruously out of step, even for these freewheeling times.

These syndicated "Side Glances" appear in newspapers throughout North America and reflect the addition of social issues such as divorce and separation to politics, war and mothers-in-law as the contemporary humorist's stock in trade.

"Somehow, it seems a shame to pay $300 for a gown that you'll wear only three or four times!"

"Bill and I were going to get divorced, but decided against it. We hate going along with trends!"

erty-settlement law. Assuming you can have the documents served on your husband, you can bring an application for division of property, support and other matters shortly after the desertion occurs. This isn't a divorce; you'll have to wait three years for that. But if you can survive economically during that time, you will save expenses by combining your property and support claims with your divorce petition.

MARRIAGE CONTRACTS

You thought your marriage contract covered every eventuality, but now that you're divorced, the property division and support arrangements don't seem fair.

This is a problem that seems certain to lead to a lawyer's bonanza following the radical change in family law. When any adult person willingly signs any contract whatever, it's regarded as the thoughtful acceptance of a legally enforceable agreement. If, for example, your new car turns out to be a lemon you shouldn't entertain high hopes of renegotiating the terms of the loan contract.

Most Western countries once banned marriage contracts lest they undermine the stability of marriage and the family. Today, these contracts are legally binding in Prince Edward Island, Ontario, Manitoba, Saskatchewan, Alberta and British Columbia, and people intending to marry, or already married, may draw up contracts outlining property rights and support obligations that shall apply during the marriage and in the event of divorce.

Power of discretion. While the terms of the contracts can be varied at any time by the courts, the reality is that judges are most reluctant to alter the terms of any contract. The law of contract is as old as literate man and if agreements between individuals—or companies, or governments—can be lightly broken, then all other transactions stand on shifting sands.

The new laws usually state that a marriage contract is subject to variation by a court if it is "unconscionable," or if it was entered into under fraud, duress, or undue influence. If, for example, one of the spouses is on welfare the court may ignore a waiver of that person's right to support. This usually concerns the wife, but because of the mutual-support obligations in some provinces, it may be the man who is so favored by the court. Thus, it could turn out that a working ex-wife is ordered to make indefinite payments to an ex-husband who decides to ride the welfare train.

Courts have power to make any orders in the best interests of children, regardless of a contract. Manitoba, Alberta and British Columbia permit marriage contracts to deal only with division of property. Prince Edward Island and Ontario say the only matter that may *not* be dealt with is the right to custody or access to children.

Many Quebec couples enter into marriage contracts that define them as being "separate as to property." What the parties own before marriage, and what they acquire during it, remains their own individual private property. Each is also liable for his or her own personal debts incurred before and during marriage.

A marriage contract may be especially appropriate for couples entering a second marriage. Each may have property that is to be kept separate in the event of separation, or for estate purposes. For example, a man may be moving into the home owned by the woman and they may agree that he will have no property rights in the house, or acquire none, unless the marriage lasts a specified term. Or a couple may prefer to limit the merger of personal property into "family assets" by agreeing that some items remain outside the contract. ("I'll marry you, yes, but my stamp collection doesn't go with the deal.")

The "palimony" payoff. Judges now are making more flexible rulings on "implied contracts" or "tacit understandings" between individuals living together but not married, which used to be regarded as immoral and illegal. Many couples are moving to protect themselves with "cohabitation contracts," hoping they'll stand up in court. These contracts can deal with "ownership in or division of property; support obligations; the right to direct the education and moral training of their children, but not the right to custody or access to their children; and any other matter in the settlement of their affairs." That last catchall clause could include almost anything—who does the dishes, who walks the dog—as long as it's not "against public policy." For example, a cohabitation agreement could not stipulate that the woman is to have an abortion if she becomes pregnant.

Courts in Prince Edward Island and Ontario can alter a support obligation in a cohabitation agreement only if the couple has lived together continuously for at least five years, "or in a relationship of some permanence where there is a child born of whom they are the natural parents."

THE DO-IT-YOURSELF KIT

You read an ad for a do-it-yourself divorce kit. Your lawyer estimates about $500 for an "open-and-shut case."

You have the right to represent yourself in any Canadian court, but it's an old saying in legal circles: he who represents himself in court has a fool for a client.

An "open-and-shut" divorce case is one in which the parties are in complete agreement and where there are no property disputes or child-custody matters to be resolved. But even in such a straightforward case there are many formalities and every "t" must be crossed and every "i" dotted, or else the case will probably be thrown out of court. Before your case reaches court you must complete a number of documents and affidavits, and though many nonlawyers have coped with this task adequately, the risk of botching the job is high. "Divorce kits" contain clear instructions all right, but merely being able to read is no guarantee you'll clear all the hurdles.

At trial there are certain crucial matters that must be proved formally, such as establishing that the court has jurisdiction to hear the case, that there is a valid marriage to dissolve, and that there are grounds for divorce. Even in uncontested cases, the paper work and the proper presentation of evidence may defeat the lay person. In a contested case, you as an amateur are bucking very strong headwinds; an experienced divorce lawyer may be representing your spouse.

If funds are a genuine problem, Legal Aid may be available.

9 You, the parent

Honor thy father and thy mother. The commandment has taken on a quality of plaintiveness in this "enlightened" age—an age that is not an easy one for mothers and fathers. The traditional concept of family seems to be under assault from all sides, encircled by those who would improve it by tinkering with details, by others who prescribe radical changes, and by some who would scrap it altogether in favor of an up-to-date institution still to be invented.

But despite the alarming and depressing statistics on failed marriages and the ensuing broken homes and shortchanged children, the majority of parents are weathering the storms and managing to raise less-than-perfect families in this less-than-perfect world. In most of these families, the question of parents' "rights" is not a frequent issue; the traditional arrangement of authority and responsibility, with some modifications, is taken for granted by mother, father and children.

At least part of the conflict and confusion that arise from discussions of parents' rights nowadays seems to be the emphasis on the individual. Little attention is paid the concept of husband and wife as a single entity—the traditional idea of "one flesh"—while much is written and spoken about the rights of the individual spouses and children.

It has become fashionable, too, to accuse parents of such a litany of sins and shortcomings that their only defense is to blame their parents. One sometimes wonders on what experience some critics base their conclusions: themselves as parents or as children?

Parents are being told on all sides that they should love their children more, guide them better, protect them more adequately, but—stop telling them what to do. They shouldn't punish them physically or mentally if they transgress, and they are to blame if the kids go wrong.

In fact, there has been such an onslaught of experts telling parents how to raise their children that some parents are reluctant to discipline their offspring for fear the law will step in, according to Judge R. H. Harris of the Manitoba Family Court. "I'm of the opinion that children have too many rights. What about their responsibilities?" Judge Harris asked a meeting of the Child Welfare League of America, in Winnipeg in October 1979.

When parents fail as parents—in their obligations to one another and to their children—it is proper that the state be ready to salvage what can be salvaged and to protect the innocent parties. But most parents are, at least, qualified successes and they earn the right to the authority that must accompany responsibility.

In spite of gloomy predictions and alarums and excursions, most Canadians still honor their fathers and their mothers. And there is no compelling evidence that coming generations will not do likewise.

PROVIDING 'NECESSARIES'

Your 15-year-old son, who has stopped going to school and won't look for a job, says you must continue to support him.

The law is on his side. Federal and provincial statutes compel parents to support their children to at least age 16. But you also have the obligation to see that he attends school until his 16th birthday, unless there are exceptional circumstances. (*See* Chapter 10, "Education.") The Federal Criminal Code requires a "parent, foster parent, guardian or head of a family" to provide "necessities of life" for a child under 16, which means the child must not be "in destitute or necessitous circumstances," or his life or health endangered.

Provincial child-support laws usually require that fathers and mothers share equally the support of their children. In Prince Edward Island and the Territories, the primary responsibility falls to the father; the mother is liable only if she can pay and her husband cannot.

Parents must continue support until a child reaches 16 in Alberta, New Brunswick, Saskatchewan and the Northwest Territories, but it becomes 19 in New Brunswick, 18 in Saskatchewan, if, through mental or physical disability, a child cannot provide himself with the "necessaries of life." There is no cutoff date for parents in Quebec: the obligation for support remains forever if the child is in need. The limit is 17 in Newfoundland and 18 in the other provinces and the Yukon. The Family Law Reform Acts of Ontario and Prince Edward Island say both parents must supply support and education whether a child is born in or out of wedlock. The duty lasts until the child reaches 18 or marries, but a child of 16 or older who "has withdrawn from parental control" frees parents from further responsibility. When parents are sued for child support, courts take into account such factors as their financial circumstances and the child's standard of living and means of looking after himself. "Necessaries of life" have been interpreted to include medical care, clothing, household equipment, food, education and training for a trade.

Under the federal Divorce Act, "maintenance" (regular payments) may be awarded to children under 16—or children over 16 who are unable by reason of illness, disability or other cause to withdraw from parental shelter or control. All provinces have "dependents' relief" laws to ensure that children are adequately provided for from the estates left by deceased parents. There's also financial support of children born out of wedlock—up to age 16 in some provinces, to 18 in others.

Ontario and Prince Edward Island impose an obligation on children 18 or over to provide support for their parents, relative to the parents' need and the children's ability to pay. In Quebec, you must not only support your children, but also, in some circumstances, your mother-in-law and father-in-law if they are in need and they must support you if you need help.

UNDERAGE RUNAWAYS

Your 15-year-old daughter has gone to live with her older sister and refuses to return home.

She is still a "child" in the eyes of the law and under your responsibility and control. You must support her until she is 16—possibly 19 if you live in New Brunswick, or even forever if she is in need and you live in Quebec—but if you can't assert your authority you will be regarded as a parent who has "lost control" and the courts can have a big say in what happens next.

Why your daughter left home and whether she's better off where she is would be investigated. She is supposed to have your consent to live outside the family home—at least until she is 16—but a judge could decide she's justified in choosing another home. He could decide that she cannot remain with her sister, but that she shouldn't be compelled to live with you either. And if your older daughter is obviously a bad influence on her sister, you could be in big trouble if you didn't strive to get the youngster out of there. You could seem to be condoning (accepting) the situation and be found guilty of the crime of "contributing to juvenile delinquency."

If persuasion has failed to get your daughter home, the Children's Aid Society (CAS) should be consulted—by any of the parties or by an outsider. The main purpose of the CAS is to try to find solutions to family problems and, if counseling doesn't work, more drastic measures are available. The CAS *must* respond when someone calls for help.

If the social worker on the case decided the child was in an environment where her health or morals were endangered, she would be considered "a child in need of protection." She'd likely be removed—forcibly, if necessary—to "a place of safety." A Family Court judge would decide where she should live. The answer might well be a foster home. The days when parents literally "owned" their children are gone. Now, the welfare of the child is the primary consideration.

CHILD NEGLECT

You go to a movie and leave your 9-year-old daughter to baby-sit your infant son. A nosy neighbor calls the police and now you are charged with leaving infants unattended.

Maximum penalty is two years' imprisonment for anyone who "unlawfully abandons or exposes a child who is under the age of 10 years, so that his life is or is likely to be endangered, or his health is or is likely to be permanently injured." However, the law is not really meant for cases of benign neglect such as this. Your judgment is obviously faulty: a 9-year-old is still legally an "infant" and too young to be left unattended, let alone left in charge of a baby.

Provincial child-welfare laws all provide heavy penalties for child neglect, but the wording of the statutes varies considerably. In Ontario the Child Welfare Act penalizes "any person having the care, custody, control or charge of a child under the age of 10 years who leaves the child unattended for an unreasonable length of time without making reasonable provision for the supervision and safety of the child."

If a charge of child neglect was laid after the neighbor's intervention, the situation would hinge on the "reasonable provision" clause. Was your infant strangling in his crib upstairs while his sister was watching TV? Some 9-year-olds are surprisingly mature and responsible, others are not. Next time get an adult, experienced baby-sitter, preferably one you employ regularly, or else skip the movie. When you do leave your children in the care of a baby-sitter, leave the address and phone number where you can be reached, or give the name and number of a friendly neighbor to call in an emergency and the emergency numbers of the fire and police departments and your doctor.

TEEN-AGE PREGNANCY

You are shocked to find out that the family physician prescribed the pill for your daughter.

Your right to know about this depends to a large extent on the age of your daughter. The lower her age (especially below 16), the

The unborn child

In 1979, a Nova Scotia judge appointed an unrelated person as guardian of an unborn child, after the guardian argued that the life of the child was endangered because the mother was seeking an abortion. The decision raises difficult, fundamental questions about the rights of the unborn vis-à-vis abortion, which has been legal in Canada since 1968.

A Dalhousie University law professor, Arthur Foote, said the Nova Scotia decision was the first such case "I know of within the Anglo-Commonwealth system." A similar request, by an unrelated person seeking to prevent an abortion, had been rejected a few weeks earlier by an Ontario judge.

Since 1968, under the Criminal Code, the decision to have, or not to have, an abortion is between the mother and the abortion committee of an accredited hospital. Neither the unborn child, the father, nor anybody else has any say in the matter. But if the 1979 Nova Scotia decision is taken as a precedent, or leads to Criminal Code amendments, the legal situation may be modified. A "next friend"—the father, or any adult—could intervene on behalf of the child.

stronger your right to know. The law is vague. It's tied in with "the age of consent"—which is not always the same as the age of majority (adulthood)—and this involves such questions as whether the girl is mature enough to appreciate the nature of what's involved and has the ability to come to her own "reasoned decision." The medical profession has only fuzzy legal guidelines to go by when determining whether parental consent must be obtained.

Courts generally distinguish between the case of a doctor prescribing medical treatment, such as insertion of an intrauterine device, and that of a doctor counseling a patient. The former involves physical contact and, if the girl is under 16 and the treatment is not urgent, the law, not to say common sense, seems to require the doctor to obtain parental consent.

But it appears he doesn't need that consent if he is only counseling or advising. However, some authorities believe prescribing birth control pills is treatment, not counseling, and parental approval should be obtained unless there is sufficient reason to dispense with it. This situation arises when the applicants are between 16 and 18. It's not necessary if the girl is of age to live legally outside the parental home, or outside of parental influence with court approval.

FINANCIAL RESPONSIBILITY

Your 15-year-old son takes your car without asking and has an accident. The other motorist is suing him and you, too.

Except in Quebec, parents are not responsible for the *torts* (civil wrongs) of their children and it's unlikely that a suit for damages against you would succeed. Exceptions can arise when, in the words of one judge, a parent "has knowledge of the wrongdoing and consents to it, where he directs it, sanctions it, ratifies it." In this situation, the parent "becomes in effect a party to it (the wrong), and as such is liable to the injured person." While your boy is in all sorts of trouble (minimum age for licensed driving is 16 or older), the fact

that the car was taken without your permission clears you of knowledge or consent.

The other driver is likely to charge that you failed to supervise your child properly; you neglected to instruct him not to take the car. But he has to prove his case "on the balance of probabilities." It's unlikely he can. Even if he succeeds in establishing the boy's negligence, and is awarded damages, how can he collect? A 15-year-old seldom has personal assets and the parents would not be under any legal obligation to pay.

You might be held liable if the other driver proved that your son had a "propensity" (tendency) to steal, that you knew of it, that you should reasonably have anticipated he might steal the car, and that there was some reasonable step you could have taken to prevent the particular theft and that you failed to do so.

Parents do have the duty to supervise and control their children properly, but the obligation diminishes the closer the children get to maturity. The test of whether a parent acted with reasonable care usually hinges on the answer to this question: could an adult reasonably have foreseen the possibility of danger arising from the child's conduct in a given set of circumstances?

SCHOOLYARD DAMAGE

Your son knocked out his opponent's front teeth in a schoolyard fight and the parents have sent you a $1,000 bill for dental work.

Unless you feel morally responsible, send the bill back by return mail. There's little chance that a suit can succeed if you are sued for damages. You do have a duty to supervise and control your son but you delegate that responsibility to the school authorities during the hours your son is in school, or while he's taking part in school activities. The parents of the other boy might well have a case against the school principal or the Board of Education for failing to supervise the children in the schoolyard properly.

To succeed in having you held liable for the injury caused by your son, the other party would probably have to prove that your son was well known as a bully, that he frequently got in fights at school, and that you were aware of this and encouraged him to use his fists. In these circumstances a judge might rule that, in effect, you were the guiding force behind the fight. This possibility would be even stronger if the action took place after school hours and off school property: then the supervisory responsibility you delegated to the school authorities is back in your hands.

CORPORAL PUNISHMENT

You took your belt to your 16-year-old son for using filthy language and he says he's going to have you charged with assault.

Parents have the right to inflict moderate and reasonable corporal punishment on their children. What is "reasonable" is a question of fact, not law, and will depend on the individual circumstances. The Criminal Code states: "Every schoolteacher, parent or person standing in the place of a parent is justified in using force by way of correction toward a pupil or child, as the case may be, who is under his care, if the force does not exceed what is reasonable under the circumstances."

But even if you have tried everything else, delay reaching for the belt until you're sure your temper is under control. If you spare the rod you may indeed spoil the child, but you're risking prosecution if you strike in anger. If you used your belt, even unintentionally, on the head or spine or any part of the body where the skin is thin, a court would very likely consider the force "unreasonable" and you could be convicted; buttocks are safest.

The bruise barometer. Our courts are ever vigilant for any sign of child abuse. Where's the borderline between physical abuse and punishment? A study of court judgments offers some guidelines: the child must "merit" punishment; the punishment must fit the crime—a few whacks of the belt on the posterior might be considered reasonable for obscene talk or insolence, but unreasonable for a dirty look or mild disobedience.

It's not illegal to cause pain. As one judge remarked: "Without pain, the whole purpose of the punishment would be lost." You may leave bruises, but you can be in trouble if they are long-lasting. "The greater the mark left by the punishment, the greater the burden on the parent," as another judge opined.

Child punishment involving the risk of permanent injury will always be regarded as excessive, even if permanent harm doesn't result. And what might be considered as reasonable punishment for a 16-year-old might well be excessive for a child of 10.

So it's possible, though rare, for a child to sue a parent in the civil courts for damages for excessive use of force. He can't sue "in his own right" (because he's under the age of majority), and must proceed through a "next friend" or, in Quebec, a tutor—an adult who will be responsible for legal costs. This can get complicated because, in most provinces, the "next friend" must be a male and is usually the father. Since the father would be, in effect, suing himself, someone else—maybe an uncle or an older brother—would have to launch the action.

ADOPTION

You gave up your infant son for adoption. You want him back.

The courts call it a "change of heart" case. The natural mother's right to seek the return of her child poses one of the most intricate and emotional issues of all family law. But the right is a limited one, depending on the terms of the law reform in your province and on the time elapsed since the adoption.

In case after case, the courts have wrestled with the extremely tough task of balancing the welfare of the child, the rights of the natural parent, and the interests of the couple adopting the child. Some legislatures have tried to make the job of the judges easier by spelling out what factors are to govern. Some statutes say that a mother can revoke her formal consent to the adoption within 30 days of signing it, some allow 21 days, others say nothing on the subject.

The variations and uncertainties create fear in the minds of adopting parents that they might lose the child, especially in New Brunswick, Quebec and Alberta—provinces that have not spelled out a cutoff period for revocation of consent. The yardstick everywhere when consent to an adoption has been revoked is what is in the best interests of the child. But different courts apply different criteria in establishing this and nothing is crystal clear.

The Supreme Court of Canada awarded custody to the natural parents in one well-known case, stating that "the welfare of the child" was the most important consideration. The justices said there was a strong presumption in favor of natural parents over "strangers"; the natural parents could lose their right to custody only by abandoning the child or by so misconducting themselves that it would be improper to leave the child with them.

The ties that bind. Adoption involves a breaking of the ties that bind a child to the natural parents and the substitution of new ties with the adoptive parents. Adoption laws require consent from specified parties and although they differ in detail, the general classes of persons whose consents are needed are similar. They fall into four groups:

■ The child, if deemed old enough to give consent (usually at about 12 years).

■ The spouse of the person applying, if the application is not made jointly by husband and wife.

■ The natural parents, unless for specified statutory reasons the consent may be dispensed with.

■ The guardian or authorized agency to which the child has been surrendered or committed as a permanent ward.

Anyone wanting to give up a child for adoption or wanting to adopt a child should get in touch with the local Children's Aid Society. Parents don't have the right simply to decide to shed their children. Yet some parents are unable or unwilling, even with the help of welfare services, to care for their children properly.

The total surrender. All provinces have statutes that permit the voluntary termination of parental rights. This may be done by means of a "surrender instrument" or by a "consent to adoption." Consent is by far the most commonly used adoption procedure in Canada. If the child was born in wedlock, the general rule is that both parents, or the surviving parent, must consent to the adoption. An exception is made in some provinces when the parents are separated or divorced, in which case the only consent needed is that of the parent who has legal custody of the child. If the child was

Foster parenting: the need and the joy

Tens of thousands of neglected children desperately need foster parents and the "experts" agree on two things: the urgency of the need, and the fact that older people—including grandparents—often make the best foster parents. Having been "through the mill" with their own families, they are able to offer what troubled children so sadly lack: love, patience, guidance and security.

There are never enough good foster homes to go around, and if you're interested you should get in touch with your nearest Children's Aid Society office. You can expect a thorough vetting of your material circumstances—what kind of physical environment you can offer a child, or children—and of your personal background. And don't expect to make money. Financial support provided through the Children's Aid Society ranges from about $80 to $250 a month per child, depending on the province and the age of the child.

Wherever you live in Canada, if you can offer a good home for a child on a temporary basis, there are sure to be dozens of children who need one—urgently. Call your local Children's Aid Society for details.

born out of wedlock, the laws usually state that only the mother has the right to consent to the adoption—although Ontario, Quebec and the Yukon require the consent of the natural father if the child is living with and being supported by the father.

The consent must be voluntary in every way. In the case of an unwed mother—the source of most adoptions—five provinces won't sanction the consent if it is given before the expiry of a specified number of days from the birth. The periods range from 4 days in the Northwest Territories to 7 in Ontario, 10 in British Columbia and Manitoba, and 14 in Prince Edward Island.

All the "change of heart" cases so far have been concerned with the revoking of the consent to an adoption, not the validity of the consent itself.

LEGACIES

Your father-in-law left sizable legacies which your children will get at age 21, but you could use some money now for their education.

You should approach the executor of your father-in-law's estate and ask for an advance. Most wills that contain this kind of delayed inheritance clause also say the executor has the right to pay some or all of the legacy prematurely, if payment will "benefit" an underage beneficiary. (*See* Chapter 33, "Wills and gifts.") The wording probably approves early payments if money is needed for the youngster's "benefit, maintenance or education." Even if "education" is not specifically mentioned, any court would agree that this is included in the term "benefit." The executor doesn't have to ante up, but he probably will if you can demonstrate the need and the benefit to the heirs.

Dead man's wishes. If the will contains no provision for earlier payment, this is not necessarily the end of the matter. In most provinces, a parent or executor can apply to the court for an order authorizing partial payment of children's shares before they reach the

stipulated age. The applicant would have to show that the deceased probably intended to allow this. Judges are fairly flexible in authorizing such payments, unless the deceased made it crystal clear in the will that this wasn't to be done. An Ontario judge allowed $2,500 a year to a 21-year-old man who was to receive $150,000 at age 30. The heir wanted some money now to help support himself, his wife and child while he attended law school.

Generally, any interest earned from the capital sum left to a child on a time-delay legacy can be obtained with little difficulty, if it's needed for maintenance or education. But the court won't release the capital sum unless it's obvious that this would be more beneficial to the child than preserving the property until the stipulated age.

Newfoundland, Saskatchewan, Alberta and the Northwest Territories will permit the sale of real estate willed to a minor upon attainment of a stated age, if a court considers it necessary for educational purposes. Ontario and Alberta permit a court-ordered sale on *any* personal property under the same general conditions. British Columbia and Saskatchewan don't go that far, but their laws permit a judge to order that stock dividends accruing for the benefit of underage beneficiaries be paid to a parent or guardian to maintain or educate the child.

GUARDIANSHIP

Your brother asks if he can name you as guardian of his children, but you have three of your own to look after.

You need not grant his request if you or your wife feel reluctant for any reason. And the question of guardianship won't arise unless *both* parents are dead. Your brother's wife—even if she is his ex-wife—automatically becomes guardian of the children if he dies. If she lives until all the children reach their majority (age 18), there will be no need for an outside guardian. You can't simply be appointed guardian—the decision is yours. If both parents die and you change your mind, the Probate Court will appoint a guardian in your place. It often happens that a yes turns into a no because time has changed things— you have moved to another province or another country, or your health is no longer equal to the task. Naming a guardian in a will merely indicates a preference; the only guardianship that has full legal effect is the one formally approved by a court, which, in the interests of the children, might appoint someone else—perhaps the public trustee.

Cost of guardianship. A guardian is not required by law to spend his own money on the maintenance of his wards, but the law imposes some obligation to maintain and educate the children, to the extent of his financial means. Ordinarily, all the income of the deceased parents' estate will be available to the guardian for the maintenance and education of the children. A guardian would be taking a risk if he dipped into the capital of the estate without the will specifically stating that he could do so. The court might give its retroactive blessing, but then again, it might not. The test would be that the expenditure was "reasonably needed." A guardian cannot take what may have been earned by the children themselves.

MAY-SEPTEMBER ROMANCE

Your 16-year-old daughter is infatuated with one of her teachers, who is in his thirties. You've asked him to stop seeing her, but he refuses.

Your parental rights in such a situation are slim indeed. Calm and concerned persuasion is about your only recourse. The law offers you no help. At 16, your daughter is no longer a juvenile. She can go out with anyone she chooses and quite possibly get court permission to marry if you withhold consent. (*See* Chapter 7, "Engagement and marriage.")

You could discuss the situation frankly with the principal or the school board. Your daughter is legally in their charge while on school property and they have a duty to safeguard her morals and welfare. They are almost certain to discourage or forbid teacher-

pupil romances as a general policy, but there's really not much else they can do. They can't forbid him to see her on his own time and they'd be asking for trouble if they threatened to fire him over the issue. But they might arrange a transfer.

KIDNAPPING

You were given custody of your son when you were divorced. He disappeared from the day-care center and you learn he's now in California with his father.

You have the clear right to "possession" of the boy, but you may have a difficult time exercising it. Your ex-husband could be guilty of the serious crime of abduction or kidnapping, as well as contempt of court. The maximum sentence in Canada for kidnapping is life imprisonment.

Only women or children under 14 can be abducted. It doesn't matter if the child consents to be taken away and the crime doesn't need to involve any confinement of the victim. Abduction of a woman relates to her being seized for the purpose of sexual intercourse or marriage. The penalty for abduction can be 10 years' imprisonment. Any other kind of forcible taking of a person is kidnapping. Whether or not a ransom is demanded is immaterial.

The Criminal Code says a person (and this includes any parent) is guilty of abduction if he or she "takes or entices away or detains" a child under 14 who is in the "lawful care or charge" of another person. But this law "does not apply to a person who, claiming in good faith a right to possession of a child, obtains possession of the child."

A claim of "good faith" may protect a parent from a charge of abduction. Take the case of the father who took his children from British Columbia to Ontario. They had been living with their mother in British Columbia, under a custody order issued in Ontario. The father was convicted of abduction but was acquitted on appeal. The Supreme Court believed he had an honest but mistaken belief that the Ontario order was not valid in British Columbia.

Judges are generally reluctant to apply the criminal law of abduction to a family conflict—especially where there is no custody order. If there is such an order, contempt of court proceedings will normally be started to force compliance.

Needs convincing proof. The defense of the parent charged with abduction is usually that it was in the best interest of the child. For example, an ex-husband may allege that the mother is not leading a moral life or is otherwise unsuitable to retain custody. But the court will hit him hard for his flouting of a judicial order unless he can show convincing proof.

In deciding one such case, a judge warned

A child's first fall from grace

There comes a sickening moment in the lives of many parents when they find out that a son or daughter has broken the law. It's much worse when the news comes from a policeman—the child has been caught and is already in the toils of the law—but it's shattering even if the child hasn't been apprehended. Many parents tend to blame themselves, wondering where they "went wrong" in their management of the child's upbringing. While parents should not be overly harsh in their self-criticism or be destroyed by a child's temporary fall from grace, it is true that they have a direct responsibility for their children's behavior. They have a duty to monitor their children's activities and to prepare them for the legal and moral temptations they must inevitably confront.

Stealing is only one of the traps into which young teen-agers (and even subteens) can fall. And shoplifting is probably the most common form of theft that youngsters attempt. Here is a checklist that parents can apply as an "ounce of prevention" against something that could lead to much grief for them and their children.

■ Be aware that shoplifting can be just the beginning of bigger trouble for children.

■ Make sure your children understand that shoplifting is stealing, and stealing is a criminal act.

■ Be certain that your children know what a criminal record can do to their chances for college education, jobs and travel.

■ Know how much money your children have and how they spend it.

■ Know what your son or daughter brings into the house. If it isn't his or hers, check on where it came from. Don't accept a pat answer.

■ Know when, where and why your child is going shopping.

■ Teach your child that it is more "chicken" to go along with the crowd than to refuse to do so.

■ Be alert to a daughter who repeatedly goes shopping with an extra-large handbag or shopping bag. These are common tools of a shoplifter.

■ Supervise any "clothes swapping."

Many parents who discover a child has been shoplifting adopt the straightforward practice of going to the manager of the store, telling him exactly what has happened, returning the goods or offering to pay for them and asking that he not proceed with charges on this occasion. If it's a first offense, the chances are good that he will compliment you on your good sense and leave the matter in your hands. But, plagued by heavy losses from shoplifting, his company may have a fixed policy of prosecuting in all instances. Other parents send the store the price of the merchandise anonymously as "conscience money." But unless the child's own money is used—or deducted from allowances or his earnings—the lesson may not hit home. One way or the other, the important thing is that you ensure your children realize the seriousness of the situation—a shoplifter is a thief; to steal is wrong, morally and legally.

that he would ensure that "swift and easy modes of travel do not make it a simple matter for a disgruntled or emotional parent to take the law into his own hands and province-hop across the country, deliberately ignoring legitimate court orders." Nevertheless, jurisdictional problems can arise over such questions as whether a federal custody order—as part of a divorce action—takes priority over a provincial custody order.

Across the border. Extradition problems can complicate the return of a child from another country. You are by no means powerless if your ex-husband has your son in California, but you'll need the assistance of a lawyer experienced in that field. The absconding parent often starts immediate custody proceedings in the jurisdiction where the child now resides. This can have the effect of freezing the situation temporarily until a ruling is given by a court in that place. Judges everywhere are usually very careful in protecting minors from being bounced back and forth like tennis balls between warring parents.

When a custody fight has been particularly bitter, Canadian courts sometimes make the parent who didn't get custody post a bond before exercising visitation rights. This is one way to deter that parent from skipping out of the province with the child. British Columbia law permits a judge to order the immediate "apprehension" of a child who has been taken away by a parent.

CHILD ABUSE

A little girl from down the street often has bruises on her body and you believe her parents are abusing her.

It's your legal duty to report any well-founded suspicion of child abuse and the law will protect you against liability for so doing. Provincial child-care laws vary in detail but this principle is now well established. Child abuse has become one of our most appalling and puzzling social problems. Thousands of children are beaten, maimed, emotionally scarred or even killed by their parents every year.

Court records show that children are whipped with belts, clubbed with baseball bats, flailed with chains, burned with electric irons, scalded with boiling water, choked, bitten, stabbed and stamped upon. One Ontario mother threw her baby son to his death from an eighth-floor balcony: she said she couldn't cope with the ordeal of raising him alone. A single-parent father handcuffed his son to a bed so that he wouldn't interrupt his reading. A 19-month-old girl was dead on arrival at hospital with more than 70 injuries, including sexual violation.

The duty to inform. Laws in all provinces, except New Brunswick and Prince Edward Island, now require that all suspected cases of child abuse be reported. Every citizen has the legal duty to call the provincial director of child welfare, a Children's Aid Society, or the Crown Prosecutor's office. The person supplying the information is exempt from any liability, unless the report is made maliciously or without reasonable grounds. Except in Saskatchewan, any alleged confidentiality of information—such as may be claimed between doctor and patient—does not erase the duty to report. And while New Brunswick law doesn't impose a duty to report, it does protect anyone who does.

In British Columbia, the person doing the reporting can be subpoenaed and required to give evidence of the abuse or neglect. A "family advocate" appointed under provincial law may require anyone he thinks has information concerning a case of child neglect to make a full report. Alberta, Nova Scotia and Newfoundland go a step further and make it an offense *to fail to report* cases of child abuse. In Ontario, professionals—doctors, public-health nurses, hospital personnel, teachers and lawyers—who fail to report incidents can be fined $1,000.

Most provinces have a confidential central register of abused children and of parents or guardians who have failed in the past to provide proper medical treatment. Studies show that child abusers come from every economic group and social class. Yet they do have definable characteristics; for one, most were themselves abused as children.

10 Education

Education is in a state of siege in Canada. The palmy days when governments opened the treasury vaults to build new universities in the boondocks (seven in Ontario alone since World War II), to hike teacher salaries and fringe benefits, to finance an unending stream of conferences, surveys and studies are over. Between 1959 and 1979, government spending on education rose from $1.1 billion to $16.3 billion. Today, "restraint" is the word of the hour.

The Canadian birthrate has fallen sharply since the mid-1960s, causing school enrollment to drop. In the face of worldwide economic recession, budgets have been slashed. The inevitable result is the reduction of our education system. The falling enrollment and budget cuts are closing schools all across the country. Several teachers' training colleges have closed down. Thousands of teachers and bureaucrats have been dismissed, or are struggling to hold on to their jobs.

For nearly two decades after World War II, the birthrate ran at 25 to 29 births a year per 1,000 of population, guaranteeing the flow of students. Since 1965, the rate has been below 20 per 1,000 and, during the last half of the 1970s, lower than 16. (Compare Mexico, at 42 per 1,000.)

In 1971, enrollment stood at 5,655,000 students; by 1978, this had declined to 5,144,000, and it is still falling. Teachers in all disciplines numbered 262,000 in 1971; there are now about 250,000, and that figure is expected to shrink to 200,000 by the turn of the century.

Government grants for education are based on school enrollment—so many dollars per student. Struggling taxpayers are asking: "If enrollment is down, shouldn't taxes be down, too?"

But education is still the biggest business in Canada. About 80 percent of the population is either receiving or dispensing it in some form.

The total bill approaches $17 billion a year. About 65 percent of this sum goes directly in salaries and benefits to ensure the hiring of well-qualified teachers, professors and education administrators. In 1979, for example, about 120 administrators at the University of Toronto were each earning $46,000 or more a year and the director of the Metro Toronto School Board was being paid $57,000. The salary range for the chief executive officer of a large school board in Nova Scotia reached as high as $45,000 annually, for the equivalent position in British Columbia as high as $50,000.

By law, Canadian children are granted the right to a quality education to whatever level they are capable of attaining—and can afford. They are assured of education to the level that corresponds with the school-leaving age of the province where they live. But there are signs that this largesse is not appreciated by a widening faction among the student body.

Millions of dollars in willful damage is being inflicted on school property each year. The Montreal Catholic School Commission, the nation's largest school board, estimates that its losses amount to an annual $2.5 million—enough to build a large new elementary school. In a recent 12-month period in British Columbia, 42 school fires—set mostly by students—caused more than $11 million in damage.

Several school boards have urged the legislatures to make parents financially responsible for damage done by their vandalizing children. Some boards, on the other hand, are proposing to pay students *not* to vandalize their own schools. It's a novel kind of reverse blackmail. For example, the Lakehead Board of Education, in northern Ontario, decided in 1979 to set up a fund for both elementary and secondary schools out of which vandalism repairs would be paid. Anything left in the funds at year-end goes to the student councils.

Teacher federations accuse parents of fobbing off the responsibility for moral and other fundamental instruction onto the harassed classroom teacher. Parents, on the other hand, accuse teachers of debasing the ideals of education through their use of the strike weapon in salary disputes. Extremism aside, the once accepted bond of trust and understanding between teacher and parent in the best interests of the learning child seems to be in peril.

EDUCATION STANDARDS

You are dissatisfied with the standard of public education and you want to teach your children at home.

During the permissive 1960s, and through most of the 1970s, education authorities appeared to go along with the mood of the times and accept the premise that students had the right to "do their own thing." School was not merely a preparation for responsible citizenship, for getting a job or running a home; it was a life-enhancing, mind-expanding "encounter." The basic subjects, the "three R's," were never abandoned, but in many cases they were downgraded.

Statistics Canada classifies anyone who has not progressed beyond Grade 8 as "functionally illiterate." This adds up to 4.5 million Canadians! A survey by the Ontario Institute for Studies in Education of 12,000 Grade 8 students in 1978 revealed that 40 percent could not adequately understand even simple newspaper reports. It has become possible to graduate from high school, supposedly prepared for university, without the skill to write a paragraph of correct English. Students intending to become English teachers are not usually required to take English courses at university. At Humber Community College in Toronto, teacher Walt McDayter once told a class in communications that he didn't expect the students to write like Hemingway. Asked one student: "Who's Hemingway?"

Ministries of education across the country began a concentrated return to the development of basic reading and writing skills in the late 1970s. Formal examinations, as opposed to the easygoing credits system, were gradually coming back in favor. The feeling was growing that students had been shortchanged for nearly two decades in their right to a well-rounded education.

In 1978, the University of Toronto ruled that all candidates for bachelor's degrees would have to pass a test in basic English composition. The test, according to the Dean of Arts and Science, would be equal in difficulty to "what used to be given at Grade 7 or 8."

Independent schools. You actually have the right to educate your children yourself if you can persuade the authorities that you can do it well enough. A national survey by The Canadian Press in 1978 showed that more and more parents, distressed by what they consider the failure of the public schools to provide proper grounding in basic subjects, were, in fact, looking for an alternative.

All provinces have regulations under which a child may be educated outside the provincially run schools. The Public Schools Act of British Columbia, for example, says a parent will not be penalized for failure to send a child to school if the child "is being educated by some other means satisfactory to the Justice or tribunal before whom the prosecution takes place." Ontario says a child is excused from attending school if "he is receiving satisfactory instruction at home or elsewhere." The key word is "satisfactory." Education authorities (or judges, if there is a prosecution) must agree that the alternative form of education—by parents at home, by tutor, by correspondence course, private school, or whatever—is generally equivalent to what a child would receive at a tax-supported school in that district.

Most private or independent schools are set up for religious or cultural reasons to serve parents who want their children to receive instruction based on principles set down at home and in church. Some of these schools received a boost in 1979 when Alberta Judge H. G. Oliver ruled that 45 Mennonite parents were justified in taking their children out of public schools and enrolling them in a school started by the sect. Judge Oliver upheld the Alberta Bill of Rights in his ruling that compulsory-attendance sections of the provincial School Act denied the parents freedom of religion.

If you plan to set up a schoolroom in your home or church, you should ask your provincial Department of Education to outline the ground rules. The ministry will probably insist on approving the curriculum, whether or not public funds are involved.

Private schooling can be expensive. Annual fees and live-in costs at some private schools run to $7,500 and more. And the parents involved must still pay the same education taxes levied on all taxpayers. Private schools in British Columbia, Alberta, Saskatchewan and Quebec fare better than elsewhere because they get provincial grants if they meet government requirements.

SCHOOL ATTENDANCE

Your daughter has been skipping school unknown to you. Now you are being charged with failing to ensure her attendance.

Education is compulsory. Parents or guardians have a legal duty to make sure their children attend school while between the ages of 5 and 16 in Nova Scotia; 6 and 15 in Alberta and Quebec; 6 and 16 in the Yukon, the Northwest Territories and Ontario; 7 and 15 in British Columbia, Prince Edward Island and Newfoundland; and 7 and 16 in Saskatchewan, Manitoba and New Brunswick.

A parent who fails, or refuses, to make sure that his child actually attends school is guilty of an offense. Fines can be imposed; in Ontario, for example, up to $100. A parent or guardian may also be ordered to post a cash bond, to be forfeited if the child is not attending class within a given number of days.

Some provinces rule that a child who refuses to go to school, or is habitually absent from school, can be treated as a juvenile delinquent. The parent can be charged with contributing to juvenile delinquency. A truant can be taken to court and tried under the child-welfare laws. If the misconduct is serious enough, he is taken from his home and put in the custody of the Children's Aid Society.

Right to know. The parent has the right to be informed of the child's truancy. As far as you may know, the child leaves for school every day on time, and is back home for supper.

School authorities must tell you about the absences and give you a written warning of the possible consequences. You should not be charged with anything if they neglect to tell you what is going on. In fact, if they fail to do this, you may be able to sue the board for damages—for the humiliation and expense you have been subjected to because of the charges. Not all kids who play hooky are simply artful dodgers. Some are very bright, ahead of their class in intelligence, and bored with the curriculum. Discuss the situation with the principal. A child may need tougher courses, or different ones—courses of a more practical or technological nature, perhaps.

Most teachers are still dedicated professionals. They have to be, to survive and progress in what has been called the "blackboard jungle." But others are less inspired. Charles Dickens recognized the problem. In the preface to *Nicholas Nickleby,* he wrote:

> "We hear sometimes of an action for damages against the unqualified medical practitioner, who has deformed a broken limb in pretending to heal it. But what of the hundreds of thousands of minds that have been deformed for ever by the incapable pettifoggers who have pretended to form them!"

PROFESSIONAL DEVELOPMENT

It seems that your children's teachers are continually having professional-development days. You feel that this is basically a rip-off.

Teachers have rights, too. A generation ago, the schoolteacher—like any other civil servant—had a safe and highly respected job. He was expected to draw a large measure of satisfaction (and not much else) from dedication to his chosen profession. His status in the community was similar to that of the clergyman, the doctor or the lawyer.

Nowadays, schoolteachers negotiate with

the school boards through federations (their trade unions) on such issues as hours of work, rates of pay and vacations. Since the 1960s, they have become increasingly militant, and some locals don't hesitate to strike in order to back up their demands.

Where salary is concerned, these negotiations have been successful. Canada's teachers are now relatively well paid. In the 1977-78 school year, the average salary for public-school teachers at the elementary level was $17,900. They earned most in Alberta

Not much to chew

It's sometimes the case that liberal-minded teachers present their own atheistic views to students—a fact that can be of grave concern to any God-fearing family. High-school students tend to be impressionable, and the subject is deep. If you are determined to counter the evident atheism of your child's teacher, you are, in theory, on solid ground; the law appears to be on your side in every province. But in practice, unfortunately, you'll have the devil of a time trying to assert your right not to have atheism thrust at your child in our public schools.

The duties of teachers in public, nondenominational schools are spelled out in the provincial education statutes. And although Judaeo-Christian ethical principles are stressed, the language is so vague that even atheism could gallop through some of the loopholes on a black horse. The Ontario Education Act, for example, says it's the duty of a teacher "to inculcate by precept and example respect for religion and the principles of Judaeo-Christian morality and the highest regard for truth, justice, loyalty, love of country, humanity, benevolence, sobriety, industry, frugality, purity, temperance and all other virtues." It sounds impressive. The lawmakers seem to have included everything except motherhood—but there's very little that you can sink your teeth into.

Controversy has raged for years over the idea of starting the school day with the Lord's Prayer. Critics roar that this is "stuffing religion down kids' throats" at an age when they are too young to make their own intellectual evaluation of formal religion.

In Ontario, teachers under contract to "separate" (Roman Catholic) school boards are in a different legal position. In 1978, the provincial Supreme Court and the Court of Appeal sanctioned the firing of two women teachers who "did not give an example of respect for the Church." Both had remarried following divorces, which Roman Catholics are not normally permitted to obtain.

Both courts agreed that the British North America Act preserved the rights and privileges that "denominational schools" had enjoyed before Confederation in 1867. This included the right to dismiss a teacher for running counter to the teachings of the Church. "Serious departures from denominational standards by a teacher cannot be isolated from his or her teaching duties," the Court of Appeal stated. "Within the denominational school, religious instruction, influence and example form an important part of the education process."

The tighter discipline and teaching values of the separate schools are attracting ever larger numbers of non-Catholic students. In 1979, the Metro Toronto Separate School Board reported enrollment of 725 non-Catholics—at an extra fee of $389 per child. Mrs. Blanche Lund, whose son Jeffrey, 13, was switched from a Toronto public elementary school to a Catholic high school, was delighted with the transfer. "The kids used to call [their old school] Happy Valley or the Holiday Inn. They smoked and didn't worry about schoolwork .... The Catholics get good academic results from the students. We feel the religious instruction will make a better person of Jeffrey."

($18,700), least in New Brunswick ($15,900). At the secondary level, the national average was $21,200, Ontario paying the highest ($22,500) and Prince Edward Island the lowest ($17,500).

Recharging the batteries. The professional-development days and sabbaticals to which you object are either Department of Education policy in your province or part of the labor contracts won by teachers and professors. One possible recourse, if you and other parents object to these schemes, is to lobby your Minister of Education and your elected school trustees, which may encourage them to reshape policy. Your best weapon is the threat of the ballot box at the next election. And, of course, the letters column of your local paper is open to you.

Professional-development days were originally granted so that a teacher would have out-of-class time to keep abreast of new ideas in education, to plan the curriculum, attend grading conferences and conduct parent interviews. Sabbatical leave—a calendar or academic year off every seven years on full or partial salary—is intended to allow eligible teachers or senior scholars time away from ordinary duties so that the intellectual batteries can be recharged.

Critics of this entrenched system point to the long summer and other breaks that already pace the school year. And to the fact that educators on sabbatical often take consultative or other lucrative work during these paid "holidays." They cite cases of professional-development days being spent on the golf course or used to stretch long-weekend statutory holidays. But educators defend the system with equal fervor.

SLOW LEARNERS

Your son is rated as a slow learner and placed in an "opportunity class." You believe this denies him a fair chance.

He has the right to an education in a tax-supported school, but the administrators have the power to decide just how that education will be delivered. It would be wrong to assume they have anything but your child's best interests in mind.

You should speak with the principal and teachers to assure yourself that your son is getting every chance to realize his full capability. If the teacher in the special class is knowledgeable and dedicated—as are most teachers who undertake this difficult work—that's where your child has most chance of success.

If you are convinced he is merely being shunted out of the normal stream for the convenience of the staff, or to make the school's grade averages look good, you can take your case either to the school board or directly to the provincial Department of Education.

Every province maintains either special schools or classes for children with "learning disabilities." This is a category that covers approximately 6 percent of all Canadian schoolchildren. In Nova Scotia, Ontario and Saskatchewan, the direction of a slow learner to these classes is mandatory. Experts in this field work closely and patiently with the student; individual tutoring is sometimes arranged.

There's the alternative of taking the child out of the publicly supported system and enrolling him in one of the many approved private schools. Some of them have a much higher teacher-pupil ratio, which may help the slow learner.

It's a good idea to have your child's hearing and eyesight checked by a specialist. This kind of unsuspected physical handicap may be at the root of the problem.

Confusing god and dog. Dyslexia, or impairment of the ability to read, is a strange and crippling affliction which prevents many otherwise bright children from learning to read or write normally. One child in every seven is thought to suffer from it to some degree. Inventor Thomas Edison and statesmen Woodrow Wilson and Winston Churchill were probably sufferers, as they had great difficulty in coping with ordinary schoolwork when they were young. The disease made Hans Christian Andersen an atrocious speller all his life.

For some unknown reason, the brain confuses the signals sent out by the senses. To the dyslexic child, the word "god" may appear as "dog." "Book" could read "koob." He may be able to copy down words, but not reproduce them when asked. Abstract ideas of time and direction can be handled only with great concentration. In all other ways, the child may be entirely normal.

Elementary-school teachers are generally on the lookout for such children today. Instead of being labeled as class dunces, these children are routed into an "opportunity" or "special" class for remedial treatment.

SEX EDUCATION

You are shocked by the explicit content of sex-education lectures. But your request that your children be excused from these classes is denied.

About one third of Canadian schools offer sex-education classes, usually as part of a "family life" program which covers not only sexual matters but many everyday problems that a child is likely to face in family and social situations.

It's a controversial subject—perhaps the most volatile in the curriculum. Many parents feel it has no place in the schools. Much of the criticism focuses on the use of material that some parents consider too explicit. Certain films, slides and literary works have raised a storm of complaints about "pornography in the classroom."

The decision as to how sex education should be handled in the public schools is made, initially, by the provincial Department of Education. Local school boards, however, have some autonomy, and considerable authority is delegated to regional directors of education, to superintendents and even to the individual principals. Therefore, the actual content of sex-education lectures can vary widely.

Educators are notably reluctant to excuse a student from a course simply because a parent doesn't approve of it. They feel that this would take the choice of curriculum out of their professional hands. For example, a socialist-minded father could object to an economics course because it was based primarily on the free-enterprise system.

But the law states, in general terms, that the parent has control of the child; the school is merely exercising delegated authority during the hours of compulsory attendance. Therefore, if you have reasonable grounds to object to the "family life" program—religious reasons, perhaps—you may be able to secure permission for your children to miss those lectures.

Increasingly, schools are selling parents on sex education in the classroom by reviewing the course material with them, arranging screenings of films for them, lending them the books their children will read. Opposition tends to shrink where this sort of communication exists.

GOING BACK TO SCHOOL

You dropped out of school years ago and now you want to go back and study for your diploma. But you can't afford to quit work.

The availability of further education is virtually unlimited, and you don't have to quit your job to get it. Thousands of Canadian adults are taking a second run at formal education by attending night school or by taking correspondence courses. Once you have that diploma, there's no reason you can't forge ahead by the same route and try for a university degree in your chosen subject.

If you're a mature student—an adult who has been out of school a long time—you should apply to a high-school principal or school-board secretary for permission to resume studies. Usually you'll be granted a certain number of credits both for schooling completed earlier and for on-the-job experience picked up over the years. You may also be granted credits for completion of apprenticeship or home-study courses. A "maturity allowance" of up to 12 credits may be given on the basis of age and the length of time out of school.

No matter how many "equivalency credits" you are awarded, the mature-student schemes usually demand that you earn at least four additional credits by completing courses normally taken during the third or fourth year of high school. You may earn these credits at day school or evening classes, through correspondence courses, or through private study.

High-school drop-outs are now graduating even from medical and law schools, thanks to mature-student programs. Senior citizens are enrolling in university courses to enrich their retirement. Other mature students are earning degrees at home, listening to taped lectures, and writing essays and examinations by correspondence. Several Canadian universities— Memorial in St. John's and Concordia in Montreal, for example—teach off-campus

credit courses by television. Lakehead University, in Thunder Bay, Ont., sends professors out by car, train and chartered bush aircraft to teach in remote areas.

SUPERVISION OF STUDENTS

You call the principal to complain about your son being bullied at recess. He doesn't seem very concerned.

If an injury occurs through lack of supervision at school, the teacher, principal and school board can be liable for damages. The largest sum ever awarded by a Canadian court in a

The report card

As a concerned parent you have a right to expect sound, articulate feedback on your child's progress. The report card may be one of the few avenues of communication between you and your child's teacher, and it's reasonable to desire the fullest account possible. When the Roman Catholic Separate School Board of Bruce and Grey Counties in Ontario asked parents what they favored in the writing of report cards, down-to-earth comments were requested and the board revamped its reporting method. This type of parental input may be equally effective in your area.

negligence action was $859,628, after a child was injured in a school gym in Prince George, B.C. A child is compelled to attend school and the school board is bound by law to "supervise, care for and educate" the pupil. The level of care demanded is usually that of a "reasonably careful parent," a somewhat nebulous distinction. The supervising teacher is not expected to keep his eye on his charges every minute but he must guard against "reasonably foreseeable risks."

The Supreme Court of Canada ruled that supervising teachers were not negligent in failing to notice when a known bully picked up another boy and dropped him on some ice. They were, however, found negligent in failing to care properly for the injured child. The teachers and the school board were ordered to pay $10,510 and costs.

In a Nova Scotia case, a boy lost an eye after being struck by an acorn thrown by a fellow pupil in the schoolyard. Four teachers were supervising 500 pupils at the time; only a few children were throwing acorns. Justice V. C. MacDonald ruled that the teachers were not negligent "in failing to see and stop the acorn-throwing activities of a handful of boys in the short period of their occurrence." Parents in a case such as this might consider prosecuting the parents of the culprits, but it should be remembered that, except in Quebec, parents are not generally held responsible for the torts (civil wrongs) committed by their children. (*See* Chapter 9, "You, the parent.")

Off school property. The school board may be liable for injuries sustained by a student away from school premises, if they were incurred during an approved activity such as a field trip. This kind of mishap would represent a breach of the duty of supervision. And provincial laws require school boards to maintain safe premises and equipment. In Ontario, a pupil was injured when he fell on a pile of rubble in the playground. He sued the school, and won. An Alberta child injured on an unsafe teeter-totter won damages from the school board.

Dangers in the lab. The duty to supervise may diminish as the student gets older. A Quebec trade-school student was severely injured in a laboratory explosion caused by another pupil. It happened when the supervising teacher was in a different room on the same floor, attending to other school duties. When the case came to trial, the school board was held responsible for the injured student, but this decision was overruled by the Quebec Court of Appeal. The case went to the Supreme Court of Canada, which also absolved the board. The damage was "not the result of a probable and foreseeable act and was not due to the lack of supervision on the part of the teacher." The interference of the other student could not have been anticipated.

In another case, a Manitoba judge ruled that serious eye and face injuries to one student resulted from the failure of a high-school teacher to give adequate instructions before a chemistry experiment. He awarded the injured student more than $25,000.

The "careful parent" test applies to cases involving supervision while students are being transported in school buses. When a school board provides transportation and controls the running of the buses, its duty of care continues until the passengers reach their home stops.

A school-bus driver was held to be negligent in letting a kindergarten child off the bus at the wrong place. The child was hurt in a traffic accident moments later. Damages of more than $60,000 were awarded.

STANDARD OF DRESS

Your daughter's principal won't permit the wearing of jeans. But can the schools still enforce dress codes?

Private schools, yes; public schools, no. School uniforms were once thought to be egalitarian, the rich girls having to wear the same tunics as the poor girls. They were also intended to foster loyalty to the school—and to identify the students in the streets. But after World War II, all this was swept away in the name of individual freedom.

Provincial education laws step very gingerly around the questions of student dress, behavior and discipline. A local school board may suggest that students meet certain minimum standards of dress. But it can't insist. The regulations probably state that a student shall "exercise self-discipline" and "be clean in his person and habits."

Suspension, expulsion. Ontario's Education Act says that a principal may suspend a student for "persistent opposition to authority" and for "conduct injurious to the moral tone of the school or to the physical or mental well-being of others in the school." That statute is similar to the laws in other provinces. The wording could catch a boy who comes to school in filthy clothes, or a girl who dresses provocatively.

A suspended student has the right of appeal. The principal must immediately send written notification of the suspension to a flock of people: the student, his teachers, parents or guardians, the school board, the school-attendance counselor, and the supervisory officer. The notice must state the reasons for the suspension, and inform the student of his right to appeal. In some cases, the parent or guardian—or the student, if he has reached the age of majority—may, within seven days of the beginning of the suspension, appeal to the school board to remove or modify the suspension.

The school board may also expel a pupil if "his conduct is so refractory that his presence is injurious to other pupils." Webster's Dictionary defines "refractory" as "hard to manage, stubborn, obstinate." Does that describe the kid who writes obscenities on the blackboard, smokes marijuana in the hallways, and hasn't completed an assignment for months? The school trustees must make that judgment. But expulsions are never ordered lightly. The criterion is whether or not the student's behavior is physically or morally injurious to students or teachers.

The expelling of any student from a public school, no matter what the offense, involves more moves than a firing in the civil service. First, it must be recommended by the principal and "the appropriate supervisory officer." The pupil and his parents or guardians must be notified in writing of the recommendation.

So must the pupil's teachers. There must be written notification to the pupil and parents or guardians of the right to make representation at a hearing before the school board.

DISCIPLINE IN THE CLASSROOM

Your son was strapped by his teacher for insubordination. You understood that corporal punishment had been banned from the schools.

And so it has—but not everywhere. The Yukon and Newfoundland explicitly authorize corporal punishment, and British Columbia just as explicitly forbids it. In all other provinces, the decision is up to the individual school board. You should check with your school board to learn whether it has abolished corporal punishment, or whether it still subscribes to the time-honored view: "Spare the rod and spoil the child" (*Proverbs*, XIII, 24).

Principals and teachers are empowered to maintain discipline and order at school. The law confers on them, in effect, the rights of parental authority during school hours. The Criminal Code, applicable equally across Canada, says that teachers, as delegates of parents, may use "reasonable" physical force to correct children entrusted to their care. What is reasonable depends on the circumstances.

The fact that they're on school property doesn't protect students from the law. Pupils who strike, threaten or abuse teachers or other pupils can be arrested and charged either as juvenile delinquents or, if older, as adults under the provisions of the Criminal Code. While a teacher in some provinces still has the legal right to punish a student physically, the student has no matching right to strike the teacher. This would be assault.

The violent student. While this seems incredible to anyone over 50, the problem of violence in the schools today centers not on the sadistic headmaster beating the children but on children beating up the teachers.

In North York, an affluent section of Metropolitan Toronto, high-school teachers prepared a report in 1979 asking for "danger pay," and leave of absence for those suffering from "battered teacher's syndrome." They also wanted "special insurance benefits." Within a 90-day period, 26 North York teachers had been physically assaulted, 3 indecently assaulted and 35 verbally harassed by students. There were 23 cases of theft, 41 of willful damage, 23 cases of possession of weapons, and 7 cases of arson.

In Montreal, students at a large high school went on strike in 1978, holding two weeks of violent protests because they were not happy with the choice of courses. With the help of police, the school was closed. In Sackville, N.S., a former student once came to his school on graduation day and threatened to shoot the principal.

Student suspensions are on the increase. The grounds include alcohol abuse, misbehavior, theft, fighting and truancy. But the average suspension is for a few days only. Hardened offenders laugh off suspensions as a welcome break from compulsory attendance.

CHEATING

You are shocked when your son shows you some mimeographed "cribs" he bought before the university exams.

If caught cheating or plagiarizing—passing off someone else's writing as his own—your son could harm his career almost as effectively

'My son, the tool-and-die maker'

A dearth of skilled workers in the marketplace and high unemployment rates for the young—14.2 percent in Ontario in 1979 for the 15-24 age group—have turned students off vague liberal arts courses and on to practical, career-related studies. While many universities are lowering their entrance requirements to attract freshmen and still posting enrollment losses, the nation's community colleges are jammed with students taking one-, two- and three-year courses in practical subjects. At Conestoga College, Kitchener, Ont., in 1979, for example, 240 applicants vied for the 25 places in the broadcasting course and 375 competed for the 50 places in a kindergarten-teacher course.

The community colleges carry different titles in different provinces; few of them, curiously enough, include the word "community" in their labels. In Quebec, they're CEGEPs (collèges d'enseignement général et professionnel); in Ontario, CAATs (colleges of applied arts and technology).

None of the community colleges can grant degrees. They all specialize in job-related courses for those beyond high-school age.

Humber College, Toronto, offers its students 120 different courses.

Manpower experts, after relying for many years on immigration to fill the demand for skilled workers in industry, are now urging a "massive overhaul" in job-training programs. They blame job snobbery—the glorification of the white-collar job over the blue-collar job— for part of the shortage. Also the federal Department of Employment and Immigration is allocating $20 million for a crash Critical Trade Skills Shortages Program to accelerate the training of highly skilled blue-collar workers.

William Cameron of the Ontario Manpower Secretariat says Canada would be in better economic shape if the average parent was as eager to boast about "my son, the tool-and-die maker" as about "my son, the doctor." To move into technological leadership, Canadian industry could use 4,000 more tool-and-die makers. These essential and highly paid blue-collar workers, Cameron asserts, "have the talent and imagination of surgeons, but they work in metal rather than the human body. They turn dreams into reality."

as if he had a criminal record. Punishment ranges downward from expulsion to rustication (temporary suspension), to a severe reprimand. A failing grade is given in the course in which the student cheated, and the offense recorded on his transcript. Transcripts must be produced to show proof of marks when a student changes to another university, seeks entrance to a professional faculty, or applies for certain jobs. The black mark can be a lifetime stain.

At the University of Toronto, the nation's largest with nearly 50,000 full-time and part-time students, about 40 cases of "academic crime" are prosecuted yearly. The university announced in the summer of 1979 that it would, in future, release the names of all students caught cheating or plagiarizing. It's a serious offense, for example, to have aids such as pocket calculators or dictionaries in examination rooms, unless they are specifically allowed.

Five bucks a page. "Essay mills" are operating profitably all over the country. The universities can't prevent them from operating, or even from advertising their wares on campus. One catalogue lists 3,000 subjects, from Agriculture to Zionism.

The essays are written by hard-up graduate students; and they usually retail for $5 per page. A paper on an obscure subject can be specially ordered for quick delivery at $10 per page. The academic quality is supposed to be high enough to guarantee a B-plus; too many A's would arouse suspicion.

It's not illegal in any way for a student to *buy* such a prepared essay. In fact, it may help his understanding of an examination subject and improve his writing ability. The offense occurs when he tries to pass off the paper as his own. The wary, cynical or lazy student usually juggles the crib essay a bit, gives it a new title, and has the paper retyped.

But some students don't make much effort. At the University of Waterloo, Ont., an English professor was handed a photocopied essay in which locations and a few names had been scratched out and replaced. He remembered a colorful phrase in the introduction. The same essay was on file with another professor.

LOANS AND BURSARIES

Two of your children are at the top of their class in your rural school. But there's no way you can afford to give them a university education.

Perhaps not, if you are considering their tuition fees and residential charges as your personal liability. Tuition fees generally cost only a few hundred dollars, but the cost of room, board and books can add two or three thousand dollars to this sum. Funds can generally be found for the deserving student, however.

For example, one of the basic principles of the federally sponsored student-loans program is that "governments at all levels are interested in supplementing the resources of the student and his family, and any resources available through education institutions or other sources where needed, thus assisting all qualified students in reaching their education potential." In other words, money is available when needed.

Each province has several schemes—grants, loans, bursaries, fellowships and scholarships—to help or totally subsidize needy students. Financial support is usually awarded solely according to the student's personal economic need, but certain awards are based on demonstrated academic excellence and others are intended to encourage study in particular fields.

You owe it to your smart children to check with the nearest university, or with your provincial education department, to find out just what aid is available in your province and how you qualify.

If the student's needs aren't met by the federal loan plan, he may be eligible for a loan, or bursary (nonrepayable grant), from various provincial programs. Quebec student loans and bursaries can run as high as $4,613 for a married student with one child. Manitoba provides bursaries of up to $1,800 a year to its residents who are either Canadian citizens or landed immigrants.

The federal Canada Student Loans Plan, which is administered by the provincial governments (except Quebec, which has its own plan), makes money available to needy students up to a maximum of $9,800. To qualify for the yearly segments, the program of study must be at least 26 weeks long.

It's not necessary to attend university. The plan grants loans for students enrolled "in a course of studies at the post-secondary level at an eligible educational institution." Eligible institutions include high schools (Grades 9-12), community colleges, schools of nursing, Bible colleges, and some private institutions, including approved ballet schools.

The student applies for the loan at any bank branch. A formal in-depth statement of parents' income is required, along with the reporting of any personal revenue-producing assets. Each province varies in its definition of "needy" and its requirements regarding family support. It's wise to inquire about this before applying.

If the loan is granted, no interest or capital repayments will be required until six months after the student ceases full-time studies. Then, the bank expects repayment over a maximum of 9½ years. If the student dies before the loan is repaid, the federal treasury will pay off any remaining debt.

The Ontario and Quebec governments may also award fellowships (grants) of up to $2,000 to students in an undergraduate or graduate program where the language of instruction is different from their own.

If funds for university remain a problem in your home, look into the scholarships and bursaries offered by large corporations, veterans' organizations and service clubs. Individual universities, colleges and private schools usually offer a certain number of scholarships, fellowships and bursaries funded by former graduates, or as memorials to former students killed in war or accident.

11 Children in trouble

Children are committing more serious offenses than ever before—and at younger ages. In the late 1970s, 14-to-16-year-olds—male and female—have committed murder in Canada. A 15-year-old boy was charged with raping an 11-year-old girl. A 10-year-old was tried for setting fire to his school. Runaway girls are found selling their bodies on the streets of major cities, and more than a thousand teen-agers—many of them single—are becoming pregnant each week.

Thirteen has become the peak age for delinquency. In Sault Ste. Marie, Ont., in 1979, a 14-year-old girl was charged with juvenile delinquency after a 19-year-old woman was fatally stabbed. A 14-year-old boy in Kingston, Ont., was found guilty of delinquency in the manslaughter of an 84-year-old widow. In Edmonton, Alta., police grabbed a gang of shoplifters in a city mall: the ringleader was an 11-year-old girl; her cohorts were 8 years old.

Each year some 80,000 Canadian children are adjudged to be "in need of care and protection." But the very laws designed to protect the immature from slipping into lives of crime or despair are used by street-smart kids, and lawyers representing them, to escape the consequences of deliberate delinquency or criminality. As an extreme example of what distracted observers call "revolving-door" justice, one Toronto juvenile appeared 28 times before the Bench without losing a day's freedom or receiving any material punishment.

For more than 70 years, reform not punishment has been the pivotal policy of the Canadian courts. Problem children are considered more the victims of poor parental guidance—or of low mental ability—than deliberate lawbreakers. Judges are loath to send young offenders to training schools or "houses of detention," because this breaks the family tie. It also throws a first offender into the company of incorrigibles. Even in such an institution, the child is not under lock and key, merely subject to an agreed curfew.

Through the relatively new "diversion program," judges in the Juvenile or Family Courts may adjourn a case indefinitely. They'll use this avenue when an accused child shows an interest in working to pay for damage he's caused or to make restitution for money or property stolen. The hope is that the youngster will be diverted from going any farther down the delinquency road. He gets a chance to help himself before he has to face the might of the court. If the child straightens up, the Crown will not proceed with the charge. About 80 percent of juveniles charged in the Toronto courts are currently being "diverted." The Quebec Youth Protection Act provides that children under 14 cannot be charged with delinquency no matter what they have done and a youth protection worker decides if a 15- to 17-year-old can be taken to court. The act aims to direct problem children from the judicial system to appropriate treatment.

Many parents blame the easy availability of sex-oriented literature and movies for what they see as permissiveness or depravity among the teen generation. They find their cleanup efforts frustrated by the muddled state of the obscenity laws and by the anticensorship lobbies. In May 1979, when aldermen in Hamilton, Ont., ruled that erotic literature must be sold in opaque covers in stores with special licenses, the city's Criminal Lawyers' Association vehemently opposed the bylaw. One member described it as "pernicious, vicious and embarrassing." A spokesman for the National Book and Periodical Development Council said the bylaw would return the city to the Dark Ages, and Mayor Jack MacDonald decided to "go back to the drawing board . . . It (the bylaw) makes the city appear to be ludicrous."

But thousands had petitioned that the by-law be retained and a modified version was enacted. In Hamilton now, only dealers with special licenses may sell erotic magazines, which must be kept in sealed, transparent covers, on high shelves or behind the counter.

THE INCORRIGIBLE CHILD

Your 15-year-old child has become unmanageable. You fear he'll drift into a life of crime.

He will be a "child" or "minor" at law until he's 18—19 in British Columbia, New Brunswick, Nova Scotia and Newfoundland—even if he's six feet tall and sporting a six-inch beard, and the parent has both definite rights and inescapable responsibilities up to that time. As parent (or guardian) you are responsible for the safety, welfare, and "quality of life" of your child. You have to ensure that he receives education until the minimum school-leaving age in your province. You are responsible for his moral and spiritual development. These obligations have been acknowledged by the international community. The Declaration of the Rights of the Child, approved by the United Nations in 1959, states in part: "The child shall enjoy special protection, and shall be given opportunities and facilities, by law and by other means, to enable him to develop physically, mentally, morally, spiritually and socially in a healthy and normal manner and in conditions of freedom and dignity."

Society generally regards the child as "belonging" to the parent. The state will intervene only when it is convinced that such action is in the best interests of the child. Even if a government agency does step in, it does so only in lieu of the parent. The arbitrary power of the parent over the child is not materially changed; it is merely transferred to the agents of the state.

Seek professional help. If you are at your wit's end about how to manage a completely unruly child, it's safe to assume that family councils have failed. For the sake of the child—and probably for your own peace of mind—you should seek professional advice.

Every school board either has a psychologist on staff or has regular access to qualified counseling. You can tap that advice confidentially by approaching the school principal, or through your provincial ministries of education or health. Or you can get in touch with the nearest branch of the Children's Aid Society (CAS), the outstanding resource for help for children in trouble.

The CAS is concerned solely with the welfare of the child. It is required to do everything possible to help the family resolve problems so that the child can remain at home. Often CAS counseling and guidance will get things back on the right track.

Don't think your situation is unique. The CAS of Metropolitan Toronto gets about 2,000 telephone calls a day through its several branches and district offices. Some 450 calls daily are received by the CAS in Moncton, N.B., and officials in Winnipeg estimate that more than five out of every 100 children will require CAS help at some point.

"Disruptive behavior." In CAS records, the largest single category of youngsters requiring help stems from what's labeled "disruptive behavior." This includes the unmanageable child, or youngsters whose welfare is in jeopardy because of sexual liaisons, truancy, job-related problems, emotional upsets, attempted suicide, alcohol or drug abuse.

If the wayward child is not turned around, there's indeed a good chance he'll soon run afoul of the law. Close to 45,000 Canadian youngsters appear in Juvenile Court each year. As many as 200,000 others come into what is euphemistically called "conflict with the law" and are dealt with outside the formal judicial structure.

No matter what crime is committed—even murder—the only charge that can be laid against a juvenile is "juvenile delinquency," and even this charge cannot be laid in Quebec if the offender is under 14 years of age. In all provinces, no charges at all will be laid against a child under 7. The provincial Attorney General can, however, in a serious case decide to proceed against a juvenile in adult court. In Quebec, a youth protection worker from one of the province's 40 social service agencies decides whether a youthful offender over 14 is taken to court. If the case does go to trial, the youth may have his own lawyer and the ordinary rules of evidence are followed but the youthful offender cannot be sent to jail.

The first court appearance of a juvenile often has nothing to do with crime in its commonly accepted sense. Juvenile Courts can send difficult, wayward, promiscuous or truant children into training schools (reformatories) although they may not have actually committed an offense. But this can't happen in Ontario unless the child has committed an offense that would earn a jail term if committed by an adult.

A scolding or a sentence. Under the federal Juvenile Delinquents Act, judges have wide powers ranging from verbally disciplining the child to sending him to training school under detention. Between those two extremes, the choices include declaring a child delinquent, placing him on probation, ordering him to perform some community service or pay a fine up to $25, and ordering him into a foster home "subject to the friendly supervision of a probation officer." Judges can also impose any further conditions upon the delinquent. This could, and often does, include ordering the child and the parents to accept counseling or other therapeutic treatment.

THE RUNAWAY

Your 14-year-old daughter runs away to a large city. You're terrified of what might happen to her.

If you haven't already done so, notify the police. Give them every scrap of information that might lead to her apprehension and return home. You could be liable to serious charges if you neglect this duty. Don't fret at this stage about *why* she ran away; that problem can best be tackled when you get her back. The police will help you to the best of their ability. It's not easy to find a young girl in a metropolis, but they know the likeliest places to look.

More than 50,000 juveniles are running away from home each year, according to figures released by the Canadian Council on Social Development. It's believed that many thousand more runaways are not reported to police. An alarming number of these children get a fast introduction into street crime, drug addiction or prostitution. But don't despair. Nine out of every 10 runaways either talk to police or telephone friends within a few days, hoping their parents will find them. Montreal police report that about 70 percent of runaways are located within three days.

Limits really wanted. Most runaways have neither money nor extra clothing. They flee in anger or despair on the spur of the moment. They lack friendly contacts in the strange city and are afraid to approach social agencies. Many are soon reduced to sleeping in bus terminals or bunking in communal "crash pads" with undesirables they meet on street corners or in the heated shopping malls. Attractive young girls are particularly vulnerable; they drift into shoplifting to sustain themselves or are steered into prostitution by the pimps that infest the bus and rail stations.

Youngsters run from rich as well as poor families. Usually, there is tension in the home, either between child and parent or between the parents. Some are fleeing abusive homes, or broken and remarried families where they do not feel welcome or wanted. The reasons they give include quarrels with parents over dating, length of the boy's hair, far-out dress, use of marijuana, poor grades in school. Some speak bitterly of uptight or narrow-minded parents who just don't understand the alleged sex freedoms. Others reel off parental sins such as excessive drinking, hypocrisy, social climbing, bickering and, especially, indifference.

Authorities on adolescents, on the other hand, say that most "runs" could be prevented if parents were *less* permissive. They believe that most juveniles really want limits set on their behavior; in a confusing world ahum with talk of individual freedoms, they'd prefer to know just what the bottom-line rules are. A psychiatrist advises: "The best way to prevent conflicts from escalating into a breakup is to listen to your child and then, between you, decide on limits you both agree on."

When a child needs protection

The Children's Aid Society (CAS), with hundreds of branches countrywide—some operating under slightly different names—is the major resource and protection for the child in serious trouble. Staffed by professionals and qualified volunteers, its help is available for swift action or confidential advice 24 hours a day.

The organization is usually listed in the "white pages" under Children's Aid. If you have any difficulty finding the number, call the nearest police station, social services bureau or school principal's office.

This chart illustrates how the CAS machinery jumps into gear when the welfare of a child is endangered.

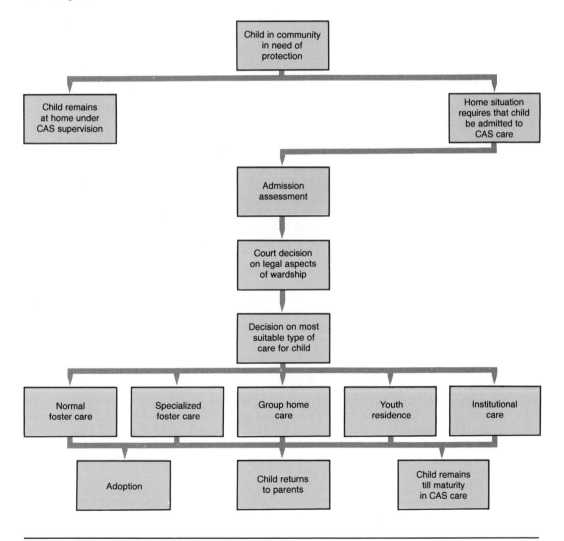

Counseling available. Parents of runaways are almost always hurt and furious over what they see as a slap in the face of the family. If the search for your child is successful, or if he or she returns voluntarily, don't vent your repressed anger. Treat the incident as a sure sign of a serious family problem, not just a child problem. You're lucky to get your child back unharmed. Now try calmly and warmly to isolate the key issues and work out a shared solution. If you don't think you are likely to be successful within the family circle, talk to your pastor or seek other qualified counseling. It's available through private consultants recommended by your family doctor or lawyer, or free for the asking from your nearest government social services bureau.

SHOPLIFTING

A teen-age gang leader demands that new members prove themselves by shoplifting. Your son was caught by a store detective.

Much depends on your son's age and the value of the goods stolen. If he's under 16 he can be found guilty only of being a juvenile delinquent. The judge can impose a fine, suspend sentence or place him on probation. In British Columbia and Newfoundland, the possibility of being charged as a juvenile still exists if he was under 17 at the time; in Quebec and Manitoba, it can exist to 18 The benefit of these age extensions may be withdrawn if the Crown prosecutor decides to treat the theft as an indictable offense. If the value of the goods stolen exceeds $200, he must do so. The Criminal Code states that anyone convicted of stealing goods worth more than $200 is guilty of an indictable offense and can get up to two years' imprisonment; if the prosecution treats the theft as a summary offense, the maximum punishment is a $500 fine, or six months in prison, or both.

Shoplifting costs retail businesses in Canada about $1 million a day, and both merchants and police are cracking down hard on offenders of all ages. Very few shoplifters are let off with a lecture.

Close to the cutoff. If your son was more than 16 at the time of the offense—even a day more—he'll be tried as an adult, subject to the same punishment as any other adult, unless you reside in one of the four provinces with higher age limits for juveniles. The judge would probably treat him leniently, however, if he was close to the cutoff age and hadn't been in trouble before. But he would still pick up a criminal record.

The judge might grant your son a conditional or unconditional discharge, which is supposed to mean that he doesn't get a criminal record. It's a bit of a sham because that discharge is recorded. The only real benefit of a discharge is that if a prospective employer asks him if he's ever been *convicted* of a criminal offense, he can truthfully answer "No." To clear the record completely, he'd have to apply for a pardon. (*See* Chapter 1, "Civil rights," and Chapter 4, "You, the defendant.")

The gang leader in this case can also be charged with theft because he counseled the commission of a crime and so became a party to it. If your son was charged as a juvenile and found to be a delinquent, the leader might well be convicted of contributing to juvenile delinquency.

One clash with the law doesn't mean your boy is a criminal beyond redemption. His day in court may teach him a very valuable lesson. You can help him in two ways: show him he has your moral support and love, and get him a good lawyer.

Rude awakening. More than 10,000 theft charges and about 70,000 "break and enter" charges are brought against Canadian juveniles each year. It takes a child's arrest to shock many parents into realizing that they don't know what's going on under their own roofs. "But why would he steal? He had everything he could possibly want," many disbelieving parents say. The misconception that only the children of the poor steal is a hangover from the Victorian age. Youngsters who "have everything" do steal. They're not deprived in any material sense, but they are bored, restless and depressed. Social workers routinely report that many of them hunger for love and understanding, a sense of direction and a purpose for living. They steal for "kicks."

Such a child is almost certainly disturbed—possibly about something in his home life. Talk to him, calmly and patiently. Don't mollycoddle him, but do your best to find out in his terms "what gives." You have to walk the thin line between rejection and abandonment on one hand and excuses and rationalizations on the other. There may be something you can correct within the family relationship. Reexamine the social and ethical standards and values you live by and impart. If psychiatric counseling appears necessary, don't hesitate to get it. If your child is sullen or uncommunicative, that is possibly only a coverup for shame, confusion or fear.

PREGNANCY

Your Grade 12 daughter has become pregnant and she can't, or won't, identify the father.

All 10 provinces and both Territories have laws that force fathers of children born out of wedlock to support their offspring. But—and it's a big "but"—those laws can't be enforced unless a man has acknowledged his paternity or has been found by a court to be the father.

As the child's parent, you have the right to start proceedings by laying "an information" (an accusation presented under oath) against the alleged father before a Superior, Provincial or Family Court judge. You can start the ball rolling before the baby is born. The provincial laws vary in some details, but action can usually be taken also by a guardian, or anyone having care of the girl, or by the provincial director of child welfare. Without the cooperation of your daughter, however, it's going to be uphill all the way. And don't just take a stab at naming the culprit. You could be blackening the name of an innocent person who might then take *you* to court.

Newfoundland, the western provinces and the Territories provide that an *affiliation order*—ruling that a certain man is the father of a certain child—cannot be made on the evidence of the mother unless her testimony is confirmed by some other evidence. Corroboration is not required in some provinces—for example, New Brunswick, Nova Scotia and Ontario—but paternity must be proven "on the balance of probabilities."

Evidence that the girl and a certain man had opportunity for sexual intercourse isn't enough to qualify as corroboration. Things that do qualify could include payments by the putative father for the mother's hospital expenses, a continued affectionate association between the parties, lack of evidence that the mother had associated with other men, an application by the putative father for family-allowance benefits, or admissions made to a third party.

Saskatchewan and Alberta permit the alleged father to be called as a witness; he can be cross-examined by, or on behalf of, the mother of the child.

Fornication—voluntary sexual intercourse between unmarried adults—is not a crime in Canada. If the girl is younger than 16, the act is regarded as rape and may be severely punished. The man may get life imprisonment if the girl is under 14, even if she consented to or solicited the act. If she is between 14 and 16, and solicited the act or gave her consent, the maximum penalty the man faces is five years' imprisonment. From 16 on, she is mistress of her own body.

If the judge decides that the defendant is the father, he makes an order declaring *paternity.* This will force the father to make payments for medical expenses, maintenance and education of the child. The order could be for a lump sum, or regular payments.

The provinces differ on the duration of maintenance payments. In Alberta, they have to be paid until the child is 16, or 18 if attending school or unable to earn a living; in British Columbia, New Brunswick and Saskatchewan, until the child is 16; in Manitoba, Ontario, Nova Scotia and Prince Edward Island, until 18, although the Ontario and P.E.I. fathers' responsibilities cease if a child age 16 or more leaves home; in Newfoundland, until 17 or as long as the child is incapable of earning a living; in Quebec there is no cutoff date. The obligation to support remains forever if the child is in need. The maintenance order may be changed from time to time as the circumstances of the child and the father change. It can work both upward and downward. If the father dies before his child reaches the cutoff age, his estate will have to continue to honor the terms of the affiliation order.

The crisis in your family is far from rare. The problem of teen-age pregnancies is reaching "epidemic proportions," according to the adolescent gynecology clinic at Toronto's Hospital for Sick Children. This is occurring at the same time as the pregnancy rate of women above age 19 is decreasing sharply. "Today's teens tend to start dating at 13½, have intercourse by 15 and are often pregnant by 16," says Dr. Diane Sacks, a pediatrician at the Toronto clinic. Of the more than 1,000 teen-agers who become pregnant each week, it is estimated that close to half will seek abortions and that nine of every 10 who continue their pregnancy will keep their babies. Most of these mothers will drop out of school. Many will require public assistance and will subsist in poverty for years. This reality belies what Dr. Robert Aikman, formerly of the Montreal Children's Hospital Adolescent Unit, describes as the media concept of the teen-ager: a beautiful, secure and sexually active adult. Dr. Aikman blames this concept for the teen pregnancy epidemic.

CHILDREN'S DEBTS

A garage allowed your college-age son to run up a bill for rental cars. The owner insists that you must pay.

Unless you allowed your son to pledge your credit, and made this known to the owner, the garage hasn't got a prayer. You are no more liable to pay a debt contracted by your child than a stranger would be. You may, of course, decide to pay up to sustain the family's good name—that's strictly up to you.

The relationship of father and son is not enough, in itself, to make you liable. But if the relationship is coupled with clear knowledge on your part that your son was running up those bills, it might be successfully argued that you gave his conduct your blessing, thus leaving yourself open to legal liability for the debt. The garage would have to prove that you knew what was going on and approved of it.

A college-age son is probably old enough to make his own contracts, and be bound by them. It depends on the age of majority in your province (usually 18). The general rule is that a contract made by an "infant" (a child, or minor) is invalid. There's an exception: a contract made by an infant for "necessaries" is binding if it's for his benefit. It's highly unlikely that rented cars would be legally classified among the "necessaries of life."

The contracts your son made with the garage are probably "voidable" if he's not yet an official adult. A voidable contract is an agreement that is not void from the beginning but remains in force until the party who has the right to repudiate it, does so. Such a contract is made binding on a minor if he confirms it when he reaches his majority. If your son is still a minor, he can confirm or repudiate the contract when he reaches his majority. If he confirms it, by promising to pay or by starting payments, he's legally responsible from then on.

A minor who lies about his age and says he has attained his majority—which would give him the right to make a valid contract—cannot later repudiate his contract on the sole ground of his minority. The merchant would have to prove, however, that he was misled by the lie. A child who merely allows another person to assume he is an adult is not guilty of fraud.

MARIJUANA

A bunch of teen-agers chipped in to buy a bag of "grass." Your 16-year-old son had the drug when the police closed in and he is the only one being charged.

After years of fervid argument, surveys, medical controversy, film documentaries, even a royal commission, the law on the possession of *cannabis* (marijuana, hemp, grass, pot) hasn't changed. (*See* Chapter 5, "The question of morals.") It still is a prohibited drug under the Narcotic Control Act. The law gives the police no choice—anyone caught with it faces a criminal charge.

You won't impress anyone, or divert the course of justice, by heatedly describing "joints" being smoked openly at parties, nightclubs or at rock concerts. The police know a lot more about this than you do. A survey commissioned by the Ontario Ministry of Education in 1978 indicated that more than 33 percent of high-school students had used marijuana or hashish.

It's quite possible that the police are trying to break up a distribution system at your son's school, or in the neighborhood. Don't expect them to admit it publicly, but they are thoroughly bored—or frustrated—with picking up teen-agers with small quantities of grass on "simple possession" raps. They are after the "pushers" (regular sellers) whom they hope to nail on charges of trafficking in drugs. When your son tells them where he bought his bag, the net can tighten.

Possession, 10/10ths of the law. In your son's case, the charge would be possession of a narcotic. It's often referred to as "simple possession," to indicate that the accused merely had it. If he had been making any attempt to sell it, the charge could escalate to "possession with intent to traffic" or "trafficking." Technically, the other youngsters are also guilty of possession because they knew about the bag, they shared in its purchase and apparently consented to your son's physical possession of it on behalf of the group. Should you or your son tell this to the police, the others might be charged, too.

You should immediately retain a lawyer experienced in court appearances. Your son needs counsel to help guard against the possibility of a more serious charge being laid, and to defend him if such a charge is brought forward. If your son pleads guilty to a charge of possession, and if it's his first offense, he is likely to get an absolute discharge. His de-

Two reports from Toronto the Good

"**P**lus ça change, plus c'est la même chose." The more things change, the more they stay the same. The thought of young children selling themselves from darkened doorways revolts and angers the average citizen. Surely that's something from Dickensian days. Not exactly. It happened on our streets 80 years ago, and it's still happening today. Read these two reports.

I have known children, actually children, solicit men and boys on the streets. One little miss, who was certainly not more than 12 years of age, met me on Jarvis Street near Carlton one night and stopped me.

"But," I objected, "where can we go?"

"There is a lane that runs through to Mutual Street, where we can go and no one will see us."

"And how much do you want?" I asked.

"Anything you like. Twenty-five cents."

– Excerpt from
Of Toronto The Good,
C. S. Clark (1898).

. . . on any given night along Yonge Street and the streets adjacent to it—the capital district of Canadian street life—there are at least half a dozen children, 11-, 12- and 13-year-olds of both sexes, soliciting. But there may be as many as 30 or 40 children—split evenly between boys and girls—engaged in this commerce, children whom almost no one sees except the customers themselves.

– Excerpt from
Street Kids,
Philip Marchand, *Chatelaine* (1979).

meanor and his willingness to assist the police can be factors. But he could be sent to prison for six months.

The Criminal Code says a person who receives a discharge, conditional or unconditional, is "deemed not to have been convicted" of the charge he faced. But he's tabbed with "a record" just the same. (*See* Chapter 1, "Civil rights," and Chapter 4, "You, the defendant.")

Just about every time the Criminal Code is discussed in Parliament—several times each session—there are promises or hints that simple possession of marijuana may soon be "decriminalized." Nevertheless, convictions for possession rose from fewer than 6,300 in 1970 to about 35,000 in 1979.

PORNOGRAPHY

Your teen-agers insist on their right to bring lurid magazines and books into the home.

They have no such "right" in law. The overriding principle is that you, the parent, as owner or occupier, have control over what comes into the home, including *who* comes in. Also, you have a definite duty to supervise the welfare of your children, including their moral welfare. With all that said, however, the policing of a teen-ager's reading matter is a ticklish subject; any disagreement is best thrashed out in friendly family councils.

When the law of the land obviously permits the open sale of magazines, books and films with startlingly erotic or violent content (*see* Chapter 5, "The question of morals"), the disapproving parent faces an almost impossible task. You may forbid your children to bring them into the house, but you have virtually no way of stopping them from studying them elsewhere. You don't want your youngsters reading "skin" magazines because you're afraid they'll damage their morals, their social and cultural values.

These publications, available almost everywhere, give a distorted view of sex, promoting the idea that the human body is nothing but flesh to be flaunted and exploited. At least, that's the opinion many of today's parents have of them. However, there's another view: that explicit portrayal of the body and no-holds-barred discussion of sexual matters blow away the sex guilts and frustrations that plagued previous generations.

Psychologists say that teen-agers, swimming through uncharted seas toward adulthood, find rules more palatable when they know why they exist. Don't stop at merely forbidding them to bring those magazines into the home, explain exactly why you are taking that stand. Be prepared for the objection: "But all the other kids are allowed to have them." Your reply is: "I don't care what others are allowed to do. Their parents are responsible for them. I care about you." However, the best defense against pornography is a sound moral education from an early age, coupled with good example in parental reading tastes.

Getting to the source. You can attempt to shut off the local supply of pornography by "laying an information" with the police against the retailer on the grounds that he is distributing obscene matter. The police will usually act upon a complaint laid by a responsible citizen but, given the confused state of the obscenity laws, it's a difficult charge to prove.

The fundamental freedoms of speech and expression are invoked by those who oppose censorship of any kind. They don't appear to be moved by questions of taste, the demeaning of human dignity, or by the alleged effect of such material on the susceptible young.

CULTS

Your son gave all his belongings to a far-out religious cult and moved into the group's "monastery." You want to rescue him.

If he's not yet legally "of age," you have every right to take every legal step to restore him to your home. If he's 18 or over, he's in full charge of his own destiny. In fact, if he's over 16, and thus no longer a "juvenile," few judges will use legal powers to force an unwilling child back into parental care. If you succeed in having your runaway child forcibly removed from his cult family, it's obvious you're going to have serious trouble in getting him to accept parental authority and normal social customs. North America abounds with bizarre cults and "churches" that have mastered the technique of reducing teen-agers and young adults to zombielike total obedience. They appear eager to commit themselves to "the cause," surrendering all their possessions, begging or selling flowers on the street.

Debriefing the deluded. Quite a few parents have succeeded in abducting their children back into the family fold, usually by tricking chaperoning cult members. The convert, whose mind is now shaped so that he doesn't want to be rescued, has to be "deprogrammed" by a psychiatrist or psychologist, or by someone who's been through the nightmare himself. It doesn't always work. The expert has to prod patiently into the captive mind and try to dislodge the dogma that's been pounded into it incessantly. Sometimes the subject resists all efforts and goes back to the cult, or is coaxed or threatened back.

If you can make contact with a child who has fallen into the grasp of the cultists, experts suggest that you don't begin by running down his new "church" or its leaders. That creates antagonism. Try to make a deal something like this: "If you plan to spend the rest of your life with this group, you owe us one week—or a month, if you can wangle it—to hear our side of the story, and to explain to us your new attitudes and plans." If he agrees to that reasonable proposition, you've got a chance of winning him back.

Be prepared for a lot of patient listening, even if the dogma sounds like absolute nonsense. Prepare your case carefully and present it warmly. Seek the guidance of a psychologist who may agree to sit in on your meetings. Ask child-welfare agencies if they know of any ex-cult members who might help.

Keep in mind that the "Moonies" and other cults will not hesitate to call in the police if you resort to physical action to rescue a child who is "of age." They will be the first to point out that freedom of religion is guaranteed to all under the Bill of Rights. (*See* Chapter 1, "Civil rights.")

ALCOHOL

In your townhouse development, there is an alcoholic widower who permits his teen-aged children to drink and run wild. You feel you should intervene.

You not only have the right to intervene, in some provinces you have a legal duty to do so in the interests of the children's well-being. Under Quebec's Youth Protection Act and Ontario's Child Welfare Act, any member of the public can be prosecuted for not reporting any case of child neglect or abuse.

You could probably have the man charged with disturbing the peace, or with contributing to juvenile delinquency. Depending on the severity of the situation, you could be instrumental in having the youngsters taken away from him as "children in need of protection." If you feel the children are being corrupted, you should give the police a detailed and corroborated report. They will consult with the Crown counsel and Children's Aid Society (CAS) officials on investigation and possible prosecution.

The federal Juvenile Delinquents Act is aimed at helping children who might, without guidance, be headed toward a criminal career. It provides for the punishment of adults who assist in the commission of a "delinquency." Any act "contributing to a child's being or becoming a juvenile delinquent" is a serious offense. Providing alcohol excessively to underage drinkers—under 19 except in Prince Edward Island, Quebec, Manitoba and Alberta where the minimum age is 18 years—would likely rate as "contributing."

The duty of protection. Parents and guardians who knowingly fail to do something that would prevent delinquency, or fail to remove conditions that are likely to make a child delinquent, are subject to stiff penalties, including two years in jail. To be adjudged delinquent, the child must violate the Criminal Code of Canada, or any other laws, including the liquor laws, or be guilty of sexual immorality, "or any similar form of vice," or be liable to be committed to an industrial school or juvenile reformatory. It's a pretty wide canvas.

The question of teen-agers drinking at home poses tough problems for the police in many instances. For example, in British Columbia, Manitoba, Ontario, New Brunswick and the Northwest Territories, a parent or guardian may supply liquor to his underage children in a "residence."

The residence could be a tent and the right extends to "the land immediately adjacent." A 1978 survey by the Ontario Ministry of Education revealed that 75 percent of elementary-school students and 87.5 percent of secondary-schoolers had drunk or tasted alcohol within the preceding six months. Nearly 30 percent of the high schoolers said they consumed alcohol at least once a week.

All provinces have child-welfare laws designed to assist "children in need of protection." The Ontario Child Welfare Act, for a typical example, gives many definitions of a "child in need of protection"—including "a child who is living in an unfit or improper place," "a child whose parent is unable to control him," and "a child whose life, health or morals may be endangered by the conduct of the person in whose charge he is." That's another wide canvas.

The act says that such children may be removed from their homes and taken to "a place of safety," pending a hearing. If the evidence is conclusive, the youngsters may be placed in the care of the CAS, perhaps permanently.

Provincial controls. Some provinces go into details about the "proof of age" that is acceptable to the authorities. Others state no standard except, in the words of one judge, "what would satisfy the honest mind of a practical and reasonable man." All provinces require young people to provide some sort of proof of age if questioned—maybe a driver's license, or student's identity card—but many youths switch these items around with the dexterity of faro dealers.

The liquor laws of several provinces state that no person apparently under a certain stated age shall be served liquor or beer in a drinking establishment. These statutes say that if a patron is prosecuted, the judge shall determine from "the appearance" of the accused, and from "other relevant circumstances," whether he or she is apparently under the minimum age.

If a 17-year-old could pass as being years older, the tavern owner might well be let off for acting "in good faith."

Not-so-sweet sixteen. In a Saskatchewan case, a youth in a tavern appeared older than the minimum age (19), except for his complexion which an observant waiter thought tabbed him as being under age. The patron signed a certificate stating that he was 21, and that, plus his mature manner and familiarity with the premises, satisfied the waiter. In fact, the drinker was 16. The waiter was charged.

At the trial, the judge observed the boy closely and agreed that he "clearly seemed older" than a witness who was 23. "Estimating ages is not a precise or exact science," the judge noted, "and wide errors in fact are innumerable." Because the law didn't spell out "a particular standard of proof," he felt the accused had acted "prudently and in good faith." The waiter was acquitted.

Proprietors of pubs and bars can be subject to severe penalties if they or their employees serve any kind of alcoholic beverage to anyone who is apparently intoxicated—no matter what the patron's age.

If a drunken customer leaves the establishment and later injures himself or someone else, commits suicide or is accidentally killed as a result of his condition, the license holder can be prosecuted. He could be sued by the victim if he lived, by his relatives if he died accidentally or by suicide, or by others who might have been injured.

Studies by the Addiction Research Foundation in Ontario revealed that close to 90 percent of high-school students aged 16 to 17 had experimented with, or were using, alcohol. Within a five-year period, 150 deaths in the province were attributable to teen-age drinking.

When Quebec police raided a tavern in Laval, after complaints from parents, no fewer than 67 minors were found on the premises. Some of them were only 14.

OBSTRUCTING THE POLICE

Your son got involved in a violent street protest. He's charged with obstructing the police.

Violence is simply not accepted in Canada as a normal part of the democratic process. We are all guaranteed the fundamental rights to free speech, association and assembly, and that usually permits orderly demonstrations and protests in public places such as the parks and streets. (*See* Chapter 1, "Civil rights.") Law-enforcement officers in the cities will often tol-

erate some jostling and even some verbal abuse generated in the heat of the moment. But if the protest breaks out into actual—or threatened—violence, either against persons or property, expect the police to drop the kid gloves.

Serious charges can follow for anyone who deliberately gets in the way of a peace officer attempting to carry out his sworn duty, or who resists the arrest and detention of himself or another person. (*See* Chapter 2, "You and the police.") The chances of getting a few bruises are pretty good, too, as the police have the right to use as much force as is reasonably

Proof of age

Anyone who has reached Ontario's minimum drinking age of 19 can complete this application for a card certifying his, or her, age. The card contains what purports to be a photo of the applicant, which is a good safeguard if the person shown in the picture is in fact the one who applied. Of course, it's an offense to "supply false information or a false photographic likeness" when applying for a card, or to use anyone else's card. Our police forces would have to be quadrupled, however, if all such regulations were scrupulously exercised.

necessary. Not much scope for "beg pardons" in the midst of a violent melee.

Obstructing police is a charge that, depending on the gravity of the circumstances, can be regarded as either an "indictable" (serious) or "summary" (lesser) offense. If the Crown counsel chooses "indictable," the maximum punishment on conviction is two years in prison. If he calls it "summary," a small fine might be the only punishment.

If the "obstruction" included, say, taking a swing at a policeman, the charge might be one of assaulting a peace officer, or of assault with intent to resist arrest. Both of those carry a top penalty of five years. The same protection covers a "public officer"—a category that includes any officer of the Customs or Excise, of the Canadian Armed Forces or the Royal Canadian Mounted Police—when executing his duty. How the courts will handle your son will depend not only upon the circumstances of the incident but on his age.

The Juvenile Delinquents Act defines a child as "any boy or girl apparently or actually under the age of 16 years, or such other age as may be directed in any province." A child under 16 who commits an offense can be convicted only of being a juvenile delinquent, with one exception. That protection is not available to anyone over 14 who has committed an offense that the authorities treat as "indictable." If a judge so orders, that child is tried in the adult courts and risks the same punishment a convicted adult would normally receive.

THE JUVENILE DELINQUENT

If your accused son is tried in Juvenile Court, no judgment will be made public. You're sure he's innocent and you'd prefer the case to go to adult court so that his name will be cleared.

You could be throwing a boomerang that might return and seriously hurt the youngster you're trying to help. Your plan is advisable only if you're virtually certain he'll be found not guilty. And how can you be so sure? No lawyer will ever offer you such a guarantee.

For the vast majority, the scramble is to keep such cases in Juvenile Court where they will normally be cloaked in secrecy and anonymity. This process is almost always preferable to trial in the ordinary courts, where publicity is the order of the day. Not only that: in Juvenile Court the only offense is that of being a juvenile delinquent—no matter what the boy is alleged to have done.

The federal Juvenile Delinquents Act says a "child" is anyone below the age of 16. The provinces and the Territories are permitted to set their own definitions of the word "child," up to age 18. New Brunswick, Nova Scotia, Prince Edward Island, Ontario, Saskatchewan and the Territories have stuck with 16. British Columbia and Newfoundland draw the line at 17; Quebec and Manitoba at 18. In Alberta, it's 16 for boys and 18 for girls.

The misguided child. The aim of the Juvenile Delinquents Act is the protection and rehabilitation of children, outside the normal criminal process. The federal law says that "the trials of children shall take place without publicity and separately and apart from the trials of other accused persons." The news media are not permitted to publish the name of a child, his parents, or any school he attended. If a 1979 decision by the British Columbia Court of Appeals can be taken as a precedent, however, this does not block the right of members of the public, including reporters, to be present at the trial of a juvenile. The appellate judges pointed out that the trial judge could still enforce the ban on the publication of evidence.

The community interest. Our judicial system does permit a child over the age of 14 to be tried in the regular adult courts, rather than in Juvenile Court. The alleged offense must be "indictable"—one of the more serious crimes. The case cannot be transferred to the adult courts unless the judge is satisfied that "the good of the child and the interest of the community demand it." Parliament, reinforced by the decisions of many judges, has made it clear that there must be compelling reasons to try a child as an adult.

The youngest juvenile ever to be charged with murder and tried in an adult court in

Canada was found guilty in 1979 and sentenced to life imprisonment. The crime was committed by a boy in Swan River, Man., when he was 14 years old. He will not be eligible for parole for 10 years.

PROCURERS AND PROSTITUTES

You suspect that a "talent scout" is really recruiting young girls for prostitution.

While the laws controlling sexual behavior will be rigorously enforced whenever children are involved, there are relatively few offenses in the Criminal Code especially defined to protect children. There are laws forbidding sexual intercourse under certain circumstances with girls under 18, and another section of the code makes it a crime for parents or guardians to procure their children to have sexual intercourse with anyone.

The federal Juvenile Delinquents Act contains a general provision for the protection of children against moral corruption. Anyone who encourages or assists a child to commit a delinquency or contributes to a child's becoming a delinquent is guilty of an offense. And "delinquency" covers sexual immorality or any other form of vice.

The Big Time. If you have reasonable grounds for your suspicion, you should notify the police immediately. Even if the attempt at recruitment failed, the "pimp" is guilty of *attempting* to commit the offense of procuring a female person to engage in prostitution. The punishment upon conviction is the same whether the attempt was successful or not.

The chance of breaking into the theater, television or nightclubs is dangled sometimes before countless pretty, inexperienced girls, talented or not. A low-pay position as hostess—that is, waitress—in a dimly lit cocktail lounge is presented as a chance for "discovery" in the big time. Too often such jobs can lead a girl into selling more than drinks. But the employment of minors—under 18—is strictly controlled under the labor laws. (*See* Chapter 25, "Work conditions.") A license must be obtained and the employer will be investigated and monitored by the Children's Aid Society.

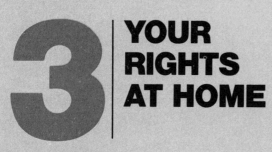

3 | YOUR RIGHTS AT HOME

12 When you buy

The family home is usually the biggest investment made in a lifetime. The average house price in Canada was recently $55,084, with Calgary tops at $72,251. Ownership can bring satisfaction and contentment (and add up to a shrewd financial deal), but it can also bring a load of trouble and heartache to the unwary.

Federal, provincial and municipal legislators over the past half century have woven an ever-growing network of housing laws—most of them aimed at safeguarding the rights of the buyer. Also, the construction and real estate industries have set up self-regulatory bodies to help the citizen get a fair deal. Building, wiring and plumbing standards, zoning restrictions, fire and environmental protection, highway access, the supply and repayment of purchase funds—all these, and many other matters—are subject to official scrutiny and control. But, in the final analysis, it is up to the individual to know the rules by which the game is played.

Before you sign anything at all, see an experienced and reputable lawyer or, in Quebec, a notary. It is possible to buy a home without legal help, but it would be unwise to attempt it. The buying or selling of real estate is a complicated matter, hoary with tradition, strewn with pitfalls.

Few of us have the qualifications to assess the true market value of real estate, but you can shop and compare. Having decided on your basic needs, study the house advertisements in the local paper, then visit all or most of the listed houses in your range. In our society, price is set by the law of supply and demand. When the economy is "soft," the buyer's hand is firmer on the whip.

Periodically, real estate boards publish summaries of sales that provide average prices realized in different areas.

Most properties are sold through real estate agents, and even if the agent is your cousin Fred, remember that his commission is paid by the seller (the vendor). The higher the price, the bigger the agent's paycheque. That does not mean that agents are likely to misrepresent property or premises (they know that misrepresentation or lying can nullify a contract), but you can be sure they will describe everything in the rosiest terms.

When you have narrowed the choice to one dwelling, call in a professional appraiser. He will assess the value of the land and buildings and give you an impartial written report. Top-line appraisers are licensed by the Appraisal Institute of Canada; they use the initials AACI (Accredited Appraiser of the Canadian Institute) after their names on their business cards. The Canadian Residential Appraiser (CRA) is also qualified for any housing up to a triplex. Veteran members of real estate firms do appraisals too, based on their expert knowledge of a local area.

You should be able to get an adequate appraisal of the average family home for $100— and the outlay could save you money later. Mortgage and insurance companies always require a hard-edge figure on market values, and they should accept the report of your hired professional. Otherwise, they'll make their own valuation and add its cost to your bill.

When you buy a home with the aid of a mortgage, you (the borrower) transfer to the lender a partial interest in the property. You grant this as security for the loan. If you should not keep up your monthly payments, the lender has the right to take possession and may sell the property over your head to get back what he is owed. As long as you do meet your obligations, you have full rights to live in and use the property in any legal fashion. You can also arrange to rent, lease or sell it. When the mortgage is paid off entirely, you get a "discharge" of the lender's claim.

SALES AGENTS AND VENDORS

Before accepting your "offer to purchase" the real estate agent asks you to write a sizable cheque in his company's favor as a deposit. You are worried about the safety of that money.

You needn't be. The certified deposit cheque ($1,000 minimum) is a normal adjunct of the formal "offer to purchase." It demonstrates both your sincerity and your financial capability. You make it out to the agent's company "in trust" and he holds it on behalf of the vendor. If the sale goes through, it will become part of your payment. If not, it will be returned to you without deduction.

Checking out the agent. Most homes are bought and sold without the buyer and the seller ever coming face to face. The job is done by the real estate agent who works for, or through, a licensed broker. The broker, acting for the owner, is almost always a member of the local real estate board.

If you have any doubts about a firm, and thus about the safety of your deposit, check with your lawyer, the real estate board, the nearest Better Business Bureau, and/or a consumer group. (*See* Section 10, "Effective complaining.")

Usually, the prospective buyer is led to the agent through a newspaper advertisement or by the sign hammered into the front lawn. But if for any reason you do not wish to deal with that broker, you can approach an agent of your choice, perhaps someone you know personally or someone who has a closer knowledge of the particular area or neighborhood. Cooperation between brokers is routine. In fact, in the larger centers, both probably belong to the Multiple Listing Service (MLS) through which all members receive details of available dwellings, including photographs. Bringing another agent in on the deal won't cost you an extra penny. If a sale results, the participating agents split the commission.

Keep in mind that no matter how many salesmen or brokers are involved, all are legally responsible to the vendor. Since it is he who will pay for their services, they must try to get him the best price they can. This holds true even if you walk in off the street and ask a selected broker to find the right house for you.

The private sale. If an owner offers to sell his home privately (that is, without using an agent), the price may be lower. After all, the vendor is saving the agent's commission (usually 6 percent).

There's nothing illegal about this, and it could indeed save you money, but you are still well advised to bring in a lawyer and a qualified appraiser. Also, consider hiring your own real estate agent to act as counselor for a stated fee (most firms offer this service).

If the private vendor is, say, a Texas oilman who has been working temporarily in Canada, take special care. The government will treat him as a non-Canadian resident, and there are certain tax provisions covering any profit he may make on the sale of real estate. If he should happen to overlook sending the government its share, then you as purchaser could be forced to pay.

THE 'OFFER TO PURCHASE'

You and the vendor have both signed what is officially called the agreement of purchase and sale. Now you want to back out.

Perhaps something completely unexpected has happened in your life. You've lost your job. There's been a family tragedy. Your rich uncle has changed his mind about helping you with the down payment. Whatever the reason, you have little chance of canceling the deal at this stage, even though the official "closing date" is in the future.

You made a legal contract with the vendor and, if the matter should be taken to court, it's likely you'd lose. A minute's thought will convince you that if things were otherwise, all business activity would come to a standstill. It is possible that the vendor (either an individual or a company) and your mortgagee (the person or institution that has agreed to lend you the bulk of the purchase money) would listen to a sincere hard-luck story and release you from your obligation—after deduction from your deposit of any costs incurred. They know they would face a bleak prospect if, in truth, you could no longer live up to your financial promises. But don't count on it.

Breach of contract. There are, however, two situations where the contract could be nullified without cost to you. The first concerns willful misrepresentation. Although the description of the property as given by the agent does not form part of the actual contract (he is allowed a certain amount of exaggeration, and you are expected to check before you buy), if you were deliberately led astray, and if you could prove it to the satisfaction of a judge, you would not be forced to go through with the deal. The relevant law is very complicated and the advice of a lawyer would be essential.

Second, one of the basic conditions in a property sale is that the vendor can produce an acceptable title deed—clear evidence of his ownership in all detail. A vital part of your lawyer's responsibility is to "search the title" at the land registry office. If your lawyer finds some flaw (such as a disputed boundary or a subcontractor's claim for unpaid building charges), the problem must be resolved by the vendor to your satisfaction. If the vendor can't or won't, the contract is null and void.

If either the buyer or the seller should die after the offer is put forward, but before it is accepted, the contract is dead also. If either of the principals dies after the offer is accepted, the contract remains binding on the heirs or successors. (In this context, an incorporated company or a partnership has the identity of a person.)

Prompt in attack—ready in defense

Edmund Burke, the Irish-born statesman, once wrote that the study of law "renders men acute, inquisitive, dexterous, prompt in attack, ready in defense, full of resources." That just about sums up why a call at a lawyer's office should be your first step in a real estate transaction. A lawyer (or, in Quebec, a notary) will protect your rights throughout the complicated deal, and his fee may be the smartest fraction of your outlay.

Your lawyer will check into, provide or advise upon the following items:
■ Legal description of the property, making certain the boundaries are clearly defined.
■ Rights over any mutual driveway.
■ Easements—that is, rights others may have on or over the property.
■ Disposal of your present property.
■ Conditions written into, or deleted from, the agreement of purchase and sale.
■ "Searching the title"; ensuring that no unmentioned claims or restrictions have been registered.
■ Mortgage conditions and obligations.

■ Registration of new owner or owners (whether husband, wife or both).
■ Fire and liability insurance.
■ Filing of required legal papers, payment of statutory fees, and sales and land transfer taxes.
■ Final and detailed report to you, listing all expenses; transfer of the door key.

Ask for at least a ballpark estimate for a "start-to-finish" fee. Regional law societies do publish a suggested fee schedule for real estate work (about 1 percent of the property price) but this does not bind the members.

If you consider you have been overcharged, you have the right to have your bill checked out by a special "taxing officer" appointed by the provincial Supreme Court. If you refuse to pay your lawyer's account, he can sue you just like any other creditor and, if he gets a judgment against you, he can issue a writ against your goods, your property, even a portion of your wages.

As Burke noted two centuries ago, the lawyer is "full of resources."

MORTGAGES

You have $5,000 for a down payment on a $65,000 home but the big mortgage institutions have turned down your application for a loan.

The banks and insurance and trust companies that provide the bulk of Canada's housing money are, from this angle, all alike: They have to be convinced of your ability to carry the mortgage.

How much can you sensibly afford to pay each month? The basic rule is that the total price of the home should not exceed three times the family's income. That means you would need a minimum of $20,000 a year gross, or $384.61 per week, to borrow $60,000. Mortgage payments, heating, repairs and property taxes should not exceed one-third of your gross income.

Raising the money. Just about any regularly employed adult can get a mortgage to buy property or to improve property already owned. A mortgage may be for 20 or 30 years, but its life is usually divided into five-year "terms."

At the expiry of each term, the mortgage must be renewed, and at that time the lender has the right to alter the interest rate. In times when inflation is high, some mortgages are "reviewed" every year.

Mortgages (legally, they are referred to as "charges"—that is, charges upon the property) are available from four main sources.

Under the National Housing Act, Central Mortgage and Housing Corporation guarantees repayment of mortgages granted by private ("conventional") lenders, such as banks and trust companies, and makes direct loans when conventional funding is not available. By the end of the 1970s there was almost no difference in the costs of private versus NHA mortgages.

However, the NHA guarantee provides much easier access to conventional mortgages because lenders don't have to worry about getting their money back and the percentage which can be borrowed can be higher.

The maximum NHA loan or guarantee in 1979 was $70,000. The maximum applied across the country, but the amount of the loan was calculated differently, depending on housing costs in specific markets.

In designated high-cost markets, such as Toronto, Calgary and Vancouver, mortgages were based on 95 percent of the first $60,000 of appraised value, plus 75 percent of the balance. In the rest of the country the loan was based on 95 percent of the first $50,000, plus 75 percent of the balance.

The maximum for a conventional mortgage was 75 percent of value, but this could be increased if the borrower bought mortgage insurance—which he had to do with an NHA loan.

The private mortgage supplies a great deal of home-purchase money. Your lawyer or an accountant may suggest individuals who lend money in this field. The most common form is the "take-back mortgage" (or "purchase-money mortgage") offered by the vendor.

The "take-back mortgage" may be for the whole sum needed above the down payment, but more commonly it is a second or "junior" mortgage—designed to make up the difference between your down payment plus the amount of your NHA or conventional first mortgage, and the sale price.

Other sources of second mortgages are private financiers and mortgage or loan companies. Second mortgages are usually for short terms. Because the lender's risk is greater, second mortgages carry much higher interest rates than do first mortgages. If you defaulted on your payments and the place was sold, the second mortgagee would have to stand in line for his money until the first mortgagee was paid off. (Large properties sometimes have third and fourth mortgages.)

When buying an older home, you may be offered the opportunity of taking over ("assuming") the mortgage currently extant on the property. In that case, you simply assume at the stroke of a pen all the obligations and rights of the original borrower. This can be worthwhile if the old mortgage has a low interest rate. The lender (mortgagee) has the final say.

This is the clincher

The label "offer to purchase," still widely used, does not make the document it describes sound as important as it should. The official title is a little longer but much better: "agreement of purchase and sale." It is by far the most important item in the transaction—so important that you should never sign one without your lawyer, or another qualified person, checking it over first.

In effect, this standard form becomes the contract between buyer and seller. It is an "offer" when you sign it as prospective buyer; it becomes an "agreement of sale" when countersigned by the vendor. Every item and aspect of the deal, every condition, must be included. The real estate agent almost invariably fills out the form, and he is the agent of the vendor. Never assume that the price includes any appliance, fixture or furnishing, even if you have been so assured.

Just because the standard form is printed and "looks official" doesn't mean it can't be amended or added to, but you and the vendor should initial any changes to avoid the possibility of later dispute. Wife and husband are both usually required to sign, whether buying or selling.

In the agreement shown here—selling a let's-pretend house in Brantford, Ont.—the sale price mentioned represents average values for a suburban bungalow in late 1979.

ONTARIO REAL ESTATE ASSOCIATION
AGREEMENT OF PURCHASE AND SALE

PURCHASER, *Richard A. Roe and Sally Roe*, offers to buy from
VENDOR, *Frederick Frost*, through Vendor's
AGENT, *Elm Real Estate Ltd.*, the following
PROPERTY: fronting on the *east* side of *Maple St.* known municipally as *100 Maple St.*
in the *City of Brantford* of *County of Brant*
and having a frontage of *60 feet* more or less by a depth of *100 feet* more or less and described as

Lot 14, Plan 1850, and having a private side driveway at the PURCHASE PRICE of

Forty-six thousand Canadian Dollars ($Can. *46,000*)
on the following terms:
1. Purchaser submits with this offer *Five thousand* Dollars ($ *5,000*)
cash/cheque payable to Vendor's Agent as a deposit to be held by him in trust pending completion or other termination of this Agreement and to be credited towards the Purchase Price on completion.

2. Purchaser agrees to
Pay the balance of the purchase price by cash, or by certified cheque, on closing.

3. Purchaser and Vendor agree that all existing fixtures are included in the purchase price except those us..
The unattached floor area rugs
and that the following chattels are included in the purchase price: *The drapes in the living room, and tracks*

4. Purchaser agrees that this Offer shall be irrevocable by him until 11:59 p.m. on the *1st* day of *July*
19 *80*, after which time, if not accepted, this Offer shall be null and void and the deposit shall be returned to Purchaser without interest or deduction.

5. This Agreement shall be completed on the *30th* day of *July*, 19 *80*. Upon completion, vacant possession of the property shall be given to Purchaser unless otherwise provided as follows:

6. Purchaser shall be allowed the *21* days next following the date of acceptance of this Offer to: examine the title to the property at his own expense, to satisfy himself that there are no outstanding work orders affecting the property, that its present use (*as a residence*
may be lawfully continued, and that the principal building may be insured against risk of fire.

7. Vendor and Purchaser agree that there is no condition, express or implied, representation or warranty of any kind that the future intended use of the property by Purchaser is or will be lawful except as may be specifically stipulated hereunder.

8. Purchaser acknowledges having inspected the property prior to submitting this Offer and understands that upon Vendor accepting this Offer there shall be a binding agreement of purchase and sale between Purchaser and Vendor.

9. Provided that the title to the property is good and free from all encumbrances except as aforesaid and except for any registered restrictions or covenants that run with the land providing that such are complied with and except for any minor easements to public utilities required for the supply of domestic utility services to the property. If within the time allowed for examining the title any valid objection to title, or to any outstanding work order, or to the fact the said present use may not lawfully be continued, or that the principal building may not be insured against risk of fire is made in writing to Vendor and which Vendor is unable or unwilling to remove, remedy or satisfy and which Purchaser will not waive, this Agreement, notwithstanding any intermediate acts or negotiations in respect of such objections, shall be at an end and all monies theretofore paid shall be returned without interest or deduction and Vendor and Vendor's Agent shall not be liable for any costs or damages. Save as to any valid objection so made by such day and except for any objection going to the root of the title, Purchaser shall be conclusively deemed to have accepted Vendor's title to the property.

10. Purchaser shall not call for the production of any title deed, abstract, survey or other evidence of title to the property except such as are in the possession or control of Vendor. Vendor agrees that, if requested by the purchaser, he will deliver any sketch or survey of the property in his possession or within his control to Purchaser as soon as possible and prior to the last day allowed for examining title.

11. All buildings on the property and all other things being purchased shall be and remain until completion at the risk of Vendor. Pending completion, Vendor shall hold all insurance policies, if any, and the proceeds thereof in trust for the parties as their interests may appear and in the event of substantial damage, Purchaser may either terminate this Agreement and have all monies theretofore paid returned without interest or deduction or else take the proceeds of any insurance and complete the purchase.

12. Provided that this Agreement shall be effective to create an interest in the property only if the subdivision control provisions of The Planning Act are complied with by Vendor on or before completion and Vendor hereby covenants to proceed diligently at his expense to obtain any necessary consent on or before completion.

13. Purchaser hereby warrants that he is not a non-resident of Canada pursuant to The Land Transfer Tax Act.

14. Purchaser shall be credited towards the Purchase Price with the amount, if any, which it shall be necessary for Purchaser to pay to the Minister of National Revenue in order to satisfy Purchaser's liability in respect of tax payable by Vendor under the non-residency provisions of the Income Tax Act by reason of this sale. Purchaser shall not claim such credit if Vendor delivers on completion the prescribed certificate or his statutory declaration that he is not then a non-resident of Canada.

15. Fire insurance shall be assigned to the Purchaser on closing subject to the consent of the insurer having been obtained to such assignment, and the vendor shall supply to the purchaser at least five (5) days before the completion date details of any such policy to be so assigned.

16. Unearned fire insurance premiums of any policy to be assigned pursuant to paragraph 15 herein, rents, mortgage interest, taxes, local improvements, water and assessment rates and the cost of fuel shall be apportioned and allowed to the date of completion (the day itself to be apportioned to Purchaser).

17. The deed or transfer shall, save for the Land Transfer Tax Affidavits, which shall be prepared and completed by the Purchaser, be prepared in registrable form at the expense of Vendor and the Mortgage at the expense of Purchaser.

18. Time shall in all respects be of the essence hereof provided that the time for doing or completing of any matter provided for herein may be extended or abridged by an agreement in writing signed by Vendor and Purchaser or by their respective solicitors who are hereby expressly appointed in this regard.

19. Any tender of documents or money hereunder may be made upon Vendor or Purchaser or their respective solicitors on the day for completion of this Agreement. Money may be tendered by bank draft or cheque certified by a chartered bank, trust company or Province of Ontario Savings Office.

20. This Agreement shall constitute the entire agreement between Purchaser and Vendor and there is no representation, warranty, collateral agreement or condition affecting this Agreement or the property or supported hereby other than as expressed herein in writing. This Agreement shall be read with all changes of gender or number required by the context.

DATED at.....*Brantford*.....................this.*29 th*.. day of.*June*.....................19*80*

SIGNED, SEALED AND DELIVERED   IN WITNESS whereof I have hereunto set my hand and seal:
in the presence of:

.....*Mary Smith*.....................   .....*Richard A. Roe*..................... Date..*29/6/80*
                                                             (Purchaser)

.....*Harry Brown*.....................   .....*Sally Roe*..................... Date..*29/6/80*
                                                             (Purchaser)

The undersigned accepts the above Offer and agrees with the Agent above named in consideration for his services in procuring the said Offer, to pay him on the date above fixed for completion, a commission of ....*6*.....% of an amount equal to the above mentioned sale price, which commission may be deducted from the deposit. I hereby irrevocably instruct my Solicitor to pay direct to the said Agent any unpaid balance of commission from the proceeds of the sale.

DATED at.....*Brantford*.....................this.*30 th*.. day of.*June*.....................19*80*

SIGNED, SEALED AND DELIVERED   IN WITNESS whereof I have hereunto set my hand and seal:
in the presence of:

....*Fredrick Frost*..................... Date..*30-6-80*
                                                             (Vendor)

.... Date.....................
                                                             (Vendor)

The Undersigned Spouse of the Vendor hereby consents to the disposition evidenced herein pursuant to the provisions of The Family Law Reform Act, 1978, S.O. 1978, c.2, as the same may be amended from time to time.

In consideration of the sum of One Dollar ($1.00), the receipt of which from the Purchaser is hereby acknowledged, the undersigned spouse of the Vendor hereby agrees with the Purchaser that he/she will execute all necessary or incidental documents to give full force and effect to the sale evidenced herein.

.... Date.....................
Witness   Spouse

ACKNOWLEDGEMENT

I acknowledge receipt of my signed copy of this accepted Agreement of Purchase and Sale, and direct the agent to forward a copy to my solicitor.

.....*Fredrick Frost*..................... Date.*30-6-80*
(Vendor)

.... Date.....................
(Vendor)

Address: ..*100 Maple Street*.....................

Telephone No. ...*200-1234*.....................

Vendor's Solicitor ...*John R Doe LLB*.....................

I acknowledge receipt of my signed copy of this accepted Agreement of Purchase and Sale, and direct the agent to forward a copy to my solicitor.

.....*Richard A. Roe*..................... Date.*30/6/80*
(Purchaser)
.....*Sally Roe*..................... Date.*30/6/80*
(Purchaser)

Address: ..*100 Elm St*.....................

Telephone No. ...*200-3214*.....................

Purchaser's Solicitor ....

Form No. 101

ZONING RESTRICTIONS

You make sure that your "dream house" is in a residential-only zone, but when you move in you discover that your neighbor is running a trucking business from his home.

That could be entirely legal. Zoning bylaws (like almost all legislation) are not retroactive. If the business was in place at the time the district was zoned as residential-only, it would be permitted to remain while under the same ownership. But it is unlikely that it could be expanded in any substantial way, such as by taking over the next-door property or by the erection of extra buildings on the lot. And it is also unlikely that a new owner would be allowed to carry on the business on that site.

Zoning bylaws are enacted and enforced to protect the rights of home buyers (and tenants), and to ensure the orderly growth of cities and towns. (*See* "Zoning" in Chapter 17.) Among other things, they regulate types of housing and use. You could find, for example, that you are prohibited from installing a swimming pool, or parking your camper in the driveway.

Taking in roomers. You may own your home outright, but you still do not enjoy the right to do exactly as you wish with it—even inside. Before you take in a roomer, boarder or any paying guest, it would be wise to check the zoning bylaws. Many urban areas prohibit boardinghouses.

If you purchase a house already accommodating roomers, you may not be allowed to continue the "business."

Adding a room. Any alterations or additions to a dwelling require a building permit. If your plans run counter to the conditions set out in the zoning regulations, you will almost certainly be refused a permit. If you go ahead "on the quiet," you run the risk of being ordered to demolish the addition, and perhaps being fined as well. Building inspectors get their tip-offs from disgruntled neighbors and from hardware and lumber salesmen and deliverymen.

The unpaid subcontractor

A mechanic's lien is something very few homeowners know anything about. It has nothing to do with your garageman leaning against the wall puffing a stogie when he should be working on your car. Ignorance of the term, however, could cost you a sizable sum of money.

All provinces try to protect the right of the workman to get his due. If the contractor building your home has not paid his subcontractors (for example the plumber, electrician and bricklayer), any one of them can slap a mechanic's lien on the project.

This action would be noted against the property's title deed at the local registry office. The house may be completed in the meantime, but until all of the tradesmen are paid, the title is not "clear." Apart from anything else, your mortgage company won't come through with the loan.

Even after you take possession of your home, tradesmen still have a prescribed period (usually a month) in which to file. During that period, you are required by law to withhold a portion of the sale price (usually 15 percent) as security against such claims. The main contractor, in turn, should withhold the same fraction from his subcontractors in case they haven't paid their bills. When your lawyer has checked that there are no liens outstanding, he advises you to release the rest of the cash.

If you disregard this question, and if your contractor is in difficulties, you the owner can be held liable for unpaid construction bills. In the last resort, the courts could order the sale of the property to pay the liens.

Customer satisfaction guaranteed

Under provincial new-home warranty schemes, the purchaser is largely protected against the unscrupulous or unsound builder or real estate developer.

Before taking possession of your new home, both you and the seller should sign a "certificate of completion and possession." It will list any work remaining to be done, or improved, at the date of possession. When those items have been completed to your satisfaction, you will still be covered for the first 12 months against any defects in materials or workmanship that show up.

HUDAC NEW HOME WARRANTY PROGRAM
Suite 702, 180 Bloor Street West
Toronto, Ontario M5S 2V6

ONTARIO NEW HOME
WARRANTIES PLAN

CERTIFICATE OF COMPLETION AND POSSESSION
(for Homes and Condominium Units)

Registration No. _99-9999_   Enrolment No. _00,000_

New Home Address _100 Maple Street, Brantford_

Legal Description: Lot/Block _79a_ Plan _15_ Municipality _Brantford_

Type of Home _Detached_ If Condominium, Unit No. _____ Plan No. _____

Date of Possession _1st July 1980_

Purchaser(s) _Richard A. Roe_   _Sally Roe_

Vendor _John Doe Homes Ltd._

Builder (if other than Vendor) _Same_

For service, the Purchaser (s) should first contact:

John Doe Homes Ltd., 200 Maple Street, 200-1234
Name(Service Contact)   Address   Telephone

Items, if any, are to be corrected or completed (describe):

Bedroom doors don't fit
Kitchen floor uneven
Kitchen counter top cracked
Bath tub chipped
Handrail missing on basement stairs
Crack in basement wall
Noisy pipes when toilet flushed
Some electric outlet plates missing

VENDOR CERTIFICATE

The Vendor hereby certifies to HUDAC New Home Warranty Program as follows:

1. The home described on the face hereof is substantially completed and is ready for possession by the Purchaser(s) on the date of possession indicated on the face hereof subject to the completion of seasonal work and items of a minor nature and to surface defects in workmanship and materials accepted by the Purchaser(s), all of which are more particularly described on the face hereof.

2. The Vendor will grant possession of the home to the Purchaser(s) on such date of possession.

Date _1st July, 1980_ Vendor _John Doe Homes Ltd._

per _John B. Doe._

PURCHASER CERTIFICATE

The undersigned Purchaser(s) hereby certifies to HUDAC New Home Warranty Program that the Purchaser(s) has/have inspected the home described on the face hereof and such home is substantially completed and is ready for possession by the Purchaser(s) on the date of possession indicated on the face hereof subject only to completion by the Vendor of seasonal work and items of a minor nature and to surface defects in workmanship and materials accepted by the Purchaser(s), all of which are more particularly described on the face hereof.

Date _July 1st, 1980_

Richard A. Roe
Purchaser

Sally Roe
Purchaser

FORECLOSURE

Times are hard and you cannot meet your monthly mortgage payment.

Every mortgage contract will permit the lender to take over your property ("foreclose") after a short "period of grace" if you don't, or can't, comply with the terms to which you agreed. The law on foreclosure is extremely involved, with several avenues open to each party, and formal legal proceedings are always necessary. If there are two mortgages, it is usually the holder of the second who will institute the action because his loan is the one at greater risk.

If a lender succeeds in a foreclosure action against you, that in itself does not give him possession of your home. He must proceed via a separate court action to obtain possession. If successful again, he can call on the sheriff to evict you.

If you have assets apart from the property in question (perhaps stocks or bonds, jewelry or automobiles), the lender might choose to launch a civil action for seizure of enough of those assets to get his money back.

Seeking a respite. Your banker or other consultant would advise you to go to the lender as soon as you are in trouble and lay your cards on the table. The lender may agree to suspend payments for a period (a "moratorium").

If you are served with a notice of foreclosure but believe you will be in a position before long to square things away, you can file a form at the courthouse stating your intentions. In most jurisdictions you will be granted a definite period (perhaps six months) in which to bring things back into line. Eventually, of course, you would have to pay not only the arrears of interest and principal but also costs incurred by the lender in instituting the legal action or in protecting the property.

A foreclosed property is sometimes sold for a sum greater than that required to satisfy all the mortgages plus costs. In that case, all funds left are handed over to the defaulting borrower. Anticipating this situation, there is a legal provision for a defaulter to ask the court to sell the property. The sale would then be carried out under the judicial eye and the borrower's rights would be fully protected.

Other rights of the lender. You will find that your mortgage contract—which is drawn up by the lawyer representing the lender—stipulates other conditions, apart from nonpayment, under which the lender can foreclose or force a sale of your property. For example, if your fire-insurance policy on the building falls into arrears, thus placing the investment in jeopardy, action can be taken against you. Nonpayment of taxes can have the same result.

If you permit the property to run down, with the buildings in disrepair or the grounds overgrown, you can be in trouble. The mortgage is based on the appraised value of the property at the time the contract was signed, and the fine print commits you to maintaining the property to a reasonable standard. The lender has the right to inspect, upon giving you proper notice. After foreclosure, he could have repairs done and sue you for the cost.

The lot may have been notable for its fine stand of mature trees. If you cut them down for firewood, or other use, the value of the property could be depreciated. Legally, this is termed "committing waste."

EARLY REPAYMENT

You have received a large, unexpected sum of money and you want to pay off your mortgage immediately. You are faced with a substantial penalty.

On a first mortgage, there is almost certainly no escape. The size of the penalty for repayment earlier than the date of maturity will depend on the size of the loan, how much time is left on the term, and maybe on other conditions written into the contract. Three months', or even six months', interest may be demanded. Three months' notice of your intention is required. And the lender may simply refuse to accept prepayment.

Investment in mortgages is a huge and complicated business. In a recent year, mortgage financing in Canada totaled $7.7 billion. The core of it is that the lender bases his prospective income on the steady receipt of payments. If you pay off your mortgage early, the lender has to make other arrangements for his invest-ment funds. There will be legal costs, perhaps brokers' fees, and office overheads. Should interest rates have dipped, he could be faced with a loss. You will be asked to meet some or all of these costs, and you will find that you will incur legal costs of your own.

Big Brother will listen

The real estate board of your community is sharply concerned about the reputation of its member firms, and you can approach it with confidence if you are in serious disagreement with a salesman or broker. But not all firms are necessarily members of a board.

If you can't get satisfaction locally, write complete details of the problem to one of these addresses:

Superintendent of Real Estate
Department of Consumer Affairs and
    Environment
Real Estate Division
Box 999
Elizabeth Avenue
St. John's, Nfld. A1C 5T7

Superintendent of Real Estate
Provincial Department of Consumer Affairs
P.O. Box 998
Halifax, N.S. B3J 2X3

Consumer Services Division
Department of Provincial Secretary
Box 2000
Charlottetown, P.E.I. C1A 7N8

Administrator of Real Estate
Department of Justice
P.O. Box 6000
Fredericton, N.B. E3B 5H1

Real Estate Brokerage Service
Department of Consumer Affairs
800 Place d'Youville
Québec, Que. G1R 4Y5

Registrar
Real Estate and Business Brokers' Act
8th Floor
555 Yonge St.
Toronto, Ont. M7A 2H6

Registrar
The Real Estate Brokers' Act
Manitoba Securities Commission
Room 1128
405 Broadway Ave.
Winnipeg, Man. R3C 3L6

Superintendent of Insurance
Room 308
1919 Rose St.
Regina, Sask. S4P 3P1

Superintendent of Real Estate
Real Estate Division
9th Floor
Capital Squares Building
10065 Jasper Ave.
Edmonton, Alta. T5J 3B1

Assistant Secretary
Real Estate Council of British Columbia
Suite 608
626 West Pender St.
Vancouver, B.C. V6B 1V9

Superintendent of Real Estate
Department of Consumer and Corporate
    Affairs
Government of the Yukon Territory
Box 2703
Whitehorse, Yukon Y1A 2C6

You do get a chance to "pay off" your mortgage at the end of each term (usually every five years—*see* "Mortgages" in this chapter). At that time the lender may renegotiate the interest rate—and the borrower has the right to retire his debt without any penalty.

Usually, not having become suddenly rich, you will want agreement with the lender for another five-year term. If he wants his money, you'll have to look for another lender. But if you have made your payments regularly, and if you have kept the property in good repair, your lender probably will renew the mortgage.

The "open" mortgage. On a second or third mortgage, the situation is usually quite different. If you need a second mortgage to swing your deal, ask your lawyer to add an "open clause" to the contract so that you have the right to pay off this expensive debt at any time without penalty. Permission is usually conceded.

There's another valuable right seldom but easily exercised. Get your lawyer to insert a clause demanding that if the lender should sell your mortgage (this is routinely done at a discount) you have the first option to buy it. (Although the average householder seldom participates, there is a steady market for mortgages between specialized brokers. You may find that halfway through your mortgage term you will be instructed to send your monthly payments to a new address.)

When you are the vendor

Unless you decide to sell your home privately—and that's a lot more difficult and time-consuming than you might think at the outset—you will simply select a real estate agent and drop the whole problem into his lap. Give him every scrap of information you possess about the property and then let him do the selling. It's his job.

But there are several considerations the vendor must ponder. You have every right to get the best price the market can offer for your property. If you've lived in the house for several years, the increase in its value may astonish you: values in growth areas increased about 100 percent over the 1970s. In the first quarter of 1978 alone, house prices in Ontario jumped by 6 percent. Study the sale statistics released regularly by the real estate board for your area.

There's the question of the type of listing: open, exclusive or multiple. In the first case, you list the property with any number of agents; in the second, one firm has sole rights for a specified time; and in the third, all the agents joined in the Multiple Listing Service (MLS) will get on the job. The rate of commission will probably be lowest for an open listing and highest for a multiple listing, although the practice varies across the country. Make sure that no commission is payable unless a deal is completed.

There's the question of your participation in the financing. When selling an older home which is still under mortgage—the most common situation—you will probably want cash for your equity (that is, the total value less the amount owing to your mortgage); you can offer the purchaser the privilege of "assuming" (taking over) the existing mortgage. He may prefer to make his own arrangements, and provide the funds for you to pay off the existing mortgage. For your own investment income, you may offer to supply your purchaser with a second, or other, "take-back" mortgage. As a general rule, this should be no greater than the new owner's down payment. Your banker or your accountant will advise you on the best course to take.

Don't be too hard to get along with if the purchaser puts a condition in his offer that he must sell his present home before closing with you. You can add a condition of your own to the acceptance giving him 72 hours, or whatever, to complete his sale.

CONDOMINIUMS

You are thinking of buying a condominium home but you have doubts about the principles of its operation.

To live contentedly in a "condo" you have to decide that in a lot of matters you are willing to bow to the decisions of the majority among your close neighbors. Briefly, the condominium permits a number of individuals to own their own homes within an apartment or a row-housing development, while shared areas and facilities—indoors and out—are owned and maintained communally. You do have the right to sell your unit, and any profit comes to you. Your buyer would have to assume all your obligations. The concept can be applied equally well to office buildings, farming settlements and summer-cottage developments.

Apart from the economies effected by sharing the cost of land, construction and landscaping, there are further savings in such things as snow removal, garage space, heating, security checks and upkeep. The pooling principle can provide saunas, tennis courts, swimming pools and gym rooms that no individual could afford.

What you can and can't do. Provincial governments require that before a condominium project can be set up legally, a declaration of the rights and obligations of the joint owners must be registered. You must abide by this "constitution" if you buy into the project. Typical conditions include: only one family per unit (no roomers or tenants); no structural alterations without the permission of the management board; no advertising signs or display notices; adequate fire-insurance policies; restrictions on garbage disposal and types of pets. You must leave a copy of your door key with the manager so that he can enter in an emergency.

The constitution usually cannot be amended without the unanimous consent of all unit owners and the mortgage lender.

There is always provision for a board of directors, elected by popular vote among the unit owners. The board's bylaws can be amended by a two-thirds vote. Usually, the board delegates day-to-day administration to a management company, often a subsidiary of the developer and mortgagee, who may be one and the same. This is usually mandatory for the first few years so that the lender, who has the major stake in the property, can be sure that the infant corporation is on the rails.

In most condos, the mortgage deeds will probably include a clause permitting the mortgagee to overrule the unit owners. He is not likely, however, to insist on exercising this right unless some very controversial or important issue comes up. When the mortgages are paid off, the unit owners' corporation is in full command.

Expenses in common. Each owner is responsible not only for his mortgage and insurance payments but for all expenses incurred within his own walls. (Those "walls," incidentally, usually mean the plastered surfaces and not the structural parts of the wall which carry wiring and piping that services everybody.) You must also pay your share of the "common expenses" of general upkeep and management. If there is a swimming pool, you pay part of the lifeguard's wages whether you swim or not. If spending exceeds the yearly estimate, you must make up a percentage of the deficit.

You probably will also be assessed a modest sum for the corporation's reserve fund. This is banked against emergency costs such as extra snow removal during a tough winter. If the majority votes to use some of the fund for tree planting or tennis courts, you are bound by that decision.

The co-op difference. Cooperative ownership buildings share the principle of exclusive rights within suites, and communal rights and responsibilities for shared areas and facilities. But in a co-op, the corporation owns the entire property and shareholders lease their units. You hold title to your home indirectly through the company. If you want to sell, you find a purchaser willing to take over your shares and an assignment of your lease.

Because there is only one overall mortgage on the building, the co-op home may carry for less. However, should any unit owner default on his monthly payments, the other owners have to make good.

In both condo and co-op developments, penalties for nonpayment include foreclosure and eviction.

CONSTRUCTION DELAYS

You were promised you could move into your new home next week. Now they tell you it won't be finished for another month.

Promises. Promises. When it comes to the crunch, nothing counts except what is written down and agreed to, with signatures, by all parties to the contract. Look again at the fine print of your interim agreement or the agreement of purchase and sale. If a firm date of possession is stated, another clause probably allows for a postponement.

The builder is sticking his neck way out if he gives you a definite completion date. The project can be hit by bad weather, nondelivery of materials, a strike in any one of several industries or services. He can't hope to control these factors.

You, on the other hand, may already have given up an apartment lease, or sold your old home and given the purchaser a fixed date of possession. If you can't stall there, you could be faced with moving in with family or friends, or paying for a hotel and storing your furniture at considerable personal expense.

The sting of the cottage bug

The first bug to bite as summer nears is the cottage bug. After another long and weary winter in city canyons or snowy suburbs, many Canadians decide that this year they'll make that dream of a hideaway by the lake come true. Back to the wilderness, all that fresh air, good fishing, the cry of the loon. . . . Great for the kids.

But the cottage bug can pack a sting. Your rights are just as much at hazard in the purchase of a summer home as in any other property deal. In fact, there are extra pitfalls in resort country.

People will still buy a cottage lot, even a dwelling, sight unseen, accepting the glowing descriptions in a brochure. Others will commit themselves in wintertime when ice and snow mask swamp and rock. Some forget about the lack of sewers, distance to the nearest hydro line, access by automobile, high and low water levels, a drinking water supply. Buyers who do not bother to check bylaws may discover they have to install septic tank and tile systems that can cost $2,500 and up.

Before you get swept away by the sunset over the rippling water, get the building in-spector of the nearest municipality to check the lot. For a modest fee ($15 to $25), he will tell you what you can build there—and he may say you can't build at all! He will explain the zoning, construction and health bylaws, or tell you where you can inspect them.

■ An old lumbering lease may restrict you from building anything within 20 metres of the water. Expensive boathouses, and even finished cottages, have been torn down or moved in these circumstances.

■ Neighbors may drive cheerfully back and forth across your lawn because they have previously gained legal right of access.

■ That row of silent shacks across the bay may boom all night to the sound of guitars when the rock set swarms in for weekends.

■ Your neighbor may be a working farmer. If he keeps livestock, you can be liable for half the cost of common fencing.

Owners in long-established resort areas usually form a cottage-owners' association for mutual aid, fund raising and the protection of their investments. The potential buyer should get in touch with the secretary or other members for on-the-spot impressions and advice.

Think twice before moving into a partially completed home. Unless you are specifically protected in writing, the act of taking possession can be regarded as a token of your general satisfaction. The builder is almost certain to insist that you pay the rest of the purchase price at that time. You could be left in the mud if he suddenly declared bankruptcy. You would have to complete the work on the building and the lot yourself, or hire someone else to do it. If all the broadloom or appliances listed in the sale contract are not in place at possession, you will at the very least be awaiting their installation somewhat anxiously.

In a buyer's market, you might be able to win a provision that, if the home is not complete by the promised date, you can pay part of the price into a trust account—enough to cover the incomplete work or missing items.

The builder might slip a clause into your agreement stating that you will take possession and pay in full when the dwelling is "habitable." Beware of that. Habitable is a stretchy word and it could mean merely "fit to live in." The lady of the house may not agree.

NEW-HOUSE DEFECTS

You loved your new house in the fall but this spring the basement flooded five centimetres deep.

Your purchase contract with the subdivider or the builder guarantees that all work and materials will be acceptable. There is always a warranty of some type, and you can push to have the fine print of the agreement make some attempt to nail down what is "acceptable."

Obviously a basement that turns into a frog pond at the first heavy rain is not acceptable. The same applies to a roof that leaks, floors that sag, plaster that cracks, plumbing that blocks up, doors that jam.

If the responsible party is still alive and in business, you should have no difficulty in getting your basement dry-proofed, or in having other repairs made. And your nearest consumer-protection agency would step into the picture to give you added muscle. (*See* Section 10, "Effective complaining.")

If you have to sue, the courts probably would hold that the work must be of a standard and quality acceptable to a reasonable person. (That doesn't mean perfection. Almost every house in the Prairies will develop cracks in the basement floor because of the movement of the subsoil during the winter.)

In 1977 Ontario led the way with a provincially backed five-year warranty plan which protects the new-home buyer (up to a maximum of $20,000) even if the builder has given up business, gone into bankruptcy or died.

All Ontario builders and vendors of new homes must be registered under the New Home Warranties Plan (NHWP) of the Ontario Council of the Housing and Urban Development Association of Canada (HUDAC), an organization of builders and developers. There are a few exceptions, including summer cottages, rebuilt homes and mobile homes not installed on permanent foundations. The NHWP does not cover rental properties.

If any problems show up during the first year, you take them directly to your builder or vendor. If he doesn't agree to make good, you call in the NHWP inspector to act as referee. This costs you $50, but you get the money back if your complaint is considered to be justified. Within 14 days, you get that decision. If either you or the builder are unhappy with the ruling, an arbitrator will review it. Beyond that, of course, you can take legal action.

During the following four years, you take any problems directly to the NHWP office. Any major structural defect will be repaired or any item replaced. (Not covered are normal "wear and tear," and "acts of God" such as floods or lightning.) But the warranty does cover down payments up to $20,000 for freehold homes and the full deposit on condominiums. If you sell the home within the five-year period, you can pass on the unexpired portion of the guarantee to the new owner.

No matter where you reside you should not take possession of a new home without drawing up a list of all apparent defects. The builder, or the developer's agent, should countersign this, guaranteeing that any extra work required will be performed to your satisfaction without extra cost.

13 When you rent

It's a common misconception that apartment dwellers rent because they can't afford to buy a house. Some do, of course—especially those first moving away from the family home. But many others are attracted by the advantages of renting.

The 40 percent of Canadians who live in rented accommodation are not pinned down by long-term commitment. Security is less a worry in a multi-unit building. Monthly costs are fixed for the duration of the lease. Major essential appliances and services are provided. You are free from most maintenance responsibilities and expenses.

All property rights come under provincial jurisdiction, and the laws in our 10 provinces and two Territories vary considerably. Nevertheless, most recent legislation favors the tenant not the landlord.

For example, some form of rent control existed throughout the 1970s right across the country. Every legislature has established basic tenant rights, and several provinces have appointed a rentalsman, or similar official, to adjudicate disputes between tenant and landlord.

The lease—the contract between you and the owner—sets out the terms and conditions under which you are granted occupation and "enjoyment" of the premises for a fixed period. Even the "standard" printed lease usually runs to three or four pages of small print, a lot of it couched in difficult legal jargon.

When you sign that document (or agree to an unwritten arrangement), you are bound by all of its conditions—except any that the current law overrides. And the landlord is likewise bound by his obligations to you. To borrow a bullring phrase, this is the moment of truth.

Don't sign unless you understand every word of the lease. Be sure you can meet the monthly rent (it should not exceed 40 percent of your net income). If any of the landlord's rules seem too onerous or restrictive, negotiate now with the rental agent. Remember that any clause can be deleted or altered—but make sure that both parties initial any changes.

Check particularly such items as a cable television hookup, parking space (size and location), security and the due date of rent. Other important issues include responsibility for repairs and redecoration, any prohibition of pets, personal injury coverage in the common areas (such as stairwells), subletting privileges (these cannot be flatly denied to you), security deposits, and "escalation" clauses permitting a rent increase based on property taxes or other rising costs. Keep in mind that, under any circumstances, the landlord will have to get a court order to evict you.

The roomer or boarder has definite rights too, whether or not a formal contract is exchanged. In fact, if your quarters are self-contained, and if you have a key to your door, you have all the privileges of the apartment tenant. If you share the kitchen or bathroom, special conditions may apply.

THE LEASE

You find an ideal apartment, but the landlord's agent asks you to sign an "application for a lease," not the lease itself.

Where the occupancy rate of apartments (or rented houses) is high, the owner naturally has a wider choice of tenants. If his agent presents an "application for a lease," he will almost certainly ask you for a deposit at the same time. This form does not bind the landlord, who may take a dozen applications for the same apartment, then choose the best among them. The rejected applicants will have their deposits returned.

An "agreement for a lease" on the other hand, when signed by both parties, is a contract stipulating that you will both sign the lease subsequently. Such agreements are likely when you reserve an apartment well in advance of your moving-in date. A deposit will be demanded, and you could forfeit this if later you change your mind.

Once the formal lease is signed, you must receive an identical copy—usually within 21 days.

Don't sign any contract the day you view the premises (unless you are determined to obtain that particular apartment). Study the papers overnight. Consult a lawyer if you are unsure on any point. No matter how "standard" the forms may appear, remember that the landlord's legal firm prepared them, and you can be sure that they protect (perhaps favor) the landlord's rights.

Periodic leases. These usually are month-to-month arrangements. Such leases may be oral only, but are no less valid if sealed only by a handshake. You agree to pay a stated sum on a certain date (probably the first of the month).

In most provinces, you can terminate a periodic lease by giving written notice to your landlord on the rent due date. If you are a weekly tenant, one week's notice is sufficient; a monthly tenant must give one month's notice (Ontario requires 60 days).

Rent-control legislation does not protect tenants with periodic leases.

Fixed-term leases. The fixed-term tenant signs an agreement to pay a specific monthly rent for a definite period. The residential term usually is one year. Most commercial leases are for five or more years.

If your lease is in the fixed-term category, most provinces require you to give your landlord 60 days' notice of your intention to leave at the expiry of the term; if you don't do this, you will be graded as a monthly (periodic) tenant. The landlord cannot increase your rent during a fixed term.

Statutory rights. Legislation protects the tenant against lease clauses which contradict a province's Landlord and Tenant Act (in Quebec the Civil Code) even if the tenant has agreed to them. For example, a landlord is prohibited from cutting off vital services such as hydro. He cannot demand postdated cheques for the rent.

DISCRIMINATION

You offer to take a vacant apartment but the rental agent cavils, apologizes and finally tells you it is no longer available.

This smacks of discrimination, which is prohibited by various provincial human rights codes. All forbid discrimination on the grounds of race, color, religion, nationality or ancestry. Some add sex, marital status, language and age.

If you feel that discrimination is the root of your rejection, file a complaint with your Human Rights Commission. (*See* "Housing" in Chapter 6.) If your complaint is well founded, the commission will mediate the dispute or bring your claim to court. Landlords found guilty of discrimination are liable for "exemplary damages" of up to $5,000.

But not all "discrimination" is illegal. A landlord may restrict his tenants to adults, allow families with children only on certain floors, or bar pets.

In practice, racial or color discrimination is rarely overt, and can be difficult to substantiate. The landlord's claim that his advertisement attracted several inquiries and that he "will let you know" may be entirely true. Unsuccessful applicants who suspect prejudice can check by telephone to see if the apartment remains vacant after they have been told otherwise.

Members of the Canadian Civil Liberties Association recently telephoned 30 real estate agencies in Ontario and pretended they had property to rent. Several respondents agreed not to "show" to members of minority groups.

Some landlords have claimed that if they rented to blacks and Asians, their existing tenants would move out. But a petition circulated in one such apartment block revealed that most tenants either did not care, or would welcome minority-group tenants.

The man who came to dinner

Background

In 1974, Brigitte Jahn and her brother rented a house in Gormley, Ont., from Monford Johnstone, an elderly man who lived with his wife in an adjacent house. Both homes were set back from the highway and were served by a single, long, gravel lane.

For two years, the two households were cordial. When the Jahns' car was stuck in the snow, Mr. Johnstone helped get it out. In the summer, Mrs. Johnstone provided the Jahns with produce from her garden.

On Aug. 7, 1976, Brenda Deroche came to the Jahns for dinner and, while there, invited a friend, Keith McGhie, to join them. Mr. McGhie, a black, arrived in his pickup truck and had barely sat down when the phone rang. A very agitated Mr. Johnstone wanted to know if Miss Jahn had "a Negro in there."

Miss Jahn said yes. The landlord ordered her to "get him (her black visitor) out of here right away or I'll call the police," and told her to move herself and her property out of the house at once.

The brief conversation upset Miss Jahn, and Mr. McGhie, realizing her distress was linked to his arrival, hastily finished his dinner. Assuring Miss Jahn that he did not want to cause further difficulties between herself and the landlord, he left the house.

His truck had barely gone from the driveway, when Mr. Johnstone arrived at the Jahn house. "What do you think you are doing to me?" he shouted from the porch. "I am boss here." Pointing a finger, he yelled: "How could you disgrace my property? You'll have to leave right now!"

Miss Jahn said she wouldn't move because she had prepaid her rent for a month. At that, Mr. Johnstone replied: "Well, you have a month to leave."

Relations between the two families were never again friendly. Miss Jahn continued to occupy the house until Oct. 14, 1976. When she returned the key to Mr. Johnstone, he said: "This is white man's country and it is going to stay that way."

In Toronto, where she moved, Miss Jahn complained to the Ontario Human Rights Commission that she was discriminated against in housing because of her guest's race and color. The commission tried to conciliate the complaint and failed.

Judgment

A Board of Inquiry heard the evidence of both sides and concluded that Miss Jahn had the right to "quiet enjoyment" of her rented property, and that her landlord could not circumscribe this right by restricting the race or color of her friends or guests. By attempting to do so, Mr. Johnstone had indeed discriminated against her.

The board ordered Mr. Johnstone:

■ to send written apologies to Miss Jahn and Mr. McGhie;

■ to give written assurance to the Ontario Human Rights Commission that he would not discriminate in the future;

■ to advise the commission of any rental vacancies he might have in the next two years;

■ to pay Miss Jahn $200 damages for the humiliation and embarrassment she suffered on the evening of Aug. 7, 1976.

DEPOSITS

At the signing of the lease, the landlord asks for two months' advance rent and a hefty "security deposit" against damage during your tenancy.

The landlord may, and probably will, ask for a lot of things to protect and enhance his investment. But there are definite limits to what he can *demand*. And he cannot demand money to pay for damage that has not yet been done.

If your lease (or oral agreement) contains such a requirement, and even if you agree to it, it is illegal.

The landlord can demand advance payment of the final month's rent. The money must be used for that purpose only. And the landlord must pay you interest on the money.

Anyone who leased an apartment before the mid-1970s and who, at that time, paid a security deposit against damage should examine recent amendments to landlord and tenant legislation. That money probably is returnable, perhaps with interest.

Because of variations in the relevant provincial statutes and the vagaries of the money market, deposit amounts and interest rates will differ from region to region.

REDECORATING

You move into your apartment and find that the walls have not been repainted and that fixtures are missing from the bathroom.

The law will ensure that you get, eventually, what your lease promised—down to the last bathroom tap. But it is up to you to demand them, and promptly. Remember that the act of taking possession implies a basic acceptance.

If you live in the same city, you should not commit yourself to the move until you have inspected your future apartment and are satisfied with it. If you are coming from out of town, you could delegate this job to a business colleague, a relative or family friend.

Schedule of dilapidations. This is the legal term for a report on the state of the premises. After you sign the lease but before taking possession, go through the apartment with the landlord or his agent, listing in duplicate anything missing, broken or unfinished. This will be the day of days when the landlord is most anxious to please you. Date the list, ask the other party to sign it, and share the copies. File your copy safely. It could be important if the question of damage should arise when you move out.

REPAIRS AND MAINTENANCE

The walls and ceilings of your apartment have developed holes and cracks. Your kitchen drain is clogged, the laundry machine is out of order, and the light above your apartment entrance has been out for three weeks. Your landlord does nothing about it.

Repairs and maintenance are thorny subjects in tenant-landlord relationships, and the relevant provincial laws differ. The problem above involves both structural repairs and everyday maintenance, both within the individual suite and in the common areas. In this situation, tenant and landlord have definite obligations, whether or not they are spelled out in the lease.

Almost everywhere, a residential landlord must keep his premises in good repair, and he must comply with all health, safety and housing code standards. Thus, the onus is on him to repair, say, that hole in the ceiling, and to keep the entrance properly illuminated. Where a laundry room is part of the agreed-to services, he must maintain the washing machines in working order.

The tenant's obligation is generally restricted to normal housekeeping. If a sink drain is clogged, most of us would free it. We replace our burned-out light bulbs.

Where you or your guests cause damage— perhaps a broken window, or a dent in the plaster—the landlord will expect you to pay for the repairs. If you went off for a winter holiday and turned off all heat, you would probably be liable for any damage resulting from burst pipes.

Applying the pressure. If your janitor ignores your complaints, write to the landlord's business address, outline the repairs you consider necessary and state the length of time you have been waiting for action. Send a copy of your letter to the rent-control agency and keep another copy for your own file.

To strengthen your hand, check the local housing standards at your city hall or township office. Ask the clerk to explain the regulations, if necessary. If there's an apparent violation (maybe the elevator seems unsafe), ask for a visit by the housing or health inspector. This would cost you nothing.

Should the landlord ignore your valid complaint, the municipality, after inspection, can issue a work order demanding compliance with local building regulations. A court order could demand that the repairs be made by an outside firm at the landlord's expense. The court might even award you a rent refund for the period during which the landlord disregarded his obligations.

If officials confirmed extremely unsafe or unhealthy conditions, you could simply move out and be free of your rent responsibilities until the problem was corrected. Your landlord would have to be advised of the move and you could sue him for your moving expenses.

Direct action. You may have been advised to have a tradesman do the repairs at your expense, or to buy the materials and do the work yourself, deducting the cost from the rent. These are chancy propositions.

In a showdown, you would have to prove that the repairs were necessary (your unsupported word might not be enough), and also that the expenditure you incurred was reasonable. You would require written estimates from several contractors, and receipts from any suppliers. You would have to prove that

How tenants get clout

Some 2,500 years ago the Greek writer Aesop is supposed to have declared: "United we stand, divided we fall." The famous aphorism can be a potent slogan for tenants who feel their landlord is giving them a raw deal.

If individual complaints produce no action, consider forming a tenants' association in your building. Might isn't always right, but the odds are high that the erring landlord will listen carefully to well-researched, concerted demands. The trade-union movement bases its strength on this principle.

Knock on doors or use the telephone to call a meeting in your suite. You don't need a formal organization—although there are numerous well-established associations, particularly in the larger cities, to serve as models. Toronto has so many tenant associations that they have formed a federation.

Have each tenant state his or her complaints in writing. Summarize these and then prepare a polite but firm letter from the group requesting early action. Send it by registered mail to the business address of the owner, or to his management agent. State—but don't exaggerate—the membership of your group, and give the name of your secretary or spokesman.

Often, a precise, well-written letter will result in the landlord discussing the issues with the tenants. He is unlikely to relish the prospect of a mass confrontation. Several large developers cooperate with tenants' associations, if only to attempt to defuse explosive situations.

If your landlord doubts your solidarity as a group, give all rent cheques to your secretary for payment through the business office. Don't rush into a rent strike without legal advice—action of this kind can boomerang.

The law everywhere protects the tenant's right to organize. A landlord cannot evict or harass you for stirring up the hornet's nest.

you had properly advised the landlord that repairs were necessary (telling the janitor would not be enough), and given him adequate time to get the work done.

A wise tenant, in these circumstances, would set aside the amount of withheld rent—perhaps in a separate savings account. This would help to convince a judge that you were not attempting to evade your lease obligations.

HEATING

Autumn comes, and with it the year's first cold weather, but the heat in your apartment doesn't come on.

Each municipality in Canada sets a minimum level of heating (usually 20°C), and dates when it must be provided. In most regions, Oct. 15 is the start date.

If you are shivering, call the janitor or the landlord's office. There may be a mechanical breakdown or a labor strike affecting fuel deliveries. If speedy action is not forthcoming, your city or county public-health agency will soon get results. If your province has a rent-talsman, he will intervene if the turn-on date has passed.

A prolonged period of inadequate heat during the prescribed heating season could be grounds to break your lease. You would need convincing documentation, however. If the matter was beyond the landlord's control, he could demand that you resume your payment obligation, when the problem was corrected. Seek the advice of your lawyer, or call your rent-control agency or ministry of housing before taking action.

DISTURBANCES

A neighboring tenant plays his stereo loudly until 3 a.m., and has noisy parties every weekend. The landlord does nothing.

Your right to "quiet enjoyment" of your rented quarters is one of the most important covenants (agreements) in your lease. But any lawyer will warn you that it's difficult, or sometimes impossible, to define that right exactly in legal terms.

In deciding to live in an apartment, or any type of multiple housing, you are presumed to understand both the drawbacks and the advantages. You know that life styles and preferences differ widely. Rock music exists along with the string quartet. A boisterous birthday party can be fun to the participants but intolerable to the family down the hall.

Virtually every lease includes rules and regulations about such things as pets, bicycles in the lobby, noise. Often, it states that "noise" must cease at 11 p.m. But what "noise" is, and what the landlord can do about it, remains imprecise.

Landlords everywhere have found if difficult to obtain the necessary court order for eviction on the grounds of noise alone. So the landlord will likely accept a promise from the offending tenant to act reasonably in future. Then, after much effort, hard feeling and cost, you are all back to square one.

If you can't sleep at midnight for the pounding of guitars or drums, and if your calls to the janitor produce no results, you might try a polite personal call on the offender. This works more often than irate threats. If it doesn't, you could complain to the police that your neighbor is committing a public nuisance—but the police are understandably leery about interfering in neighbors' squabbles. Your last resort is probably to buy a set of earplugs, and plan to move.

RIGHT OF ENTRY

Without your permission, the landlord allows an electrician to enter your apartment to repair a faulty fuse box.

Privacy in your rented accommodation is one of the fundamental rights set out in your lease. And even if your lease somehow skipped this clause, the law guarantees it anyway. You are master or mistress behind that front door.

Nevertheless, apartment living requires some concessions for the good of all. A fire in one suite endangers everyone in the building. In an emergency, the landlord always may enter and he retains a key for this purpose. This is one reason why neither tenant nor landlord can change (or add) door locks without the other's consent.

Apart from an emergency, the landlord may not admit anyone to your apartment in your absence and without your prior consent. If he does, you can bring an action for trespass.

The landlord (or his agent) may inspect your apartment in daylight hours—but only after giving written notice of his intention to enter. Almost all apartment leases contain this proviso. It's worth noting that many municipalities oblige landlords to ensure overcrowding does not exist within their building, that noxious or dangerous chemicals or liquids are not present, and that certain businesses are not conducted there.

During the month before you vacate, the landlord may show the apartment to prospective tenants at reasonable hours. Courtesy demands that he phone you beforehand.

Fairly recent legislation, or widely accepted custom, says that landlords cannot prevent candidates for public office from entering and canvassing in their buildings.

Landlords sometimes permit designated

How high can they hike your rent?

It's a paradox that while most Canadians object to the state setting any limit to their personal earnings, they prefer that the rents they pay for houses or apartments be controlled. That is, that the earnings of those who provide the accommodation be limited by law. And politicians everywhere have usually been willing to oblige.

In this application for a rent review, the tenant is protesting a rental increase which is much bigger than the 6 percent permitted in Ontario. Unless the landlord can justify the extra dollars before the rent review agency, the increase will be cut back.

tradesmen—milkmen or dry cleaners, for example—to trade in their buildings. The tenant, however, may do business with a tradesman of his choice, unless his lease specifically denies this freedom.

THE ABSENTEE LANDLORD

A large company owns the building in which you live. You want to lodge a complaint but you can't get in touch with "the proper authority."

Corporations, or perhaps family trusts, own the great majority of high-rise complexes. They appoint agents to represent them in everyday contact with tenants. The most visible agent usually is the resident manager, or janitor.

The company, or individual, described as "the party of the first part" in your lease, represents the owner, or owners, and is empowered to speak for them. Most jurisdictions impose stiff fines if the legal name of the landlord is not posted conspicuously within the building. The business name might not identify the individuals who own the place (and there could be thousands of shareholders), but your rent-control agency or Better Business Bureau should be able to assist. Newspapers such as *The Financial Post* periodically publish lists of company directors and these lists are available to the public.

In most areas, owners must provide on-the-site reference copies of the Landlord and Tenant Act, or of the statute (the names of these laws vary) relevant in that province. This applies also to proprietors of mobile-home parks which rent units.

RENT INCREASES

Your lease is due for renewal and you feel that the proposed rent increase is excessive.

In every province, you have recourse to an impartial government agency which will examine the landlord's claim and decide the fair rent for the next term of your lease. Manitoba has an appointed rentalsman; British Columbia and Quebec have enacted rent-control laws. Check with your ministry of housing to learn which laws apply, or what agency can help, in your province.

It's sensible to accept that as property taxes, hourly labor rates and the price of just about everything else increases, the price of renting a dwelling must rise as well. The question is: what's fair? In the residential lease—seldom longer than two years—the landlord takes likely cost increases into account when setting the initial rent. With each renewal, he repeats the process. Almost inevitably, you face a rent increase for your next term.

The landlord will notify you (usually 90 days before your lease expires) of the increase and the reasons for the hike. If you feel the sum is unreasonable, check with your provincial rent-control agency. It probably has a rule-of-thumb percentage of permitted increase.

If the increase is at the base rate for your area, your protests are unlikely to succeed, unless you can prove that the landlord has allowed the accommodation to deteriorate, has not made essential repairs, or has withdrawn services (such as free parking) previously provided.

If you are determined to contest the increase, your rent-control agency will have you fill in an application for a hearing of your complaint. Send a copy to your landlord by registered mail 60 days before your lease expires.

Intimidation can be subtle. Before the dispute about the rent increase has been settled, the landlord may ask you to renew your lease in order to protect your tenancy. Don't sign. You can't be evicted on this issue alone and you have the right to stay on as a periodic (month-to-month) tenant pending a ruling on your case.

The landlord whose increase exceeds the provincial base rate must supply the rent-control agency details of his expenditures and income from that particular apartment block. You or your representative have the right to check this statement for accuracy. Has the landlord, as he declares, repainted the lobby and hallways? Was the landscaping redone last spring? Is the security guard really on duty 24 hours a day?

Should the rent-control officials okay the demanded increase, you may appeal to the courts.

In subsidized housing, where normally rents are geared to family income, you will be required to fill in a form every year stating your income and expenditures. (*See* Chapter 45, "When in need," and Chapter 48, "Retirement.") This information will determine the level of your rent for the next term.

RENEWING THE LEASE

You have been a model tenant but the landlord decides not to renew your lease.

He can't make this stick unless (a) he needs the premises for himself or for a member of his family, or (b) he intends to demolish the build-

ing or to so rebuild or convert it that vacancy is necessary.

In any case, written notice of his intention not to renew is required—usually 90 days ahead of time. And he must give reasons. If you choose, you can contest the matter in court.

If the lease expires, and if you continue to pay the rent on the due dates, you automatically become a monthly tenant. In effect, you are protected against eviction pending a judicial ruling.

SUBLETTING

You are being transferred out of town and wish to end your lease. Your landlord objects.

This happens to thousands of persons each year. It's one reason why the subletting clause of the lease is so important.

In all provinces, tenants have the right to

When you are moving out

In most jurisdictions, you are required to give your landlord notice of your intention to move out upon expiry of your lease. This gives him a fair chance to search for a new tenant. If you overlook this responsibility, you may find that the law regards you as a monthly tenant, and your rent obligation could continue past the termination date of your lease. A notice such as this will suffice.

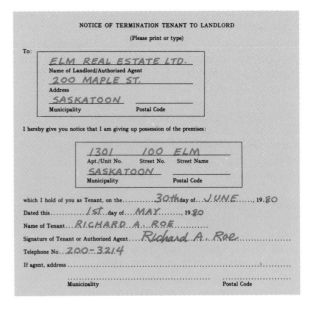

NOTICE OF TERMINATION TENANT TO LANDLORD
(Please print or type)

To:
ELM REAL ESTATE LTD.
Name of Landlord/Authorized Agent
200 MAPLE ST.
Address
SASKATOON
Municipality   Postal Code

I hereby give you notice that I am giving up possession of the premises:

1301   100   ELM
Apt./Unit No.   Street No.   Street Name
SASKATOON
Municipality   Postal Code

which I hold of you as Tenant, on the............30th day of....JUNE......, 19.80
Dated this............1st..day of....MAY........, 19 80
Name of Tenant....RICHARD A. ROE.............
Signature of Tenant or Authorized Agent....Richard A. Roe...............
Telephone No...200-3214
If agent, address..
............Municipality....................Postal Code

sublet for the unexpired term but remain responsible for the rent and for any damage to the apartment. The landlord may not reject your subtenant without substantiating his grounds for the refusal. This means that if you find someone willing and financially able to take over your contracted obligations, the landlord has to accept him.

If you want to move out before the lease has expired, the ball is in your court. Don't expect the landlord to find a replacement—although he may do so. Many desirable apartment blocks have waiting lists and the landlord or his agent may find you a subtenant if you pay any reasonable expenses of the changeover. Most provinces prohibit subletting fees ("key money"), or restrict them to token amounts.

Since rents always increase, it may well suit the landlord to cancel your lease and write a new one for your successor. If this happens, then your obligations will cease.

If the landlord refuses permission to sublet, you can bring him to court. But you might avoid this time-consuming and costly route by discussing the situation with your rent-control agency (or rentalsman), or consulting your provincial ministry of housing.

Breaking the lease. To win a favorable court ruling without finding a suitable subtenant, you would have to prove that the landlord had committed some important breach of his written obligations—such as failing to provide heating in the winter—or that the premises had fallen into noticeable disrepair. If the elevators hadn't worked for some weeks, or if the hallways were not cleaned regularly, the court might consider that you had reasonable grounds for checking out.

You might hear suggestions that, to break your lease, you should make yourself so objectionable to the landlord (to your neighbors, really) that he will be glad to see you go. Some people advocate noisy, nightlong "lease-breaking parties." But most lawyers would advise you not to count on this tactic. The landlord's commitment to provide "quiet and enjoyment" to his tenants is difficult to pin down in legal terms.

Do not refuse to pay the rent (the "rent strike") without legal advice.

Normally, residents of subsidized or "public" housing may not sublet. But since there always is a long waiting list for these units, there should be no difficulty in arranging a new tenancy.

DAMAGES DURING SUBLETTING

The person to whom you sublet held a wild party during which the apartment was badly damaged. The landlord is suing you.

And he may well collect! Even though the landlord permitted you to sublet, you still are responsible for the rent and for damage other than normal "wear and tear."

So think twice before subletting to just anybody. It could cost you a lot of money. Even if the landlord agrees to the subtenancy, he isn't really taking much of a chance. After all, he still has you on the hook.

Housing agency files are well stocked with cases of subtenants not only overlooking normal cleaning and sanitary procedures, but also removing and selling broadloom, draperies, light fixtures and appliances. A thriving bordello was operating in a downtown Toronto high-rise within weeks of a subtenancy agreement.

14 You and your neighbors

Just a step or two outside one's own family circle is the neighborhood. On this stage, frequently, the clashes and concerns of everyday living unfold.

A single volume of solutions to the most common problems of neighborhood life would probably be as well thumbed as the pioneer family Bible. In fact, the Bible *does* emphasize a neighbor's rights and duties. The Ten Commandments (Exodus, 20) exhort: "Thou shalt not bear false witness against thy neighbor," and "Thou shall not covet thy neighbor's house . . . nor anything that is thy neighbor's (including his wife)." Six separate books of the Bible urge us to "love thy neighbor as thyself." Even though most of us probably fall short of this last ideal, the commandments as given to Moses on Mount Sinai are the basis of the laws we must obey today. And often it is true that disputes between neighbors are basically similar to those over which nations go to war.

Friendly and satisfying relationships between neighbors frequently break down because the parties are unaware of their rights and obligations. Petty situations escalate into fisticuffs or legal confrontations. In an era of big and impersonal government, community values wither and we tend to forget that most "next-door problems" can be solved over a beer or a cup of coffee. This is even more true for apartment dwellers than for suburban or rural families. The closer we get, the farther we move apart.

In a prairie city not long ago a householder, alerted by his daughter, surprised his neighbor's only son up on a ladder, peering into the girl's bedroom. Instead of calling the police, the man invited the flustered and ashamed teen-ager into the house for a chat. Conversation revealed that the boy totally lacked sex education. His strict parents couldn't discuss the subject openly with their son.

Next day, the man invited the boy's father for a beer in the local tavern. There, he tactfully reported the occurrence and the shocked father agreed to talk frankly to his son, "man to man." There was no repetition of the offense. The spirit of the age-old biblical precepts made good neighbors good friends.

BOUNDARY LINES

You and your neighbor agree to share the cost of rebuilding the fence between your properties, but you don't agree on the exact property line.

"The old line-fence dispute" used to be a lawyers' toast. Intractable arguments about exact boundaries kept lawyers in clover. Although land-registry requirements now include exact measurements and descriptions of real property, many of these disputes still reach the courts. Land title deeds in Canada date from the 17th century.

The earliest landmarks were mere blazes on big trees. Dividing fences, or stone walls, were often erected to conform with the meandering of a stream or an access road along the easiest terrain rather than to any surveyor's line. Even compass bearings can be uncertain because of the ever-changing magnetic declination.

If a row of maples straddles your boundary, should the fence run on your side, your neighbor's side, or through the middle of the trunks? First, examine your title deeds. They will include written descriptions—but the measurements may be in outdated terms such as chains, links or perches. And where exactly does the measurement begin from? That point could have been the bank of a stream, long since diverted into a culvert, or from a stone cairn removed years ago.

The deed to the larger residential lot, farm or commercial property may well include a plan showing all boundaries in detail, with color shading outlining the perimeters. But this is seldom the case in the suburbs. And again, unless the plans have been drawn or checked in recent years, the start points may be obscure. If a bank or mortgage company holds your title deed, they will allow you to examine it upon request.

Drawing the line. When you bought your property, it was your lawyer's duty to "search the title," and that includes checking the lot lines. (*See* "The 'offer to purchase' " in Chapter 12.) If these were in doubt, he should have employed a surveyor, to protect your rights. Only these chartered professionals, licensed by the provinces, are qualified to establish boundaries.

The real estate broker handling a sale usually tries to ensure that the lot lines are properly described, but he is not liable if they are not. Any *easement*, permitting another some use of your property, should also be revealed. But calling for a fresh survey—and paying for it— is strictly up to you.

Your deed may be explicit enough to establish verifiable boundaries, ownership of all fences, and the responsibility for their repairs. Slight imperfections in title deeds are common, however, and suspected errors or misalignments seldom justify the expense of a lawsuit. Judges often decide that a fence, wall, or other divider, that has stood unchallenged for 20 years, has become the legal boundary.

If both you and your neighbor are determined to press the issue, share the costs of a new survey and abide by the result.

Who pays for the palings? Unless the title deeds specify the ownership of a dividing fence, neighbors usually share the costs of reconstruction or painting. The widely held view that ownership (and responsibility) lies on the side that bears the supporting posts has no legal basis.

Without consulting your neighbor, you may erect at your own expense any fence that conforms to your municipal building code. But make sure that the fence is on your side of the lot line.

Don't build a fence or wall on the boundaries, expecting your neighbors to reimburse you for half the cost. There's no way you can enforce such a demand.

If there is a *covenant* (a formal agreement) on shared ownership and responsibility for a fence, a co-owner can unilaterally rebuild or replace it if it is obviously derelict. If you are considering this course, get several written estimates and submit the chosen estimate to your neighbor. If he remains silent or obdurate, you can have the work done, and send him a bill. If he ignores that, you can sue him for his share. But don't expect an invitation to his next party!

ENCROACHMENT ON YOUR LAND

After a new survey, you find that your neighbor's garage (built years ago) encroaches 18 centimetres onto your land. He refuses to move it back.

Property rights have always been close to sacred in Canadian law—and you possibly could win this one in the courts.

Few lawyers would agree to handle such a suit however. Unless the encroachment causes a recognizable hardship, the judge might consider the action *frivolous* (a waste of the court's time), dismiss your action and levy costs against you. You will certainly lose the goodwill of your neighbor if you proceed.

The court could rule that an *easement by prescription* had been created if the garage had stood unchallenged for several years. A legal privilege also exists if some use of your property by others, whether paid for or not, has been condoned for a time. The usual term is 20 years, but this varies with circumstances, including the system of land-title registration in your area.

If the intrusion of the garage was marked on your lot plan, and if you accepted it at the time of your purchase, then you've got no case now. Similar situations can arise with driveways, gardens, boathouses and docks. Previous owners of adjoining lots may not have been so fussy about trifles.

If you (or your mortgage lender) want to establish your right to those centimetres of land, but do not wish to disturb the garage, your lawyer can arrange for you to grant a provisional easement to your neighbor. The garage then could stand, as is, but it could not be rebuilt inside your property line. An easement grants the "right to use"; it does not grant possession.

The "hangover" problem. On the smaller city lot, encroachment from next door commonly takes a different form. Balconies may appear to overhang your property if your neighbor adds a second story to his house. Water runoff from a new roof might pour onto your flower beds. The natural light that you have enjoyed for years could be shut off from your windows at certain hours of the day.

The law does not require your neighbor to discuss his building plans with you. But he must give details to the municipality before he, or his contractor, will be granted a build-

ing license. Before work begins on the addition, the license must be displayed publicly at the street line.

If you anticipate problems, you should examine the plan at the building inspector's office. The inspector must ensure that the municipality's zoning and building bylaws are obeyed, and that the rights of other property owners are respected.

Any reasonable protest at this stage should trigger a second look by the inspector. If he does not agree that your rights are in danger, you can have the work stopped by court injunction, while your lawyer examines the case.

The right to light. From English common law we have an inheritance of the right to daylight. It is known as the principle of *ancient lights.* In Britain, if your windows have been unobstructed for 20 years, you can maintain your right to continued enjoyment of the sun's rays. While current Canadian law does not guarantee this as securely,

---

'Good fences make good neighbors'

Homespun poet Robert Frost wrote that rather bitter line. On balance, though, the literary record is weighted heavily in favor of the good neighbor.

Thou shalt love thy neighbor as thyself.
—Leviticus 19:18

Thou shalt not bear false witness against thy neighbor.   —Exodus 20:16

A bad neighbor is as great a misfortune as a good one is a great blessing.   —Hesiod

Call in law when a neighbor breaks your fence.   —Browning

That community is already in the process of dissolution where each man begins to eye his neighbor as a possible enemy.
—Learned Hand

I am as desirous of being a good neighbor as I am of being a bad subject.   —Thoreau

What we've got to do, is keep up our spirits and be neighborly.   —Dickens

The same reason that makes us wrangle with a neighbor causes war betwixt princes.
—Montaigne

It is other folks' dogs and children that make the most of bad feelin's between neighbors.   —E. P. Butler

In the field of world policy, I would dedicate this nation to the policy of the good neighbor.   —F. D. Roosevelt

. . . To practice tolerance and live together in peace with one another as good neighbors.   —UN Charter

the principle is no less arguable. Construction of the huge Eaton Centre in downtown Toronto was delayed in the mid-1970s while lawyers, engineers and even astronomers thrashed out the daylight rights of Holy Trinity Church.

OVERHANGING TREES

A double row of maples lines your boundary driveway. Your neighbor threatens to cut off all overhanging branches and the roots under his land.

The "tree problem" rivals the "fence problem" in urban areas. Friction can arise when the leaves of your deciduous trees carpet your neighbor's lawn, or when branches break off and litter his driveway.

As is often the case, the law has two opposing faces. First, it states that the tree belongs to the person on whose property it grows and that he is responsible for any injury or damage it might cause, providing he knew (or should have known) of its dangerous condition. He isn't liable, for example, if lightning splits his tree and it falls on the neighbor's automobile. That's an act of God, and legally the tree owner is "judgment-proof."

Second, the neighbor does have the right to lop off overhanging branches, or dig up roots at his property line. If he has a contractor do this work, the courts probably would force you to pay the bill. But—and here's Catch-22—you can sue him in turn if he damages your tree. And the removal of a limb or the cutting of a main root can be fatal to any tree. It amounts to a "saw-off."

Anyone who buys a property bordered by trees is assumed to have noticed the *status quo* (existing state of affairs). You also will be aware that leaves tumble in the fall, and that trees slough off unwanted wood. It's naive to complain about these natural occurrences afterward.

Forbidden fruit. You retain the right to all the produce of your fruit trees, even fruit overhanging or fallen onto your neighbor's lawn. However, you cannot force your neighbor to return the fruit or to permit you to collect it.

The sensible compromise is to offer your neighbor any fruit on branches overhanging his land or any windfalls on his property. That way, it's unlikely he'll complain about raking up the autumn leaves.

CHILDREN CAUSING DAMAGE

Children playing in your yard kicked a football through your neighbor's window. He demands that you pay for the damage.

That understandably irate neighbor may not necessarily be entitled to compensation from you. If a child causes damage, then the *child* is generally held liable. "Child" is not a legal definition; all youngsters are either "infants" or "minors" until they turn 18. (*See* Chapter 11, "Children in trouble.")

Your neighbor could sue the youngster who kicked the ball, or perhaps all of those in the game, but it would probably be pointless; few minors have funds of their own. And a child normally is not expected to act with the prudence or maturity of an adult. Customarily, parents voluntarily pay for damage done by their children. Perhaps you could telephone all the parents involved and suggest equal contributions.

The parental burden. In some circumstances the parent (or legal guardian), while not responsible for damage done by the child, will nonetheless be liable. The judge may decide you failed to exercise reasonable supervision and control of your child. This raises the principle of *negligence*, and we can all be forced to compensate for damage caused by our careless acts.

It might seem unfair and unrealistic that a parent should have to pay for damage caused by his 16-year-old, six-foot-tall son booting a football over the fence. But the age of adulthood is set by Parliament and legislatures, not by the courts.

Your liability would be almost certain if your aggrieved neighbor could show that youngsters customarily gathered in your yard to play ball games. And more certain still if you had been seen coaching them.

You could be liable for compensation even if your own child was not playing when the window was broken. The players would be regarded as *licensees* or *invitees* on your property—even if you have never laid eyes on them. You are responsible to some degree for the actions of your "guests" of all ages.

Moral: send the kids to the park to play football. And keep up your liability insurance.

HAZARDS TO CHILDREN

Your children are fascinated by a deep well on a neighbor's property. He refuses to cover it securely and warns you to keep your children off his land.

The neighbor is on shaky legal ground, even if it is his ground.

The law recognizes that children are irresis-

A parent on every block

From inauspicious beginnings in 1964, the Block Parent program has taken root across North America. Essentially, it is a neighborhood anticrime campaign—a determined move by ordinary folk to assist the police.

The organizers, with police supervision and encouragement, hope soon to place the familiar red-and-white Block Parent sign (*right*) on every urban street in the country. Already, they claim some 350,000 participants. Although the volunteer "parents" offer assistance in just about any emergency, their prime objective is to stamp out the sexual molesting of children.

The Canadian program got under way in 1968 after a man lured a 7-year-old Toronto girl into the subway by telling her that her mother was in hospital and was asking to see her. That same year a 9-year-old London, Ont., boy was sexually assaulted and murdered, his body thrown into an icy creek. Today, London has 9,000 Block Parents, covering about 95 percent of that city.

When a Block Parent sign is displayed, children know that help is available against molesters or bullies. The Block Parent will try to obtain a description of the offender and immediately call the police. If an accident has occurred, parents are notified or an ambulance is summoned.

Block Parents are not detectives, law en-

forcers or first-aid orderlies. They provide only a close-at-hand haven and swift contact with the authorities. But their very existence, the proliferation of the placards, appears to be cutting street crime.

All Block Parent volunteers and their adult families are carefully checked by local police. Privacy is protected by sealed applications being sent directly to the police.

If you would like to be a Block Parent on your street, information can be obtained from the Canada Safety Council, 1765 St. Laurent Boulevard, Ottawa, Ont. K1G 3V4.

tibly curious. A well fascinates all youngsters, and they are likely to try to sneak a peek down it even if they have been ordered to keep away. The prospect of peril merely adds spice.

Over many years, the courts have established the doctrine of the *attractive nuisance*, sometimes called *allurement*, to provide protection for the wandering child.

The property owner who has anything on his place that attracts children, and is dangerous to them, must protect them from that danger. It's not enough to post a "Keep Out" notice.

An open well, or one covered only with a few loose boards, would likely be considered an attractive nuisance. So would a derelict automobile, a ladder set against a wall, open cans of chemicals, sharp tools or instruments left within reach of a child. That's why the backyard swimming pool must be fenced, protecting even those children who have been ordered off the property a dozen times already.

Another prime nuisance is the abandoned refrigerator. Every year, there are tragic deaths from asphyxiation, when small children get locked inside these old appliances. If you place an old fridge anywhere outside, remove the door and store it separately.

PET DOGS

Your dog is normally a friendly mutt, but your neighbor claims it bit him severely.

There is some legal substance behind the old adage that "every dog is allowed one bite," but "dog's rights" are minimal if more than a playful nip is involved. The Vicious Animals Act in your province provides for the death penalty in all serious cases.

Almost everywhere in Canada, you are allowed to keep pets in humane conditions on private property. You can probably keep even a wild animal—a tiger, boa constrictor, monkey, or buffalo—unless your municipal bylaws state otherwise. In adopting such exotic and obviously dangerous pets, you are virtually asking for costly trouble should they injure anyone—even a burglar.

Most of us settle for a dog, with the cat running a close second. It's a rare owner who will admit his dog is dangerous, but it's equally true that nearly all dogs are capable of inflicting injury, sometimes without provocation.

With some exceptions (seeing eye dogs for the blind; working dogs on a farm), you must purchase an annual license for each adult dog on your property. The person named on the license, generally speaking, is responsible for the proper care and feeding of the animal and liable for any injury or damage it may cause. If your dog wanders off your property, it may be considered to be "running at large," and can be seized by the police or your local dog-catcher, held in a pound, sold or eventually destroyed.

You in the doghouse. Let's say that your neighbor claims he was walking toward your house when your dog rushed out of the bushes, bit him in the leg and tore his trousers. Without an impartial witness, it's basically an irrefutable complaint. Even the most intelligent pet can't argue that he was merely protecting his own, or his master's, territory.

As a property owner, you must exercise reasonable care toward those who come onto your land. The standard of care varies with the legal status of your visitor, but some care must be exercised toward *everybody*—including the trespasser. You can't sic your dog on the door-knocking politician, the persistant encyclopedia salesman, or even the tax collector. You can't shrug off even the mildest attack.

If a suit for damages ensues, you will seldom be excused because you had posted a "Beware of the Dog" notice. That can actually weaken your case. It is evidence that you knew your dog might be dangerous. You shouldn't assume, either, that everyone has good eyesight or can read English (or French).

If you keep a large dog with known aggressive instincts—such as the Alsatian, Doberman pinscher, English bulldog—your opportunities to put forward the "one bite" defense are obviously limited. You'll need a convincing witness if you argue that your normally friendly pooch must have been provoked.

If your guard dog was penned, or on a

chain, you are on firmer ground. The prudent visitor should simply keep clear, a legal principle expressed in Latin as *volenti non fit injuria*: "no harm can befall a willing person." However, this would not necessarily exonerate you if a child climbed into the dog pen and was bitten. The child may think that all dogs welcome affection, like Lassie.

If a dog's owner is under 18, the parent or guardian is responsible for any damage or injury the pet might cause. If the dog was left in the charge of another person—say, at a boarding kennel—then that individual temporarily takes over the duty of care, and any liability.

If your neighbor's Newfoundland dog makes a habit of defecating on your lawn, check the dog-restraint bylaws in your municipality. Some municipalities impose stiff fines for such offenses. If you are tempted to get out your shotgun, don't: cruelty to any animal is a crime—and "improper killing" rates as cruelty.

If your dog comes out a winner in a neighborhood dogfight, you can't be held liable for any injuries to another dog—unless, of course, it could be proved that you encouraged it to attack or did nothing to restrain it.

Protecting livestock. Every year, some pet owner is outraged when a farmer shoots the pet for "worrying" his livestock. The farmer is within his rights, even if none of his cattle, sheep or fowl are actually killed or seriously injured. Farm animals easily panic or stampede when chased by untrained or unsupervised dogs, and financial loss can be high.

Provincial laws provide for compensation to farmers whose stock is injured by a dog running loose. The stock owner can sue the municipal corporation which, in turn, recoups the allotted sum from the ratepayers.

Rights (and wrongs) of keeping pets

On a pleasant leaf-strewn street in Toronto's Rosedale district, a stroller ducked for cover as some two dozen dogs—give or take an Airedale or two—burst through the front windows of a neat brick home. The neighbors never could get an accurate count of "the Dog Lady's" menagerie.

Eventually some 200 of her neighbors petitioned Toronto City Council for help. The breakouts were only occasional, but the noise and the stench were constant in the well-to-do community.

The council responded by proposing a bylaw restricting each owner to two dogs. Then the roof fell in. The councilor who sponsored the clampdown was receiving 50 calls a day, most accusing her of hating "man's best friend."

It is a paradox of our time that while one man fiercely defends his right to keep pets, the right of his neighbor to peace and tranquillity (and a clean footstep) is at hazard. And the dogs appear to be winning.

With an estimated two million dogs defecating outdoors, something close to 650 tonnes of feces falls every day on our parks, streets and private lawns. Yet the cities that try enforcement of dog control—including "stoop and scoop" rules—soon slip back into apathy. Dog owners tend to belong to higher-income groups, with more political savvy and clout. The "antidog lobby" usually finds itself identified with cranks and kill-joys.

The Canadian Council for Animal Welfare claims that 10,000 *unwanted* dogs are born each day. Destiny for them is usually cuffs and kicks, hunger and early death.

The staff at your local animal shelter advocates the spaying or castration of all pet animals not intended for breeding. These are simple neutering operations, carried out under anesthetic by a veterinarian. Both dogs and cats usually recover fully within 48 hours.

As things stand, the animal shelters are putting to death thousands of abandoned animals every day.

NOISE

The teen-agers next door play rock music day and night.

The law does not concern itself overmuch with musical tastes: it labels repeated excessive noise as a *nuisance*, and provides a ready remedy.

The first step, of course, is to ask politely that the volume be turned down. A fair measure is that you should be able to be heard without shouting within your own boundaries. If this approach is unsuccessful, or received derisively, don't take an ax to the offending instrument. Your recourse is to the law.

If your family and your guests are the only sufferers, then your complaint is one of *private nuisance*. You can launch a civil action as a citizen to restore the level of reasonable "peace and quiet" to which we are all entitled.

If you make your case, the court will issue an injunction—an order that the offender "abate" the nuisance. If he still pounds you with the Rolling Stones, he will be in contempt of court, and could face jail.

If the whole street is subjected to the din, then perhaps a *public nuisance* is being committed. In that case, the police could intervene, because committing a public nuisance is a crime in Canada.

More neighborhood nuisances. Your neighbor must cease any action which interferes substantially with normal use of your land and premises. Apart from excessive noise of any kind, actionable nuisances can include gases, smells, smoke, vibration, any type of environmental pollution.

If your "nuisance" complaint reaches the courts, the test of "reasonableness" will be applied. The law does not demand that we avoid all annoyance or inconvenience to our neighbors at all costs. The circumstances will be studied.

If a new house is being built next door, you will have to tolerate the hammering. If the brewery across the street wafts the smell of hops through your windows, well, all breweries smell like that and Canadians are unlikely to give up their beer. However, if your neighbor continually is fermenting a mash in his basement to make home-brew, you could have grounds for civil action.

The biker next door who shatters your quiet when he leaves for work, or when he returns, is not committing a nuisance. But if he and his buddies tune up a half-dozen Harley-Davidsons every Sunday morning, and practice takeoffs on the driveway, you have a pretty clear-cut case.

UNKEMPT PROPERTIES

On your well-kept street, there's one place with peeling paint, broken windows, an uncut lawn, and a rusty automobile in the front yard.

Quite apart from the offense to civic pride, the Tobacco Road dwelling can lower the market values of other homes in the neighborhood. Even persons with a "live and let live" philosophy may think twice when they put their showplace home on the market.

The righteous neighbor is not powerless in this common urban situation. Action will depend on your municipal bylaws and the efficiency of your civic officials, particularly your housing standards officer.

In all probability, your municipal bylaws include a grab-bag zoning or planning clause, enabling the council to "preserve existing property from depreciation." Ontario municipalities, for example, can demolish, repair or renew—at the owner's expense—any "ruinous or dilapidated" building deemed to be in an unsafe condition, or a fire or accident risk. Because it is seldom exercised doesn't mean the authority has expired.

If you suspect that sanitation, fire hazard, overcrowding or child-care problems exist, several municipal and provincial authorities would quickly investigate.

If an accumulation of garbage ("any worthless, unnecessary or offensive matter") is attracting insects or rodents, the health inspector can order it removed. If this is ignored, he'll get a court order compelling the property owner to obey.

SHARING MAJOR FACILITIES

For 10 years you and the folks next door have shared the cost of their swimming pool and the upkeep of your spacious garden. But now they're moving.

Unless your neighbors grant you a normal *easement* permitting you continued use of the swimming pool, the incoming owner is not obliged to continue the arrangement. If you instituted legal action, you'd lose.

It is unlikely, too, that a potential purchaser of the property (or of yours, for that matter)

would be eager to assume such a legal obligation. Mortgage lenders would look askance at such an arrangement.

Even if you are willing to make your garden available to any new neighbor as a *quid pro quo* ("something for something") privilege, that cuts no ice. Who's to say that the existing friendship will continue with the newcomer? He may be the hermit type.

Even among the best of friends, it's wise to have cost-sharing arrangements in writing.

The ubiquitous easement. It's a common device. Where neighbors share a mutual driveway, or access to a beach, their respective title deeds note easements granted. The in-

---

Edmonton *en garde!*

When the Edmonton Social Planning Council titled its 86-page community self-help manual *Rape of the Block*, wide public attention was assured.

What it was all about, really, was rallying citizens against dubious "progress."

"Don't wait until a high-rise or a freeway threatens your backyard," the editors urged. "Begin to get together with your neighbors *now* and formulate a plan for an ideal community ... It is of utmost importance that citizens begin to plan their own communities, and not merely react to the plans of others."

Organized neighborhood action can start at the coffee klatch level, then move with minimal expenditure to a public meeting in a church hall or schoolroom. Advise all existing community organizations of the date, time and venue of your meeting, and seek their active support. Distribute publicity leaflets door to door. Pin up posters in local stores, laundromats, restaurants, apartment-house lobbies, on the street fences of willing homeowners. Deliver a typed announcement to newspapers, radio and cable-television outlets (some of them will publicize nonprofit meetings *free*).

Plan your meeting carefully. Accumulate zoning maps, aerial photographs of your area,

up-to-date public transport charts, data on parks, present and projected. Try to attract responsible officials and local politicians who will be ready to answer questions from the floor.

Have everyone who attends sign a roll, noting address and phone number, plus any professional or other skills. This becomes the basis of your membership.

Select a leader with some experience of public gatherings to chair the meeting, but don't try to be too "structured." Passion, excitement and commitment are essential to provide the spark of inspiration. You want everyone to talk freely.

Arrange for a couple of shorthand secretaries to record all the gripes, worries and suggestions from the floor—perhaps prompted by your core executive. This material can be edited into a crisp statement of aims and objectives.

Incorporate your movement as a provincial nonprofit society (the fee is $25-$50). Nonprofit societies will get government grants whereas individuals won't get a dime.

Now you are ready to decide on priorities. As the Edmonton activists say, it's time to "hustle your bustle."

coming purchaser thus is informed of the neighbor's rights before committing himself.

Public utilities frequently seek easements to accommodate power, telephone, oil, gas or water lines. They pay for the privilege and, usually, the property owner can resume almost total use of the land when construction is complete.

Easements can be granted as favors, for payment or for other reasons. If a subsequent owner wants to erase an easement on his land, this can be arranged by mutual consent between the parties, or by the courts, if there are sufficient grounds. The owner might be ordered to pay compensation.

If you fear that neighbors habitually using your property as a shortcut might establish a right-of-way easement, you should bar the route periodically—say, one day a year—in the presence of witnesses. A chain, wire or rope across the path or roadway would clearly demonstrate that you were interrupting the passage. It usually requires 20 years of uninterrupted, or unchallenged, use of another's property for an easement to be established "by prescription."

GOSSIP

A busybody in the neighborhood is spreading tales that you have been drinking to excess.

In a general way, it's best not to gossip—and not to pass it on, however juicy. Gossiping is a pastime of psychologically maladjusted people. The mature citizen is expected to brush off a certain amount of verbal abuse. Nobody who knows you is likely to believe such stuff, anyway.

A stage can be reached, however, where repeated gossip may resurrect that old bromide "Where there's smoke, there's fire."

You have a right to compensation if your character has been harmed in the minds of reasonable people.

The law classes malicious gossip, unfounded or not, as *defamation of character*. If spoken, it is known as *slander*.

Shakespeare wrote (*Othello*, Act II):

Who steals my purse steals trash . . .
But he that filches from me my good name
Robs me of that which not enriches him,
And makes me poor indeed.

Who heard the story? Publication is a necessary ingredient of a slander suit. The offending words have to be told to someone other than the intended victim. If the alleged defamation gets into print, or any permanent form, it is known as *libel*.

If you are determined to protect your reputation in court, be warned that, even if you seem to have a watertight case, you are going against one of the most cherished democratic liberties: freedom of speech. If the allegation is true, you have no case unless you can prove malicious intent. To be awarded compensation, you will likely have to prove that you have been actually damaged, not just embarrassed.

Your lawyer will advise you that a court action over slander (or libel) publicizes the offending material even more. The gossip might be halted though, if the lawyer writes a letter to the scandalmonger, warning of possible legal consequences.

Although family honor may be outraged, Canadian courts will not hear defamation cases based on insults to the dead.

# When crimes occur

At the core of our concept of citizenship lie the security and privacy of the home. But crime respects neither place nor person and more crimes (offenses under the Criminal Code, as opposed to civil offenses) occur in and around the home than anywhere else. In the most recent census year, Canadians reported 963,748 cases of breaking and entering, theft and other offenses against property; by comparison, traffic violations under the Criminal Code that year numbered only 239,737. Proven and suspected cases of arson totaled 6,636.

What right have you to protect yourself?

Section 40 of the Criminal Code states: "Everyone who is in peaceable possession of a dwelling house, and everyone lawfully assisting him or acting under his authority, is justified in using as much force as is necessary to prevent any person from forcibly breaking into or forcibly entering the dwelling house without lawful authority."

The question of how much force is "necessary" is certain to be controversial if anyone is seriously injured. Of course, under the ancient principle of self-defense, you have the right to protect yourself from physical harm, and the duty to protect your family. But no item of your property is to be set in value against life and limb.

Thousands of crimes involving narcotics, homicide, assault, and sexual and gambling offenses also occur on private property. Any one of us can become the victim of a crime, and many of us will commit crimes—whether accidentally, through negligence, or deliberately. A crime is no less a crime because you commit it on your own private property.

The homeowner's comprehensive package insurance policy is a near-essential in a society where property crimes double (and sometimes triple) each decade. For little more than $200 a year, you probably can cover your home against almost any eventuality, including mindless vandalism and the loss of your wristwatch while you are abroad on vacation.

Where crime is concerned, Canada is very much a united country. While all 10 provincial legislatures, two territorial councils and the federal Parliament pour forth a flood of varying laws, regulations and ordinances, the Criminal Code applies evenly and equally to every person in the land.

INTRUDERS

In the early morning hours you surprise a burglar ransacking your home.

It's a shocking and frightening experience. You feel a sense of outrage at a stranger invading your privacy and attempting to steal your hard-won things. You are face to face with imminent physical peril and you see yourself as the guardian of others still sleeping in the house. Despite the fact that the Criminal Code allows for a penalty of life imprisonment for breaking and entering a dwelling, the incidence of this crime doubled during the last census period.

You were awakened by the sound of a window being opened, or something being knocked over in the living room. You grab the war-souvenir pistol that's been in your bottom drawer for years. Slipping into the living room, you see a dark moving figure. You shout, and there's the flash of a knife blade in the moonlight. You raise the gun . . .

But wait! This is not some gangster movie on the late, late show. It's real life. No matter how panic may distort your values at such a moment, the court will dispassionately weigh the consequences of every act and, if blood is shed, the law could rule that *you* have committed the greater crime.

You may use force against another person only if you have absolutely no other recourse. And if you do resort to violence you must use no more force than is absolutely necessary. In the scene just sketched, you would be justified in shooting the intruder only if he attacked you, or you were sure he was about to attack you. Only 8.6 percent of all crimes involve violence.

If you blasted away in the dark with your gun, or struck out with a crowbar, you might be horrified to discover when you turned on the light that you have maimed or killed a 14-year-old boy. Theft in its many variations leads all other offenses among juveniles.

Even when you can justify your use of violence, you must not have the intention to cause death or grievous bodily harm. The law permits you to use only the degree of force required to defend yourself or your family. In other words, you can't "shoot to kill" indiscriminately.

All handguns are restricted weapons in Canada. The law prohibits the possession of a handgun without a valid registration certificate.

Break the silence. The urge to act to safeguard your property is instinctive, but when physical danger threatens, discretion may well be the better part of valor. The burglar listens intently for any indication that he has been discovered. He doesn't want a confrontation, even if he is carrying a weapon. His object is to steal and depart without detection.

Any sudden commotion, or turning on of lights or radio, even in another room, will usually set a thief running. He may abandon anything heavy or bulky he has gathered. Most burglars have a police record; they know that their punishment if caught will be progressively more severe. The crime of *theft* escalates to *robbery* if there is any violence, actual or threatened—including the brandishing of a toy gun. Again, the maximum penalty is life imprisonment.

The most sensible single move by the householder—if circumstances permit—is to telephone the police. In an emergency, just dial "0" and the operator will immediately pass your address on to the police. This can be done almost silently if you have a "touch" phone. If you can call the police on a bedroom extension phone, bar the door of the bedroom and wait for their arrival. Tipping a chair back under the doorknob can provide an effective lock. It is comforting to recall that your theft insurance is paid up.

If you decide to confront the intruder, keep your cool, and never forget that it is the cornered rat that fights. Snap on the lights, get a good look at him, and let him escape by the easiest route. Await the police, and give them a clear description.

The good Samaritan. The law will condone a "breaking and entering" if the motive is pure. You return from a shopping expedition and discover that a serious car accident has occurred in front of your house. An onlooker broke into your home to call the police and an ambulance.

To be a crime, breaking and entering must be accompanied by the actual commission of a criminal offense, or by the intent to commit such an offense. The good Samaritan only used the telephone and then left.

Who pays you for the damage done to your house? Probably the person held liable for the accident. The law could maintain that the good Samaritan acted on behalf of the injured persons, and they could include your claim in theirs.

SEARCH WARRANTS

Police barge into your home and turn everything upside down searching for drugs. They brush you aside when you ask to see a warrant.

It's a myth that you can refuse the police admittance to your home at all times unless they produce a search warrant. Under several circumstances they can, and will, charge the door down if necessary—and possibly charge you with obstruction. In a few of these situations, no search warrant is required; in others, the householder may not have asked to see a warrant before barring the door.

The chances of this happening to the law-abiding citizen are remote. Most people will assist the police when asked, and the innocent householder will usually invite them to enter. The police themselves take great care to follow the letter of the law. But law enforcement sometimes requires fast action, and there isn't always time to observe all the courtesies. In the heat of the moment, or by simple human error, police make mistakes. Following a hot tip to an incorrect address, police have been known to kick down the wrong apartment door.

Operation Identification

If an earnest student calls on you offering to place identifying marks on all your valuable portable property, don't slam the door. He may be there as a representative of Operation Identification—a burglary deterrent and property-recovery idea that could pay off for you a thousandfold. The accurate identification of stolen property (such as your color TV or your son's bicycle) is often very difficult, and both the thief and the dealer in stolen goods can go scot-free when conclusive evidence is not forthcoming. Supported in the past by several Kiwanis International service clubs, Operation Identification is no more complicated than tying labels on your suitcases—but it's miles ahead in technology.

In certain cities over past summers the federal Department of the Solicitor General has supplied funding for student teams to canvass the suburbs. The students carry credentials from either the police or your local Kiwanis branch. A phone call to either body will provide verification. The students also carry two identification tools. One is a pen-type device that writes with invisible ink on just about any surface, including a camera lens. The other is a small electric engraver that leaves a permanent mark on solid property.

The pen, which does not deface an item, is preferred for marking anything that you may later sell. Its writing can be read only with the aid of ultraviolet light. Every police station has an appropriate handheld reading device.

You can choose just about any identification symbol, but your social security number is preferred since it is easily traceable to you.

If you don't fancy the idea of a stranger seeing or handling your valuables, you can buy one of the pen marking sets—they retail for around $10—and do the job yourself.

When your goods are marked, you receive a small colorful sticker (*below*) for the front door or window of your home or shop. The cruising burglar will think twice before he breaks into premises where his potential loot can be identified easily by the police.

Bell Canada has adopted the system for all its company property, and lends marking tools to its employees. Bell's security division reports that instances of theft and break and enter are 66 percent lower when valuables are marked.

WARNING
Articles Inside Are Invisibly Marked For Identification By Police

ATTENTION
Les objets à l'intérieur sont marqués à l'encre invisible et peuvent être identifiés par la police

Normally, a policeman who wants a search warrant swears before a justice of the peace that he has reasonable and probable grounds for believing that he will find certain things relating to the commission of a criminal offense. He should not get the warrant on mere speculation, or for a "fishing expedition." In practice, the issuing of search warrants by a J.P. is fairly routine. If a policeman shows up at your door with a warrant and you refuse him entry, he can use whatever force is necessary to execute the warrant.

Writ of assistance. This curiously named document is a special kind of search warrant now issued by the Federal Court of Canada solely to RCMP officers to assist them in their hunt for illegal narcotics. Until recently, it was also issued to customs officers looking for smuggled goods of any kind.

A named officer of at least two years' experience can apply for a writ of assistance, empowering him to break into any premises at any hour of the day or night if he believes he will find illegal drugs. A specific writ holds good for two years. The officer does not have to prove that he has "reasonable and probable grounds." It's not hard to imagine what a drug pusher would do with his cache of cocaine, hashish or marijuana if the police, having tracked him down over a period of months, had to engage in a long palaver at the door.

But the policeman granted a writ of assistance has to make reports to the court on his use of it. And RCMP regulations require a sworn statement from the officer in cases where use of the writ does not provide evidence of an offense.

Damage to property is inevitable in any forced entry, and the police are not held responsible for damage caused in executing a search warrant. This assumes, of course, that the householder, if present, refused them entry. Floorboards may be ripped up, and furnishings torn, in any search for drugs. The pusher seldom leaves his stock on the kitchen table.

If nothing is found, or a mistake of address occurs, the householder may have cause to sue for damages. A lawyer would probably advise, however, that this would be a waste of time and money. The legal costs would probably exceed the amount awarded as damages.

In one case in Ontario, the occupant of the searched premises could not afford the expense of litigation and took her case to the provincial ombudsman. The RCMP, after a long delay, paid her $400. In another case, brought by an apartment tenant for illegal entry, false imprisonment and assault, the trial lasted three days. The tenant won, and was awarded $500. That did not nearly cover legal costs.

Grass in the attic. The police are at your door. They have information that your teenage son sells marijuana at his high school, and they present a search warrant. Can they enter your home to seek evidence for another's crime?

The answer is "yes." Police can obtain a warrant to search any given premises for items connected with a crime believed to have been committed by a person or persons other than the legal occupant.

Where do you stand if the police find a stash of grass concealed in the rafters of your house? Can you be charged with and convicted of possession of narcotics? The answer is again "yes," if the prosecution could convince a judge that you knew the drugs were there and that you either hid them yourself or allowed someone else—including your son—to put them there.

If discovery of the cache came as a shock to you (this has occurred to thousands of unsuspecting parents), it's unlikely a charge of *possession* against you would stick. Judges realize that parents in today's permissive social climate cannot be held totally responsible for all the actions of a teen-ager under their roof.

Although a warrant may authorize a search for narcotics only, the police can seize any item of evidence which they believe is related to a criminal offense. A separate investigation, or charge, would ensue. The same thing applies even if the police enter your home illegally—perhaps because of a mix-up in apartment numbers.

No warrant required. The federal gun-control legislation of 1978 grants police the right to search for and seize firearms without first obtaining a warrant, when circumstances do not allow time to process an application. This extension of police powers is intended to encourage the swiftest possible action in dangerous situations. Most murders occur in the home.

When the police seize a firearm they must take it to a judge for disposition; the court and the public are thus reassured that the police acted on reasonable grounds. The use of a firearm during the committing of an indictable offense now brings a mandatory sentence of from 1 to 14 years for the first offense, and from 3 to 14 years for subsequent offenses. The offender must serve such a sentence on top of any other sentence imposed for the crime.

Police may also enter any premises without a search warrant when in hot pursuit of a criminal, or when they have reasonable grounds for believing that a crime is being committed or is about to be committed.

THEFT

A diamond ring is missing from your home and you suspect the cleaning woman.

Suspicion is one thing, proof is another. Even if a domestic is the only person believed to have had the opportunity, it doesn't follow automatically that she is the thief. Also, the fact that the jewelry—or any household valuable—is missing (that is, not in its accustomed place) does not prove that a theft was committed. Rings, brooches, bracelets, earrings, watches—all are small and easily misplaced.

Your cleaning woman has the same right to protect her reputation as the governor general's lady and you should be careful before you make any allegations, especially in the presence of a third person. If you report the matter to the police they are not likely to begin an investigation based on your mere suspicion. (They may suspect that you are doing an "insurance job.")

A private citizen can arrest only those persons he finds committing a crime. If you catch the cleaning woman walking out the door with your ring you are justified in detaining her (which is an arrest) and summoning the police. But if you have only a suspicion, regardless of how reasonable it may be, you are taking a chance in arresting her. If it turns out that she did not steal the ring, or that you cannot prove she stole it, she can sue you for false arrest.

If you see her remove the ring from its place, or if you see her two weeks later with an identical ring (which may not be yours), your best course is to demand the ring, failing which you should call the police.

If you do not recover your ring you should immediately report the matter to your insurance company, assuming your property is insured. If the company is satisfied that it was lost or stolen, they will compensate you. If the ring is valuable they will probably begin their own investigation, including checking up on the cleaning woman.

What is theft? Stealing, embezzlement, robbery, burglary, shoplifting, possessing or dealing in stolen property—all of these and more are "offenses against property and the rights of property." To most people, they all fall under the heading of *theft*. It is the one crime most likely to affect the average citizen. Every code of law from ancient times to the present protects the right of ownership of property.

The interpretations of theft have become very finely detailed. For example, if a valuable statue was bolted to a pedestal and a would-be thief removed the bolts so that it could be taken away, then that is theft, and not merely attempted theft. The same general theory could apply to someone removing a ring from a jewel box in a bedroom and placing it, say, on a porch to be picked up later.

The unauthorized placing of a long-distance telephone call, or use of a telex machine, is theft. Even hydro power can be stolen.

Anyone who takes something out of the garbage put out by a householder for pickup is guilty of theft. If, however, the stuff is thrown onto a municipal garbage pile by the owner, or otherwise abandoned, it cannot be stolen. Things not owned or possessed by anyone become the property of whoever takes them.

Proof of loss

PROOF OF LOSS (Other than Fire)

This form is provided to comply with the Insurance Act and without prejudice to the liability of the Insurer.

I.B.C. CLAIM FORM NO. 8
4-73

CLAIM NO. *1234-5*

INSURER *Royal Insurance Co.*

INSURED *Richard A. Roe* *157 Charles St., Kamloops, B.C.*
Name   Address

under Policy No. *7411210* in force until *May 31, 1979*

against loss or damage by *Theft* to the amount of *contents 20,000* Dollars according to the terms and conditions printed therein, including all forms and/or endorsements attached thereto and forming part thereof.

TIME AND ORIGIN: A loss occurred on the *12th* day of *March*, 19*79*, at *10 P.* M, caused by *break-in to house*

LOCATION: The said loss occurred at *157 Charles St., Kamloops, B.C.*

POLICE: Authorities at *Kamloops Police Dept.* were notified on the *12th* day of *March* 19*79*

TITLE AND INTEREST: At the time of the loss the interest of the Insured in the property described was sole and unconditional ownership and no other person or persons had any interest therein, lien or encumbrance thereon, except *none*

CHANGES: Since the above policy was issued there has been no change in use, possession, location or exposure of the property described, except *none*

INSURANCE AND LOSS: A particular account of the loss is attached hereto and forms part of this proof. The actual cash value of the property insured, the actual amount of loss or damage, the total insurance thereon at the time of the said loss and the amount claimed under this policy are as follows:

Item Involved	Replacement Cost	Cash Value	Total Loss or damage	Total Insurance	Amount named in this policy	Claimed under this policy
SEE SCHEDULE ON REVERSE SIDE						

TOTALS

OTHER INSURANCE: There is no other contract of insurance written or oral, valid or invalid, e
amounts). *No exception*

The said loss or damage did not occur through any wilful act, neglect, procurement, means or conn or this declarant.

Payment of this claim to *Richard A. Roe* is hereby authorized and in consideration of such payment the Insurer is discharged forever from reason of the said loss or damage. All rights to recovery from any other person are hereby transferred is authorized to bring action in the Insured's name to enforce such rights. All right, title and interes hereby assigned to the Insurer.

I, *Richard A. Roe* do solemnly declare that the foregoing claim and statements are to the best of my knowledge and particular, and I make this solemn declaration conscientiously believing it to be true and knowing t force and effect as if made under oath, and by virtue of The Canada Evidence Act.

DECLARED severally before me at *Kamloops*

this *25th* day of *April*, 19*79* *Richard A. Roe*

G. C. Bremner, Comm.

Commissioner for Oaths in and for the Province of
Wadham Publications Limited, 109 Vanderhoof Ave., Suite 101, Toronto, Ont., M4G 2J2

SCHEDULE OF LOSS

DESCRIPTION OF PROPERTY	WHEN AND WHERE PURCHASED	ORIGINAL COST	REPLACEMENT COST	DEPRECIATION	AMOUNT CLAIMED
Color TV — Zenith	*Circle TV 1975*	900 00	1,100 00	200 00	700 00
Stereo System — Dual	*Hitchen's Radio 1970*	785 00	1,000 00	150 00	635 00
Sterling Silver 8 piece set	*Stroud's Gift Shop 1965*	1,300 00	2,600 00	—	2,600 00
Downhill Skis — Fischer	*Leslie's Ski Den 1978*	280 00	325 00	140 00	140 00
TOTALS					4,075 00
DEDUCTIBLE					$100 00
NET CLAIM					3,975 00

APPORTIONMENT OF LOSS

Insurer	Policy No.	Insures	Pays
All with Royal Insurance			

TOTALS

The form that an insured person must fill in when making an insurance claim after a house burglary is similar to the form used for a claim resulting from fire damage to a private home.

This does not apply to a wallet or handbag found in the gutter, because the owner has merely lost, not abandoned it.

The archaic term "color of right" can refer to the taking of property under the reasonable belief that the owner would not object. This has obvious relevance to the unilateral borrowing of a neighbor's towrope or an office typewriter. The act is not likely to be judged fraudulent if the taker honestly believed the owner would not have objected if he had been present. If you took someone else's umbrella from a restaurant under the belief that it was the one you brought from home, it is likely that it would be considered you had "color of right" and were not acting "fraudulently." However, better take it back next day!

Permanent or temporary? "I just wore it to that one party, Your Honor. I was going to take it back unharmed." Every court in Canada has heard that tearful plea from a woman accused of shoplifting a dress or coat. But it is still theft because the owner has been deprived of possession of the property "temporarily or absolutely."

A husband and wife cannot commit theft of each other's property while they are living together ("cohabiting"). But if one of them was planning to desert, or to separate from the other, then the taking of any property legally belonging to the other would be theft.

The maximum penalty for routine theft is 10 years' imprisonment if the stolen property is worth more than $200; under that figure, two years or a fine. There are many special penalties. For example, a public servant who fails to deliver property entrusted to him can get 14 years.

INJURY AND MOLESTATION

Your young child is crying bitterly when you return home, stammering that the baby sitter "hurt" him.

Injuries to a child caused by a baby sitter, a parent or by anyone else in the home are both regrettably frequent and regrettably difficult to prove in court if the child's word is the only

evidence. There are so many ways in which a "hurt" can be inflicted that the authorities are understandably wary. But if your suspicions are reasonably aroused, call the police.

The court will accept the evidence of "a child of tender years" (under 14) without an oath being sworn if the judge considers the child intelligent enough to understand both the occurrence and the duty of speaking truthfully. However, the law requires some other material evidence that backs up (corroborates) the child's testimony. The corroboration must establish not only that a crime was committed, but that it was committed by the accused.

Let's say that an 8-year-old boy complains that the baby sitter attacked him with a knife and cut his arm. He shows you the wound. He says that in his attempt to get away he bumped into a table knocking a vase to the floor, breaking it. The broken vase is found, just as the child said. He also says that the baby sitter grabbed him, and there is blood on the sitter's clothes.

All the evidence appears to confirm the boy's story—but none of it is corroborative. He could have been playing with a knife and accidentally cut himself. In running to the baby sitter, he bumped into the table and knocked over the vase. The sitter could have got the bloodstain in assisting him. All of the confirming evidence turns on what the boy says. None of it stands independent of him. And perhaps he is motivated by fear of punishment for breaking the valuable vase.

Let us give these facts a twist. Suppose that the boy ran into the street, where he is found crying by passersby. His flight, and his agitated state, tend to corroborate his story. Suppose also that the sitter says the boy cut himself and that nobody else touched the knife. The sitter's fingerprints are later found on it. The lie could be corroboration. Both these items of evidence are independent of what the boy says and both tend to indicate not only that someone injured the child but also that that person was the baby sitter.

Sexual molestation. A child left with a baby sitter might complain, or indicate, that some kind of sexual activity has taken place. This would be classified as *indecent assault*. (It could, of course, happen with either sex, but the law is much more solicitous about the female.) Assuming that the sitter—or any other older person involved—denies the accusation, the problem is once again to corroborate the unsworn testimony of a child of tender years.

Call the police immediately. You may not be able to see any physical evidence of moles-tation but the police can arrange for a special medical examination. Sometimes, this will reveal injuries or signs of a nature that can corroborate the child's story.

A separate offense, the "corruption" of children, carries a punishment of two years' imprisonment. This includes the practice in the home of any form of immorality or vice en-

How to protect your home

With reported cases of breaking and entering, and theft of all types, hovering at the million mark yearly in Canada, your chances of being hit are far from remote. Yet many thousands of us take only the most rudimentary precautions to protect our homes. It's estimated that thieves make a quarter of all illegal entries into homes through unlocked doors. The careless person is both victim and accomplice.

Unmown lawns, snow-filled driveways, crammed mailboxes, piles of newspapers, drapes drawn in the daytime, open and empty garages, lack of sound or lighting—all of these signal opportunity. High fences and hedges, big shrubs and tall woodpiles offer useful concealment to the intruder.

The apartment dweller whose name and apartment number are displayed in a lobby offers any thief with a telephone directory the chance to check by phone to see if anybody is home.

Avoid any display of affluence, such as all-night lighting around your swimming pool. Be discreet about personal publicity. A pinup note for tradesmen is a classic giveaway. Don't leave keys "under the mat."

The average burglar isn't smart enough to pick locks: he uses a "spreader" (a small crowbar) in the crack between door and frame to release the lock bolt or tongue. A snugly fitting door, preferably metal or solid wood, makes his job tougher. No part of any door hinge should show on the outside.

The widely used chain lock is useful but it won't bother the professional. He has a bolt cutter or hacksaw.

Keyed window locks are inexpensive compared to your color TV set. If a sash window is used for ventilation, large nails driven into the upper tracks will prevent it from being opened high enough to admit anyone. Metal storms-and-screens are not difficult for the burglar to remove, but they slow him down considerably. To secure sliding patio doors, cut a broomstick to fit into the floor track.

Second-story artists usually just go into the toolshed or garage and get your ladder. Put strong padlocks on all outbuildings.

Always leave at least one lamp alight, and a radio playing, when you leave home at night. You can buy a modestly priced timing device to turn them on in your absence. A good hardware store can also provide all manner of ingenious economy devices that make noise or switch on lights when a door or window is surreptitiously opened.

Beware the ruse to get you out of the home. A woman who mislaid her handbag during lunch at an expensive restaurant was delighted to get a call that afternoon from an apologetic girl who said she had picked up the bag by mistake. She couldn't leave her downtown office for more than a few minutes. How about a meeting outside the post office to return the bag? The lady of the house set off joyfully for the rendezvous. There was, of course, no one there, although she waited for an hour. Meanwhile, using the door key in the bag, the thieves entered the house and rifled it.

dangering a child's morals. This would presumably require either the presence, or the involvement, of the child to some degree. The relevant section of the Criminal Code defines a child as anyone who is, or appears to be, under the age of 18.

A prosecution under this heading requires the consent of the attorney general of the province unless the charge is laid by a Children's Aid Society or an officer of a Juvenile Court. If the accused person is under 16, any charge will be laid not under the Criminal Code but under the Juvenile Delinquents Act—unless the circumstances are exceptional.

TRESPASS

For years, people have been cutting across your land to get to the park. Now you want to cultivate that ground.

You have the right to evict any persons who are illegally on your property after ordering them to go. You can, in the extreme, use whatever force is reasonably necessary. (*See* "Sharing major facilities" in Chapter 14, and "Intruders" in this chapter.) Tenants or lessees have the same authority.

Persons who have been taking a shortcut across your land are doing so under your license—that is, with your permission, stated or unstated. You can revoke that license either by word of mouth, by erecting "No Trespassing" signs, or by constructing a fence.

The same actions will strengthen your hand in keeping snowmobilers off your country property. It's worth noting that if you take no action against snowmobilers or hikers, should one of them be injured on your property, you could find yourself being sued.

Trespass in a storm. Although an owner may exclude others from his property, this right is limited by laws that permit other persons to enter the land in certain situations.

The right of the police to enter in execution of a search warrant is discussed in "Search warrants," this chapter.

Common law recognizes that a person who would otherwise be a trespasser can enter your property under great necessity. In an Alberta case, a snowstorm blocked the public highway. The defendant drove his car across the plaintiff's land and through a barbed-wire gate, and was charged with trespassing.

The judge ruled: "Where a highway becomes impassable, travelers are entitled to deviate from the established road on to adjacent land, taking care to do no unnecessary damage." The plaintiff lost his case.

Summer boating parties, under the impression that they have a right to use the shoreline, often picnic on privately owned property. The owner can order them off, and charge them with trespassing if they refuse to go.

Someone borrowed your lawn mower and refuses to return it after a quarrel. Can you march over to his house and take back your mower? No. You must seek your remedy in court. If you go into his toolshed uninvited you are trespassing.

SQUATTERS

Some people have moved into an empty house you own, and they refuse to leave.

If you are the legal owner or occupant of the premises and you have ordered the intruders (they are sometimes called "squatters") to leave, you are totally within your rights to eject them. If they resist, you may use whatever force is reasonably necessary to get them off your property, although it would be wiser to summon the police and let them do the job.

If the trespassers have damaged your property they could be charged with *mischief*, but that would not compensate you financially for the damage done. You could launch a civil action for damages but squatters would be unlikely prospects for payment. Another move, if the squatters are put on probation, is to present a bill for repairs to the Crown counsel and ask him to seek restitution under the terms of the probation order. The criminal courts will order restitution if the dollar value of the damage is not obviously beyond the accused's ability to pay.

"Damage" covers more than just material injury such as broken doors or fixtures. It could include loss of prospective rental and other factors.

The degree of force you can legally employ in the protection of property rights is difficult to determine. You cannot physically attack the trespasser, yet if he resists a legal attempt to remove him he is technically committing *assault*. The amount of force that may be used to prevent or defend against an assault is governed by the ordinary principles of self-defense, discussed earlier. Hot words, insults or provocative gestures do not constitute an assault, although the use of them might be considered in any subsequent trial. You must not take the law into your own hands. You can't beat up a trespasser just to "teach him a lesson" or because he did not leave the premises immediately.

Squatter's rights. As a legacy from pioneer days, many people retain a misty concept of "squatter's rights." If they see that land or a building is unoccupied, and if they believe they need it for shelter, they argue their "right" to move in.

There is in Canadian law some vestige of the principle. It is known as *adverse possession*. For a squatter to establish his right to take over empty or unused real estate, he must maintain "open, peaceful and undisturbed" possession for a span of from 10 to 30 years, depending on the province. (In British Columbia, Manitoba and parts of Ontario the possibility does not exist at all.)

"Open" means that a squatter cannot sneak in and out to avoid the notice of the owner. "Peaceful" means that he cannot get there or remain there by force or threat. "Undisturbed" means that he has never been ordered off by the owner.

On crown land—any part of Canada to which a title has not been granted—the squatter has a fighting chance. He or his successors can hope to establish legal ownership if they have occupied the parcel of land for 60 years without the payment of rent. The occupant, in this case, must put the empty land to productive use by farming, raising buildings, and so on. He must pay any taxes levied against the property. He can't just fence it off and claim it.

If a person who had legally obtained a grant of crown land failed to clear or develop it as required by the terms of his grant, another person could move onto it. If the newcomer did comply with all the requirements, he could expect to obtain "squatter's rights" after 20 years.

'PEEPING TOMS'

A neighbor's balcony overlooks your apartment and he spends his evenings staring at you through binoculars. Your friends say that you can charge the man with being a "peeping Tom."

There is much confusion about the "peeping Tom." For a start, there's no such criminal classification. Looking in other people's windows is not a crime. The closest offense is trespassing at night, more commonly called prowling.

According to the Criminal Code: "Everyone who, without lawful excuse, the proof of which lies upon him, loiters or prowls at night upon the property of another person near a dwelling house situated on that property is guilty of an offense punishable on summary conviction."

If you are bothered by someone under these circumstances, your obvious solution is to call the police.

But even if a man stops on the street or sits in his car or on his balcony, or adjusts a telescope or binoculars in his apartment to watch a woman undressing before a window he cannot be charged with prowling because he is not on private property near a dwelling house.

On the other hand, a woman who repeatedly undresses before a window with the drapes open, well aware she can be seen by neighbors or by any passers-by, is committing an indecent act. She could also be charged with nudity because, although she is on private property, she is exposed to public view. But such a prosecution in these days of topless waitresses is most unlikely.

FIGHTING

You tried to stop a fight at your New Year's Eve party and now you are charged with assault.

When you invite guests to your home you cannot warrant that one of them is not going to attack another, and little criminal or civil liability attaches to a host because of the acts of his guests.

One exception is when guests start mixing it up. As host you should intervene, not as a referee but as a peacemaker. If the altercation does not cease you should order the offenders off your property. If they refuse to leave, call the police. Your demand that they leave turns them into trespassers. You are then justified in

---

Secondhand 'bargain' or stolen goods?

Trying to sell stolen items personally in taverns or bars is too risky for the professional criminal. He might bide his time and then advertise certain objects in the classified ads, but it is more likely he will trade the stuff off to a "fence"—a dealer in stolen goods—at a fraction of its value. By this route, valuables stolen from your home can appear in a secondhand store, in an antique shop, or as part of an auction consignment. The seller may be completely unaware of the origin of his merchandise.

Suppose that in a secondhand store you noticed a mahogany chest that had been stolen from your home months earlier. You can claim the chest from the store, provided you can prove that it is yours. There's the rub. Only a few householders place identifying marks on their portable goods.

You inform the storekeeper that the piece of furniture is yours, and you may be able to point out certain scratches or imperfections in confirmation. That's seldom enough. You may consider your $1,000 stereo to be an exclusive, but there are thousands just like it. Even expensive diamond rings are mass-produced.

If you can identify your stolen property, call in the police. If the storekeeper hurriedly offers to hand it over to you, summon the law anyway. If he is a "fence" you could help others to recover their valuables, and perhaps set the police on the trail of the thief.

Should the police consider there is sufficient evidence, they will lay a charge of possession of goods obtained by the commission of a criminal offense. The offense of *possession* is related not only to stolen goods but to those obtained by fraud. If the storekeeper is convicted, the court will probably order that your goods be returned to you.

The maximum penalty for possession of stolen goods exceeding $200 in value is 10 years' imprisonment; under $200 value, two years' or a fine or both. Even if one never sees the stolen property but assists in some way with concealment or disposal, the charge can stick. Nobody can just "close his eyes" to the possibility that property may be stolen.

Assume that the storekeeper purchased your mahogany chest from another person, honestly believing that it belonged to that other person. He paid fair market value for it. You can still demand the return of your property and, if the innocent storekeeper refuses, you can sue him for it.

The storekeeper's only recourse would be to sue the person (thief or not) who sold the property to him. He would probably have more luck trying to pass through the eye of a needle.

Suppose you purchase a house and discover a silver tea service in a box under some sacks in the hedge. The person who sold you the house knows nothing about it. Presumably, the silverware was stolen and concealed by thieves.

You would have a title good against all the world except the true owner. And he would have to identify it positively as his own.

using whatever force is reasonably necessary to remove them.

If you intervene in a fist fight at home or elsewhere, you risk being charged with *assault* yourself, either by mistake or because you went beyond mere peacemaking. Before you intervene, make sure that witnesses can say you got in the action to stop a fight or to come to the rescue of one of the combatants who was in danger of being injured.

The booze factor. Drunkenness is often an element in physical flare-ups at parties. So is jealousy. In the cold light of the "morning after," apologies all around are usual. But sometimes the law has to enter as a reluctant third party.

The fundamental issue when intoxication— by alcohol or drugs—is a factor is the ability of the aggressor to form the intention to commit an offense. The law refers to this as *mens rea.* The onus is always on the prosecution to establish the "guilty mind." It is not a question of how drunk a person was but of whether he meant to do what he did. Simply "being drunk" is by no means a passport to crime. Juries often tend to require the accused to give convincing evidence of his incapacity to form criminal intent.

Jealousy is not a state recognized in any court. It is an emotional state existing between private individuals and must be worked out on that level. (*See* Chapter 9, "You, the parent.") If, however, provocative actions at a party lead to an assault, they could be considered in mitigation of any punishment.

ARSON

A mysterious fire damages your garage and car. You suspect a malicious neighbor.

The deliberate setting of any fire to destroy a building (even by you on your own lot without legal sanction) constitutes the crime of *arson.* Because of the great risk of injury or death, the law takes a serious view of the offense. The penalty upon conviction can be up to 14 years' jail, and up to a life sentence if lives are endangered.

If you suspect that someone maliciously burned your garage, you have the duty to report the matter to the police. Any insurance companies covering your house and your car will also be sharply concerned. Perhaps you have had a bitter dispute with a neighbor or a business associate? Perhaps there have been threats? Is someone "out to get you"? It may be that your neighborhood has a pyromaniac, a deranged person who sets fires for his own gratification. In any case, the fire department officers who put out the blaze will automatically check the possibility of arson.

The prank that backfired. A fire set "for a lark" is arson. Four youths near Kingston, Ont., crept up to a dairy barn in the small hours of the morning and lighted a small fire. They were playing a prank on a crusty farmer. The dry timbers of the old barn flared up and the structure was destroyed. The pranksters were caught, sent to prison for short terms, and have long since been released. The farmer, who was underinsured, was wiped out financially and may never recover.

While it is, to quote some authorities on criminal law, "clearly an offense in most circumstances to set fire to one's own building," you can destroy personal property (an old sofa, unwanted documents, fallen leaves) by fire—unless there is a fraudulent purpose or you run afoul of local regulations.

WILLFUL DAMAGE

While driving home from work, you have an altercation with a member of a motorcycle gang. The next night, rocks shatter your front window.

No matter how certain you feel that the biker or his leather-jacketed pals did a job on your window, the breakage and your suspicions do not add up to evidence against anybody. When you summon the police they'll make that clear to you.

It would be different if the youth had threatened you or your property, and if this was followed by a series of incidents. You could go before a justice of the peace and

Heavy breathing on the phone

We take the telephone for granted and thus we are startled and shocked when, once in a while, a heavy-breathing voice spills obscenities in our ear, or makes abusive or threatening remarks. Sometimes you answer the phone and get no reply—yet you "know" someone is there.

Anybody who is repeatedly bothered by such calls should write up a log like the one shown here. Blank logs can be picked up from the business offices of telephone companies. The collected information might establish a pattern that, matched with other research, could identify the bothersome caller.

Annoyance call log

1. Does what the caller says change when different members of the family answer the call?
Caller always asks to speak to mother.

2. Has your family had any recent publicity (marriage, promotion, etc.)?
My volunteer work was the subject of recent pictures and story in local paper.

3. Can you hear any background noise when you receive an annoying call? If so, describe it.
Music, possibly a radio, is playing in the background.

4. Is there anyone who might want to annoy or "get even" with any member of your household?
No.

5. Have you reported these annoyance calls to the police?
No.

Bell Canada

Annoyance call log

Name: *Sally Roe* Tel. No. *200-3214*

Occurrences	1	2	3	4	5
Date	March 8	March 9	March 12	March 15	March 20
Time	9 p.m.	11.30 p.m.	6 p.m.	6 p.m.	10 p.m.

HOW LONG DID THE CALL LAST?

	2 minutes	seconds	seconds	seconds	seconds

TYPE OF CALL

	1	2	3	4	5
Obscene	✓		✓	✓	✓
Harassing					
Threatening					
Other					

THOSE AT HOME

	1	2	3	4	5
Husband					
Wife	✓	✓	✓	✓	✓
Daughter	✓	✓			
Son	✓	✓			✓
Other					

NOT AT HOME

	1	2	3	4	5
Husband	✓	✓	✓	✓	✓
Wife					
Daughter			✓	✓	✓
Son			✓	✓	
Other					

DESCRIPTION OF CALLER

	1	2	3	4	5
Man	✓	✓	✓	✓	✓
Woman					
Boy					
Girl					
Other					

CALLER'S VOICE

	1	2	3	4	5
High					
Low	✓	✓	✓	✓	✓
Strained					
Camouflaged					
Other					

swear that you feared injury from the biker. The J.P. would probably issue a summons requiring the youth to appear before him. If the proceedings indicated that you had reasonable grounds for fear, the accused would be required to make a bond to keep the peace. If he refused to sign it, or if similar incidents continued, he could face a year in jail.

HARASSMENT BY TELEPHONE

Your wife is upset by obscene telephone calls while you are away at work.

It is a crime to make harassing or obscene phone calls, but tracking down perpetrators is difficult. Such persons are seldom known to their victims, whom they often select at random from phone directories.

Unless your wife recognizes the voice over the wire, she is probably better off trying to ignore the calls. The person calling hopes to get some reaction, perhaps just to instill fear, and if he draws a blank, or gets the phone slammed down in his ear, he'll probably desist.

If you are reasonably certain about the caller's identity, inform the police. Don't storm around to his house and clobber him—you're dealing with a sick person and the police are experienced with the breed. Even if it was only a misguided prank, a visit by a constable can have a salutary effect.

If the calls persist, you can arrange to have your telephone number changed, and to be kept out of the next directory.

If you consider such calls as more of a nuisance than a threat, your wife might try the following remedy. Purchase a loud whistle and keep it by the phone. The next time an obscene call comes in, hold the receiver away from the ear and blow a shrill blast into the mouthpiece. It is reported to have an effect like a spike driven into the head.

The telephone companies offer the following suggestions to help you handle high-pressure salespersons who call you by phone:
■ Don't feel obligated to answer any questions just because the caller sounds "official."
■ Don't tell a stranger over the phone anything you wouldn't tell him on the street.
■ Always ask who is calling. Get the name of the caller and of the company he or she represents.
■ If you are not interested in the product mentioned by a salesperson, or in participating in a survey, simply say so—and goodbye.

If you receive a physical threat, hang up. Then call the police immediately.

GAMBLING

Friends come to your place on Friday nights for some serious poker. Your wife says you'll be charged with running a gambling den.

Gambling itself is not a crime in Canada. No law says you can't have a poker game with your friends, regardless of the stakes. Or a bet on a hockey or football game. But several offenses relate to gambling.

It is a crime to keep a common gaming house. Gaming is defined as playing or operating a game of chance or of mixed skill and chance. A "common gaming house" is any place that is kept for gain to which people come for the purpose of gaming (gambling), or in which the keeper makes money by charging a fee or receiving a portion of the wager.

The law will take an interest in your Friday night poker party if one of the players is accused of dealing from the bottom of the pack. Cheating at play is an offense.

If police making an authorized raid are obstructed in entering, that in itself can be enough to provide proof that the place is a common gaming house. The finding of gambling equipment serves the same purpose. Any person found without lawful excuse in a common gaming house is a found-in and is liable to a $500 fine or six months' jail. This applies to the owner, occupier or tenant of the house, whether or not he has been playing.

It is an offense to participate in a game of chance in a public conveyance such as a train, bus or plane. Some ships, especially on cruises, have casino licenses.

A famous French safety study concludes: "Accidents are not accidental. Each one is the result of a chain of causes, and most of them can be avoided." Our legal system takes the same view. When serious accidents occur, the law sifts through the facts and accepted custom and usually establishes who was negligent.

The primary thrust is to ensure that the hapless victim suffers as little as possible. The law can't prevent pain (from a physical injury) but it can apportion financial compensation.

Most accidents occur in the home—even if traffic accidents claim dubious pride of place in national statistics. Most home accidents go unreported; only those where people are hospitalized or police are involved get into the records. Governments and service agencies now deluge us with warnings and advice on how to save our skins. We have, presumably, to be instructed not to drink poison, to butt out our cigarettes, and not to jump into the lake if we can't swim.

Before sinking under this well-intentioned media blitz, we can grasp another life belt. Insurance. Comprehensive personal liability coverage—usually included in every householder's package policy at modest cost—can prevent financial disaster if you are judged liable in an accident case. With that, and insurance on your life and property, you are reasonably secure from the buffets of fate and the carelessness to which we all are prone.

While you can never shrug off the duty to act with reasonable care toward everyone, what about accidents that occur at your home when you are miles away at factory bench, office desk or plowing on the back forty? Your teen-age son backs the family car over the neighbor's bicycle. The house painter splashes the mailman's clothes. The handyman trips over the hose and breaks his leg. The inveterate borrower cuts himself with your power saw.

The range of possible accidents is limitless, and your rights are in the balance every hour. You can't take refuge in the words of the Duke of Wellington: "I care not one twopenny damn." Better to heed that more learned general, Marcus Aurelius: "Be not careless in deeds, nor confused in words, nor rambling in thought."

FALLS

A furnace repairman breaks his hip in a fall down your basement steps. He claims you are liable because there was no handrail.

Falls account for the largest number of home accidents by far, and for some 14 percent of Canada's fatalities. Seven out of every 10 fatal falls occur within the over-65 age group, and a great many of the accidents involve steps or stairs.

Every homeowner or tenant has a legal responsibility to take reasonable care of anyone in his home or on his property. This extends to the actions or neglects of his family. Whether or not you were personally at fault is immaterial. In the eyes of the law, you should have foreseen the possibility of peril and taken measures to forestall it.

In our problem, you should have realized that it was dangerous to descend those steps without hanging onto a rail. No matter that others had been up and down them a hundred times without incident or complaint. In essence, the law has evolved this way to ensure that accident victims are compensated for their suffering, or loss of working time.

Disputes over a situation like this are rare because the prudent householder carries personal liability insurance, either as a separate policy or as one segment of his homeowner's or tenant's package policy. It works the same way as the third-party liability section of your automobile insurance. Without such coverage a serious mishap could ruin you financially.

Your first action after the accident should be to get medical attention for your repairman. Then you should contact your insurance agent. An adjuster is seldom called in for such a straightforward (if regrettably frequent) occurrence, but there will be forms to complete if the repairman lodges a claim.

Care in climbing. Most home falls occur from steps and stairs, ladders and scaffolds. Children tumble from windows and porches, off roofs and out of trees. Tripping over obstacles causes thousands of injuries every year.

It's good sense to install handrails on each side of staircases, and to show children, by example, that you use them. When there are toddlers in the house, place a safety gate at the top of stairs. Keep all stairs, and the steps to the basement, free of clutter. Check the lighting on your stairs, and have switches top and bottom. When carrying things up or down stairs, don't let the load obstruct your view.

Polished floors may delight the housewife but they can be a hazard to hurrying feet, especially if covered by scatter rugs. Use nonskid finishes, and back your rugs with rubber matting. Wipe up all spills immediately. Long electric cords are like tripwires; install more base plugs to minimize the cord lengths.

The tidy home is the safe home. Be a martinet and insist that everybody in the house picks up toys, magazines, shoes.

POWER EQUIPMENT

A boy cuts your grass with a power mower. A stone ricochets off the blade and he loses the sight of one eye.

If you did not have personal liability insurance coverage, you could face a steep bill. When awarding damages, juries are notoriously sympathetic toward young victims. A 9-year-old girl in California recently was awarded $1.7 million after a backyard accident left her brain damaged. A person in Ontario won $800,000 when struck by a piece of masonry.

There are perhaps a million power mowers in Canada, and they injure—often cripple—some 7,000 persons a year. A middle-aged Toronto man felt "a stab in the chest" while using his mower; an X-ray revealed a piece of wire embedded near his heart. A 2-year-old was watching his father cut the grass when the mower struck a hidden rock. The blade splintered and a fragment entered the child's forehead, a fatal wound.

The blade in the average hand-propelled rotary mower whirls at 4,000 revolutions per minute, and can amputate toes or fingers as easily as it cuts grass. The heavier "ride-on" tractor-type mower can be just as dangerous. Several terrible cases on record involve small children being literally cut to ribbons.

Read the manual. All new power tools marketed in Canada must meet strict government standards. You would have a right to damages from either the manufacturer or his sales agent if injury to a person or property occurred through some basic defect in a powered machine, whether or not you noticed the defect at the time of purchase. But substantiating its existence could be difficult.

Before using the mower, or allowing anyone else to operate it, read the manufacturer's instructions. Many don't, at their peril. The instructions are sure to state that you should clear stones or other objects from the area to be mowed.

If you borrow a power tool, you accept the responsibility of operating it safely. And you must return it promptly, and undamaged.

DANGEROUS TOYS

Your 5-year-old son is badly gashed by a toy. You think the manufacturer should be held responsible.

All toys and baby products must meet government standards of safety before going into the stores. Toys are submitted to "torture tests" to uncover any hidden hazards; all chemicals, paints and construction materials are analyzed. Many items are modified or withdrawn from sale after testing, yet thousands of Cana-

The bargain bodyguard

Without comprehensive personal liability and personal property insurance you are playing Russian roulette every day in an accident-prone world. Even when you are blameless—even if you were miles away when the accident occurred—you could be held liable for injury to someone or for damage to his property.

The homeowner's or tenant's routine residential package policy (sample below) is one of today's few bargains. The personal liability premiums are about $8 per year for every $100,000 of coverage. Insurance of $15,000 worth of personal property costs between $60 and $125 per year. If your district is served by fire hydrants, or if you are within eight kilometres of a fire station, the lower rate probably applies.

dian children are injured by their playthings every year, and some die.

You can sue for damages if you believe that the toy that injured your child was dangerous. Discuss the situation with your lawyer. Perhaps you think the item should be withdrawn from sale, and that other parents who have bought the same toy should be warned of danger. Either the Department of National Health and Welfare or the Department of Consumer and Corporate Affairs would welcome your report, and advise you on any further action. The Hazardous Products Act is frequently updated after complaints and fresh research.

But the ruling fact—as every mother knows—is that no toy is "child-proof" for long. An energetic youngster will bash it, bathe it, chew it, suck it or throw it down the basement steps. If it is small enough, he may swallow it. However zealously government laboratories and conscientious toy makers work for maximum safety levels, accidents will continue to happen.

Who hasn't given a child a balloon? But young children have choked to death with balloons stuck in their windpipes. In trying to inflate them, they suck instead of blowing. Few would advocate the banning of balloons—but you should not give an uninflated one to a child under 5. Small boys have died after swallowing model soldiers, toy car wheels, and just about everything else you can imagine.

Toys decorated with lead paints once posed a serious poisoning hazard to chewing infants. Canada bans them now, but you should be on guard against all toys brought into the country as presents by travelers.

The duty to protect. Every minor has the right to the protection (and supervision) of the parent or guardian. The injured child can sue the parent for damages; this legal procedure might be followed in insurance claims to ensure compensation for the child, even when the parent is blameless.

The Department of Consumer and Corporate Affairs promotes these six safety tips to prevent accidents with toys: Buy a toy that is right for the child's age and know-how; keep in mind who else in the house might play with it; check the instructions and really look the toy over; show the child how to use the toy; if a toy breaks and sharp edges are exposed, throw it away; watch the child at all times.

FIRE DAMAGE TO A HOUSE

A fire destroys your house and you learn that the rebuilding cost far exceeds the amount of your insurance.

It can happen to you—a fire occurs in a Canadian home every 10 minutes. Practically everybody takes out fire insurance when they purchase a house, a condominium, cottage or mobile home. All mortgage lenders insist on sufficient coverage at least to protect their investment.

You can suffer a crippling financial blow if you don't study the policy carefully and review it periodically, making sure the premiums are paid. Any insurance agent will advise you, without obligation—it's part of his highly profitable business. To find a qualified agent in your area, look in the Yellow Pages of your phone directory for a Chartered Insurance Broker (CIB) or Fellow of the Insurance Institute of Canada (FIIC). An agent has passed tough exams to get those credentials, and the industry is closely supervised by a government agency.

Insurance is founded on very simple principles. Essentially, it is the sharing of a relatively small incidence of risk among a large number of persons.

For fire-insurance purposes, the appraised value of your home does not include the value of your land.

If your house burns to the ground and it is insured under a standard "no frills" policy for $50,000, then you can count on getting only that sum, less depreciation. Yet the replacement cost can be easily $75,000 or more.

A guide to the rising cost of home replacement is the index of construction costs available from Statistics Canada. Ten percent per year has become routine. Remember that you will still owe any outstanding mortgage payments on the house that no longer exists. You could find it difficult to arrange a new mortgage to cover the gap in the cost of replacement.

The solution: ensure that the basic insured value of your dwelling does not fall below 80 percent of its current replacement value. If you pay premiums to cover up to that vital percentage, most residential fire-insurance policies will cover the bill for total replacement. It's called the "new-for-old" clause. Review the face value of your policy at least every two years.

If you have paid for "broad" coverage—one step up from the standard—your policy can cover your swimming pool, pump house, any outbuildings and things in outside storage (such as storm windows). In fact, you can insure just about anything, at a price.

Partial damage. Few fires, in urban areas at least, result in dwellings being burned "to the ground." It becomes a matter of repair or reconstruction. Don't expect to wind up with a better house than before. Insurance adjusters know every trick in the book. Many fires start in the kitchen and if only that room was destroyed or damaged, only that area would be rebuilt under your insurance cover.

If fire destroyed your shingle roof and you were not insured up to at least 80 percent of total replacement value, the insurance company would be liable only for the depreciated value of that roof. If the roof's useful life was 30 years, and 10 years had expired, the insurance company could offer two-thirds of the original value.

Damage caused by firemen in gaining access to a burning building or in extinguishing the blaze is covered, even if the fire itself is held to a small area.

The wise homeowner, reviewing his fire insurance, remembers improvements made since he took out his policy. The new forced-air heating system, the extra bathroom, the bedroom in the attic—all these have added real value. If you haven't listed them in your policy, or increased its face value, you won't recoup that expenditure.

How did the fire start? If it resulted from *arson* (deliberate setting of a fire) you would

be covered unless you, or the family under your control, were responsible for that crime. Arson is punishable with up to 14 years' imprisonment.

Carelessness causes most fires, and the cigarette smoker is the prime villain. Smoldering butts lead to millions of dollars in damage and many deaths every year. Next in line are defective furnaces and electrical appliances, and overloaded circuits. But no one expects us to be paragons of virtue. Insurance companies will pay off, unless there is evidence of gross negligence.

Structural damage to the home can be caused by many things besides fire. The homeowner's insurance package, which has replaced most separate residential fire policies, offers coverage for damage by vandalism, lightning, gale, riot, water escape, impact by vehicles or aircraft. Flood damage is invariably a separate risk.

FIRE DAMAGE TO POSSESSIONS

In a fire you lose some valuable antiques—furniture, books and paintings. The insurance company rates them only as "furniture and furnishings."

Your right to full recovery of the value of prized possessions rests upon your own head. After a fire, the onus is on you to prove their value. If you don't list them—together with values from a qualified appraiser—on the policy form, you cannot expect compensation. The policy that covers the contents of your home against fire or other damage can include a "rider," or "schedule," specifically designed for such details.

On average, the unspecified contents of a home are considered to be worth about 40 percent of the value of the structure itself. This varies, of course, with the size of the dwelling and the number and life style of occupants. But it is all "furniture and furnishings" unless set forth in separate detail. And your insurer will regard the value of the contents as having depreciated with time.

Money (up to $100) and securities (up to

$500) kept in the home are insured under the householder's package policy.

You should evaluate and list all "out of the ordinary" items in your home; if a fire or other calamity occurs, it's unlikely you'll have time to rescue anything. Indeed, it is generally unwise even to attempt such a move—smoke inhalation can render you unconscious in three minutes.

If you've been a householder for some years, the value of your possessions is probably much greater than you would guess. It adds up through gifts, legacies and purchases. Your grandmother's porcelain dinner service may have had hard use for generations but its value may have increased a thousandfold. Pieces of 18th-century furniture—many stand unsuspected in Canadian homes—are now very valuable indeed. Rough pine kitchen cupboards, fashioned in New France, often sell for four figures.

Silverware, china tea services, crystal, imported carpets, jewelry, watches, furs, old firearms, collections of coins, stamps, documents and old photographs—all of these appreciate with time. You must expect to pay an extra premium to cover such items.

Keep an inventory. It doesn't take long to compile and, if you suffer a house fire, it will be invaluable. Most insurance companies supply blank inventory booklets, but any handwritten or typed list will do. Remember, after a fire or burglary, it's up to the homeowner to *prove* the value of expensive items.

Draw a plan of your home, allotting a sheet of paper to each room. List items systematically, not forgetting the contents of drawers, cupboards, attic and basement. You might take snapshots of each wall, indexing them against your plan.

Have jewelry, antiques and any other valuables assessed and file the appraisal with your inventory. A separate policy will cover your automobile and your camper even if standing within an attached garage, but list all portables (such as snowmobiles, or bicycles).

Overseeing the underwriters

Insurance is possibly the most closely regulated business in Canada and any dissatisfied consumer has a wide choice of action.

If you are not satisfied with policy service or with the settlement of any claim in the general insurance field, the Insurance Bureau of Canada (IBC) wants to hear from you. It represents 120 insurance groups, and some of those groups control up to 10 companies.

"General insurance" includes all property insurance (fire, theft, public liability) covering automobiles, boats, machinery, and farm policies. The IBC members collect more than 90 percent of premiums in their field. Life, accident and sickness policies are not included.

If you are stalemated in a dispute with your insurance agent, or broker, supply the number of your policy, the name of the insuring company, and the basic details of your problem to the IBC. It will take it from there.

Each province appoints a Superintendent of Insurance who acts as public watchdog over the companies within his jurisdiction. The office usually is part of either the provincial ministries of justice or consumer affairs. In Ottawa, the Superintendent of Insurance for Canada performs the same function for more than 400 insurance companies and societies registered with the federal Department of Insurance.

Notwithstanding all those lines of soldiers, your best protection is to read all the small print before you sign. Even if you have to borrow a magnifying glass.

The IBC maintains offices at:
181 University Avenue, Toronto M5H 3M7
1080 Beaver Hall Hill, Montreal H2Z 1S8
409 Granville Street, Vancouver V6C 1W9
10080 Jasper Avenue, Edmonton T5J 1V9
1505 Barrington Street, Halifax B3J 3K5

Finally, keep your inventory file and your insurance policy in your desk at the office, or in a safety-deposit box at your bank or trust company. You would be astonished at how many of these essential documents are burned up inside the homes they are designed to protect.

Possessions in your summer cottage, or second home, must be insured separately or by an extension to your householder policy.

The tenant's package. In nearly every case, the landlord insures his building but the tenants are responsible for their own property. All insurers offer package coverage for fire, explosion and smoke damage. The package may or may not include loss from theft.

To ensure full reimbursement for loss, follow the same course as the homeowner. All fire policies require the policyholder to exercise reasonable care in protecting his property. For example, you are expected to operate household appliances in accordance with the manufacturer's instructions. If you don't clean out the lint filter in your clothes dryer, combustible material might fall onto the element and cause a fire.

The condominium owner's insurance package is fundamentally the same as the tenant's.

Contents insurance covers not only the possessions of the policyholder, but also the property of his relatives living in the household, and of persons under 21 who are in the policyholder's care.

Moving. If you move, your insurance remains in force once you are installed at your new address. Be sure to advise your agent of that new address. Goods in transit are insured by licensed carriers.

FIRE INSURANCE RENEWAL

Fires badly damage your home twice in the same year. Your insurance company won't renew the policy.

There are 900 insurance companies and societies in Canada—all in business for profit. What they lose in claims they must make up by premium income and investment. About half of them handle only *casualty* (other than life) policies. Although closely supervised by government agencies, they are entirely free to insure whom they choose.

They do not have to give you any reason for declining to accept you as a client. And no law forces a householder to take out insurance to protect his dwelling.

If your current insurer turns you down you can go to another agent of the company or to a broker for another insurance firm.

The reasons for refusal are manifold. But the obvious ones are suspicion of arson or gross negligence, potentially dangerous construction, use of defective appliances and equipment, or lack of financial capability to pay the premiums.

Arson is difficult to prove, but the overall circumstances, and the record or reputation of the policyholder may suggest it, even if no charge is laid. Insurance adjusters tell some chilling tales.

Decrepit houses (and back-street stores) are bought for minimal down payments and insured to the hilt. A higher-than-average percentage of fires is likely in those premises. The fire risk also leaps above the norm where there is overcrowding, excessive use of drugs or alcohol, or where parental supervision is lax or nonexistent. Sometimes, in row housing or old frame buildings, the life style of neighbors can be a factor. Adjusters tell of fires being deliberately set in buildings that contain sleeping children.

Before issuing any policy covering fire damage, insurers will ask for a written answer to the following question: Have you had any fire loss during the past three years?

SMOKE DETECTORS

None of your family smoke, and you have recently equipped your home with smoke detectors. You feel you have the right to cheaper fire insurance.

Check with an insurance broker and you will probably find that you can indeed reduce your insurance costs. The electronic smoke detec-

Make an inventory

It's difficult to tell how much you own or what it's all worth unless you make an inventory. Insurance companies provide inventory booklets designed to help you. When you complete all the pages, you will know how much insurance you should have on your household goods and personal property, and you'll have a record that may be invaluable to you, especially in case of a fire loss.

LIVING ROOM

No.	Articles	Estimated Cash Value
250	Books	$ 500
1	Bookcases	150
2	Chairs, occasional	175
2	Chairs, upholstered	350
	Clocks	
	Curtains and Draperies	200
	Desk	
	Fireplace accessories	75
4	Lamps	350
	Mirrors	
2	Pictures	250
1	Phonograph *(Stereo)*	750
73	Phonograph Records	300
	Radio	
	Rugs *(Wall to wall)*	500
1	Sofa	450
4	Tables	550
1	Televi...	

BEDROOM NO. 1

No.	Articles	Estimated Cash Value
1	Beds and Springs	$ 400
	Blankets and Spreads	225
2	Bureaus	650
2	Chairs	175
1	Chests	150
1	Clock	20
	Curtains	45
	Desk	
	Dresser	
	Dressing table	
3	Lamps	200
	Mattresses and Pillows	275
	Mirrors	

DINING ROOM

No.	Articles	Estimated Cash Value
1	Buffet	$ 400
1	Candelabra	150
	Centerpiece sets	
6	Chairs	300
1	China Cabinet	375
	Chinaware	250
	Clocks	
	Curtains and Draperies	150
	Electrical Appliances	
	Glassware	250
	Lamps	100
	Linen	175

BASEMENT

No.	Articles	Estimated Cash Value
1	Ping-pong table	$ 100
1	workbench	135
	Hand tools	250
1	Electric drill	40
	Xmas decorations	50
1	Skis	400
	Winter clothing	600
1	Couch	100

tor (ESD) is the greatest advance ever in the saving of life in residential fires. The Canadian Association of Fire Chiefs believes that the relatively inexpensive gadgets (from $20 up) have halved deaths from smoke inhalation—the major killer in house fires.

All provinces will soon make ESDs mandatory in new houses and apartment buildings. Some of these inconspicuous, ceiling-mounted units can detect smoke an hour before flames appear.

Don't count on the smoke detector alone to protect you. You should reduce fire hazards in your home; on request, a fire prevention officer will call to advise you.

All approved smoke detectors carry the label or stamp of a recognized testing laboratory, such as the Underwriters' Laboratory of Canada (ULC). Electrically operated units should bear the seal of the Canadian Standards Association (CSA).

Fire in the high-rise. Tall concrete-and-steel apartment blocks pose their own special fire hazards. The bones of the building may indeed be fireproof, but the contents of the apartments definitely are not.

If a fire occurs in your apartment, shut the door of that room, and operate the fire alarm in your corridor. Telephone the fire department. Don't try to put a blaze out yourself. Don't start grabbing your valuables. Hurry—don't run—to the signposted fire exit.

If the fire is elsewhere in the block, and the corridor is impassable from smoke, stay behind closed doors, and let the firemen do their job. Wait on the balcony or by an open window, and wave something white—a pillowcase or towel.

DAMAGE TO A VACANT HOME

You go south for a week in the winter and come home to burst pipes. The insurance company refuses to compensate you for the damage.

You should inform your insurance company beforehand when your home is to be unoccupied for more than 30 consecutive days ("un-

occupied," in this instance, means that your household goods remain in place and you intend to return).

When your home is unoccupied for more than four days (96 hours), you must take certain precautions to keep your insurance against "water escape" in force. You can satisfy the requirements of this clause in your policy by having someone visit your home daily to make sure no pipes have sprung leaks, and that the heating system is working so that a freezeup can't burst the pipes.

To be absolutely safe (even reliable friends might forget the daily check, or be unexpectedly prevented from making it by problems of their own), you can shut off the water supply where it enters your home and drain the entire system. This is tedious, but it's a foolproof way of avoiding damage through water escape.

Remember that while your home is unoccupied, the homeowner's routine comprehensive insurance will not cover any damage done by vandals.

POISONING

While your teen-age daughter is baby-sitting in your home, her charge eats a dozen headache tablets. The baby recovers but the parents are suing you.

The parents had the right to assume their infant would be protected under your general responsibility to take reasonable care of guests under your roof. More than that—and especially if money was exchanged—there was an implied contract that your daughter offered "expert" services.

But it is generally recognized that a person under 18 usually has no means to pay, if he or she is found to have been negligent. So, even though parents are not liable for their children's illegal acts, a judge would probably decide nonetheless that the baby sitter's parents—you—are vicariously responsible for damages ("vicarious," in this case, meaning "substitute").

Almost all common pharmaceutical products can be dangerous if taken in excessive amounts. A young child is especially vulnerable. Headache tablets, and many similar pills, can look like candy to a child. As few as 10 "baby Aspirin" (one-quarter adult strength) can cause serious illness; a bottle of 50 can kill. Toddlers have swallowed mothballs thrown in the garden to discourage rodents from eating flower bulbs. The bulbs themselves, and many other plant leaves, stems and berries are extremely dangerous if eaten by children. One leaf from the poinsettia plant, so popular at Christmas, can kill a small child. Azaleas, daphne, larkspur have all caused death.

Children are not expected to read or understand any warning labels. Those warnings, demanded by the health authorities, often stipulate that the product be kept out of reach of children.

Most people are careful with prescription drugs but surprisingly easygoing with household cleaners, sprays, solvents, insecticides and other toxic products, which often are more dangerous to a child. Death can lurk in that cupboard under the kitchen sink.

The federal Health and Welfare Department has recorded 20,000 poisonous substances—most of them bought in drug or hardware stores—taken by children. A survey of 15,000 common household products found nearly 50 percent to be toxic.

Medicine containers with "child-proof" safety caps are not yet mandatory everywhere in Canada. Safety experts advise that in homes with children you keep all drugs under lock and key. A small inexpensive padlock can be installed easily on a cupboard. Throw away all medicines or products you no longer need.

Health authorities have a nationwide network of more than 300 poison control centers, usually at general hospitals, to treat cases of accidental poisoning. The telephone number

Fourteen ways to protect your child from poison

Every 15 minutes a Canadian child swallows a potentially toxic household product, with harmful—even fatal—consequences. Yet, almost always, such mishaps could have been prevented.

1. Take an inventory of potential poisons in your home. It may shock you.
2. Keep by the telephone an emergency list of your nearest poison control center, hospital, doctor, ambulance service, police station and fire department.
3. Keep in a sealed envelope an emergency fund for taxis and medicine.
4. Always lock up drugs, and don't let your children see where you keep them.
5. Never give or take medicine in the dark.
6. Don't tell children medicine is candy.
7. Don't let children chew painted surfaces or paint flakes that may contain lead.
8. Teach your children never to eat strange berries or other plants.

9. Flush old drugs down the toilet and rinse empty cans of toxic substances before you throw them out.
10. Keep poisonous household products locked up or out of a child's reach, even when you answer phone or doorbell.
11. Don't transfer hazardous products to other containers, especially food or drink bottles.
12. Store products such as gasoline, pesticides, fertilizers and fire starters in a locked cabinet, and declare the garage and toolshed off limits.
13. Insist that baby sitters, visitors and relatives keep potential poisons out of reach. Watch your child closely when visiting friends.
14. Start a neighborhood or club campaign to promote poison prevention in prenatal classes, schools and other public places. Enlist the help of your local poison control center, hospitals, drug and grocery stores, newspapers, radio and TV stations.

will be prominently listed in your phone directory. Make sure that any baby sitter in your home knows that number.

MAKING REPAIRS

While repairing your washing machine, a serviceman suffers a severe electric shock. You are worried about your liability.

You have the right to assume that any tradesman offering professional services is both competent to perform the given task and aware of dangers inherent in the work.

Although you are never free from liability arising from your own negligence, you are not called upon to warn an electrician about the danger of high-voltage power. All provinces license the professions and trades to protect the public from the incompetent. These regulations also serve to protect the workman: He may not undertake potentially dangerous work until he has proved, by written examination and practical testing, that he has the requisite knowledge and experience.

The tradesman who agrees to put up your television antenna, to point the brickwork on your chimney, to reshingle your roof or install new eavestroughs is aware that the contract exposes him to heights, and he should know how to guard against the possibility of injury from falling.

Workmen's compensation. Legal action arising from the injury of a workman on the job is comparatively rare, because legislation in all provinces now provides for compensation to injured workers. (*See* Chapter 25, "Work conditions.") Various workmen's compensation acts oblige most employers to pay into a central fund, which makes almost automatic payments to the injured worker. He, in turn, gives up the right to sue the employer for any negligence.

You should pause before asking your kindly neighbor to fix your faulty electrical appliance, or to give you a hand in painting your house. Workmen's compensation laws do not cover casual labor.

In such cases, if injury occurred, you would need personal liability insurance. It's probably included within your householder's comprehensive insurance package. Check your coverage before employing that daily cleaning woman!

Where do you stand if a tradesman borrows your ladder to reach your roof and a rotten rung breaks? If you have any reason to suspect the ladder is unsafe, you should warn him. But the general application of the law is that any borrower assumes responsibility for common perils. And again, in these circumstances, the law expects the qualified tradesman to exercise a level of expertise above that of the ordinary householder.

POOLS

A wandering child is drowned in your swimming pool. You weren't even home at the time, yet you are blamed.

Nightmares like this trouble conscientious homeowners or tenants whose property includes a water surface—pond, swimming pool, river or beach. Drownings account for about 5 percent of all accidents in the home environment. Small children can, and do, drown in a few centimetres of water. In one study, one-third of drowning victims were under the age of 6. Half of all drownings occur within six metres of safety.

The law demands that you offer a reasonable standard of care to anyone who comes onto your property for a lawful purpose. And this responsibility increases if the visitor (or trespasser) is a child. (*See* "Hazards to children" in Chapter 14.)

You are not required to provide total protection for anyone—that obviously is impossible. But if you are aware of some perilous situation on your property, and especially if you created that situation, you should make a reasonable effort to protect the visitor from that danger. The mandatory fencing of backyard swimming pools illustrates this law in action.

Safety precautions. "Swimming Prohibited" notices at your pond or waterfront would be evidence of your concern for safety. Provision of a life belt attached to a light but strong rope, or a long pole with a rigid wire loop at the tip, would serve the same purpose—and perhaps save a life. Your potential liability would be lessened if you could prove that you had made strenuous and continued efforts to keep children off your property. This could involve enclosing your entire grounds with stout fences, and posting "No Trespassing" notices. But the law doesn't usually require you to go to such extremes.

At all times, parents and guardians bear legal responsibility to protect their children. Allowing a young child to wander abroad can bring a charge under the Criminal Code. A famous judgment states: "Parents cannot shift the burden of looking after their children onto the shoulders of those who happen to have accessible bits of land."

Prevention is better than cure. The best safety protection against drowning for your own family is to encourage all members to learn to swim. Lessons are available at little or no cost at YMCA and other community-sponsored pools. Even toddlers can be taught. A study of 1,309 drownings found that only 1 percent of the victims were good swimmers. The humble dog paddle can get you to safety.

The relatively new technique of "drown-proofing" saves even those who can't swim a stroke. It is based on the natural buoyancy of the body with lungs inflated, even when fully clothed. Four- and 5-year-olds master the system with a few hours' practice. The idea is to relax and float vertically; in calm water the nose will be only centimetres below the surface. The head is raised only to inhale, then submerged again. Persons have survived more than eight hours in open seas by this method. In the majority of incidents, the ability to stay afloat for one hour would almost guarantee rescue.

Morally—and, in some cases, legally—we are required to aid an injured person to the best of our ability. If you were the injured party you would demand no less from others. In a drowning accident, the ability to apply artificial respiration can mean the difference between life and death.

Fighting city hall

In Canada, as in other Western societies, there seems to have been a growing discontent with bureaucracy since World War II. Some philosophers argue that this rises naturally from the tremendous increase in higher education—more of us simply know more about government, about the levers of power at all levels.

"Fighting city hall" has taken a new impetus. When we want road, park and business improvements, more-generous welfare, better water, brighter lights, more frequent buses, tougher policing, cheaper utilities, or historic buildings preserved, the hometown politician, the council and other local authorities are right on the firing line.

The British North America Act places responsibility for local government on the provincial legislatures. They set up the network of semi-independent corporations—the county (or region), township, metropolis, city, town and village—which usually provide transportation, police protection, recreation, environmental controls, health services, education and public utilities within their respective districts. These services are financed from taxes on real property and on businesses and amusements; from licenses or other fees for permits and concessions; from rents, fines for bylaw violations, and from provincial grants.

Each municipal corporation resembles a miniature parliament. It does not have legislative control of works or services such as railways or shipping, which are a federal responsibility. But it can pass bylaws, ordinances and regulations binding upon all residents of the municipality.

The prefix "by" signifies habitation or locality and is thus used specially for municipal (from the Latin *municipalis*, "belonging to one place only") government. A bylaw can be quashed or changed on several grounds, unlike a law passed by a legislature, which can be challenged only on the grounds that it is unconstitutional (contrary to the British North America Act or its amendments). A bylaw cannot be enforced if it runs counter to provincial legislation.

There is usually a six-month limit on any action for damages against a municipality or similar body. You must lodge your claim in the terms laid down in the ruling bylaw or other legislation. You sue the corporation—not the civil servant you consider responsible. In some cases, however, both the official (or agent) and the corporation are codefendants. The corporation (the "master") can be held liable for the negligent acts of its "servants" unless the statute under which it operates specifically grants it immunity. The "injury" involved does not have to be physical. It could involve your property, your reputation or your civil rights.

A "class action" can be brought against the municipality on behalf of all ratepayers, or one specific group. Although the word "ratepayer" seems to define itself, sometimes it has been interpreted to include any inhabitant. Also, you can be liable for "rates" (property taxes) without being an inhabitant of the municipality.

City hall remains the most important element of government in our daily lives. Every day its bylaws and decisions affect you to some extent.

MUNICIPAL SERVICES

Your neighborhood needs a park, more frequent garbage pickup and better street lighting.

Almost everybody wants more and better services from the local authorities—and just about the same number objects to any tax increase.

An overcautious, unimaginative or smug council needs the sharp prod of the social activist. And if the reformer researches his case well, and assembles a body of supporting opinion, he (or she) has a much greater chance of success. Shock tactics can draw brief attention to a cause or problem, but persuasion and logic usually win the day.

Local improvements don't always require higher taxes. They can be achieved, perhaps, by more efficient control or reallocation of revenue.

Many projects can count on financial support from the provincial or federal treasury, from lottery corporations, even from wealthy, public-spirited families. Toronto's High Park was a gift to the city from philanthropist John G. Howard.

Even if a major item of progress—a new swimming pool or hockey arena, day-care center or citizens' advice bureau—does involve extra expenditure, the public acceptance of the cost would probably surprise both the passionate advocate and the cautious council. Your fellow ratepayers don't really object to taxes—provided they are convinced that their money is being well spent.

Stirring up city hall. Public opinion can spur city hall into considering the local improvements you desire. Try to make your case constructively, and don't be overcritical of the political incumbents. Remember that they have been elected by your fellows, in open contest.

Meetings, letter writing or telephone campaigns, media advertisements, letters-to-the-editor—all these avenues are open to you. The general sessions of the councils of all municipal corporations are open to the public, and you have the right to present petitions. Every mayor or reeve will look hard at a petition carrying a lot of names, specially if those include prominent persons. The smaller municipalities frequently permit a temperate advocate "to address council."

The strident "guerrilla" tactics that surfaced in the 1960s are often counterproductive. Sit-ins might still be effective at, say, a university or college, where the rights of the public are not directly affected. Similar tactics at city hall probably will result in a charge of trespass. Tossing an egg at the mayor can bring a conviction for assault.

That's not to say that demonstrations, boycotts, or attempts to embarrass public officials are always ineffectual. But if you go too far, you can expect the moderates—sometimes called "the silent majority"—to swing against you.

The law does change for the better. The most superficial study of the Canada of a century ago will convince you of that. One of Canada's most respected jurists, Dr. J. A. Corry, once wrote: "High-minded reformers are often disappointed and frustrated by the seeming obstinacy of the community about accepting ambitious legislative or social advances. The law must obviously be set at a level that the bulk of the people find tolerable. Man's reach, however, should always exceed his grasp, and we must continue to reach for the stars."

THE TAX RATE

Your property tax has nearly doubled since you bought your home. Now you are informed that it's going up again.

Benjamin Franklin said that nothing in the world is certain but death and taxes. Most homeowners would agree that it's just as certain taxes will increase. In many urban areas, property taxes double every decade. You should count on an increase of from 5 to 8 percent a year.

Ironically, the more you improve your property, thus increasing its value, the higher taxes you will pay. Realty tax—Canada's third largest source of government revenue after income tax and sales taxes— brings in nearly $5 billion a year. The landowner pays for the road outside his door, the schools, local policing, parks, public libraries and local welfare programs. Education almost always is the greatest single expense. Although elected trustees control school expenditures (including teachers' salaries), the municipality has the unenviable job of collecting the money.

Real property tax (realty tax) is levied ei-

How to dispute your property tax

This sample notice of assessment contains the details of the property valuation. If your property has an assessed value of $5,550, and if the mill rate is 100, your taxes will be $555. Complaint procedures are outlined on the reverse side of the notice. You should complain promptly, if you feel you have been improperly assessed; otherwise, your taxes will be calculated from the valuation shown. And your taxes are not subject to review, whereas your valuation is.

NOTICE OF ASSESSMENT
(This is not a Tax Bill)

MUNICIPALITY:
SIDNEY TOWNSHIP

DATE MAILED	For Taxation Commencing	ROLL NUMBER	CNTY.	MUN.	MAP	SUB	PARCEL	"PRIM/SUB"
DEC. 04/79	JAN. 01/80		12	34	000	012	123-00	0000

OCCUPANCY STATUS	NAME AND MAILING ADDRESS OF PERSON(S) ASSESSED
OWNER	ROE RICHARD ALBERT R R 3 FREDERICTON N.B.
*RU	

DIRECT QUESTIONS TO:
THE REGIONAL ASSESSMENT OFFICE
BOX 520, 80 DIVISION ST.
FREDERICTON N.B.

SEE REVERSE SIDE
FOR COMPLAINT PROCEDURES

LOCATION AND DESCRIPTION OF REAL PROPERTY

CBF L12PT   L34SPT
N OF 2 HWY
                    A   1.234

MAIL COMPLAINTS TO:
THE REGIONAL REGISTRAR OF
THE ASSESSMENT REVIEW COURT
2378 HOLLY LANE
ROOM 123
FREDERICTON N.B.

LAST DATE
FOR COMPLAINT   JAN. 09/80

REAL PROPERTY TAX—The Tax Bill will be calculated by applying a Residential or Commercial mill rate to the assessed value of the real property as indicated in the box(es) below.

BUSINESS TAX—Your Tax Bill will be calculated by applying the Commercial mill rate to the business assessment as indicated in the Total box below.

REAL PROPERTY	RESIDENTIAL/FARM	COMMERCIAL	EXEMPT	TOTAL
	$ 5550.	$	$	$ 5550.
				TOTAL
				$

COMPLAINT PROCEDURES

(Section 52 of The Assessment Act, R.S.O. 1970, Chapter 32)

If you believe you have been improperly assessed in any way, you or your agent may give notice of the complaint in writing to the Regional Registrar of the Assessment Review Court. See the front of this Notice for the address of the Regional Registrar and the last day for lodging a complaint.

NOTICE OF COMPLAINT

IF YOU WISH TO USE THIS NOTICE for lodging a complaint against your assessment, state your reason(s) in the space below, sign and forward to the Regional Registrar.

...... My neighbour has a similar lot and his assessment ....
...... is $1,000 less than mine. I believe I am entitled to ....
...... equal treatment.—...

Name of Owner or Agent (Please Print)....... RICHARD A. ROE ....
Telephone No. Residence.. 200-3214   Richard A. Roe ....
                                SIGNATURE OF COMPLAINANT OR AGENT
        Business................. 100 ELM ST., FREDERICTON, N.B.
                                MAILING ADDRESS

IF YOU WISH TO LODGE A COMPLAINT AGAINST YOUR ASSESSMENT AND RETAIN THIS NOTICE, include the following information on a separate sheet of paper headed 'Notice of Complaint', and forward to the Regional Registrar:

1. Name, Mailing Address, and Telephone No. of Complainant.

2. Location and Description of Property under Complaint (see front of Notice of Assessment).

3. Assessment Roll Number (see front of Notice of Assessment and set down in the order in which they appear on the Notice of Assessment the numbers shown under the headings 'CNTY. (County or Region), MUN. (Municipality), MAP (Map Division), Sub. (Subdivision), PARCEL, TENANT').

4. Reasons(s) for Complaint.

5. Signature of Complainant or Agent.

ther by the region, county, township or city in which you reside. It is, in most cases, a percentage of the assessed value of your land and buildings. Additional taxes may be levied for local improvements such as street lighting or sewers. Contributions from the provincial treasuries ensure rough equalization of services across each province.

The protest procedure. Most property owners receive a yearly "notice of assessment." This form identifies the owner or occupier, gives the official description and the location of the land, and the assessment value. It is not your tax demand!

Now is the time to protest, if you think your assessment is too high. Normally, the reverse side of your "notice of assessment" bears a printed "notice of complaint," and the address of your regional assessment review court. Officials there will examine your objection, if you fill out the form (you can attach extra details if necessary) and lodge it within the time limit.

The most common grounds for protest are that the property has been valued unequally to similar properties in the area, or that the assessment is above market value. If your complaint is dismissed, and you still think you are being wrongly treated, consult a lawyer about appeals to higher authority or action through the courts.

A lot of homeowners believe that they have the right to challenge their property taxes. Not so, in direct terms. It is the yearly assessment that is open to review. If you don't lodge a protest to that figure, then your tax bill will follow (after the tax rate for the ensuing year has been struck).

Read your tax demand with great care. Many municipalities require either advance payment in full or payment by installment, and they levy interest charges after each due date on unpaid balances.

You can lose your home if you don't pay your realty taxes. The procedure is much the same across the country. If you owe three years' taxes, your property will be listed for sale in the provincial *Gazette*. But even if someone buys your house, you can redeem it within one year by paying all the overdue taxes plus a service charge.

Monthly payment. To protect their investments, some mortgage lenders pay the realty taxes themselves. Then they divide the yearly tax by 12 and add that sum to your monthly mortgage payment.

Should your home be destroyed or damaged by fire (or other disaster), ask city hall for interim tax relief.

BUMPY ROADS

On a poorly lit roadway you drive into a deep pothole and damage the front end of your car.

If you feel that the responsible local authority failed to keep the road in reasonable repair, thereby causing significant damage to your vehicle or injury to yourself or passengers, you can claim financial compensation.

The relevant provincial statutes set out the responsibility of counties, regions, cities, towns, villages and other local authorities for the roads over which they have jurisdiction. Not only do those laws differ across Canada, but the precedents set by judges in deciding cases brought under those laws also vary widely.

Almost everywhere, the law states that every roadway shall be kept "in repair." The responsible authority is bound to make every reasonable effort to keep its streets or highways free from obstructions or defects—such as deep potholes—or, at least, to install suitable warning signs. Unless otherwise specified, the municipality must make all reasonable efforts to maintain its roads so that a traveler, using them in the normal way, can do so in safety. But the law does not demand that the roads be safe *at all times*. Weather is an important factor. Would you work outdoors in a blizzard?

Where did you hit the pothole? If your car is damaged by a pothole on a four-lane highway, your chances for compensation are greater than if the accident occurs on a back-country concession. Provision of mirror-smooth surfaces everywhere would bankrupt your province.

Is the road hilly or flat, the country rocky or smooth? The wealth—and thus the tax-paying ability—of the area is also a factor. If the pothole has been filled with loose gravel, that might be all the council can afford. It need not use the most expensive means of repair. This doesn't offer an automatic cop-out, but it is among excuses that courts have accepted.

If a hazard had not been reported by anyone within, say, the previous 48 hours, compensation might be ruled out. The public works department can't patrol every metre of perhaps hundreds of kilometres of streets and highways every day. And it can't remove dangers it doesn't know about. If you hit, or notice, a deep pothole, call your city hall or township office, or the police.

How deep is dangerous? It might seem like the Ungava Crater when your front wheels drop, but the depth of the pothole is seldom the clinching factor in a compensation case. The configuration of the hole, its edges, its position on the road—all these can be important. A hole less than eight centimetres deep has been deemed to be unsafe.

Your speed at the time of the incident can make a lot of difference. Even a huge washout won't break your springs or shocks if you go through it at 15 km/h.

Warning signs and barriers. As soon as a dangerous hole or other obstruction is discovered, work crews erect either a battery-operated flashing light, painted sign or some kind of barrier or fence. These are familiar to everyone who drives the highways, especially during road-widening or resurfacing operations. If you hit one of these, you are out of luck.

If you steer off the normal "traveled portion"—that is, the usual traffic lanes—to avoid obstacles, you are driving *cum periculo* (at your own risk). Ontario prohibits suits against governments for damage or injury caused off the traveled portion by any "obstruction or erection or any situation, arrangement or disposition of any earth, rock, tree or other material or object adjacent to or in, along or upon a highway." The "traveled portion" includes bridge approaches, boulevards between road surfaces and sidewalks, median strips and the shoulders of the road. But not roadside ditches. "Traveled" should not be read as "travelable."

Railway grade-crossings can get dangerously eroded. The municipality must keep them, and the approaches, in a safe condition even if the railway company neglects its responsibility.

However, municipalities need not erect guard fences along all drainage ditches. Also, any fences or barriers erected do not have to be strong enough to fend off a car, truck or motorcycle. Some provinces even have protective legislation against damage claims arising from the absence or frailty of guardrails.

How to get compensation. Most municipal corporations and similar bodies carry liability insurance. You pay the premiums on those policies through your taxes.

First, write a letter within 14 days of the incident. Address it to the municipal clerk (*not* the mayor). State all the relevant facts—date, time, place, details of damage or injury. If you have witnesses, give their names, addresses and telephone numbers. Include a photocopy of a garage mechanic's appraisal of the damage to your vehicle.

Your letter will go to the adjuster for the insuring company. His investigation might include photographs and measurements of the obstruction, and interviews with you and possibly others about your driving speed, weather conditions and other factors. His report will influence the decision to offer, or refuse, compensation.

If your claim is rejected or you consider the offer insufficient, you have three months to issue a writ (notice that you are suing).

You may also be able to press your claim through your province's Small Claims Court. Prepare your case well; less than 25 percent of liability suits against city hall succeed.

PEDESTRIAN HAZARDS

You trip on a cracked sidewalk and fall, fracturing your arm. The city now rejects your claim for compensation.

Your local authority has the obligation to keep its sidewalks in repair and free of obstructions such as broken utility pipes. You should not have to pick a path with great care, as through an enemy mine field. But you cannot assume the sidewalk will be in perfect condition, or even safe for walking, at all times.

In an oft-quoted case, fought in the Toronto courts in 1926, the presiding judge found that: "Pedestrians are not entitled to expect sidewalks to be as smooth and level and as free from defects as a billiards ball."

Sidewalks are often constructed of precast concrete slabs, and soil movement can result in differences of level from one slab to another. All of us have tripped over these "lips," not necessarily with serious results. In court cases, "lips" (or edges) up to three centimetres have not been rated as "disrepair." The pedestrian is expected to proceed prudently at all times.

The icy sidewalk. Aunt Martha hurries for the bus to the pre-Christmas sales. She slips on a stubborn patch of ice and there's another ankle—or worse, a hip—fractured. This tale is told in just about every city, town and village in Canada each winter.

In some circumstances the victim has the right to compensation from the municipality, or from the business or individual responsible for maintaining a designated frontage in a reasonably safe condition.

Appropriate compensation will be awarded by the courts if the individual sues the municipality and proves that it was negligent. The individual's need could also be a factor in the court's decision.

The local authority's finances are a factor in the condition of its traveled surfaces. City hall is not called upon to spend unreasonable amounts keeping its sidewalks continually safe from perils of ice and snow. To avoid liability, it is usually enough for a municipality to have a snow-clearing scheme in operation, and to be "doing its best" to maintain safe conditions.

In most provinces, the successful plaintiff must prove gross negligence before the municipality can be held liable for injuries caused by sidewalk ice or snow. This can be next to impossible to prove. Nothing new about it: the most quoted precedent is a case brought—and lost—in Ontario in 1894.

It is not "gross negligence" if ice covers part of a sidewalk. And the fact that an accident causing injury occurred on sidewalk ice does not, in itself, rate as proof of negligence. But if the hazard had been reported to the municipality, and if sufficient time had elapsed to allow for inspection and sanding, liability might be fixed.

In public buildings. In a general sense, the liability for repair and safe operation of public roads and sidewalks extends to all public buildings, grounds and activities. Although the relevant provincial and federal laws may differ in degree, this obligation is passed on to any commission, board or agency empowered to act on behalf of the ruling authority.

If you were hurt by an unguarded mop and pail at your liquor store, you could sue the governing corporation in the same way you could sue any individual citizen who injured you through negligence. But the fact that the defendant (the liquor board, in this example) is a public body does not make it any *more* liable than the individual citizen. Bluntly, you shouldn't hope to get extra compensation.

On the other hand, there is virtually no limit to the size of a cash judgment against a municipality. If there were not enough funds, or insurance was inadequate, legislation exists for striking a special tax on the ratepayers to provide the funds. In Alberta, a creditor can have a municipality's income garnisheed.

ACCESS TO YOUR DRIVEWAY

Six times this winter, road-clearing crews have left a sizable snowbank blocking your driveway.

Perhaps no other aspect of winter living raises the Canadian ire more than this. The law defines such an obstruction as a *nuisance*—and it certainly is that.

After every heavy snowfall, the householder gets out with shovel or snowblower and clears his driveway. For many, it is the heaviest physical chore of the year. Then along comes the plow, lights flashing: the result—a windrow of snow or ice chunks that effectively bars entry to your property. If you charge through it with your car, you can damage your oil pan or wrench off your exhaust system.

It is even more infuriating if you have already paid a stiff bill to your local garage for plowing your driveway. Garages never seem to get their visits synchronized with the snowplow runs.

Can you insist that city hall refrain from blocking your driveway with snow? The answer is, no. The local authority must keep its road reasonably safe for travel in the winter as in other seasons. It has no such obligation toward your private, or mutual, driveway.

In carrying out its duty, the local authority must use "the means at its command." That boils down to the juggernaut snowplow and perhaps the application of salt. The amount of snow that falls on Canada—even the inhabited fraction of the land—each winter is colossal. Some average annual snowfalls in centimetres are: St. John's 363.7; Charlottetown 305.1; Halifax 210.8; Saint John 204.7; Sept-Iles 432.2; Montreal 243.1; Toronto 141; Kapuskasing 321.8; Winnipeg 131.3; Regina 114.8; Calgary 153.9; Edmonton 132.1 and in the Rockies 969.5.

Any attempt to sue the municipality because it blocked your driveway with snow while keeping the road "in repair" would be doomed at the outset.

Right of access. When your land adjoins any public roadway (except a limited access road) you do have the right of access to that roadway for any vehicle necessary for the "reasonable enjoyment" of your property. You are not, however, guaranteed access across every metre of your frontage, nor safe entry for a 16-wheel trailer rig. No law forces a municipality to provide a culvert where a rural driveway meets a highway (although such culverts are usually provided during reconstruction). If a rebuilt roadway is significantly higher than the old, you may have to regrade your driveway. If the law denies you the right to sue for damages in these cases, you

You can beat city hall

They say it can't be done; Edmontonians proved the opposite in 1978. The issue was the salary which the city's aldermen voted themselves.

The previous December, a newly elected, 13-member council announced, after secret meetings, that the aldermanic pay was raised from $12,000 to $19,200 a year, a 60-percent increase. At the same time, the council insisted that its unionized workers were limited to a 6 percent wage increase, under federal anti-inflation guidelines.

A civic uproar ensued, fired partly by the size of the aldermen's increase, and partly by the backdoor style of the move. Broadcaster Phil Fraser suggested that his listeners get up a petition demanding a plebiscite.

The Municipal Act of Alberta obliges councils to act on petitions signed by at least 3 percent of the population. In short order,

24,669 irate citizens signed Fraser's petition—about 7 percent of the population.

The Edmonton aldermen merely "received" the petition as "information" and continued to bank their cheques.

The publisher of *The Edmonton Journal*, Patrick O'Callaghan, entered the fray. Acting as a private citizen, he took city hall to court, seeking a ruling that a vote of the citizenry must decide the issue. District Court Judge John Bracco upheld this view six months later.

Eventually, council repealed the pay increase, and decisions on salary scales were left to an independent commission headed by Justice Arnold Moir of the Alberta Supreme Court. The commission recommended an aldermanic salary of $16,000, a rollback of $3,200 a year. The city fathers, noted the commission in its report, had "acted in a high-handed and arrogant manner."

still can press the department of highways for arbitration of your claim. If this fails, take your case to the ombudsman.

Your battered mailbox. If you live on a rural route, with your mailbox planted on the roadside where it can be reached through the side window of the mail delivery vehicle, you can look forward glumly to the box being wrecked sooner or later. As the snow is piled ever higher, the box may not even be visible from the cab of a hurrying plow.

Almost always, the edge of the roadway, for some metres beyond the shoulder, is public property. Your mailbox is really just being tolerated in that space.

Rural householders set up all kinds of ingenious devices, including long cantilevered metal arms, to keep their mailboxes out of the snowplow's reach. But if the winter is tough enough, the abominable plowman gets them all eventually.

ZONING

City hall has agreed to the construction of a shopping center that clearly breaches the zòning restrictions in your suburb.

You bought, or built, in that zone because it offered the seclusion or social characteristics that you preferred. Now your rights are being abrogated. No doubt about that. Your elected representatives have been persuaded that the public benefits in this case override your individual rights. Population expansion, transportation difficulties, any number of things seem to dictate the provision of more convenient shopping. City hall is prepared to amend the controlling zoning bylaw, or create a new one, to allow the construction and operation of the shopping center. It's called "spot rezoning," to indicate that the classification of your zone remains unchanged—except in this instance. What can you do about it? Plenty.

The council must move openly along a strictly defined course. Even if the developer already has the land for his shopping center, or holds options on it, his plans—and how these will affect safety, traffic and the local environment—will be subject to council scrutiny.

A "shopping center" has acquired a separate legal definition over the past 20 years and, depending on the wording of the zoning bylaw, its construction may not require an amendment to the bylaw. Most residential zones contain neighborhood "convenience" shops. And the legal definitions of "shop" run to several closely printed pages in the lawbooks. Usually, however, an amendment is required.

The public hearing. The municipality must give public notice of the proposed zoning change. Failure to so notify residents in Halifax and Winnipeg resulted in a higher authority declaring the amendment invalid. The public notice (in the newspapers or by letter) has to describe the proposal in such terms that the ordinary reader would understand the effect of the change on him and his interests.

Although the various provincial planning and municipal acts lay down different procedures, in every instance the householder has the right to protest at this juncture.

Prepare your case thoroughly. You can be sure that the development company will have done just that. Obtain copies of its proposals, and examine them for "hype" or bluff. You don't need a lawyer to present your objection, but if a sizable group of your neighbors agree with your views, you could band together and share legal costs.

Politicians have to hark to public opinion— if they value their jobs. Start a letter-writing campaign in your local newspapers, write and telephone your alderman, the mayor, your MPP and MP. Call a neighborhood meeting and present your views forcefully enough to catch the attention of the media.

Emphasize the traffic hazards the new shopping center would create, especially to children walking to school or playing in your quiet streets; the business losses to established merchants; the prospect of vandalism and noise by loungers attracted to the mall's late-night lights and air conditioning.

If, in spite of the protests, the developers get the go-ahead through spot rezoning, you can appeal to the provincial cabinet—either by a

The armchair warriors of city hall

The bureaucratic army of a metropolis seems formidable indeed. This chart shows one such organization, the six-municipality federation that is Metropolitan Toronto. Federation members share 37 seats on the central council that rules 620 square kilometres of the most populous area in Canada. Metropolitan governments in Vancouver, Winnipeg, Montreal and St. John's, Nfld., are composed of similar municipal federations.

But these armchair warriors are not invulnerable. The ranking officers (top tier on chart) are elected politicians, subject to dismissal at the drop of a vote. Since they appoint or control the rank and file, you really can fight city hall—and win. Ballots are the best bullets.

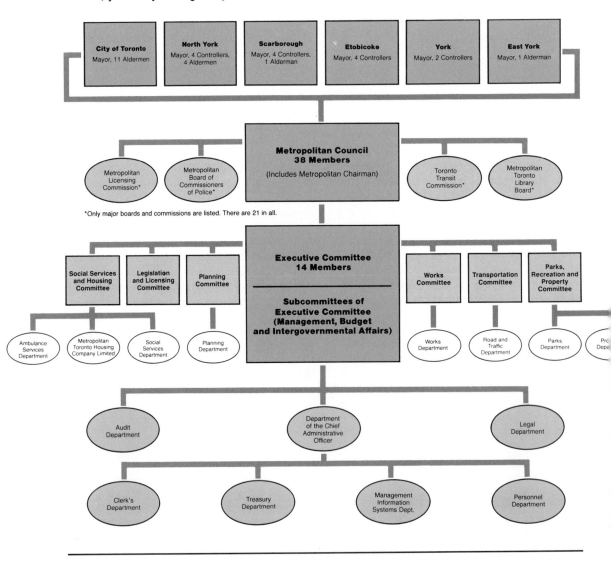

letter to the secretary, or by a formal writ filed by your lawyer. After a sustained outcry by a numerically small protest group, the Ontario cabinet blocked the extension of an expressway into the heart of Toronto.

The public good. The shadow of "special interests" often hovers over spot rezoning decisions. The embattled citizen sometimes suspects a payoff in a crucial political decision that can earn large profits for a company or its major shareholders.

Partly to counter such foreboding, the law ensures that the repeal, amendment or creation of zoning bylaws is subject to examination at a level above the municipality concerned. Decisions at each level of authority can be appealed, ultimately to the Supreme Court of Canada.

Municipal lawmaking must not favor or discriminate against any one individual or corporate entity. But the local authority may amend its bylaws (by spot rezoning for a shopping center, for example) when it can demonstrate that such an action is in the public good.

It is equally true that if you can prove your rights are affected you can have a bylaw or an amendment rescinded. In Manitoba, the courts ruled a bylaw amendment invalid because it was passed "in the interest of an individual" and not for the benefit of all the ratepayers. A similar precedent was set in British Columbia in 1967.

If all efforts to prevent a spot rezoning fail, and if you still believe that the development harms you (perhaps by reducing the value of your property), you have the right to seek compensation under the head of *injurious affection* (being affected harmfully).

EXPROPRIATION

The city expropriates your property for an access road to a new shopping center. You think that the compensation offered is far too little.

Expropriation is the official action whereby property is taken from an owner without his consent. It is sometimes called "the power of eminent domain." In most cases the property consists of land with or without buildings; it can be the total lot or just a strip.

Expropriation is always preceded by an attempt to purchase. If you think the compensation is inadequate, you have the right to hearings and then to appeals, in some cases all the way to the Federal Court in Ottawa.

Before expropriation goes into effect, you have a right to fight the impending action irrespective of the purchase price that may have been offered. Your objections will force a public hearing. Both federal and provincial statutes grant the owner the right to argue his case before a commission appointed by the Minister of Justice or the Attorney General. Where several homeowners (or property-owning companies) are involved, they should combine forces and hire an experienced lawyer. By this stage, though, your chances are slim. Your opposition argues that it is advancing the best interests of the public at large.

After an expropriation order is issued, it is pointless to contest its validity, however angry or distressed you may be. The question then is—how much should you be paid?

You probably expect to get the going market price for your property, plus "something extra" for the inconvenience of relocating. If you have owned your home for a few years, you may be pleasantly surprised at the offer and choose to accept it. Most do. After all, expropriation valuers aren't spending their own money and they don't want to get involved with long expensive hassles. On the other hand, it's human nature to seek top dollar, especially when we know "the government" is picking up the tab.

The expropriators. It can shock the homeowner to realize that—despite the popular conception—he does not control his "freehold" land. No individual or company owns a metre of Canada absolutely. The Crown (the Queen of Canada as represented by her elected governments) retains a vital interest. Your title deed will state that you hold your piece of land *in fee simple*. It's just a hangover from medieval times in England when the king granted *fiefs* to his barons and knights. The basis of expropriation laws is that what the Crown gives, it can take back again.

Thousands of agencies in Canada can expropriate all or some of your land. Eleven different federal statutes confer expropriation powers on government departments and Crown corporations. When the federal government (through the Department of Transport) needs land for new airports (such as Vancouver's Sea Island, and Montreal's Mirabel), it can order the surrender of the required property—after, of course, giving proper notice, hearing and weighing any protests, and paying compensation. Each province has its Expropriation Act, conferring takeover powers on several agencies. This authority filters down to lower levels of government, including the municipality that wants to punch a new road to the Shady Oaks shopping center. Land for schools, hospitals, post offices, jails, parks, council offices, even parking lots for civil servants, can be acquired in the same way.

Many private or semiprivate corporations can be granted expropriation powers also. Hundreds of acts of Parliament have conferred this right on railways (about 1,500 cases), pipelines, airlines, and on broadcasting, water, gas, hydro, telephone and other companies.

Fair and reasonable. Establishing compensation for the expropriated property would seem to require merely an examination of the recent selling prices for comparable properties in the vicinity. It's not that simple. The "going market price" is everywhere accepted to be what a willing buyer would pay. Your lot might be the only one in the area to include a pretty stream or a fine stand of birch. Assuming that any large-scale impending expropriation has been publicly announced, the supply of "willing buyers" would have vanished. Plans to expand Vancouver's airport were announced more than six years before expropriation proceedings were launched.

Compensation can differ when the owners are young and likely to move in response to

---

Saving the historic house

Is there an interesting old house in your neighborhood that's threatened with demolition? If so, listen to John Sewell, who became mayor of Toronto in 1978.

Sewell suggests you list the address and the lot size, and get a professional assessment of the structural soundness of the building. Check at city hall to see if a building permit has been issued for the site.

Inform your alderman, or rural councilor, and seek political support. Seek out the names of the potential developer and of your town planner. If there is a historical board in the area, apply to have the building listed as being of historical interest. This board can usually delay demolition while studies are made.

Call a meeting of other concerned citizens— you won't get far on your own—and invite a representative of the developer. Perhaps he can proceed with his overall plan and still save the building. For him, it's usually a matter of money. After all, he doesn't really want to spoil the neighborhood.

If there's no immediate threat, get copies of your municipal bylaws controlling redevelopment. You might be able to get the bylaws tightened.

Remember that even if you succeed in staving off the wreckers, the building can't just sit there and rot. You will need a plan to preserve, repair and use the house in the public interest. It might be adaptable for a folk museum, art gallery, day-care center, consumer-aid agency—all of these purposes can be supported by provincial (or private) grants.

Funds might be found to help you buy the property, then rent it to a sympathetic occupant willing to cooperate with cultural agencies that want to "show" the place or use it for research or educational programs.

career or family demands, and when they are older and consider themselves settled for retirement. Companies forced to shift quarters can suffer economic loss. The many hardships and problems of relocation are referred to legally as *disturbance* and *injurious affection*. If you feel that compensation offered you is unfair, list your problems and send them to your provincial Land Compensation Board. Should this fail to bring a satisfactory offer, you can pursue the matter through the courts.

In court, the principle of *equity* (basically, fair play) probably will color a judge's decision. In the Supreme Court of Canada, Mr. Justice Rand decided: "The question is what would he [the dispossessed owner], as a prudent man, at that moment, pay for the property rather than be ejected from it." The words "prudent" and "at that moment" are worth emphasis. You won't get far by insisting that in another 10 years the property would double in value. The future use of an expropriated property has no bearing on its current value.

On the other hand, there are legal precedents for the payment of extra compensation for the loss of such things as swimming in a lake off your own property, and for docking facilities for your boat. Make sure that you get your just due.

Some provincial laws set the payment of "disturbance damages" at a 5 percent allowance above the agreed-upon value figure, provided that the owner can prove inconvenience (not a difficult task, usually). This would come as a bonus above reasonable relocation costs. Although legal precedents differ across the country, a tenant who has to move out of his rented accommodation because of expropriation can also press to collect "disturbance" compensation. Likewise, a landlord who lost tenants in such a move should be in a position to seek adjustment.

Let's say that a local authority expropriated neighboring land—or a part of your own lot—and turned it to some use (say, the construction of a sewage plant) that you believe has damaged your property. Although this would not fall strictly under expropriation law, you could well have a good case for proving "injurious affection," and thus a claim for compensation.

Personal property. A further shock. Several federal laws permit the expropriation of property, or goods, other than land or buildings. Examples include the War Measures Act, the Radio Act, the Cape Breton Development Corporation Act, the Atomic Energy Control Act. The property can include stocks of coal or other minerals, patent rights, machinery, and indeed any items of any kind.

As with expropriation of land, the individual or company concerned has clearly defined rights to first protest the seizure and then argue about the level of compensation.

Finally, your acceptance of the offered compensation for any type of expropriation does not extinguish your right to seek an upward adjustment at a later date.

4 | YOUR RIGHTS AS A CONSUMER

18 Food and drugs

Everybody is a consumer—of energy, entertainment, education, even transportation—but when we buy goods such as food and medicines for our personal needs, we are consumers in the truest sense.

Food and nonalcoholic beverages accounted for about 22 percent of all disposable personal income in Canada in 1979. But don't sigh for "the good old days": in 1951 the figure was 24 percent.

The wide range of products and retail outlets makes annual sales of prescription and nonprescription drugs difficult to assess, but all market analysts agree it's a fast-growth industry. Sales in drugstores and specialty stores alone exceed $1.5 billion yearly.

The federal Department of Consumer and Corporate Affairs was created in 1967 partly to protect consumers' rights. Through its powers of inspection, of quality and price monitoring, of providing information and of imposing regulations, the government intervenes in the marketplace. Similar provincial ministries also exist.

The federal department checks labels and food advertising to ensure that products are exactly what they claim to be. "Extra large" eggs must be really large, "Lean" ground beef must be lean, and those "Canada No. 1" carrots have to be top grade. If you have a complaint about what you think are deceptive food standards or labeling, this department wants to hear from you.

Canada has been a world leader in the quality grading of foods and the checking of canned goods. Nova Scotia was branding barrels of butter as "prime," "second" or "third" in 1790. Shortly after Confederation, the adulteration of food and drugs was outlawed. Today some 20,000 food samples are analyzed each year and only 2 percent are proven to have foreign or impure ingredients.

A wide-ranging Food and Drugs Act—regulating foods, medicines, cosmetics, household chemicals and contraceptives—was enacted in 1920. Through its enforcement, Canadians can be confident that any food or drug offered for sale in the stores is what it purports to be.

It is illegal to sell food containing any foreign material. The penalty for the "presence of any filthy, putrid, disgusting, rotten, decomposed or diseased animal or vegetable substance" in a food or drug product can be a fine of up to $5,000 and three years in prison.

The Province of Upper Canada, now Ontario, began grading food in the early 1800s. Bread had to be "sound, good and well made." By 1867, all four provinces that combined to become Canada had rudimentary laws governing the grading, packing and inspection of food, and standard grades for meat, fish, poultry, eggs, grain, dairy products, fruits, vegetables, honey and canned goods have existed now for some 60 years.

Your breakfast egg, for example, is graded either A, B or C to standards set by the federal Department of Agriculture. Grade A eggs are subdivided into: extra large, large, medium and small.

Grade A eggs must be fresh. This is determined by the size of the air space at the big end of the egg. The bigger the space, the older the egg. An A egg must have a smooth, clean shell and a yolk that is centered and of the proper color.

B and C eggs are smaller, of poorer quality and liable to be not as fresh.

And hamburger must be all beef and can be sold under three names only: "Regular" if it contains up to 30 percent fat; "Medium" if it's up to 23 percent fat; "Lean" with 17 percent fat or less.

Some consumer activists want the government to become even more involved in consumer protection but many retailers argue that consumerism has already taken too negative a direction. A representative of one national retail chain, which has had a "goods satisfactory or money refunded" policy for generations, says the media and government have nurtured a "rip-off syndrome." But retail competition is fierce in Canada, she points out, and sensible shoppers will always go where they get the best deal.

Consumerism, however, was not invented by government, nor is it something new. The Consumers' Association of Canada, the biggest and best-known of the dozens of private agencies going to bat for the shopper against the manufacturer and merchant, was founded in 1947. Its bimonthly magazine, *Canadian Consumer*, presents no-holds-barred evaluations of new products and services.

The Better Business Bureau (BBB) has been around since the 1920s and now maintains offices in 14 cities. It has plans to double that number. The BBB is a self-regulatory agency for business, handling complaints from consumers and general inquiries about the track record of its corporate members, whose annual dues finance the bureau.

In the final analysis, the consumer who demands that all purchases be satisfactory is the best marketplace policeman. That's not counterfeit money you're spending.

LABELS

While unpacking your groceries at home you notice that the recommended date for use of the cold cuts has expired.

The supermarket does not have to take a product off the shelf just because its recommended date for use has expired. It's up to you to check the date on the product before you buy it. Getting that date there in the first place took years of consumer agitation. If you disregard it, you're on your own—although the food must still be fit for your table.

Except for fresh fruit and vegetables, most prepackaged perishable foods with a life of 90 days or less must have a "best before" date. The dates are minimums and although the

food may not be at its peak after the printed date, it will still be nutritious and edible. If you are old enough to go shopping alone, it's assumed you can tell a rotten apple when you see one.

Fresh or previously frozen meat, fish and poultry with a life of 90 days must have the packaging date on the label. Signs, or the label itself, must tell you how long the goods can be stored in the home. If the product requires storage at other than room temperature, the label must say so.

All labels on food products must show the common name, the net quantity, and the name and address of the manufacturer or distributor. Ingredients in prepackaged food must be listed in descending order of proportion, or by percentage. If artificial flavoring has been used, the label must say so.

When the label states that the package will provide a certain number of servings, it must give the size of each serving. If you don't understand metric measurement, pin up a conversion chart in your kitchen.

And even though you are not entitled to either a refund or an exchange for those aging cold cuts, discuss the matter with the supermarket manager. It's possible that he or she finds goodwill gestures preferable to disgruntled customers.

BAD FOOD

The butter you bought was rancid and you threw it in the garbage. Your grocer doesn't want to compensate you.

Unless you are a regular and reliable customer, a storekeeper is unlikely to accept your unsupported word about spoiled produce and he will want evidence to back your complaint. How can he be sure you even bought it from him?

If you take rancid butter back within a reasonable time, your grocer should replace the item or refund your money. If one or the other is not forthcoming, inform your local consumer services bureau.

The retailer is not required to put a "best before" date on a pound of butter, but he must provide proper storage facilities for perishable products. Failure to do so is a violation of the Food and Drugs Act.

ADDITIVES

Hot dogs and hamburgers are your family's favorites, but you are concerned about what additives they contain.

An active adult needs 48 grams of protein a day. You would have to eat about 10 wieners to meet that requirement. Ground beef, with twice the amount of protein per pound, is a better buy.

A few years ago, the soybean was seen as an ideal "stretcher" protein. Millions of World War II soldiers had munched on unappetizing but nourishing soy sausages, and by 1957 soya fibers could be reconstituted to resemble any meat—from beef to bacon.

In the United States, the government permitted the substitution of soy protein for meat in meals provided through school luncheon programs. In Canada, several firms put soy-extended meat products on the market.

Today, the soy-extended products have all but vanished from the grocery shelves. Consumers simply won't buy them, even though soyaburger costs about 30 cents less a pound than hamburger.

If wieners are described as "all beef," you can buy them with confidence. (Hamburger *must* be all beef to meet government regulations, and inspectors check to make sure. In 1979 federal officials caught more than 50 stores with cheaper pork products mixed with hamburger.) The health protection branch of the federal Department of Health and Welfare has strict regulations controlling the "additives" in meat products.

The regulations define a food additive as "any substance, including any source of radiation, the use of which results or may reasonably be expected to result in it or its by-products becoming a part of or affecting the characteristics of a food." *Thus vitamins, seasonings or flavoring, or agricultural chemicals are not included.*

Before permitting a manufacturer to use an additive, the health protection branch considers the physical and chemical properties of the substance, the amount to be used, safety and labeling and the benefit to the consumer in nutritive value or acceptability of the food.

Any additive used must be listed on the label—which may not be of much help if the substance has a long chemical name. Sodium chloride is the chemical name for salt, sugar is sucrose.

Here are a few common additives: silicon dioxide—an anticaking agent used in icing sugar; potassium bromate—a bleaching, maturing and dough-conditioning agent used in bread and flour; annatto—a coloring agent used in butter and cheese; acacia gum—a texture-modifying agent used in beer; papain—a meat tenderizer; aluminum sulfate—a firming agent used in canned salmon and tuna; mono- and di-glycerides—an antifoaming agent for jams; glycerol—used in sausage casings to prevent drying out; sodium stearoyl-2-lactylate—a whipping agent for topping mixes.

As old as the Pyramids. Additives are controversial in an era of cancer scares, yet there is nothing new about them. The ancient Egyptians added coloring to their food. In China, bananas were ripened with burning kerosene. The Romans preserved food and extracted spices by soaking in oil.

Some additives keep food from spoiling and others make it look and taste attractive. Canada permits nine synthetic food-coloring agents.

Scientists don't always agree on additives and one considered harmless this month may be classed as harmful next month. A new additive is generally tested on lab animals in amounts 100 times as great as those to be used in human food.

Benefits versus risks. People in the food business say the benefits of additives outweigh the risks—that crossing the street is more dangerous than consuming additives all your life. Organic-food buffs will argue about that all the way to the nature-food shop.

Industrial food technology has doubtless eliminated more risks than it has created. Nevertheless, be alert to possible dangers from additives. If you have doubts about anything—including the amount of filler in your wieners—go to one of the more than 40 Consumer and Corporate Affairs centers that monitor safety, weights and other food matters.

HOMEMADE FOODS

The farmers' market and charity bake sales in your community seem to ignore regulations on handling and keeping food.

Ontario food inspectors raised a furor in 1979 when they charged that church suppers weren't meeting the standards of the provincial Public Health Act. They wanted the affairs banned unless they met the same standards as stores and restaurants. The officials soon found that they were meddling with a sacred rural institution. Fearful politicians jumped in to assure their constituents that the inspectors would tread slowly and carefully in enforcing their tough standards on community halls.

The enforcers acknowledged that the church and charity groups would be hurt, but argued there could be no double standard about serving food. Some health services personnel even wanted to monitor food cooked at home and brought to a sale.

Said one home-baker: "We are cooking the food in our own homes and wrapping it carefully before we take it to the church, and you know what happens there, don't you? We have to eat it as well."

At last report, the potluck suppers and farmers' markets were flourishing.

The takeout tests. Inspectors check hundreds of restaurants, bakeries, factories and grocery stores each week to ensure the food laws are obeyed. Food must not be "manufactured, prepared, preserved, packaged or stored under unsanitary conditions."

The inspectors may enter any commercial food outlet and take away any food they think is bad, or they may close any establishment on the spot. The padlock stays on until conditions are improved, unless an appeal against the closure is successful.

Although "greasy spoons" seem to pop up overnight, it's not easy to get a restaurateur's license. Inspectors must pre-check—and approve—the sanitation and ventilation systems of the premises, the washroom facilities and the equipment for disinfecting utensils.

Although the raw materials for your dinner are trucked to the food manufacturers by the

Grasshopper: an acquired taste?

Scientists are searching for substitutes for conventional meat protein, and if they succeed, our traditional meat-and-potatoes dinner may become as rare as buffalo hump and syllabub. Dr. Robert Elliott of the University of British Columbia is experimenting with grasshoppers. This traditional nemesis of western farmers is considered a delicacy by the Japanese, who are already paying up to $1.70 a pound for dried Canadian grasshoppers.

Dr. Louis Zsuffa, a scientist with the Ontario Ministry of Natural Resources, claims poplar leaves may become an important source of protein. He says the leaves contain a higher percentage of amino acids, the building blocks of protein, than oats, wheat, maize or rice and are almost as nutritious as meat.

Scientists in Australia are adding tropical foliage to yeast, which is fed to sheep. It's a more efficient way of producing protein than feeding forage directly to animals. The scientists think the enriched yeast might be adapted for human consumption.

Ever heard of dandelion salad, or wine? Pigweed, with a bit of butter and salt, is not unlike spinach. A Toronto botanist makes a drink from leaves of purslane, a weed often found in gravel driveways.

carload, all are subject to rigid checking. The same can't be said for the meat pie at the church social.

ROADSIDE STANDS

The apples you purchased from a roadside stand contain evidence of worms but the vendor refuses to refund your money.

The state doesn't permit anyone to sell inedible food, but it doesn't guarantee perfection. It's a fact of life that insects attack fruit. It's also generally agreed that if you buy outside normal trade channels you accept the goods "as is." You select your apples and you're stuck with them.

No farm-gate fruiterer could guarantee that his apples will not reveal worm damage. Even with the most rigorous pest-spraying program it is virtually impossible to produce worm-free apples. The apple maggot, sometimes called the railroad worm, also attacks plums and other fruits. The codling moth lays its eggs on apples and pears.

There's a host of other marauders, including the weevils that lay eggs on apples, pears, plums, cherries and peaches. Other insects attack leaves and stems. Although an orchardist may take every known precaution against insect damage to his fruit, one single unsprayed tree in the vicinity makes it practically impossible to keep his trees totally uninfested.

The old apple tree can be a menace in the garden for all its sentimental or ornamental appeal. More than most trees, it attracts insects and crop diseases.

IMPURITIES

Your mother found a caterpillar in a box of cookies you had just bought. This is destroying her enjoyment of food.

Complaints about foreign matter in commercial food products have tripled over a three-year period. Reported incidents now number about 7,500 a year.

The health protection branch of the federal Department of Health and Welfare says 44 percent of complaints are about foreign objects, 19 percent concern chemical contaminants, 15 percent allege insect infestation and others relate to packaging and labeling. About 85 percent of the complaints are justified.

This doesn't necessarily mean that the quality of our packaged food is getting worse but rather that consumers are more aware of their rights and know where to lodge their complaints.

A beer drinker found a grayish mass in his bottle. It turned out to be a cigar butt.

A woman bit into a pork chop and her tongue was pierced by a fragment of hypodermic needle. It had presumably been used to vaccinate the hog.

A variety store employee found a sliver of glass in a soft drink.

A housewife discovered a mouse in a bottle of salad oil.

A consumer complained of "funny tasting" milk. The returnable container had been used by another consumer to store gasoline.

It is illegal to sell food that "has in or upon it any poisonous or harmful substance" or "is unfit for human consumption." If you buy food that matches these descriptions, get in touch with the retailer, or the manufacturer, your provincial district health office or your local consumer services bureau and keep the contaminated food, bottle or package as evidence.

If the product causes mental or physical injury, get witnesses to the incident and see your physician as soon as possible. A medical report could be invaluable evidence in any claim for damages or compensation.

Another helping of worms? It would seem that not everyone would be appalled by a caterpillar in a box of cookies.

George Main of Richer, Man., raises earthworms. He thinks they will be the wieners of the future. "They are crispy when fried," he says. "Really, a very bland taste."

Revulsion for unusual foods is all in our heads, Main insists: a gourmet balks at eating worms, but considers snails (*escargots*) a delicacy.

Farmer Main offers this recipe for applesauce surprise cake: combine butter, sugar, flour, cinnamon, cloves, nuts and applesauce. The *surprise* is a level cup of chopped earthworms.

PRICE STICKERS

The can of peas has two price stickers and the checkout clerk insists that you pay the higher figure.

The law is quite clear: if an item has two price stickers, you pay the lower price. Speak to the manager if the cashier argues.

The storekeeper can put on a new price, but only one should be shown. Adhesive stickers make it simple for the merchant to apply new prices over the old.

Some larcenous shoppers strip off the new tab and sometimes they pull stickers off low-priced items and place them on more expensive products. If questioned, they lie: "Well, that was the price on the thing on the shelf so I assumed it was correct."

Don't try it. Most of the larger stores are under surveillance of some kind and you could be sorely embarrassed if the cashier buzzes for the floor manager. Besides, it's attempted fraud.

WEIGHTS AND MEASURES

Your meat purchases weigh less on your kitchen scale than they did in the shop.

If your scale is accurate, take the meat back and complain to the manager, and to the nearest consumer services bureau, so that others won't be gypped.

Learn the signs of danger

There are some 50,000 poisonings in Canada every year and most of the victims are children under four. More than one-third of the accidents are caused by ordinary household products.

Hazardous products must carry symbols and words warning of danger. The label must name the product's most hazardous chemical and describe the recommended first-aid treatment. Some substances must be contained by "child-proof" caps to deter curious toddlers.

In the event of an accident, get the victim to the nearest hospital without delay and take along the container of whatever substance was ingested. Specially equipped poison centers are listed in your telephone book.

Newfoundland has a novel way of making children more aware of poisonous products. A cartoon character, Officer Ugg, identifies products children must not touch, taste, inhale or swallow. Parents are encouraged to tour the house putting stickers on bottles of pills, co-logne, detergents, shaving lotion, cleansers, glue, sprays and pesticides.

The Officer Ugg Poison Prevention Kit (including a brochure on first aid) can be obtained free from the Janeway Child Health Centre, Newfoundland Drive, St. John's, Nfld., A1A 1R8.

It's illegal for the storekeeper to short-weight you because of faulty scales.

Canada's first Weights and Measures Act was proclaimed in 1872. It has been updated frequently to keep pace with packaging and labeling legislation. Government inspectors verify the accuracy of *all* commercial scales *before use* and run regular spot-checks in the marketplace.

The same inspectors check the accuracy of weights and volumes shown on all packaged products, such as ice cream and detergents, corn flakes and frozen shrimp. Electricity and gas meters are inspected on a fixed schedule, and for a small fee the consumer can have any such meter inspected.

Gas pumps and fuel-oil tank meters are inspected, too. Self-serve gasoline meters are marked: "In case of disagreement between this register and the cashier's register, this register shall be taken as correct." A fuel-oil meter must be set at zero before a delivery commences. A new ticket may not be put in the meter until it reads zero.

As Canada moves closer to complete metric measurement, more and more commodities are offered in decimal units. The sooner you learn about those kilograms, litres, and metres, the better protected you'll be in the marketplace.

LAETRILE

Your father hopes Laetrile will cure his cancer and wants you to get the drug from Mexico.

It is illegal to manufacture or distribute Laetrile in Canada, but it is not illegal to bring it into the country for personal use. Mexico permits both manufacture and treatment, and you should have no problem bringing in enough for an individual treatment, although it's very unlikely your father would find a Canadian doctor willing to administer this drug. The Ontario College of Physicians and Surgeons warns that doctors who treat their patients with Laetrile could face malpractice suits.

Laetrile is a chemical substance extracted from the pits of apricots and peaches, from bitter almonds and from other plants. It has been around since 1952 and has been tested many times by medical authorities, who found no evidence that it has any effect on cancer.

Many medical practitioners say Laetrile is a cruel fraud that raises false hopes among sufferers, luring them away from conventional treatments that might help them. Yet testimonials continue to appear from people who say it has cured or arrested their cancer. Their authors accuse the medical establishment of a conspiracy to suppress it.

In all this there's one sure fact: Laetrile production and treatment is highly profitable. On the black market, it sells for up to 700 percent above the base cost. A course of treatment in Mexico costs about $1,000.

ERRORS BY DRUGGISTS

Your mother got a prescription filled at your local drugstore. Now the pharmacist has phoned to say that he dispensed the wrong substance.

Assuming your mother has not taken the medication, all is well. You can expect the drugstore to deliver the prescribed medicine and retrieve the other. But if your mother has already ingested the wrong medicine and suffers in any way as a result, she'll have an iron-clad case for damages for malpractice.

Pharmacy is a tightly regulated profession, requiring a four- to five-year study program after high-school graduation. Licensing and supervision (as with all professions) is within provincial jurisdiction, but it's largely a self-regulating profession. All the provincial associations work with the Canadian Pharmaceutical Association.

We all take it for granted that the prescription received from our physician will be correctly filled at the drugstore. But all humans are fallible, and mistakes do occur. However, the druggist must keep the prescriptions he has filled on file. And the container in which you receive drugs includes the name of the drug and the dosage instructions. If disputes arise, the unused portion of the medicine can be matched with the prescription and a simple analysis will determine the ingredients.

DRUGS

Members of your family get little or no relief from a well-known over-the-counter cold remedy.

An old adage states that the common cold, untreated, lasts for seven days; with treatment, it takes about a week to run its course.

There is no cure for the common cold: at best, popular cold remedies alleviate the symptoms. And North Americans spend more than $1 billion a year seeking this relief. Advertising triumphs over science.

Quiet revolution? The Quebec Order of Pharmacists has been warring with patent medicine manufacturers for years. One college spokesman, concerned by the advertising claims of drugs with little proven value, wants all drugs to be available only on prescription by a doctor.

Prescription drugs are subject to vigorous

The Universal Product Code

Only a laser beam can read the Universal Product Code (UPC) seen on most prepackaged food items. The code—a row of numbers surmounted by vertical bars—is computer shorthand. The first five digits and the corresponding black lines identify the manufacturer. In the sample shown, this would be Vallée. The second set of numbers and vertical lines describes the product—name, size, color, flavor, quality and grade—which in this case is apple juice.

Manufacturers developed the code as part of a proposed computerized system which would include automated checkout counters in the supermarket.

Some 30 stores, mostly in Ontario, were using the UPC system as of 1979. Its use is expected to be widespread by the mid-1980s.

official testing; over-the-counter (OTC) drugs are not. The Food and Drug Administration in the United States is forcing manufacturers to withdraw OTC products which have been proven ineffective. In Canada, federal Food and Drugs regulations require manufacturers to supply "all studies conducted to establish the safety of the drug and to provide substantial evidence of the effectiveness of the drug for the purpose and under the conditions of use recommended by the manufacturer." But, policing of drugstore shelves is mostly left up to provincial health departments.

In July 1979, a committee of the health protection branch of the federal Department of Health and Welfare recommended that nonprescription pain relievers be sharply restricted and some ingredients (especially codeine) prohibited.

Other recommendations included:

■ Removal of caffeine from acetylsalicylic acid (ASA) compounds such as Anacin.

■ Gradual removal of codeine from OTC remedies.

■ Banning advertising of products containing acetaminophen, a pain-killing ingredient in Tylenol and some citrus-flavored cold remedies.

■ Adding warning labels to drugs containing ASA, cautioning against their use in the last three months of pregnancy, and advising consumers they should not use such drugs for more than five days consecutively, without a doctor's advice.

■ Inserting warnings with drugs containing such ingredients as ASA, acetaminophen and others telling consumers of possible side-effects, reaction when used in combination with other drugs, and how to deal with an overdose emergency.

■ Limiting the size of products with codeine to 24 tablets per package and 100 tablets per package for those containing acetylsalicylic acid.

The price of tranquillity. It's estimated that enough tranquilizers are sold each year to keep a quarter of a million Canadians in a perpetual state of "tranquillity." Tranquilizers are only available by prescription, but doctors have been under fire for overprescribing these depressants.

Used sparingly, tranquilizers can relieve tension and anxiety, but they can also create psychological dependence. There are already far too many people who must have a tranquilizer to get through the day.

If your doctor prescribes tranquilizers, or any proprietary medicine (that is, a medicine whose brand-name patent is owned by a company), shop around for the best price. A Toronto reporter recently took the same prescription to 12 different drugstores and was quoted prices that varied by 320 percent between highest and lowest.

Drugs bought under their generic names—those names given to them by chemists according to rules that are agreed upon internationally—should be substantially cheaper. Generic names cannot be protected by patent, but pharmaceutical manufacturers may register—and patent—names for the compounds they make. Manufacturers resist any trend by doctors to prescribe by a drug's generic name. Consumer groups, on the other hand, are pressing for legislation to make prescribing by generic name mandatory.

19 Furniture and clothing

About three million new appliances—refrigerators, ranges, freezers, dishwashers, washing machines, dryers, vacuum cleaners and air conditioners—are bought in this country every year. The domestic furniture industry racks up annual sales of more than $1.25 billion. (And the furniture-appliance business generates more consumer complaints than any other product field.)

Consider these statistics: 99.4 percent of Canadian homes have a refrigerator, 86 percent have electric stoves (others have gas models), 98 percent have radio and television sets, 76.5 percent have electric washing machines, and vacuum cleaners gulp the dust in 88.7 percent of the nation's households.

Most of us have only a hazy idea of how these complicated devices work, but we buy them confident that they will perform as advertised. We expect that if something does go wrong prematurely, it will be fixed or the product will be replaced or our money refunded.

Our confidence is based on the strong safety net of consumer laws woven by government during the past two decades. The old Roman maxim *caveat emptor* (buyer beware) may soon be displaced by *caveat venditor* (seller beware).

This welcome swing does not relieve the consumer of responsibility for his or her own decisions. Far from it. Every adult in the marketplace is assumed to be acting with reasonable judgment. For example, it is not reasonable to demand a refund from the retailer if you operate an appliance contrary to the instructions supplied.

Too often, buyers don't even look at the warranty until there's a problem with the product. The warranty may well disclaim any responsibility in the given circumstances and you agreed to that condition when you made your purchase. Or the warranty may specify that it is valid only if the owner follows the instructions for use and maintenance of the appliance.

The vast majority of the millions of consumer transactions that take place daily are concluded to the satisfaction of both parties. But, you have the right to a fair deal at all times—not just most of the time. If you have a legitimate gripe, demand satisfaction. The rules and regulations are on your side.

DEFECTIVE PARTS

The timer on your stove has broken down for the third time and your year's warranty recently expired.

Look first to the dealer's "express warranty," which puts in writing exactly what is guaranteed. Verbal promises by a salesclerk may not be reliable and are always difficult to prove.

Manufacturers have traditionally limited their liability with a standard form of warranty stating, for example, that the product is covered for "one year, parts and labor." In Saskatchewan, under new legislation which may become a model for other provinces, such time-limit clauses may no longer be valid.

Your warranty indicates what free service will be provided and the expiry date. Check the details carefully. Different parts of an appliance may be covered in different ways and for varying lengths of time.

If the stove already has a documented history of unsatisfactory performance, you still have a good measure of protection even though the warranty has expired. Under each province's Sale of Goods Act, there's an "implied warranty" that all goods sold be of "merchantable quality." While this may sound just vague to the consumer, it has, through many years of legal argument, come to have a fairly well defined meaning to lawyers and judges and to reputable manufacturers and retailers.

If you have kept records of the earlier servicing of your stove timer—and probably even if you haven't—the implied warranty should stand up, if you are forced to sue either the dealer or the manufacturer. A stove of "merchantable quality" should work well for much longer than a year. Ten years, more likely.

Just about everything you buy carries an implied warranty. Your new stove, washer or vacuum cleaner must do the job the vendor says it will do. A freezer must freeze and a mixer mix. Otherwise, you are entitled to repairs, a replacement or a refund.

Changing laws. The first phase of Saskatchewan's Consumer Products Warranties Act became law in late 1977. Its purpose was to create new and tougher standards for the sale of manufactured goods.

The innovative law allows consumers to have an appliance such as an electric stove repaired without cost, or even returned for a refund, if either seller or manufacturer is found to have breached the warranty standards set out in the act. It does not matter whether the complaint is excluded from the merchant's guarantee or other sales agreement, or whether that guarantee has expired. In fact, it is illegal in Saskatchewan to limit the remedy for breach of warranty.

The new law establishes a contract at the point of sale between the consumer and the manufacturer as well as with the vendor (the retailer). Previously, the courts had ruled that buyers had no contract with the manufacturer and must take action against retailers in any dispute about a product.

The new standards apply only to consumer products. These are defined as items purchased by the average householder for personal, family or household use. All merchants in Saskatchewan are subject to the law, as are manufacturers who directly or indirectly supply the provincial market.

Saskatchewan consumers are entitled to take legal action if an appliance or any of its parts are not "durable for a reasonable period of time." Judges and manufacturers were soon asking what "reasonable durability" means.

The government's answer: "The product must last for a reasonable length of time taking into account the price and description as well as how the product has been used and maintained."

Judges in the civil courts are arbiters of disputes but the legislation also provides for mediation by an official of the Department of Consumer Affairs and for arbitration by an impartial outsider.

By mutual consent. Although the Sale of Goods Act demands that the vendor supply goods of "merchantable quality," the buyer and seller are free to modify the terms implied by the law. Take care that you don't nullify even the minimum protection of the act by accepting an express warranty, with fewer guarantees, from the seller.

While some provinces are imposing a stricter liability on the manufacturer and the merchant, the national situation remains in a state of flux. Most provincial consumer laws still permit the vendor to include disclaimers, limiting liability to a fixed period of time or to certain parts of an appliance.

Of course, if the vendor's sales pitch can be shown to have been deliberately misleading, it's a different story. Such action by the vendor constitutes a fraudulent act for which he bears responsibility, whether or not he has limited his warranty.

The law aims to protect the consumer, even if the defect was not specifically known to the retailer or manufacturer.

REGISTERING THE WARRANTY

You forget to mail the warranty card for your clock radio and now the manufacturer won't listen to your complaint.

Many manufacturers require that you register your warranty to make it valid. You may be able to do this at the dealer's where you made the purchase, or you may have to fill out and mail a card. If you fail to validate your warranty, the manufacturer may not be obliged to honor it.

If you can prove the date of purchase, you

A warranty checklist

Make sure you know the answers to these questions before you accept any guarantee or warranty.

Is the product described in full detail, with all registration and model numbers?

Is the entire product covered, or only certain parts?

Are both parts and labor covered?

How is the guarantor's liability limited? What is the product guaranteed against? What is not covered?

Is the guarantee or warranty transferable if the item is resold?

What must the buyer do to benefit from the warranty? Must the warranty be registered in some way?

Who is behind the guarantee or warranty? The manufacturer or the retailer or both?

What local servicing is available?

When does the warranty go into effect and how long does it last?

If the need arises to claim under the warranty and you get a runaround from retailer and manufacturer, don't give up. Complain to your consumer services bureau, or the Better Business Bureau, or a newspaper Action Line columnist.

For a small fee, you can drag the dealer and manufacturer into the Small Claims Court. It's a long road, but rights are never won easily. If you've got a sound case, your chances of winning are good—and if the judge agrees you've been stung, you'll get your court costs back too.

WARRANTY

1. This Proctor-Silex appliance is warranted against defects in workmanship or material for one year from date of original purchase.

2. This warranty provides for a comparable replacement or repair at our option:

    (a) Without charge when the defective appliance is hand carried to and from the dealer from whom it was purchased or a Proctor-Silex Authorized Service Centre.

    (b) With a charge only for return transportation when mailed prepaid.

3. The warranty does not cover (a) misuse (b) use for commercial purposes (c) shipping damage (d) broken glass or plastic parts (e) cord wear (f) use on electrical circuit other than specified or use for purposes other than those intended.

4. Cheques for return transportation, accompanying the appliance will save return C.O.D. charges.
   Proctor-Silex Authorized Service Centres are independent businesses (not owned or operated by Proctor-Silex). They are listed in the Yellow Pages under "Electrical Appliance—Small".

5. Be sure to save your sales slip or other reasonable facsimile to establish date of purchase should your appliance prove defective under terms of this warranty.

SCM **PROCTOR-SILEX**
DIVISION OF SCM (CANADA) LTD.
PICTON, ONTARIO K0K 2T0

Customer Portion   **Section du Client**

Appliance model   Modele de l'appareil

Serial No and Date purchased   No. de serie + Date d'achat

Dealer's name   Nom du vendeur.

Braun kitchen appliances - 5 year warranty
Braun personal care appliances - 3 year warranty (including portable heaters and air cleaners).
In the event a Braun Appliance fails to function within the specified warranty period because of defects in material or workmanship, and the consumer returns the unit to an authorized service centre, Braun Canada Ltd. will, at its option on either repair or replace the unit without additional charge to the consumer. This guarantee does not cover any product which has been damaged by dropping, tampering, servicing performed or attempted by unauthorized service agencies, or misuse or abuse.

The provisions of this warranty are in addition to and not a modification of or subtraction from the statutory warranties and any other rights and remedies contained in any statute applicable in this Province.

Appareils menagers Braun - garantie de 5 ans.
Appareils pour soins personnels Braun (incluant chaufferette portative et purificateurs d'air) garantie de 3 ans.
Dans le cas ou un appareil Braun s'avererait défectueux, durant la periode specifiee par la garantie, a cause d'un défaut de fabrication ou de matieres premieres, et que le consommateur le retourne a un centre de service autorize, Braun Canada Ltd., a son choix, réparera ou remplacera l'appareil sans aucun frais additionnel. Cette garantie ne s'applique pas pour tout appareil que nous jugerons avoir fait l'objet de tentative de réparation par des personnes non autorizes ou qui aura été endommagé par suite d'une chute, d'un messuage ou d'abus.

Les stipulations de cette garantie s'ajoutent aux garanties statutaires et à tous les autres droits et solutions contenus dans tout statut applicable dans cette province, et ne constituent pas une modification ou une soustraction de ceux-ci.

may get your faulty radio repaired or replaced without charge. Did you get a receipt when you made the purchase? This is basic drill for the careful shopper. The receipt should provide the essential data—the dealer's name and the date. If you used a credit card, there will be a record of the purchase, or your canceled cheque will show that you paid a certain amount to the store on a certain day.

Manufacturers often limit warranty coverage to the original purchaser, and they may specify that the warranty is void if anyone but one of their authorized servicemen repairs the product. If you try to repair an appliance yourself, you may not only fail to fix it, but you may render the warranty void in the process.

If "strict (or total) liability" of the manufacturer ever becomes the national standard, warranty rights would be extended to those getting the item as a gift, as well as those buying it second- or thirdhand. Theoretically, the buyer of a used car could then sue the manufacturer if performance was faulty and the vehicle had not given adequate service for a reasonable length of time.

THE 'FLOOR MODEL'

Your "demonstrator" floor polisher is a lemon but the appliance store refuses repair, refund or replacement.

In each province, legislation provides that every article sold carry an implied warranty that it will do what it's supposed to do. But this protection does not apply if the parties freely make some other arrangements in the sales contract.

Often a "demonstrator" or "floor model" is offered "as is." It is not a new item, though it may be only slightly used. It is sold at a discount with all its good and bad features. When you snap up such bargains, you may have no warranty protection whatsoever.

Of course, the merchant must not misrepresent any product. You might have a case if you could prove that he misled you about the condition of the floor polisher.

PARTS... AND LABOR?

Your dryer broke down while under warranty. The store replaced the faulty part but billed you for labor costs.

Your warranty protection depends largely on the province where you live. For the majority of consumers, what you'll get is stated in the express warranty handed to you when you bought the dryer. If the manufacturer guarantees the parts but makes no mention of labor, you can expect to pay that charge.

In Saskatchewan, you are entitled to have faulty products repaired at no cost, regardless of what the express warranty says. If the seller fails to make the repairs to your satisfaction, and within a reasonable time, you can have the work done elsewhere and he'll have to pay the bill. And you're entitled to compensation for any losses you suffered because of the appliance breakdown.

In the other provinces and the Territories where consumer laws may be changing, call the government department concerned to check the current situation.

The installation catch. Perhaps the appliance salesman said the store would install your dryer, but the deliveryman merely put it in the basement and refused to connect it. You may as well brace yourself to pay a hefty service charge if you have only the salesman's word.

Salesclerks live on enthusiasm. Whenever they promise anything, do your best to get it in writing. And no ambiguous phrases! For instance, does "install" mean "connect"?

Verbal promises can form part of an enforceable contract, but they can also be regarded merely as "representations" made by the salesman to clinch the sale. Unless those representations can be interpreted as misrepresentations (deliberate lies, in other words), they are not actionable. A judge might rate a salesman's claims as mere opinion, or estimates of future performance. Many such claims are regarded as "puffery," exaggerations upon which no reasonable person would rely.

If in doubt, question the store manager

about installation of any major appliance before you buy. Have your receipt endorsed: "Complete installation."

DEPOSITS, RETURNS, EXCHANGES

You made a $50 deposit on a television set. Then you find a model that you prefer at another store. You want your deposit.

The merchant is under no legal obligation to return your money. A deposit commits you to purchase the item; accepting the deposit commits the merchant to holding the item for you. You may forfeit your deposit if you decide to back out of the deal. Perhaps the item could have been sold to someone else in the interim or, counting on his sale to you, the merchant may have entered into other contracts.

Ask for a guarantee in writing if you want to be assured that you can get your deposit back. Don't accept a verbal promise. Be prepared to forfeit any deposit if you don't go through with a purchase by a reasonable date.

Technically, sales are final unless other conditions are specified at the time of sale. Many merchants do take merchandise back and give refunds and others will return deposits to customers who have changed their minds, but it all depends on the policy of the individual store.

That policy may be modified as, for instance, when "All Sales Final" notices are displayed during department-store clearances. You are being notified that the store's usual policy of allowing refunds or exchanges has been suspended during the sale.

A good return. You're never entitled to a refund simply because you're unhappy with a

---

Standing on guard

If a toilet flushed satisfactorily four times a day for 170 years, would you consider that a fair test? Yes? Then you should appreciate the work of the Canadian Standards Association (CSA). Before the association label is affixed to any product, its safety and serviceability are put through a torture test.

The CSA was founded in 1919, primarily for the engineering industry. It is still an independent association, grouped with other standards-writing bodies in the Standards Council of Canada. The CSA's particular field now is product safety and performance. Almost 500 persons work at the head office and testing laboratory in Toronto and regional branches in British Columbia, Alberta, Manitoba and Quebec.

They throw weights against television screens, smash steel balls into bathtubs, and flush toilets 250,000 times. A steam iron goes through 20 tests for 700 hours before it earns the CSA label. Kitchen counter-tops are scrubbed 12,000 times. Plumbing fittings are exposed to a corrosive spray and immersed for 96 hours. A 4,500-pound weight is pressed against a hockey helmet to see how well it will protect the head and spine.

The CSA is best known for its testing and certifying of electrical equipment. All household electrical appliances offered for sale must carry the CSA emblem.

The nonprofit CSA is financed through membership and testing fees and revenue from its publications. There is no direct cost to the consumer.

---

purchase. Merchants are not obliged to take goods back unless these are defective or have been sold under misleading claims.

However, they will often give refunds in the interest of retaining customer goodwill. Many of the largest retailers advertise that they'll return your money—cheerfully, even—if you are not satisfied with a purchase. You can't do better than that. Make sure the store's policy on refunds is clear to you at the time of purchase.

When you must ask for a refund for personal reasons (that is, you are not claiming that the goods are defective), never lose your temper and be ready to negotiate. If you present a good case, the manager may exchange the purchase, or give you a refund, even though the store doesn't do this as a rule.

It's particularly important when buying gifts to determine the store's refund policy. Ask that the right of return or exchange be written on the sales slip.

Salesclerks act as the agents of the proprietor who must, within reasonable limits, back up their statements or promises. However, sales staff have been known to become overzealous, especially when they get a bonus on sales volume. So have a witness or, better, get everything in writing.

But when faced with a shopper who is obviously determined to lay a formal complaint with the consumer watchdogs, most store managers will come to terms, as long as the item is in its original condition and you have proof of purchase.

The sale syndrome. Nothing annoys a careful shopper more than to see last week's expensive purchase advertised for sale this week at "20% off."

Careful shoppers know that there's a predictable cycle of sales in almost every field. Favorite times are toward the end of seasons and just before the introduction of new models. And sales must offer genuine reductions. Otherwise, the merchant is risking prosecution and a heavy fine.

If you are planning a major purchase, why not ask if the store has any plans for a sale. Helpful clerks will tip you off if any clearances or price cuts are imminent. If you can get the

store to accept a deposit on the item on the understanding that you will buy it at the sale—that's consumerism!

LATE DELIVERY

You're living in a motel because the department store hasn't delivered your furniture and appliances on the date promised.

Promised delivery dates have to be reasonably flexible. Many things can affect the delivery of your bedroom furniture, including factors beyond the control of the store. Even if you believe the delay is unreasonable, you can't just cancel the contract on your own. The store may agree to a cancellation, but don't expect it to pay your motel bill. And if it balks at canceling because of late delivery, you'll probably have to take legal action to nullify the contract. The judge would then have to decide if the store had breached the contract.

Protect yourself at the time of purchase: make the delivery date a condition of sale by inserting it in the contract.

Gremlins in the sofa. If you think you're having delivery troubles, consider the case of Lawrence Selby of Shawbridge, Que., who ordered $3,800 worth of furniture and appliances from a Laval, Que., firm.

To start with, the order didn't arrive on time and when some furniture was finally delivered, the shipment included several pieces that Mr. Selby hadn't ordered. Another delivery was made a month later—only this time none of it was Mr. Selby's furniture. The whole shipment was somebody else's order.

Meantime, Mr. Selby had difficulty getting a hearing at the store. By now, both the original salesman and the store manager had been replaced.

The new manager eventually got Mr. Selby the right sofa and rocking chair, but the kitchen set was still wrong—and scratched, as well. The store sent a repairman out.

The refrigerator and stove were not the models ordered either, but the customer gamely decided he could live with them. However, the living-room pieces were of different wood, color and style. The right ones were delivered—after three tries. Mr. Selby was less successful with a floor lamp. It was changed three times but the store never hit on the right model.

But when Mr. Selby held back payment of $200 until his order was completed properly, the store gave his account to a collection agency.

That was the last straw. Mr. Selby then

Warp and woof

Knowing your fabrics and materials is important, when shopping for curtains and drapes and upholstered furniture. Match the material to the job you want done.

DRAPERY. The first four in the following checklist are natural fibers, the others are synthetics:

Cotton. Strong, with good resistance to abrasion, but will weaken in prolonged exposure to sunlight.

Linen. Has durability, crisp texture and natural luster; can be dyed easily in rich colors.

Silk. Lustrous, with excellent draping quality, but weakens in sunlight.

Wool. Resists sunlight, wrinkling and creasing; often combined with other fibers for draperies.

Polyester. Strong, with excellent resistance to wrinkling, damage from heat or sunlight, and abrasion.

Nylon. Wears well, easily cared for, resists wrinkling; will deteriorate under lengthy exposure to the sun.

Fiberglass. Resists damage from sunlight and heat; doesn't shrink or wrinkle. Not resistant to abrasion and must be hand-washed.

Acetate. Luxurious soft feel and silky appearance. Average resistance to fading, but will wrinkle and fray if fabric rubs on a surface.

Rayon. Lustrous and largely colorfast; often substitutes for silk.

Acrylic. Resists fading, keeps its shape and can be machine-washed.

Modacrylic. Resists wrinkling and fading. It won't burn but will melt under too hot an iron.

UPHOLSTERY MATERIALS. A home filled with teen-agers needs material that will take hard knocks and spills. That calls for synthetics—vinyl, polyester, nylon and olefin. Silks, cottons and brocades are stylish, but won't stand rough treatment. Blends of synthetics (say, nylon and acrylic) can offer the best features of each. Synthetics and natural fibers (polyester and cotton) blend well and serve many purposes.

CUSHIONING. Consumers don't often spend much time checking cushioning materials, yet these are a prime factor in comfort and durability. There are nine common materials:

Foam rubber. Resilient, crush- and mothproof, it retains shape well.

Polyurethane foam. Lightweight, soft, yet with high tensile strength. Nonallergenic and resistant to insect and mildew damage.

Polyester staple. Resists alcohol and acids; feels like down. Often used as outer wrapper for foam-rubber seats.

Acetate staple. Soft, resilient and mildewproof; low inflammability and moisture absorbency.

Kapok. These fibers from the seeds of the kapok tree don't mat when wet. Good for outdoor furniture.

Cellulose. Bonded wood fibers primarily used as firm padding.

Down. Luxury filler (from goose and duck feathers) for cushions and pillows.

Hair. Durable, odorless, verminproof; used as filler on backs of sofas and chairs.

Cotton. Resilient, odorless, manufactured as batting or felt; often combined with foam rubber.

wrote to a newspaper's Action Line column. After the paper named the company, everything Mr. Selby had ordered was delivered within a week.

Quebec's 15-day deadline. Around the time of the Shawbridge fiasco, the Quebec Furniture Retailers Corporation (QFRC), which represents 300 independent stores, was showing all Canada a lead by proclaiming its own code of ethics. At member stores, consumers can now cancel any purchase and get full refund if delivery is not made within 15 days. Consumer complaints against any QFRC member will be heard by a conciliation committee, which can expel any store that refuses to abide by its decision.

If new goods are delivered in damaged condition, send them back. When delivery is part of the sale contract, your warranty really begins when you get the item into your physical possession.

Don't get caught in the middle of any disputes about "goods damaged in transit." That's strictly a problem between the shipper and the trucker.

DURABILITY OF CLOTHING

Your child's snowsuit split at the knees after only a few hours of wear. You are convinced the fabric was faulty.

You are entitled to a refund or a replacement if a garment does not stand up to reasonable wear and tear. This right is provided under your provincial Sale of Goods Act.

You will have to show the retailer that you used the merchandise with care and complied with any instructions on how to protect it from damage. Understanding the terms and conditions of refunds and exchanges can head off many problems.

Kids are tough on clothes. The Retail Council of Canada offers these suggestions, when buying children's clothing:

■ Estimate how much wear the garment will get and how long you expect it to last. Obtain the Canada Standard Size information (a federal brochure is available from your nearest consumer services bureau) and assess your child's weight, measurements and growth pattern.

■ Look for stretch fabrics, elastic inserts, wide seams that can be altered, tucks and pleats that can be let out.

■ Fiber content should be shown on all fabric labels. Check the instructions for washing, drying, bleaching, ironing and dry cleaning. Keep all tags.

■ Fabrics for child wear should be soft, absorbent and lightweight, firmly woven for durability. Look for reinforcement at points of strain, such as the knees and armholes. Is the stitching short and even with strong thread? Seams should be flat and smooth. If the garment is meant for active play, it will require heavy-duty fastenings.

■ Check for easy care. Is the garment soil resistant? Colorfast? Preshrunk? Perma-press? Will it stand up to machine washing and drying?

Nylon-thread stitching. The garment industry is fond of nylon thread. It's cheaper than cotton or linen thread and it doesn't break on the machines, meaning less loss of production time. But nylon thread has one great disadvantage to the consumer. Its "chain stitch" unravels easily. All the thread slides out when that key stitch lets go. Cotton thread doesn't do that.

Under the Sale of Goods Act (or, in Quebec, the Civil Code) the vendor is obliged to sell goods which are fit for the purpose for which they were bought. A flaw or defect means the goods do not meet the legal standard. This warranty is guaranteed by law, regardless of what the seller told you, orally or in writing.

If an expensive, nylon-stitched garment falls to pieces, the retailer or the manufacturer has a responsibility to compensate you.

But you can avoid such hassles by buying only cotton-stitched items, or clothes sewn with the new polyester-cotton thread, which combines the best factors of nylon and cotton threads.

It has been estimated that use of this thread would add only 10 cents to the cost of the average garment.

QUALITY OF FABRICS

Bright drapes recommended by the store's interior decorator are badly faded after one summer. You want to exchange them.

Unless the store gave a written guarantee that your drapes would not fade, you're probably stuck with them. You might be able to build a case for a partial refund or exchange, if you could prove that you were misled by the decorator's advice.

Even fabrics with a high resistance to the sun's rays will eventually deteriorate if overexposed. Colors may fade and threads weaken. Unconditional warranties on drapes, curtains and other fabrics are rare indeed and you are expected to shop with this in mind.

Your best protection is to learn something about modern fabrics and try to match the special properties of each type of cloth with the job you want it to do. This information is readily available from provincial consumer service bureaus, and usually from department stores and specialty fabric shops. (Your public library should have reference works under "textiles.")

Manufacturers have devised so many synthetic fibers and combinations that they have created what is often called the "fabric explosion." The advent of polyesters, nylons and acrylics created fabrics with new nonwrinkling qualities, resistance to dirt and mildew, staining and fading and with increased "wearability."

Federal regulations require manufacturers to label textiles with the generic name of each fiber they contain, along with the percentage by weight. This label must also carry the name of the manufacturer (or his identification number).

Take it to arbitration—if you can afford it

Voluntary arbitration can be as binding as a judge's ruling. When the amount in dispute is greater than the maximum allowed in Small Claims Court, arbitration can be an alternative to a slower and more expensive civil suit in the regular courts.

Almost unknown in Canada until recently (except in the labor-management field), arbitration is used to settle about 25,000 disputes a year in the United States.

The Arbitrators' Institute of Canada (AIC), chartered in 1974 as a nonprofit organization, now offers the services of about 200 independent arbitrators. They are people experienced in banking and finance, construction and engineering, consumer contracts, insurance, labor, landlord and tenant rights, real estate, accidents, transportation and other fields.

Arbitration works this way: One or both of the parties in the dispute write to the AIC (45 Richmond Street West, Toronto, Ont., M5H 1Z2). The institute examines the problem and suggests a single arbitrator or a panel, which the disputants may choose. Three arbitrators may be used in a complicated case. Each side chooses one and the two chosen select a third as chairman.

Arbitration is a judicial function with a decision based on evidence, but it is not bound by the legal technicalities that exist in a court of law. Unlike mediation, arbitration provides a decision, and the parties have agreed in advance to accept it, whatever it may be.

All provinces have some provision for the legal enforcement of private arbitration, and all except Newfoundland and Quebec have separate arbitration acts. The AIC presses for national acceptance and a uniform code of procedure.

Arbitrators work for a fee negotiated privately with the parties in the dispute. The minimum rate is about $200 a day. The AIC gets a referral charge amounting to 10 percent of the fee.

CARPETS AND FITTING

Your fitted carpet does not fit. The dealer and the independent installer blame each other.

The surest way to avoid carpet-fitting woes is to buy at a store that will take responsibility for measurement and installation and guarantee satisfaction.

Measuring a room for carpeting or rugs is easy. For a 12-by-15-foot room, fitted wall-to-wall, you'll be shopping for 20 square yards of carpeting.

Multiply length by width, in feet—then divide by nine to get square yards, the way most carpet is sold. (Carpet measurements were to become metric in 1980, but dual sizing is likely to continue for a long time. The basic width of broadloom is to remain at 12 feet or 366 centimetres.)

If you buy 20 square yards of nylon broadloom at rock-bottom price to install yourself, make sure that the measurement is stated on the sales receipt. You'll have the proof you need for replacement or adjustment if it turns out that the cutter has made an error. This standard size in popular colors and weaves is very often precut and sold at a unit price.

If you hire an independent installer to lay and perhaps sew your broadloom, he will be responsible only for the quality of his services. If he makes a mistake, he'll have to make it good. If it's a serious mistake, he could be forced to replace a spoiled length of carpet.

Magic carpet clues. In the summer of 1979 the Canadian Carpet Institute responded to the problems of carpet buyers by setting up a new quality grading system. It's a voluntary scheme but the institute soon reported that all but two of Canada's major manufacturers were cooperating.

Most broadloom bears a coded label which indicates the carpet's ability to retain its original appearance after installation. The label will show one of three capital letters: P, M or L. The "P" label stands for "plus," the best there is; the "M" is for "medium," the carpet is good for more than three years, even in heavy-traffic areas; the "L" is for "low," up to three years retention of original look. Normal maintenance is assumed in all cases.

To catch out any cheaters who might sew a "P" label on an "L" carpet, the institute has an annual budget of $25,000 to buy random samples for checking against the standards.

Price isn't everything. A carpet at $10 a square yard can sometimes give you better service than one selling at $30. It all depends on how it's made, where you put it and what you want it to do. In high-traffic areas, such as hallways, durability is more important than beauty.

The trade rule for carpet quality is: "the denser and the deeper, the better." Most of the carpeting offered in reputable stores today is solidly backed and well constructed; the difference in price reflects the depth and weight of the pile. Style and color are minor cost factors.

ANTIQUES

An expert on antique furniture assures you that your 18th-century armoire is a modern reproduction. You paid a dealer $8,500 for it.

Anyone able to pay $8,500 for an armoire (a large wooden cupboard or wardrobe) should have enough business know-how to demand that the dealer supply a written description of the piece, its style or period and approximate date of manufacture. With that "provenance" in your pocket, you will be in a strong position to get your money back (or sue for damages) if the item turns out to be *circa* 1976 instead of *circa* 1776.

Legislation forbids deception or misrepresentation in the sale of goods or services. And although *circa* means "about," a judge would frown upon an error of 200 years.

Most of Canada's hundreds of antique dealers (there are 326 listed in the Toronto Yellow Pages) will give you a written warranty attesting that the item you have bought is an antique. If they won't, it isn't.

What is an antique? The law is silent on the matter, but it is generally accepted in the trade that an antique must be more than 100 years old. Only a fraction of the goods in the average antique shop are genuine antiques.

Antique fairs for specialists usually won't show furniture built later than 1830—about the time machine shops ousted the craftsman—but it takes expertise to recognize the shady tricks used to make newly built stuff look old.

To cash in on the nostalgia trend, clever and serviceable reproductions are pouring out of factories in North America and Europe. Wood can be instantly "aged," or "distressed," in a number of ways: new wood is beaten with a rusty chain, or stained and sprayed with muriatic acid to pit the surface; burns and gouges are skillfully inflicted.

Treasure in the attic. Antiques will usually outdistance stocks or bonds as an investment. A Quebec diamond-point armoire was worth $1,500 about 15 years ago. Now it brings up to $15,000. ("Diamond point" refers to the carving on the doors and sides.)

A small pine cupboard picked up in Quebec's Eastern Townships for $30 went to a Belleville, Ont., dealer for $60, then to a dealer in Niagara Falls, Ont., for $120 and finally to a Toronto antique show priced at $380. The escalation took place in less than two weeks without the slightest change in the cupboard. Maybe you should check out the dim recesses of your attic, or the barn on the family farm.

AUCTION ACTION

The auctioneer mistook a gesture of yours as a bid and insists you're now the owner of a dining-room suite you don't want.

If you object immediately it's unlikely that a reputable auctioneer will threaten to take you to court to make the sale stick—or that a disreputable one will have much success if he tries. The usual remedy when there's any confusion about bids is for the item to be resubmitted for sale immediately.

The efficient auctioneer will often name the last bidder or, when the bidder is a stranger, indicate the person concerned with some identifying remark such as: "Twenty-five dollars I'm bid . . . the lady in the blue coat."

An auctioneer can be required to reveal the source of the latest bid, to prevent him pumping up the price with phony bids. An auctioneer in high gear can be taking bids from Mars for all the rookie observer knows.

The vendor is permitted to start off the bidding for any item with what he estimates is a fair price, and genuine bids submitted in advance by persons not present at the auction can be fed into the bidding stream.

A reserve price is often placed on a quality item by the owner. If the bidding does not reach that figure, it is "passed in" (withdrawn from sale). The auctioneer may jump the bidding up to that reserve figure. It's probably not strictly legal, but since he has contracted not to accept less, there's no victim.

Carried away by wheelbarrow. An auctioneer will forgive a genuine mistake, but an overbid made in the heat of the action will remain in force. Believe it or not, some auction addicts get so carried away they bid against themselves.

People buy the strangest things in the excitement of the moment. A 20th-floor apartment dweller in Vancouver once found himself the owner of a large, rickety wheelbarrow.

Most auctions allow time for the goods to be examined before the sale starts. Salesrooms often set aside two or three days for the preview and this is your chance to see the stuff up close, to check the upholstery on that elegant loveseat and to make sure appliances are in working order. Remember that all goods at an auction are sold "as is." There's no warranty or other consumer protection of any kind, unless specific factual statements or promises are made in the catalogue or sales pitch. When the auctioneer drops his hammer, the wheelbarrow is yours—even if the wheel falls off in the elevator.

20 Advertising

Protecting and exercising the rights of the consumer in the sometimes glamorous, sometimes shady world of advertising has become almost an industry on its own. Consumer agencies, the provincial and federal governments, the Canadian Advertising Advisory Board, the provincial press councils, some disenchanted advertising agency executives, and advertising managers of television and radio networks, newspapers and magazines are all moving into the picture.

With the recent sharpening of the misleading-advertising clauses of the federal Combines Investigation Act, the consumer bureaucracies bared their watchdog teeth. One proof of their zeal is the bulletin of convictions published quarterly by the federal Department of Consumer and Corporate Affairs.

One such bulletin reported that:

■ A national department store chain had advertised 100-percent down-filled parkas, which contained only 20 percent of down feathers.

■ A weekly newspaper had claimed more than twice its actual circulation.

■ A bakery chain was fined $675 for selling improperly labeled cherry cake.

■ A real estate company, which advertised abandoned mine workings and scrub swamps as prime resort land suitable for retirees, was fined $21,000.

■ A chartered bank was prohibited from advertising its acceptance of utility account payments from senior citizens, unless it was prepared to accept *all* utility accounts.

For serious offenses, transgressors are liable to a maximum of five years' imprisonment and unlimited fines (at the court's discretion). Lesser offenses can bring one year's imprisonment or a fine of up to $25,000 or both.

The liability for misleading statements in advertising now includes not only the merchant but also the agency that prepared the advertisement. Blind reliance on the advertiser's tests and statements is not enough. If the smiling television housewife says that Snowite detergent washes the ground-in grease from hubby's coveralls, then everyone who has a hand in the suds had better be able to prove the claim.

Marketing, an advertising trade journal, comments: "It is no excuse for the advertiser to say that the agency prepared the copy. It's no excuse for the agency to say that it relied on the advertiser's tests and technical representations." Even if the statements about goods and services are technically accurate, a prosecution may still be launched if the "general impression" is misleading in any material aspect.

Nevertheless, the creative advertiser will still find ways to whet our appetites for all sorts of products. The truth is that successful advertising is all persuasion.

EXAGGERATION

Your battery-powered calculator, guaranteed for 1,000 hours, has ceased functioning. You feel its life span was only a quarter of that advertised.

When making a purchase, you are expected to exercise the care and judgment of a reasonably intelligent person. You know that the seller will present his product or service in the best possible light, maybe even exaggerate a bit: it's sometimes called "puffery." If stuck with a bad deal, you have to prove beyond a reasonable doubt that you were victimized. The same challenge faces the numerous government watchdog and investigatory agencies.

But there's a new climate in today's courts. The old stance of *caveat emptor* (let the buyer beware) won't do. It's no longer safe for a manufacturer to advertise, say, that a watch will be accurate within a minute a year and then reap a harvest of sales secure in the knowledge that the claim can't be challenged until a buyer has tested the watch for 12 months.

In the landmark 1977 conviction of an agency for misleading advertising in a television commercial, the judge stated: "Television advertisements deliver a swift punch. It must be delivered above the belt. Winds of change in our society apply to the law as well and the law now requires statements of honesty, frankness, truthfulness and disclosure that were unknown in years gone by."

Was your calculator bought just a few months ago? The lapse of time since purchase can indicate the hours of use. Even at 20 hours a week, the machine should last almost a year. If it doesn't, discuss the matter with the store manager.

If you fail to get satisfaction, get in touch with your nearest Consumers' Association of Canada (CAC) branch. You may not be the only disgruntled purchaser, and action against those involved with the calculator promotion may already be in the works. Even if it isn't, the CAC may be able to advise on the best approach for your case.

There's considerable overlapping in the federal and provincial misleading-advertising laws. Prosecutors tend to prefer the federal Combines Investigation Act, which forbids an advertiser to make claims for his product without "adequate and proper tests." It provides for up to five years' imprisonment or unlimited fines or both. What's adequate? What's proper? The judge will decide.

The brush-on face lift. Would you believe that creams brushed on the skin would produce "a face lift without surgery or peeling?" Enough Toronto women believed in this miracle to pay $160,000 a month to a group of beauty salons. Judge William Rogers didn't, and he fined the promoters $2,000 for misleading advertising. Said the judge: "There shouldn't be profits made from people who try to find the fountain of youth. Obviously, the customers would have been better off to buy a Halloween mask. It would have looked better and lasted longer."

An important precedent was the 1979 Ontario Supreme Court award of $28,550 to farmer Glen Murray whose harvester, advertised as capable of processing 45 to 60 tons of silage an hour, failed to exceed 16 tons an hour. Until then, farmers were regarded as businessmen and, as such, exempt from consumer legislation protection.

TOO MANY COMMERCIALS

Commercials saturate evening viewing on your local television station. You complain to the manager, who says you can always turn to another station.

The percentage and type of advertising in any television time slot is regulated by the Canadian Radio-television and Telecommunications Commission (CRTC). Currently, 12 minutes of commercials are permitted in each hour of adult programming.

If your local station dismisses your objections, compile some facts and figures. If you still feel that the station is exceeding the permitted amount of advertising, write to:

The Chairman, Canadian Radio-television and Telecommunications Commission, Ottawa, Ont. K1A 0N2.

Give the station's call sign, and outline your objections clearly. List dates, names of advertisers and the times of commercials.

Don't waste the CRTC's time if you simply object to all advertising on the air; that point of view should go to your MP.

If you object to specific commercials on either the public Canadian Broadcasting Corporation or private CTV and Global Communications Ltd. networks, don't expect the commission to go to bat for you; it can't regulate taste. Complain first to your local broadcaster and the advertiser. If you are dissatisfied with the response, write to the head office concerned. Address your letters to: The President, Canadian Broadcasting Corporation, P.O. Box 8478, Ottawa, Ont. K1G 3J5; or to: The President, CTV Television Network, 42 Charles

Street East, Toronto, Ont. M4Y 1T5; or to: The President, Global Communications Ltd., 81 Barber Greene Road, Don Mills, Ont. M3C 2A3. Each network has an internal screening process and is vitally concerned with wide public acceptance of all its programming.

Another avenue of recourse is the Canadian Advertising Advisory Board, a self-regulating body with considerable power. Viewer complaints are handled by its Advertising Standards Council, 1240 Bay Street, Suite 302, Toronto, Ont. M5R 2A7.

If you feel that deception or fraud or undue persuasion is involved in a commercial, notify the police or your provincial consumer affairs ministry or the federal Department of Consumer and Corporate Affairs.

Those bathroom breaks. A Canadian Media Directors' Council survey of viewing behavior during commercial breaks and studio credits found that:

■ Up to 25 percent of women viewers and slightly fewer men do not watch the commercials.

■ The more that viewers like a program, the greater the number who leave the room during commercial breaks.

■ Commercials at the beginning get less attention than those during and following a program.

Cutting down on beer. Enforcement may be spotty but consumer action is forcing restraint on commercials suggesting that booze and good times go together. In 1978, Ontario cut the amount of beer and wine advertising permitted on radio and television. The weekly maximum for each company became 55 minutes (down from 120) on any one radio station, 30 minutes (from 90) on television.

The tobacco industry voluntarily suspended advertising from the national airwaves in 1971. In the print media, cigarette advertising is still king-size. But health authorities almost everywhere demand that consumers be warned of the hazards. Here's a sample of the international finger-wagging:

Canada. "Warning: Health and Welfare Canada advises that danger to health increases with amount smoked—avoid inhaling."

U.S.A. "Warning: The Surgeon-General has

Subliminal seduction

Wilson Bryan Key was teaching at the University of Western Ontario in London in 1974, when he alleged that ice cubes in a gin advertisement outlined the word "sex."

The charge was in *Subliminal Seduction*, a book in which Key claimed that we are all victims of subliminal stimuli by the media, advertising and public-relations agencies, corporations and governments.

Subliminal selling, Key said, deprives us of our right to a free choice of products. Moreover, it's an invasion of the privacy of the unconscious mind. (Subliminal persuasion involves deliberately induced sensations or perceptions of which we are not consciously aware but which subconsciously influence our actions.) Key was not the first to warn of subliminal advertising. American author Vance

Packard had done so in *The Hidden Persuaders* in the 1950s.

One critic described the subliminal technique as "the most alarming invention since the atomic bomb." *New Yorker* magazine warned that "minds and not just houses could be broken and entered."

Many down-to-earth people refuse to believe that subliminal communication exists. And the advertising world generally dismissed Key's charges, repeated in a later book, *Media Sexploitation*. Here Key charges that agencies are producing innocuous-looking advertisements containing hidden pornographic messages.

Key says the fact that no advertiser has ever sued him is evidence he's right. It could also mean advertisers think his allegations are ridiculous.

determined that cigarette smoking is dangerous to your health."

Britain. "H.M. Government Health Department's Warning: Cigarettes can seriously
damage your health."

In Ireland, where circumlocution is a national art, the warning is uncharacteristically
blunt: "Smokers die younger."

Tempting the toddlers. When the colored lights go up in the stores and the Santa
Claus parade jingles through town, the toy
manufacturers begin promoting full blast for
their biggest sale season of the year. And, just
as surely, a hard core of consumer activists
steps up the campaign to ban all advertising in
all media aimed at young children.

One leading figure in the struggle, Prof.
Marvin Goldberg of McGill University, Montreal, suggests that television advertising is
likely to make children materialistic, and can
set up conflicts in the home when children ask
for advertised toys that the parent doesn't approve of, or can't afford.

A nine-year survey by researchers from the
University of California, made public in 1979,
indicated that 4-year-olds who watch TV eat
up to 50 percent more sugared cereal and
snacks between meals than those who don't
watch. Manufacturers on both sides of the
border argue that the would-be regulators underestimate the intelligence of the modern
child. A major cereal producer points out that
the generation that grew up with Popeye the
Sailor cartoons did not acquire his famous ap-
petite for spinach.

In Canada, children's TV programming is
tightly regulated. The CBC excludes commercials from children's programs. All private
stations comply with the Broadcast Code for
Advertising to Children. They do not carry
advertising aimed at preschoolers during
weekday mornings, and at all times forbid any
direct incitement to buy; they also forbid endorsements from athletes or other celebrities.
All medication or vitamin commercials are
outlawed.

Quebec's wide-ranging consumer-protection law prohibits all television advertising
aimed at the pre-teen audience. A board scru-
tinizes all commercials.

'BAIT-AND-SWITCH'

Attracted by an advertisement for a bargain-priced sewing machine, your wife is talked into buying a much more expensive model.

One of the most notorious marketing tactics is
"bait-and-switch" selling. The "bait" is usually a cleverly written advertisement for a bargain-priced product. Once you are in the store,
the sales staff push a higher-priced product.

The salesman may confide that the advertised product is not really a good buy: for a
few more dollars you can get a much better
appliance, a product better suited for use in a
superior household.

Bait-and-switch advertising is illegal. But it
is usually extremely difficult to prove. To get a
conviction, you will have to convince a court
that the advertiser had no intention of selling
the bargain sewing machine.

To protect himself from a bait-and-switch
accusation, the merchant will probably have a
reasonable quantity of the advertised item at
hand. What number is "reasonable" depends
on whether he's advertising grand pianos or
pantyhose. However, if you believe the operation is illegal, you should get in touch with
your local police. Your evidence will be valuable if they press charges.

LIMITED SUPPLIES

You were in the opening lineup for a sale on brand-name power saws. When you reached the counter, you were told the bargains had all been snapped up.

The "Sorry, sold out" gambit is a variant of
"bait-and-switch." Complain to the department head or the store manager. Threaten to
go to the Better Business Bureau or a government consumer agency. The bargain saw may
suddenly materialize. If it doesn't, carry out
your threats.

It's quite possible there were only a few "on
sale" saws and that they have been sold. In

this case, the reputable merchant should still make good on his advertisement.

A Montreal man rushed to a department store that had advertised mattresses at a discount. They were all gone, but when he complained to a local Action Line columnist he was supplied with a mattress at the advertised price. A store spokesman explained that the mattresses were, in fact, sold out when the customer arrived, but that he should have been given a more expensive one at the advertised price.

The customer had accused the store of false advertising. He was told that if the store had only one mattress at the advertised price, its promotion was still within the law. False, no; misleading, maybe.

Door-crasher specials. Some stores protect themselves by stressing that there are only a few items available at the sale price. These "door crashers" or "opening specials" are gambits to get shoppers into the store in the hope they'll make other purchases. Such stores ensure they have a strictly limited supply of the bargains.

PHONY 'SALES'

A supermarket is advertising a special on New Zealand lamb chops. You know the price is lower elsewhere.

The federal Department of Consumer and Corporate Affairs has repeatedly warned business about "sale" prices. If they don't represent a genuine reduction, trouble can follow. Referring to an "ordinary selling price" that is not the regular open-market price is an offense.

If a product is advertised at a sale price of $10, "regular price $20," when the regular price on the open market is really $15, the store can be prosecuted, even though the customer is saving $5.

A Toronto store that advertised, "Here's that $300 camera you've always wanted . . . $159" was fined $1,500 when it was proved that the camera usually sold for $175.

One of Canada's largest rug merchants was fined $22,500 in 1978 for false and misleading advertising four years earlier. The company had advertised 10 nonexistent sales with such slogans as, "Pre-inventory sale," or "Buy for as low as one-half price," even though there were no real reductions throughout that year.

A Calgary furniture store tagged a sofa and chair set: "Our low price, $599," and "Why pay $899?" The regular price for sets of comparable quality and style was much lower than $899 and the company was fined $2,500.

Any prosecution is bad for the public image of a business or even of a whole industry. Almost everyone agrees that self-regulation is preferable to increased government surveillance and regulation. The Advertising Standards Council (ASC), a standing committee of the Canadian Advertising Advisory Board, encourages the industry to regulate itself better.

In a recent six-month period, the ASC ruled that in 24 of 157 referred cases, the advertising was misleading. One example was a sports store advertisement for an item at the "lowest price ever," when the store had sold the item for less at a previous date. The store agreed to supply the item at the lower price.

In cases where the merchant is noncooperative, the CAAB advises the media not to accept his advertising. They are almost certain to take the advice.

A supermarket is entitled to advertise a lamb-chop sale if the price (say $1.89 a pound) is less than the regular, open-market price (say $2). The fact that another store has a better sale on lamb chops that week doesn't make your supermarket guilty of an offense.

The outcome can be different if the open-market price is $1.89 and the supermarket maintains that its $1.89 is a sale price. You should first discuss the matter with the store manager. If your charges are right, he is unlikely to risk the penalties for false and misleading advertising and will probably correct the misinformation—or lower his prices—promptly.

If you don't get satisfaction, you could provide details of the "sale" to the federal Department of Consumer and Corporate Affairs in Ottawa and to the ASC.

The advertiser's code

Many industrial and retail organizations and all major advertisers, advertising agencies and media groups, including the Canadian Association of Broadcasters and the Canadian Daily Newspaper Publishers' Association, subscribe to this Code of Advertising Standards.

The code avoids the subjective area of taste, which is difficult to pinpoint, and in which personal judgment plays an important part. But participating organizations agree to discourage advertising of questionable taste, or advertising that is deliberately irritating in its content or method of presentation.

Violations are arbitrated by the Advertising Standards Council. Uncooperative offenders may be deprived of normal advertising outlets.

False or misleading advertising. No advertisement shall be prepared, or be knowingly accepted, that contains false, misleading, unwarranted or exaggerated claims—either directly or by implication. Advertisers and advertising agencies must be prepared to substantiate their claims.

Public decency. No advertisement shall be prepared, or be knowingly accepted, that is vulgar, suggestive or, in any way, offensive to public decency.

Superstitions and fears. No advertisement shall be prepared, or be knowingly accepted, that is calculated to exploit the superstitious, or to play on fears to mislead the consumer into the purchase of the advertised commodity or service.

Exploitation of human misery. No advertisement shall be prepared, or be knowingly accepted, that offers false hope in the form of a cure or relief for the mentally or physically handicapped, either on a temporary or permanent basis.

Price claims. No advertisement shall be prepared, or be knowingly accepted, that makes misleading or inaccurate presentations of actual and comparative prices.

Testimonials. No advertisement shall be prepared, or be knowingly accepted, that contains false or misleading testimonials, or that does not reflect the real choice of the person giving the testimonial. Advertisers and agencies must be prepared to produce evidence in support of the claims made in any testimonial advertisement.

Disparaging claims. No advertisement shall be prepared, or be knowingly accepted, that unfairly disparages products or services of other advertisers. Substantiation is always required where comparisons are made with competing products or services.

Professional or scientific claims. No advertisement shall be prepared, or be knowingly accepted, that distorts the true meaning of statements made by professionals or scientific authorities. Advertising claims should not be made to appear to have a scientific basis they do not truly possess. Scientific terms, technical quotations, etc., should be used in general advertising only with a full sense of responsibility to the lay public.

Guarantees. No advertisement shall be prepared, or be knowingly accepted, offering a guarantee or warranty, unless the guarantee or warranty is fully explained as to the name of the guarantor or warrantor, conditions and limits, or it is indicated where such information can be obtained.

Advertising to children. No advertisement shall be prepared, or be knowingly accepted, that would result in damage—physical, mental or moral—to children.

Imitation. No advertisement shall be prepared, or be knowingly accepted, that deliberately imitates the copy, slogans, or illustrations of other advertisers and is apt to mislead the consumer.

Bait advertising. No advertisement shall be prepared, or be knowingly accepted, that does not give the consumer a fair opportunity to purchase the goods or services advertised at the terms or prices represented.

TESTIMONIALS

A sports celebrity tells you privately he never touches the beer he praises in advertisements. That sounds like outright fraud.

Testimonials and endorsements promoting the sale of merchandise can be probed under the Combines Investigation Act. The public is particularly susceptible to representations by prominent persons, and such advertising could be questionable, and possibly illegal, if the person giving the endorsement is not using the product regularly at the time.

The advertising would be even more open to question if the endorsement suggests an entire line of products is reliable, when the celebrity has been using only some of the company's goods.

When a hockey star gives a testimonial, the public assumes he is being paid for it. It's not misleading, therefore, that the advertising copy doesn't mention the payment. It would be misleading if he gave the impression he was giving his endorsement voluntarily.

Snacks for champs. Olympic champion skier Nancy Greene Raine advertises candy bars, skis, ski boots and ski holidays. She endorses only products she has used, and insists on personal contact with the people behind them. Her candy endorsements earned her about $20,000 a year.

Olympic decathlon champion Bruce Jenner, criticized for endorsing a breakfast cereal, headed off a false-advertising action by proclaiming publicly that he did, indeed, eat the stuff for breakfast.

British Columbia sportscaster Ted Reynolds made commercials for Dupex Energy Ltd., a Port Coquitlam insulated-window firm, after being shown written endorsements from satisfied customers and seeing samples of the company's work. When the firm folded, leaving dozens of customers with no windows and no refunds, Reynolds said:

"I really don't think it's fair for anybody to blame me for what happened. I've been duped as much as anybody, except I didn't lose any money. I was taken in—my services were taken in. I'm very upset about the thing . . . but there's absolutely nothing I can do. I'll be very, very cautious about such things in the future."

A spokesman for the Department of Consumer and Corporate Affairs, pointing out the difficulty of obtaining proof of the truthfulness of personal endorsements, cites these hypothetical examples of an actor promoting a cold remedy:

■ The actor says that nine out of 10 persons recommend the remedy for a cold. The company will have to prove this statement of fact or face prosecution for misleading advertising.

■ The actor, in character as a doctor, recommends the remedy to his patients. This implies that members of the medical profession endorse the product. The advertiser will have to show that there's a doctor somewhere who holds that opinion. If most doctors say the remedy is useless, the opinion of one will not be considered representative of the profession.

■ The actor, posing as a consumer, says he always takes the cold remedy because it works. It will have to be proved that this opinion is held by more than one actual consumer.

INVOLUNTARY 'ENDORSEMENT'

Your daughter once visited a local disco. Now her photograph is being featured in the club's advertisements.

Unless your daughter gave written authorization for the commercial use of the photograph, she could sue for what amounts to an invasion of her privacy. At the very least, she can insist that the advertisement be withdrawn, or that she be paid a fee.

If a photographer had taken her picture for use in a news story, she would have no recourse. Nobody holds copyright to his or her likeness. If you are physically harassed by a photographer, that's different. It could be grounds for an assault charge.

Personalities in the public eye are conceded the right to profit from exploitation of their fame. It's part of their business. They can (and do) sue for damages when their photographs are used commercially. But even they don't always win. One such was football player Bobby Krouse of the Hamilton Tiger-Cats.

He was photographed by a newsman, who sold the photo to a car manufacturer, who used it in a promotion. Krouse knew nothing of the deal, had given no consent, and received no compensation. The shot didn't show his face—but it did show his number (14).

The player sued on the grounds that his recognizable back was being used to sell cars, and that no other company would now hire him for a similar purpose. He claimed he was being deprived of potential earnings.

After long litigation, the appeal division of the Ontario Supreme Court ruled that the photograph had not exploited Krouse's personality; it was merely a shot of participants in a team sport.

A subsequent suit involved George Athans, Jr., a world water-skiing champion. In 1971, Athans had a promotional photograph taken, which was widely used around the world. Four years later, a water-ski camp sought his promotional services and the camp's advertising agency made a drawing of the now famous photo. The deal fell through but the agency used the drawing on the camp's brochure anyhow.

Athans, who was not identified on the draw-

Getting action

The Department of Consumer and Corporate Affairs investigates complaints about false or misleading advertising and prosecutes offenders. Another avenue for complaints is the advertising industry's self-regulating Advertising Standards Council, which provides complainants with this form. Advertisers are likely to abide by rulings of the council: It advises the media not to accept advertising from those who don't.

Complaint Notice

Français au verso

Product or service: _ABC Coats_

Date advertisement appeared: _May 22 to 25, 1979_

Where it appeared: ☑ TV ☐ Newspaper* ☐ Magazine* ☐ Radio ☐ Outdoor ☐ Transit ☐ Other
(*Please attach clipping)

Name of Publication or Station: _CXYZ TV_

Please investigate this advertisement which in my opinion breaks the Canadian Advertising Standards Code because: _The commercial claims that everything in the store is reduced by 30% to 60%, but price tags on most coats show reductions of only 5% to 10%._

Name _Sally Roe,_

Address _100 Maple Street,_

City _Mississauga,_ Zone _____ Province _Ontario._

Advertising Standards Council, 1240 Bay Street, Toronto, Ontario M5R 2A7

ing, sued for loss of potential earnings and won. The judge ruled that damages were deserved for "an aspect of the tort of appropriation of personality."

The key difference between the Krouse and Athans cases, explained the judge, was that football is a team effort, whereas water-skiing is an individual sport. In the car promotion, the manufacturer sought an advantage, not in association with Krouse as an individual but with the game of professional football.

The judge noted that in neither case was there an attempt to associate the athlete with a company's product. But Athans's exclusive right to market his personality had been invaded. He was awarded 10 cents for every brochure distributed.

DECEPTIVE ILLUSTRATIONS

You are misled by a refrigerator-sale ad showing a higher-priced model than the one on sale.

In the highly competitive marketplace, the merchant is granted the right to "puff." Only the most naive shopper would plank down her money for a refrigerator on the basis of an illustration alone; you are expected to inspect the item—unless you are relying on an iron-clad money-back warranty.

A glance at your local paper should convince you that if every retailer had to hire a photographer to depict each advertised item, the cost of the product would soar. Many advertisers use a newspaper's stock library of commonly used items.

When an advertiser uses a picture of a more expensive item than the one he's selling, he usually protects himself with some phrase such as "Not exactly as shown." If the print is too fine, or placed too far from the picture, it could be considered deceptive.

And it's when the advertisement, or its illustration, deliberately intends to deceive, or would be classed as deception by the average reasonable consumer, that the question of misleading advertising crops up. While this is a gray area legally, the Canadian Advertising Advisory Board tells all advertisers to avoid

it by illustrating the actual item on sale. And the board wields enough quasi-legal power to bring repeat offenders to heel.

If you feel that you were deliberately deceived by an illustration in an advertisement, detail your experience when you tried to buy the item, and send this information and the advertisement to the Marketing Practises Office of the Department of Consumer and Corporate Affairs in Ottawa, or to any of the regional offices in St. John's, Halifax, Moncton, Quebec, Montreal, Toronto, Hamilton, London, Winnipeg, Regina, Edmonton or Vancouver.

The Ontario office receives some 3,600 complaints a year, and in a recent nine-month period won 37 convictions out of 40 prosecutions.

Wardair, Canada's largest charter airline, was prosecuted in 1979 for false advertising in that it failed to supply reasonable numbers of seats on overseas flights after advertising bargain fares. When some passengers tried to book on specific departure days, they were told these flights were already full.

Judge Robert Dnieper dismissed the case because the advertisements had advised potential clients to check for flight availability. There was a fine-print warning: "Some flights may be sold out."

Said the judge: "I don't know what else they could have done. This would not mislead even the ignorant if the person reading the advertisement took care to read all of it."

MISPRINTS

A department store advertised a sale on lawn mowers at $19.99. When you rushed to grab the bargain, you were told there had been a typographical error and the price was really $99.99.

There's a popular misconception that when an error in the price of an item appears in an advertisement, the retailer is obliged to sell at least one item at the erroneous price.

Not so, says the Canadian Advertising Advisory Board. "An advertisement is not a contract. There is no contract until a purchase has been made and money handed over."

We are all fallible—and that includes the typesetter and the retailer. Who hasn't seen typographical errors in the press? You have an obligation to be fair to the vendor just as he has to be fair to you. It's not a one-way street.

An error in an advertisement, especially when a price is involved, is usually corrected as quickly as possible. When a store makes a mistake, an apology and correction are customarily given the next day. If a newspaper is at fault, the error is usually corrected in the next edition.

INDECENCY

Your weekly newspaper sells advertising space for X-rated movies, strip clubs, and dubious dating services.

Freedom of the press is specifically guaranteed by the Canadian Bill of Rights and so, subject only to the law, a publisher, writer or broadcaster may "publish" anything he likes. This includes advertisements. Most advertising departments will reject advertisements that they think are highly exaggerated or in bad taste.

According to the Code of Ethics of the Canadian Advertising Advisory Board: "No advertisement shall be prepared, or be knowingly accepted, that is vulgar, suggestive or in any way offensive to public decency." Advertisements cannot "exploit the superstitions or play on fears." But it can be difficult—if not impossible—to lay down firm legal definitions of contemporary public taste and "decency." (*See* Chapter 5, "The question of morals.")

The several provincial press councils will investigate complaints about anything that appears in print—in either editorial or advertising pages—in their member newspapers. The councils have no enforcement powers but considerable moral suasion.

In recent years, human rights legislation has put many curbs on advertising ("charwoman" is out; "cleaning person" or "building maintenance person" is in) and has led to some interesting civil and criminal actions.

When *The Vancouver Sun* refused to run an advertisement for Gay Liberation, the local homosexual alliance pursued the case to the Supreme Court of Canada—which ruled in favor of the paper. Earlier, *The Toronto Star* had refused a similar advertisement, but eventually published it after the Ontario Press Council sided with the gays.

Most daily papers currently compromise—

Does sex sell?

The *Journal of Advertising Research* examined this question in 1978. Five advertisements were shown to a group of male volunteers. The first advertisement was a pastoral scene. The rest contained illustrations of a girl in increasing degrees of nakedness.

The volunteers remembered more brand names from the first advertisement than they did from the others. It seemed that the sexy advertisements distracted them from that all-important brand detail.

Do nude girls, as in *Playboy* or *Penthouse* magazines, promote better brand recall than a partly clad model? There was no significant difference in this test result.

Finally, the study separated the volunteers into two groups. One consisted of people with a liberal attitude toward nakedness. The second group was fundamentally opposed to nudity in public.

Again the tests revealed no substantial difference in the evaluation of the selling impact of the advertisements.

So, if sex doesn't sell, are those advertisements that show bikini beauties in sports cars really just a waste of money?

The storm at the Pepperpot

Background

Several decades ago, it was not unusual to see signs: "No Jews Need Apply" or "House for Rent—No Negroes." Today, society views such sentiments with great distaste and few people would dare express them publicly. Moreover, such signs are now illegal. But the defenders of human rights are maintaining an eagle-eye watch and one case that raised a furor involved a drive-in restaurant called Sambo's Pepperpot in Creighton, Sask., a small town near the Manitoba border.

In August 1974, Barry Singer, a white man, complained that the entrance sign—the restaurant's name with a small black figure in a chef's hat and a grass skirt—contravened the province's Human Rights Code. The restaurant's advertisements, including matchbooks and automobile stickers, also depicted the Sambo caricature with the phrase: " 'jez ain't none better!' "

The Saskatchewan Human Rights Commission asked the owners, Pennywise Foods Ltd., to change the name and the caricature. The company refused, and the commission appointed a Board of Inquiry. Hearings began in December 1975.

It was all a tempest in a teapot, the restaurateurs told the inquiry chairman, Judge Tillie Taylor. The sign was just a name; the figure, a catchy, well-recognizable symbol. Neither malice nor discrimination was intended toward anyone.

The commission lawyer argued that Sambo was a negative stereotype of a plantation slave—docile, stupid, irresponsible, lazy and chronically given to lying and exaggeration—and as such discriminatory to black people.

Indians from a nearby reserve testified that the Sambo sign belittled all minority groups with dark skin. Laura Erikse said that the sign made her feel "put down" or inferior.

The caricature demeaned all blacks, said complainant Singer. It made him ashamed of being a member of white society.

Judgment

The Sambo caricature reinforced prejudices of blacks as childish, funny, and inferior, Judge Taylor found. Such negative stereotyping endangered a black person's opportunity of finding a responsible job. She ordered that the Sambo sign be taken down.

Pennywise Foods Ltd. asked the Court of Queen's Bench to quash the order on the grounds that improper evidence was presented. In May 1977, the appeal was upheld, thus setting aside the Board of Inquiry ruling.

The Human Rights Commission then turned to the Saskatchewan Court of Appeal and on May 29, 1978, the three-member court restored the Board of Inquiry ruling.

dates of homosexual organizations' meetings are published; promotional advertising for such groups is not.

Classified columns now often contain explicitly worded appeals for "companions." No advertising manager would have accepted such advertisements 10 years ago.

Of course, just about every newsstand today displays glossy magazines containing advertisements that might have been rejected by a Sodom and Gomorrah *Times*.

All health-product advertisements come under close scrutiny. If an advertiser makes extravagant claims for a remedy, the advertising departments of all media will probably want documented proof before accepting the advertisement. The word "cure" is forbidden.

Dancing in the dark. In 1979, a dance studio in Ottawa was fined $171,000, and the manager was jailed for a year, for exploiting the studio's clientele. The prosecution, by the Ontario Ministry of Consumer and Commercial Relations, was for violations of the Ontario Business Practises Act. Thirty-two charges involved sex, lies, deceit, misrepresentation, use of undue pressure, exaggeration, innuendo and ambiguity.

After two or three "teaser" lessons, lonely "students" were pressed to buy courses costing from $800 to $6,000. In 29 weeks, more than $300,000 was taken in. One woman spent $15,000 in three months; another was advised to sell her house to pay for lessons.

The dance instructors, who were not individually charged, "had no scruples whatever" in pressuring clients to buy the courses. "They were thieves and fraud artists," said Judge Jean-Marie Bordeleau. One former instructor testified that they were told to "snuggle in to get that body contact" and that some instructors had sexual relations with students to help sell lessons. One 37-year-old was told he would have his pick of beautiful women if he learned to dance. After the trial ended, the Ontario ministry issued a consumer-guidance booklet entitled *Beware the Dream Merchants*. Self-improvement courses could be positive, it stated, but they could also be used to exploit those made vulnerable by loneliness, insecurity or a sense of inferiority.

Buying on credit

Consumer credit is the oil that keeps the wheels of modern industry turning. At the end of 1979, Canadians collectively owed about $30 billion in this kind of debt.

Citizens and their governments have embraced the concept of paying later for goods and services to be used and enjoyed right now. This had always been the privilege of the thin slice of society known as the "upper classes," to whom the butcher, baker and candlestick maker allowed generous credit terms while demanding cash on the barrelhead from the "common masses."

Dramatic changes took place after World War II. Military demand had multiplied our industrial plants and they needed a new army of peacetime consumers. Millions of young Canadians had been wrenched out of traditional backgrounds and life styles by the war, and homilies such as "A penny saved is a penny earned" fell on increasingly deaf ears. Consumer-credit agencies proliferated, allowing individuals to obtain goods, services or cash on a deferred-payment basis. ("Consumer credit" does not include commercial loans and mortgages.)

Financing today is provided by a web of banks, credit unions, caisses populaires, finance companies, department stores and other retailers, and by the credit-card companies. The latter are increasingly controlled by the chartered banks with their Chargex-Visa and Master Charge cards. The American Express card is now accepted in lieu of cash in 72 countries.

As the use of "plastic money" spread, it was met by the countervailing forces of the new "consumerism." Governments were spurred to tighten surveillance and regulation of the money flow. Provinces regulate the credit industry within their borders and Ottawa keeps a stern eye on all federally chartered companies including banks. Distribution of unsolicited credit cards is strictly controlled.

Consumer activists insist on saying "debt cards" rather than credit cards. It's true that many consumers use their cards as a variety of personal loan—at 18 percent per annum.

Banks, having energetically exploited the consumer loan field for years, finally introduced their cards to increase their share of the consumer credit market. From the consumer's point of view, the only major difference between taking out a loan and running a debit balance with a credit-card company is that the interest rate is higher for the latter.

All credit contracts must provide certain basic information in language understandable to the average borrower. Keep in mind that all credit deals—the loan for your new car as well as the $100 you borrowed from your Uncle Harry—involve contracts, whether written or not.

Any firm advertising loans or installment payments must make clear to you both the full cost of borrowing and the annual interest rate. You may think you can handle an interest charge of 2 percent a month on an outstanding balance, but realizing that's 24 percent a year may cause you to think twice about making a purchase.

The federal Small Loans Act restricts moneylenders other than the banks to a maximum scale of interest on loans up to the $1,500 level. Over that figure, it's every man for himself. Installment-plan schemes such as a "revolving charge account" at a department store are not regulated.

All provinces restrict to some extent the right of the creditor to demand full payment of an installment debt immediately, or to repossess the goods involved, if payments are late. Your provincial consumer affairs department will explain your rights in detail. If you had arranged an installment-payment plan, then decided to pay it off after cash became available unexpectedly, you must be granted a rebate of a portion of the precalculated interest charges.

Almost everyone has some life-insurance protection but many persons don't realize that insurance companies will loan money up to the cash-surrender value of the policy. The interest rate is usually lower than that obtainable elsewhere because the company has a vested interest in keeping the policy in force. Usually, you will be offered additional term insurance, which will pay off the loan in the event of your death.

But the plastic-money revolution rolls on. A motorist in British Columbia pulled into a gas station one wintry day and asked for a 59-cent windshield scraper. He found he had no cash in his pocket. "Why not use your credit card?" the attendant suggested.

"Good idea," said the motorist. He fished out a card and used it as a scraper to clear his frosted windshield. Then he handed the 59-cent scraper back to the attendant and drove away.

CREDIT RATING

You have no debts and a good income, yet your application for a loan has been turned down.

This is an occasional paradox in today's marketplace: you pay all your bills on time, use cash when you buy, and own no credit cards. You have baffled the computers of the credit bureaucracy. You have no credit rating, the track record on which moneylenders judge your ability and willingness to repay.

Of course, if the company knows you as someone who always pays his bills, your application for credit will be granted immediately. But, outside the small towns, most business today is done between strangers and you will have to go through a detailed check. Firms usually hire credit-investigation agencies to do this, and it can take a long time.

The investigator will check out where you live and whether you own your home. Your work record is vital. The employee who has held a job for five years is a better risk than

one who was hired six months ago. A recent study showed accountants were the best bet for paying off debts. Farm laborers came at the bottom of the scale. Policemen ranked right in the middle, with lawyers and judges only slightly higher.

Credit agencies base "ratings" on the three Cs: character, capacity and capital—character being the willingness to pay, and the others having to do with the ability. Some creditors add a fourth C: conditions. Is your work environment likely to change in a way you can't control? Is the trade, industry or plant that provides your "capacity" stable or in decline?

A national network of affiliated credit bureaus keeps a file on the paying habits of most adult Canadians and sells this information to prospective lenders. The system is used by insurance companies and banks, as well as by retailers, and its files can have a tremendous impact on your life. Your local credit bureau must show you your file (or mail you the information), and tell you where the information came from. In most provinces, you can dispute any wrong or questionable information. The bureau must verify details or add to them to make your file accurate and complete, but you can't force the bureau to destroy it. Except in Quebec, Alberta, New Brunswick and the Territories, credit granters must notify customers that a credit investigation will take place.

If you are having credit difficulties, you'll find that the most ready lenders are the consumer finance companies. These companies make some 1.5 million loans—averaging $600 per loan—to Canadians annually. Their interest rates on sums under $1,500 are controlled under the federal Small Loans Act, but they are not cheap. Rates are on an inverse sliding scale: maximum interest allowed on a $300 loan is 24 percent annually; a $1,500 loan will probably cost you about 15.2 percent a year. In a recent year, finance companies reported profits of $1.5 billion before taxes.

Apart from rich relatives, the best people to borrow from are credit unions or chartered banks. Their interest rates fluctuate—but will almost certainly be lower than elsewhere. (*See* "Bargains in borrowing" in Chapter 30.)

LATE PAYMENT

You went to Europe for a holiday and missed installments of your car loan. Now the bank wants the balance paid in full.

Loan contracts generally stipulate that the entire loan becomes due and payable if payments are missed. The law demands that these conditions be clear to you at the time the loan is negotiated. We are all bound by the terms of the contracts we sign. Carelessness or poor memory are not legitimate excuses.

If you are two payments behind, call at the bank, explain the circumstances, and work out arrangements to catch up. If you have a steady job and the ability to pay, the chances are the crisis can be averted—maybe by extending the term of the loan.

If you were withholding payment because of dissatisfaction with your car, the law may help you. At one time, a moneylender could dissociate himself from any complaint about a product. And the maker of the product, having received payment from the lender, could not be brought to task either. But under amendments to the Bills of Exchange Act, a lender cannot sue without honoring the terms of the purchase, which might include the satisfaction of the customer under any warranty.

INABILITY TO MEET PAYMENTS

You have accumulated too many debts and won't be able to meet all your installment payments next month.

Don't hide the true state of affairs from your creditors. If one obligation is particularly threatening, arrange to meet that creditor and discuss your difficulty. Don't let him learn of it through missed payments.

Since he doesn't want the sale to turn sour or to lose you as a long-term customer, he may suggest that you refinance your purchase. He may allow you to make smaller payments over a longer period of time, which means you'll pay more interest in the long run, but your credit rating remains intact. *One of the sad facts of our "credit" society is that the less you can afford to pay, the more it costs.*

Debt consolidation may be your answer. In Ontario, judges of the Small Claims Court have the power to make what is known as a consolidation order for defendants before the court: an officer of the court will pool your bills and decide how much you can afford to pay each week or month. This amount will be divided among your creditors according to their share of your total obligation. As long as the court order is in effect, those to whom you owe money will not be allowed to take any other steps to recover it from you (such as forcing you into bankruptcy).

Under The Bankruptcy Act, debtors in Alberta, British Columbia, Manitoba, Nova Scotia, Saskatchewan, Prince Edward Island and the Northwest Territories can apply for a similar consolidation order to a special clerk of their County or District Court, thus avoiding the full impact and penalties of bankruptcy. Some provisions of the Code of Civil Procedure (provisions previously known as the Lacombe Law) help debtors in Quebec. Here a debtor may deposit a sizable portion of his salary into a court office within five days of being paid. The money is distributed periodically among creditors until the debt is cleared. In New Brunswick and Newfoundland, a debtor can *propose* to pay off only a portion of his debt over a specified time. If the creditors accept the proposal, the balance of the debt is wiped out.

This system has many advantages. For one, it's simple. You are dealing with only one collector—the court. You don't have to juggle your bills, paying an installment here and another there to keep your creditors at bay. It also protects you against harassment by professional bill collectors.

Free financial advice. You are legally bound to honor all debts legally contracted, and the law is on your side as long as you are making a sincere effort to pay. In a bankruptcy, everyone loses.

A wide range of free financial counseling is available. Provincial consumer departments provide assistance to debtors. (*See* Section 10,

How to get plastic money

This Master Charge application (Bank of Montreal, Provincial Bank of Canada, Canada Trust, Victoria and Grey Trust) is self-explanatory. Anyone who fills out one of these is placing just about all relevant details of his background and finances into the Credit Bureau files forever.

Note particularly the marital questions. They ask for the "nearest relative not living with you"— just so they can floor the thief who may steal your card. That's not information the thief could have.

In Canada alone, Master Charge is honored at some 125,000 stores, restaurants and service stations, and some 2.2 million Canadians prefer to use this card, for which there is no fee, rather than carry large amounts of cash.

TEAR OFF HERE BEFORE MAILING
PLEASE PRINT CLEARLY AND COMPLETE IN FULL

Master Charge Application

The First Canadian Bank
Bank of Montreal   E9

□ Mr. □ Mrs. □ Miss □ Ms.	First Name	Middle Initials	Last Name	Social Insurance Number

Address	Apt. Number	City	Province	Postal Code

Yrs. at Present Address	Own □	Rent □	Other □	Monthly Rent or Mortgage $	Home	Telephone	Office (Ext.)	Date of Birth /D /M /Y

Previous Address			How Long?	□ Married □ Single	□ Divorced	☑ Separated □ Widowed

Present Occupation	Gross Monthly Salary $	Other Monthly Income $	Spouse's Name	Number of Dependents Ex. Spouse

Name and Address of Present Employer	How Long?

Previous Occupation	Previous Employer and Address	How Long?

Spouse's Occupation	Name and Address of Spouse's Employer	How Long?	Gross Monthly Salary $

Bank	Address of Branch	Account Number Type

Name of Nearest Relative Not Living With Me	Address	Relationship

Credit References

Name	Creditor Address	Account Number	Original Amount	Balance owing	Monthly Payments

Home Mortgaged By:	Estimated Value $	Mortgage Amount $	Amount Owing $

Life Insured □ Yes □ No	Car Year and Make	Province	Driver's Licence Number

A card for your spouse? Check here and have your spouse sign below □	Correspondence □ English □ French	Send Statement to □ Home □ Office

The undersigned or each of them, if more than one, certifies the above information to be true and correct, requests your Master Charge card and renewals or replacements thereof from time to time at your discretion, **by signing below accepts as notice in writing of and consents to the obtaining from any credit reporting agency or any person such information as the Bank may require at any time in connection with the credit hereby applied for** and consents to the disclosure at any time of any information concerning the undersigned to any credit reporting agency, or to any credit grantor with whom the undersigned has financial relations and if a Master Charge card is issued, agrees to abide by the terms and conditions of the Bank of Montreal Master Charge Card Agreement accompanying the Master Charge card and set out on the reverse hereof. If card is requested in spouse's name, each of the undersigned applicants shall be jointly and severally liable for indebtedness incurred through use of charge cards issued pursuant to this application.

X _____ X _____

Signature of Applicant	Signature of Spouse (if Applicable)	Date

FOR MASTER CHARGE USE ONLY

S. _____	No. of Cards _____	Credit Officer _____
6/77 R. _____	Transit No. _____	Credit Limit Assigned _____

"Effective complaining.") Your banker has a stake in your solvency and your union officers can probably help. Many communities have professional credit counselors who will help you organize your finances and fight your way out of trouble. If you are one of the five million Canadians who belong to a credit union, you may be able to get a loan on favorable terms to pay off your high-interest debts.

Dunned for debt. It is never pleasant. The first time you don't meet a payment you'll get a polite reminder. Then the letters become more insistent, even peremptory. You will be reminded that your credit rating is one of your most valuable assets. Lose it, and you'll find yourself being forced to pay cash for almost all your purchases. You may also be hit with a late-payment fee which can range from 18 to 24 percent in yearly interest.

If the account is still not paid, it will probably be turned over to a collection agency, which receives a commission on what it collects. The agency's tactics will include blunt letters and telephone calls, and it will not hesitate to take you to court where it is almost certain to get a judgment with costs against you.

It is far easier and more pleasant to deal with the retailer's credit manager, who has an incentive to renegotiate your contract so that your installments are manageable and you remain a customer.

About the worst thing you can do is rush out and borrow more money to get you through the next couple of months. That kind of money is usually not too hard to find, but the interest rate is high. If you are having trouble paying your present installments, adding to your costs won't help.

The collection game. Bill collectors are not likely to win any popularity contests, although they believe they are much maligned and that their role in the national economy is not understood and appreciated. They point out that agencies collected $68.2 million in Ontario alone during one recent year, putting cash in the coffers of some hard-pressed companies.

The largest of the agencies—FCA International of Montreal—charges retailers 33.3 per-

cent of money collected if the last payment was made less than 12 months ago; beyond that, it's 50 percent. The company's profit in a recent year was $1.9 million.

Even though the collectors worry about their image, relatively few written complaints about harassment are received by the provincial licensing departments. In Ontario, where some 30,000 telephone calls are placed by the 100 registered agencies every day, regulators receive an average of 160 written complaints a year, half of which are found to be justified. Statistics are not available on the number of verbal complaints.

Bill-collecting agencies may not collect more than the amount owing; may not cause the debtor undue anxiety or distress; may not communicate with the debtor's employer about the debt and may not call the debtor in the middle of the night.

REPOSSESSION

You couldn't meet the installment payments on your furniture and it was repossessed. Now the company claims you still owe $500.

When your grandparents wanted a new stove or a dining-room suite, they saved until they had enough money to buy it. If a customer furnishing a home paid cash today, most retailers would be startled.

Some retailers offer to divide the list price into installments, with no "carrying charges," or to delay the start of payments for several months. But the sensible shopper realizes that the vendor must somehow recover his financing costs.

When credit terms are offered, the law requires the seller to state the full costs, including the annual interest rate, in straightforward language. The retailer who offers a no-carrying-charge installment plan will sometimes substitute a discount off the list price for cash.

Installment buying, even with its pitfalls, can be a boon. The amount of cash needed for a down payment is small. You get immediate possession, and can enjoy the use of the item while you pay off the balance. In times of steep inflation it can make good financial sense. The price of a major article may spiral, but your payments remain fixed.

Usually, the item passes into your possession when you sign an agreement to pay the remainder of the cost plus interest at regular intervals. It's called a conditional sale. But ownership remains with the seller (the "vendor" in legalese) until the entire amount has been paid. If you fail to pay your installments, the vendor can take back ("repossess") the furniture (or whatever) and sell it elsewhere. He may also be entitled to damages for any loss he suffers on the resale.

If you had bought $1,500 worth of furniture and defaulted after paying $500, the vendor might be able to resell it for only $500. He would be out $500 on the transaction.

Whether you could be sued successfully for that remaining $500 would depend on where you live. Ontario, Saskatchewan, Alberta, British Columbia and Quebec have what are known as "seize or sue" regulations. In those provinces, the creditor can take back his goods *or* sue for the balance owing. He can't do both. The defaulter may also be liable for the vendor's costs for cartage or reselling.

Similar to the conditional sale but not much used these days is the sale by chattel mortgage: from the buyer's point of view, it's much the same. Instead of retaining ownership of the goods, the seller "lends" the buyer enough to complete the purchase so the buyer has legal ownership—but he mortgages the goods back to the seller as security for the loan. If the buyer defaults on the installment payments, the vendor calls the mortgage and repossesses the goods.

Young working couples often fall into a special kind of installment-buying trap. A large percentage of their joint income is committed to time payments for house, furniture, a new car. Then, because of pregnancy, an illness, a layoff or a strike, one partner ceases working and all those payments must be met from a single pay cheque.

Band on the rocks. A new rock group bought a $10,000 sound amplification system on time and had repaid $6,000 when the group

disbanded. The leader asked for extra time to re-form the group and resume payments, but the creditor repossessed the equipment.

The equipment was bought on a conditional sales contract and, although the governing regulations differ from province to province, this vendor had the right to take back the goods and try to resell them to someone else. If $7,500 of the debt had been paid, the seizure would probably have been blocked by the courts. In most provinces, after a certain portion of the total cost (usually two-thirds) is paid, merchandise cannot be seized without a judge's permission.

Once goods are repossessed, the vendor must hold them for a period during which the defaulting buyer can recover them by paying the outstanding balance plus expenses. If there's to be a resale, the original buyer must be given written notice, including a description of the goods and a statement of what is still due.

Assuming that the repossessed sound system was eventually sold for $5,000, the vendor would then have received $11,000 in all. He would be required to rebate $1,000, less his costs for repossessing and reselling, to the original buyer. Those costs would have to be strictly documented.

RESALE OF GOODS

You want to sell your television set, on which there are still payments outstanding.

You probably bought the set on a conditional sales contract or with a chattel mortgage. In the first case, you will not own the item until you have made all payments. In the second, the seller has loaned you the money to buy the set and taken a mortgage on it. In either case, your title to the set is not clear and the contract or mortgage will have been registered with the clerk of the County Court to protect the vendor should you try to sell the set.

If you made a sale, the person to whom you sold would have to give up possession on demand. It doesn't count that you neglected to mention that you lacked clear title to the set.

265

Your buyer could sue you, but he might not recover his money. The law holds that he should have made sure you had clear title. The company that sold you the television set would probably let him keep it if one of you paid the amount owed.

The moral is that if you buy secondhand items privately, be sure that the seller can pass clear title to you. Check at the courthouse if you're not sure.

BILLING ERRORS

On your most recent credit-card statement, there is an $85.06 charge that you did not incur.

The first credit cards were given to select customers in the 1920s by leading department stores and by the 1960s Diners Club and American Express were widely accepted. The

The retailer's ante in the credit card game

The company that accepts your credit card pays a fee to belong to a bank-card plan and rents the machine that prints the sales slip from your embossed card. The card company gets a commission—from 2.5 to 5 percent—on every sale charged to a credit card.

Formerly, many bank customers received unsolicited cards through the mail with letters saying that unless the bank heard otherwise, the cards would be considered valid. Some provinces now prohibit this practice; others require the issuer to offer the service in writing and get an affirmative response before sending out the card.

Card companies have erected a "computer curtain" to protect themselves against theft and fraud.

Merchants have a limit per purchase (usually $50) which they can allow without authorization from the nearest data center. When a purchase exceeds that sum, the merchant phones the card number, his own account number and the amount of the purchase, to an operator who punches the figures into a computer. If you are within your personal credit limit (the average is $800) and there are no other problems, the transaction will be approved. If the card being checked had been reported lost or stolen, the data-center operator switches the call to the security department.

This checkup goes through so quickly that the customer barely notices the time lag. If a Canadian cardholder makes a purchase in a European city, the query can be flashed across the Atlantic and the answer received in a matter of seconds. Major department stores and other retailers operating their own card systems have private linkups which respond just as quickly.

If your card is stolen in Vancouver (and you report the loss immediately), anyone attempting to use the card in Florida a day or so later is risking arrest by the local police. The data center whisks a coded warning to the merchant, and he will probably start taking as long as possible to "complete" the transaction. Meanwhile, the data center's security force is getting through to the local police headquarters. A radio call goes out to the nearest squad car, and the astonished thief may be apprehended before he can walk out of the store with his parcel.

Random checks are made to deter card thieves who try to beat the game by keeping purchases under $50. The card companies require some stores to get authorization for all transactions.

Some dishonest cashiers run off extra impressions from a credit card, forge the signature and exchange the forged slip for cash from the till. The forgery surfaces on the customer's next monthly statement, by which time the cashier has quit and vanished. The card-issuing bank then has to adjust the customer's balance and take the loss.

major Canadian banks introduced Chargex-Visa and Mater Charge in the 1970s and today more than 60 percent of Canadians own at least one credit card. Chargex now has 6.7 million cardholders and Master Charge 2.2 million. Millions more cards are issued by department stores and oil companies. The bank cards alone account for $5 billion a year in purchases and cash advances. The average transaction is for $30.

Chargex and Master Charge supply instructions and regulations, which include a customer-service telephone number for the data center, for use if your card is lost, or stolen. If you are disputing any entry on your statement, that number is your first complaint recourse. You should follow up with a written complaint—headed by the account number embossed on your card and including the reference number and date of the disputed transaction—within 15 days.

Dealing with any computerized operation can be frustrating but if your facts are right, you'll eventually win. The onus is on the credit-card company to prove that you did make the purchase listed—and it must be documentary proof. It must dig out of the files its copy of the retailer's sales slip—with your signature—and make it available to you for inspection. If it can't produce this document, it must remove the charge from your account.

Firms such as travel agencies and florists accept a reliable customer's credit-card number over the phone, and complete a sale without running the card through the little machine that produces the official sales slip. The firm relies on its customer not to challenge this charge on the credit-card statement, or to demand that the data center produce a signed sales slip.

Theoretically, it might also be possible to do the same thing if you found yourself without wallet and credit card when the time came to settle your bill in a restaurant or bar. If the manager was convinced of your identity and good character, and if his phone call to the data center confirmed that your account was in good standing, he might write in your account number (supplied by the data center) and have you sign the sales slip.

LOST OR STOLEN CARDS

Your credit card is stolen, and before you miss it, the thief forges your signature and runs up charges of more than $600.

If your card is lost, misplaced or stolen, you are obliged to inform the data center (or the issuing bank) as quickly as possible. You are responsible for the first $50 of unauthorized use, but card companies generally write the whole amount off. The merchant who accepts the card is responsible for verifying the signature on the sales slip against your sample signature on the back of the card.

Companies won't divulge figures for forgery losses, but the total is believed to be only one-tenth of 1 percent of annual volume.

CASH ADVANCES

You used your credit card to get a cash advance. Even though you repaid the amount a week later, your current statement shows that daily interest is still being charged on the amount of your advance.

There is a cost difference in using your credit card to get a cash advance and using it to make a purchase. Interest charges for a cash advance begin immediately, but for a purchase they don't begin for 25 days. In other words, if you pay off a purchase within 25 days, you pay no interest; if you pay off a cash advance in 25 days, you pay 25 days' interest.

To get a cash advance, produce a valid card at a member bank and you can draw cash whether or not you have an account at that bank branch. (Some travel cards, such as American Express, offer cash advances at hotels and some other establishments that honor the card.) If you want to pay off a cash advance quickly, you should take your payment into a member bank and ask the manager to handle the matter for you.

Normally, the data center's computer applies any payment received to outstanding interest charges first; to the oldest unpaid balance second; and to the current charges on your account last.

GARNISHEEING OF WAGES

Unexpected expenses compelled you to allow some bills to pile up and now one creditor is threatening to garnishee your wages.

An impatient creditor (or the agency to which he has passed your overdue account for collection) will generally launch a barrage of increasingly tough "dunning letters" and telephone calls. If that doesn't work, the last resort is to take your unpaid bill to court and ask that you be summoned to appear. Under oath, you must answer questions about your income and your ability to pay. If the overdue debt is proved, the magistrate will order you to settle up.

Your creditor may seek a garnishment (from Small Claims Court if the amount is within the court's limit) ordering your employer to deduct a certain percentage of your salary to be paid into court and applied to your debt. Other assets, including your bank account, may also be included in the order, and court costs will be added.

Having your wages garnisheed may jeopardize your position with some companies, although some provinces—British Columbia and Quebec, for example—will not permit a worker to be fired for that reason. All provinces regulate the percentage of your total wage that can be deducted to pay your debts. Generally, it's 30 percent, although it may vary, at the discretion of the judge, according to your marital status and personal circumstances.

Salaries of federal civil servants and judges cannot be garnisheed and neither can federal pensions, teachers' superannuation allowances, alimony, unemployment insurance or welfare payments.

POST-DATED CHEQUES

You forgot about a post-dated cheque you wrote three months ago. Now it has bounced and the creditor is threatening to sue.

It is an offense to issue a worthless cheque, but you can probably avoid criminal action by issuing a new cheque, assuming you have funds to cover it.

Issuing post-dated cheques can be a convenience for buyer and seller. Landlords often ask for a series of post-dated cheques to cover rent for a year. Some merchants use the system to cover payments under an installment plan.

Keep a record of any post-dated cheques which you issue. It's unpleasant to find your chequing account suddenly depleted by a forgotten cheque—and embarrassing if it bounces.

If the person to whom you issued a cheque misplaces it, then comes across it much later and presents it to the bank for payment, it will be refused as "stale-dated" if more than 180 days have passed.

When anyone accepts a cheque as payment of a debt, the payment is conditional on the cheque being honored by your bank. If it is not honored for any reason, the debt stands. If you refuse to issue a new cheque, your creditor can take legal action to recover his money.

22 Buying in the home

Consumers buy tens of millions of dollars' worth of goods and services every day—mostly from firms or individuals they know by experience or reputation. The share of this huge expenditure spent by consumers right in their own homes has been growing fast and may soon reach 20 percent of general merchandise sales.

In-home sales are generated by mail-order catalogues and brochures, "flyers" tossed on your porch, telephone campaigns, and door-to-door salesmen—our latter-day peddlers. It's a useful service for those who can't get to the stores regularly or who live far from metropolitan centers where sales volume reduces costs and increases the choice of goods and services.

Time for leisurely shopping has decreased since two wage-earners in a family became the rule rather than the exception. Many families now find it convenient to shop through catalogues and brochures, mailing in their orders and paying by personal cheque or by quoting account numbers from their credit cards. Some use time payments, despite the high cost of this kind of financing.

A cable-TV system in some North American cities allows consumers to inspect sale merchandise on their television sets at home. Order forms are distributed in newspapers, magazines and brochures and supplemented by free long-distance telephone calls to a central sales desk.

It's inevitable that the quick-buck artist, the shoddy-goods merchant, and the outright con man are attracted to this new Eldorado. When decisions to purchase are based on advertising materials or stage-managed demonstrations by door-to-door salespeople—rather than on the traditional tests of taste, smell, touch, and tryout—the opportunities for the unscrupulous multiply: families mortgage their homes to pay for new roofs they don't need; hopeful neurotics shell out hundreds of dollars for a new personality by mail, and prepaid magazines never arrive.

Over the past decade federal, provincial and even municipal governments have increasingly tried to protect the consumer, including those who choose to buy in the home. Most cities and large towns have a consumer services bureau—either a government agency or one staffed by local activists. Also there is the federal Department of Consumer and Corporate Affairs, as well as the provincial consumer ministries. They will take up your complaint if you have been deceived or victimized. The law insists that home-bought goods must be what they profess to be and perform as advertised, in every particular. Even if the basic claims are true, prosecution can follow if the "general impression" is misleading.

The mail-order industry itself is eager to clean up the act. The Canadian Direct Mail/Marketing Association, 130 Merton Street, Toronto, Ont. M4S 1A4, which represents about 80 percent of the trade—publishers, catalogue companies, book clubs, fund-raisers, department stores, financial institutions, insurance firms, correspondence schools and even some governments—invites complaints and offers a free booklet of consumer advice.

If requested, the association will remove your name from its members' address lists. Some 3,200 persons recently asked to be taken off the lists, while 1,440 asked to be put on.

HIGH-PRESSURE TACTICS

A door-to-door salesman sold you an expensive vacuum cleaner which you really can't afford.

Every province and Territory has a consumer law that allows some form of a "cooling-off" period during which you can cancel the sales contract without cost. But the period of time varies widely across the country. It is 10 days in Newfoundland and Nova Scotia, seven in British Columbia, Prince Edward Island and the Yukon, five in Quebec and New Brunswick, four in Alberta, Manitoba, Saskatchewan and the Northwest Territories, and two in Ontario.

Your right to cancel must be exercised within a prescribed time after you receive a copy of the sales contract. This will either be handed to you at the time of sale or mailed to you within a legally defined period. It must state the name and address of the vendor, describe the goods, the total price and terms of payment (including all interest charges), any security given for payment and any warranty.

If the goods are not supplied within a certain time (usually 120 days), most provinces extend the time for cancellation to as much as a year. The period is also increased if the seller is not licensed, has violated his license, or has not given the buyer a copy of the sales contract or an information sheet.

All jurisdictions except Newfoundland, Quebec and Ontario provide a form outlining cancellation rights, which the seller must give the buyer. (Quebec plans to introduce such a form.) Protective legislation is not much help if the customer is ignorant of his or her rights.

A registered letter is the best notice of cancellation. No written notice is required in Quebec if the buyer simply returns the goods.

Holding back delivery. An unscrupulous door-to-door salesman may withhold delivery of goods until after the cancellation period has expired while pleading that he's temporarily out of stock. If you're convinced that he's waiting out the "cooling-off" period, cancel at once. If you live in Ontario or British Columbia, you have no cancellation rights if you paid cash and got immediate delivery of goods or services. Some provinces offer protection on contracts only up to a certain amount and some allow the seller some compensation for services rendered before the contract was canceled.

Upon cancellation, the vendor must return any deposit paid. Your provincial law may permit you to retain the goods until your money is refunded. Vendors in most provinces are entitled to compensation if the goods have been damaged.

WORK-AT-HOME PLANS

You bought a sewing machine and material from a company that promised to buy the finished garments from you. But now the company rejects your work as substandard.

While genuine work-at-home schemes provide supplementary income for many shut-ins, they are also one of the con man's most popular gimmicks—and one of the hardest to police. Thousands are gypped every year, most of them senior citizens, widows, or others who need extra money.

Back away from any deal—in or out of the home—that requires you to advance money, or that offers to buy back merchandise at high prices, or claims there is unlimited demand for the goods or services you are going to produce or sell by telephone.

Sewing at home is one of the most popular deals. The client is promised a handsome profit for sewing aprons, place mats, rugs, seat covers or other items—but there's a catch: the customer must first buy a sewing machine and material from the company. All too often the machine is defective or hard to use, or the worker lacks the skill to turn out a salable item. Whatever the reason, the products are unacceptable or so time-consuming as to be unprofitable. However, there will be a legal sales contract covering the purchase of the machine and material and the customer is stuck with the payments.

In these cases, the company is interested in selling, not buying. Chances are it doesn't even have a market for home-sewn products.

Victims of another common fraud respond to a newspaper advertisement and receive a form letter saying: "For $20, to show your good faith, a starter kit will be sent telling how you can make up to $100 a week." The kit may be nothing more than a booklet advising the respondents to place similar advertise-

The right to cancel

All provinces now permit the consumer to have second thoughts about any sales contract, or any membership or other obligation, he may have entered. As long as the right is exercised within the time limit set out in the relevant law, no reasons need be given for cancellation.

Generally speaking, such notice will end any financial obligation and bring a refund of any money paid in advance, by deposit or whatever.

In Alberta, the following notice must be attached to any direct-sale (sale in the home) contract. In certain cases, Albertans have a whole year to change their minds.

THE DIRECT SALES CANCELLATION ACT
STATUTORY NOTICE
Right of Cancellation by Buyer

1. This is a sales contract to which **The Direct Sales Cancellation Act** of Alberta applies.

2. The buyer may cancel this contract by giving notice of cancellation within four days after the date on which the buyer's copy of this contract is received by him, by personal delivery or by mail, without giving reasons for cancellation.

3. The buyer may cancel this contract by giving notice of cancellation within one year of the date on which the buyer's copy of this contract is received by him, by personal delivery or by mail, in any of the following cases:

If the goods or services to be supplied under this contract are not supplied within 120 days after the date this contract was signed by the buyer and no date for delivery is specified in or ascertainable from this contract.

OR

If the seller herein was during the period in which this contract was solicited, negotiated and concluded, required to be licensed under **The Licensing of Trades and Businesses Act,** but was not so licensed.

4. The buyer may cancel this contract by giving notice of cancellation within six months after the date on which all of the goods or services are to be supplied under this contract where that date is a fixed day stated in this contract or is ascertainable by reference to the fulfillment of the buyer's obligations to the seller and where the goods or services are not supplied within 30 days after that date.

5. A notice of cancellation under paragraph 2, 3 or 4 may be delivered to or sent by mail to

XYZ Novelties Co., 100 Maple St., Red Deer, Alta.

(insert name and address of the seller or other person)

and if sent by mail, is deemed to be given at the time of mailing.

6. The buyer is advised to make and keep a copy of the notice of cancellation for his own use and to note the date on which it was delivered or mailed, if it is not sent by registered mail.

7. This statutory notice indicates in a general way only the buyer's rights of cancellation. **The Direct Sales Cancellation Act** should be consulted as to the right of cancellation and other rights of the buyer in respect of this contract.

ments in their local newspapers. Even if you have signed a legal contract for products or services, the "fair business practices" legislation of your province may protect you if you've been high-pressured or victimized. In Ontario, firms convicted of using unfair methods can be fined up to $25,000 and individuals can be fined up to $2,000, or can get up to a year in jail, or both. Check with the nearest consumer services bureau for details of the legislation in your province.

Seniors are vulnerable. The over-65s—about 8 percent of Canada's population—are prime targets for unscrupulous door-to-door salespeople. The aged tend to stay close to home and they usually welcome a knock on the door and a smiling face. Unable to tackle heavy repair jobs about the property, they are especially vulnerable to fly-by-night home-repair swindlers.

Here's what can happen. A 65-year-old part-time laborer opened his door to a salesman offering a black-and-white portable TV for $150, with a bonus of a free turkey or Christmas cake. He bought the set but never received the bonus, which wasn't mentioned in the contract. When he complained, he was informed that the special offer had ended, that he was too late. And, instead of paying $150, he eventually paid some $263. He hadn't noted that the contract included insurance and carrying charges. The same set was selling in many stores for less than $100.

TELEPHONE SALES

You agreed over the telephone to subscribe to a new magazine that does not measure up to the sales pitch.

The law tries to protect the consumer by insisting that most sale contracts are valid only if they are in writing or if a "consideration" (such as a down payment) has been exchanged. Since these conditions cannot be met over the phone, you can usually back out of a telephone deal. But a telephone acceptance has the same legal standing as any oral agreement and may be binding. If it came to a court

hearing, the judge would decide whom to believe.

Since the magazine does not match the description you were given, you can almost certainly cancel without making any payment. Cancellation would also be justified if, for example, one in a group subscription deal of alleged family periodicals turned out to be a sleazy "girlie" magazine.

If you have already paid for the goods, write demanding your money back. Reputable firms will probably comply. If this fails, you can sue through Small Claims Court but the amount of money at stake may not justify the time and trouble involved.

Many people regard telephone soliciting as an intrusion on their privacy. If you're among them, a brisk "No thanks" will generally end the matter. Unless you know a product by reputation (say, the name of a national magazine), telephone buys are risky. You cannot see the seller or his merchandise. You are virtually taking his word about the value offered.

"Cancel my subscription." Most periodical publishers include money-back guarantees in their offers, so even if you have paid for a subscription in advance, you can cancel at any time for any reason and get a refund. You'll probably have to pay for any magazines actually delivered. Some publishers send unsolicited trial subscriptions. If you don't pay (and you needn't, since there's no contract), the "trial" will end. Sometimes a periodical is delivered without any request for payment. These are "controlled circulation" publications. The objective is to create a specialized audience for advertisers interested in zeroing in on those likely to be most interested in their goods or services.

All Canadian publishers seeking subscriptions by mail or telephone subscribe to industry regulations. If you have any difficulty with an individual publisher or subscription agency, complain to one of the following: Canadian Central Registry of Subscription Representatives, 3 First Canadian Place, Toronto, Ont. Periodical Press Association, Suite 508, 100 University Avenue, Toronto, Ont. M5J 1V6; Magazines Canada, Suite 300, 1240 Bay Street, Toronto, Ont. M5R 2A7.

PURCHASES BY CHILDREN

Two door-to-door salesmen have talked your 16-year-old son into signing a magazine subscription contract.

Such a contract signed by anyone under 18 years of age is invalid—in some instances the contracting parties must both be 21 or older—and parents are not legally responsible for debts incurred by their children. You can't be forced to pay. Inform the publisher of the circumstances and cancel the subscription.

Some salespeople don't check the ages of their youthful customers, banking on indulgent parents picking up the tab.

There are two exceptions to the age rule in the validity of contracts. If a parent cosigned or otherwise specifically guaranteed a minor's contract, it would stand up in law. Or if a contract was for "the necessities of life," you could be called upon to pay. "Necessities" are hard to define in precise terms, but it is not likely a commercial publication would qualify.

However, if your son lied about his age, and appears to be an adult, the contract could be ruled valid. The vendor can plead "good faith" in accepting answers to verbal or written questions. Subscription order blanks for "adult" magazines require the purchaser to confirm that he is over 18. The vendor is not required to check the customer's stated age.

Persuader on the porch. Every salesman knows there's nothing like a bargain or a bonus to clinch a deal. Book clubs may offer several good books at a low price to get you to agree to buy several more books at the "regular" price. Some publishers will include a free lottery ticket or a chance on a trip around the world in the subscription price.

These sales gimmicks are fair trading. Any prizes or special bonuses offered publicly can be assumed to be genuine. That trip around the world must be awarded to someone—and not to any agent, employee or relative of the vendor—even if the promotion is a sales failure. Contests or lotteries must be decided by tests of skill or by random chance. The law will step in quickly if there's anything false, misleading, deceptive or unconscionable (against the public interest).

But there's one area where consumer law is virtually powerless. When you answer your doorbell, or your telephone, you may be told that the caller is conducting a survey, or that you are the selected representative in your area—anything but the fact that your visitor is selling something.

It's strictly up to you whether you continue such conversations. There's nothing illegal in knocking on doors and trying to do business, even where "No Canvassers" signs are posted. And although such salespeople will seldom risk an outright falsehood, they won't hesitate to play on your sympathy, cupidity or compassion.

Consider this example: Householders were offered a "free" set of encyclopedias in return for filling out a questionnaire and paying a marketing service charge of 77 cents a week for 10 years. That adds up to some $400 and the Ontario Ministry of Consumer and Commercial Relations finally stepped in and issued a "cease and desist" order.

LATE DELIVERY

The mail-order firm cashed your cheque but informs you that the goods you ordered will not be available for several weeks.

Unless the vendor offered immediate delivery, there's not much you can do except wait for a reasonable time. Most mail-order firms advise customers to allow some weeks for delivery.

If the waiting time becomes unreasonable, you can cancel your order and demand your money back. If the goods arrive after your cancellation, write "Refused" on the package, sign it and return it to the post office.

Cash on the doorstep. The post office's cash-on-delivery (C.O.D.) system is an answer to the time-lag problem. If the vendor offers this option, you pay nothing until the goods arrive at your door. The value of the merchandise determines the C.O.D. fee, which is currently as low as $1 for goods worth up to $20 and increases with the value of the goods. You also have the right to refuse acceptance, and return the shipment to the sender.

Think before you leap. Mail-order shopping began in 1884 when the T. Eaton Company distributed a 32-page advertising brochure to visitors at the first Canadian National Exhibition in Toronto. It generated so many orders from rural areas that it became necessary, as Lady Eaton noted in her memoirs, for "one woman to devote her entire time to the filling of orders, with the aid of a small boy to do the parceling." Within a few years,

---

Saints and sinners

In Ontario, in the mid-1970s, a confidence ring used religion to win the trust of the elderly. Once inside the house, they would hold impromptu prayer meetings, then offer to carry out home repairs. These were vastly over-priced and often quite unnecessary.

Two retired sisters in Brampton, Ont., ran up a bill for $16,850 for the installation of siding, windows, doors and awnings and for shoddy wallpapering and roofing. The "contractors" drove them to a finance company to arrange a mortgage of $14,000 to pay part of the cost.

A Portuguese woman, who didn't speak English, paid out $10,420 to a contractor who promised to install air conditioning, plumbing and wiring in the immigrant's home in Windsor, Ont. All he did was disconnect the existing furnace and plumbing.

Tracked down by the police, the contractor was convicted of six counts of fraud. He received a "weekend" jail sentence and was ordered to make restitution. In that same year, he committed five more home-improvement frauds and got another jail sentence, which his lawyer appealed. Freed on bail, he skipped the country. None of his victims ever received a cent.

Among the con men who might knock on your door are the shady chimney repairman and the phony inspector. The former is likely to suggest you are endangering your children's lives if you don't fix your chimney immediately. Don't panic: chimneys don't deteriorate overnight and there is always time to make a thorough check. The "inspector" may advise you to fix your furnace at once or risk asphyx-iation. Any genuine inspector, however, will come by appointment and with credentials.

The Alberta Department of Consumer and Corporate Affairs canceled contracts for home improvements entered into by five elderly people. One—a 79-year-old woman—signed a contract for $5,986 after being high-pressured for two hours.

The young can fall into these traps, too. A 29-year-old Toronto man signed a $6,403 contract to have a basement built. He was left up in the air when the contractor jacked up his house and then went out of business. The consumer had to pay off a $4,000 loan he had undertaken to pay for the job.

A Manitoba couple's story had a happier ending. They signed a $4,000 contract with an aggressive aluminum siding salesman, made a $1,500 deposit by cheque, then decided to cancel the contract the next day:

"All persuasion attempts by the company failed to make us reconsider. Finally, the seller said that by law we still owed 20 percent of the contract price because of expenses incurred on our behalf.

"At this point we contacted the Manitoba Consumers' Bureau which discovered that the sellers were not licensed as required under the Consumer Protection Act. The bureau was successful in getting our $1,500."

Cancellation rights, for any reason (including a simple change of mind), vary widely from province to province. A telephone call to your provincial ministry—it's listed in your phone book—or a personal call at the nearest consumer services bureau will advise you of your rights.

Eaton's mail-order sales were rivaling those of its stores.

Mail-order shopping, now about 18 percent of all general merchandise sales, is increasing. "Goods satisfactory or money refunded" policies have largely resolved the problem of the customer not being able to examine the product before buying.

But no sales system is foolproof from the consumer's point of view. Run through this checklist before you order goods by mail:

■ Does the advertising sound too good to be true? Then it probably is.

■ Do you really need the merchandise? A digital clock that shows the time in Tokyo is of limited practical value.

■ Is the article any dearer in your local store? If the price is close, remember those postage and handling charges.

■ Do you have the choice of paying C.O.D.? That way, your money doesn't leave your savings account until you get the goods.

■ Does the advertising give you enough specific information? It should provide the company's registered name and permanent address. Beware of box numbers and foreign dealers from whom redress might be difficult.

■ Is there a money-back guarantee? Unless this is clearly stated, you'll have little legal recourse unless the goods don't match the advertised description.

■ What do you know about the company's reputation? If you know nothing, check with your Chamber of Commerce, Better Business Bureau or other consumer agencies.

■ Never send cash. Use cheques, bank drafts, credit-card numbers or money orders to ensure the payment is recorded.

UNSATISFACTORY GOODS

The mail-order nursery delivered your seedlings too late for spring planting and all of them appear unhealthy.

If the delivery was unreasonably late, and especially if a more seasonable delivery time was specified in the catalogue or newspaper advertisement, you can demand a refund.

Most mail-order firms will refund or exchange goods. Their terms of business are stated in their advertising, which forms part of the sales contract. All consumer authorities urge you to read the terms and conditions—the small print with the large—before you sign anything. You may be committing yourself to buy other merchandise over a period of time. The merchant may disclaim responsibility in advance if the goods are "out of stock."

While the law will crack down hard on any deliberate deception, it is generally agreed that when you mail your order, you are accepting the seller's offer as stated, and that a deal has been concluded. This is especially so when you pay in advance, whereas with the cash-on-delivery system, if your spring planting doesn't arrive until July, you can simply refuse to accept the package.

However, if you do pay C.O.D. and find the goods unsatisfactory, the post office won't return your money or help with your complaint. Write immediately to the vendor and if you do not get satisfaction, get in touch with your local consumer services bureau or the Canadian Direct Mail/Marketing Association.

In what is called "sale by description," it is implied by the vendor that the goods on arrival will correspond with the written or illustrated description. If goods are sold by sample as well as description, they must correspond with both description and sample. If they do not, they may be rejected. Some businesses operate by "negative option." Series of books are often sold this way. Once you have signed up, you continue to receive merchandise unless you inform the seller you no longer want it. An alternative is the preview card sent in advance of a book selection. Unless you return the card indicating that you don't want the book, it and the bill will follow.

Right of rescission. If your mail-order deal turns sour and you believe you have been "taken," your final solution may lie in seeking "rescission" of the contract. This, however, is a time-consuming process but, if your case stands up, you can expect total satisfaction in the end. The steps are explained in Ontario's Business Practices Act, fairly typical of similar legislation across the country.

275

Step 1. Within six months of entering into an agreement (the sales contract, be it by coupon or other order), send a letter by registered mail or by hand to the company concerned asking that the transaction be declared null and void. This is rescission. It's also a good idea to send copies to the salesperson involved and to the sales manager of the company. Keep a copy for yourself.

Quote the relevant clause of the act whose protection you are seeking. A telephone call to your nearest consumer agency will supply the details. In Ontario, it's Section 4 of the Business Practices Act.

Step 2. If the merchant ignores your complaint, or does not offer you satisfaction, ask your provincial Department of Consumer and Commercial Relations to mediate the case.

The consumer officials will listen to both sides of the argument—and they have punitive powers. In Ontario, for example, the director of the Business Practices Division can issue a "cease and desist" order against a doubtful practice. The order remains in effect for at least 15 days; it becomes permanent if the company doesn't file an appeal with the Commercial Registration Appeal Tribunal.

UNSOLICITED GOODS

You received a box of unsolicited Christmas cards in the mail. At the end of January, a bill arrives.

If you didn't order it, don't pay for it. You are under no obligation to return the cards, or anything else that arrives at your home out of the blue. The post office requires that unsolicited goods, such as Christmas cards, be accompanied by a statement that you needn't return them or pay for them, even if you use them.

The Post Office Act makes it illegal to send goods C.O.D. if they have not been ordered. At one time, ghoulish crooks studied the death notices in the newspapers, then sent C.O.D. packages to the deceased persons. They counted on the grief of relatives to deter them from checking on whether the goods had really been ordered.

Some direct-mail vendors will fill your mailbox with unsolicited offers and unasked-for goods. Perhaps a set of steak knives will be sent to you "on a trial basis," along with a prestamped card which states that you must

Charity begins at home?

Nine out of ten Canadians contribute to charity, often through door-to-door canvassers. Swindlers know this very well and don't hesitate to exploit our generosity.

When anyone comes to your door soliciting, ask for identification. If a product is being sold, the canvasser should be able to produce a current door-to-door vendor's permit for your province or Territory. A license is not valid outside the jurisdiction in which it is issued. Don't let a salesman into your house unless a satisfactory identification document is produced. Thieves sometimes pose as salespeople to "case" your home for a burglary.

All canvassers for the major charities will give you a receipt for any cash donation. Do-

nations to recognized charities are deductible from your taxable income.

A handicapped canvasser may say he "represents" an organization for the handicapped. But, profit-making firms often hire the handicapped to do their soliciting. The charitable organization will get a percentage of the sale price but the lion's share will go to the firm.

The Better Business Bureau of Metropolitan Toronto has an A to D rating system. It awards an "A" to the true nonprofit charity. The "D" rating is for the outfit that sounds like a charity but is actually taking a profit. If you have any doubts about a canvasser's "charity," call your consumer services bureau, or the police.

fill it out and mail it back if you want no more such items. You forget the card or you lose it and the goods keep coming. Again, you are under no obligation whatever and can simply tear up any bills.

Miniature automobile license plates are mailed by war-amputee organizations, whose mailing lists come from provincial vehicle registrations. Many drivers attach these to their car-key rings so that they'll be returned if the ring is lost. To send or not to send a donation, however, is strictly up to you.

The mysterious package. Once an article is put into the mails it becomes the property of the person to whom it is addressed. If you get such an article and you don't want it, you can throw it away, or write "Refused" on it, sign it, and return it to the nearest post office. If it bears a return address, it will be sent back. If it doesn't, the parcel will be opened and anything of value will go to the Receiver-General of Canada.

While the post office has no authority to interfere with ordinary business carried out by mail, certain types of mailings are offenses under the Criminal Code. These include any immoral, obscene or dangerous materials, fraudulent or false advertising. The post office will investigate any complaint about objectionable use of the mails. Prosecution may follow. Use of the mails is a privilege, not a right—and that privilege can be withdrawn, effectively shutting down any mail-order business that abused the privilege.

HOME REPAIRS

Large cracks have appeared in your two-year-old paved driveway, apparently because of settling. The contractor disclaims responsibility.

The contractor may not be responsible under the terms of his contract with you. Check the agreement carefully, especially the clauses dealing with the warranty. If he fulfilled all terms and conditions, you're going to be stuck with a major repair bill; if he didn't, you can take him to court to force him to do the job

properly or to compensate you for failing to deliver the product that he promised and for which you paid.

Installing a paved driveway is a major investment which demands that you do some homework and acquaint yourself with the basic techniques and materials. For example, if your present driveway tends to be muddy, you may have to pay more for base and drainage in order to ensure the paving won't settle into the ooze. And crushed limestone makes a better base because it compacts better than gravel, which is cheaper.

The contract should specify the depth of the base, the thickness and grade of asphalt, the drainage arrangement. Home driveways usually require a grade of asphalt known as HL3A, which is coarse but durable.

A contract and a guarantee are only as good as the person or firm standing behind them. There's little consolation in having an airtight, gilt-edged warranty if the fly-by-nighter who issued it has decamped. The simplest way to check out a contractor's credentials is to talk with people whose driveways he has paved. And, in most towns, there is competition in the business; so get a "second opinion" and a second (or third) cost quotation.

If it isn't possible or practical to inspect your prospective contractor's earlier work at first hand, check with your consumer services bureau, police, Board of Trade or Better Business Bureau.

Above all, make sure that you understand what is required in the way of workmanship and materials to make a good, sound driveway and that the contract spells everything out clearly. Write the contract yourself, if necessary. This is critical—it will be the document on which your claims are based if the product proves unsatisfactory.

The siding story. Putting siding on your house falls into the category of major undertakings, even more so than paving your driveway. Survey the choices carefully before taking the plunge. There are many reputable firms selling and installing siding, but there are also fly-by-nighters in the business, so choose your contractor carefully.

Applying siding is costly and unless you're

one of the fortunate few who have five or six thousand dollars set aside, you'll require financing. That may take the form of a second mortgage, or a low-cost home improvement loan guaranteed by Central Mortgage and Housing Corporation. Don't rush into signing up for the financing plan that may be offered by the contractor. Shop around at your credit union, bank and trust company.

Don't pay the whole amount in advance. A 10 percent down payment should be sufficient, then 75 per cent upon satisfactory completion and the balance when you have made sure no liens have been placed against your property by a subcontractor or supplier who hasn't been paid by your contractor.

Read carefully the fine print in the warranty offered for any siding installation, be it aluminum, steel, vinyl or wood. Siding products are usually guaranteed against defects in man-

---

Two sides to the coin

Property law in Canada is under provincial jurisdiction, but the federal government has found ways to build consumers' rights into the written law. These rights, as expressed by the Department of Consumer and Corporate Affairs, apply to all residents in Canada:

■ The right to truthful and honest information about the goods and services you buy. This must, by law, appear in advertisements of all kinds and on labels and packages.

■ The right to choose among products and services that we require to satisfy our needs, offering different qualities and prices. You have the right to choose a level of quality and performance equal to the price you are prepared to pay.

■ The right to safety in the goods and services you buy. The right to expect that household products and children's toys, when used according to manufacturer's instructions, will not explode, set your house on fire, or cause personal harm in any way.

■ The right to be heard. The right to complain to a retailer who, you feel, has not given you your money's worth. If the retailer won't "hear" you, you should try the manufacturer, and if he won't "hear" you, try any one of the many consumer agencies across Canada.

But the department, warning that it can't play fairy godmother to a nation of Cinderellas, also publishes a list of consumer responsibilities:

■ The responsibilities to protect yourself by shopping carefully and wisely, understanding the terms of the sale, reading and following instructions, getting guarantees in writing and saving receipts, asking questions at point of sale and keeping informed about new products.

■ The responsibility of carrying out your transactions in a businesslike way—such as reporting unsatisfactory products to retailers and manufacturers, in order that the products may be removed from shelves and future production.

■ The responsibility to tell other consumers about any unfair treatment by a retailer or manufacturer so consumers can protect themselves in future dealings.

■ The responsibility to report apparently unsafe merchandise to the Department of Consumer and Corporate Affairs in Ottawa so that it can be tested and, if necessary, removed from the market or be more specifically labeled. If you discover dangerous items and simply toss them into the garbage, you are shirking your responsibility as a consumer.

Federal protection of all Canadian consumers is specifically embedded in the Combines Investigation Act, and in the following acts: Hazardous Products, Consumer Packaging and Labeling, Fish Inspection, Food and Drugs, Textile Labeling, Weights and Measures, Electricity and Gas Inspection Acts.

ufacture but not against damage or faulty installation. Most metal sidings carry a 20-year guarantee from the manufacturer. Check to see whether your siding is guaranteed against fading, chalking or pollution, the most frequent causes of problems. Some warranties require that you clean the siding regularly.

Get at least three written price quotations and make sure all work, such as installation of new eaves troughing, screen and storm doors and windows, is specifically included.

Insulation's $-factor. Siding provides little insulation by itself and even though new siding cuts down on drafts, it isn't really the answer. The experts say that proper insulation can save you up to 25 percent of your annual heating bill. Central Mortgage and Housing Corporation has approved about 120 types of insulation. Additional information on insulation (and do-it-yourself instructions) is in the federal Department of Energy, Mines and Resources book, *Keeping the Heat In* (available from P.O. Box 900, Westmount Postal Station, Montreal, Que. H3Z 2V1).

Savings on the heating bill may make it worthwhile to borrow, if necessary, to insulate your home. Central Mortgage and Housing Corporation offers insured loans for house improvement, below the current market rate. The maximum is $4,000 for a single-family home or the first unit of a multiple-family dwelling, with an extra $1,500 for each additional unit. Discuss the matter with your bank or credit union.

Large loans can be obtained under the Residential Rehabilitation Assistance Program in designated Neighborhood Improvement Areas—mostly in older sections of a city. The maximum loan is $10,000 and up to $3,750 may be forgivable (in other words, it need not be repaid), depending on the income of the applicant. The federal government offers taxable grants on the cost of materials used to reinsulate older homes.

The all-important contract. When you hire a contractor to do a renovation job on your home, don't take any oral commitments. Get everything in writing.

Key clauses in this kind of contract include:

■ The starting and finishing dates.

■ A detailed description of the job, including dimensions, quantity, quality, and types of materials.

■ A guaranteed price—or at least a guarantee that the cost won't run more than 15 percent over the estimate.

■ Details of the warranty on labor and materials.

■ A clause stating that the contractor is responsible for cleaning up after the job is done and restoring lawns, shrubbery, and so on, to their original condition.

Only when the entire job and cleanup have been done to your satisfaction should you sign a completion certificate. This is like putting your name on a cheque. It's your agreement that the work has been done well and that you'll pay the agreed price.

23 Troubles with service calls

ew consumers today fail to exercise their rights to the warranties that most manufacturers offer. Those who buy from major retailers have learned that slogans such as "Goods satisfactory or money refunded" generally mean what they say. But when you call a serviceman, tradesman or technician to your home to carry out repairs or renovations, you can be sailing into troubled waters—even when the call involves repairs apparently covered by a manufacturer's or retailer's warranty.

There is a dearth of qualified service personnel and it can be traced to the multiple career choices offered to students in the 1960s and 1970s. Many students turned away from trade and craft courses and householders soon began to notice a shortage of qualified repairmen and technicians. According to the 1976 census, there were only 2,159 appliance repairmen to service Canada's millions of electric stoves, washing machines, dishwashers, refrigerators and vacuum cleaners.

Into the gap rushed many former handymen, laborers and other semiskilled people offering to do everything from structural renovations to painting, plastering, wallpapering, bricklaying, carpentry, roofing and excavating. Householders often came to regret the clumsy or careless efforts of these incompetents.

The tide appears to be turning as the financial rewards and steady jobs exert their pull. Provincial education departments report a sharp swing from liberal arts to vocational courses. The community colleges are gaining enrollment while many universities are scouring the high schools for freshmen. There's renewed interest in apprenticeship schemes.

Meantime, the wise consumer will examine closely the credentials of his serviceman. Don't buy by price alone when you need a job done. The honest workman is worthy of his hire.

EXCEEDING ESTIMATES

The carpenter says lumber costs have skyrocketed and his bill for wainscoting your basement is double the written estimate.

An estimate, either written or oral, is not a contract. Besides, the carpenter's preliminary calculations may have been realistic—at the time. Many things, including a rise in the price of lumber over which he has no control, can increase the price. But there's also the chance that he simply quoted low to beat the competition.

If his estimate was oral, you have little recourse, although you can ask him for an itemized account with his bill which might flush out any padding. Of course, you can also refuse to pay and let him take you to court, where the facts will be aired. A written estimate, on the other hand, can be compared with the carpenter's final itemized account. If lumber prices didn't increase, as he claimed, confront him with your findings.

Since the laws of supply and demand rule the marketplace, get at least two estimates. When a contractor knows he is competing, he'll sharpen his pencil.

Even the most conscientious estimate is only an approximate cost of your renovation. That's why it is important you sign a contract before the work begins. Get all the details in writing, even down to the kind of wood to be used and the brand names of other material. Make sure that all the subcontracting—plumbing or electricity, for instance—is covered. If a large amount of money is involved, ask your lawyer to review the deal.

The contract should guarantee that costs will not run over the estimate by more than a certain sum. The amount suggested by most consumer organizations is 15 percent.

Two million a week. Home-improvement frauds are believed to cost Canadians up to $100 million a year. The unscrupulous contractor may give you a low estimate on a renovation, then deliberately build in "unforeseen problems" that double the price.

Your best defense is to negotiate a fixed-price contract by which the builder undertakes to do the work in accordance with certain architectural and engineering drawings for a fixed sum within a specified time. This forces the contractor to hire efficient workers, reduce his overhead and complete the job on time.

An alternative is some variation of the cost-plus contract. You pay all costs, plus either a fixed sum, or a percentage, or a bonus for work completed on schedule, or you withhold a bonus if the work is late.

DAMAGE DURING REPAIR

Your bathroom carpet was damaged during plumbing repairs to your apartment. The landlord and the plumber each says it is the other's responsibility.

Dig out your lease and also check your provincial landlord-and-tenant laws. Rights and responsibilities can vary substantially. (*See* Chapter 13, "When you rent.")

Contrary to popular belief, the onus has been on the tenant in most provinces to look after major repairs. But the law is changing. In Ontario, for example, the landlord must offer and keep premises in good repair. It's not a concrete definition but, basically, the tenant has only to act as a good housekeeper, keeping the place clean and safe. This provision can override clauses written into individual leases.

Quebec landlords are obliged to make whatever repairs are necessary to keep rented accommodation in a habitable condition.

Don't move into an apartment until the landlord has made any necessary repairs, or guaranteed in writing that he will make them to your satisfaction. Once you're in, if you want to install a bidet or a sunken Roman tub, the cost is yours—and the lease will almost certainly require that you get the landlord's permission.

Many large apartment blocks have a tenants' association. If you join up, it will go to bat for you to get compensation from either the landlord or the plumbing contractor.

Damage to your furnishings is covered under an all-risk or homeowner's policy. If you have such a policy, your insurance company will have to sort out the squabble whenever you lodge a claim.

DRY CLEANING

When you had your rugs shampooed, your most expensive carpet was discolored. The cleaner denies liability.

A cleaning company—as any other company or individual—is responsible for any damage it causes to your property, either through ignorance, inadvertence (accident) or negligence. In accepting the job, the cleaner professed the expert ability to carry it through to the satisfaction of a reasonable person.

However, if you fail to get satisfaction from management and the dispute goes to court, you will need evidence of the rug's condition beforehand. You will need a witness who will vouch for its condition before it was cleaned. You must prove that the damage occurred during the cleaning process.

Complaints about fabric cleaners are many and their resolution is often difficult. Even though a cleaning company's expert knowledge of its field is implied by the charge for service, a court may rule that the customer is obliged to point out that an unusual fiber or color requires special attention or treatment. The cleaner may argue that the manufacturer failed to label the item properly.

Examine the work ticket you get when you send articles to the cleaners. It may state that the company will not be responsible for loss or damage. Even if this carries no legal weight, it warns you that you'll have a fight on your hands if anything goes wrong.

If you are handing over a carpet worth hundreds or even thousands of dollars, take the same care that you would with, say, an heirloom gold watch.

The carpet that shrank. A Winnipeg housewife wanted her fitted broadloom drycleaned before moving into a new house. The cleaner warned her that up to three centimetres of shrinkage was possible. She gave him the job.

When returned, the carpet was warped and, in some places, had shrunk by as much as six centimetres. The cleaner rejected her claim for compensation, she sued through the Small Claims Court and was awarded $400 plus costs. When the cleaner did not come through with the money, she went back to the court to have the judgment enforced. Finally she got her money—and the cleaner learned not to specify the amount of possible shrinkage.

Fiberglass drapes came back from a Toronto cleaning company with frayed edges and faded color. Their texture "was now like sacking," said the owner, who asked the Better Business Bureau to mediate when the cleaner ignored a written complaint.

A panel of dry-cleaning experts examined the facts and decided the company should never have accepted the drapes, since fiberglass should be hand-washed only. The company's cleaning was done largely in machines that handled some 180 kilograms of fabric at a time. It had not acted with the expertise that could reasonably be expected.

Nine months later, after a lot of prodding, the customer received a $100 cheque, three white roses, and a note that read: "Sorry for the inconvenience."

Clean, cleaner, cleanest. If you toss your polyurethane-treated coat into a coin machine and it comes out with the sleeves fused, there isn't much you can do about it. Vinyl fabrics are a problem even for the professionals. Your local dry-cleaning depot probably won't guarantee results. If a valuable fabric has an unusual stain, you should take it to a custom cleaner.

When your goods come back, check immediately for discoloration, deterioration and for missing buttons or other fasteners. Inform the cleaner immediately, preferably in writing, if something is wrong. Your chances for compensation are far better if you tell him within a week than if you wait for a month. Most householders simply hang those plastic-sheeted suits or dresses in a closet without inspection.

If a cleaner loses your garment and if you

Hiring a contractor

Before you hire a contractor for any substantial job, find out how long he has been in business and inspect personally some of the jobs he has done. If he has been around a long time, the odds are favorable that he'll stay around a lot longer and that your remodeling will be completed satisfactorily.

The Better Business Bureau or Chamber of Commerce will give you its assessment of the contractor's reputation. Both are bound to inform you of any black marks. If you know the names of any subcontracting companies (perhaps the brick or concrete supplier), you could inquire if your contractor is keeping up with his phase payments.

If some doubts remain, call the Workmen's Compensation Board. Every contractor must pay dues to the board to protect his employees in case of injury. If your contractor is behind in his payments, that's often a pointer to money troubles.

Once you have agreed to a deal, the contractor's financial status is of primary concern to you. If he should declare bankruptcy, your contract becomes void. Should that happen when your job is only half-completed, that's where it will stay until you make fresh arrangements with another firm. Any unspent portion of an advance payment would probably be unrecoverable.

can produce your claim ticket, you have a cast-iron case for compensation. You'll probably get a percentage of the replacement cost, depending on the age of the garment.

TELEVISION REPAIRS

You have just finished paying a whopping TV repair bill and now you're told you need a new picture tube.

More than one half of the 10 million television sets in Canada are color sets, which range from $400 to $1,200 each. And when the picture flickers or fades, you have to depend upon the skill and integrity of the television technician.

If the manufacturer's warranty is still running (a year is the usual span), your problems should be minimal. It's after the warranty expires that "the box" can cause you trouble.

A Montreal pensioner selected a serviceman from the Yellow Pages when her set "went dead." He said that $10 to $15 should cover the repairs and, with the customer's consent, took the set to his shop. Next day the woman was told by phone that the set would be returned on payment of $80. She protested, but grudgingly agreed when given a technical explanation about extra parts and labor. Another serviceman inspected the returned TV and found that one new tube had been installed. The job, he claimed, should not have cost more than $15 and could easily have been completed in the home.

Today, the pensioner could probably recover $65 through mediation by the provincial Consumer Protection Office or via the Small Claims Court.

Under Quebec's new consumer protection legislation, a written estimate of costs must be offered by every appliance serviceman unless the customer formally waives that right. It must include the estimator's name and address, a description of the appliance and the nature and cost of the repair. When the job is done, the replaced parts must be presented along with an itemized bill which states the hourly cost of labor. A 90-day warranty on

the new parts and workmanship must be given.

"Everything went black." The Manitoba Consumers' Bureau was told of a Winnipegger's color television screen suddenly going black while he was watching his favorite Sunday football program. He called a TV repair shop that advertised 24-hour, seven-day-a-week service and a technician arrived promptly, but said the set required shop repair. Over the anguish of the armchair quarterback, he took it away.

Six days later, the set was delivered, along with a bill for $164. The invoice did not show what parts had been replaced or how much was charged for labor, but it did include a six-month warranty on the repair work. The owner didn't want to miss the next game. He asked no questions and paid the bill.

Three days later, the screen blacked out again. Once more the set was picked up and checked. This time, the owner was told it needed a new picture tube. He assumed the tube had been serviced earlier and would be included in the warranty. Wrong. Although the serviceman admitted he knew the tube was weak, he had not serviced it on the first call.

Nevertheless, considering the large number of TV repairmen offering service, the percentage of "fast-buck" operators appears to be relatively small. But no amount of skill equips the serviceman to take one look at your complicated color TV and diagnose the trouble immediately. The set must often be taken to the shop for bench tests. Then you must depend on the firm's integrity not to replace parts needlessly or run up phony labor charges. You should get back any replaced parts, but how many of us have the inclination to have them tested?

MINIMUM CHARGES

The plumber replaced a washer in your kitchen tap in five minutes and now bills you for $35.

Plumbers and other qualified servicemen charge for a minimum hour or half-hour on each call. Their rates are based on union contracts and there's little you can do about them. Self-employed plumbers usually charge the same scale. You can expect to pay the minimum even if the job is done in five or 10 minutes. You should try to line up enough small jobs around the house (is there a noisy toilet?) to get your money's worth.

The service contract. If you buy a major appliance from a local firm that maintains its own repair shop, you may be offered a full-service contract to run with any manufactur-

er's warranty or to extend beyond it. Optimists tend to refuse them but they're worth careful consideration. Warranties expire anywhere from 30 days to a year, and they are seldom free from conditions.

As with any other contract, read before you sign. If trouble occurs, you'll be able to demand only the services or parts specifically promised. A Quebec man signed up for a free-service-and-parts contract for his furnace. In October, when the house temperature climbed

Your furnace is on file

To forestall house fires from faulty furnaces and to protect the homeowner from fly-by-night salesmen and installers, all provinces require heating contractors to obtain permits before installation. When the work is complete, approval is probably required by an inspector from the provincial fire marshal's office.

If a contractor is installing a new furnace in your home, he should be able to produce a permit, similar to this one from British Columbia.

FIRE SERVICES ACT

OFFICE OF THE LOCAL ASSISTANT TO THE FIRE COMMISSIONER

ANYPLACE , B.C.,
JANUARY 8 , 19_80_

Permit to Install Fuel-oil Burner and Oil-burning Equipment

Permission is hereby granted to _HYGRADE HEATING_
725 1ST AVENUE (The installer.) _ANYPLACE, B.C._
(Address.)

to install the following fuel-oil burner and oil-burning equipment:—

Manufacturer _AIRCO HEATING PRODUCTS_ Address _ANYPLACE, B.C._

Trade-name of burner _AIRCO_ Model _FA 90_

Type: Range. ☐ Domestic. ☑ Commercial. ☐ Control _AUTOMATIC_

Capacity of tank _350_ gals. Gauge of tank _12 (SEE SECTION 3.04)_

Location of tank _OUTSIDE – UNDERGROUND_ Grade of oil _2_

Address of installation _900 1ST AVENUE, ANYPLACE, B.C._

Name of occupier _RICHARD A. ROE_

This permit is issued in accordance with the provisions of the regulations pursuant to the Fire Services Act, and shall be subject to cancellation at any time for failure to comply therewith.

(Signed) _Samuel Snow_

Local Assistant to the Fire Commissioner.

For City
District
Town
Village
Fire District } of _ANYPLACE_ , B.C.

1 Issuing Office Copy.

out of control, the repairman fixed the thermostat wiring. Within two weeks it was acting up again. Another visit from the repairman brought things back to normal for a month. When the problem recurred, the serviceman said a new part was needed. The consumer got a bill for $125 for a part available wholesale for $53.75.

Even though prodded by a newspaper columnist, the repair firm stuck by its original billing. The part was not covered under the service plan, which called only for replacement of about two dozen specified parts. While agreeing the charge was $70 more than the wholesale price of the part, the company insisted this was justified by labor costs and a reasonable profit margin.

WARRANTIES

The store agrees to send an electrician to repair your stove which is under warranty, but will not specify the time or the day.

Some firms still haven't adjusted to the fact that all the adults in most households are holding down jobs. While it's unlikely that the terms of the warranty cover this situation exactly, you have the implied right to receive the promised service within normal business hours at your reasonable convenience. Any unreasonable delay would give you grounds for formal complaint.

The store will probably not guarantee the exact arrival time of its serviceman, but you can insist that it specify the day and whether it will be in the morning or afternoon. Even if it is busy, it should be organized well enough to be able to telephone you, say, 12 hours in advance of your "appointment." In fact, some companies insist on making such a call to be sure that there'll be someone home.

If you have continued trouble getting service under your warranty, get in touch with the manufacturer. (*See* "Defective parts" in Chapter 19.) He can bring pressure to bear on the retailer. If this doesn't work, report the matter to the nearest consumer services bureau.

When the deadline approaches. You've got a lot of money locked up in the household machinery you take for granted—perhaps $5,000 in the average family residence. Keep track of the warranties that protect that investment. Once they expire, your family budget can be wrecked if serious trouble strikes.

Modern mass-production techniques often dictate that an entire ailing motor or other major part be replaced rather than any repair attempted. This can be so costly that you may be forced to consider buying a new machine at short notice.

Review your warranties regularly and if any appliance is showing signs of trouble, lodge a service call before the expiry date on the warranty. Don't rely on a telephone call to the dealer. Write a dated letter. If the expiry deadline is closing in fast, register the letter so that you may have a dated receipt to silence any argument.

Although many of the larger dealers guarantee the customer's satisfaction, it is the warranty itself that spells out the protection and warranties can vary widely. Ask the salesman to explain the warranty in detail before buying an expensive appliance.

UNAUTHORIZED WORK

The electrician was called to check your dishwasher connections. He persuaded your housekeeper that a big rewiring job was essential.

Angry disputes often arise when a tradesman does a lot more than he was asked to do, especially in your absence. You are presented with a fait accompli, and with a much steeper bill than you anticipated.

You may be unlucky enough to strike a rip-off artist who grabs a chance to pad his account. The wiring on that circuit was in a dangerous state, he claims—would you want to run the risk of a house fire? Your technological knowledge is scanty and, even if you sense that you've been "taken," you feel helpless and outwitted.

Consider the reverse. He is a licensed, qualified man. He may have done you a big favor. His services are in strong demand in the community. These days, in the high tide of consumerism, would he risk involving his firm in a shady or illegal practice?

The problem in such cases often is that the householder, having hired an expert, instructs him in general terms to make repairs. When the electrician takes the dishwasher apart, he quickly realizes that the problem lies deeper. As he checks along the power line, he discovers what he considers a potentially dangerous situation. His integrity demands that he do something about it; his license could be in jeopardy if he ignored it.

He explains the facts to the housekeeper and installs the new wiring that he considers necessary, not only so that the dishwasher will get its power but that the whole circuit will be safe. Most people would regard his action as both justified and reasonable.

Nevertheless, in black and white terms, the electrician has exceeded the bounds of the contract. You could have grounds for refusing payment for anything more than repair or replacement of the appliance connections. Almost always, the "contract" for such jobs is verbal. The consumer describes the problem and then says: "Make sure it's all okay," or, "Do whatever is necessary." In a dispute over payment, the serviceman could reasonably argue that he took your instruction literally.

The agency relationship. A housekeeper can be assumed to be in charge of your home as your servant during your absence. Therefore she can be seen as your *agent*, empowered to act on your behalf, unless there has been some statement to the contrary.

In business, an agent is usually appointed by written contract and is paid for services performed. But the law also presumes an agency relationship exists in other cases even if neither party realizes it. For example, if you had previously honored obligations incurred in your name by the housekeeper (maybe she orders your groceries), she could be regarded legally as an *ostensible agent* and so you could not repudiate this present debt.

Then there is *apparent authority*. If you (as the "principal") place another person (the "agent") in a position that normally carries certain rights or authority, a court may rule that you have "vested" that person with the authority that usually goes with that position. The test is not whether you can prove that the housekeeper did not have the requisite authority but whether the serviceman reasonably thought she did have it.

A concise, exact contract between you and the serviceman is your best protection against

The best beefer of them all

Who is the world's most successful complainer? No, it's not Ralph Nader, the famous thorn in the side of Detroit. The *Guinness Book of World Records* hands the palm to Ralph Charell, who not only advises consumers (the "small guys") on how to battle the manufacturers and retailers (the "big guys") but makes a small fortune in the process.

With two best-selling paperbacks, Charell has fired countless thousands of consumers to pursue their rights. In *How to Turn Ordinary Complaints into Thousands of Dollars* and *How to Get the Upper Hand*, he not only gives practical advice to consumers fighting such titans as telephone companies, the government bureaucracy and big business, but also tips on how to get better food on airplanes, how not to be kept waiting in the corridors of power and how to get fast action about defective merchandise.

In speeches all across North America, Charell has instructed and amused audiences with his ingenious techniques for outsmarting the "big guys." His light touch has earned him the Mark Twain Society award for an outstanding contribution to humor.

similar situations in the future. Instruct him to do the specific job and nothing else. Tell him to phone you, or to leave you a note and a cost estimate if he uncovers further problems.

What needs to be done. Few cases of unauthorized work are clear-cut. Typical is the customer who took his car for an overhaul that, in years past, had usually cost about $100. The mechanic filled out the work order: tire rotation, grease and oil, a general safety check and a remedy for the "bumpy ride." He gave no estimate and the owner didn't ask for one.

Later, when he phoned to see if the car was ready, the owner was told he needed a new $26 part. He told the mechanic to "do what needs to be done," then, when he picked up the car, he got a bill for $350. He balked at the charge and the mechanic said: "You told me to do what needed to be done and I did it." And he showed that the repairs were necessary.

You run similar risks every time you give a serviceman such instructions. Had the motorist known all the details beforehand, he might have preferred to postpone some of the work, or even trade the car in on a new model.

One safeguard is to sign a work order and specify that you don't want the cost to exceed, say, $100. You could then refuse to pay a bill beyond that figure.

Better to specify what you want done, and ask to be called for authority to go ahead if more work seems to be necessary.

POOR WORKMANSHIP

You had your house redecorated but the paint is streaky and the wallpaper doesn't match.

Poor workmanship is a common consumer complaint.

In Calgary, where the Consumer and Corporate Affairs office gets about 50 calls a day, one woman complained that the paneling she had ordered for her recreation room looked so bad it made her "seasick." An investigator agreed the job was far from perfect, but there was nothing he could do. In her arrangement with the decorators, the woman had not specified either the thickness or support of the paneling. In effect, she had received roughly what she paid for.

The incident highlights the fact that you must accept responsibility to guard your rights. When you have your house redecorated, specify exactly what you want in wallpapers or paint—the color and grade, perhaps even the brand names. Be sure that the firm you hire has the track record for achieving the result you want by inspecting similar work it has done. Get several written estimates so that you can "comparison shop." If the company, or individual tradesman, promises "All work guaranteed," pin down just what that guarantee covers. Know that it's notoriously difficult to be sure from the store's paint samples or wall-covering books just what the stuff will look like on your walls.

Remember to hold back 15 to 20 percent of any substantial contract price even when you are satisfied with the workmanship. The Mechanic's Lien Act provides for such holdbacks to protect you from workmen or creditors whom the contractor may not have paid. If they have not been paid, such creditors have about 30 days (it's 37 in Ontario) to "place a lien" on your house.

You may not feel it necessary to go by the book when dealing with an established firm. It couldn't stay in business long if it were being dunned by its suppliers or subcontractors. But when you cut corners by hiring some one-van outfit, it's better to be safe than sorry.

DELAYS

A contractor began installing air conditioning in your home two months ago. Two heat waves have since come and gone, the place is a mess and the job is still incomplete.

If the crew doesn't turn up regularly, it's likely the firm has several jobs going at once. Everybody in town has decided at the same time not to swelter through another hot summer. It's cash-in time for the few local installers.

Even if you understand the reasons for the delay, don't be too sympathetic. The customer who presses aggressively is likely to be satisfied first. Your contract entitles you to expeditious completion, even if a finish date was never exactly promised.

Let's assume you have tried repeated calls to the contractor to speed him up. The next step is to get the local office of the federal or provincial consumer services bureau to intervene.

If you get fobbed off or lost in the corridors

A consumer diary

You could say that the Manitoba Consumers' Bureau goes looking for trouble. Nearly 40,000 telephone calls were received in a recent year, many generated by a TV advertising campaign advising consumers of their rights and by the bureau's outreach program, by which officers visit communities across the province. Some typical cases:

■ A consumer had a sofa custom-built with velvet covering that he was told was suitable. Within a short period, extreme wear was noticeable and the retailer did some remedial work on one of the cushions, then refused to do anything more.

Both the retailer and the manufacturer told the Consumers' Bureau that the buyer had made a bad choice. Velvet was great to look at but didn't wear well on a sofa. The buyer was adamant that he had been told at the time of ordering that the material would be okay.

The argument finished up in the Small Claims Court. The judge sided with the consumer. Under the terms of Manitoba's Consumer Protection Act, the goods had to be reasonably fit for the purpose in question. The buyer was awarded compensation of $400.

■ A farmer paid $900 for a color television set that was repaired twice by local servicemen in its first year, while still under warranty. It was still unsatisfactory.

The Winnipeg manufacturer then took the set back for repairs, even though the warranty had by now expired. Returned to the consumer, it still acted up.

When the Consumers' Bureau entered the picture, the manufacturer at first declined to carry out any more repairs but finally replaced the set with another model of comparable value.

■ Seven months after a consumer purchased a vinyl-leather reclining chair and ottoman, something went wrong with the base of the chair. He returned it to the retailer for repairs.

Several months passed with no chair and no promise of when repairs would be completed and he appealed to the Consumers' Bureau. It learned that the chair had been sent to the manufacturer in Montreal.

Eventually, the manufacturer replaced the faulty chair with a new one. But the buyer was still unhappy: the replacement did not match the ottoman. He asked for a full refund of his total purchase price.

He didn't get it. Instead, the manufacturer exchanged the old ottoman for one that matched the new recliner.

■ A householder contracted to have an old set of steps replaced by a prefab unit. He expected a workman to break up the old set with a jackhammer but the contractor sent a truck with a winch and pulled it out. In the process, the asphalt driveway was badly damaged and the contractor quoted a net $1,200 for its repair. (He allowed $300 for the damage done by the truck.) The consumer got some other estimates, then had the driveway fixed with concrete for less than $600. He asked the first contractor for a cash adjustment, but was refused on the grounds that the work had been done in concrete rather than the original asphalt.

But after letters and a visit from an officer of the Consumers' Bureau, the contractor finally paid up.

of bureaucracy, legal action is your final recourse. If the court decides that "time was of the essence" (that is, vital to the contract), the contractor would probably be ordered to complete it forthwith. Further delay would entitle you to cancel the contract and seek damages, such as extra expenses incurred in hiring a new contractor.

Installation of air conditioning is a major and costly undertaking and your contract should specify both starting and completion dates. Try to insert a default clause—although few tradesmen will accept such a dire condition—by which the contractor agrees to pay for any damages or financial loss caused if the job is not completed on target. The clause could set a penalty to be charged for every extra day.

Pay no more than 10 or 15 percent of the contract price at the start and the remainder in stages as work is completed. Then there's an incentive to keep the crew on the job.

BONDING OF EMPLOYEES

During your vacation, an agency looked after your houseplants and pets. Several valuable items of jewelry are missing.

You're looking at the crime of theft over $200 value. The maximum penalty is 10 years' imprisonment. So don't jump to conclusions. Whatever your immediate suspicions, the fact that someone had entry to your home doesn't add up to anything more than circumstantial evidence.

Breaking and entering is a common crime and others besides agency employees probably knew that you were on vacation.

Before you give any agency entry to your home in your absence, check its credentials with the police, Better Business Bureau or Chamber of Commerce. If there have been complaints against the company, you'll be told. You can also get basic information about how long it's been in business, its registered address and the names of the company officers.

You should not hesitate to ask for references. And you should follow up by checking those recommendations back to the issuers.

Security of the bond. If a firm's employees are bonded, a sum of money has been put up against the possibility of an employee's dishonesty. Bonding establishes a contract among three parties—the employer, the employee and the bonding company. The bonding company, in effect, guarantees the honesty of the employee.

If it was proved that a bonded serviceman had stolen the missing jewels, the owner would be compensated under terms of the bond.

Instances of theft by bonded employees are relatively rare. It's much more likely that your jewelry was stolen by a break-and-enter individual or gang. The mobile housekeeping service van in your driveway may have been a tip-off to your absence.

Sadly, crime does pay. Only one-third of reported thefts result in capture and prosecution of the offender. The fraction of stolen goods recovered is smaller still.

5 | YOUR RIGHTS AT WORK

24 Job security

Does the worker, once hired, "own" his job? Or is the boss free to hand out the pink slip? The answer—to both questions—is "Yes" and "No."

Employment standards legislation and the human rights codes demand that all workers be treated equally and fairly. Union contracts invariably set a procedure by which members may lodge dismissal grievances. Provincial labor laws provide machinery by which the sacked worker—unionized or not—can seek reinstatement or a cash settlement for loss of income. Finally, the civil courts are open to suits for compensation or damages.

The employer, on the other hand, retains the right to fire any employee on the spot for "just cause." After giving notice, he can also lay off staff for a given period, or indefinitely, citing business reasons.

But what, exactly, constitutes "just cause"? The days when, without fear of redress, an autocratic boss could fire a man for a single cheeky remark or for not wearing a collar and tie, or send a female employee packing for wearing tight slacks, have gone the way of the 48-hour week. Production quotas, compulsory overtime, staff uniforms, calling the boss "sir" or "ma'am"—these things are only unhappy memories in most workplaces today.

A worker who knocked his foreman to the floor during an argument was reinstated by a government-appointed arbitrator who held that firing was too tough a penalty for an act done "in the heat of the moment." In Kamloops, B.C., in 1979, a bank was forced to allow staff agitating for a union contract to wear union lapel buttons on the job.

On the other hand, the list of employee offenses or shortcomings that rate as "just cause" for dismissal is still a long one. It can range from deliberate misrepresentation on the job-application form to repeated insolence or abuse, inability to do the work allotted, violent or aggressive behavior, ignoring safety measures, and even behavior off the job that harms the employer's reputation.

Nevertheless, today's boss may face a tough, protracted battle when he decides to hand an employee the traditional pink slip. More than one million Canadians now work for one or another level of government, and they are virtually free from threat of dismissal, so intricate and lengthy is the process of job termination. Professors and teachers who achieve "tenure" are generally invulnerable. Under closed-shop agreements, which cover some 68,000 Canadian workers, the union virtually controls all hourly paid hiring. Management almost invariably advises the union representative of dismissal decisions—and weighs the possible reaction before coming to such decisions.

DISCRIMINATION

You are refused a job at a new factory despite your experience in similar work. Most of those hired are inexperienced.

Many legitimate factors can influence a hiring decision. The employer may claim that you aren't really among the best qualified for the job, despite your experience. He isn't compelled to spell out his reasons. If you decide to press the issue, and he can show valid reasons for not hiring you, the matter will likely end right there.

Federal and provincial laws prohibit discrimination on grounds of race, color, religion, sex, national or ethnic origin, and marital status. The physically handicapped may not be discriminated against in British Columbia, Manitoba, Nova Scotia, New Brunswick, Prince Edward Island, Quebec or Saskatchewan.

If you have reasonable grounds to suspect discrimination when you were turned down for a job, you can ask the federal or provincial Human Rights Commission to investigate.

If the investigator decides that you were probably rejected because of, say, your sex or color, then the commission will step in. First, it will try conciliation; if that fails, it will set up a tribunal to hear your case. The tribunal may be only one person. Even so, he will have the power to order the company to hire you, or to pay you damages. If you live in Quebec, the commission will seek relief for your case through the courts.

Woman in the guard. The employer will usually settle, rather than face the effort and expense of a hearing. To some critics, this seems close to official blackmail. But it can also indicate that the employer came to realize the company's personnel policies were mistaken. In one such instance, the employer was the Department of National Defence.

In December 1978, the newly established federal Human Rights Commission appointed a tribunal to rule on a complaint by Nathalie Bedard that the department had discriminated against her because of her sex. She had been refused a summer job in the changing-of-the-guard ceremony on Parliament Hill. A month later, the Minister of Defence, Barney Danson, announced that women would be permitted to participate in the ceremony.

Apart from the clout of human rights laws, fair-employment-practices legislation in most provinces specifically forbids employment agencies to practice discrimination. In referring candidates to companies with job openings, these agencies can affect the employment chances of thousands of Canadians and legislation has been framed accordingly. Alberta forbids discrimination by "an employer or person acting on behalf of an employer." Ontario specifies that no employment agency shall practice discrimination in receiving applications or referring people to jobs.

"Affirmative action" is the bureaucrat's buzzword for schemes that try to head off discrimination before it occurs. Canada hasn't gone as far as the United States, where employers who receive government contracts must employ stated percentages of females and minority groups. Canadian authorities prefer to ask major employers to adopt voluntary affirmative-action programs to make their managers conscious of the legal obligation to treat all individuals fairly and equally. Nova Scotia's Human Rights Commission asks employers to sign affirmative-action agreements with the commission. It makes periodic checks to ensure that the agreements are being honored. The federal government has established a pool of affirmative-action consultants whose job is to seek voluntary compliance from Crown corporations and firms with government contracts worth $200,000 or more.

QUALIFICATIONS

The biggest firm in your town requires applicants to be high-school graduates, even for manual work.

Employers have the right to set standards of education and skill. If these rigidly exclude otherwise suitable applicants, then the company is the loser. Some employers ask for high-school diplomas simply because they regard them as a symbol of motivation and perseverance, even though that level of learning may have nothing to do with the demands of the job.

The setting of unreasonable standards can amount to subtle, if unintentional, discrimination. For example, if arbitrary height or weight minimums are specified for certain jobs, shorter or lighter people, however competent, are excluded. These minimums often discriminate against women. Or the personnel officer may insist on the ability to speak French and English well for a job that doesn't require bilingualism at all.

Such requirements serve to bar certain groups from employment and you may be able to argue discrimination before your Human Rights Commission. Your Member of Parliament, provincial legislature representative or city alderman may intervene on your behalf. Other sources of assistance could include the

The magic of the lawyer's letter

Do you really believe you've been sacked unfairly? The courts are open to you to launch a suit for wrongful dismissal, if your union or professional association won't go to bat for you. Of course you'll need a lawyer to prepare and argue your case. But maybe you won't have to go the whole way. If you have a reasonable case, the employer is likely to think twice when he learns that you're preparing to go to law. In many instances, a preliminary letter from your lawyer will be enough to do the trick. A Toronto lawyer who has represented a number of fired executives pries loose many thousands of dollars without resorting to litigation. He has a portfolio of four action letters from which he chooses the one that best fits a client's circumstances.

The *rush for legal help* letter: This one is addressed to a senior executive of the "enemy" company. It quotes technical legal precedents that will send the ex-boss running to his lawyer. When lawyers for the two sides get together, an out-of-court settlement is always in the cards.

The *I can't believe you really intended this* letter: This is effective against a company—say, a bank or trust company—that is very sensitive about its public image. It gives the company an open chance to make amends—and save face.

The *demolition* letter: Shock tactics. Not mincing words, it ruthlessly destroys the credibility of the opponent. Used only when you've "got the goods," it leaves just a crack under the door for him to crawl under and pay up.

The *man to man* letter: For use in writing to other solicitors when all the cards are on the table. It sets up the platform for an agreed cash settlement. Letter No. 4 frequently follows Letter No. 1, of which the following is a prime example.

January 7, 1980

Without Prejudice

Mr. I.F.B.
Executive Director
XYZ Company Ltd.
Peterborough, Ontario

Dear Sir:

Re: Miss J.T.

On May 17, 1979, you wrote to Miss J.T. dismissing her from her office with your company. She asked for reasons for her dismissal, but you gave none. You just dismissed her with one month's pay and without explanation.

Having spent some time with Miss J.T. and gone over carefully her employment history from the time she first became a qualified nurse till the day that she was dismissed by you, it has become clear to me why you were not able to give any rational explanation for her dismissal. There isn't any.

Miss J.T. is an intelligent, extremely well-qualified, courageous and dynamic person. She is a person who has received public acclaim for her work in many areas of endeavor. In all these fields she was driven by her sense of dedication to the human cause.

A review of decided Canadian cases shows that one month's pay is totally inadequate in the case of a person in Miss J.T.'s position. Here are some of the cases you should look at:

          (a list of seven court decisions in
                favor of the plaintiff)

Unless you take prompt action to right the wrong that you have done to my client, she will have no alternative but to commence legal proceedings.

Yours truly,

provincial ombudsman, the local Manpower office, or your district labor council.

One of the unfairest forms of discrimination is the reluctance of many firms to hire anyone who has been unemployed for a long time. It springs from the boss's fear that the person lacks drive or doesn't really want to work. This "welfare bum" syndrome helps to keep some of the unemployed unemployed. To combat this, Manpower placement officers suggest that you do any kind of work available, while you're looking for the right job. With a few extra dollars in your pocket, and the record of recent activity, you'll present a more competent front to the personnel officer assessing your aptitude for work in his company.

APTITUDE TESTS

You have done poorly on the mandatory aptitude test and your job application is rejected.

Aptitude tests are one of management's prerogatives and the law permits a company to refuse, on the basis of your test results, to hire you. The employer is not obliged to tell you the results, and most won't. The applicant does have some protection, however. Personality or psychological tests may be construed as an invasion of privacy. Questions about your sex habits or religious beliefs can be challenged.

Aptitude tests can sometimes infringe on fair-employment-practices legislation. You have the right to complain to your Human Rights Commission if the tests seem discriminatory. Some tests, for example, make it difficult for people without language skills to be hired even when that factor has no relevance to the job. Or the tests may be culturally oriented and may discriminate against certain ethnic groups or the "disadvantaged." Tests may be aimed mainly at men and made difficult for women to pass.

The freeze-up factor. Even though legislation doesn't clearly define what may or may not be included in an aptitude test, the employer could find himself in trouble for using a test whose impact, intentional or not, is discriminatory. Some people freeze up when faced with paper testing, though they may handle similar problems easily in real life. For this reason, sensible employers don't rely on aptitude testing alone. A test should only be part of a screening process that also includes the traditional job interview, references and assessment of work experience.

On the other hand, an aptitude test isn't necessarily a barrier. It can give a qualified person a better chance than he might have if he were judged solely on the basis of an interview with a personnel manager who may be biased or simply not a very good judge of competence.

There are thousands of aptitude tests on the market, some of them poorly prepared and handled by people unqualified to evaluate the results. Psychologists warn that members of minority groups often achieve poorer results than members of majority groups on tests used for employment, regardless of how they may perform on the job. Any aptitude test should meet these criteria: it should be related specifically to the job; be fair and reasonable; be administered in good faith; be properly evaluated, and not be used as the sole determining factor.

If the test you failed doesn't meet these standards, you can appeal for help to your elected representatives, the ombudsman or your provincial Human Rights Commission. If the company is unionized, appeal to the union secretary. Arbitration boards have upheld some union claims that particular aptitude tests were improper and some unions have won agreement that only certain tests will be used by the company concerned.

INVASION OF PRIVACY

You refused to answer some personal questions. Your application form was thrown in the wastebasket.

You have the right to refuse to answer any question that seeks information in areas in which discrimination is forbidden by law. An obvious example is that a prospective employer cannot ask you your religion, or seek to establish it by indirect questions, unless the job itself is with a religious organization. On the other hand, it's perfectly reasonable for an interviewer to ask whether your family commitments leave you free to travel. The test is whether the question is really related to the job.

The main exception to this rule occurs when you apply for a position where security clearance is an occupational requirement. Then, the federal government and its agencies may legally ask you to complete a personal history form containing questions an ordinary employer may not ask.

If you face a question on an application form that you feel is discriminatory, refuse to fill it in. If the employer says you can't have the job because you didn't complete the form, call the Human Rights Commission. The alternative is to answer the question under protest and then, if you don't get the job, go to the commission and lay a charge of discrimination. Although the mere asking of questions may not be unlawful, the commission is apt to assume that the asking is done for a discriminatory purpose. It may bring charges if people are denied jobs after they fill out forms containing questions about topics that are considered private matters.

THE 'CLOSED SHOP'

A major construction company can't hire you because you don't belong to the union, and the union is not accepting new members at this time.

You're caught in the middle and in this case, your individual employment rights aren't worth a dime. If the company has a "closed shop" contract with a union, then you can't get the job until you become a member of that union.

In times of high unemployment, unions with closed-shop agreements usually refuse to take in new members. Their argument is that there isn't enough work for those already signed up. It makes no difference if you have a special skill to offer.

The closed shop is still uncommon outside the construction industry. It began there as a move to bring some order into an industry to which almost every able-bodied man could turn when he needed a job. The unions started insisting on closed-shop contracts and thus, in effect, took over much of the hiring. When a construction boss wants 10 or 20 men for a job he calls the union hall. The union dispatcher sends workers out on a rotation system based on seniority and on a check of who has had work recently.

The closed shop, with compulsory payment of union membership dues by all workers, provides virtually total union security. All workers in a closed shop must join the union when they are hired, or when their probationary period ends and they become permanent employees. A variation of this system is "the Rand formula," named after Mr. Justice Ivan Rand who chaired the arbitration board that devised it in 1946: all employees in a bargaining unit where the formula applies must pay union dues, but are not compelled to become union members.

If a union refuses you membership for reasons other than that there are already enough of their members in the field, you may be able to bring a charge of discrimination before your provincial Labour Relations Board. The law places the same onus on unions as it does on employers to treat people fairly. The board could order you accepted into membership, or award damages.

PROMOTIONS

You have been passed over repeatedly for promotion, although your supervisor has frequently praised your work.

No one has an automatic right to promotion, unless such a provision is written into a personal employment agreement or union contract. It may be that in your company, promotions go first to relatives, or to those who are in the "old boys' network."

Actionable discrimination in promotions is difficult to prove, but not impossible. A company may hire a member of a minority group as a "token," but have no intention of permitting him to move upward.

If you suspect that's the situation in your case, the Human Rights Commission will listen to your story. Its investigators may be able to persuade the company to treat you better. Sometimes a pattern of discrimination in a company is not difficult to identify—if, for example, women never get management jobs. If discrimination is revealed, and your employer doesn't act voluntarily to correct the situation, the case can go to a tribunal and your employer may be compelled to promote you.

LAYOFFS

You are laid off from your job at the factory because the sales force can't move the product.

There is a difference between being laid off and being fired, although the material result is the same. A layoff, essentially, is ordered for business reasons and doesn't reflect on your work performance. A firing is "for cause"; your employer doesn't want you on the staff any more.

It's an important distinction if you are applying for unemployment insurance, because an employee who is fired may have to wait for an extended period before he is eligible for

There is harm in asking

The Human Rights Commissions issue guidelines to employers warning them of questions they should not ask job applicants. Discrimination is everywhere forbidden on grounds of race, religion, color or sex. Questions on these subjects are "not acceptable." The federal government and several of the provinces also include marital status, political belief, and place of origin among the prohibited inquiries.

The *Recruitment and Interviewing Guide for Employers* issued by the federal Department of Employment and Immigration clearly outlines the forbidden territory. An interviewer, or a job-application form, may *not* ask:

■ About a person's mother tongue unless the language inquiry is job-related.

■ About military service other than that in the Canadian forces.

■ Any questions that would indicate race, color, complexion (including color of eyes and hair).

■ About the clubs or organizations to which you belong.

■ About religious affiliation, except to ask about willingness to meet a specified work schedule—and, even then, the employer has to accommodate the religious observances of the applicant if this is reasonably possible.

■ About physical handicaps or limitations, unless relevant to the job and the safety of other workers.

■ Questions relative to sex, marital status, children or pregnancy.

Companies cannot demand photographs of applicants before hiring, but photos may be required later for identification purposes. Under federal guidelines, the only inquiry an employer may make relating to birthplace, ethnic origin or nationality is the question: "Are you legally entitled to work in Canada?"

The federal government and some of the provinces frown on questions about criminal convictions, unless the particular conviction is relevant to the job qualification. For example, the federal guide says theft and fraud convictions are relevant to a job requiring honesty, but possession of marijuana is not. If references are required, it is just as wrong for an employer to ask someone else forbidden questions about you as it would be to ask you directly.

benefits. In December 1979, the waiting period for unemployment-insurance benefits was two weeks if you were laid off, but could be as many as seven weeks if you quit or were fired. (*See* Chapter 27, "Salary and benefits.")

All provinces except New Brunswick and British Columbia require that notice be given if an employee is being laid off permanently. Depending on years of service, amount of notice, or pay in lieu of notice, ranges from one to eight weeks. Additional notice is required when employment of a group of workers is to be terminated. The Canada Labour Code provides for severance pay for employees with more than five years' service who are permanently laid off. The maximum is 40 days' pay. It applies only to undertakings in the federal jurisdiction, however. None of the provinces have severance-pay legislation.

Federal law protects workers who are fired but have no union to take up their cause. The Canada Labour Code was amended in 1978 to permit any employee to complain to the Canada Labour Relations Board about unfair dismissal. The board will appoint a conciliation officer who'll try to settle the case. If the employer won't take you back, and the officer feels you have a good case, you can appeal to an adjudicator for a final decision.

Make sure when your job is terminated that you get any money due to you. The legal requirements vary from province to province. In Ontario, for example, you would be entitled to either a week's notice or a week's pay if you've worked for your firm for less than two years; to two weeks' if you've been there from two to five years; four weeks' for five to 10 years' service; and eight weeks' pay, or notice, if you've been with the company for more than 10 years.

Under federal law, and in Manitoba, Newfoundland, Nova Scotia, Ontario and Quebec, employment-standards laws require employers to give advance notice or idemnity to workers when planning either a group termination of jobs or a group layoff. This legislation generally applies when more than 50 workers are affected. When between 50 and 100 workers are involved, they have to get eight weeks' notice; between 100 and 300, the period is 12 weeks; larger groups get 16 weeks' notice. The underlying principle is that the larger the group being released on to the unemployment rolls with relatively the same skills, the longer time they'll need to find jobs.

The law is normally waived for temporary layoffs—for example, up to 13 weeks in Ontario. A worker isn't entitled to get notice if he has refused alternative work.

NOTICE OF RESIGNATION

You lose out on a good job because your present employer insists that you give two weeks' notice of resignation.

The employer's right to insist on his employees' giving notice of resignation depends upon which province you live in. Employees working under federal labor legislation are not obliged to give any notice at all. This includes some 600,000 workers on international and interprovincial railway, highway, air transport and telephone and broadcasting systems, and employees of banks, feed warehouses, flour and feed mills, grain elevators and Crown corporations. The same freedom applies under the laws of British Columbia, Alberta, Saskatchewan, Ontario and New Brunswick. The other five provinces compel an employee to give notice of resignation.

In Manitoba and Newfoundland the notice has to be equivalent to the pay period; if you are paid weekly, you have to give a week's notice. In Nova Scotia, if you've been employed for up to two years, you have to give a week's notice; if you've had the job for longer than two years, two weeks' notice. Prince Edward Island demands a week's notice, except for farm and construction workers and domestics, who don't have to give any. In Quebec, all employees have to give notice of resignation—a week if hired by the week, two weeks if hired by the month, and one month if hired by the year.

However, most union and individual contracts everywhere will contain a clause stipulating a notice period before you can quit. It's wise to give notice, even when no law or contract requires this. It's a common courtesy, appreciated by your employer—and he's probably the person who'll write your most valuable reference.

REFERENCES

The letter of reference from your former employer mentions a row you had with a supervisor.

While there's no established body of law as yet granting wide access to private files, legislation on the opening of credit files and on freedom of information has set the stage favorably. Some large companies—including International Business Machines, Eaton's, and Bell Canada—permit their employees to read their personnel files and to challenge what's in them should they see fit. Employees of the federal government also have the right to see their personnel records.

Traditionally, personnel files and letters of reference based on those files are the private and secret property of management. But public concern over the amount of personal information in the hands of authorities—everything from credit information to medical records—is beginning to lift the veil of secrecy.

If you think a derogatory reference is blocking your chances of getting a better job, you should approach your provincial consumer services bureau. (There's a branch in just about every sizable town.) Laws dealing with secret credit ratings may be so interpreted as to protect you from damaging information in your personnel file.

The rotten reference. Ontario's Consumer Reporting Act applies to any report containing personal information prepared at someone else's request, with or without fee. If an Ontario worker believes he's been turned down because of an unfavorable reference, he has the right to ask within 60 days where the reference was obtained. He can then approach the person who prepared the reference, demand to see it, question its contents and ask who has seen it.

The act says that any agency preparing a report must make reasonable efforts to corroborate any unfavorable references. Consumer-agency officials say that, in several cases, they've persuaded a former employer to change an unfavorable report simply by pointing out that if the ex-boss can't back up what he has recorded, trouble could ensue. Personnel reports in Ontario may not mention bankruptcy, or a criminal conviction more than seven years old, nor make any note of your race, creed, color, sex, ancestry, ethnic origin or political affiliation.

CHANGING JOB DESCRIPTIONS

You lose your job as a cocktail waitress when you refuse to work topless.

If working topless was one of the original terms and conditions of your employment, you have little chance of succeeding with a complaint of unfair dismissal. If it wasn't, you may have a case.

In Toronto, the Bartenders' and Waiters' Union, Local 280, waged a successful fight against employers who changed requirements after hiring union members. Where waitresses had been required to be both servers of food and drink and topless entertainers, the union's complaints forced some employers to become licensed to operate places of entertainment. This move brought them within the orbit of the standards that must be met under certain provisions of the liquor licensing system. The vital licenses can be suspended or canceled when the holders fail to meet the set standards.

If you oppose the topless trend on moral grounds, seek assistance from local women's and church groups, the district labor council, and your elected representatives.

INJURIES ON THE JOB

You suffered an injury on the job. You are disabled for life.

Every province grants substantial rights to the injured worker, whether or not he is to blame for the accident. The Workmen's Compensa-

Industrial illness

The Workmen's Compensation Board (WCB) pays benefits as long as the worker is kept off the job by illness or injury. But it can be difficult to prove that an illness is directly related to your job. Some diseases develop over many years, and you could have changed jobs several times. However, the WCB doctors recognize that certain lung and skin diseases, and conditions such as bursitis or hernia are often job-caused. Each board has its own list of recognized industrial diseases. Here are some of those accepted by the WCB in British Columbia.

SCHEDULE B
(Section 7 (4))

Description of Disease	Description of Process or Industry
Lead poisoning	Any process or operation where there is an exposure to lead or lead compounds.
Mercury poisoning	Any process or operation where there is an exposure to mercury or mercury compounds.
Arsenic poisoning	Any process or operation where there is exposure to arsenic or arsenic compounds.
Silicosis	Metalliferous-mining or coal-mining industry.
Injury to the lungs	Fire-fighting.
Injury to the heart	Fire-fighting.
Occupational deafness	Any industry involving prolonged and continuous exposure to excessive noise.
Asbestosis	Any industry or process where there is exposure to air-borne asbestos fibres.
Carcinoma of the lung, when associated with asbestosis	Any industry or process where there is exposure to airborne asbestos fibres.
Mesothelioma (pleural or peritoneal	Any industry or process where there is exposure to airborne asbestos fibres.
Asthma and respiratory irritation	Any process or operation where there is excessive exposure to irritants ordinarily ... ... where there is excessive exposure to toxic gases, vapours, mists, or fumes.
Pneumoconiosis	Any process or operation where there is exposure to silica dust.
Tenosynovitis, tendinitis	Any process or operation requiring excessive use of the arm, leg, hand, or foot.
Vascular disturbances of the extremities	Any process or operation where there is prolonged exposure to excessive vibration at low temperatures.
Radiation injury or disease	Any process or operation where there is exposure to radiation.
Psittacosis	Any industry where there is established contact with ornithosis-infected avian species or material.
Undulant fever	Any process where there is contact with animals, carcasses, or animal by-products.
Staphylococcus aureus, Salmonellosis	In employment where close and frequent contact with a source or sources of the infection has been established and the employment (a) necessitates the treatment, nursing, or examination of or interviews with patients or ill persons; or (b) necessitates the analysis or testing of body tissues or fluids; or (c) necessitates research into salmonelleæ or pathogenic staphylococci.
Tuberculosis	In employment where close and frequent contact with a source or sources of tuberculous infection has been established and the employment (1) necessitates the treatment, nursing, or examination of patients or ill persons; or (2) necessitates the analysis or testing of body tissues or fluids ... ... free ... ... of tuberculosis; and (b) who continued to be free from evidence of tuberculosis for six months after being so employed (except in primary tuberculosis as proven by a negative tuberculin test at time of employment). In the case of an employee previously compensated for tuberculosis, any subsequent tuberculosis after the disease has become inactive and has remained inactive for a period of three years or more shall not be deemed to have occurred as a result of the original disability for the purpose of the Act, unless the worker is still engaged in employment listed above or the Board is satisfied that the subsequent tuberculosis is the direct result of the tuberculosis for which the worker has been compensated.
Tooth erosion	Any industry where there is exposure to acid fumes or mist.

tion Board (WCB) makes payments if you are injured on the job, or if you contract an industrial disease. If a fatality occurs, a pension is paid to surviving dependents. Just about every worker in Canada is covered except domestic servants and, in some provinces, farmworkers. The latter are protected in Ontario, for example, but generally excluded in Alberta.

Self-employed persons and professionals are by and large excluded from compulsory coverage, but they can join if they wish. A lawyer can get some protection for himself and coverage for his staff by agreeing to pay the employer's contribution. Many educational institutions and hospitals have chosen to pay workmen's compensation, thus getting coverage not only for their professional staff but for hourly paid workers, too.

If you have an accident on the job, or contract an illness peculiar to your work—a nurse who catches chicken pox from a patient, for example—then you must report your injury or disease to your employer. The company is required by law to report the incident to the WCB. In most provinces, doctors or dentists involved in your treatment are also obliged to report to the board.

You qualify for benefits on the second day after your injury or illness begins in all provinces, except Nova Scotia, where it is on the fourth day. Even if you are off work for only a short time, you're entitled to payment for that period. If your employer continues to pay your salary while you're away, the company gets the WCB payments.

No blame laid. WCB benefits cost employers approximately $2.07 for every $100 of payroll; in return, they are freed from individual claims for compensation. The amount each employer pays depends on the industry involved and whether it has a good or poor accident rate. There's no question of fault. The WCB pays temporary benefits as long as the worker is kept off the job by illness or injury, or permanent pensions if it appears he will never be able to work again or that his working capacity has been permanently reduced.

The amounts paid vary with the extent of illness or injury, and the level of your wages at the time. Nine of the provincial boards pay a maximum of 75 percent of your income at time of injury. In Quebec, the maximum payment is calculated on the basis of 90 percent of your net earnings after taxes. In all provinces, the indemnity varies according to the number of your dependents. If your disability is considered to have become permanent, you will be paid a permanent pension on a monthly basis. For an injury that is permanent but not totally disabling, you will be granted a partial pension. The loss of an eye, for example, entitles you to a 16 percent pension. WCB doctors will examine you and recommend the type of pension you should get.

If you have a fatal accident at work, or die of an industrial disease with a proved relationship to your job, your dependent spouse will get a pension, an immediate lump-sum payment, plus burial expenses. The amounts vary from province to province. In Ontario, for example, both the lump sum and the burial expense are $800; the spouse's pension is $365 a month, plus $99 a month for each child under 16 at school. If the spouse remarries, there's a lump sum equivalent to two years' pension, but payments continue for children until they are 16 or are no longer at school or college.

You can't get unemployment insurance if you are on workmen's compensation. However, WCB payments do not affect other sources of income. This means that you can also collect disability benefits from the Canada Pension Plan, if you were a contributor. If your WCB pension is very low, you may qualify for municipal welfare as well to bring your income up to a reasonable level.

If you disagree with any WCB decision, you have the right of appeal, first to the claims review branch, then to an appeal board.

SEXUAL HARASSMENT

A friend quit her factory job because the foreman continually made passes at her. Now he's making a move on you.

Sexual harassment, as it has become labeled, is a difficult problem to deal with legally. There can be a very fine line between flirtation and

How to get that job

The search for jobs is now such an integral factor of the marketplace in these times of high unemployment that it has created a bureaucracy of its own. The federal government, through the Employment and Immigration Commission, maintains a Canada Employment Service office—still widely known under its former title of Manpower—in all cities. It strives to direct the registered unemployed to known vacancies. Private employment agencies also abound; in 1979, one Toronto agency was placing about 7,000 men and women in temporary work every week, and a lot of those appointments became permanent. There's a regular army of professional job-finding officers, executive-placement consultants, and agencies that produce tailored résumés. Forty-Plus of Canada concentrates solely on helping displaced executives find new careers in the high-pay brackets. Whole pages of display advertisements offering specialized jobs appear in the larger city newspapers.

Even so, the job applicant must first become a successful salesman. The product? Yourself. The individual seeking either a first job, or a better one, should approach job-hunting as a job in itself. It's estimated that the average Canadian worker under 35 will go job-hunting once every 18 months; over 35, once every three years.

The initial task in a job-search is often the hardest: self-appraisal. What kind of job do you want, and what do you have to offer? You'll need to learn how to list your qualities, experience and potential in a written résumé. This document is your chief sales tool. A job advertised at an attractive wage may bring in several hundred applications. Almost invariably, a short list is drawn up after the résumés are sifted. The résumé should be your bid, not for the vacancy itself, but to win you an interview. It should be brief, positive and honest—but that doesn't oblige you to include anything detrimental.

Two pages is the magic number for your résumé: one looks a bit skimpy, three, verbose. Begin with your current or most recent job, and work backwards; anything more distant than 10 years should merely be summarized. Use active words. Don't puff, but don't hide your light under a bushel, either. "Secretarial duties," for example, doesn't convey much. "Private secretary to the sales director, responsible for all appointments" gets the message across. A salesman should describe how he built up his monthly figures or brought off a particular coup.

The employer doesn't care which grade school you attended. If you didn't go to university or other post-secondary school, it's enough to state "high-school graduate." The younger applicant should mention summer jobs if they are related to the vacancy or indicate energy and initiative. Night-school or correspondence courses can attest to your motivation. An interesting hobby or community activity is worth a line or two.

Read up on the target company if you know little about it. You'll be better equipped then to state in a brief covering letter *why* you'd like to work there and what you hope to achieve. Don't include letters of reference but, if you have some positive ones, say they are available upon request. Make sure you include a telephone number where you can be reached, or where a message will be received on your behalf.

When called for an interview, don't smoke, chew gum, or eat a highly spiced lunch. Dress and grooming *are* important—and sometimes vital. The business world is, by and large, conservative. Hawaiian shirts or deep decolletage are not advised. Try to relax, but look the hiring officer in the eye without staring. Don't fluster if asked awkward questions: an honest answer about a shortcoming usually disarms the questioner. If you were perfect, nobody could afford to hire you.

coercion. In a 1979 survey of employees of the Department of Housing and Urban Development in the United States, women claimed that sleeping with the boss was a requirement for promotion and higher pay for many of them in clerical and subprofessional jobs. Only 15 percent reported this harassment to higher management. Some 33 percent of this group had gone along with the boss's demands—and in four cases out of five they said it paid off.

The relatively few cases brought before Human Rights Commissions in Canada have been dealt with under the provisions forbidding sexual discrimination. While this appears to stretch the original intent of the wording of the legislation, several successful prosecutions are on record. Settlement is usually reached by voluntary agreement as both parties shrink from the publicity of an open hearing.

How can you prove that the foreman's approaches exceeded harmless flirtation, or that you didn't encourage him by your own attitude? What you need is evidence of repeated, unwanted and unsolicited sexual advances. Take your problem to your foreman's superior or have your union representative intervene. No company welcomes the prospect of an investigation by a Human Rights Commission.

The publicity penalty. Fair-employment-practices legislation generally says that no employer shall discriminate against any employee in any term or condition of employment. If repeated sexual advances should become a special condition of employment for a woman, she could lay a formal complaint with the Human Rights Commission. If you could prove that refusal of sexual favors caused you to lose your job, or forced you to quit, you'd have a strong case.

The commission, or the Labour Relations Board responsible in your province for fair employment practices, will probably investigate and try to settle the complaint quietly. If that doesn't succeed, the charge will go to a tribunal that has the power to reinstate workers, to order certain actions to cease, or to impose a cash settlement.

25 Work conditions

Today, virtually everyone is joining the campaign for better working conditions—even the strippers. Supported by the Canadian Labour Congress (CLC), the exotic dancers—or ecdysiasts—are putting everything into their fight against poorly lit and badly constructed stages in taverns and burlesque houses. "I know girls who have sprained their ankles or broken their legs falling off some of these stages," complains Diane Michaels, president of the Canadian Association of Burlesque Entertainers. Some dancers have even suffered burns from strong floodlights.

The women are taking the right tack. Dramatic improvements in working conditions are generally won by bringing potential or existing safety and health hazards to official attention. Unions have the leverage to negotiate continual progress for their members, and although they represent only about a third of the national work force, the changes they fight for can affect all workers.

Statistics on occupational accidents and health hazards show there's still a long way to go. Victor Rabinovitch, health and safety officer of the CLC, released in 1979 a congress study indicating that 70 million working days were lost in Canada in a single year through job-related injuries and illness.

Improved safety and health standards can be costly, but no government can afford politically to be overly price-conscious about workers' well-being. And many employers have learned that a healthy and contented work force means higher productivity and lower expenditures for workmen's compensation and health-care costs.

The majority of nonunionized workers tend to be employed in low-income jobs—clerks, shop assistants, typists, cleaners, farm laborers, hotel and restaurant staff and domestics. About 20 percent of them are paid the provincial or federal minimum wage. Having little or no bargaining power, they must rely on government for protection and progress.

Governments respond by tightening employment standards and financing studies aimed at enhancing the "quality of life" in the workplace. The underlying philosophy is that work must not be merely the penalty one pays to survive; the job itself should have some dignity and meaning. An Ontario law, proclaimed in 1979, makes it mandatory for labor-management committees to be set up by most companies employing more than 20 workers. These committees initiate and supervise all health and safety procedures and the law gives them plenty of clout.

RIGHT OF REFUSAL

A workmate was injured on an old forklift in your plant. You refuse to operate the machine, and the foreman warns you that you will be suspended.

As of 1979, workers in six provinces—Nova Scotia, Ontario, Manitoba, Saskatchewan, Alberta and British Columbia—had the right to refuse to perform unsafe work. The same holds true in any job covered by federal law or regulation.

Generally, these "right to refuse" laws say the employee has to have "reasonable" grounds to believe there is "imminent danger" before he can disobey a supervisor's order. Relatively new, they are a response to the concern over the human and financial costs of industrial accidents and diseases. Every 17 seconds of worktime, someone is killed or injured on the job. The cost of industrial accidents and diseases averages about $1.5 billion a year. Says Art Bray, manager of the occupational section of the Canada Safety Council:

"Fifty percent of all occupational accidents could be prevented by rigorous safety programs. It's no exaggeration to say that some of our factories and offices are as dangerous as battlefields."

Filthy facilities. Some workers, notably policemen, firemen and prison guards, don't have the right to refuse to perform tasks they may consider dangerous. Ambulance drivers and workers in hospitals and psychiatric institutions may refuse only if their refusal doesn't jeopardize someone else's life or safety. Even though teachers generally can refuse to do unsafe work, the exemption does not apply to teachers employed in correctional institutions. Others can refuse work if they think any machine, equipment or condition in the workplace puts them in imminent danger.

Four Ontario construction workers refused to work at an underground mining site at Hagersville because the toilet allocated to them was in a filthy condition. When they demanded the right to use the facilities provided for the miners, they were fired. Their complaint came before the Labour Relations Board, which awarded them compensation of about $6,000 each and ordered the company to give them "first consideration" for future vacancies.

Upon refusing a task, a worker must report the reasons for his action to the employer or supervisor, who investigates in the presence of the worker and a union representative or a health and safety representative. If the situation isn't resolved, a provincial inspector is called in to decide whether the work should go ahead.

Employers are not allowed to dismiss, threaten, suspend, discipline or intimidate workers for exercising their right to refuse. Disputes go to the Labour Relations Board for final settlement, or to arbitration if a union contract exists.

Saskatchewan gives the employee, who refuses to work because of alleged dangers, the benefit of any doubt. Unless the boss has clear evidence to the contrary, the claim that the situation is unsafe has to be accepted at face value. Under most arbitration regulations, the onus is on the worker to prove that his refusal to obey a supervisor's order is justified. A firing, or suspension, for refusal will likely be upheld if, say, another worker takes over the job and is not injured.

Before the introduction of "right to refuse" legislation, employers had the final say over what procedures or conditions were not safe.

Generally, in law, employers are not held responsible for accidents in the workplace if they can prove every reasonable precaution has been taken. In fact, where the Workmen's Compensation Board Act applies, employees are prohibited from suing their employers for accidents in the workplace. But any violations of specified safety and health standards, or neglect of reasonable precautions, can bring court convictions. In Ontario, an employer who contravenes the Occupational Health and Safety Act is liable for a fine of up to $25,000 and a jail term of up to 12 months, or both.

HEALTH AND COMPENSATION

Several workers in your foundry have developed respiratory troubles. You think something should be done about hazardous conditions at the foundry.

No employer is permitted to compel employees to work unprotected in conditions harmful to health. Your first move is to find out what standards or laws your boss may be violating in allowing work to proceed under apparently hazardous conditions. Legislative progress in this area is continuous, but uneven from one province to another. There may be no absolutes under your provincial law; the Department of Labour will advise—and inspect.

Many potentially harmful substances, whether physical, chemical or biological, are not strictly regulated by law. Instead, guidelines on permissible levels are issued by the federal or provincial governments for the use of health and safety inspectors. However, the incidence of cancer and other diseases among uranium and asbestos workers is prodding governments to impose stricter control on toxic substances. Landmark legislation permits health and safety directors to prohibit or limit the use of certain such substances. Employers must post the orders, inform workers of any dangers, and keep them informed of any exposure to certain biological, chemical or physical agents.

The International Labour Office in Geneva reported in 1978 that as many as 40 "practically indispensable" chemicals and compounds used in industry can cause cancer. The Ontario Occupational Health and Safety Act (1978) lists seven such toxic substances and harmful physical agents: lead, asbestos, silica, mercury, vinyl chloride, isocyanates, and noise.

Ontario has established an "exposure limit" for workers using methyl dianiline, a hardening agent in paints. In uncontrolled use, it can destroy liver cells and cause toxic hepatitis. In Manitoba, women of childbearing age are no longer hired for the huge smelter at Flin Flon. Research has shown that a mother's contact with lead can harm a fetus.

If clear legal standards have not yet been established in your province, your best recourse is to ask the labor department to determine what is causing the health problem where you work. If you are working under a collective agreement, your union should already be in the picture. Where joint health and safety committees are in place, they'll take up your complaint.

No benefits for smokers. Any worker sick or disabled from an occupational disease has the right to collect workmen's compensation. (*See* Chapter 24, "Job security.") The difficulty may be to provide reasonable proof that the problem is indeed job related.

Some boards are conservative about accepting compensation claims for industrial health problems, perhaps fearful of opening the floodgates to thousands of claimants. Miners seeking compensation for cancer and other diseases that can be caused by radiation and particles in uranium, or for lung disease caused by coal, asbestos and other minerals, have known long battles.

Workmen's compensation boards tend to insist on a cause-and-effect relationship, difficult to prove since cancers often take up to 30 years to develop and the worker may have had

several jobs in that time. He may also be a heavy smoker.

A man who spent 37 years in the coal mines of Canmore, Alta., after 14 years as a miner in Wales, was refused benefits for "black lung" (pneumoconiosis) on the grounds that his medical problems were caused by cigarettes. Black lung is caused by coal dust trapped in the tubes of the lung, impairing the transfer of oxygen to the blood. The president of the Canmore local of the United Mine Workers claims that 50 percent of all workers who have spent 20 years or more in the mine have some degree of this disability. The number of successful claims is growing, however, providing precedents upon which ailing workers can base demands for financial assistance.

SAFETY VERSUS COMFORT

The back-street garment factory where you work is too cold in winter, stifling in summer, and dirty the year around.

Provincial regulations for workplaces are much more concerned with health and safety than with comfort. However, they should protect workers against excessive cold, where it may cause ill health or hazards in using machinery. Excess humidity and heat are considered uncomfortable, but not dangerous.

Employers are generally required to maintain the temperature at not less than 20°C (68°F). Exceptions are made for places such as garages or warehouses where doors are constantly opening. The authorities find it impractical to regulate upper heat limits. Workers in glass factories, for example, may have to work all day in temperatures averaging 43°C (110°F).

If summer heat is intolerable, you can always ask your employer for air conditioning. If ventilation is poor, provincial inspectors will require that it be improved.

Washroom discipline. As for washrooms, the employer must provide them, and keep them in reasonably sanitary condition. Cleanup is his responsibility, but, in practical terms, he can't really be expected to clean up after each careless user. The legal number of washrooms varies with the size of the labor force.

One toilet and one basin are usually specified for fewer than 10 workers; five toilets and five basins (with separate washrooms for each sex) if there are up to 100 workers—and so on in this ratio.

A separate lunchroom must be provided for 35 workers or more. Where dangerous substances such as lead or mercury are in use, separate eating places are mandatory, regardless of the number of workers. Any place employing 10 or more females must provide a room with reasonable privacy, equipped with one or more cots for lying down.

Hard hats and earmuffs. Every employer must ensure that work buildings are safe. This is the primary consideration. Your plant must have proper fire escapes and extinguishers; walls, ceilings, floors and stairs must be rated to stand all stress put upon them. All materials and equipment must be maintained in good condition. If there are any safety hazards, the boss is required to ensure that workers wear eye protection, hard hats, earmuffs, or safety shoes. Most employers underwrite the cost of protective gear.

Call in the provincial inspectors if you consider your factory unhygienic or unsafe. They won't ask your name but will appear as if they were making a routine call. Staff at the regula-

tory offices is limited and the inspectors often rely on complaints to put their time and effort to most effective use.

DOWN ON THE FARM

You are working on a tobacco farm. The accommodation provided by the owner is substandard, and the food is worse.

Clarification of the farmworker's rights is just beginning. Traditionally, he has either been forgotten or deliberately excluded from legislation that protected other workers, such as minimum wage and labor standards laws. And he was denied the right to join unions.

This isn't deliberate exploitation. The system evolved in the days when the farmworker (the "hired hand") typically lived alongside the owner's family, often sharing the family's food and often the same living conditions. But as farms have become big business, the old concept has become outdated. The tendency now is to include agricultural workers in new labor legislation.

In 1977, the British Columbia Labour Relations Board certified the first union in Canada to represent farmworkers. The contract covered 16 workers on a 12,000-acre spread in the Peace River country.

In its ruling, the B.C. board said that oppo-

Monkeys mind the noise, too

The din and clamor of man's busy workaday world also drives monkeys bananas. Such was the finding of scientists at the University of Miami when they subjected rhesus monkeys, which possess a heart and circulatory system similar to man's, to noises heard by the typical blue-collar worker.

The monkeys began their day with the clatter of an alarm clock, the buzz of an electric shaver, and television's *Today Show*. Traffic noises and half an hour of chatter from a

car radio followed. The recorded noises of pile drivers, diesel generators and bulldozers simulated the workplace. In the evening, the monkeys listened to a televised football game, punctuated by the sounds of low-flying aircraft.

All the noises, taken individually, were rated as safe under U.S. government standards. Yet, over a three-week period, the monkeys' blood pressure increased by as much as 42 percent.

sition to bargaining rights for farmworkers had been grounded in "an anachronistic image of the family farmer which is increasingly less accurate." While the Canadian farm work force had shrunk by about 50 percent during the 1970s, there had been a marked increase in the size and capital investment of the average farm.

A report issued by Canada Manpower in 1975 listed serious problems among Canadian farm laborers: poor sanitary facilities, substandard accommodation, evidence of child labor and of whole families working but only the head of the family being paid, sick and elderly adults working long hours for low pay.

Four years later, some farmers, in Alberta and Ontario particularly, were giving a different story to newspaper reporters. Said dairy farmer Jim McPherson of Cochrane, Alta.: "Hired hands are a thing of the past. It sounds like slave labor. You must treat people on an equal basis now." Farmhands are called managers, associates, foremen and herdsmen. At a time when unemployment was running at 8.4 percent of the national labor force, Alberta farmers were desperate for workers. Gary Doyle of Canada Manpower's Calgary office explained that Canadians "don't want the hard work and long hours." Meanwhile, the majority of the 3,000 farmers in Ontario's Essex County were relying on imported seasonal labor, most of it from the Caribbean. Fruit farmer Fabian Gross reported, "I have trouble getting Canadians to work. When I've hired them, they're here for a day or two—and then they're gone." He himself had hired one man from Barbados for 10 straight summers.

To catch a cheater. A farmworker faced with substandard conditions can turn to several agencies for help. If you found the job on your own, the nearest municipal authorities are probably your best bet. If the housing is bad, municipal inspectors have power to force the farmer to provide healthy and sanitary conditions. A fouled water supply or inedible meals would require immediate action by health authorities.

If your employer cheats on the wages he agreed to pay—or tries to pay less than the minimum wage in provinces that include

farmworkers in that legislation—you should call the Labour or Employment Standards Branch—the name varies—of your provincial Department of Labour. There are definite limits on how much an employer may deduct from your wages for accommodation.

Federal labor officials keep a watchful eye on workers hired through Canada Manpower offices and drawn from the Canada Farm Labour Pool. The farmer will have stated the wages he's paying and any other benefits, such as transportation, food and room. If he doesn't live up to the deal in every way, report the situation to the local Manpower office.

ROOM AND BOARD

Wages paid by the company on Baffin Island are high, but you think the charges for food, lodging and arctic clothing are exorbitant. You weren't forewarned.

The employer isn't permitted under law to surprise you with extra or higher charges that weren't specified in your original agreement. Don't let him deduct anything from your paycheque except mandatory withholding tax and statutory deductions, unless you had previously agreed to other deductions in writing.

Under provincial laws, employers may deduct only for things that are ordered by statute: taxes, unemployment insurance, union dues, Canada Pension Plan payments. For anything else, you have to agree in writing in advance. For example, you may agree that the cost of special work gear bought at the company store will be deducted, or that your accommodation or food costs will be docked. But the boss can't put a provision in your contract for the deduction of indefinite amounts, and you can't be forced to sign a contract saying that he can deduct for any loss or damage you may cause.

Depending upon the province or Territory in which you are working, the price of room and board may be set out in labor legislation. If there's a problem on that score, in any province, you can appeal to the provincial Labor Standards Branch.

Generally, however, your best protection in a remote area lies in the agreement you sign with your employer before departing to work there. Check it carefully before you sign. Look particularly for exorbitant charges for food and board, or for transportation. You have only yourself to blame if you don't. Everyone is bound by contracts openly entered into, as long as there's no misrepresentation.

If an employer doesn't live up to his part of the contract, you can bring a lawsuit against him for damages. If he cheats on your wages, you can launch proceedings under the "master and servant" laws of the provinces to obtain what is owed to you.

When the job involves traveling far from your home, make sure the contract includes transportation to and from the site. Otherwise, if the job should fold, you may find yourself stuck for the fare home. Should that happen, see if the nearest Manpower office will help to pay for your journey back.

In rare cases, employees have successfully sued employers who left them stranded. When the Avro Arrow jet fighter was scrapped in 1959, an American engineer who'd just moved to Malton, Ont., with his family brought suit against the manufacturer and won six months' wages to cover his expenses.

EMPLOYER'S PREROGATIVES

Taped big-band music is piped to all areas of your plant. You object to that old-fashioned beat.

As long as your employer meets health and safety standards, the other conditions in the plant or office where you work are pretty much his prerogative. If he's not a rock aficionado, that's tough luck.

If the music is loud, you might get it turned down a notch with the help of the Labour Standards Branch for your province. An inspector can carry out a noise-level survey to determine whether the din is loud enough to be a hazard. Allowable decibel levels in a workplace vary from province to province, but in general you cannot be subjected to a noise higher than 90 to 98 decibels over an eight-hour period.

A research team led by Peter Alberti, professor of otolaryngology (diseases of the ear, nose and throat) at the University of Toronto, stated in 1979 that thousands of industrial workers suffer hearing damage every year from excessively noisy machinery. The deafness was irreversible but preventable through the proper use of scientific protection equipment. Alberti noted that increasing numbers of claims for job-related hearing loss were coming before the provincial workmen's compensation boards. The cause was prolonged exposure to high levels of noise. The cost in pensions was running into millions of dollars.

If you have to raise your voice to be heard by the person next to you, the boss is probably exceeding the allowable noise standards. An office with lots of typewriters has a noise level of about 72 decibels. Discotheques come in at 110 to 120 decibels, well above the safe levels.

The unblinking eye. But if your boss is not violating the industrial standards, you may have to live with his taste in everything from music to the color of the walls and the menu in the company cafeteria.

You may also have to live with excessive surveillance. The boss can insist on checking your work every few minutes and use television cameras or raised platforms to watch for theft, and even ask—but not order—you to take a lie-detector test to prove your honesty.

The use of closed-circuit television to monitor the workplace infuriates unions. They consider surveillance degrading to human dignity. In Toronto, in 1978, women textile workers escalated the use of television monitoring into a strike issue, and they succeeded in getting rid of a camera trained on the washroom doors. But other cameras still monitored the production area, parking lot and shipping docks.

The Canadian Union of Postal Workers fought a long, and only partly successful, battle against the use of cameras to survey workers handling the mail. The union wanted the cameras excluded totally, but the most it was able to achieve was an agreement that they would be used only to watch for theft, not to measure worker productivity or to gather evidence for discipline cases.

THE LAW DECIDES: A WORKER'S RIGHT

Hope for the handicapped

Background

In 1975, David Jefferson, an employee of the Department of National Defence, applied for work with the British Columbia Ferries Service. A ship's oiler at Esquimalt, B.C., Jefferson had a hook-like apparatus, replacing a hand lost in 1955, and an artificial foot, replacing a limb amputated in 1966. Interviewed by George Baldwin, the company's superintendent engineer, Jefferson said the amputations and artificial limbs were never a handicap. He had never had an accident at sea, nor ever slipped, tripped or lost his footing.

Baldwin was not convinced that Jefferson could either respond to emergencies on a passenger vessel, or perform some of the strenuous tasks the job required. He did not put the oiler's name on the eligibility list, from which employees were selected.

Jefferson complained to the Human Rights Commission. The B.C. Human Rights Code says that no employer may discriminate against prospective employees "unless reasonable cause exists," and a board of inquiry was convened in Victoria to determine whether or not a physical handicap constituted "reasonable cause."

Judgment

Agreeing with Jefferson that he should be judged on his abilities, not prejudged on his disabilities, the board ruled that physically handicapped persons have a right to equal opportunity in employment. Nevertheless, it reluctantly dismissed Jefferson's complaint. The board chairman, Sholto Hebenton, explained that Baldwin was a fair man whose greatest concern was the safety of the passengers aboard vessels owned by B.C. Ferries. His decision not to hire Jefferson was a "reasoned decision" based on managerial discretion: it was not, in essence, discriminatory.

THE TYRANNY OF TIME CLOCKS

Your office requires all junior staff to punch the time clock. You find the system demeaning.

An employer has the clear right to install time clocks and use them to check punctuality and to provide a record for hourly wage computation. Where workers have objected to the system, this management prerogative has been upheld at arbitration. If you really hate punching in, you should consider changing jobs. Generally, only the larger firms make use of time clocks.

Management isn't supposed to make any major alterations in the terms and conditions of a permanent employee's work without giving reasonable notice. If time clocks are suddenly imposed, there may be grounds for a complaint to your provincial Labour Standards Branch. But the most you'll likely achieve is a temporary respite.

The boss can't dock you more pay than for the actual time you were late or absent, as recorded by the time clock. He can't, for example, penalize you by deducting an hour's pay for each 30 minutes that you are late.

Quality of life. The elimination of time clocks and of all "dictatorial supervision" is among the aims of the relatively new "quality of working life" programs. These innovative approaches, originating mainly in Europe, hope to attack the twin problems of worker alienation and declining production as caused by absenteeism and lack of motivation.

In 1979, the Ontario government established a "quality of working life center," similar to those pioneered by Sweden two years earlier. It was designed to encourage companies and their staffs to eliminate the barriers that cause alienation in the workplace. Says Director Hans van Beinum, a former postal worker in Holland: "It means a change in social values. If you treat people like experimental rabbits, you alienate them. You can't be the expert coming in to do things for people. You have to do it *with* them and, in the end, they have to do it for themselves."

Flexible working hours, which allow employees to choose their own starting and leaving times within a certain range, are one of the best-known experiments. Job-rotation schemes are also in operation.

Van Beinum advocates direct "industrial democracy," meaning that plant and office workers themselves plan how their jobs will be done. Supervisors would no longer be required to check each worker's tasks and, further, new factories would be so designed as to eliminate the traditional supervisor's walkways along the assembly lines.

"A lot of organizations," says Toronto management consultant Peter Moon, "would be better off with far less management. We've got to remove barriers to productivity, foolish things like time clocks, punch cards and outdated rules and regulations. If members of the work group plan and manage their own jobs, they become more concerned about their personal effectiveness."

When Aluminum Company of Canada removed time clocks from its Kingston, Ont., plant—and also the bells that signaled lunch hour and coffee breaks—production increased, staff turnover decreased, and the quality of the product rose. Fred C. Whitney, an Alcan industrial relations manager, commented, "People respond if you get rid of some of these inhibitors."

DRESS CODES

The boss makes it plain he wants certain standards of dress observed. Can't you work in jeans if you want to?

Employers do have the right to set and enforce reasonable regulations about dress and appearance, but they had better be prepared to justify any discipline based on those regulations. Anyone fired for noncompliance stands an excellent chance of being reinstated—possibly with cash damages as well—unless the boss can prove that his restrictions were definitely job related.

Under federal law, which allows nonunion workers to protest a firing to the Labour Relations Board, you will probably win a case for wrongful dismissal if you can show your appearance really isn't important to the job. In provincial jurisdictions, your only recourse in most jobs is to launch a suit for unjust dismissal in the courts. The union member can lodge a grievance and go to arbitration if necessary.

Unions have taken to arbitration many cases arguing workers' rights to wear beards, mustaches and long hair. They usually win unless the employer can prove he has sound reasons for laying down the restrictions. Arbitrators balance the employer's right to set appearance standards against the employees' rights to personal freedom. Even if management expresses a strong concern for its image in the marketplace, arbitrators point out that public standards have become more lax in the area of personal grooming and attire.

An employer may be able to show that public safety or sanitation is involved. Restaurants, for example, require chefs to wear nets over long hair to avoid contamination of food. Winnipeg has a bylaw requiring waiters and cooks to be cleanshaven. It's not really all that difficult for an employer to argue reasonably that certain hair styles and attire can be held to affect his company's business image adversely. For example, a department store cannot be expected to tolerate jeans on its saleswomen in the fur salon. A bond salesman in headband and beads would raise eyebrows, not profits.

Hirsute holdouts. Even though male shoulder-length hair slipped out of style in the 1970s, the sausage manufacturer J.M. Schneider Ltd. was ordered by an arbitration board to rehire four men who were suspended for disobedience of a company ban on beards, sideburns and mustaches. Of the meatpacker's 2,300 workers, there were only these four hirsute holdouts. After five weeks' suspension, they returned to the plant in triumph, still sporting their facial foliage. The arbitrator held that the company's ban was "not reasonable."

When the Ontario Ministry of Natural Resources ordered its 210 game wardens to shave off their beards in 1978, there was such an uproar among employees that the instruction was quickly revoked. But this management right is still doggedly defended. In the fall of 1979, Syncrude Canada Ltd. began enforcing a no-beard rule at its giant oil-sands plant in Alberta. It's a safety precaution; if the wearing of a gas mask is required against the hazard of hydrocarbons, it's difficult for a bearded man to get a proper seal. Mustaches are permitted as long as they don't hang lower than the edge of the upper lip. A guard at Toronto's Don Jail resigned when his job was under threat because of his refusal to cut his locks. The jail authorities maintained that his long hair and beard could easily be grabbed by prisoners.

ASSEMBLY LINE WOES

The quality-control manager on the assembly line is a perfection fiend. You get continual reprimands.

Production standards in any plant are set by management and enforced by the lead hand on the assembly line. If the plant is working under a collective agreement, the union has probably negotiated such things as the speed of the assembly line, the number of work breaks and the rights of foremen or supervisors.

If it's an individual problem, it's possible you should be looking for other work. But if your fellow workers are also in trouble, there is recourse. Perhaps a speedup has reached the point where safety or health is endangered. Nonunion workers in this situation should ask the Industrial Safety Branch of the provincial labor department to check the operation. Excessive production demands can cause the quality of finished items to deteriorate.

To maintain a fast pace of production, management often decides to accept the fact that a certain number of the products will be faulty or broken. An individual hand may quickly get in trouble if the pace at which he can work slows down the rest of the assembly line, or results in an above-average number of breakages.

Proving incompetence. Generally under the labor laws—and specifically if there's a union contract—management's right to change the terms and conditions of the work-place is restricted. This safeguards the worker against unreasonable demands by, say, a time-and-motion enthusiast who suddenly decides you must work faster. Any incompetent work-er can be fired but if you have completed your

The way things were

In 1898, a decade after the Canadian Pacific Railway reached Vancouver, binding the nation with a band of steel, the company de-cided to push a branch line from Lethbridge, Alta., through the Crow's Nest Pass into the coal-mining country of southern British Co-lumbia. Working conditions for the men who laid that track in the winter of 1897-98—up to 4,000 "navvies" at a top wage of $26 a month—appear incredible today. When two sick laborers died at Pincher Creek after a three-day trip in an open sleigh in mid-Janu-ary 1898, without medical attention of any kind, Ottawa set up a royal commission to in-quire into conditions on the project. It was solemnly recorded that one of the men had worked only 10.5 days; after deductions for food and bunkhouse, and for his sick time, his estate received $5.35. The following testimony from a gang overseer is excerpted from the transcript of the commission's report. It de-scribes the workers' winter accommodation and the sick-call routine.

Q. Would you call the camp a very comfort-able one for the men—the bunkhouse?

A. I would, very comfortable.

Q. What sort of floor did they have?

A. No floor at all . . . the ground.

Q. What sort of roof?

A. It was cedar dug-out trough shape so as to keep the rain out.

Q. No leakage there?

A. No, it was too cold in the first place.

Q. What ventilation?

A. Well, there was the door.

Q. That is what you call comfortable quar-ters for the men?

A. It is as comfortable a camp as I have seen for railroad men and I have been railroading for 20 years.

Q. When the men did not turn out to work, what was your duty?

A. My orders were to fire them.

Q. Whether they were sick or not?

A. Well, if they were sick and wanted to go to the hospital, we were supposed to send them.

Q. And if they were sick and did not want to go to the hospital, what then?

A. Well, if they would not go to work, I would tell them they would have to go out.

Q. Even though they were sick, is that right?

A. Yes, sir.

Q. Sickness was no excuse?

A. No, sir.

The commission heard that labor recruits from the East were charged railfare to Mac-leod and then on to the current railhead in the mountains. Some men, with families at home to support, found that after working for two months in these atrocious conditions, they had not a cent coming. In fact, because of pur-chases of working gear, they were in debt to the company.

Complainers were fired on the spot as trou-blemakers, and other CPR camps were ordered not to feed them. A North West Mounted Po-lice officer reported that angry men were wan-dering in the high valleys without blankets, or even boots.

The unions of the late 19th century weren't interested in fighting against the brutish condi-tions that were imposed on the navvies. Nearly all of those men were seen as unstable tran-sients, too difficult to organize. The royal commission recommended that Ottawa send inspectors to the rail camps to insist on higher standards.

A union paper later reported that the in-spectors had no more effect than "the wind blowing from the south."

probationary period—usually three months—your boss can be called upon to prove your incompetence in order to establish just cause for dismissal.

If a dismissal for incompetence becomes the subject of a grievance, handled through the normal union channels, it's possible an arbitrator may find that the lack of skill is not entirely your own fault. He could order the employer to assign you to other tasks that you are capable of doing. The same result might be reached in a lawsuit for wrongful dismissal.

THE HOURS YOU WORK

You are concerned that having to work the overnight shift is ruining your health.

Armed with a written opinion from your doctor, you should ask the boss to switch you to the day shift. Your union representative may be able to help, although he may be bound by an agreement that all workers must take turns on the overnight shift. If you are unsuccessful, you'd be wise to try for a job in a plant that doesn't operate on a multishift rotating basis.

More than a quarter of the entire labor force is required to work outside the normal 8-to-5 routine. For some, this can pose health problems. But the system is not as yet considered an occupational health hazard or a violation of workers' rights.

A survey by the U.S. National Institute for Occupational Safety and Health indicates, nevertheless, that shift workers suffer "severe disruptions of physical and psychological well-being." The problems include chest and stomach pains, cramps, colds, fatigue, alcoholism and dependence on sleeping pills. Shift workers are involved in more accidents than workers on a regular daytime routine.

The Public Service Alliance of Canada—the federal civil servants' union—has studied the question and concluded that, in the long run, shift work is "detrimental to health, efficiency and the enjoyment of life."

Doctors refer to the breaking of circadian rhythms, the normal daily body cycles of getting up in the morning and going to bed at night. Shift work, especially the shift from midnight to 8 a.m., reverses the flow. Some people simply can't adjust. Says Paul de Biasi, a lathe operator for the Steel Company of Canada, "Being on rotating shifts is like having jet *lag*, week in and week out, all year long."

The International Labour Organization recommends that night workers have shorter hours, more days off and longer holidays than day workers in order to recover from the stress of working to an unnatural rhythm.

26 Labor relations

Labor disputes were responsible for 949 work stoppages—strikes and lockouts—in 1978. This, says Statistics Canada, deprived the national economy of 7,480,020 workdays. In an economy struggling with unemployment, soaring energy costs and record interest rates, many voices are asking if the time has not arrived when the old adversarial stance of management and labor should be superseded by new ideas.

Says one former federal Minister of Labour, Bryce Mackasey: "No doubt each union sees itself as fighting against an employer. The plain truth is that they're fighting against society. It's no longer a labor-management conflict where management loses when labor wins. It's a labor-nation conflict with the public interest at stake. Instead of fighting society for a bigger slice of the pie, and thus preventing the pie from being baked, I think the unions should be fighting for a hand in the baking . . . for a more democratic workplace."

Joe Morris, former president of the Canadian Labour Congress, advocates "three-party planning" to cure the nation's industrial ills. He says that national economic policies should be hammered out by representatives of government, business and labor. "It offers the only chance for reasonable dialogue in this country. But nobody has had the guts to try the idea out."

The right to strike having been so hardly won, many unions remain implacably opposed to delegating any of their powers—even to their own central organizations. The "social democratic" collaboration between worker and boss that seems to work so well in the burgeoning economies of West Germany and Japan is ruled out for Canada.

Andy Stewart, president of the Public Service Alliance, which represents federal civil servants, said in December 1978 that his union had the right to negotiate pay and benefits "without legislated limits or ceilings other than those dictated by reason and common sense." If that right was removed, unionists had the "responsibility and obligation" to protest "even to the point of civil disobedience."

Among those who favor Morris's approach is John Fryer, general secretary of the British Columbia Government Employees' Union. "If the concept of three-party planning were explained properly, I think there would be widespread support for the idea of trying to sit down and work out some of our economic problems together."

Such ideas appear to be making little headway, however. The industrial scene actually darkened as the 1970s ended with the spread of strike action in service fields once automatically considered essential to the public interest. Firemen, policemen, nurses, social workers, teachers, air-traffic controllers, transit operators and the men funneling prairie grain to world markets—all these, and others in vital junctions of the economy, invoked the sacred right to strike while hard-pressed governments sought to damp the fires of inflation.

ORGANIZING A UNION

A union is trying to organize your plant. You are told that, if you take part, you will not be considered for promotion.

To prevent employers using their economic power—however indirectly—to block the legal right of workers to organize, the law forbids the exercising of "undue influence." Once a union announces it is attempting to organize a group of workers, labor department officials will look very carefully at the actions taken by the employer. While the boss does have the right to talk to employees about a proposed union, the law puts strict limits on what he may say or do. Just making known his opposition to the union can be enough to make workers fearful for their jobs.

The employer may well try to forestall unionization by making wages and working conditions just as good as, or even better than, those in union shops. Many nonunion businesses try to ward off union drives in this fashion. If the workers are already getting union scale or higher, why pay dues for no material gain? For many employers, the real concern isn't that a union will drive up wages, but that it will mean some sharing of authority in the workplace.

One not-so-subtle gambit is to promote those employees who seem most interested in unionization. Or the employer might reverse the psychology. If the company has two plants, it might increase wages in the plant showing little or no sign of union interest, while leaving things as they are at the location where cards are being signed.

No carrots, no threats. Nearly all the provinces and the federal government prohibit employers from promising future benefits in order to keep employees from joining a union. The boss is allowed to point to his past or present record as a fair employer, but he can't dangle any carrots or make any threats, however veiled. Once the union formally applies to the Labour Relations Board for certification as bargaining agent, things get tougher still. Most labor laws state that the employer cannot then alter conditions of employment, except with the union's consent. The freeze lasts until the union's application is approved or refused. In Quebec, the freeze applies until either a collective agreement is signed or the employees strike.

Similarly, once a certified union serves notice to bargain for new wages and working conditions, the freeze continues to the point at which a strike becomes legal. If the employer does try to make changes—promotions, for example—the Department of Labour will likely forbid them unless they can be shown to have been normal practices before the union organizers came into view. If the boss always gave you a Christmas turkey, he can still do so—but he had better not announce that from now

on, the company will provide gas for your drive to work.

Fighting the union. Most problems arise, of course, not because the boss is being too kind in the face of a union drive, but rather because of his opposition. If his activities are too blatant, the union could get in faster. Under federal law, and in Ontario and British Columbia, the Labour Relations Boards can certify a union without a vote if it appears the employer has interfered in such a way that his workers might fear to make their true wishes known.

This happened twice in Ontario in 1977. Managements of Dylex Limited and Viceroy Construction Company Ltd. in each case had circulated brochures; in them, newspaper clippings implied that actions of a union had led to the recent permanent shutdown of a large mill in the area.

All labor laws stipulate that an employee may not be discriminated against for union activity. Once you join, you are protected if your boss fires or demotes you—or in any other way treats you unfairly—just because you support the union. It may not be easy to prove that that was your employer's motive. But, all provincial and federal legislation puts the onus on the employer to prove he had a reason other than your union activity for his actions against you. No employer can ask employees at any time to sign a contract precluding union membership. In the colorful jargon of the union hall, that's known as a "yellow dog" contract.

The employer has every right to make his opinion about unions known, as long as he does not use coercion, intimidation, threats, promises or "undue influence." He can't, for example, start talking about closing down, moving his plant or office elsewhere, being driven out of business, ending certain employee benefits, or firing or laying off those who join the union.

The union, for its part, must also play by certain rules. It is forbidden to use intimidation to compel anyone to join up, to interfere with anyone's right to free decision-making, and to disrupt business by trying to sign people up during their working hours.

CERTIFICATION DELAYED

About 60 percent of the staff at your plant signed union cards, but by the time the application for certification is heard, the number has dwindled.

Many organizing campaigns have failed because they cooled out during a lengthy wait for a hearing. Despite the legal protection afforded during an organizing campaign, success is more likely if the union can move swiftly and doesn't have to contest employer activities over a prolonged period. When enthusiasm dwindles, workers who have signed cards may change their minds and withdraw. Most unions will return a card if requested, or if the employee signs a "statement of desire" informing the Labour Relations Board that he does not wish the union to be certified. The board may require the employee to testify that the statement was voluntary and not the result of pressure from the boss.

Aware of the dangers of delay, unions prefer to get a comfortable majority signed up in hope of gaining automatic certification without a vote. All jurisdictions except Nova Scotia provide for outright certification on the basis of initial membership support.

Counting the cards. If a union has signed cards from a majority, it can go confidently to

Handling a grievance

All union contracts provide a grievance procedure by which disputes between an employee and the boss, as in this example, can be given a fair hearing. If an amicable agreement cannot be worked out, the case will go to an arbitration board for settlement.

GRIEVANCE REPORT

USWA Local Union No. _0000_ Grievance NO. _____

Location _Maplesville, N.B._ Date _Nov. 9, 1979_

EMPLOYEE'S NAME	IDENTIFICATION NO.	DEPARTMENT	JOB TITLE
Sally Roe	5432	Shipping	Inspector

Use space below to write in other important Grievance information

When my father-in-law died two years ago, I was granted three days' paid bereavement leave

Nature of Grievance

I had to take three days off work on Oct. 8, 9 and 10 to attend my mother-in-law's funeral. The boss said I could only have time off on Oct. 10, because we were short of staff at the time. I took the time anyhow, since this is the period approved by the company for such a bereavement, but I was docked two days' pay in my next paycheque.

Settlement requested in Grievance I request that I be paid straight-time pay also for Oct. 8 and 9 — thus the company will fulfill the three-day bereavement leave clause in the collective agreement.

Agreement Violation _19.05_ Bereavement Pay

Signature of Aggrieved: Signature of Union Representative:

Sally Roe

Form USWA 122 COPY FOR LOCAL UNION

the board and ask for certification as bargaining agent. The board determines whether the group of workers involved is an appropriate bargaining unit—either a craft unit of workers with the same skills or an industrial unit representing all the employees of a company. The cards are usually counted as of the day the union applied for certification. At one time, they were counted as of the day of the hearing, putting the union at a disadvantage. For example, banks could easily transfer enough employees out of small branches to foil organizing attempts.

If a union does have the required majority of cards signed, it will usually be certified without calling a vote. If there isn't a majority, or there are doubts about the employees' true wishes, the board will order a supervised vote. When a union wants to force a vote because many employees are hanging back from making a decision, it can do so with less than a majority. In British Columbia and Ontario, it can request a vote when it has 45 percent signed up; in New Brunswick and Nova Scotia, 40 percent; in Quebec, and sectors under federal jurisdiction, 35 percent. (The federal government has jurisdiction over many industries, including radio and television, interprovincial transport and many other undertakings that operate across provincial or national borders. About 600,000 workers come under federal jurisdiction, in which the Canada Labour Code is the federal counterpart of provincial labor codes.)

UNION JURISDICTION

The union you want to join tells you it has no jurisdiction in your industry.

In union terms, "jurisdiction" refers to the slicing up of the workplace among the members of the country's two umbrella labor organizations: the Canadian Labour Congress (CLC) and the Confederation of National Trade Unions (CNTU), the latter existing mainly in Quebec. These bodies have general "guidelines" saying which union should operate in which field. But unless the union as-

signed jurisdiction in your industry has already declared an interest in representing you, other unions might consider you fair game. This is particularly true if you are in a largely unorganized field. When some bank employees began organizing in the 1970s, the tellers turned to the chemical workers' union. Then the steelworkers', retail clerks', and office employees' unions competed for the bank jurisdiction. Later, the CLC set up a special affiliate to represent bank workers. Such a squabble is seldom settled until one union proves it can dominate the field.

The labor raiders. Basically, jurisdiction isn't a question of law, but of agreement among the unions. The "raiding" of a weak union's jurisdiction by a stronger or more aggressive union indicates that winning the membership battle can swing more weight than any agreement made on paper. The powerful Teamsters, for example, are an independent union and they don't acknowledge anyone else's rules about jurisdiction. They represent a broad spectrum of workers apart from truck drivers and are usually quite willing to sign up any interested group of workers—or, for that matter, raid a union that shows signs of being too weak to hold its members.

Most unions in Canada are affiliated with the Canadian Labour Congress. In 1978, there were 3,277,968 union members—roughly a third of the work force—and 67.2 percent of these were represented by the CLC. When quarrels break out between the affiliated unions about which one represents which workers, the CLC arbitrates the issue.

White-collar unions. Jurisdictional tangles are unlikely to affect anyone in the "white collar" or service industries where most non-union workers can be found. There are some general rules, however: federal government employees are members of the Public Service Alliance of Canada, provincial government workers have a separate union in each province, and municipal workers are generally members of Canada's biggest union, the Canadian Union of Public Employees.

When several unions operate in the same field, it is not unusual for employees to hold more than one card. In the entertainment field, for example, a performer might want to belong to the actors' union, the broadcasters' union, and—if he is also a writer—to the guild that represents news writers or reporters. Paying dues to more than one union can be the price for working in more than one field. Some people are "dual unionists," holding cards in more than one union for sentimental reasons—keeping the connection with a former union when a change of job means they must belong to a new one. Dual unionism is acceptable but you can't designate more than one union as your bargaining agent.

EMPLOYEES' ASSOCIATIONS

You have been told your new company is "unionized," but the union turns out to be an employees' association. And it is asking you to support a demand you don't like.

The employees' association—often called a "company union"—can represent you in collective bargaining with the boss, just like a regular union. It can call a strike, if that's the membership decision. But there's one big difference: most employees' associations have no status in labor law. If the employer refuses to meet demands, you're on your own. Unless you are recognized by a labor board, you will get no assistance from labor department conciliators, mediators or arbitrators.

An employer anxious to avoid having a real union represent his workers may lean over backward to meet requests from the association. But that's simply what they are—requests. The term "company union" reflects that fact that if the employer didn't play a role in setting it up, he was at least compliant.

You don't have the same voice in an association that you have in a union. You may vote to elect your representatives, but you may not have a vote to approve or disapprove bargaining requests. Certainly, you don't have the legal protection under which a union has the duty to give every member fair representation in disputes with the employer.

Employees' associations shouldn't be confused with professional associations, which represent groups such as doctors, lawyers and architects. Most members of professional associations are self-employed and possess skills in great demand. They're virtually able to write their own tickets. Through their self-governing bodies, they set their own fees and every set of income statistics shows them to be among the highest-paid Canadians.

CONCILIATION

Contract negotiations at your shop have been stalemated for weeks. You think the government should send in a conciliation officer.

The labor department won't intervene unless either side asks for help. Once a request is received, a conciliation officer will be assigned to the case to try to prevent a strike or lockout. When the parties aren't far apart, conciliation has a good chance of success. More often, though, conciliation is abandoned, unless the officer recommends the appointment of a conciliation board. But if he recommends that no board be appointed, then the strike countdown begins. Under federal and most provincial laws, there can be no strike or lockout until the conciliation procedure has been tried.

Taking off the brakes. In the strictly formal ritual that is collective bargaining, real negotiations often don't begin until the conciliator is on the scene. Negotiators may feel little pressure to settle until the possibility of conflict is imminent. Conciliation boards, however, are frequently bypassed. If a board is appointed and the parties reject its recommendations, the result is similar to a conciliator reaching a "no board" decision: a legal strike can begin within a prescribed number of days. Under federal law, the period is eight days; the provinces set various deadlines.

An alternative is to put the dispute to voluntary arbitration if the parties want to avoid a work disruption. This means the two sides choose an impartial outsider—usually an experienced arbitrator—to hand down a binding settlement. Once you agree to arbitration, you give up your right to strike or otherwise protest if you don't like the results.

Voluntary arbitration differs from compulsory arbitration in several ways. The latter can be imposed on disputants by the government—as in the 1978 postal dispute—if the quarrel is harming the public interest.

In some cases, the law forbids certain types of workers to strike because their work is deemed essential; special legislation provides for arbitration of their disputes. This is the case with policemen, firemen and nurses in most provinces.

In private industry, unions and managements both try, usually, to avoid arbitration because they prefer to settle on their own terms. They may request assistance from the government in the form of a mediator, who enjoys more status than a conciliator although he does much the same job. The mediator is called in on the eve of a strike, or even after one has begun. If he's unsuccessful, there can be a strike or a lockout once the legal waiting period has expired. Then the fight becomes a test of economic power.

LOCKOUTS

Although a strike date has not been set, management has shut your plant down following an isolated work stoppage.

The boss has just as much right to lock his workers out as they have to go on strike. Literally, he locks the plant gates or office doors

---

Bargaining 'in good faith'

The key word in any labor dispute is "bargaining." Essentially, it's a haggle that will be decided, in the normal run of events, in the economic arena. Some disputes escalate into strikes over doctrinaire issues—say, a union demand for a closed shop, but these are comparatively rare. The boss can even try to take back concessions granted in previous contracts. But the law steps in the minute either side is accused of refusing to bargain in good faith.

It can take a Solomon to decide what bargaining "in good faith" really is. If both sides have agreed to meet and go through the formal motions, it can be very difficult to prove that one side isn't playing fair.

The Ontario Labour Relations Board broke new ground by ruling that going through the formalities of meeting isn't enough; the party complained against must be seen to be making a determined effort to reach agreement. The board can issue a "cease and desist" order and, if the named party still refuses to bargain fairly, an enforceable court order will be issued.

In any negotiations, though, the two sides may be hanging tough on matters of principle, and nothing in the law says either union or management has to concede anything it is determined not to concede. The duty to bargain in good faith does not amount to a duty to give in. Either side may consider an issue important enough to be worth a strike or lockout—and then a test of strength determines who wins.

Refusal to bargain occurs most often when a union is negotiating for a first contract. The employer may simply be ignorant of the law or his motive may be a desire to destroy the union. Both the federal and Quebec governments have legislation providing for arbitration of first-contract disputes. The federal Labour Relations Board is empowered to dictate terms if bargaining for a first contract drags on with no sign of fair settlement. In Quebec, difficult first contracts may be sent to arbitration. The effect of both laws is to protect unions against efforts to destroy them at birth.

against them. Strikes are much more common than lockouts, however, because it is seldom in the employer's interest to shut down his business. A lockout may occur if the company has stockpiled enough products to supply customers for some time. More often, lockouts happen when the employer perceives that union tactics, while falling short of a full strike, will prove so disruptive that a total shutdown is preferable. In the fall of 1978, for example, Air Canada locked its employees out when "rotating" strikes by machinists appeared likely to throw air service into chaos.

The exact terminology is important. Only those who are direct parties to a contract dispute can legally be "locked out." Because they are involved in a labor dispute, they are not entitled to unemployment insurance while the dispute lasts. A worker cannot be forced out of a job permanently simply because he has participated in a legal strike or lockout.

Aiding and abetting. Workers not directly involved in the dispute are really "laid off" rather than locked out. (*See* Chapter 25, "Work conditions.") They cannot lose their jobs because of the labor trouble and are subject to recall at any time. They probably won't get paid but they are eligible for unemployment insurance. However, they won't get benefits if the Unemployment Insurance Commission decides they are aiding and abetting the strike and stand to gain by the eventual settlement.

A lockout is frequently the employer's response when a union advocates "working to rule." In this tactic, the workers slow production down by scrupulously obeying every rule to an absurd degree. Rotating strikes—in which different groups walk out on different days without notice—are also likely to prompt the employer to shut down completely.

The employer has the right to try to operate during a strike or lockout. He is unlikely to do so during a lockout, but when the union controlling most of the workers calls a strike, many employers attempt to get their product out by using nonunion staff.

A very determined employer may hire new people to do the work. But this is the most inflammatory action possible, and almost certain to result in serious trouble. The union movement calls this "strike breaking" and anyone who takes a job in these circumstances is dubbed a "scab." In union circles, this is the equivalent of a criminal record. Quebec law forbids the hiring of outside workers to fill vacancies during a strike. Other provinces have considered such legislation, but none have followed suit.

Even if someone is hired to take your job while you're on strike, you have the right in all provinces to have your job back when the strike ends.

THE 'WILDCAT' STRIKE

Your employees have walked out to protest the suspension of a union member. The "wildcat" strike results in damage to your machinery.

Any strike or stoppage of work is illegal during the life of a contract, or when bargaining is under way for a new agreement and the conciliation procedure hasn't yet concluded. The offense doesn't have to be as serious as damage to machinery. Any kind of concerted action that interferes with production—slowing down, booking off sick, a study session or other tactics of union pressure—amounts to an illegal strike. An employer can retaliate with actions ranging from mild discipline against the offending workers to suing the union for damages. One such suit by management was finally resolved in 1979 when the Quebec Superior Court ordered the Confederation of National Trade Unions to pay $5,981,424, plus interest, to Canadian Reynolds Metal Company. During an illegal strike 12 years earlier at Baie-Comeau, Que., the workers had left the smelter unattended, and molten aluminum solidified in the furnaces.

Penalties usually stop short of legal action. But the law is clear that employees can be held responsible for illegal work actions, and so can their union if it calls, authorizes or counsels the action.

Chaining the wildcat. Labor boards and courts look at all the circumstances when determining the consequences. Wildcat action sparked by unsafe or unhealthy conditions, or by employers' provocative behavior, may well make severe penalties seem unjustified to an impartial third party. Both the federal and Ontario governments have passed amendments making it legal for a worker to refuse to do any job he considers unsafe.

While an illegal strike is in progress, the employer can go to the Labour Relations Board seeking relief. The route used to take him to the courts, where he would ask for an *ex parte* injunction ordering the workers to stop their illegal action. But most provinces now say the labor board is the proper forum and *ex parte* injunctions—obtained on the evidence of one side only—are in disfavor.

The usual procedure now is for the employer to ask the labor board to declare that the walk-out or other action is illegal. The board then attempts to resolve the matter or directs the workers to return to work through a "cease and desist" order. If the employees refuse, or if damage has been caused, the employer can ask the board for consent to prosecute both workers and union for damages.

Employees unlawfully locked out of their jobs can take the same route to the labor board and the courts, seeking an order ending the lockout and claiming lost wages. In less serious situations, the usual recourse is found in the grievance procedure outlined in the collective agreement. The employer can file a grievance against the union, seeking damages for actions during an illegal strike. If he can prove the union's involvement in the illegal activity, an arbitrator might well penalize the union. Similarly, if the boss disciplines his workers for their actions during an illegal walkout, the union may take the matter to an arbitrator.

THE PICKET LINE

Strikers at the plant lock arms and prevent you and other non-union employees from entering.

It's a classic clash of rights. Crossing a picket line is one of the cardinal sins in the creed of the union movement. At the same time, any-one invited by management has the right to enter and to go to work, whether or not there are pickets posted at the plant gates.

What you do will depend on how you feel about the strike and how badly you need your wages. As a general rule, few workers cross legal picket lines. If it seems possible that you might get beaten up, or suffer long-term penalty as a "scab," the boss is unlikely to blame you. But if your employer has made it clear he expects you to get in to work, and if you want to go to your job, then you have every right to do so.

The legal status of a picket line is that it's not a barricade; it's there to inform the public generally and other workers in particular that a strike is in progress. That's why placards are carried, and why pickets approach anyone in the vicinity to attempt to explain the issues. If the pickets are aggressive, the company often provides transportation for those who wish to enter. Even helicopters have sometimes been used.

Cops in the middle. Police are often on the scene during strikes, although most of them heartily dislike getting in the middle between labor and management. They have their own unions and legal police strikes are occurring in some provinces. With police officers sometimes walking their own picket lines, their entry into other labor disputes becomes paradoxical, to say the least.

However, police have a duty to protect property and to ensure the unmolested passage of the citizenry on public property—such as the sidewalks and highways. If you fear either physical harm from strikers or disciplinary action from your employer for refusing to cross the picket line, you have the right to request a police escort. In a chaotic or threatening situation, the employer can ask the courts for an injunction limiting the number of pickets and defining where they may picket without causing obstruction or disruption.

Traditionally, pickets must keep walking and not form a blockade. Everyone is accustomed to press and television pictures showing that these rules are not always obeyed. Vehicles attempting to enter strikebound plants are sometimes damaged, and strikers are injured when they take matters into their own hands.

If you are a union member, but not a member of the striking union, you have a legal right to refuse to cross a picket line as long as your union has a "picket-line clause" in its contract. It will say members are not obliged to cross any picket lines set up by other unions. As truck drivers and deliverymen, the Teamsters often find themselves involved in other unions' strikes and therefore they've made a point of negotiating picket-line clauses.

When a bitter strike is in progress, or outside workers are brought in, the picket lines may grow as other unionists and sympathizers come to the strikers' aid. Other locals of the same union may stage "sympathy" strikes. They'll attempt to close down other plants that are essential to the embattled company's operations. Boycotts are sometimes organized, urging the public not to purchase products of either the strikebound firm or those that do business with it. All of these actions are illegal, but whether the company involved presses charges depends on its assessment of the impact on its public image and on future labor relations. The parties frequently prefer to bury the hatchet.

POLICE WALKOUT

You work in a shop on the main street. There is a police strike, and you think the mayor should order the strikers back to work.

Television viewers were upset in 1979 to see store windows being broken and cars racing through red lights in the center of Canadian towns, while striking police stolidly walked their picket lines. That year, three Nova Scotia towns were simultaneously bereft of local

Caught in the middle

Today's foreman is caught between union members protected by their contracts and top management which does the real decision-making. Often required to work hours just as long as the union members, but without their contractual right to overtime and other benefits, he sometimes feels he is getting the worst of both worlds. Lots of responsibility, but no authority. His predecessors often had the right to make their own decisions, hiring, firing and disciplining the workers they supervised.

Surveys among supervisors and middle managers reveal common complaints: status is lower; job security is weakened because of frequent reorganization and because this is the easiest group to cut in bad times; salaries often haven't increased as fast as union wages and benefits. By contrast, the unionized worker may have a much higher degree of protection against arbitrary action from the executive level.

In some provinces, the law now allows foremen and lower-level supervisory personnel to join employees' unions, as long as the supervisor has no access to confidential labor-relations information. In Quebec, the wording of the legislation dealing with managers is ambiguous and has encouraged the formation of full-fledged managers' unions. There are managers' unions within the provincial government and Hydro Quebec. Engineers have formed separate unions at Canadian Marconi and Northern Telecom.

Changes in the federal Labour Code and the labor law of British Columbia have given labor boards explicit authority to create separate bargaining units for supervisory and management personnel, or to include them in bargaining units with other employees. The boards are left with the tricky job of determining who is really management and what the line of demarcation should be.

police protection for a short time. It was a sobering reminder of the vital role our police forces play—not only in the solving of crimes but in the everyday "keeping of the peace."

Controversy continues on the question of whether police and other "essential" workers should enjoy the same right to strike as others in the labor force. As of 1979, only British Columbia, Manitoba, New Brunswick, Nova Scotia and Saskatchewan allowed police to strike, and then only unionized municipal policemen. But whatever the law in your province, your mayor can't "order" policemen or anybody else to stop striking. It would be up to the provincial legislature to pass a special back-to-work law. Your mayor can, at best, ask the provincial Attorney General to order the RCMP or provincial police to provide emergency protection.

Wholesale firings threatened. In recent years, postal, railway, airline and many other workers have been ordered back to work by their governments. The tradition of obedience to the law is strong in Canada and strikers usually obey. However, in the fall of 1978 striking postal workers refused to obey a parliamentary back-to-work law. When threatened with wholesale firings, the 23,000-member postal workers' union finally called off the strike. In the aftermath, the postmaster general recommended that 10 of the strikers be fired, 759 suspended for varying periods, and another 4,092 reprimanded by letter. Union president Jean-Claude Parrot received a jail sentence for counseling disobedience to the government. Grievances were subsequently filed on many of the disciplinary measures, and the Supreme Court denied Parrot's application to appeal his jail sentence.

'SUCCESSOR RIGHTS'

A company known for its anti-union sentiments has bought the plant where your union recently won a first contract.

Most provinces have a "successor rights" clause in their labor legislation to protect a union's position if a company is sold, merges with another organization, or changes its name. Some employers, particularly in the construction industry, had found it useful to disband and then reappear under another name to escape payment of union wages. Or the new owner of a business was unwilling to deal with the union already certified to represent the employees.

Unless there's been a complete transformation of the nature and purpose of the business, provincial laws protect both the union's bargaining rights and the existing collective agreement. If a new owner refuses to deal with the union, a labor department conciliator will try to settle the issue. If that fails, the Labour Relations Board will examine all the details of the transaction and if it finds that essentially the same business is being carried on, it will order the new owner to recognize the union and the existing collective agreement.

Different name, same boss. In one complicated business shuffle, the supermarket giant, Loblaw's, sold some of its stores to Gordon's Markets, which is a division of Zehrmart, which is in turn a wholly owned subsidiary of Loblaw's. The Ontario Labour Relations Board found that what had really happened was that the business had simply been transferred from one unit of Weston Corporation, the Loblaw's holding company, to another. The board ruled that the Loblaw's union still represented Gordon's workers.

Even trickier complications arise if a new owner already deals with a different union, or if former employees of the new owner now become part of the same bargaining unit. In such cases, the board has discretion to amend the original bargaining unit, or to terminate the bargaining rights of one of two competing unions. Or, if the board finds that a substantial change really has taken place in the nature of the business, it may terminate the rights of the original union.

A union also has recourse to the labor board if it finds itself dealing with an employer who carries on operations under several different names. When applying for certification, the union may ask the board for a declaration that the corporations, firms, or individuals involved really are one and the same employer.

BLACKLISTING

You have been drummed out of your union for crossing a picket line and are thus effectively prevented from earning a living.

While this may seem a denial of natural justice—your right to work in your chosen field—the union does have power under its constitution to discipline you. And that discipline probably extends to cancellation of membership. You accepted those terms freely when you joined up. Apart from appealing to the union head-office executive, your only recourse is through the courts. But when a union closely controls a trade, such as construction or seafaring—where the unions actually run the hiring halls—you'll have a hard time fighting a union blacklist.

It's in your interest to make yourself familiar with your union's constitution. When you join a union, you become a member of an unincorporated association. The law says that no actions can be taken against you that weren't a part of the agreement when you joined. In effect, that means your union cannot take any action against you that isn't stipulated in the union constitution, and even then only after the proper procedures for discipline have been followed.

Reinstatement ordered. The Canadian Union of Postal Workers (CUPW) learned this lesson after a strike in the 1970s when union leaders expelled some members who had crossed picket lines. Two Toronto CUPW members took the issue to court. The judge ruled that the workers hadn't been properly tried and weren't given the opportunity to defend themselves, as the union constitution provided. Accordingly, he ordered CUPW to take the two workers back into membership immediately.

Most union constitutions provide for disciplinary measures: fines, suspensions of membership and, for severe offenses, expulsion. Being kicked out will cost you your job only if the union has a contract with your employer providing for a union shop or closed shop—meaning you have to be a union member to work there.

The compulsory checkoff. If the union has an agreement with your employer that everyone in the bargaining unit, union members or not, must pay dues, you could lose your job for refusal to pay. However, in Saskatchewan and Ontario anyone who objects on religious grounds to paying union dues may pay the equivalent amount to a charity. In British Columbia a person who objects on religious grounds to becoming a member of a union must still pay dues; likewise in Manitoba, unless the union agrees to forego collecting dues.

In most provinces, the law says that a union can't deny you membership, or expel you, for engaging in "reasonable dissent" within the union, supporting a rival union, or refusing to pay "unreasonable" union dues or assessments. Nor can any union discriminate against you; your Human Rights Code backs up that protection.

While labor law varies from one province to another, unions generally can be forced to "fairly represent" all members of a bargaining unit. If the union operates a hiring hall or dispatching system to send people to jobs, it has to give an equal chance to everyone covered by the collective agreement. You can lay a complaint with the Labour Relations Board if the union subjects you to treatment that is arbitrary, discriminatory or in bad faith.

The same rules apply if you are complaining about some action taken against you by the boss. The union certified for your bargaining unit is obliged to give you fair representation in handling any grievance you may have. The labor boards have wide powers to make sure your union obeys.

27 Salary and benefits

F rom factory floor to executive suite, the work force of Canada numbers 10 million. Every one of these individuals, worker and boss alike, union member or free soul, is vitally interested in take-home pay. It's the bottom line in our free enterprise system.

While the extra-talented, the brave, or the serenely confident aim at the heady rewards of the tycoon, most of us accept our paycheques thankfully and look forward to steady financial advancement based on merit, loyalty or seniority. Since even the strongest unions represent only a minority of workers, we look to government as our ultimate safeguard from the vagaries, and the potential tragedies, of the open market. And, over the past half-century, the politicians have responded with minimum-wage laws, equal-pay legislation, seniority protection, overtime requirements, sick-pay provisions and, since 1941, the cushion of unemployment insurance.

The Unemployment Insurance Act has as its basic objective the provision of financial assistance to cope with interrupted earnings resulting from unemployment, including unemployment through illness. It covers virtually everyone in Canada who works under an employer-employee relationship. The core idea is that the scheme should pay for itself through compulsory contributions when the unemployment rate is at normal levels. When it is not, the state steps in and picks up the overrun tab.

In line with restraint on state spending, eligibility for Unemployment Insurance Commission (UIC) benefits was tightened in 1979. The federal government expected to save $580 million in a two-year period. The provinces reacted sharply because a cutback in unemployment benefits was expected to push more people onto the general welfare rolls. Ottawa meets only 50 percent of those costs. The federal response was an assurance that fewer than

5 percent of those cut off UIC benefits would actually shift over to the provincial and municipal welfare rolls.

Among those not collecting government benefits, however, it's a rare employee indeed who believes that he should not be paid more. The breathtaking salaries earned by a handful of top Canadian executives provide a Mount Everest incentive (in 1978, *The Financial Post* reported that at least six corporation moguls earned more than $300,000 a year). And the figures usually reported don't include "benefits" such as share-purchase options which can be very lucrative if the stock market is up, special insurance plans, low-interest personal loans, club memberships, use of company cars and aircraft.

High-level Canadian bureaucrats are also running fast in the salary stakes. It's a long time since personal status and the exercise of power were accepted in lieu of hard cash. The top rung in the federal civil service (DM3) allowed a maximum of $73,200, before a scheduled increase in 1979. About 2,000 deputy ministers and senior advisers were earning more than $70,000 a year. By comparison, the Prime Minister's salary was $35,400, plus the regular MP's "sessional allowance" of $28,600 and expenses. All parliamentary salaries are increased annually by 7 percent or more.

The average Canadian wage in mid-1979 stood at $285.15 per week.

DOMESTIC WORKERS

Your sister, a live-in housekeeper, is being paid less than the provincial minimum wage.

Although the rights of domestic workers are the subject of continuing study, almost all governments have concluded that it's too difficult to regulate the wages of those who work in private homes, either as live-in housekeepers or as "dailies."

Home help in Canada is provided mainly by unskilled women, or by those who either can't work structured hours or want to pick up a modest extra income. A live-in housekeeper usually receives free room and board, in much the same way as a family member. Most daily cleaning women get meal benefits, and often transit fares or a travel allowance. Others undoubtedly are treated shabbily.

Domestic service in private homes is excluded from minimum-wage legislation in all provinces except Prince Edward Island. In Ontario, the domestic worker must be paid at least the minimum wage if she was hired through an employment agency; and she can't be required to work more than 10 hours a day. A 1979 report by the Canadian Advisory Council on the Status of Women claimed that immigrant women were the most exploited members of the work force, with many of them working in Canadian homes for as little as $50 a week for up to 80 hours' work.

Minimum wages were once based on the income required by a male breadwinner supporting a wife and two children. Today's minimums have little to do with that concept; most families need at least two minimum-income earners to maintain their home. The minimum wage is now set by governments mainly as a basic protection for the unorganized and unskilled worker. It has become the "floor" above which unions bargain with management for a higher standard.

The hourly rate you'll get as a minimum-wage earner varies, depending on whether you are working under federal or provincial jurisdiction. The federal minimum, $2.90 an hour in 1979 for adults over 17, applies to about 500,000 workers in shipping, railways, airlines, communications and banks.

Other workers must be paid at least the ruling provincial minimum wage. In 1979, the hourly "floor" rates were: British Columbia $3, Alberta $3, Saskatchewan $3.50, Manitoba $3.05, Ontario $3, Quebec $3.47, Prince Edward Island $2.75, New Brunswick $2.80, Nova Scotia $2.75, Newfoundland $2.80, the Northwest Territories $3, Yukon $3.

Commissions and gratuities. Domestics aren't the only ones not protected by the minimum-wage laws. In all provinces except Newfoundland, farm laborers are also excluded. Others not covered are apprentices and trainees, students and door-to-door salesmen, who work on a commission basis.

Labor department inspectors can be counted upon to investigate any complaints of violation of the wage laws. Some employers tell workers they aren't entitled to the minimum wage if they receive tips. The federal, and most provincial, laws rule that any gratuities come on top of minimum wages.

It's obvious to any diner-out or bar patron, however, that some hotel, restaurant and tavern staff collect a sizable sum in tips. Doormen and receptionists in posh establishments may well enjoy a take-home pay greater than that of many of their patrons. In Ontario, the minimum wage for those who serve alcoholic beverages as part of their job is set lower—at $2.50 per hour.

If an employer tells you that you won't get the minimum wage because you are on "piecework"—you get, say, a certain amount for each collar you sew for a blouse—tell him to think again. Your piecework rate must be equivalent to the minimum hourly wage, or the boss owes you the difference.

Even if you work in your own home for an employer—making jewelry or knitting sweaters, for example—you are still entitled to the minimum wage. Employers who hire homeworkers are usually required to get a special permit. They must keep a record of all hours worked by each employee, and make sure the piecework payment equals at least the minimum wage.

EQUAL WORK, EQUAL PAY

You discover a fellow-worker is being paid a lot more for doing exactly the same kind of work as you.

The labor laws permit different rates of pay if the difference arises because of a seniority system, a merit system, or a system that measures earnings by the quality or quantity of performance or production. In fact, for just about any reason—with one large exception.

Equal-pay legislation demands that the female employee doing the same work as a male cannot be paid less just because of her gender, and this principle is backed up by the anti-discrimination provisions of the Human Rights Code. Employers used to pay women less—and some still do—because they weren't the heads of households and were "only working for pin money." But as more women entered the work force—many of them single, or the sole supporter of a family—equal-pay laws were passed right across the country.

The woman worker who thinks she is not getting a fair shake can therefore do something about it. Be sure, however, that the situation arises only because you are a woman. When factors other than sex account for the pay difference, you may not win out. If your plant or office is unionized, the union office may step in and take over your complaint under the contractual grievance procedure.

A female employee under federal jurisdiction—a field that includes half a million Canadians—can take her complaint to the Canadian Human Rights Commission in Ottawa. (*See* Section 10, "Effective complaining.") If the employer proves stubborn and won't agree to pay you the same rate, a tribunal can be appointed to adjudicate. It would have the power to order that you get equal pay, plus any back pay owing. Some provinces—Quebec and Alberta, for example—also process such complaints through the Human Rights Commission. Others conduct their investigations through the labor standards branches of the provincial Department of Labour.

Most provincial governments have women's bureaus. They'll advise you where to go to fight your case, and probably help you with it.

Under federal law, the female worker doesn't have to be doing exactly the same job as a male co-worker, but "work of equal value." This wording was introduced after women's groups complained that employers were getting around the "equal pay for equal work" law. If there was even a slight difference in the jobs, if the man lifted a heavier weight, for example, the employer didn't have to pay equal wages.

Employers sometimes hand out different titles to justify different wages. Female nursing aides in hospitals, for example, had a hard fight to get the same pay as male orderlies.

A problem still to be solved is the situation where the employer pays a woman less for doing a different job that requires a lot more brains and skill than other tasks performed by males. A female bookkeeper, for example, might not be receiving as much pay as a truck dispatcher.

Most of the provinces have followed the federal lead by adopting the "work of equal value" wording, or some variation of it. In Ontario and Saskatchewan, the employer is prohibited from paying a female at a lower rate than a male (or vice versa) for similar work performed in the same establishment when the work requires equal "skill, effort and responsibility."

OVERTIME HOURS

Instead of hiring part-time help, the boss offers the full-time staff extra shifts, but at straight time.

It's cheaper to ask for more work from the present staff than to hire new bodies to do extra work; the employer doesn't have to pay vacation and other benefits he'd owe new workers. He must pay you overtime, however, if he asks you to work more than the legal hours—and there's a limit on how much overtime he can force you to do.

Under federal law, the standard work hours are 8 hours a day and 40 a week. You can be required to work up to 48 hours in a week, but you must be paid time-and-a-half overtime after 40 hours. Some categories of workers—farm laborers, for instance—that are not covered by minimum-wage legislation are also outside the hours-of-work laws.

In an industry where the nature of the work makes regular scheduling difficult, the employer may be permitted to average out the hours over a period of weeks. This means you may be called upon to work fewer than 40 hours one week, but many more the next, and so on. But the boss still has to pay overtime if you exceed 40 hours on the average. If the averaging period is 10 weeks, a worker must be paid overtime for any hours worked in excess of 400 hours.

If you are ordered to work more than the standard hours, and not paid overtime, consult the nearest office of your provincial Department of Labour.

Long hours on the road. In some specified industries, an employer is permitted to demand longer hours because of the nature of the business. For example, an interprovincial truck driver may be asked to work for up to 15 hours a day and up to 60 hours a week at straight time. Maximum driving time is 10 hours per shift. Drivers don't work 60 hours every week and they are relatively well paid on the basis of tonnage and mileage.

Provincially, the standard hours are 8 in a day and 40 a week, and some provinces—British Columbia, Saskatchewan and Manitoba among them—require overtime to be paid after 40 hours. In Ontario and Alberta, it's after 44 hours. Only in the Yukon and Northwest Territories can you be obliged to work more than 48 hours a week.

In some provinces it's illegal for an employee to agree to work more than 48 hours a week or more than 100 hours' overtime a year. Ev-

Staking your claim

Although virtually every Canadian who draws a wage is covered by unemployment insurance, the ins and outs of eligibility can at times be complex. If you do qualify for benefits, it is understood that you are "available for work"—and that you are making "continuous," "reasonable" or "customary" efforts to find a job.

The release form is the first step in claiming unemployment benefits. Signed by your employer, it gives a record of your recent work history, your total insurable earnings, and the reason for your present unemployment.

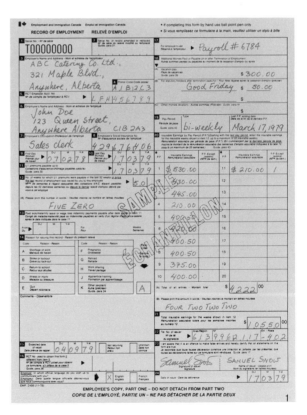

ery union has this information; it's also available from the Department of Labour.

In all provinces, the law permits a compressed workweek, so that employers don't have to pay overtime after 8 hours a day if their employees are on a four-day week. Overtime, however, must still be paid if the weekly hours are exceeded. Extra time off in another week is not a legal substitute for cash payment for overtime.

Straight time for overtime. As always, there are exceptions to rules. In Ontario, for example, local truck drivers and sewer and water line workers don't get overtime until after 50 hours a week; highway construction workers work 55 hours weekly at straight time. Overtime regulations don't apply to landscape gardening, mushroom growing, or taxi driving.

If you do piecework in a factory or shop, the overtime legislation still applies. After the standard hours, the piecework rate should go up to time-and-a-half. When the piecework is done in the home, the legislation won't protect you. You can count only on the minimum wage for work done at home.

Overtime rules apply whether you are paid weekly or monthly. But once you get into the higher salaried or managerial classes, you are no longer protected by the labor standards laws.

EMPLOYED OR SELF-EMPLOYED?

You've signed on to drive for a taxi company, but your new boss hedges when you tell him that you want a guaranteed weekly salary.

As an employee, you have the right to be paid the legal minimum wage, no matter how many hours you work. But deciding just who is an employee, according to the law, and who isn't can be a tricky business, especially if you work on commission or if you have signed an individual contract with your firm.

Taxi drivers, in general, receive a gratuity with just about every fare read off the meter. The size of the tip probably increases in pro-

portion to the quality of the service. The harder a driver hustles, the more tips he gets. It's virtually impossible for labor-standards officers to come up with a satisfactory wage base in these circumstances.

The Ontario Employment Standards Branch has studied the taxi industry to determine whether drivers should get the minimum wage. Its test involved questions of who controlled the profit and loss of the business, who set the conditions of work, and whether the hours put in amounted to full-time employment. The branch ruled that most taxi drivers were employees and thus entitled to the provincial minimum wage. They were not, however, eligible for overtime pay or extra pay for working public holidays.

Some taxi drivers, though, are clearly self-employed. In this category is the driver who owns his own car (or perhaps several) and who rents his services (and perhaps those of other drivers) to a company on specified contract terms. Such a driver is exempted from the labor-standards legislation.

A framework for free lances. The Ontario tests are typical of those applied in other provinces and in the federal sphere to determine who is and who isn't an employee. The federal Department of Labour has wrestled with the question of free lances in the broadcasting industry. The ruling is usually based on the terms of the individual agreement, or contract, between the employer and the performer, journalist or temporary executive. A "free lance" who really does all his work for one boss may be classed as an employee, while another, who sells work or services to several employers, will not.

Labor investigators are skeptical when an employer asks workers to sign contracts that would relieve him of benefits he'd otherwise have to pay to employees. This was once common in the cleaning business. Some companies hired immigrant workers to clean buildings, gave them individual contracts and told them they were self-employed. In Ontario, several of these firms have been ordered to pay the minimum wage and overtime.

An Ontario jug-milk "convenience store" group, open 24 hours a day, maintained that the managers of its neighborhood branches were self-employed people on contract. But because the rules and conditions under which the stores operated were controlled from head office, the managers were ruled to be employees.

The six-figure salesman. Sales representatives on commission provide another difficult problem for the inspectors. In certain fields, hot-shot operators make six-figure incomes, while others barely scrape by.

The general rule is that those who do their selling on the employer's premises, under his conditions, are entitled to labor-standards protection. But the salesman who operates on the outside, paid solely or partly on commission, takes a personal risk as an entrepreneur.

Driver-salesmen for companies selling food or other products fall into the same general categories. The regular driver for the bread company is an employee; the driver who owns his own van, and maybe buys the product he is selling, is self-employed.

BONUSES AND BENEFITS

Your boss announces that the customary Christmas bonuses won't be paid this year because net profit has decreased.

He giveth, and he taketh away. Any employer who makes gifts to his employees, even 20 years in a row, has the right to cease at his sole discretion. It doesn't make any difference if it's a fat turkey or a fat bonus. Workers planning on the accustomed arrival of Santa Claus are likely to enter the New Year disgruntled, but they can't look to any office of the government for assistance.

Any extra provided by your employer can be revoked by him if it isn't one of the minimum benefits provided by law or a part of the terms of employment—for example, a bonus for higher productivity, or a provision in the union contract.

You're entitled annually to certain minimum benefits under the law. They vary from province to province. The federal benefits are the most generous, setting a standard the provinces are usually in time forced to follow. Among those covered by the Canada Labour Code are employees in banks and Crown corporations, as well as in broadcasting and air transport.

An employee working under federal jurisdiction is entitled to the following: nine paid "statutory" holidays, plus two weeks' annual vacation, paid for at the rate of 4 percent of gross earnings during the year or, after six years' employment, three weeks at 6 percent of earnings. After one year's service, a woman can claim 17 weeks' maternity leave. If there's a death in the family, you can claim up to three normal working days of bereavement leave.

Benefits negotiated under collective agreements are often much more generous than these minimums. For example, one Newspaper Guild contract grants maternity leave up to six months (26 weeks) on request, the employee determining the beginning and end of the term. The United Auto Workers (UAW) persuaded employers to grant paid educational leave—education, that is, at the UAW's education center at Port Elgin, Ont.

A month's annual paid vacation is no longer a rarity.

Sharing the wealth. If a condition of your employment is that your employer pays a higher rate for workers who produce faster, or a higher commission for salesmen who sell over a budgeted figure, that bonus cannot be discontinued unilaterally. And any substantive change in the conditions of employment at the time you were hired must be negotiated.

If your company has a profit-sharing scheme, designed to motivate employees, be prepared to take losses as well as gains. The employer cannot, however, use a profit-sharing scheme in a recession to escape paying at least the minimum wage.

Any benefit in a union contract is yours until the contract runs out. During a strike, employers can take benefits away; in fact, they commonly stop paying their share of health-insurance and pension schemes.

If a boss provides meals and a room as part of the wage, there are legal limits on how much he can deduct from your paycheque for those benefits. For example, an Ontario waitress making the minimum $3 an hour who gets a meal at work can't be charged more than $1.15 a meal, or more than $24 a week. An employee who gets a room from his employer can't be charged more than $35 a week.

There are controls on how much a boss can deduct if you should lose some of his money. If you alone use the cash register, you can be held responsible for all losses and they can be deducted from your pay. But if more than one person uses the till—and separate cash drawers are not provided—an employer can't make assumptions about who is responsible for a shortage and hold a whole group liable.

Deductions for extra benefits can't be made from your paycheque without your consent. The only items that can be deducted without your consent are taxes, unemployment insurance contributions and other benefits covered by a statute, and money owed under a court judgment. (*See* "Garnisheeing of wages" in Chapter 21.) If your boss wants to deduct parking charges, for example, he must get your written permission.

The pervasive perk. You'll have to pay taxes on some benefits. If an employer pays all or part of the cost of your health-insurance scheme, you must declare that on your T4 form. If your company provides a car, you pay tax on the value of the mileage for your personal use. The company will reimburse you

Reaping the benefits

Your application for unemployment insurance benefits should be filled out as soon as you find yourself out of work. Keep in mind that even if your claim is accepted without question, there is a compulsory waiting period of two weeks before benefits are payable.

for your car expenses while on the job and gets a deduction on its corporate taxes for that as one of the costs of doing business.

Valuable privileges, or "perks" (perquisites), play an important—if seldom discussed—role in the whole structure of labor and management. Airline employees threatened to strike in 1979 when management tried to rescind their privilege of flying first class. The many thousands of women behind the counters of department stores rely on their allowed discount (15 to 20 percent) to keep up their wardrobes. The executive treasures the spinoffs from his business entertainment.

SICK LEAVE

You haven't been sick all year, so why can't you now add the equivalent paid time to your vacation?

Nice try, but you've no right to time off or extra pay if you don't use your sick leave.

You aren't necessarily entitled to sick leave at all unless you are a civil servant or are otherwise covered by a public-service act that includes sick-leave provisions. Of course, this negotiated benefit may be written into your personal or union contract.

Some private plans reward those enrolled with extra pay, or even early retirement, if they build up a good work-attendance record over the years.

Sick-leave provisions are intended to protect you from losing pay, or your job, because of illness. For example, the plan that applies to federal government employees allows a day and a quarter off each month for sickness. After that time is used up, the employer can deduct pay for time lost. A worker who stays healthy can accumulate this time indefinitely. Then, if a major illness occurs, he is entitled to all the accumulated time off before any pay can be deducted.

Layoffs when ill. Revised federal legislation passed in 1978 says an employee with at least three months' service can't be laid off for illness or injury, provided the absence doesn't exceed 12 weeks.

Any federal worker taking treatment under the auspices of the Workmen's Compensation Board for a job-related illness or accident is entitled to get the job back, no matter how long the treatment takes.

Provincial laws are not so generous. They don't provide job protection if you are absent due to illness or injury. Unless this has been granted under a union contract or individual service agreement, an employee can be laid off simply for being ill. Depending on the employee's length of service, the boss probably has to give either a period of notice before termination, or pay in lieu of notice. (*See* Chapter 25, "Work conditions.")

Anyone who has worked 20 weeks in the last 52 may apply for unemployment insurance benefits if unable to work because of illness or injury. An ill person may get up to 15 weeks of such benefits.

LEAVE OF ABSENCE

You need a year's leave of absence from your job to complete your university degree.

Except in the education field, the leave of absence or "sabbatical"—either paid or unpaid—is not a widespread right. It may be granted by a cooperative employer if your temporary absence does not unduly handicap the department or business. However, the Canadian Labour Congress is behind a drive to build paid educational leave into union contracts, as recommended by the International Labour Organization in 1974. A few large unions, notably the United Auto Workers, United Steelworkers and the Canadian Union of Public Employees, have already made gains in this field. John Munro, the federal labor minister from 1972 to 1978, insists this principle is not new. "Sabbaticals, seminars and classes for bureaucrats, professionals and business executives have been provided freely for years," he pointed out while in office. Employers, on the other hand, argue that education is a government responsibility in Canada and business should not be asked to pick up the tab.

Sabbaticals for everyone? When a university teacher has put in four or five years and been given "tenure"—a permanent job unless he is proved incompetent—he becomes eligible for sabbaticals. (*See* Chapter 10, "Education.") Common practice is for a professor or lecturer to be granted a sabbatical, at two-thirds pay, every seven years. A considerable number seek an additional grant from a foundation or government agency and take the sabbatical year off for research or travel.

Newspaper Guild members at the Toronto *Star* can ask for up to a year's leave for educational purposes with the security that their jobs will be held for them. The contract specifies that management permission "will not be unreasonably withheld." That's another way of saying that management has to show sufficient cause why the leave should *not* be granted.

Schoolteachers at all levels are granted "professional development" days—up to 16 days a year in some cases—to upgrade skills and look into new programs and teaching materials. Secondary-school teachers in some Ontario school boards have negotiated a "salary hold-back plan," under which they get every fifth year off at 80-percent pay. Twenty percent of their salary is accumulated in each of the preceding four years to pay them during the fifth year.

Only one cent an hour. More employers are beginning to offer leave to employees who wish to improve their qualifications. They hope that productivity will increase as a result. At one large engineering plant, the company pays one cent per hour for each worker into a fund for educational leaves; over the three-year contract, the fund will total $60,000.

If you are a union member seeking leave, check the contract. It might grant you that right. You would probably lose some or all of the seniority that would have accumulated, but you would keep the rights you had when you left. Should your course of study be of benefit in your job, the boss might be willing to pay for all or part of your tuition or training costs.

Many large companies, about one in four, provide in-house training courses to help employees upgrade skills directly related to their jobs. Under the Canada Manpower Industrial Training Program, the federal Department of Employment and Immigration subsidizes employers to take on workers, at trainee pay rates, and teach them new skills.

UNEMPLOYMENT INSURANCE

You have held temporary jobs only and the Unemployment Insurance Commission says you're not eligible for benefits.

Bluntly stated, the fact that you are now unemployed does not mean that you have the automatic right to collect cash payments from the Unemployment Insurance Commission. A temporary jobholder—or any other claimant—is not entitled to benefits unless he worked between 10 to 14 weeks in the year before the claim was lodged. The four-week difference comes into play, depending on the unemployment rate in your area. Where unemployment is low, it takes 14 weeks to qualify; where work is hard to get, only 10 weeks. The whole country is cut up into five regions with headquarters in Moncton, N.B., Montreal, Belleville, Ont., Winnipeg and Vancouver. These regions are subdivided into unemployment areas.

If you are joining the work force for the first time, or if you are reentering after a couple of years, then you have to work 20 weeks to qualify.

The entire issue of who can and who cannot collect unemployment benefits boils down to *entitlement*. In other words, if you can satisfy the complex conditions laid down in the Unemployment Insurance Act, you'll get your cheque; if you can't, you must look elsewhere for financial help. (*See* Chapter 45, "When in need.")

There's probably more controversy, and more misunderstanding, about unemployment insurance—popularly known as "pogey"—than any other intervention by government in the social welfare field. While just about everyone who draws a wage or salary is covered, just about every second contributor has a different conception of his "rights" to unemployment insurance benefits. Trying to keep the system on the rails employs a bureaucracy of over 12,000 civil servants.

One frustrated Saskatchewan claimant took a gun with him into the Regina Unemployment Insurance Commission office to persuade officials to grant his pogey. His problem was solved, in a way, when the state provided him with room and board—behind prison bars.

Money for not working. It required an amendment to the British North America Act to get the national scheme started in 1941. Ever since, the simplistic concept of spending very large amounts of public money to support those who are not working—or, worse, those who don't want to work—has stuck in the throats of individuals raised under the stern principles of the "work ethic." The idealistic, humane principle behind the scheme seldom gets equivalent publicity.

Even the name is a bit of a misnomer. It's not truly an "insurance" plan, as economists see it. Compulsory contributions drawn from employee and employer at the rate of $2.5 billion a year cover only about 60 percent of the costs. The massive shortfall is made up from the public treasury. In times of high unemployment, that calls for many millions a month in taxpayer subsidy.

Beating the cheaters

You don't have to be a genius to think up dodges to cheat the Unemployment Insurance Commission (UIC). Some claimants assume several different names and start claims with different offices. Some simply fake a search for jobs to get around the qualifying requirements and take off on holidays to the Bahamas. A group of the happily unemployed were once discovered enjoying the ski slopes at Banff.

The reality is that although you must fill in numerous forms, swearing that your information is accurate, the system works largely on good faith at the outset. But if the UIC police (known as "benefit-control officers") get on your trail, punishment can range from penalties—up to three times the weekly benefit payment—to criminal prosecution for fraud.

At regular intervals, the benefit-control officers run off the computerized payout records against employment records to detect suspicious overlaps. Claimants have to keep records of the names, dates and addresses of places they've gone to seek employment. Even failure by the claimant to report a change of address has been considered grounds for assessing a penalty.

In 1977, some 7,000 persons who had claimed benefits were prosecuted and found guilty of fraud. Another 62,000 less flagrant offenders were assessed fines by Canada Employment; they also had to pay back the extra money they'd taken.

Even if the UIC sends you an overpayment through clerical error, it can get the money back through legal channels. After three years have passed, though, no such collection is possible.

The commission adopts the basic attitude that it will prosecute anyone who is collecting unemployment benefits while working full time. The charge is usually based on alleged false statements by the claimant. Convictions are often widely publicized in the hope of deterring other would-be cheaters.

Employers who fake employees' records to show more insurable weeks or higher insurable earnings than was actually the case can also be prosecuted. The penalty is a fine of up to $5,000 or double the amount of benefits paid by the UIC as a result of the false information, or *both* of these fines plus up to six months in jail.

The boss can also be fined for failure to keep proper records, or for failing to forward contributions to the UIC office.

Adding to confusion, the qualifications for entitlement and the rate of payment are subject to frequent change. Your nearest UIC or Canada Employment (Manpower) office will always provide details of the most recent revisions. At the time of writing, UIC regional offices were offering 12 different brochures explaining the system. They were all available by mail in English and French, and some of them in Portuguese, Italian, Greek and Chinese.

Tougher on repeaters. In 1979, the rules for the "repeater"—someone who's already received unemployment insurance benefits during the preceding 12 months—were made stricter to discourage those who work for short periods solely to become eligible for benefits. The longer an applicant had benefits the first time during the year, the longer it now takes to requalify. However, if the repeater lives in an area where the unemployment rate is above 11.5 percent, he gets the benefit of the doubt and will only have to work the normal entrance requirement, 10 weeks.

If you are an hourly paid or salaried worker, you have to work a minimum of 20 hours a week to be insurable in the first place. Those paid on a piecework or commission basis have to earn at least 30 percent of the maximum weekly insurable earnings. (In 1979, that meant earning at least $79.50 a week.) These minimums were established to prevent people who can get high hourly rates for only a few hours' work from doing a bare minimum of work in order to qualify for benefits.

You are not entitled to benefits unless you are making efforts to find a job—and are available for work. You don't qualify if you are leaving the country, if you are 65 or over, or if you put strict limits on the kind of work you are willing to do.

Up to 15 weeks' special benefits are available to workers who are injured or ill, provided they have worked 20 weeks in the previous 52. You have to be off work eight days or more, and there's a standard two-week waiting period.

If you are getting Workmen's Compensation Board payments that total less than UIC benefits, you can ask Canada Employment for the difference. Maternity benefits (15 weeks) can be taken any time between the 10th week before the expected birth and the 17th week after.

When a claim is turned down, there's the right of appeal to the local board of referees, made up of people who are not UIC employees. Beyond that, you can appeal to the "umpire"—usually a judge of the Federal Court. His decision is final.

The waiting period. Once your claim is accepted, there's a two-week waiting period before you start to receive payments. If you have vacation pay or any other benefit coming from your previous employer, this has to run out first. This means that if you got two weeks' vacation pay, you'd have to wait a total of four weeks. From Jan. 1, 1979, the benefit rate was 60 percent of your average pay during the last 20 weeks of your employment. But there's a maximum on how much of your earnings you could insure: in 1979, it was $13,780 a year. The maximum payment was $159 a week; the minimum, about $32.

Once the waiting period is over, you are entitled to one week of benefits for each week you worked, up to a maximum of 25 weeks. If you worked longer than 26 weeks before claiming, you can then start to get one more week of benefits for each two weeks more that you worked, up to a maximum of 13 weeks more. If the unemployment rate in your area is between 7.5 and 8 percent, an extra 16 weeks can be allowed. The maximum anyone can collect is 50 weeks' benefits.

Under the Human Rights Act, you have the right to see your unemployment insurance files, and to make corrections if you can prove they contain mistakes.

FORFEITED BENEFITS

You quit after a dispute with the foreman. It wasn't your fault, so why shouldn't you get your unemployment insurance benefits?

It would be just too easy to get the benefits if all you had to do was decide to leave your job. A disagreement with the foreman isn't hard to arrange.

You run the risk of forfeiting benefits if the officials at your local Canada Employment Center decide that you quit without "just cause." The penalty is usually six weeks' loss of benefits. It's another check on those who take jobs just long enough to qualify before quitting.

The penalty isn't automatic. The test is whether the officer handling your claim thinks that any reasonable person would have quit under the circumstances. He must believe that you left only after doing everything possible to remedy an intolerable situation.

The penalty can be reduced if you show that you were not wholly to blame. The full six-week penalty comes on top of the normal two-week waiting period for benefits. If you disagree with the ruling, you can appeal.

Six weeks for misconduct. When you are fired for "just cause" (*see* Chapter 24, "Job security"), the ex-employer will be asked for proof that you lost your job because of your misconduct. If the Unemployment Insurance Commission agrees that your boss had good reason to fire you, you'll be assessed the six-week penalty. But if you were just laid off because the boss was reducing staff for business reasons, there would be no penalty; you would begin to receive your benefits after the two-week waiting period.

Unemployment insurance benefits are not paid to workers involved in a labor dispute that leads to a strike or lockout. Canada Employment Centers have experts on staff whose job is to assess disputes, decide who is directly involved and who may be affected as innocent bystanders. If you were not involved in a strike, but were laid off because the business couldn't operate because of picketing, you might be entitled to benefits. It's complicated, because the experts have to decide whether you are aiding the striking group in any way, and whether you stand to lose or gain because of the industrial action. For example, you may not get benefits if you refuse to cross a picket line.

THE FAMILY BUSINESS

Your family-run café fails when a fast-food chain opens up next door. You have paid your taxes for 20 years, but can get no benefits.

It may seem unfair after you've paid all those contributions to the Unemployment Insurance Commission (UIC), but you aren't entitled to a cent of benefits when, as the proprietor, you are now out on the street.

All employers are required to pay 1.4 times the employee rate, but only employees who have paid UIC premiums at their jobs are eligible for benefits; managers and employers are excluded from receiving benefits. Official reasoning is that the insurance is for those who might find themselves suddenly without work through no fault of their own. You are self-employed and are deemed to have assumed total risk for your own employment or unemployment. As master of your own fate, you can't be laid off or fired by someone else.

If your business has gone bust, you can get help from Canada Employment by telling them you want to find other work. They'll register you as seeking employment and do their best to help you find something suitable.

Nearly 25,000 employers in Canada pay reduced UIC premiums because their workers are covered under approved wage-loss plans for illness. If the plan pays employees a certain rate of benefit when they're off work because of illness, it means that those workers may not have to collect UIC benefits, or that they will collect for a shorter period of time. This saves the UIC money.

Some employers have supplemental unemployment benefit plans approved by Canada Employment. These allow employers to pay certain benefits to their employees when they are off work because of temporary shortage of work, illness or maternity. The benefits are paid in addition to the UIC benefits.

Your own business

The federal Small Business Loans Act defines a small business as one whose gross annual revenue does not exceed $1.5 million. That's not especially illuminating until one realizes that about half the Canadian work force is employed by small businesses. These modest enterprises range from the mom-and-pop corner store to the manufacturing or service industry employing 15 or 20 persons. Taken together they comprise the base of the country's economy, their diversity and flexibility providing stability against the feast-or-famine cycles of big businesses.

It's the rare person who has not dreamed of being his own boss—doing what he wants when he wants; becoming modestly rich through his own skill and energy; winning respect and status in the community. Small-business men who made it into the "big time" are not part of our folklore, but perhaps they should be.

Take the story of immigrant Timothy Eaton, who started his dry-goods business in the village of St. Mary's, Ont., but expanded it to reach across the country, and the Massey family's development of a small foundry into one of the world's greatest farm-implement businesses; or the rags-to-riches sagas of Garfield Weston, Harvey McMillan, Armand Bombardier, Roy Thomson and Sam Steinberg.

Most of those who set out to chase the dream, with a little capital and a lot of courage, learn the hard way that it's a rocky road indeed. Only about 30 percent succeed, and most end up making little more money—if not less—than they would have as employees, where their ambition and talent would have earned them promotions.

However, if the dizzying rewards of the tycoon escape all but a few, there is the satisfaction of "ownership." Every Main Street and shopping plaza displays the evidence of this on proud storefronts. Less visible is the testament of thousands of small manufacturers, food processors, textile operations, service industries, and farmers, fishermen, writers, sculptors, and prospectors who hunt for gold or uranium or oil.

Federal and provincial governments temper their encouragement to independent entrepreneurs with warnings of the shoals ahead, yet many still plunge in recklessly—only to see their savings trickle away as the dream turns sour. Starting your own business from scratch, buying a going concern, purchasing a franchise—these ventures are full of booby traps.

Obligations to government, employees, suppliers and customers can break the stoutest of spirits. To get started, you'll need determination, enthusiasm and a willingness to work hard for small pay. To succeed, you'll need thorough research of markets and methods, sufficient operating capital, and the guidance of professional accountants, lawyers and bankers—and a lot of luck.

ONE IS COMPANY

You are the sole proprietor of a small business and are thinking of forming a company, but you don't want to take in outsiders.

You can incorporate a company with yourself as sole director. You can be president and general manager—and the only employee. You can give it any name you choose, provided you don't come too close to an existing registered business name or one likely to confuse or hoodwink the public. You can't call your company Pierre Elliott Trudeau Consultants Limited, unless you are Pierre Elliott Trudeau.

The law used to say that any company had to have a minimum of three directors, so "dummy" directors, who really had nothing to do with the company, were often named to satisfy the regulation. The requirement was eventually dropped for federal and most provincial incorporations.

Most small private companies are incorporated provincially. The fee is $200. It's not a complicated procedure and you can probably handle all the details yourself. A lawyer will charge about $500.

Whether you are wise to form a company depends on how profitable your small business is. You're probably better off to remain a "sole proprietor" if earnings are modest. However, if things are starting to boom, there are several advantages in incorporating, especially the income-tax break. Personal income tax is graduated, the percentage going up as income goes up. The corporate tax rate on the net income of most small businesses is between 25 and 29 percent, depending on your province. Dividends can be paid with little or no tax effect on a shareholder. Forming a company will cost you some of your freedom because your activities will be regulated by additional government departments. However, besides the small-business tax rate, you may be eligible for a "manufacturing and processing" deduction of 5 percent if you are a manufacturer or a processor.

You can employ your spouse at a reasonable salary, thereby splitting income for tax purposes. The spouse also becomes eligible for benefits under the Canada or Quebec Pension Plan. (*See* Chapter 48, "Retirement.")

Limit of liability. The financial liability of a shareholder in a corporation is limited to his investment in shares, plus any personal guarantees he provides. Small companies, particularly new ones, are usually required to have individuals provide personal guarantees for bank loans, and suppliers of raw materials or merchandise sometimes seek the same protection. Sole proprietors have unlimited liability, but are relatively free from regulation. Registration of a business name usually costs only about $10. In fact, if you simply decide to set up in business as, say, a self-employed house painter, you *are* a sole proprietor. If you trade under your own name, you don't even need to bother registering. Just start, and best of luck!

A provincial corporation must be licensed in each province in which it does business. If you plan to cross borders, you should consider federal incorporation under the Canada Business Corporations Act.

PARTNERSHIPS

Your business partner died suddenly and his widow is demanding payment in cash for his half.

Unless a partnership agreement specifically states otherwise, your equal partner's heir is entitled to his half—in cash—if the widow prefers that to continuing the partnership. In fact, the death of a partner automatically dissolves the original partnership and can lead to liquidation of the business—often at fire-sale prices. At best, the business is likely to receive a major setback.

A partnership closely resembles a sole proprietorship, except that two or more persons share profits and losses. If a partnership fails, creditors can seize the personal assets of any or all of the partners. As in a sole proprietorship, all net earnings are taxed as personal income. A partnership agreement should include the key proviso that if one partner dies, the business will continue. It can also set the date and terms on which the partnership will end.

The unhappy heir. But a surviving partner can still be in a ticklish situation if his deceased partner's heir needs cash immediately. Perhaps the heir couldn't force liquidation, but partnerships soon go on the rocks unless the partners are in easy accord.

When incorporation is permitted by law (doctors, lawyers and many other professionals can't form limited companies to sell their services), it's often better for two partners to set up a company, each taking half the shares. Heirs of a deceased partner cannot then get at the company's assets. It's likely that whoever inherited your partner's shares will ask you to buy them, but you can't be forced to and the company can't be forced into dissolution.

Whether you register as a partnership or form a small private company, you should formulate a "death agreement" with your partner right at the beginning. Often, each takes out a life insurance policy, naming the other as beneficiary, to an amount sufficient to purchase the deceased partner's share from his estate. The agreement stipulates that the estate must sell and the surviving partner (or partners) must buy. If either partner has a health problem, there may be some difficulty getting insurance. But in most cases you can buy a term policy. (*See* Chapter 32, "Life insurance.") For protection against the possibility that one of you becomes disabled, you could also have an insurance plan to pay off the disabled partner's share by installments over several years. That would provide steady income for the retiree and save the business from major disruption.

The powerless partner. If partners employ their spouses in the business, only half of their salaries is deductible as business expenditure, unless they can be proved to be *bona fide* partners. You'd have to convince your District Tax Office of the spouses' qualifications and the services they perform.

There is a special "limited partnership" which must be registered as such with the provincial registrar of companies. It usually consists of both general partners and "special partners." The latter have no power to act individually on behalf of the partnership, and their liability for losses is limited.

The essence of the run-of-the-mill general partnership is that the actions of any one of the partners bind all the others irrevocably. So, know your partners.

OPERATING CAPITAL

Your small company needs some operating capital, but you fear losing control if you sell shares to outsiders.

You can sell 49 percent of the voting shares in your private company and still retain effective operating control. Absolute control requires that you keep two-thirds of the voting stock. That voting majority is needed to amend the company charter—its constitution. In fact, you may even need a 75-percent majority to pass certain proposals—for instance, to reorganize the company's capital.

Your best bet is to look for people who see the long-term potential for growth of your company—and their investment in it. They're not interested in a quick return, nor in becoming outright owners or managers of the company. They may buy non-voting common or preferred shares, or settle for the right to elect one director in order to keep in touch with the company's operations.

It's difficult for a private company to induce people to invest money in it without giving them some share of control. Selling common shares is called equity financing; borrowing is debt financing. The obvious advantage of equity financing is that the company doesn't have to pay heavy interest charges, nor meet repayment schedules.

Security demanded. Generally speaking, lending institutions would not be interested in buying part of your company. They usually offer only short-term "demand" loans at fluctuating interest rates. (*See* Chapter 30, "Saving and borrowing.") The small-business man will probably have to back these up with personal promissory notes. Lenders take the position that you should be prepared to risk *all* your own assets when you ask them to risk *some* of theirs.

Banks always require as much solid security as they can get for any loan or "line of credit," which is an agreed amount upon which the borrower can draw as required. If you have no real estate or other suitable assets to pledge, banks can lend on such things as your inventory and accounts receivable. Banks will accept modest temporary risks, but the interest rate will be high, several "points" above the rate charged to preferred customers. The local bank manager has a considerable margin of discretion, and his evaluation of you and your business could well be the key factor.

Under the terms of the federal Small Business Loans Act, designated lending institutions can lend at favorable rates for the establishment or improvement of businesses whose estimated annual gross revenue does not exceed $1.5 million. Approved businesses include manufacturing, wholesale or retail trade, construction, transportation, communications and service industries. The maximum loan outstanding cannot exceed $75,000 and must be repaid within 10 years, in annual installments. These loans must be secured in the normal way, even though they are guaranteed by the federal treasury.

Every large city has financiers who specialize in providing what is known as venture capital. In the hope of striking a bonanza, they'll invest in promising small companies—sometimes, in just an idea. Normally, however, they demand some management control in return.

GOVERNMENT ASSISTANCE

Your bank manager has turned down your request for an extension of your line of credit.

Many small businesses face recurrent financial crises because they lack reserves of operating capital to ride out sales slumps, problems with suppliers, factory breakdowns or labor troubles. Statistics show an increasing number of bankruptcies; in 1978 alone, 4,954 businesses failed. About 70 percent of new businesses go under within the first five years.

You can look for help to a whole series of

Climbing the paper mountain

Statistics Canada, formerly the Dominion Bureau of Statistics, has the right to demand that any business fill in its snowstorm of forms. In fact, you can be fined if you dump Statscan "requests" in your wastebasket. When the data reach Ottawa, they are keypunched into computers for tabulation and instant recall. Statscan collects information on prices, wages, industries, agriculture, transport, communications, construction, imports and exports, and dozens of other categories. It produces more than 1,000 publications a year, all of them available from Ottawa headquarters or designated bookstores or you can peruse them at your local library. There's a free weekly publication, too, *Infomat*.

It's emphasized that the individual source of any information is held in strict confidence. No other government department can learn the names involved—not even the eager taxmen at the Department of National Revenue. To help reduce the "paper burden," small businesses—about a 10-percent sample—are required to fill out only the abbreviated short form. If you employ fewer than 20 workers, you are rated "small."

Statscan will endeavor to prepare special tabulations more closely tailored to an infor-

mation seeker's needs: perhaps, for example, the number of fast-food outlets in your region plus the average turnover. Typical inquiries from small businesses include these:

■ A small manufacturer wanted to compare his wage rates with similar manufacturers.
■ A retailer was planning expansion in another city and wanted information on population, economic levels, average incomes, number of competitors.
■ A retailer wanted to compare her sales to the national average and find out if she was keeping up with the market.
■ A manufacturer of refrigerator parts wanted data on the number of refrigerator makers and the annual sales of complete units by province.

The Ottawa head office and eight regional offices have a "User Advisory Services Division." You can phone or write, or drop by. There's no charge unless your request calls for staff overtime, special graphs or tabulation. You'll find Statscan in the white pages of your telephone directory, under "Government of Canada." Or you can write or call Statistics Canada, Central Enquiry Service, R.H. Coats Building, Ottawa, Ont., K1A 0T6.

federal and provincial programs and agencies. Governments are well aware that about half the total work force is employed in "small" business.

The Federal Business Development Bank, formerly called the Industrial Development Bank, is a Crown corporation established in 1944. It has loaned $3.6 billion to 56,000 small and medium businesses—the average loan is $50,000. But you can apply to it only *after* you have been turned down by the usual commercial lenders. Loans are made on terms judged reasonable to the kind of business and risk involved, but normal collateral and guarantees are usually required. However, the FBDB is prepared to grant loans that are undersecured if the business appears to have good earning prospects.

For those needing advice as well as money, the bank runs a management-counseling service and offers a wide selection of publications for small businesses from its 5 regional and 90 branch offices.

Taxpayer to the rescue. Federal agencies offer about 100 different financial-aid programs to eligible groups, including the fishing, footwear, textile and apparel industries, industrial design and research, shipbuilding, farming, film development, and small-business management training. The Export Development Corporation provides loan guarantees to finance export sales. The Department of Regional Economic Expansion offers development incentives and loan guarantees to manufacturing and processing industries in designated "have-not" regions.

Federal initiatives are often matched by provincial programs, as the provinces battle for jobs and corporation tax revenues. All of them have small-business lending operations, with special help for such seasonal operations as tourist resorts, which could be wiped out by one bad year.

None of these programs are giveaways. They are guided by normal banking practices, even though some decisions have resulted in very expensive white elephants. Some disappointed small-business applicants complain that it's easier to get a million from government agencies than it is to get $50,000.

EXPERT ADVICE

You need advice on how best to handle your rapidly expanding business, but you would like to avoid the costly services of accountants or consultants.

Few enterprises can survive without expert advice. There are informal sources where you can get assistance at no charge, and formal ones where the fee is nominal. For example, your suppliers probably know a lot about the problems in the field, and how others are dealing with them. Your bank manager can be another good source of advice. Suppliers and bank both have a stake in your company's success. Almost every line of business has its central trade organization, and members can draw on that pool of know-how. Trade journals in your field exist on their ability to keep subscribers abreast of new developments.

More formally, the Federal Business Development Bank (FBDB) offers Counseling Assistance to Small Enterprises, which can provide a retired executive as a consultant for a nominal fee. This service has a pool of 1,800 experienced retirees on call. Many are former financial counselors, bank managers, civil servants, plant superintendents, union executives and the like. The FBDB publishes *Small Business News*, a quarterly broadsheet full of information, tips and warnings. Written in matter-of-fact, down-to-earth style, it's available free from Federal Business Development Bank Management Services, P.O. Box 6021, Montreal, Que., H3C 3C3.

The National Research Council offers its Technical Information Service. Its personnel will come and assess your production process, and advise on new products or processes to upgrade your capability.

Taxing the taxman. Through its 28 District Taxation Offices, the Department of National Revenue provides free information to small businesses on corporate and personal taxes. Staff experts will explain the law and its maze of regulations impartially. Common questions asked of them include: At what earning level does a business have to start paying tax? Can I choose what my financial year will be? What kind of expenses can my business claim? Can I make installment payments? Exactly what taxes do I have to pay? What records must I keep for tax purposes?

More involved questions are passed to the district office's audit division. Here is a sample of typical inquiries: My garage prepares used vehicles for sale; can this be considered as processing? What provisions are there for merging two partnerships that were totally unrelated previously? I'm a single proprietorship and want to sell my assets to my new corporation; do I have to pay taxes on the sale of the assets?

Provincial governments also provide various counseling services for businessmen, and most university business schools have a free or inexpensive counseling service which draws on the skills of senior or postgraduate students. Your local Chamber of Commerce and the Canadian Manufacturers' Association are both likely sources of guidance. They may know of senior businessmen in your town who are willing to act as consultants. In Hamilton, Ont., a council of active senior executives will donate half a day of their time to help small enterprises get on their feet.

TRADEMARKS, PATENTS

You've received a lawyer's letter ordering you to stop using your business name.

Everyone has the right, without any permission, to trade as a "sole proprietor" under his or her own name as shown in birth-registration records. But you must use exactly that name—and nothing extra.

If you are Richard Roe, you can begin trading under that name, even if there are a hundred other Richard Roes in business already. If you add anything else to the name—such as "Richard Roe Antiques"—you must register with the appropriate provincial department. If another "Richard Roe Antiques" is already registered, you are out of luck. The department will search the records in advance for a nominal fee; there are also private search firms in the field. This precaution can save you quite a lot of money—store signs, brochures, stationery—and perhaps some embarrassment.

Deceiving the public. Every incorporated company and business partnership has a registered trade name. It's an integral part of the process of setting up officially. Whether you incorporate federally or provincially, the records will first be searched to assure that there's no likelihood of the public being deceived. Sole proprietors and partnerships cannot register federally.

Once registered, your trade name is largely protected by law. But if a competitor, most likely a sole proprietor, sends a letter ordering you to cease using the trade name because of "prior right," it could require a court decision to sort things out. The judge would have to decide which name came first and whether the names were so similar that one was chosen to deceive customers. An unregistered sole proprietor, using his own name, could have been in business so long that he really has established prior right.

To protect yourself if you intend to trade outside your home province, it's wise to register with the federal Department of Consumer and Corporate Affairs. If you are incorporated under federal law, your trade name will be protected across the country.

Provincial or federal registration also protects you against foreign companies coming into the market and using "your" name, provided that you started using the name in Canada first. The small-business man is seldom concerned with international protection of his trade name, but Canada is signatory to several pacts by which countries agree to honor one another's registrations. The computer revolution makes it possible for hundreds of thousands of registrations to be checked quickly. And the system really works. A Canadian citizen who owns a small string of bookshops in Britain had to cut through a lot of red tape in Ottawa when he wanted to incorporate a separate company in Canada under a similar name. The computer kept saying: "No way. There's a company in the United Kingdom with prior right." It was hard to convince it that the proprietor in each case was the same man.

What is champagne? Often, there's confusion between trade names and trademarks, and the law in this field is complex indeed. The simplest explanation is that the trade name identifies your business, while the trademark distinguishes the goods or services of your company. It costs $100 to register a trademark in Canada; protection lasts for 15 years and can be renewed indefinitely.

The trademark can be a word, a symbol or a picture. "Coke" is a registered trademark of the Coca-Cola Company, as is the distinctively shaped bottle. One of the oldest and most famous trademarks is Nipper, the black-and-white terrier cocking his ear at a phonograph horn: the symbol of RCA record players for almost 100 years.

Well-known trademarks are obviously very valuable and they are zealously protected. The Supreme Court in 1974 ordered Canadian winemakers to stop using the word "champagne" on their labels. The complaint was lodged by the vintners of the famous French province of Champagne. But Canadian manufacturers argued that "champagne" was used in this country to describe any sparkling wine, and in 1978 the federal government canceled a 1933 agreement between Canada and France protecting each other's trademarks. The French vintners have been vindicated, to some extent, by the labeling requirements of Canada's Department of Consumer and Corporate Affairs—"champagne" originating in this country must be clearly labeled "*Canadian champagne*."

Levi Strauss and Company, makers of the original "Levi's," successfully sued to prevent other jeans manufacturers from using the name. Carling O'Keefe Ltd. of Toronto changed the name of its "Highlite" beer to "Trilight" when the Miller Brewing Company of Milwaukee complained the first choice was too close to its "High Life" brand. Over $1 million had been spent in advertising the "Highlite" brand name. The Metropolitan Toronto Police emblem was registered as a trademark to protect it from unauthorized use in advertising or on such items as cuff links.

Patent and copyright. In applicable circumstances, the Intellectual Property Branch of the federal Department of Consumer and Corporate Affairs provides several other ways to protect the uniqueness of your business. After exhaustive examination by experts, a patent may be granted giving an inventor the right to keep others from making, using or selling his invention within Canada. The total fee is $450 and the term is 17 years.

Patents are not renewable. The common term "patent pending" means merely that an application for a patent has been filed. Until the actual patent is granted, anyone can make use of the invention. If you invent a better mousetrap and get it patented, Ottawa cannot stop a foreign manufacturer from copying it. You must take out patents in each country.

The author of any original literary, dramatic, musical or artistic work—books, plays, photography, painting or sculpture—acquires copyright by the act of creation itself. Registration is voluntary, but the certificate of ownership of the copyright (literally, the "right to copy") can be very useful if a dispute about authorship should develop. When an author is hired or employed by another person or a company to create the work, the employer owns the copyright. The Reader's Digest Association (Canada) Ltd. holds the copyright of the book you are reading. A copyright lasts for the lifetime of the creator, plus 50 years.

Industrial designs can be protected for five years, renewable only once for another five. Only the aesthetic features of a manufactured article can be guarded, not its function.

PRICE-FIXING

Suppliers are refusing to provide merchandise for your discount store for fear of being boycotted by established merchants.

New sections in the federal Combines Investigation Act give you the right to take legal action against other companies that interfere unduly with your ability to compete. The act should protect you against a refusal of supplies, but the details differ in almost every case and if both parties stand pat, legal action is the ultimate recourse.

The Restrictive Trade Practices Commission is empowered to rule on situations where: a "person" is substantially affected in his business because he can't obtain supplies on usual market terms; there's insufficient competition among suppliers of the product; a supplier sets unfair conditions for buyers of his product so they can buy only from him or his nominee; customers are compelled to buy another product from the supplier as part of a package deal. There's a long list of other prohibited actions designed substantially to lessen competition. And remember that an incorporated company, a partnership or a sole proprietorship is a "person"—a recognized separate identity—under the law.

If you believe that you are being treated unfairly in the marketplace, you can apply to the Director of Investigation and Research, Department of Consumer and Corporate Affairs, for an inquiry. If this body decides your suppliers are breaching the regulations, the Restrictive Trade Practices Commission can issue an order to the effect that you must be treated on equal terms with other customers. If you have not yet been accepted as a customer, the suppliers in question must admit you to the trading circle on the usual terms.

Foiling the price-fixers. Another section of the statute prevents suppliers from controlling the prices at which dealers sell the product. In 1978, the Restrictive Trade Practices Commission showed its teeth when Levi Strauss and Company pleaded guilty to eight counts of price-fixing on its jeans, and to charges of refusing to supply some merchants who offered the company's Levi's at a discount. The company was fined $150,000 in Canada; similar charges in the United States cost Levi Strauss more than $3.5 million in settlements.

All offenses against fair competition—or a refusal to obey an order from the commission—can lead to criminal charges. Sentences

Voice of the retailer

The Retail Council of Canada (RCC) speaks nationally for the sellers, as the Canadian Association of Consumers speaks for the buyers. Members of the RCC sell us 75 percent of the $40 billion worth of goods and services we buy in retail stores every year. The council represents the large department and chain stores, but it also has a division to speak up for the small retailer. A telephone "hot line" (416: 363-8507) is always open to the council's head office at Suite 525, 74 Victoria Street, Toronto, Ont., M5C 2A5, to handle any questions or problems in retailing—*except* where to buy.

Founded in 1963, the council was originally intended solely to lobby the federal government on behalf of retailers. Now it acts as the national trade voice in all areas and conducts a vigorous educational program. A short list of interests includes business practices, consumer protection, health and safety, warranties, competition policy, advertising and taxation. It runs seminars in major centers, which are open to nonmembers, on such topics as management skills for small retailers, how to prevent in-store losses, fashion merchandising and buying techniques. Its monthly publications, *Canadian Retailer, Retail Food Report* and *Fashion Information*, are available to members. Education programs are built around training manuals on sales promotion, staff training and retail metrication. Several RCC insurance packages are available to members at discount rates, covering group life, accident, disability and extended care, fire, theft, malicious damage and public liability.

Membership fees are charged on a sliding scale, depending on the size of your business. If your sales are under $1 million, membership costs you between $50 and $120 per year.

can range up to five years' imprisonment and up to $1 million in fines. If the commission doesn't consider that your case is strong enough, or that the matter doesn't warrant a prosecution, you'll have to decide if it's worth the expense of bringing a civil action yourself. If an order favorable to you has been made, and disobeyed, you can sue for damages, alleging a breach of the Combines Investigations Act. If more than one company is involved, there could be charges of conspiracy. Your best bet as a small operator is that the filing of a complaint with the commission will be enough to make the offending suppliers begin treating you fairly. It usually is.

PRICE-CUTTING

Your fledgling business is being pushed to the wall by the price-cutting of the firm that had a monopoly in your town for years.

It used to be said that all's fair in love and war—and business. But like most adages, that's only partly true. Governments seldom interfere in a straight "price war" because when merchants fight it out cleanly, the public is usually the winner. But when the market is being manipulated with the intention of starving out competition, the big battalions have all the bullets. Section 34 of the Combines Investigation Act is aimed at those who try to maintain a monopoly by selling at unduly low prices. Once the upstart competitor is out of the way, prices usually return quickly to previous levels.

You can apply for an order from the Restrictive Trade Practices Commission against any person, or company, engaging in a policy of selling products at prices unreasonably low, or at prices lower in one area of the country than those he charges elsewhere in Canada—when this policy has the effect or tendency of substantially lessening competition or eliminating a competitor.

Everybody is in favor of lower prices, and it won't be easy to prove that your competitor is breaking the law. A lawyer will advise you as to your chances of winning a suit, and whether the cost of winning would be worth the fight. To sustain a charge against your competitor for unfair competition because he is maintaining—or trying to protect—a monopoly, you must prove that the monopoly is operating against the public interest.

INSOLVENCY

The major creditor of your new and still struggling business is threatening to petition you into bankruptcy.

After reasonable notice, your creditor can say "pay me" and, if you can't, he can petition you into bankruptcy to try to recover his money. You can't buy insurance to protect you against this eventuality. A petition for a "receiving order" is usually granted if the creditor is owed $1,000 or more and you are unable to pay. It's a serious move and the creditor must step carefully. If you aren't really insolvent—just temporarily strapped—he could be unnecessarily and unfairly destroying your business. For that, you can sue.

To head off unilateral action, make an appointment with your creditor, place all your cards on the table, and try to work out a tolerable settlement. Driving you into bankruptcy would be expensive, because of the costs of lawyers and trustees, and it might be cheaper for him to negotiate with you on an amicable basis. If you go under, he'll be a loser; but if your business is still viable, he'll have gained by helping you stay afloat.

However, many suppliers and financial institutions take the position that they can't afford to become involved with the internal problems of their numerous clients. In many cases, they are themselves using money borrowed at high interest rates.

Calculating your chances. Any qualified accountant will tell you whether your struggling business is viable—or soon likely to be. The accountant can help you draw up a forecast and accompany you to a meeting with your impatient creditor. If your business is really in trouble, don't go farther in the hole through stubbornness or sentiment. Even large companies close down when profitable operation is impossible. To avoid the penalties and complications of bankruptcy, you can still go to your creditor and propose an informal settlement. If you can't cover all your debts, you can offer to pay some fraction in return for being allowed to have one more try at making the business a success or to close up shop quietly.

Another choice is to declare voluntary bankruptcy. This will halt any legal actions against you and eventually get you released from most of your debts. Your assets will be seized to pay off creditors. But this is the final solution, of course. For it, you'll need the services of a bankruptcy trustee, licensed under the Bankruptcy Act. If you can't afford the fee of a trustee, apply to the assistance program of the federal Department of Consumer and Corporate Affairs. You'll then be asked to contribute $50 toward administrative costs, and a civil servant will be authorized to act as trustee. Any money from the sale of assets will go first to pay the department's standard trustee fee, and whatever is left over will be distributed among your creditors. If your threatening creditor decides to force you into bankruptcy, he will have to advance the trustee's fee.

Secured creditors have first call on any money realized when the trustee sells off your assets on which they have rights. A bank or trust company that had given you a mortgage would be a secured creditor. Having first claim, a secured creditor may prefer to petition you into bankruptcy, knowing he will get his money from liquidation of your assets, while other creditors will have to scramble for what's left.

BUYING GOOD WILL

Your life savings have gone to buy a restaurant as a going concern. Now the seller is opening a smart new bistro in the next block.

Looks as if you have fallen for a very old dodge, and the law can't help you. The only way to avoid finding yourself in competition with the businessman you just bought out is to write an airtight purchase contract, covering all possibilities. Obviously these should include a prohibition against his reentering the same trade or profession in your hometown, or within a stated radius of the old location.

It's not easy to close all the loopholes, however. The seller may try to slip past your contract by opening a slightly different business. A tavern is not the same thing in law as a restaurant or café; a British-style pub or a French-style bistro could be different again. But they all serve food.

And even if buyer and seller did agree on some geographical protection, the terms would have to be reasonable. For example, in a small town it could be reasonable to have a clause saying the seller won't reopen; but if the transaction took place in a big city, you might be asking too much if you try to ban him from the whole metropolitan area. If he challenged you later, a judge could decide that the contract stipulations were unfair and invalidate the whole agreement.

You probably paid a certain sum for "good will." That's hard to define, too, but it usually refers to the custom the former owner built up over the years. It could include anything from the trading name to the location or even to the existing staff.

The value of the good will is negotiated as additional to the actual value of the physical assets. It should reasonably assure you of continuity of the kind of earnings that the business formerly enjoyed. If the restaurant had a declining trade, you shouldn't pay much for good will. When good will is the main attraction, make sure it is the key element in your written agreement. Thus the former owners may agree never to use the established trade name, nor anything similar if they open a new business.

In the restaurant business, the owner—perhaps the chef—can be the main attraction and, if he is, he'll take his clients with him wherever he relocates. You could suggest that he remain in the business for a while as an adviser, or even as part of management. The contract should also state that the former owner won't raid your staff for a stipulated period. It can't bind employees to stay with you, but you can try for individual agreements with them to retain their services for a given time. That contract is really your only protection and you must think of all aspects of the business you wish to preserve. Without an explicit contract, you can find you've bought only the shell of a business, not its substance.

FRANCHISES

You buy a fast-food franchise that is profitable until another one starts up not far away.

When you signed the contract for a franchise, it probably gave you protection against the granting of another franchise within a certain distance. Fast-food franchises tend to cluster on a commercial strip that attracts a lot of automobile traffic. If your competitor is affiliated with another company, there's nothing you can do about it. But if his franchise is from the same company as yours, you may well have a case for a civil action. It all depends on whether the franchisor has breached your contract.

Even if you don't have direct protection in your contract, but the franchisor misrepresented the situation, you could have a case under your provincial business practices act. When you obtain a franchise, you are in the position of being a consumer of the franchisor's goods. If he gave you a high-powered sales pitch, or if his statements were deceptive or misleading, you may be able to get help under provincial consumer protection law.

Hot dogs and hotels. Franchising is a booming business. It covers anything from hot dogs to hotels, real estate to record shops. The franchise owner is responsible for his own sales and survival, but he must buy his raw materials or specified services from head office. Many individuals do very well at the game, but buying a franchise can be risky. Investigate carefully before buying, and be sure to hire a lawyer and an accountant to vet the deal. Delineating the territory is perhaps the most important part of agreeing to buy a franchise. With a highly salable product, a close

competitor may not matter all that much. But if your franchise is a specialized operation, a tough competitor could ruin you.

Will the traffic stay? It's a good idea, when considering a franchise, to check with the municipality about development plans that could affect you. For example, a location on a busy highway won't be much good if the main traffic route is going to be relocated after you buy.

Check with your lawyer to make sure that the contract you're asked to sign won't involve you in forbidden practices, such as retail price maintenance or "tied selling." The latter condition, in effect, forces you to buy another of your supplier's products as part of the deal in the original purchase. For example, your supplier may force you to buy something you do not want in order to get something you do want—or need.

PROFESSIONAL LICENSING

You were a successful dentist before you came to Canada. Now you're told you must take further training.

Galling, even embarrassing, but unavoidable. Just about every professional—from veterinarian to lawyer—must meet the standards of the profession's governing body when moving to this country. And since Canada's professionals practice under provincial control, the rules will depend on where you settle. Dentists actually face less red tape than most. As a matter of law, you must be licensed to practice dentistry anywhere in Canada and the license is granted by the College of Dental Surgeons, after you've proved your qualifications.

The Ontario regulations are typical. After applying to the College, the incoming professional must pass the national dental examinations. You'll be permitted to take the exams if you are a graduate of a university dentistry course recognized by the United Nations World Health Organization. Once you've passed, you must show the registrar of the college your certificate, your landed immigrant's visa and a letter from your university dean proving that you actually studied dentistry. Only then will you be licensed to practice.

The watchful eye. If you decide to move from one province to another, the procedure is simpler. Assuming you graduated recently—and are reasonably up to date—the college will accept your fourth-year graduation from an accredited university dental school as the equivalent of the national exams.

What is an invention?

In careful Ottawa phraseology, an invention is "any new and useful art process, machine, manufacture or composition of matter, or any new and useful improvement in an art process." An idea or a scientific principle is not an invention. Most of us have million-dollar ideas in bed when we've had too many dill pickles with a late supper. If you dream up a new cocktail, you can drink it—but you can't get a patent on it. In fact, getting a patent from the federal Commissioner of Patents establishing your exclusive right to market an invention can be a long and complicated affair.

Rather than attempt the impossible by trying to indicate what among our brainstorms *can* be patented, here's the Canadian Patent Office's list of what *cannot*:

■ A device that has no use
■ A device that won't work
■ An improvement to a known device that would be obvious to a person skilled in the art
■ A device or material whose only difference from older devices is a mere change in size, shape or degree
■ A device that has an illicit object in view
■ Printed matter
■ A method of doing business
■ A new variety of horticultural plant
■ New works of art
■ A method of treating patients
■ Trademarks
■ Recipes for dishes or drinks
■ Designs
■ The discovery of a naturally occurring substance
■ A computer program
■ A process (or the product of a process) that depends entirely on artistic skill and leads to an ornamental effect

If your invention survives this test, you either file for a patent personally with the Patent Office, Place du Portage, Hull, Que., or use the services of a registered patent agent. Because the process is only slightly less difficult than squaring the circle, you are advised to hire an agent. If an invention can be illustrated, drawings will be required; a model may even be demanded. Either way your agent's advice will be invaluable.

Before you rush out to buy a yacht on your probable profits, you should make a search of previously granted patents at the Hull office. Somebody has already beaten you to the mousetrap and the alarm clock. If an invention has been reported anywhere—but not necessarily patented—more than two years before your application, you're probably out of luck. Anyone can make a personal search at the Patent Office without charge; it's a fascinating experience, in fact. A classification officer will point you in the right direction amid the massive collection. However, you may not recognize the significance of prior patents. That's another good reason to hire the professional agent.

You can write for copies of all patents in your field of interest, for a nominal charge, and a copy of a specific patent in detail can also be purchased cheaply. If you win through, your patent will be good in Canada only for a nonrenewable term of 17 years.

New works of art, such as books, plays and photographs, are protected by copyright. That's a different process altogether.

When you are in practice, charging excessive fees is one form of misconduct that could cost you your license. Each provincial dentistry association publishes a fee guide for the profession. If you charge more, and don't warn your patients you are exceeding the guidelines, you could be in trouble.

These conditions apply to just about all the recognized professions, in all provinces. Some professional bodies are more rigid than others. Lawyers normally have to sit bar exams again when they move from one province to another—certainly if they relocate in another country. Since the great bulk of law in Canada is under provincial jurisdiction—just about everything except the criminal law—that's understandable. But all qualified Canadian lawyers can appear in federal courts.

The specialist's dilemma. Doctors of medicine face the toughest restrictions. A doctor from the United States, Australia, Great Britain, Ireland, South Africa or New Zealand may be treated like a Canadian graduate, except that he or she will have to sit exams set by the Medical Council of Canada. If the migrant doctor did not do internship in an approved hospital, a year's internship in Canada is essential before the exams are taken. For candidates from all other countries, two years' Canadian internship is required.

Even a world-recognized psychiatrist with many years of practice in another country must still sit qualifying medical examinations in Canada. These may deal with basic general medical lore the applicant hasn't studied for years. This problem has made it difficult for foreign specialists to practice here, although they can more easily come here to teach.

PERSONAL INCORPORATION

As an incorporated free-lance artist, you've been claiming the small-business tax rate. Your accountant warns you that you no longer qualify.

With the aim of discouraging self-employed persons from setting up sham companies just to benefit from the favorable business tax rate,

Parliament changed the federal tax laws in 1978. In 1979, a great hubbub arose from those professionals who felt they were being treated harshly by an insensitive bureaucracy.

The situation began to bug the taxman around 1970 when the Department of National Revenue lost a case it brought against Ralph Sazio, coach of the Hamilton Tiger-Cats. He had incorporated himself and collected fees—not salary—from the football club. Sazio was able to prove to a court's satisfaction that he had valid nontax reasons for forming his corporation and hadn't done it just to avoid paying income tax at the personal rate.

After that case, the formation of personal service corporations snowballed. The reason was that a corporation paid tax at 25 to 29 percent—considerably less than that imposed on an individual in the medium or upper tax brackets. So, if the individual could persuade his employer to sign a management contract, a corporation would be formed at modest cost. It would then pay tax at the 25- to 29-percent rate, or leave part of its earnings in the corporation, deferring taxes for the future.

National Revenue cracked down on personal service corporations that, in its judgment, were formed merely to avoid higher taxes. It was announced that 95 percent of genuine small businesses would not be affected, a figure heatedly disputed by scores of high-income individuals who stood to suffer financially from the crackdown.

The government's official definition of "active businesses" still qualifying for the small-business tax rate shuts out most doctors, dentists, accountants, architects, writers, painters, athletes and other professionals. It smiles on small firms engaged in manufacturing, processing, mining, construction, farming, fishing, logging, transportation or the wholesale and retail trades. The explanation is that this type of small firm needs to be able to accumulate capital to expand and create more jobs.

The new law sets out two conditions, and you have to meet at least one to qualify as a legitimate corporation. Either you must have five employees, or you must demonstrate that no more than two-thirds of your annual income comes from one source. The first condition is intended to prevent professionals from setting up corporations in the names of their wives or other relatives. However, that test might destroy many small ventures that start out as one- or two-man firms, so the other condition allows these firms to qualify.

The two-thirds-of-income provision no doubt eliminates some people who are really covert employees, but it penalizes free lances who work on long-term contracts, longer than, say, eight months' duration. The writer or artist who might be eager to tackle a project that could take years to finish is now tempted to select less onerous tasks.

MALPRACTICE SUITS

The accountant who handled the financial side of your small business has made a serious error and now you face bankruptcy.

If you are convinced that your accountant, or any professional offering himself for hire, has caused you financial or physical harm through lack of skill or care, you may seek compensation through the courts in a malpractice suit. You must prove that your accountant's work or advice fell below the standard expected of an accountant. You will probably have to find another accountant to testify as an "expert witness" in order to establish what the standard is.

If you can show that your accountant was negligent, you must also prove that the loss you are claiming arose as a result of his bad advice. If your business was on the brink of bankruptcy—even if you didn't realize it—and his mistake pushed you over the brink, you cannot claim all of your loss from him because much of it was probably due to other factors.

Most professions and trades are regulated and licensed by the provinces. Candidates are examined, usually by private organizations of their peers, and only those who qualify are entitled to display degrees or technical certificates. The public has the right to expect that these persons will work with reasonable care and with at least average competence. This standard applies to anyone who undertakes such specialized work, or gives such advice, whether or not he is technically qualified, as long as it is intended that you act on that advice.

Doctor in the dock. The standard of care for a medical practitioner is similar to that imposed on any professional, even if a physician's mistakes may have more disastrous results. (*See* Chapter 46, "Doctors and dentists.") In order to establish negligence on the part of your doctor, you must show that his skill or knowledge was below that professed by other doctors, or that what he did, or failed to do, was outside of accepted medical practice. You can't impose the standard of a specialist on a general practitioner, unless he professes to be a specialist.

Let's say you believe your doctor made a mistake in his diagnosis that resulted in a permanent disability. To prove your allegation, you must obtain the "expert" testimony of another doctor or doctors as to accepted medical practice. Usually, the provincial medical association will arrange for a specialist to review your case and advise you. It's up to you to prove that the doctor was negligent, not to the doctor to disprove negligence; yet the evidence lies within the professional sphere of the doctor. Nevertheless, the doctor has a duty to account to you—and to a judge—for what he has done.

A wrong diagnosis does not necessarily result in liability. A doctor diagnosed a woman as having a tumor in her uterus. On exploratory surgery, the tumor turned out to be a fetus. In the subsequent civil suit, the doctor was cleared of liability. He had used skill and had followed ordinary practice in making his diagnosis. The woman's complaints and symptoms were consistent with the presence of a tumor.

In another case a physician was treating a patient's fractured ankle. The ankle developed complications which the ward nurses duly reported to the doctor. He failed to correct the problem and the patient's leg had to be amputated. The court awarded damages against the doctor, ruling that he should have called in a specialist when complications developed.

6 | YOUR RIGHTS AND YOUR MONEY

29 Your income tax

British Columbia levied Canada's first income tax in 1876; Prince Edward Island followed in 1894. The federal income tax was introduced as a "temporary measure" to meet World War I costs, and Ontario and Quebec entered the field in the 1930s. About 13 million Canadians filed returns in 1979, when the federal levy brought in some $28 billion—more than double the figure for 1976.

Whatever the taxman demands, you must pay—and by the due date—or suffer penalties or interest charges, or both. After you pay you can dispute the assessment through a chain of appeal procedures, but the government holds the stakes.

You have the right to claim every deduction and allowance written into the regulations, although they won't always be allowed:

In 1977, a Newfoundland schoolteacher claimed her newborn son as a deduction for 1976 on the grounds that the fetus was "wholly dependent" on her during part of that year. Revenue Canada didn't buy that.

The Income Tax Act (it runs to 700 pages) and other relevant legislation are usually revised annually and important changes occur frequently. Read the annual guide carefully to make sure the ground rules you followed last year haven't changed.

If you think you pay iniquitous income taxes, try these international comparisons, published by the Canadian Tax Foundation in 1979. The figures are the percentage of earnings taken in income taxes by different countries from a $15,000-a-year production worker with three dependents—a spouse and two children: Canada, 13.6 percent; Denmark, 28.6; the Netherlands, 10.6; Sweden, 33.6. In frugal Switzerland the rate is 7 percent.

And pity the poor Swedish author who howled when her income tax rate was set at 102 percent after book royalties were added to her regular salary.

FILLING IT IN

You find the annual income tax form confusing and difficult and you resent having to pay a fee to have it completed.

Revenue Canada says you should be able to complete your income tax return easily and accurately yourself, using the standard guide. But a recent poll of taxpayers indicated that only 34 percent filled in their returns unaided and about one in four made mistakes—sometimes three or four mistakes. More than half of the errors resulted in payment of more tax than was due.

Expert help is available—free—at any of Revenue Canada's District Taxation Offices. Telephone or call at the office and a clerk will assist you. The official may not complete the form for you, but will advise you, as you do it right there yourself.

There are also plenty of tax preparers for hire. Fees and competence vary widely, so shop carefully.

The walk-in wizards. The most familiar name in consumer tax preparation is H. & R. Block. This American firm has 800 offices in Canada and claims to handle up to 22 percent of all individual returns filed in this country. It and its many competitors will handle your basic return for a flat fee of $15 to $30. Most will guarantee their work, but there are a few fly-by-nighters who disappear before their sloppiness becomes evident. Accounting and legal firms charge hourly rates of $50 to $150, and handle complex business or investment returns.

The amount you spend on the preparation of tax returns can be a deductible expense. Fees are deductible if you have income from a business, or investments that are sufficiently complex to require professional assistance.

This rules out people whose only source of income is wages or salary.

The refund buyers. In recent years the practice of offering immediate cash for your income tax refund has gained ground. It's really nothing more than a loan and the discount charged is interest. If you accept an offer of $90 cash for your $100 refund and the refund comes through in two months, you have paid an annual rate of interest of 60 percent! You can do a lot better than that if you go to a credit union, trust company or bank and get a short-term loan—at about a quarter of the cost.

LATE FILING

You were on vacation and failed to file your tax return by the due date. Now Revenue Canada is demanding interest.

D-day for filing your income tax form is April 30. This return is for the calendar year ending the previous December 31. Revenue Canada does not accept excuses.

Interest is assessed at an annual rate of 11 percent on the balance of unpaid tax. When an individual (usually self-employed, or a person receiving more than a quarter of all his income without tax being withheld at source) is required to make quarterly installment payments, interest will be levied on installments that are late or deficient. Installments are due March 31, June 30, September 30 and December 31.

When information is delayed. Perhaps you have already filed your return and then you receive some relevant information. If you have not yet received your notice of assessment, write to Revenue Canada in Ottawa, enclose the new information and ask that your return be adjusted. If you have received your assessment, write to your nearest District Taxation Office (DTO). Include your social insurance number (which is now your taxation "surname") and your account number.

You must pay the sum demanded in your notice of assessment but you have 90 days from its date of mailing to dispute the amount. Generally, if the additional information is purely documentary—perhaps another tuition or pension receipt—the return will be adjusted beyond the statutory time limit. However, if the information changes an interpretation of fact—maybe changing some funds to a capital gain from a fully taxable gain—you should obtain professional advice about filing a Notice of Objection.

This is a formal disagreement with Revenue Canada's assessment. It protects you from an official refusal to change your return based on new information. Once Revenue Canada has received the objection it will be reviewed by your DTO.

If you are not satisfied with the decision you have the right of appeal, beginning with the Tax Review Board and then the Federal Court of Canada. In some instances, you can appeal even to the Supreme Court of Canada.

Court costs and legal fees can be massive—especially if you lose—but they are deductible expenses on your next return!

Bureaucracy can bend. Revenue Canada is usually reasonable when there's obviously no intent to defraud or evade. Nearly all differences can be settled without resorting to the courts. You have up to four years from the end of the tax year in question to request a refund.

LATE PAYMENT

Unforeseen expenses have left you broke and you simply can't pay your tax bill on April 30.

Call the nice people at Revenue Canada before they call you. The Income Tax Act requires that your tax be paid by midnight on April 30. If it is not, Revenue Canada has the power to proceed to collect by legal action. If you have to take out a loan to pay your tax bill, the interest charge (at 1979 rates) will be at least 17 percent a year, whereas the federal government charges only 11 percent on past-due taxes. In Quebec, there is a penalty of 5 percent of the amount unpaid and an interest charge of 10 percent a year.

If you can convince Revenue Canada that immediate payment in full would cause you undue hardship, it will usually accept post-dated cheques. However if it thinks you can reasonably afford to pay up, it will proceed with legal action to collect.

The writer's cramp. A free-lance journalist miscalculated how much money to put aside to meet her tax bill and found she was nearly $1,000 short. Her district taxation official suggested that she send in five postdated cheques for $200 each, but she couldn't be sure she'd earn the money to cover them.

Eventually, they agreed on payment in full within a year. The writer reported that the tax official was "really considerate. He even told me that if I had difficulty making my payment some months to let him know."

However sympathetic the occasional taxman, he is bound by law to make every effort to get the state's ordained slice of your earnings. If necessary, he will not stop until every asset you own is seized and sold.

Pay as you earn. All those whose income is wages or salary have payments deducted at source by the employer and remitted to the government treasury. All provinces except Quebec have a tax-collection agreement with Ottawa. Residents of Quebec file a separate provincial return. (Residents of the Territories, or diplomats and others who work abroad, pay an impost that corresponds to provincial income taxes.)

The first step in determining how much money is withheld from your paycheque is to fill out Form TD1, which is kept by your employer and details the deductions and exemptions, such as personal exemption, married (and supporting spouse) exemption, dependent children. These exemptions determine your tax category, which the employer must follow when he calculates your pay. In addition, he also deducts amounts you are paying into the Canada Pension Plan, to unemployment insurance and to your company's pension plan. These are not the only deductions you may make on your tax return, but they are the only deductions allowed when calculating your withholding taxes.

If you have no other source of income and no additional taxes were paid during the year, the amount deducted each payday should come to within a few dollars of your total tax liability for the year. This is the "pay as you earn" concept.

If you do have other income from which no tax is deducted and it is not greater than one quarter of your total employment income, you can instruct your employer to withhold more tax. It requires completing yet another form, but it can help you avoid a large tax bill in the spring.

If that extra income is greater than 25 percent of your employment income, you must pay installments.

If you do not have the cash to pay the balance due on your tax bill, file the return on time anyway so as to avoid any penalty. The tax department will charge you interest on the unpaid tax but this is better than being hit for a penalty as well.

TRANSFERRING DEDUCTIONS

You and your wife earn almost identical salaries. She uses her maiden name at work and wants to keep her financial affairs separate from yours.

As far as her income tax is concerned, there is no choice. All income-earning Canadians must file their own returns. The concept of "joint" returns exists in the United States but the closest Canada has come to this is the right to transfer certain deductions between husband and wife when one has no taxable income. In 1979, a spouse could earn up to $2,530 net without being liable for income tax. The unused portion of the following deductions may be transferred:
■ Age exemption (65 years or over)
■ Interest plus dividend and capital-gains deductions
■ Pension-income deduction
■ Blind or infirm deduction
■ Education deduction

When a spouse does not require any of the above deductions to reduce taxable income to zero, they may be used to calculate the other's taxable income.

Valuable marriage lines. When it comes

to income tax, the government can be quite sexist. It does not allow a marital exemption for common-law partners, and child-care expenses are usually only deductible by the mother. The only time a man can claim these expenses is when the mother is either separated from him, in jail, or mentally or physically infirm.

In normal cases, the mother must be working and earning income before child-care expenses are allowable. Earned income is defined to include all wages, salaries and gratuities, income from carrying on a business, or an adult training allowance, scholarship or research grant.

Payments made for baby-sitting, day care, boarding school or camp qualify as child-care expenses. Receipts must be filed. Payments to individuals must include that individual's social insurance number on the receipt.

TIPS AND SIN'S WAGES

Your wife pays tax on her wages as a waitress but won't declare the tips she receives.

Failure to declare tips and gratuities is a frequent cause of trouble and strife with the authorities. Tips received because of your job, whether from your employer or some other party, are taxable: a gift of $50 for finding your neighbor's dog is not.

Self-employed people must declare tips as part of their total business income. For example, the owner-driver of a taxicab often gets a tip from his customer. It's taxable because it is related to the job.

If you win the lottery or some other game of chance, your prize is not taxable. It does not meet any of the legal definitions of income. Americans don't get the same break. Lottery winnings and game-show prizes are taxable in the United States.

But even in Canada there comes a point where windfall gains are taxable. Most of us fritter away a few dollars on football or baseball bets, the horses, cards, or in the office hockey pool. Any winnings from this occasional gambling are not taxable and the losses

are not deductible. A person who gambles for a living, however, is in a different category. All his earnings will become taxable and the losses allowable deductions. Revenue Canada considers them business earnings.

On the shady side. The same reasoning is applied to illegal activities such as prostitution or drug dealing. Earnings from these sources are taxable and must be declared. But here there is both good news and bad news for those who earn their living outside the law. The good news: anything you report on your tax return is confidential and cannot be used by the Justice Department for anything other than the enforcement of the tax laws. The bad news: it's not easy to get away with not reporting illegal income. The taxman has a device known as "net worth assessment" by which he can measure changes in your net worth over a period of years. That's not difficult for professional valuers and any increase is assessed as income. Then it's up to you to prove otherwise. It's one of the few instances in law where you're guilty until proven innocent. The only defense is to produce records that substantiate your innocence. This presented problems for a well-known madam in Vancouver who swore she had had to pay heavy bribes in connection with her bordello. Strangely enough she couldn't produce receipts.

The law requires you to keep records of all business dealings. In fact, if you are self-employed, you are supposed to obtain permission from Revenue Canada before destroying them. Revenue Canada has the right to reassess your tax for any given year at any time within the next four subsequent years. If it suspects fraud, it can go back as far as it wishes.

DEPENDENT'S EARNINGS

Your son, a college student, has been doing part-time jobs for the last three years and has never filed a tax return.

If he did not owe any tax, there was no need for him to file a return, but it might pay him to do so because it is the only way to obtain the various provincial tax credits. But if Revenue Canada demands that he file a return, he must obey, even if he is not liable for taxes.

Chances are that your son owes no tax. In fact, he's probably owed a refund for the taxes withheld from his paycheques and he must claim it within the statutory time limit of four years.

Status as dependent. If you're concerned about claiming your son as a dependent, remember he's allowed some earnings that won't affect your claim.

For most people the word "income" means the total amount of money earned, but when the law speaks about income it means *net* income, that is, gross income less the applicable deductions. These include such items as contributions to the Canada Pension Plan (CPP) and the Unemployment Insurance Commission (UIC), standard employment expenses and tuition fees. It is your son's net income that is important in calculating your allowable exemption.

In 1979 the total allowable net income that your son could earn before you began to lose this exemption was $1,840. The exemption vanished totally once his net income went over $2,750. These amounts are indexed to infla-

Child tax credit benefits

In 1979, for the first time, income-tax payers could claim a "child tax credit" to help them support their children. With the birthrate at an historic low, it's a direct subsidy of parenthood. It applied, in the first instance, to the total family income in the calendar year of 1978. The table shows the amounts to which families of different sizes and incomes are entitled.

The basic credit of $200 is reduced by 5 percent of the amount of income above $18,000. The credit is subtracted from "tax payable." Families that have no taxable income receive a cheque for the amount of credit for which they qualify. A family with eight children and no taxable income would get a cheque for $1,600.

But to claim the credit, the person who receives family allowance benefits—normally the mother—must file an income tax return. She would simply report no taxable income and claim a $200 cash rebate for each qualifying child.

FAMILY INCOME	NUMBER OF CHILDREN					
	1	2	3	4	5	6
$0-18,000	$200	$400	$600	$800	$1,000	$1,200
20,000	100	300	500	700	900	1,100
22,000		200	400	600	800	1,000
24,000		100	300	500	700	900
26,000			200	400	600	800
28,000			100	300	500	700
30,000				200	400	600
32,000				100	300	500
34,000					200	400
36,000					100	300
38,000						200
40,000						100

tion each year and you should get in touch with your District Taxation Office (DTO) to discover the current income limit. The exemption for dependent children is usually eliminated once they reach the age of 21, except when they are either in full-time attendance at a school or university, or infirm.

Transferable deductions. Let's say your son is 22 and attending university full time. You paid $840 in tuition. In the summer, he made $2,400 from which was deducted $38 CPP, $34 UIC and $186 income tax. He could request a tax-exempt status on his TD1 form as his income from all sources is less than $2,890, which is the 1979 basic personal deduction. If he had done this there would have been no tax withheld at source, but he would still be required to make the CPP and UIC contributions.

The tuition fee is only deductible by the student, but there is an additional $50 deduction for each month or part of a month that he remains in full-time attendance and this deduction is transferable to a supporting parent. You can transfer your son's education deduction if, as in this case, his basic personal exemption leaves him no taxable income.

Let's look at a variation. The basic facts are the same but during the last two summers your son earned another $1,200 in tips, from which no deductions were made. The taxman regards those tips as part of his income. Even with a gross income of $3,600 his deductions still result in no taxable income and a total of $500 can be transferred to your return if he attended school for 10 months.

In the example above, $186 of income tax would have been withheld and your son is entitled to get it back. The only way he'll get it is by filing a return. The same applies to his provincial tax credits. In Ontario, if your son lived in a university residence in 1978, he would be entitled to a property tax credit of $25, even if he had no income.

At what point does the parent lose the deduction for a child? In 1979 children under 17 could earn up to $1,750 and the full deduction of $500 was still allowed. If they earned more, but less than $2,750, the deduction was $500 less one half of earnings over $1,750.

Children 17 and over could earn up to $1,840 and the full deduction of $910 was allowed to the parent. If they earned more, but less than $2,750, the deduction was $910 less the amount over $1,840.

Earning limits are changed periodically in relation to the Consumer Price Index. A phone call to your DTO will give you the current levels.

EVASION AND AVOIDANCE

You decided to hire an accountant to handle your returns and he has informed you that you have been "evading" taxes for years.

Most of us see a clear distinction between tax *evasion* and tax *avoidance*. The taxman sometimes sees it differently.

Tax evasion is the commission or omission of an act, knowingly and with an intent to deceive, whereby you pay less tax than you should. Conspiracy to commit or omit such an act is also evasion. It will almost always be prosecuted and severe penalties applied. Unlike the Internal Revenue Service of the United States Treasury Department, Revenue Canada doesn't pay informers rewards.

Organizing your affairs in order to pay the least possible tax is not illegal. However, if you enter into any scheme with the sole or main purpose of reducing, deferring or avoiding taxes, even though it is not specifically prohibited by law, you could be in trouble.

The Special Investigations Section of Revenue Canada deals with evasion, and the Tax Avoidance Section reviews avoidance schemes. Because there is often a very fine line between evasion and avoidance, certain apparently legitimate schemes are eventually turned over to the investigators. The unclear distinction between evasion and avoidance can create uncertainty even for your accountant or other consultant. If you are in doubt about your personal plan, you would be wise to request an advance tax ruling from your District Taxation Office.

The primary responsibility for the return is yours even if you follow exactly the advice of your accountant. Your adviser could suffer heavy penalties if he was professionally negligent in advising you, or if he knowingly assisted you in making a false statement on your return.

But when you sign that return it's yours, not his. Make sure you understand it completely, because ignorance of the law is no excuse.

WINDFALL GAINS

Your husband's uncle gives each of your children a $1,000 gift. You are told that this affects your taxable income.

It doesn't. Gift tax is levied on the giver, not the getter. In any case, Quebec now is the only province with either a gift tax or succession duties. (*See* Chapter 33, "Wills and gifts.")

Any income earned from this gift by your children (under 18) would be deemed to be income of their uncle. There would be no effect on your deduction claims for dependent children.

There are several windfall gains that are not taxable: personal injury awards, life insurance proceeds on death, damages paid or awarded as a result of a threatened or successful lawsuit, lottery winnings, and so on.

The Tax Act specifically excludes from income certain pensions paid to the military and RCMP, workmen's compensation awards, welfare payments and the salary of the Governor General.

FOREIGN EARNINGS

You receive a small income from an old trust fund in the United States, but tax is deducted before you get it.

Taxes due to the United States are withheld on such items as trust income, dividends, interest and rental income.

Canada follows the common principle that the country where the income was earned has the first right to taxation. The amount withheld is usually set by tax treaties between states. Treaties between Canada and the United States, and Canada and Britain, require a 15-percent withholding tax on outgoing dividends and interest.

The Canadian Tax Act requires that the gross amount of all your foreign income from whatever source be included in your return. That includes even the withholding tax levied by another government. You are then entitled to claim a foreign-tax credit. This credit directly reduces your Canadian tax; it usually equals the total amount that was withheld from your foreign income.

Only those resident in Canada are liable for tax in Canada. Non-residents have to pay tax here only if they work or carry on a business in Canada, or if they sell certain types of capital property.

The tax law does not define "residency," but the courts have set certain guidelines. These include the length of time spent in Canada; the ownership of a home in Canada; and possession of Canadian citizenship. Members of the Canadian armed forces and individuals who are not normally resident in Canada, but who were present here for 183 days or more during a year, are deemed to be residents.

Then there is the part-year resident. This is a person who becomes or ceases to be a permanent resident of Canada, either by immigrating or emigrating. The part-year resident is taxable in Canada only on the income earned while he was actually still a resident here. The part-year resident must also prorate permitted personal deductions on the basis of the length of time he resided in Canada.

BUSINESS DEDUCTIONS

You run a one-man business out of your home, but your claims for expenses have been disallowed.

You have the right to deduct legitimate expenses incurred in earning income, or in reasonable expectation of earning income. The overriding limitation is that the expense must be reasonable in the circumstances.

"Reasonable" would include traveling expenses such as hotels, meals and automobiles while you were away from your home. You can also deduct a portion of your house expenses—interest on the mortgage, property taxes, insurance, utilities and upkeep. The portion deductible would have to relate closely to your business; it is usually calculated on a per-room or square-footage basis.

If you are going into business for yourself, the choice of business year-end can provide you with immediate tax savings. Individuals are taxed on income earned during the calendar year, but business reports its income on an accrued basis and may have a year-end other than December 31.

Let's assume that you start up a business on June 30, 1980. You can pick a year-end at any time up to June 30, 1981. The business earns $10,000 to December 31, 1980; $11,000 to March 31, 1981; and $22,000 to June 20, 1981. A good year-end in these circumstances would be Feb. 28. For 1981 you would include only income earned up to Feb. 28, 1981. You would not be taxed on a full 12 months until 1982 (March 1, 1981 to Feb. 28, 1982). A substantial tax deferral can be arranged in this manner.

TAXABLE INCOME

You are an amateur artist and receive a surprise honorarium of $1,000 for a portrait. You don't see why Ottawa should get a cut of that.

You might not have to pay taxes on the $1,000 if you can prove that when the painting was done you had no expectation of making a profit. And you won't be subject to capital-gains tax since the sum is not in excess of $1,000.

When you enter into a venture with a reasonable expectation of making a profit, any income made is taxable and any legitimate expenses are deductible.

The standard of "reasonable profit" can be difficult to establish. It depends on your experience, the effort expended and the amount of money invested. If you have a history of selling paintings, you will have to include the

"honorarium" in your taxable income. It would not matter whether you received the payment in cash or in kind—such as a free cruise in the Caribbean.

Of course, tax would be assessed only against the net profit. You would deduct your expense in painting the portrait—the canvas, the paints and brushes, your traveling costs, and so on.

Any pie in the sky? An expense could still be deductible even if you had no income, as long as there was reasonable expectation of future profit. Revenue Canada will challenge deductions where it doesn't believe future expectation exists.

A man who spent a large sum on car racing had his expense claims disallowed because the prize money he was competing for was so small that there could never be any reasonable chance of profit. The same reasoning is applied to the executive with his hobby farm.

If the amateur artist dabbling away with no intention of making a profit was acclaimed overnight as the new Picasso, he would create a tough problem for the taxman. He could claim his millions were not income from a business and so not subject to income tax.

TAXABLE BENEFITS

You were shocked to learn that you must pay tax on the new car provided by your employer.

Outright gift or permanent loan of an automobile by the employer is seen by Revenue Canada as a "taxable benefit." Lacking convincing evidence to the contrary, it assumes the gift or "perk" comes to you in lieu of an increase in wages or salary upon which you would normally be assessed tax.

The most common case of "taxable benefit" is when you have the personal use of a company car. Apart from your business use of the vehicle, a minimum monthly charge will be added to your taxable income. It is calculated as 1 percent of the car's original cost (not the depreciated cost) or one-third of the lease payment.

Any payment you make to your employer

Give the taxman his due

Here's the way a fictional Ontario resident completed his return for 1978.

Richard A. Roe earned $16,000 and paid $169.20 to the Canada Pension Plan (CPP), $187.20 to the Unemployment Insurance Commission (UIC), $25 in union dues, $2,800 in income tax, $1,000 to his company pension plan, $500 to a Registered Home Ownership Savings Plan (RHOSP) and a further $500 to a Registered Retirement Savings Plan (RRSP). He took a university course that cost $125.

Mr. Roe had a small inheritance that brought in $800 in interest, and another $100 in dividends from Bell Canada. He

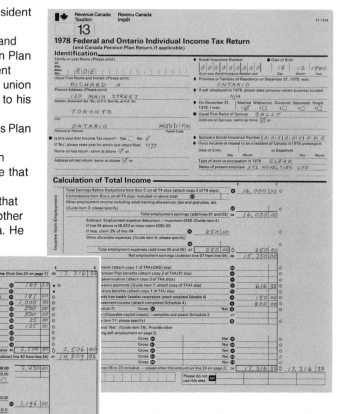

pays $300 a month in rent. His wife, Sally, earned $1,400 in 1978. Her deductions were $10 for CPP and $14 for UIC. She also received $616.32 in family allowance.

First Mr. Roe deducted the allowable employment expense, which left him a net employment income of $15,750. He added the $613.32 in family allowance, $800 in interest and $150 in dividends—for tax purposes, dividends may be "grossed up" by 50 percent in order to claim a higher tax credit—for a total income of $17,316.32.

His deductions were $2,506.40, leaving a net income of $14,809.92. His basic personal exemption was $2,430, the adjusted exemption for his wife was

$1,196, and exemptions for his children totaled $1,300. To this he added the standard $100 deduction for medical expenses and charitable donations. His dividend and interest payment (being under $1,000) was tax free, so Mr. Roe deducted $950 ($800 + $150). His taxable income—his total or gross income less deductions and exemptions—was $8,833.92.

Because of that $150 from taxable dividends, Mr. Roe had to use the "Detailed Tax Calculation." Using the rate chart at the bottom of Schedule 1 rather than the tax tables, he arrived at tax payable of $1,536.07, and a dividend

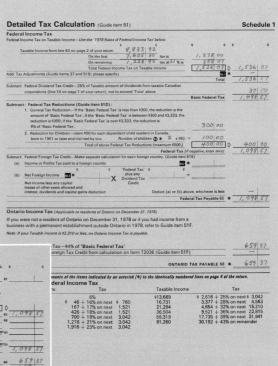

credit of $37.50 (25 percent of the "grossed up" $150). He had a federal tax reduction of $300 plus a $50 reduction for each of his children. (This particular reduction is no longer allowed.)

Mr. Roe calculated his Ontario income tax at $659.37. Additional calculations on page 4 of the return showed the total tax payable was $1,757.94. But the income tax withheld from his salary plus the Ontario tax credit of $124.59 (claimed on a separate form) amounted to $2,954.59, so Mr. Roe claimed a refund of $1,166.65.

(See "Child tax credit benefits" in this chapter.)

for your personal use of the car will reduce the taxable benefit that you must include in your April 30 return.

Perks you can keep. There are numerous "fringe benefits" of definite cash value to the recipient that escape the taxman's clutches. Revenue Canada draws a distinction between the "taxable benefit" and the "tax-free privilege."

Tax-free privileges include: travel passes issued to employees by such companies as Canadian Pacific and Air Canada; discounts on merchandise; subsidized meals; membership fees to business or professional associations where it is advantageous to the employer for you to belong; moving expenses paid by the employer. (*See* Chapter 27, "Salary and benefits.")

Taxable benefits provided by the employer on which you will be assessed, at least in part, include: car provided at little or no cost; free or low-rent housing; free board and lodging; trips and other prizes; tuition fees; traveling expenses of your spouse; premiums paid to provincial health plans.

Traveling expenses. People traveling on company business spend millions of dollars annually which are generally nontaxable. An allowance is often paid over and above salary and the employee is not called upon to account in detail for the amount received. In other instances, a fixed daily allowance is provided.

Any reasonable allowance is tax free. What is "reasonable" is a question of judgment and, in the last analysis, Revenue Canada—or the courts—will be the judge.

TAX SHELTERS

A business friend suggests you should put some funds into a "tax shelter." The whole idea sounds vaguely crooked.

You have the right to enjoy your total earnings, or other income, to the extent permitted by law. Substantial tax savings can be effected by using "shelters." Far from being crooked, some of them have been introduced by the government to assist individuals in planning for retirement or when saving to buy a house. They are also used as a financial tool to encourage housing starts and development of the oil and gas industry.

The most common type of shelter is the Registered Retirement Savings Plan (RRSP). This plan supplements the Canada Pension Plan and company pension plans and is the major vehicle for self-employed people to save for their retirement. (*See* Chapter 48, "Retirement.")

An RRSP is a private pension plan that has been registered by Revenue Canada. Contributions to this plan are deductible from taxable income. There is no tax on the earnings while the contributions remain in the plan. Upon retirement the plan is paid out in the form of an annuity, which is taxed as you receive it. The concept is that you make deductible contributions when your tax rate is higher, but receive the income during retirement when your income is lower. If you have to borrow to make the contribution, loan interest charges are also deductible.

The contributions can be made at any time during the calendar year and up to 60 days after the end of the year. The maximum allowable in 1979 was $5,500, with a further limitation that it could not exceed 20 percent of your earned income. "Earned income" includes salary, wages, gratuities, and income from a business, but does not include dividends, interest or rental income. In 1979, the maximum allowable contribution for a person who is also a member of a registered company pension plan was $3,500 or 20 percent of earned income, whichever is less.

Sheltering the spouse. One good tax planning idea is a "spousal contribution." This allows you to split the retirement income between yourself and your spouse (legal wife or common-law partner). You accomplish this by making the contribution and naming your spouse as the beneficiary. In this way, you obtain the benefit of the current deduction but your spouse receives the income when the plan is terminated. (This assumes, of course, that you are in a higher income tax bracket than your spouse.) Interest paid on a loan to make a "spousal contribution" is not deductible.

Shop around for the best RRSP. Many financial institutions offer them and investment yields and fees can vary considerably.

Another popular plan, and one that is particularly beneficial to those saving for their first house, is the Registered Homeownership Savings Plan (RHOSP). If you want to sound like a professional, this is pronounced "rosp."

The purpose of this plan is to allow individuals who have never owned a home before, in Canada or elsewhere, to contribute up to a maximum of $1,000 a year (including the year that you buy a home) to an RHOSP. The contribution is deductible from your income and must be made before the end of the year. As with the RRSP, the interest earned while in the plan is not taxed. The big break comes when the plan is terminated. If you use the money to purchase an "owner-occupied home" then the total amount of the plan, including the earnings, is tax free. This makes the RHOSP an attractive savings instrument.

What is an "owner-occupied home"? It is defined in law to include a house, cottage, apartment building or condominium.

There are a few catches. The maximum amount that you can contribute over the years is $10,000 and the maximum length of time that you can keep such a plan alive is 20 years. At the end of the 20 years, the total amount sitting in your RHOSP is brought into income in the 21st year and taxed—if you don't use it to buy a home.

Tax averaging. Some folk find themselves with a high income one year and a low one the next. Our progressive income tax rates would make taxation heavier over the two-year period than if the same amount had been earned in each year. Enter the tax-deferral system called income-averaging. This allows "qualifying income" to be averaged over a future period and thus leveled into an even income stream for tax purposes.

Qualifying income is deemed to be any amount received from athletic, artistic or musical endeavors, the taxable portion of your net capital gains and lump-sum payments received from employers.

AUDITS AND INVESTIGATIONS

An official from your District Taxation Office (DTO) arrives at your home to carry out an audit. You think this is an infringement of your rights.

The common "desk audit" is carried out at the local DTO to investigate a certain occupation or specific type of expense claimed. In the normal case, a letter is mailed to you to ask that you produce certain information or receipts within 15 days, or to arrange an appointment with the tax auditor.

But audits can be carried out at your office or home. This can include a review of your account and record books and an examination of supporting documentation. You will be given advance notice of any audit.

Anatomy of an audit. If Revenue Canada suspects an evasion or avoidance scheme, it will conduct a reassessment. Investigators can seize and remove records, but they must have special authorization. Records must be returned within 120 days unless a court order for retention is obtained.

The investigator is not allowed to search your premises; he can only seize *available* records. A warrant must be obtained to conduct a search. A lawyer may claim client-solicitor privilege on certain documents which will then be held by the sheriff until a court rules on the question.

You have the right to have your legal or accounting advisers present during questioning. Revenue Canada can also hold an official inquiry and summon witnesses; your testimony at an inquiry could be used in a criminal court unless you claimed protection of the Canada Evidence Act. The inquiry may lead to prosecution by the Department of Justice.

Prosecution may be by summary charge or by indictment—the Attorney General makes the choice. Penalty on summary conviction is a fine of from 25 to 200 percent of the tax evaded, or a two-year jail term, or both. Penalty on conviction of an indictable offense is a mandatory jail sentence of not less than two months and not more than five years.

30 Saving and borrowing

anadians are canny savers and determined borrowers. Even the doubling of interest rates over the past decade didn't dampen the borrowing boom.

Between 1967 and 1977, consumer loans by chartered banks rose from $3.6 billion to $20.2 billion and the banks' mortgage lending increased from $840 million to $11.6 billion. At any given time, loans of all types make up about 70 percent of the chartered banks' total assets. Many billions more were loaned by trust companies, credit unions, specialist mortgage companies and consumer-finance companies.

But Canadians also continue to save. At the end of the great Depression of the 1930s, the average individual savings account was $365. It was $805 in 1967 and $1,854 in 1979—although two-thirds of all savings accounts were under $1,000.

Federal legislation regulating major money markets is under almost continual scrutiny and the Bank Act is revised every 10 years. But in spite of these precautions, organizations such as the Consumers' Association of Canada (CAC) are apprehensive at the increasing takeover by the computer of most day-to-day banking business. The CAC argues that an electronic funds transfer system means that most financial transactions will be done with a plastic card and that a considerable volume of personal information will be available to anyone with access to a computer. Other groups fear electronic theft. The Canadian Bankers' Association insists the system will protect the customer's privacy and that its speed and efficiency should result in lower service charges.

Women's rights activists say the banks' predominantly male loans officers are reluctant to grant a personal loan or credit to a woman, and often ask female applicants to get a man to act as guarantor. The trouble is that many women have no credit record upon which a lender can gauge his risk. This is changing, however. In Ontario, for instance, the Consumer Reporting Act enables a woman to request that a credit history be maintained in the names of both husband and wife.

Banks in North America are more "public" than in much of Europe and most of Asia and Africa, although the situation overseas is rapidly changing. It isn't all that long ago since an individual could not open a bank account in Britain until satisfactory references were presented to the manager.

In 1867 there were 35 banks in what is now Canada and 83 more have been chartered since Confederation. The most recent is the Continental Bank, opened in 1979.

Several mergers and amalgamations occurred over the years and today Canada has 11 chartered banks which operate more than 7,500 branches and have assets of about $170 billion. Two-thirds of their 150,000 employees are women. About 85 percent of all business is handled by the five largest chartered banks.

The Bank of Canada regulates the nation's money supply, controls the total volume of credit, maintains the value of the dollar and holds a fixed percentage of every bank's cash reserve.

The office of the Inspector-General of Banks keeps tabs on all facets of banking, gets detailed monthly reports from all banks and examines the banks' head-office books at least once a year.

SECURITY

Your father-in-law, who recently arrived from abroad, is worried about entrusting his savings to a bank.

Newcomers are sometimes doubtful about the safety of the Canadian banking system. The fact is that no Canadian bank has failed since the Home Bank of Canada went broke in 1923. Further, in the extremely unlikely case of bank failure, individual deposits are guaranteed by law up to $20,000. This guarantee also applies to trust and mortgage companies and some other financial institutions.

Immigrants' attitudes to North American banking are often colored by unsettling reports or rumors about American bank failures. But the banking picture in the United States is very different from Canada's. Generally, American banks are not permitted to operate beyond state boundaries. This means that, mostly, they are smaller and more numerous than Canada's chartered banks. Some are purely local in character. And their record of failures has been a depressing one. Since the 1920s, there have been more than 14,000 bank failures in the United States, some causing substantial losses for depositors.

Operations abroad. Prospective immigrants may well find that a branch of a Canadian bank is already operating in their home countries. The major banks have more than 300 branches in 50 countries, plus reciprocal arrangements with about 5,000 foreign banks.

Along with services to exporters and importers and substantial foreign investment programs, Canadian banks abroad offer just about every imaginable financial service to the individual with Canadian connections: they can take care of an immigrant's funds before he leaves home, paying him competitive monthly interest; on his arrival, his money will be waiting for him at the local branch.

Security? If your father-in-law is worried about his nest egg, he'll be reassured to know that the foreign exchange assets of Canadian banks currently exceed $50 billion.

THE 'CATHEDRAL' ATMOSPHERE

You feel that your modest transactions do not entitle you to all the customer services of one of Canada's gigantic banks.

Not so very long ago, banks and trust companies seemed very forbidding places with stern tellers enclosed in wire cages and all the counter personnel partially concealed behind high glass or wooden screens. They were deliberately designed like fortresses to give an impression of solidity and security. Money was a very serious business. Some of the large city bank offices were very imposing edifices with marble floors and pillars. Many a would-be customer was overawed and felt that his small deposit was of no importance. In those days, managers often gave the impression that they were doing you a favor by allowing you into the building.

Today buildings are functional and bright. Schooled by public relations experts, managers welcome prospective customers with open arms; advertisements invite you to drop by to borrow or deposit and, at times, coffee is served and gifts are handed out when new accounts are opened.

Managing your money. The basic services to the individual are savings accounts and personal chequing accounts.

The *chequing savings account* pays a low interest rate, but permits writing cheques; the *non-chequing savings account* pays a higher interest rate, but does not permit writing cheques, although withdrawals or transfers can be made in person at any time. The *joint account* allows two or more persons to use the same account. A special agreement can be made by the individuals and the financial institution which allows any one of them to make deposits, or write cheques and make withdrawals. Without this agreement the signatures of all are required.

A new kind of savings account, by which interest was added to the balance at the end of each day, was introduced in 1979. This *daily interest savings account* is particularly suitable for those whose savings accounts fluctuate widely during the month, but the interest rate is lower than on regular savings accounts.

You will still have to do some comparison shopping because some banks will credit earned interest every month; others only twice a year. Some offer daily interest payments in all branches; others only at branches connected with their central computer.

The *personal chequing account* is useful for payment of regular expenses. This type of account doesn't earn interest, and there is a service charge for each cheque written. You receive a detailed monthly statement and your canceled cheques, which are generally accepted as legal proof of payment. And the monthly statement is a help in keeping personal finances in order. Some banks and trust companies allow free chequing if a specified minimum balance is maintained.

CREDIT UNIONS

Your son is starting his first job and plans to open an account in a credit union. You think he would be better off dealing with a bank.

The larger credit unions offer almost identical services as the banks—chequing and savings accounts, term deposits, personal loans and safety-deposit boxes. When your son joins, he will become a shareholder with a vote in the operation of the credit union. (A qualifying share usually costs $5.)

Member deposits make up almost 80 percent of the assets of credit unions, which is the reason that the smaller ones don't have large amounts to lend. Surplus annual operating profit is distributed among members in the form of dividends and rebates of loan interest.

Most credit unions are more liberal and flexible than other financial organizations, even if not as secure, often lending money for projects that banks might not consider feasible. Credit unions allow accelerated repayment of loans without penalty and management has greater freedom to extend or refinance loans.

Your son isn't the only one who feels these services are worthwhile. Statistics Canada reports that in 1977 almost 8.5 million Canadians were owner-members of credit unions and caisses populaires. That's one credit union member for every third person in the country. The Vancouver City Savings Credit Union, Canada's largest, had 55,000 members and eight branches.

There are two credit unions for every three branches of chartered banks and about five credit unions for every trust company branch.

Quebec has more caisses populaires than branches of chartered banks and trust companies combined.

RETURNS ON SAVINGS

You want to invest your savings to obtain the best return at the least risk.

You might put part of your savings in a term deposit. This offers a higher rate of interest than a savings account if you are prepared to leave the money for a fixed term. This can range from 30 days to six years. Credit unions, banks and trust companies offer term deposits, and you'd be wise to shop around for the best deal. Generally speaking, the longer the fixed term, the higher the rate of interest.

If you place $10,000 on deposit for 12 months you will get a term-deposit receipt for this amount. You can still withdraw your cash before the year is up, but there will be a reduction in the original interest rate. Interest on term deposits can be paid at maturity, monthly, or on the last days of April and October.

The juicy GIC. Trust companies and other "near banks" compete for your surplus money with guaranteed investment certificates (GICs). While these generally pay a slightly higher rate of interest, they cannot be cashed before the due date. Should you die before the date of maturity (it's normally a five-year term), the GIC can be redeemed by the executors of your estate.

MUTILATED MONEY

You accidentally dropped a roll of bills into the fire. They were partly burned before you could snatch them from the flames.

Take mutilated currency to any bank branch, which will forward it to the Bank of Canada for replacement. This could be at 50 or 100 percent of value—or nothing. It depends on how much of the damaged currency the Bank of Canada can identify. Your credit union or bank branch manager might even replace it for you on the spot, if he believes the Bank of Canada will go along with his judgment.

You must have the physical remains of your cash before replacement will be considered. For example, if you drop your bulging billfold over the rail of a cruise ship in the middle of the Caribbean, you can wish it bon voyage unless, of course, you are insured against such loss.

Backyard burial. Two technicians work full time at the Bank of Canada's headquarters in Ottawa determining the worth of damaged currency. (The Bank's provincial offices can handle many replacement requests, but the tough ones go to the Ottawa laboratory.)

Fire damage is the most common problem,

but others include water or chemical damage, mildew and injury by worms or insects. People have buried thousands of dollars in tin cans, only to find the cash reduced to compost by worms and dampness. The Bank of Canada's technicians use spectroscopes and other sophisticated equipment to identify the contents.

Years ago damaged bills were replaced on the basis of how many "corners" had survived. Each corner carried the signature of the governor or deputy-governor of the bank, or a serial number. Replacement was based on 50 percent for two surviving corners and 100 percent for three. Crooks began turning three bills into four by clipping a different corner off

The kindly father of the 'people's banks'

At 46, journalist Alphonse Desjardins of Lévis, Que., had been official reporter of debates in the House of Commons for eight years. Inspired by stories of loan-sharking related in a debate on interest rates, he determined to start a cooperative "people's bank" to provide loans at the lowest possible rates to the ordinary working man.

A well-read man, Desjardins knew of the growing success of the cooperative movement begun in Britain by Robert Owen in the late 18th century. In December 1900, he drew 128 persons to a meeting in Lévis and 80 of them agreed to become charter members of *La Caisse populaire de Lévis*. They contributed $26 in nickels and dimes, and the Canadian credit union movement was launched.

Within six years, the funds of the Lévis *caisse* had swelled to $49,000. Desjardins devoted the last 20 years of his life to promoting and organizing the spread of the people's bank. The idea took particular root in rural areas where the small farmer could seldom amass the assets demanded by the chartered banks as security for loans.

At last report, the total assets of Canada's 4,000 credit unions stood at $19 billion. While

the number of active units is decreasing, the larger units are becoming stronger. In their local spheres, they offer most of the same facilities for personal banking as the branches of Canada's 11 chartered banks. With total assets of $189 billion, and over 23 million personal savings accounts, the banks aren't sweating.

The central difference—apart from national coverage and strength—between the credit unions and the banks is that the former are owned and operated by the member-depositors. It's a "one man, one vote" situation. All loan or investment decisions are made by a credit committee elected annually. Surplus profits are intended to be returned to the members in the form of rebates or lower interest rates on loans.

Credit unions are often formed for mutual financial assistance among workers at large plants. They have the "closed shop" advantage of being permitted to arrange the deduction of members' regular deposits from the payroll.

Alphonse Desjardins died in 1920 but his name lives in the Quebec federation of some 1,200 *caisses populaires* named after him, and in the huge Complexe Desjardins shopping center in downtown Montreal.

three good bills and presenting the clippings as the remains of a nonexistent fourth. It was a short-lived game even in its heyday and it's impossible now.

CASH OR CHEQUE

You've always dealt in cash and remain suspicious of cheques.

The complex world of modern business simply could not operate without the "negotiable instruments" of finance, of which the most common is the cheque. When you write a cheque you order the bank to pay that amount out of the money which you have deposited with it.

We pay more than three-quarters of all our bills with cheques. The chartered banks process more than two billion cheques a year. In fact, the person who pulls out a wad of money to pay for a major purchase—such as a car— would probably raise an eyebrow of suspicion.

However, you can insist that cash ("legal tender") be accepted in payment of any debt, although there's a restriction on the amount of coinage you can dump on your creditor. He is not forced to accept more than 25 cents' worth of pennies, $5 worth of nickels or $10 worth of dimes or quarters.

The vital signature. There's nothing old-fashioned about being cautious about cheques. A cheque is worth nothing until it is accepted at the branch of the bank or trust company upon which it was drawn. Even in the electronic funds transfer era this can take 48 hours or longer.

When a cheque is received, the bank staff debits the amount to the customer's account. If the bank rejects the cheque, it is up to you to collect. You'll be safe if you demand a certified cheque. In this case, the financial institution "freezes" the amount in the issuer's account to guarantee payment of the cheque.

When you cash a cheque, or accept it in payment, look carefully at any endorsement on the back. A cheque must be endorsed by the person to whom it was originally issued. Don't endorse any cheque made out to you until you are ready to cash or deposit it. Once endorsed, it is easily negotiated by another party. If you accept a cheque and the bank upon which it is drawn refuses to honor it, the loss is yours. If the bank accepts a cheque with its customer's forged signature, it has to take the loss. If you accept a postdated cheque, remember that the issuer can stop payment any time before the due date.

Lost or stolen. Government cheques— pension, family allowance, income-tax refunds—are favorite targets of thieves, who forge the endorsement and use false identification to cash them. If your pension cheque does not arrive on schedule, notify the postal authorities, your bank and the firm or government department from whom you receive the cheque. If the cheque has been stolen, and you don't take these steps, you might be held negligent and thus ineligible to recover the money. You will probably be asked by the people who send you the pension to sign an affidavit (a sworn statement) that your cheque was not received. They will instruct their bank to stop payment on the missing cheque and then send you a duplicate payment.

BAD CHEQUES

You were embarrassed and annoyed when your bank bounced one of your cheques.

Your bank must honor any properly drawn cheque you issue—as long as you have enough money in your account or have made an arrangement in advance. The same holds good for any financial institution that allows you chequing privileges. If you have not enough money to cover the cheque, it may be returned to the payee marked NSF (Not Sufficient Funds).

It is an offense under the Criminal Code to intentionally write a rubber cheque. A genuine mistake or careless personal bookkeeping still carries a penalty—the bank will charge a fee for the extra work involved in returning the cheque and a bouncing cheque may adversely affect your credit rating.

Most bankers know the customer who is a chronic offender is not a criminal; he's careless, overoptimistic or overextended. When cheques were sorted by hand, some hard-pressed customers wrote cheques they knew could not be covered by their funds but hoped they could deposit sufficient money before the cheque completed its passage through the sorting process. Computers now scan more than a thousand cheques a minute, worsening your odds of cashing a rubber cheque. The computer reads the magnetic ink character coding—those strange, spindly numbers pre-printed on your personalized cheques. Looming closer is the personal identification number system which will replace your signature. Even the teller may become obsolete.

To err is human. Even the flinty-eyed banker is aware that everybody makes mistakes. When a dependable customer issues a cheque that exceeds his balance, chances are it will be honored. The bank will post a debit to the client's account—in effect granting him a personal loan.

It sometimes happens that a bank "bounces" a customer's cheque by mistake. A computer error can set off a string of problems that may take weeks to find and correct. An Ontario government commission studying banking electronics pictured the average bank customer as "a small, shaky digit quivering before a colossal unfeeling machine."

If you are the victim of a bank error, insist that the manager write a letter of apology to the person to whom you wrote the cheque (with a copy to you).

Remember that all banking is just business. Nothing sacred about it. If you don't get satisfaction, take your problem to your consumer services bureau. Banks have been brought to heel and fined for misleading advertising just like other merchants.

BARGAINS IN BORROWING?

You can pick up a real bargain in antiques but you haven't enough cash to swing the deal.

The same principles of comparison shopping apply to borrowing as to any other purchase. Money is, after all, just another commodity and competition makes for "deals."

Banks and other financial institutions have always made personal loans to individuals, but it is only in recent years that this kind of business has been actively solicited. Today, we are almost bombarded with offers of loans. The chartered banks are by far the largest source of credit of all kinds. They have about four million loans "on the books" at any given time.

Anyone under the legal age of majority (in some places 18 years, in others 21) can have a chequing or savings account, but can't get a loan from a bank because minors cannot enter into contracts. (Many credit unions will lend money to minors who are members in good standing.)

The Bank Act was amended in 1978 and the banks were given greater leeway in the types of security they could accept. This cleared the way for their drive to dominate the personal-loan market. A major change was to allow them to take chattel or collateral mortgage security over assets such as motor vehicles, *at the time of making the loan*. Only the finance companies had been able to do this previously.

If you have a good credit rating and a steady job, you should have no difficulty in negotiating a personal loan from your credit union, bank or trust company.

Looking at loans. There are many types of loans available. For instance, the *demand loan* bears a lower rate of interest than the installment loan and can be paid off at irregular intervals. However, the bank manager will normally ask for collateral, such as the pledge of stocks or bonds or the cash-surrender value of a life insurance policy for loans of this kind.

The rate of interest can fluctuate during the term of a demand loan and, as the word implies, the bank has the right to demand repayment of a demand loan at any time, although this seldom happens.

The interest rate charged is usually quoted as a percentage "above prime"—this percentage can range from ½ percent upward. Prime rate is what banks charge their "best risk" corporate customers and is based on the Bank of Canada rate.

Various government-sponsored loans include farm-improvement loans, student loans and small business improvement loans.

If you have balances outstanding on several charge accounts and credit card loans, it may be advisable to consider consolidating them under one personal loan. Ask a bank manager to calculate the comparative interest costs and keep in mind that the banks *want* to make loans—it's a very profitable business.

If you don't belong to a credit union and can't get a loan from a bank, there are circumstances where it could be profitable to borrow from a consumer-finance company.

Suppose you use your Chargex-Visa or Master Charge credit card to purchase goods worth $1,500 from a department store. You

Earning and paying interest

When you deposit money in a bank or credit union, you lend the institution the money. It, in turn, lends that money to others—perhaps even yourself. Financial institutions make money because their lending rates are higher than their borrowing rates. For the individual dealing with these institutions, the situation is just the reverse.

ANNUAL INTEREST PAID ON $5,000*

Chartered Banks

3%–3½% (chequing savings accounts)	$150–$175
9½%–10% (non-chequing savings accounts)	$475–$500
9¾%–10¾% (term deposits)	$487.50–$537.50

Trust Companies

10%–10½% (non-chequing savings accounts)	$500–$525
10¼%–11⅛% (term deposits)	$512.50–$556.25

Credit Unions

5½%–10% (non-chequing savings accounts or unit shares)	$275–$500
10%–11% (term deposits)	$500–$550

Canada Savings Bonds

Series 33 (Nov. '78–Nov. '85, 9½% for 7 years)	$475

ANNUAL COST OF BORROWING $5,000*

Chartered Banks

12%	$600

Trust Companies

12¼%–13½%	$612.50–$675

Credit Unions

11¾%–12¼%	$587.50–$612.50

Consumer Finance Companies

17½%–18%	$875–$900

Rates are what lenders would charge the borrower with a first-class credit rating and gilt-edged collateral. The latter might include a first mortgage on property, a frozen savings account or term deposit certificate of the same amount as the loan.

*Rates quoted were in effect in August 1979

will pay 21 percent interest. If you buy the items through a store installment plan, the interest rate will also be 21 percent.

But the Small Loans Act will not permit finance companies to charge more than 15.4 percent on a loan of $1,500. So it would be cheaper to borrow the total sum from the finance company and pay off the department store.

LOAN APPLICATIONS

You are both angry and upset because the bank turned down your application for a loan.

You have the right to be told why your application was rejected—and you can apply at any one of a dozen other lending offices. But, pause to consider that the bank makes money by lending money; if it won't give you what you want, perhaps you are overreaching yourself financially.

The harder up you are, the poorer risk you are from any lender's point of view. Therefore, the higher rate of interest you will have to pay. The cost of a consumer-finance company loan is not permitted to exceed the aggregate of 2 percent per month on any part of a loan not exceeding $300; 1 percent per month on loans of $300 to $1,000, and one-half of 1 percent per month on loans of $1,000 to $1,500. Above $1,500, the sky's the limit. The finance company will also want you to pledge salable assets as collateral.

Collateral and character. Most lenders' personal loan applications include questions about your employment record, income, marital status, debts, and any assets that could be pledged as *collateral*—that is, things the lender could seize in case you failed to live up to your promise to pay back the loan.

They may ask that you provide a *guarantor* who would guarantee to pay your debt if you couldn't or wouldn't do so. You will be asked for permission to check your background and credit rating through the local branch of the Credit Bureau. (*See* Chapter 21, "Buying on credit.")

Bank branch managers have set limits be-

yond which loans cannot be made without head office approval. Not all managers have the same upper limit.

Personal judgment of the local manager can have something to do with rejecting your loan application, especially in a marginal situation. Another manager might well consider the same set of facts and arrive at the opposite conclusion.

MORTGAGE LOANS

You're in the market for a new home and wonder about the best source of mortgage money.

Trust companies and banks are the major sources of mortgage funds and, in this competitive market, you would be well advised to shop around.

The Bank Act now permits chartered banks to make mortgage loans, in competition with trust companies and other traditional mortgage lenders. Previously, banks had been restricted to loans of comparatively short term. Total mortgage loans outstanding are limited to 10 percent of each bank's Canadian dollar deposits and debentures. Between 1967 and 1977 total mortgage lending by banks increased fourteenfold to almost $11.6 billion.

Banks can offer a straight mortgage or one guaranteed under the National Housing Act (NHA). The interest rate on NHA mortgages is marginally lower and the loan-to-value ratio is higher, but the $70,000 maximum loan may be less than you require. (*See* Chapter 12, "When you buy.")

TRUST COMPANIES

Many advertisements of trust companies and banks lead you to believe they are identical.

From the average consumer's point of view, the differences between trust companies and banks are minimal. Some of the larger trust companies operate under the federal Trust and Loan Act and are subject to rigid controls. They offer such banking facilities as savings accounts, fixed-term deposits and current accounts. These are almost entirely individual rather than business accounts. Provincially chartered trust companies administer estates, invest money held by them in trust, or look after the affairs of minors or incapable persons. Their interest rates, chequing facilities and service charges are in line with the banks'. Most must have Canada Deposit Insurance (as do banks) which protects individual deposits up to $20,000.

The federal Bank Act is revised every 10 years and, as guardians of the public interest, politicians tend to be eager to restrain the powers of the 11 chartered banks and to expand the rights of the "near banks"—trust companies, mortgage-loan firms and societies, credit unions (*caisses populaires* in Quebec). There are always more votes in the streets than in the board rooms. One result is that the banks have developed their ownership positions in the trust companies. For example, the Bank of Montreal is connected with the Royal Trust Company, and the Royal Bank—Canada's largest—is associated with the Montreal Trust. By law, a bank's holding in a trust company is limited to 10 percent of the equity.

Trust companies make personal and commercial loans; the latter are generally modest compared with those of banks. Trust companies act as trustees and executors, which banks cannot do. They act on a bank's behalf in such dealings. One of the few trust companies to go broke was British Mortgage and Trust Company of Stratford, Ont. However, no depositor lost money.

That collapse was one of the reasons Canada Deposit Insurance Corporation came into being in 1967.

CONFIDENTIALITY

You worry about entrusting your bank manager with all the details of your financial affairs.

A strict rule of banks is to keep private business private. A bank should only divulge details with the customer's written consent, or by court order. Employees who break the rule risk dismissal, regardless of position or seniority.

Major financial institutions are members of the nationwide Associated Credit Bureaus of Canada. (*See* Chapter 21, "Buying on credit.") They use the bureaus in assessing risk and they supply the bureaus with general information about their customers. Rather than the dollar amount of a customer's loan or balance, they make use of expressions such as "An excellent record of meeting obligation," "Dependable," "Good paying record," or "Slow payer."

If you have a legitimate reason to seek a bank reference on an individual or company, you'll probably be told how long an account has been open and given a fairly vague comment on the stability and integrity of the client. It's up to you to read between the lines. The credit bureau itself rates credit risks on a scale from 1 (pays on time) to 9 (poor risk). You won't be given any information by phone, even about your own account, unless you are a customer the bank employee can identify.

The safety-deposit box. For an annual fee you can maintain strict privacy over your personal property, papers and valuables within the security of the bank premises, protected even from the bank's knowledge or scrutiny. Boxes can be rented in banks, trust companies and some credit unions.

It takes two keys to open a box, the bank's and yours. If you lose yours the box will have to be drilled open by a locksmith and a new lock fitted—at your expense.

The automatic $20,000 insurance policy on your deposits does not cover the contents of your safety-deposit box. The bank or trust company will not hold itself responsible for any loss from the box either by theft or through fire, although it will take elaborate precautions against both.

Keep an updated list of the contents of the box, including the numbers of any securities and a detailed description of other important documents. The rental contract you sign covering the use of a safety-deposit box forbids the storing of cash. If you ignored this and the box—and cash—was stolen, you would have no hope of being compensated for its loss.

Investments

In a free society you have the right to spend your money any way you choose. If you are convinced that the hula hoop or the yo-yo is about to make a comeback, or that topless bingo parlors are going to sweep the country, then you can snap up those shares and start dreaming of your castle in Spain.

But whenever you try to make your surplus funds earn more money through investment, remember, there's no way that the innocent, the gullible or the greedy can be entirely protected from the pitfalls of ignorance, the snares of the unscrupulous or the vagaries of a supply-and-demand market.

The lawmakers do their best. Each province has a securities act which regulates the sale and distribution of stocks and bonds, monitors offers made to the public and prevents open deception. All stockbrokers, investment dealers and their salesmen must be licensed. All public companies are required to disclose fully all pertinent facts.

The administrator of your provincial Securities Commission has many of the powers of a judge. He can compel the attendance of witnesses, take evidence under oath, seize any relevant documents or records and launch prosecutions. If the commission cancels or revokes the registration of any company, partnership or individual, that's just about curtains as far as further practice is concerned in Canada or the United States.

In Alberta, Saskatchewan, Manitoba and Ontario, the law allows any purchaser of a new securities issue a two-day "cooling-off period" during which he can cancel the order. A telegram to the broker is acceptable. Within 90 days, the purchase contract can be rescinded if the offer contains an untrue statement of a material fact, or omits any fact that amounts to misrepresentation. British Columbia also has legislation that includes this rescission provision.

On top of all this, a network of self-regulatory professional organizations rides herd on all aspects of the money market. Canada's stock exchanges are jealous of their reputation for fair dealing and can crack down swiftly on transgressors. In 1978, The Toronto Stock Exchange levied a $25,000 fine on a member firm. That same year, two other Ontario stockbrokers went to jail for conspiring to manipulate the stock of a petroleum company.

About a million Canadians participate in the financing of the free-enterprise society through the purchase of common shares in public companies. They "own a piece of the action" and hope—or pray—that the value of their stocks will grow and become a hedge against inflation. They know that a dollar bill left under the mattress for 20 years comes out as four quarters.

For the small investor, the brokerage fees that erode the net return after any sale or purchase are no small matter. The stock exchanges set minimum commission rates, and they forbid any under-the-counter rebates or discounts. Last revised in 1977, these commissions differ for sums under and over $5,000.

Minimum commission is $5 if trade is $50 or more. The base rate depends upon the price of the stock bought or sold. For example, if 100 shares were sold at $4.99 each, commission would be levied at 3 percent; for 100 shares at $15 each, 1 percent plus 20 cents per share. For transactions between $5,000 and $500,000, there's a sliding scale that any stockbroker will be glad to explain.

Whether you put your money into the bluest of the "blue chips," into Uncle Joe's bakery, into penny stocks or the stoutest bonds, land, Quebec pine tables or pre-Confederation postage stamps, there's a single simple rule which you ignore only at your own peril: "Investigate before you invest—and after."

FIRST INVESTMENTS

Inflation is eroding your savings, but you know very little about the stock market and you're uneasy about investing.

The "little guy" is much more important in the stock market than the stories in the financial papers may lead you to believe. No stockbroker will slam the door on the person who has, say, $1,000 to invest. The private investment club in your office, plant, club or neighborhood may let you start with $100 a month, or even less. But a novice is right to feel uneasy. The stock market—indeed the whole world of investment for profit—is complex and never absolutely safe. The essential rule for the investor is: "Never risk more than you can afford to lose."

If you are lucky enough to be looking at surplus cash for the first time, don't be seduced by dreams of getting ahead by "playing the market." You must get to "know the territory," even though you can generally trust your stockbroker, the bank or trust company investment officer, your lawyer or chartered accountant to do his honest best to advise you how to place your money to profitable advantage. In addition, government licensing and other regulatory bodies are looking over their shoulders. And, on the bottom line, they make more money, in commissions or fees, if they help you realize a profit.

The jargon barrier. The mysteries of the money market will soon dissipate if you are willing to study the rudiments of the system. It's not nearly as tough as algebra. Even a little knowledge—far from being a dangerous thing—will prepare you to understand the jargon of the professionals and equip you to make sensible decisions.

Before you try to choose among the bewildering array of "vehicles"—common or preferred shares, convertibles, bonds and debentures, mutual funds, mortgages and so forth—learn what these things are, what they can do for you, how you can use them to build up that nest egg, and how "the market" works.

Investment information is freely available in the business section of your public library. Much more is obtainable from the major stock exchanges in the large cities, the Investment Dealers Association, the Canadian Securities Institute, and through correspondence courses or seminars offered by some of these and by the commerce departments of many universities. Community colleges provide business or investment courses, usually taught by local professionals. Most stockbrokers and bond dealers will give you useful, up-to-date literature or place you on their mailing lists for regular market newsletters.

INTEREST AND INFLATION

You are told that your bonds are "as safe as a church," but the interest rate is fixed while inflation continues to soar.

Well, how safe is the church these days? In the wacky 1960s radicals were crying, "God is dead!" Nevertheless, the church remains a symbol of stability and security and bonds remain the most stable and secure investment. Literally, the issuers "bond" or pledge themselves to pay a stated interest at regular intervals on any money you invest, and to repay the loan in full on a given date.

Bonds are issued by almost all governmental bodies and agencies, from the federal government to the smallest municipality, and by some public utilities. All are secured by the taxation rights granted to these bodies by law. In other words, "you the taxpayer" pay the stated interest to "you the investor."

When a corporation floats a bond issue—usually to raise extra capital for expansion—it is, in effect, issuing a promissory note backed up by the assets of the company. Your bond does not give you any say in the management of the company, but neither do you have liability for any losses. If the company is one of, say, *The Financial Post*'s top 300 Canadian corporations, you shouldn't stay awake at night worrying about your investment.

When a company needs extra capital for less than 12 months, it normally goes to a chartered bank. If it wants money for a longer term, it sells bonds to the public through an investment dealer. As with all sales of securities, the terms of the offer and the background of the offerer are scrutinized by the regulatory agencies. These bodies do their best to guard the investor's right to a fair deal.

Money locked in. The whole point about bonds is the security. You know exactly what income you'll get half-yearly or yearly and that you'll get your money back intact. But what will be the purchasing power of that money when you get it back? This is a major consideration. Look at the Composite Price Index, or other measuring tools, which show the erosion of the dollar in the accelerated inflation of our times.

The term of a bond is a period of years—maybe 5 to 20 or more. Your money is locked in and your interest rate remains the same, no matter what happens in the swiftly changing world. If you sell during the term, you may lose a fraction of the sum you invested. If the corporation backing your bond goes belly-up, you'll be among the first in line when assets are distributed.

Market forces sometimes determine the interest rate on demand bonds. Canada Savings Bonds (CSB), issued by the federal government to tap the savings of the average person, provide a case in point. In late 1979 the interest rate on previously sold bonds was hiked to 12 percent from 9.25 on a one-year basis. If Ottawa had not made this move, CSB holders would have cashed their bonds to buy higher-yielding investments. Capital will always flow toward the better return.

If you want to sell your commercial bonds to realize quick cash—there are times when this can be done at a profit—you'll find that the stock exchanges don't figure in the deal. You can find out the current value of your bonds in the "bid-ask" columns of the larger daily newspapers, but these securities are traded "over the counter." The business is generally done over the telephone and the dealers need not be members of a recognized stock exchange. By and large, stock exchanges trade mainly in common or "ownership" shares in large corporations.

Whether stocks are listed or unlisted, you'll still have to pay brokerage commissions when you sell or buy. Brokers are not eager to trade in very small or broken "lots," simply because their overhead expenses rule out reasonable profit. A normal "lot" is the number of shares of that stock normally traded—it can be anything from 10 to 100. But brokers will generally handle awkward packages if they smell more business down the road.

Spreading the risk. Some critics who worry about the future of the free-enterprise system frown on the tendency of the small investor to put his surplus money into mutual funds. While it makes good sense for the inexperienced, they say it's rather like trusting Big Brother to take care of problems too complex for the individual.

The idea of mutual funds is more than a century old, however, and it's still gaining ground. A group of money managers, either operating on their own or as employees of a trust or investment company, offer its shares (or "units") to the small investor. There are about 300 mutual funds in Canada.

The pool of money created is then invested in either a wide or narrow range of securities, depending on the philosophy or skills of the managers. Many of them operate in the bond market; some mix the fund's portfolio with both stocks and bonds. Some operate solely in the real estate market, offering their clients small slices of many mortgages. A few specialize in providing venture capital to new businesses.

When you buy into a mutual fund, common sense tells you that brokerage and management fees must be paid. This "front-end load" can amount to your first two years' profit on your investment.

The buying and selling prices of most of the mutuals (professionals say "bid" and "ask") are quoted in the financial pages of the daily newspapers, but few are listed on the stock exchanges. Some of the funds sell units only through their own organizations, whereas others make use of the normal broker-dealer channels. Either way, like all stock transactions, they're monitored by your provincial Securities Commission.

HIGH-RISK STOCKS

You know someone who made a killing in penny stocks, but these investments look risky to you.

If you can buy stocks for pennies, don't. This high-risk end of the stock market is not for the average investor—certainly not for the novice.

Unless you possess expert knowledge of the particular field, it's more like buying a lottery ticket than investing. Of course, you'll hear of the lucky ones who "made a killing," but there's only a hurt silence from the great ma-

jority who are licking their financial wounds.

Common shares promise no capital repayment or dividend. They provide, however, the investor's best chance of fighting inflation because the worth of the shares of a successful company—and the size of dividends paid on them—should grow faster than the rate of inflation. The income tax rate on dividends paid by Canadian corporations is reduced by up to 50 percent, and you pay tax on only half the profit you make—your "capital gain"—when you sell the shares.

Most Canadian public companies have their common shares listed on one or more of the

Canada's your best bet

Late in 1979, as interest rates hit record highs everywhere, the federal government decided to offer a guaranteed 12-percent return on the first year of its new Canada Savings Bonds (CSB) series. At the same time, to dissuade holders of earlier, less remunerative bonds from cashing in or switching to other investments, it bumped up the interest rates on all outstanding bonds.

Held for the full term of seven years, a $100 CSB now grows to a value of $204.82. Individuals can buy up to $25,000 worth each. Unless inflation gallops clear out of control, the CSB offers the safest and best bet for the average Canadian who wants to put surplus money to work.

five Canadian stock exchanges. The law requires that shareholders receive annual reports on companies whose shares they own.

The preferred position. Preference shares make up the second main type of equity stock offered to the public. Literally, they occupy a "preferred position." The holder is usually entitled to a fixed rate of dividend as long as the company is able to pay. While that decision is always at the discretion of the directors, the dividend on the "preferred" will always be paid before the "common" get any.

Preference shares can be cumulative or noncumulative. In the first case, should the dividend be passed in any year, it will accumulate as "arrearage" and must be paid in full before any dividend is paid on common stock and before the preferred share is called in—that is, redeemed or bought back by the company. The noncumulative share entitles the holder to the specified dividend only in the year in which the dividend is declared; if the dividend is passed that year, he has no comeback.

The "convertible" preferred carries the extra value in that it can be exchanged, on certain conditions, for the issuing company's common shares. There's usually a time limit on the conversion.

Preferred shares do not as a rule give the holder the right to vote on management decisions at the annual or any special meetings of the company. But if the dividends are passed, these individuals frequently do acquire certain rights—perhaps including the right to elect a given number of directors.

When a company is wound up, holders of preferred shares usually have a prior claim on any assets, ahead of the common-share holders but behind the company's creditors, which include any bond and debenture holders.

PLAYING SAFE

You would like to own some "blue chip" stocks, but they seem so expensive.

Most everyone has heard the apocryphal story of the nephew who was given one share in the infant automobile industry as a Christmas present. Several Christmases later, after all the mergers, stock splits and bonus issues, that one share had fattened to a value of a million dollars. Well, in the rarified world of the "blue chips," it could have happened.

In the game of high-stakes poker, the blue chips are the most valuable. The term is now universally recognized as applying to the most highly rated stocks, the market leaders boasting long and steady dividend and growth records. The price of the stock invariably reflects this strength.

The investor with limited means will obviously be able to tuck fewer of these shares into his portfolio—his collection of investments—than if he invests in more moderately priced issues. But if he is looking for income, hoping for growth, and demanding security, the blue chips are probably his first choice. Each July, *The Financial Post* lists Canada's 300 top stocks; *Fortune* magazine lists the top 500 in the United States.

Bank of Montreal has paid dividends on its common stock every year without a break since 1828, and The Bank of Nova Scotia since 1833. An annual return of about 8 percent is not difficult to ensure. Then there's the factor of growth as a counter to inflation.

Moore Corporation of Toronto, the largest manufacturer of business forms in North America, "split" its stock in 1959 and again in 1967. (*See* glossary, page 383.) A split usually results in an increase in the holder's original investment. In the 1950s, one Moore common was worth about $5; twenty years later, it was worth $35. That was a 600-percent increment for the lucky, or well-advised, holder, far exceeding the ravages of inflation.

Instant action. When mergers or takeovers occur among the industry giants, there's usually enough money involved to offer a very favorable price for the outstanding shares the aggressor may need. The takeover may not delight everyone, but it can put a lot of cash into shareholders' pockets.

The "marketability" of the blue chips is another plus. Any time you want to sell to collect your capital gain, you'll get instant action on the stock exchanges. Perhaps within two minutes.

MARKET ETHICS

You phoned your broker to sell some stock when the price jumped. By the time the sale was completed, it had slumped. You have actually lost money.

You have the right to expect that your stockbroker, acting as your *agent*, will execute your instructions diligently and faithfully. His sole interest lies in earning his commission, and he has every reason to act as swiftly as circumstances allow.

You are financially liable, as the *principal*, for any actions the agent carries out on your behalf. For example, to repudiate any deal you would have to prove that you had been deceived or manipulated—in short, that, like any other licensed professional, he was guilty of malpractice.

The price quotation you saw, probably in the daily press, referred to the "bid" offered by a buyer during the previous day's trading on a stock exchange, or maybe at the present day's 4 p.m. close. (The western exchanges open earlier and close earlier to keep pace with the trading times of the much larger eastern exchanges in Toronto and New York. For example, The Alberta Stock Exchange trades from 8 a.m. to 2 p.m. Calgary time.) There's no guarantee that at the next day's opening, your "ask"—offer to sell—can be executed at yesterday's peak.

Shout it out. Your broker transmits your order by telephone or telex to the stock exchange floor, either through his own head office—if it owns a "seat" at the exchange—or through an associated firm. The trader at the exchange makes known your offer to sell "in full outcry" at one of the "trading posts," where certain classes of stocks are regularly traded. The "outcry" is traditional to ensure that no undercover deals are made. Electronic gadgetry aside, it's not basically different from a country auction.

Your "ask" cannot be completed until it has been matched with a satisfactory "bid." If there are plenty of buyers around, the transaction can be made in minutes from your original phone call. If trading has turned sluggish, it can take much longer. But either way, the trader will automatically shop around as the bids are shouted and written up on boards by the clerks, to get you the best price, even to a fraction of a cent.

Unless instructed otherwise, the trader will take the best price he can get this day, either selling or buying. It's called an "at the market" order. But you can order him not to accept less than a stated figure; to sell all your shares or none; and to buy another stock immediately with the proceeds of the sale, if the "ask" price falls to a stated point. The deal is consummated when a "floor ticket" is written up and initialed by the traders concerned.

The governor rules. To protect the public against sharpies, there's a rigid code of trading rules on the stock-exchange floor and in all other markets where securities are traded. Disputes in the bedlam between rival traders are settled on the spot at the exchange, either by the floor governor or the floor committee, or by a vote of the traders present—and sometimes even by the toss of a coin.

The Securities Acts of Quebec, Ontario, Alberta and British Columbia allow the governing bodies of the stock exchanges, and the powerful Investment Dealers Association of Canada to exercise a large measure of self-regulation. Unethical conduct is described as any conduct of business, or omission, considered to be not in the public interest or in the interest of the exchange. Penalties range from fines to suspension and, in extreme cases, to expulsion.

To protect further the rights of the investor, the stock-exchange committee and the Securities Commission are empowered to delay or halt trading in any security, temporarily or permanently. This infrequent action is taken at the request of the company concerned or by the exchange itself if, say, there's an unusual rush of buy or sell orders for a particular stock, or if there's news pending of a merger or a big change in dividends or earnings that could send prices skyrocketing or plummeting. The exchange may merely feel the need for clarification of a turn of events, or it may think a company is failing to live up to the

Bulls, bears—and lambs

Trading has been with us since the Stone Age hunters began bartering mastodon chops for firewood or flints, and it has bequeathed us a language all its own. Some of the original meanings of stock-market jargon are lost, the expressions bent into other uses. New terms are coined continually, especially in response to technological change.

The "bull" in the market is an optimist—he's convinced that prices are on their way up; the "bear" is his opposite—he expects a slump. The rookie investor will lessen his chances of becoming a sacrificial lamb by learning the key terms in this glossary.

Annual report. The formal financial statements and report on operations issued by a corporation to its shareholders after the end of the fiscal year.

Arbitrage. The simultaneous buying of a security on one stock exchange and the sale of the same security on another exchange at prices that yield profit to the arbitrager.

Assets. Everything a company or a person owns or is owed.

Balance sheet. A financial statement expressing the nature and amount of a company's assets, liabilities and shareholders' equity on a given date.

Bank rate. The rate of interest at which the Bank of Canada will make infrequent loans to chartered banks or investment dealers who participate actively in the money market.

Bankrupt. The status of a person or company legally declared unable to pay creditors.

Blue chip. An active, leading, well-seasoned equity issue, usually with a long-time dividend record and strong investment features.

Bond. Evidence of a debt on which the issuer guarantees to pay the holder a set amount of interest for a specified period of time, and to repay the loan on maturity or expiration date. Technically, assets must be pledged as security for a bond. However, the term is often used loosely to describe any debt security.

Book value. The amount of net assets belonging to owners of a business, or shareholders of a company, as fixed by balance-sheet values.

Collateral. Securities or other property pledged by a borrower to guarantee repayment of a loan.

Commercial paper. Short-term negotiable securities issued by corporations that call for the payment of a set amount of money at a fixed time.

Commission. The amount charged by a broker for buying or selling securities on behalf of a client, based on a scale that applies uniformly for all stock exchanges across Canada.

Common stock. Securities that indicate ownership in a corporation and usually carry voting privileges.

Convertible. A bond, debenture or preferred share that may be exchanged by the owner, usually for the common stock of the same company, in line with the terms of the conversion privilege.

Coupon. A detachable portion of a bond certificate granting the holder an interest payment of a specified amount when it is detached and presented at a bank on or after its due date.

Current asset. An asset that, in the normal course of business, would readily be converted into cash or consumed in the production of income, usually within a year—for example, cash itself, accounts receivable, inventories.

Current liability. A debt that is due to be paid within a year.

Debenture. A certificate of indebtedness of a government or company secured only by the general credit of the issuer and not by mortgage or lien on any particular asset.

Depreciation. Systematic charges against earnings to write off the cost, less salvage value, of an asset over its estimated useful life.

Dividend. An amount paid to preferred and

common shareholders in cash or stock, determined by a company's board of directors.

Fiscal year. A corporation's accounting year. Because of the nature of their particular businesses, some companies do not use the calendar year for their bookkeeping.

Insider report. A report of all transactions in the shares of a corporation by those considered to be insiders of the company and submitted each month to the Securities Commissions of the provinces concerned.

Investment trust, company, or fund. A company that uses its capital to invest in other companies. There are two main types: *closed-end* and *open-end* or *mutual* funds. Shares in closed-end investment trusts are readily transferable in the open market and are purchased and sold like other shares. Capitalization of these companies is fixed. Open-end funds sell their own new shares to investors, are ready to buy back their old shares, and are not listed on stock markets. Open-end funds are so named because their capitalization is not fixed; they issue additional shares in response to market demand.

Load. The portion of the offering price of shares of most open-end investment companies (mutual funds) that covers sales commissions and all other costs of distribution. The load is incurred only on purchase since, in most cases, there is no charge when the shares are sold or redeemed.

Long. Signifies ownership of securities. "I am long 100 Alcan common" means that the speaker owns 100 common shares of Alcan.

Manipulation. An illegal practice. Buying or selling a security to create a false or misleading appearance of active trading, or for the purpose of raising or lowering the price to induce purchase or sale by others.

Margin. The amount paid by a client when he uses credit to buy a security, the balance being supplied by his broker against acceptable collateral.

Money market. The part of the capital market in which short-term financial obligations are bought and sold.

Mutual fund. See *Investment Trust.*

Net asset value. Total assets of a corporation minus its liabilities.

Net earnings. The part of a company's profits left after all expenses and taxes are paid, and out of which dividends are payable.

Option. A right to buy or sell specific securities or properties at a set price within a specified time.

Over-the-counter (OTC). A market for securities made up of securities dealers who may or may not be members of a recognized stock exchange. Over-the-counter is generally a market conducted over the telephone. Also called *unlisted market* and *between-dealer market.*

Paper profit. An unrealized profit on a security still held. Paper profits become realized profits only when the security is sold. A *paper loss* is the opposite of this.

Penny stocks. Low-priced issues, often speculative, selling for less than $1 a share.

Portfolio. Holdings of securities by an individual or institution.

Preferred stock. A class of share capital that entitles its owners to certain preferences ahead of the common shareholders, such as a fixed rate of prior dividend and return of the stock's par value in a liquidation.

Price-earnings ratio. A common stock's current market price divided by its annual per-share earnings.

Prime rate. The interest rate that chartered banks charge their most credit-worthy borrowers.

Prospectus. A legal document that describes securities offered for sale to the public. It must be prepared in accordance with requirements of the applicable provincial Securities Commission.

Proxy. Written consent given by a shareholder to someone else—who need not be a shareholder—to represent him and vote his shares at a shareholders' meeting.

Puts and calls. Options giving the holder the right to sell or buy a fixed amount of a certain stock at a set price within a specified time. A put gives the holder the right to sell the stock; a call the right to purchase the stock. Puts are generally bought by those who think a stock may go down; calls by those who expect a price increase.

Real Estate Investment Trust (REIT). An investment company that specializes in real estate, investing either in mortgages or in real property and, in some cases, in a combination of both.

Retained earnings. The portion of annual earnings that have been retained by the company after payment of expenses and taxes and the distribution of dividends.

Right. A temporary privilege given to existing common shareholders to purchase additional shares of a company from the company itself at a stated price.

Short sale. The sale of a security the seller does not own. This is a speculative act done in the belief that the price of a stock will fall and the seller will then be able to cover the sale by buying it back later at a lower price, thus making a profit on the operation. It is illegal for a seller not to declare a short sale when placing the order.

Split. The subdivision of a company's outstanding common shares into a larger or smaller number of new common shares. A 2-for-1 split by a company with one million shares outstanding would result in two million shares outstanding; each holder of 100 common shares would own 200 shares after the split. In a 1-for-2 split by the same company, each holder of 100 common shares would own 50 shares of the 500,000 shares outstanding after the reverse split.

Spread. The gap between bid and asked prices.

Stock dividend. A *pro rata* payment to shareholders of additional stock. Such payment increases the number of shares held, but does not change a shareholder's proportional investment in the company.

Street certificate. A stock certificate registered in the name of an investment dealer or stock broker rather than in the name of the individual owner so as to increase its negotiability.

Warrant. A certificate granting the holder the right to purchase securities at a set price within a specified time limit, or in perpetuity. Warrants are normally issued with a new issue of securities to increase the marketability of the new issue.

Yield. Return on an investment. A stock yield is determined by expressing the annual dividend as a percentage of the current market price of the stock. A bond yield is a more complicated calculation. It involves annual interest payments plus amortization of the difference between its current market price and par value over the life of the bond. This yield can be obtained from a bond-yield table.

formal agreement—its statutory sworn declaration, filed before the stock was accepted for listing on the exchange.

BUYING LAND

You'd like to put some surplus funds into land, but changing tax rates and government regulations make you hesitate.

The beginning investor nearly always gets into land even before he has a surplus of cash. That's because taxation regulations tend to favor the homeowner. (*See* Chapter 12, "When you buy.") Owning your own home outright—or having the mortgage well in hand—is the first advice you'll receive from any reputable stockbroker. In fact, the Registered Home Ownership Savings Plan (RHOSP), which allows you to deduct up to $1,000 a year from your taxable income, is regarded as Canada's number one tax shelter. Further, if you use the money eventually to buy and furnish a house or a summer cottage, the whole sum is tax-free. The shrewdest investor on the stock market can't beat that deal.

Although population growth in Canada has slowed noticeably, freehold land in desirable locations is still in great demand. The conventional mortgage provides security and interest income in excess of most bank-deposit rates. First-mortgage rates stood at 14 to 15 percent in 1979. The mortgage-lender has, for security, the borrower's house and land; if the latter fails to repay the loan or interest, he stands to lose it all. The mortgage is held by the lender until the loan is repaid, then canceled or destroyed.

In Canada, there is no organized market in which to trade small amounts of mortgages so, for the small investor, such deals are usually arranged privately through lawyers, accountants, or mortgage brokers. If you have sizable funds available, however, there's no reason why you shouldn't advertise personally for borrowers. Be sure you have the expertise to check credit ratings and a thorough knowledge of local property values. Several of the country's large mutual funds give the small

investor a chance to get into this field. The price of these fund units is probably quoted in your daily paper.

TAX-FREE EXCHANGES

You want to channel dividends to your wife to cut your tax bill, but it looks like a complicated maneuver.

A Canadian taxpayer can split his investment income between himself and his wife or children so that he can maximize the $1,000 dividend, interest, capital gains deduction that is available to each taxpayer. (*See* Chapter 29, "Your income tax.")

For example, you can make an interest-free loan to family members, who can buy stocks or bonds with the money. In most provinces, any income or capital gains realized from the use of this loan would not be attributed to you as the lender. The situation is somewhat different in Quebec where loans in excess of $60,000 would not be regarded as interest-free for tax purposes.

If a spouse has investment income but cannot use the full $1,000 exemption, the other partner may apply the unused part of his or her exemption on investment income, as well as using the full amount of his or her own personal $1,000 exemption.

Investors routinely plan their transactions to minimize or defer tax. This planning can include the gift, sale or transfer of property, including securities, between spouses prior to death. The law is clear on the point (*see* Chapter 33, "Wills and gifts") and, as long as you remain within the law and report your income correctly, you don't have to worry about complications.

Specific advice on tax planning is available from accountants or consultants specializing in tax law. But any investor can profit from some simple moves. The government looks with some favor on the active investor as a contributor to economic progress, while frowning on those who hide their money under the mattress or send it to Switzerland or Grand Cayman. You can borrow money to invest in Canadian companies and the interest you'll pay is tax-deductible.

Careful timing of the sale of securities and the subsequent loss or gain is important. Losses must be considered prior to the end of the calendar year to offset any capital gains realized that same year. Capital gains may be deferred until early in a new year so that the maximum of deferred tax can be achieved. Ideally, gains and losses should be matched.

Tax on your capital gains—say, your net profit in the market—can be deferred by buying one of the income-averaging or deferred annuities sold by the trust and insurance companies. Income-averaging spreads your income over a period of years when you may have peaks and lows. Since income tax is progressive—the higher the income, the higher the percentage of tax—you'll come out better with averaging if you've had a lucky strike with Miracle Mines or another of those tempting "penny stocks." With a deferred annuity, you arrange to accept payments at a later date. Tax on the interest portion is postponed until the payments are actually received. Perhaps by then your income will be smaller and you'll be in a lower bracket.

One half of capital gains and one half of capital losses must be taken into account when computing your total annual income. Individuals can deduct from other income a maximum of $2,000 per year of allowable loss—that is, one half of a total loss of $4,000 or more. If Miracle Mines didn't strike gold, your financial loss over the $2,000 annual maximum may be carried back one year, or forward indefinitely, subject to that annual limit.

SHAREHOLDERS' POWERS

You own only a few shares in a very large corporation but you are incensed at the huge salaries and bonuses paid to the top executives.

Even if you hold only a single share, you are a part-owner and thus have the right to express your views on how the company is run. You'll get your chance to criticize at the annual meeting. All public companies must, by law, provide you with annual reports, and adequate notice of annual or special meetings of the shareholders. Each share of voting stock is entitled to one vote.

Companies are not, however, run by the shareholders. Management is in the hands of the board of directors, which is elected by a majority of the shareholders. The minority stockholder gets the opportunity to vote on the slate of directors proposed at the annual meeting, or to propose a director outside that list. Almost invariably, that cannot amount to more than a formal protest, to be recorded in the minutes of the meeting—unless your viewpoint is supported by a reasonable number of the other shareholders.

Battling the big battalions. Normally, the slate of directors put forward by management is assured beforehand of the support of a solid majority. Even if your cause is doomed, you may stir up enough controversy among waverers to force a vote allowing your criticisms to be aired. You don't have to win to register a sharp rebuke to the existing board.

Only a fraction of the shareholders of a large public company attends annual meetings. Votes are often cast in blocks large enough to ensure that the big battalions will win. When people can't attend in person, they assign their voting rights to others by signing a proxy (permission to vote in another's name).

Proxies can be used in any type of vote that must be put to the shareholders. When there is widespread dissension—over management remuneration, say, or dividend policy—a bitter fight for proxies may develop in advance of the crucial meeting.

The shareholders must appoint—again by majority vote—the company's auditor, usually a firm of independent chartered accountants. It's a key resolution, as the auditor is obliged to reveal publicly any excesses or weaknesses in the financial setup.

Share and share alike. Any new bylaws passed by the directors during the past year must be approved. This can open several doors to discussion from the floor of the meeting. In brief, the directors are not permitted to change materially the purposes or structure of the business without the approval of a majority of the shareholders. Besides, a minority group has access to the courts if the board is acting in violation of the company's charter of incorporation, or behaving in a manifestly unfair way. For example, all shareholders of record must share equally in dividends whether or not they approve of the actions of the ruling management block.

Moreover, federal or provincial corporation laws override the bylaws of any incorporated company. And, of course, you hold the final sanction. If you don't like the way the company is being run, you can sell your shares and invest elsewhere. If enough shareholders take that route, the value of the stock falls, and directors don't like that.

CONTROLLING SHAREHOLDERS

You are asked to become a director of a small company in which you have invested. Doesn't that make you liable for its future debts?

Not as a rule, unless one of the company's creditors—perhaps the bank or a major supplier—requires you to guarantee personally one or all of the company's debts. Your personal debt liability is generally restricted to the amount of money you have invested. That's the basic reason for the incorporation of a limited company. Banks or other lenders almost invariably demand that the controlling shareholders or officers in small companies, however, pledge their personal assets as security against any company borrowing above an initial limit.

Even when there's no personal guarantee, the responsibility of the director is greater than that of the ordinary shareholder. The directors of any company must always act "in good faith," because they have accepted election to serve the interests of the shareholders. They can be held liable for acts of gross negligence by management.

Any illegal acts committed by the corporation with the knowledge and consent of the directors—things like improper loans to any director, or the payment of dividends when there's not enough cash in the treasury—can rebound on the board. Ontario's Business Corporations Act is typical in demanding that company directors must exercise "the degree of care, diligence and skill that a reasonably prudent person would exercise in comparable circumstances."

The directors are responsible for appointing the officers of the company, even if the directors are themselves the chief officers. It's always necessary to remember that a company stands apart as a separate legal entity from its owners and that the directors have very definite responsibilities toward it.

COMPANY TAKEOVERS

There are rumors that the company you've invested in will be taken over by a multinational corporation, and you fear the new owners may shut it down.

The small investor can usually rub his hands when a takeover of David by Goliath is in the wind. The reason is that once the multinational has decided that the move will result in a higher long-term profit or other advantage, it is likely to offer an attractive price for any outstanding shares it hasn't already corraled. You may be offered a combination of cash plus shares in the aggressor's company, or any one of several other choices. But it is almost certain that, unless your company is failing, you're going to profit from the deal.

Of course, if you are opposed to takeovers, mergers and commercial bigness on principle—that's another story. The basic assumption is that the investor is trying to make his surplus money work as hard as possible for the best possible return.

Even if the original business is absorbed and shut down, this action should be regarded unsentimentally within the whole supply-and-demand philosophy of the marketplace. It is not, admittedly, the home turf of the idealist.

When two moguls were competing in 1979 for control of the 300-year-old Hudson's Bay

Company, the offers to the uncommitted shareholders were sweetened almost daily. When the family holding company set up by Roy Thomson of Timmins, Ont.—the late Lord Thomson of Fleet—won out, the value of the common shares had jumped from a previous trading price of $20 to $37 a share.

SELLING 'SHORT'

A business friend tells you that selling "short" is a great way to make money when prices are falling. Sounds crazy.

In bluntest terms, selling short is the selling of securities that you don't actually *own* at the moment. The trick is that you think the price of the stock will continue to fall, and you will be able to buy it in a short time—for delivery to your purchaser—at a lower price than that at which he bought it from you. The difference is your profit. And it's completely legal. You are, in market jargon, a *bear*.

The mechanics are interesting. The short seller must provide his broker with ample security to cover the transaction. The broker gets permission to borrow enough of the stock from another owner, or from other brokers. When the shares are finally purchased by the short seller, the borrowed stock is returned to the portfolio of the lender. The short seller takes any profit, less commissions. If the deal goes bad—that is, if the stock rises instead of falling—the short seller must make up the difference. The short seller's broker can demand at any time that his client actually buy and pay for the shares involved at the going price.

Your ticket to profit—or loss

If you make any transaction on the stock market—buying or selling shares—your dealing will be recorded on a ticket similar to one of these. The tickets indicate the number of shares (200); the price; MKT since it is a market order; the name of the stock; the name and address of the client; and the identifying numbers of the account and salesman for the broker.

387

This may sound crazy, but—like the bumblebee—it does fly. Incidentally, if you are "long" rather than "short," it simply means that you actually own the stock concerned.

DAY OF RECKONING

You've seen offhand references to "V-Day" in the financial columns and are worried that it could affect you because of some inherited bonds.

Well, it could. Valuation Day ("V-Day") was established by the Department of National Revenue to permit the accurate assessment of capital-gains tax on all property, including stocks and bonds, as of the beginning of 1972. (*See* Chapter 29, "Your income tax.")

A capital gain results when property is sold for a price higher than its original cost. All income-tax payers must report one half of their net capital gains; and losses may be deducted. There are some statutory maximums.

Until 1972 capital gains were not taxed in Canada. Because of this, a chalk line had to be drawn for valuation purposes. V-Day for shares traded in Canadian public companies was December 22, 1971. This included foreign stocks traded on a Canadian stock exchange. For all other Canadian property, the date was December 31.

A complete list of the V-Day valuations of stocks is available free of charge from the Department of National Revenue. The relevant bond prices can be obtained from *The Financial Post*, 481 University Avenue, Toronto, Ont., M5W 1A7, or from the Bond Traders' Association in Montreal or Toronto.

INVESTMENT CLUBS

There's an investment club in your condominium. You'd like to get started in the market, but for $40 per month you surely can't buy much.

Your ten bucks a week won't buy very much, but if there are 20 members, that's $10,400 a year. With that amount, an investment club is definitely in business.

The average investment club meets once a month to review the club's portfolio, examine new financial research and make investment decisions by majority vote. The larger clubs may leave buy-sell decisions to an elected committee. A membership of more than 40 contributors is likely to become unwieldy. Because the stockbroker will charge commissions on each transaction, there's an obvious advantage in pooling funds and investing in the name of the club.

The Canadian Association of Investment Clubs, c/o Mr. A. D. H. Smith, Davidson Partners Ltd., First Canadian Place, Suite 3700, P.O. Box 122, Toronto, Ont., M5X 1EG, will help you form a club in your condominium, office or plant. The nonprofit Investment Dealers Association of Canada (IDA) will provide guidance literature. Its head office is in Commerce Court South, Toronto, Ont. The IDA conducts correspondence courses in English and French. A pass in its *Canadian Securities Course* is the basic requirement for registration to sell stocks and bonds to the public. Completion of advanced courses leads to the qualification, Fellow of the Canadian Securities Institute.

32 Life insurance

anadians own $300 billion in life insurance—a household average of more than $40,000. And this doesn't include the value of the more than one million annuity plans written by life insurance companies.

We spend $4.5 billion a year for this coverage, more per capita than any other country.

Despite this mammoth expenditure, most of us have scant knowledge of insurance laws or of our rights under a policy. At the same time, life insurance is one of the most closely regulated businesses. The 150 companies doing business in Canada must get government approval each year. Provincial superintendents of insurance supervise all operations and control licensing of insurance brokers, agents and claims adjusters. A federal superintendent oversees foreign companies and others operating under federal charters.

Your local life insurance agent's income comes mainly from commission on sales of some 50 types or combinations of policies. There's plenty of competition and, if you're not satisfied with his proposals, scores of other agents will jump at the chance to give you a second opinion, without any fee or obligation.

Consulting fees are usually restricted to complex estate planning or business insurance services.

Most veteran agents have a broad knowledge of taxation and laws that can have a bearing on your affairs, but even a rookie must have passed a stringent provincial examination and should be knowledgeable in his field.

The Life Underwriters Association of Canada offers professional training to its 18,000 member agents. A Canadian Life Underwriter (CLU) has successfully completed a three-year study of estate planning, taxation, accounting, commercial law and other subjects.

Insurance companies range from the coast-to-coast giants to smaller, provincial and regional firms. Your money is safe with any of them. Since the first "made in Canada" life insurance contract was issued in 1833, not one company has ever failed to live up to its financial obligations.

ASSESSING YOUR NEEDS

You have $50,000 of group life insurance at your workplace, an accident plan and your Canada Pension Plan benefits. Your wife says this isn't enough protection for your family.

Calculate the financial needs of your survivors if you died, say, at 35. Would present insurance coverage and Canada or Quebec Pension Plan benefits be adequate support for a wife and three children, ages 3, 6 and 9?

First, the immediate picture. The $50,000 insurance payout, invested at 10 percent, would provide an annual income of $5,000. Canada or Quebec Pension benefits, at 1979 rates, would provide about $3,400 a year, until the children reach 18. That's a total annual income of $8,400, a sum that wouldn't likely support the family's present life style.

Looking at the overview, pension benefits up to the time the youngest child is 18 will amount to about $50,000. There will be an additional $20,000 if each child attends school full time to age 25.

The figures are a rough estimate: the government pension plans are tied to the Consumer Price Index and benefits could be higher. But it's safe to estimate maximum benefits at $100,000.

That, plus the principal and interest from the insurance payout, adds up to about $300,000.

But if you live to normal retirement age, you will probably earn considerably more than $1 million. Even after income tax, chances are you will contribute between $600,000 and $700,000 to your family.

So your wife is right when she says your present coverage isn't enough to replace your income in the event of your untimely death.

Groups not permanent. Your group insurance plans are good value and have a place in your program. However, they should not be the sole foundation of future financial security; they are not permanent and not under your control.

Your $50,000 group life insurance coverage could be canceled if you changed employment or if your employer or the insurance company terminated the master group contract. You would have the option of converting all or part of the coverage into an individual policy without medical proof of insurability, but the premiums would be based on your age at the time and might be too expensive.

Only the insured can cancel an individually purchased and owned life insurance policy; the insurance company cannot cancel the policy, regardless of changes in your health, occupation, habits or behavior, as long as you pay your premiums.

THIRD-PARTY INSURANCE

Your husband suggests insuring your life for a large amount. You are a full-time homemaker and mother and you'd sooner spend the money on a vacation.

If you died suddenly, what would it cost to replace you—as cook, home economist, dietitian, hostess, housekeeper, and chauffeur?

A jury in Washington, D.C., recently decided that $905,000 was the value of the services of a 27-year-old mother of three boys, who was killed in a traffic accident. The calculation was a projection of existing wage rates for domestic help until her youngest son would reach age 18.

Economists estimate that it would cost between $15,000 and $20,000 a year to hire help to replace the mother's services in the average family home.

A "working wife" contributes to the Canada (or Quebec) Pension Plan and if she dies, her husband receives more than $1,000 in benefits plus monthly payments toward the cost of a housekeeper while the children are growing up.

An insurance policy on the full-time homemaker—and about half of all married women do not work outside the home—can provide at least equal benefits. A term insurance policy with a family-income rider is not expensive for the younger woman.

It's a mutual decision. If the policyowner and the insured are not the same person, it's called a "third-party" contract. Except in Quebec you may not insure any other person without that person's knowledge and consent, supported by his or her signature on the application form. The only exception occurs when the insured is under 16. In that case, consent may be given by either parent or by a legal guardian. In Quebec, you may insure any person in whose life you have an insurable interest, without that person's knowledge or consent. This could include your consort, your descendants and those of your consort, any person upon whom you depend for support or education, your employees and staff and anyone in whose life you have a pecuniary interest.

Parent and child. If an agent presses you to take out an education policy on your child's life, look first at the family's overall priorities.

The child's chances of surviving through to college entrance are twice as good as his parents'. Assuming the father is the main earner in the family, an education policy on his life would probably be better.

If you don't live to see your child complete his or her education, such a policy would ensure money for college without using up funds earmarked for other purposes—such as wiping out the mortgage or providing your spouse with a reasonable income. A term policy would provide cash if the father died; a short-term endowment policy would mature at the time needed.

If you choose a policy on your child's life, add a "payor insurance benefit." For a few extra dollars the premiums would be waived in the event of your death.

Protecting your family

The main purpose of life insurance is to provide your dependents with an income if you die. This applicant is married, has a young son, and is steadily employed at an average salary. On his 30th birthday, he arranges increased protection for his family.

His insurance agent proposes a whole life policy with a face value of $20,000, for an annual premium of $456. But should the worst happen (say the young husband dies in a hunting accident two years later), there would be a considerably greater estate.

The basic policy provides $20,000 of immediate death benefit to the benefi-

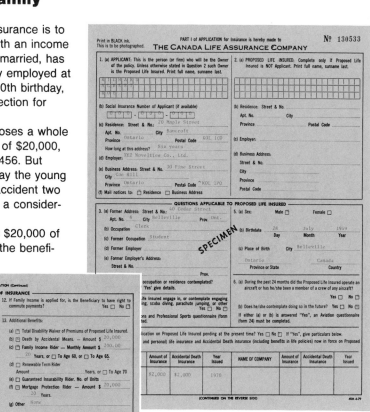

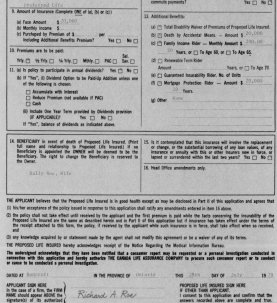

ciary (his wife). Then, because the policy offers additional benefits, his wife would also receive $20,000 for the accidental death benefit together with another $20,000 to pay off the mortgage on their new bungalow. Then, the family-income rider would provide an additional $200 a month for 18 years (balance of the 20-year benefit). That's a total possible payout in excess of $100,000.

NAMING A BENEFICIARY

Your marriage ends in divorce and you'd like to change the beneficiary on your life insurance policy.

Former spouses can't always be excluded from insurance benefits and don't automatically cease being beneficiaries when a marriage breaks up. Even if a man specifies that his beneficiary is "my wife, Mary Smith," and is subsequently divorced, Mary Smith continues as beneficiary: the designation "my wife" only serves to distinguish that Mary Smith from all others.

The legal situation is a little complicated. If you reside in a province other than Quebec, and you named your wife as beneficiary on or before June 30, 1962, she would then be in the "preferred" class, which included spouse, child, grandchild or parent. Your divorce on or after July 1, 1962, would move her from the "preferred" to the "ordinary" class, and you can freely change an "ordinary beneficiary" designation. If your ex-wife was named as beneficiary on or after July 1, 1962, and if the designation was "revocable," you still have nothing to worry about. Just as with the "ordinary" designation, you are free to name a new beneficiary. Get a "change of beneficiary" form from your agent or simply make the proceeds payable to your estate. If your ex-wife was designated as an "irrevocable" beneficiary, your rights are strictly limited. You cannot alter or revoke that designation—before or after divorce—without her consent.

In Quebec, the name of a spouse as beneficiary is irrevocable unless a revocability clause is written into the policy at the time of purchase.

TERM INSURANCE

Your neighbor contends that term insurance is the best deal. There must be some drawbacks.

"Term" provides protection for a stated period of time. If the insured dies within the term, the company pays the full amount of the policy. If you live beyond the term, the policy expires and it's worth nothing. It's a year-by-year gamble, and the cost jumps as you get older. You should buy insurance to cover a need: if you don't have an identifiable need, don't buy any insurance. If your needs are temporary, they're probably best covered by term.

Typical temporary needs are mortgage protection, income replacement while children are still dependent, and debt insurance—if, for example, you borrow $100,000 to start a business.

If you're the newest dentist in town, you will likely owe a large sum on your office equipment, so you should consider buying the biggest block of term insurance you can afford. If your wife is pregnant, the need is obviously greater still. You might even buy term with the idea of converting some of it to permanent insurance later on.

On the other hand, if your wedding's next month and you are earning a fairly good income, a whole-life policy might be more appropriate. This type of policy builds up a cash value and pays off whenever you die. If you remain in good health, you can always tack on an inexpensive term rider when temporary needs arise.

Term insurance can be made renewable and convertible; that is, the term can be extended quite cheaply and the policy subsequently converted to permanent insurance.

Before you switch. If your neighbor's policy sounds better than yours, you should still look carefully before you switch. Compare them item by item.

Note the features that are lacking in your policy. Jot down the premium. Is it payable yearly in advance or by installments? Make sure you know your neighbor's age at the time that his policy was issued; that's the key to all premium prices. If he was younger than you are now when he signed up, he'll be paying less for the same coverage. There's no way you'll get the same deal.

Tell your agent you are dissatisfied and want to be advised on whether your policy could or should be amended to include benefits similar to those of your neighbor.

Extra conditions (riders) can be added to your insurance to provide additional benefits in the event of death or disability. One such condition might be supplementary monthly income for the family should you die while your children are still young. Other riders might provide for doubling or trebling the policy's face value in the event of accidental death, or a monthly income if you should become totally disabled for more than six months. One or more such riders might put your policy on a par with your neighbor's.

By and large, all life insurance companies offer similar coverages. Should your circumstances change and you need a quite different type of policy, your present insurer will normally amend your existing contract to suit your needs. This will preserve the value of your premiums to date and the rate advantage of your original "age at issue," while avoiding any interruption in your insurance protection.

INSPECTION REPORTS

You are insuring your life for a large amount and the agent advises you that inquiries may be made about you. You take a dim view of such an investigation.

Unpleasant, but routine, it's called an inspection report. The insurer is mainly concerned with verifying the nature of your work and discovering your drinking, driving and other habits that may affect your life span.

The personnel office where you work will

The computer looks at John Doe

Life insurance is based on numbers, not personalities. The computer doesn't care if you are king or clown, Titan or tinker. You are just a statistic.

Nearly 300 years ago, the English astronomer Edward Halley drew up the first mortality tables, based on the life span of the average person at a given age.

Today, the computer, once given the essential data, takes only seconds to print out the costs and benefits of a life insurance plan.

The implacable tables tell the insuring companies that John Doe, Canadian, now age 30, has a further life expectancy of slightly more than 42 years. It has about doubled since Halley's time.

If John Doe is among the minority who don't make the full span, his insurance will be there to help his dependents. If he survives to retirement age, he can surrender the policy for cash, or take a monthly income to bolster his old-age pension.

CANADA LIFE

```
AN ILLUSTRATION FOR MR.  J  DOE              MALE AGE 30        JUL 10,1979

PLAN              PREFERRED LIFE

PREMIUM PAYABLE

    ANNUAL PREMIUM FOR SUM ASSURED OF        $10,000.00        $165.70
    FAMILY INCOME OF    $200.00 PER MONTH FOR 20 YEARS         $85.00
    WAIVER OF PREMIUM BENEFIT                                  $3.50
    ACCIDENTAL DEATH BENEFIT                                   $39.80

    TOTAL ANNUAL PREMIUM                                       $294.00

    MONTHLY PAC PREMIUM                                        $25.39

ACCUMULATION OF RETIREMENT FUND

    END OF      GUARANTEED      PAID-UP *      CASH VALUE*      TOTAL *
    YEAR        CASH VALUE      ADDITIONS      PD-UP ADDNS      CASH VALUE
      1            0.00           17.20           4.80             4.80
      2            0.00           48.50          14.00            14.00
      3          110.00          100.20          29.70           139.70
      4          240.00          174.60          53.30           293.30
      5          380.00          263.80          82.80           462.80
     10        1,100.00          932.90         337.70         1,437.70
     15        1,900.00        2,036.90         847.40         2,747.40
     20        2,780.00        3,620.80       1,719.90         4,499.90
     25        3,620.00        5,707.40       3,064.90         6,684.90
  AGE 60       4,490.00        6,357.50       5,022.90         9,512.90
  AGE 65       5,350.00       11,639.40       7,728.60        13,078.60

THE GUARANTEED CASH VALUE AT AGE 65 WILL PROVIDE YOU WITH A
MONTHLY LIFE INCOME - 10 YEARS GUARANTEED - OF                  $34.35

THE CASH VALUE OF DIVIDENDS AND INCOME DIVIDENDS
COULD INCREASE YOUR MONTHLY INCOME TO *                        $107.38

* THESE FIGURES INCLUDE DIVIDENDS WHICH ARE ILLUSTRATIONS BASED ON THE
  CURRENT DIVIDEND SCALE.  THEY ARE NEITHER GUARANTEES NOR ESTIMATES
  FOR THE FUTURE.  THE ACTUAL DIVIDENDS PAID WILL VARY WITH COMPANY
  EXPERIENCE.

BRANCH 0757      AGENT 99995                   E. & O. E.          F82

THE CANADA LIFE ASSURANCE COMPANY
```

probably be asked if your occupation is as described in your application and if it involves any serious hazards.

If the report indicates you are a highway menace on Friday evenings, practice high-wire walking in your backyard, or that your work requires frequent use of dynamite, the company will pause and reflect: its premiums are based on the kind of life the average person leads.

The Medical Information Bureau. Since 1902 this bureau has been exchanging medical information among member life insurance companies, enabling them to detect deceit or the nondisclosure of pertinent material.

The companies claim that the bureau and the inspection reports safeguard other policyholders by reducing the chances of a poor-risk individual getting insurance on the terms and rates offered to the good-risk applicant: when undue insurance losses occur, premiums will rise for all.

Provincial laws require that life insurance applicants must be told that an inspection report and a Medical Information Bureau inquiry may follow.

Inspection reports are not confined to life insurance applicants. A similar investigation will probably be carried out on your son when he first applies for automobile insurance.

PRESUMED DEAD

Your husband disappeared six months ago, on a wilderness fishing trip. His life insurance policy has a $50,000 accidental death rider.

As the beneficiary, apply to the courts for what's called a "declaration of presumption of death," but you will probably have a long wait for the money.

Your claim can ultimately be based on one of two sets of circumstances: evidence of death or probable death exists; or the insured is not seen or heard from for seven years and there are no indications he may still be alive.

The insurance company will probably advise you that if search parties or other sources find no evidence suggesting death, a seven-year wait is probable. It's important that the policy be kept in force. If you are financially pressed, ask your agent whether the premiums can be continued by way of a loan from the policy's equity.

If your husband's life insurance is a term policy, there will be no such equity. Then it's wise to pay each premium within the prescribed 30 days of grace. But policies vary, and in Quebec, for instance, the insurance may be reinstated under certain conditions if the policyholder applies to the insurer within two years of the date it was canceled for nonpayment of the premium.

Double indemnity. In order to collect double indemnity, it must be proved that the death was accidental.

Even if the body is discovered and identified, accidental death may be difficult to prove. Exposure, hunger and thirst are more likely causes of death in the wilds. Even an apparent drowning may have resulted from a heart attack, following such unusual (but voluntary) exertion as paddling through rapids.

INCOME OPTIONS

Your wife is a soft touch and you worry that, if you die, her spendthrift brother will persuade her to "lend" him some of the insurance payout.

Appoint an executor or trustee with authority and instruction to pay your wife a regular income instead of the lump sum.

You can also block the predatory brother-in-law by stipulating, at the time of purchase, that the balance of insurance remaining after capital expenses are met be paid only as monthly income. This is done by your selection, at the time of purchase, of a settlement option and by withholding, in writing, any right by your beneficiary to "commute"—that is, take a cash settlement in lieu of part or all of the income.

Settlement options vary. You could direct that the income be payable throughout your widow's lifetime, or that a stated monthly

Who gets the money?

When you insure your own life, you have the right to decide who will get the money if you die while the policy is still in force. And you also have the right to change your mind, unless you "irrevocably" named your spouse as beneficiary. In Quebec, you can't write a spouse out of your policy at all, unless you made a special stipulation at the time of signing up.

SUN LIFE ASSURANCE COMPANY OF CANADA
HEAD OFFICE: MONTREAL

Change of Beneficiary
(Death Benefit)

| POLICY/POLICIES | 000 000 | *Richard Albert Roe* |

With reference to the above-numbered Policy or Policies issued by Sun Life Assurance Company of Canada, I, the owner, change the beneficiary presently nominated to receive the proceeds as they become due by maturity on the death of the life assured/annuitant as follows:

See over for illustrations

PRIMARY BENEFICIARY OR BENEFICIARIES Show relationship to the life assured or the owner.	*My wife, Sally Roe*
CONTINGENT BENEFICIARY OR BENEFICIARIES IN THE EVENT OF THE DEATH OF ALL PRIMARY BENEFICIARIES Show relationship to the life assured or the owner.	*My son, Robert Roe*
SPECIAL PROVISIONS See over.	*In the event of the death of both of the above, the principal sum payable to my estate.*

Unless otherwise specified, surviving beneficiaries within a class (Primary or Contingent) will share equally. In the event of the death of the above-mentioned beneficiaries, the said proceeds will be paid to the owner, if living, otherwise to the estate of the last survivor of the owner and the beneficiaries.

If any of the alternative methods of payment has heretofore been elected for the proceeds arising from the death of the life assured/annuitant, such election is hereby revoked. The right to change the beneficiary and to elect a method of settlement is reserved.

Signed at *Bancroft, Ontario* this *28th* day of *July*, 19 *79*
Witness *Samuel Snow*   *R. A. Roe*
Occupation *Salesman*
Address *123 Central St.*

CAUTION — This form has been prepared by the Company for your convenience but is not suitable for all purposes. Make sure it will carry out your intentions before signing. The Company cannot be responsible for the effect or sufficiency of the completed form.

EXPLANATORY NOTES

Some specimen designations are printed below. More complex designations should be referred to Head Office for preparation of the form.

I	Primary Beneficiary or Beneficiaries	My wife, Mary Doe	II	Primary Beneficiary or Beneficiaries	My wife, Mary Doe
	Contingent Beneficiary or Beneficiaries			Contingent Beneficiary or Beneficiaries	My son, John Doe
III	Primary Beneficiary or Beneficiaries	My wife, Mary Doe and my son, John Doe	IV	Primary Beneficiary or Beneficiaries	John Doe as trustee under Trust Agreement dated July 1, 1970. Payment to the trustee will discharge Sun Life Assurance Company of Canada.
	Contingent Beneficiary or Beneficiaries	My parents, Harry Doe and Jane Doe		Contingent Beneficiary or Beneficiaries	
V	Primary Beneficiary or Beneficiaries	My wife, Mary Doe			
	Contingent Beneficiary or Beneficiaries	The children, if any, born of my marriage to the said Mary Doe			

SPECIAL PROVISIONS: This block is reserved for Common Disaster (Time Delay) clauses, appointment of a trustee for a beneficiary, etc. The exact wording for any such instructions should be obtained from Head Office or the Regional Service Centre.

amount be paid until the capital and applied interest are used up. Another choice might be monthly payments until she reached 65, when Old Age Security benefits would begin.

Before you restrict payment of the insured lump sum, allocate the amount required to pay off any capital debts. If you have a sizable mortgage, or if you're renting but you'd like your widow to have the security of a debt-free home, cash will be needed. Assign a policy, or part of your group insurance, to that purpose.

INSURABILITY

You have quit smoking since you applied for life insurance. You feel you should get a better rate now.

You'll no doubt be feeling better, and you may live longer, but spurning the weed is not grounds, on its own, for a premium reduction. Use or abuse of alcohol or tobacco is, however, among several factors that determine your degree of insurability. In rating you as a risk, insurance companies consider:

■ Age and sex.
■ Type and size of requested policy, including special benefit riders.
■ Occupation.
■ Places of residence and employment, including degree of travel.
■ Hazardous activities such as vehicle or boat competition, aviation, scuba diving.
■ Personal habits; extent of use of alcohol, tobacco or drugs.
■ Height and weight, with reference to fluctuations.
■ History of any serious illness or surgical operation.
■ Ailments as a child.
■ Your family's medical history.
■ Particulars from medical examination or statements made in the applicant's general declaration.

From these data, the company determines the class of the risk: (a) standard, (b) substandard or special, and (c) not insurable.

Since agents weed out unlikely candidates in the early stages, about 98 percent of applicants fall into categories (a) and (b). A third of the remaining 2 percent are pronounced uninsurable because of heart disorders.

If you have already been rejected by other companies, or are recently released from hospital after major surgery, the agent will probably suggest a retirement or other "non-insurance" type of plan. Maybe he'll propose a two- or three-month delay before you submit your application.

Abstainers' benefits. If you were rated as a substandard risk because you were a heavy smoker with possibly related bronchitis or habitual coughing, you might now be able to have the extra premium removed. This would most likely occur if you reapplied and were accepted as a standard risk.

Similarly, if you are paying an extra premium because of an occupational hazard—such as deep-sea diving—and you've now changed to less dangerous work, speak with your agent. Most companies delay one or two years before altering a rating because of a change of jobs, to ensure that the hazard is permanently removed. Many dangerous occupations offer high wages and insurance companies believe there is a cash temptation to return to that kind of work.

A similar waiting period will be imposed by your insurer if you give up sky diving or other risky pastimes.

Extra premiums are not permanent; they can and will be removed on submission of proper evidence. Frequently, an insurance company will make the removal retroactive if you had forgotten to provide details about your medical, occupational or recreational improvements earlier.

On the opposite score, if you are paying regular rates for your life insurance and later you join a flying club, your policy won't be affected. You would have been asked originally if you engaged in, or intended to engage in, activities such as boat racing, scuba diving, parachuting, sky diving, or flying other than as a passenger on regular airline flights. If you truthfully answered "no," your later decision to learn to fly cannot affect your existing insurance.

To increase your premium, the company

would have to prove that, when you applied for insurance, you had the *intention* of taking up private flying.

DETERRENT TO SUICIDE

Your neighbor committed suicide and his wife is worried that his insurance company won't pay.

Generally, the company will pay the full face value as long as the policy had been in force for two years at the time of the tragedy. The two-year stipulation is to discourage people who are contemplating suicide from buying insurance. Those who are serious about such a plan are unlikely to wait out a 24-month exclusion period.

It sometimes happens that a person who is in difficulty allows life insurance to lapse and then reinstates the policy by paying the overdue premiums. Federal regulations give policyholders 24 months to renew lapsed insurance and anyone whose insurable status has not worsened must be reinstated. The two-year exclusion for suicide begins on the date of such a reinstatement. If a policyholder commits suicide within this period, the beneficiary will collect only the premiums paid.

INSURANCE AS COLLATERAL

Even with your 20-year-old life insurance policy as collateral, the loan interest rate demanded by the bank still seems excessively high.

Dig out your old policy and read all the fine print. Unless the sum you need is considerably higher than the value of your life policy, chances are you can do a lot better by borrowing directly from your insurance company.

Your insurer is bound by the policy's original commitments. These include the offer of loan advances, usually up to 95 percent of the total cash value including dividends, at a set rate of interest. The interest rate was probably 7 percent or less when you bought your insurance 20 years ago. And with the interest rate on consumer loans running as high as 17 percent in November 1979, you can almost certainly more than halve the prospective interest rate on your loan by getting the money from your insurance company rather than from the bank.

Even if your policy's total loan value is less than the cash you need right now, it should still be worthwhile to borrow what you can

The contested claim

An insurance company has the right to assume that you fill out your application form truthfully and accurately. So if you lie or make misleading statements, the company can cancel the policy. But an unintentional misrepresentation is a different story. Say you forgot to mention a serious childhood illness, which comes to light five years later. At that stage, the company can't back out.

After a policy is in force two years, nondisclosure or misrepresentation—in the absence of proven intent to defraud—does not make the contract voidable. Those two years are known in the trade as the "period of contestability."

If you had understated your age by a few years, thereby paying less than the proper yearly premium for your life insurance, the company must pay the claim on your death. But it would not pay out the full amount of the policy's face value.

The law says the insurance payout shall be the amount that the premium you paid would have provided, had the policy been issued at the correct age. In other words, your beneficiaries will get just what you paid for. On the other hand, if you had overstated your age, thus paying a higher premium than necessary, there would be an increase in the payout.

from the insurance company at the low rate and then negotiate for the balance with your credit union or bank.

Numerous policyholders borrow from high-cost lenders, forgetting they have a lower-cost source of cash in their life insurance policies.

Out of creditors' reach. The policyholder who goes into debt needn't worry about creditors getting at the cash values building up in his life insurance, or at the policy proceeds if he should die, and leaving his beneficiaries out in the cold.

Creditors could certainly reach for those funds if your estate were designated as beneficiary of your insurance. But you will be safe on both counts if you name your wife or someone else as irrevocable beneficiary. That designation can't be altered without the beneficiary's written consent.

If you have specified either your spouse, child, grandchild or parent as a revocable beneficiary—alterable at any time without the beneficiary's consent—the funds are still beyond your creditors' reach.

However, a revocable designation of other than these relatives provides no protection against creditors *while you are alive and the policy is in force*. But when the insurance money becomes payable, either at maturity or at your death, it becomes an asset of the beneficiary and is not subject to the claims of *your* creditors.

CLIENT RECOURSE

Your life insurance application has been declined and you want to know the reasons. The agent insists he can't tell you.

Your insurance agent doesn't have access to the medical and inspection reports. These confidential documents go directly to the company's underwriting department and are kept there.

You'll waste your time if you badger the company for medical details. Instead, speak with your own doctor.

Getting impartial advice. If you have a problem or a complaint and you don't want to approach your local insurance branch office or agent, you can call The Life Insurance Information Center free of charge from anywhere in Canada. In British Columbia the number is 112-800-268-8663. From all other provinces, dial 1-800-268-8663 (English), or 1-800-361-8070 (French).

If you prefer to write, the address is The Life Insurance Information Center, Suite 1400, 55 University Avenue, Toronto, Ont. M5J 2K7. Letters in French should be sent to Association canadienne des compagnies d'assurance-vie, Service de l'éducation, bureau 1407, 666, rue Sherbrooke ouest, Montréal (Québec) H3A 1E7.

The Canadian Life Insurance Association operates the center as a public service. It has no sales affiliation—it won't even recommend any individual agent or company—and its staff is qualified to advise clients or to investigate complaints or grievances.

WAIVER OF PREMIUM

Your uncle has terminal cancer and encounters difficulty continuing the premium payments on a $35,000 whole-life policy taken out 10 years ago.

The objective should be to keep the policy in force for its full amount at the lowest possible premium outlay.

Check the policy for a possible total-disability benefit. This would allow for waiver of premium. At least one large Canadian company automatically includes the waiver-of-premium benefit with its whole-life policies and many companies recommend it where it's not automatic. Premiums are usually waived after six months' disability.

Also make sure your uncle has applied for the Canada or Quebec Pension Plan disability pension.

If a premium has not been paid within the 30 (or 31) days of grace, the policy will have been kept in force by automatic premium loans from the built-up cash value.

In the United States, most companies use a nonforfeiture benefit called "extended-term insurance" to continue a policy at full face value for a period dependent upon how long the policy has been in force. Most Canadian policies allow this extended-term insurance provision, but you must apply for it. On a 10-year-old policy, the extended term would be about 14 years without further premium.

This means that if your uncle survived the next 14 years, the term of insurance would be over and the company's liability ended. In essence, this scheme uses the policy's cash surrender value to buy term insurance of the same face value.

Better than borrowing. Assuming your uncle's policy contains the extended-term provision, and his life expectancy is short, using that provision makes better sense than payment by the automatic premium loan, which has to be repaid out of the proceeds at death.

Don't confuse "extended-term" with "paid-up" insurance—another nonforfeiture provision that cancels further premiums but substantially reduces the face value while retaining a cash value. In your uncle's case, retention of the cash value is unimportant because it becomes part of the $35,000 face value, paid when death occurs. Extended-term puts that cash value to work by extending the $35,000 policy for up to 14 years, which more than likely is longer than he will live.

Additional benefits contained in the policy are terminated when the extended-term option is exercised.

RESCISSION RIGHTS

You've increased your insurance but discover that you cannot afford the extra premium. You'd like to back out.

Most companies provide a "cooling-off" warranty called "rescission rights." This allows you to return your policy without explanation within 10 days of its receipt. Your premium will be refunded. Or you can ask to have the face value of the policy altered so that the reduced premium is more in line with what you can afford. Your agent would far sooner adjust the contract than permit the policy to become void. Lapses are expensive for the insured, the agent and the company.

Proceed with care if shortly after you buy insurance, another agent presents what appears to be a more attractive plan. If he knows you have just bought a policy from a competitor, he is flouting the industry's code of ethics. His tactics (called "twisting") are not always in the best interest of the insured. The Life Underwriters Association of Canada and provincial superintendents of insurance may even regard them as the offense of "replacement." Your best course of action is to ask for a written description of the alternative plan so that you can discuss it with the original agent. That way, you'll easily verify or disprove any claimed advantages.

33 Wills and gifts

Nothing in this book is more certain than this chapter to touch the life of every reader. Death awaits us all and we must leave behind family and friends. The making of a will is therefore a universal responsibility. If you die without family or friends—or if they're already well provided for—there are many worthy charities that would make good use of any gift.

Simple and inexpensive as it is to draw up a will, an astonishing number of adults still put it off—and off—and then accident or sudden illness intervenes. Those who die without a will are legally "intestate," and the law must move in to divide and distribute the estate according to a rigid formula, which can produce results far from the deceased's intention. Worse perhaps is the family squabble that can arise so easily over who gets the car, the heirloom silver teapot or the summer cottage.

It's a common error for an ordinary worker or pensioner to think that there's little of value to leave anyone. You shouldn't come to that conclusion without sitting down and making a thorough list of your possessions, your income and social benefits, your insurance and your prospects. For instance, is there any likelihood of your inheriting money or property? A retired waitress in San Jose, California, was left property worth $250,000 by a man she had smiled upon while serving him a hamburger. She didn't know his name or even remember the incident.

Naming a trusted executor to carry out your wishes is simple common sense. A lawyer who specializes in estate planning advises: "The smaller your estate, the more you need to plan. Big estates can often afford to make mistakes. Small estates can't."

Provincial legislation everywhere now recognizes the validity of the "holograph" will—a simple handwritten and dated document, written on just about any material and signed by the testator. (Such wills have always been accepted in Quebec.) But this reform may turn out to have been ill-considered. Lawyers and judges are either rubbing their hands or quailing on the Bench at the thought of thousands of persons—especially the elderly—scribbling new wills whenever the whim moves them. The distracted administrator of an Ontario senior citizens' home knows of one resident who wrote five holograph wills within the span of a few weeks.

DO IT NOW

Your son is pressing you to make a will and you feel his insistence is in very bad taste.

In a way, you should thank him. He's doing you a favor. Don't put off this vital task or you may leave your family, especially your spouse, in a bind. If you die without a will, the administration of your estate will be complicated by the fact that you have not appointed an executor. In most provinces, the Probate or Surrogate Court of your district must appoint someone. Obviously, it would be better to select someone you know and trust. Death without a will could result in your assets passing to people you don't wish to benefit—maybe relatives you can't stand. Also, people you would want to benefit, and who you thought would inherit, may receive less than you intended—or nothing at all.

In drawing up a will, you exercise the right to have your wishes carried out with a minimum of expense and delay. No matter what its size, you worked hard to build up your estate and you should call the shots. If you die without a will, your provincial government will act according to the inflexible Table of Intestate Succession, or on dispositions of the Civil Code if you are domiciled in Quebec. For example, it's a common error to believe that if a married man dies without leaving a will, all his property will pass to his surviving wife. It could work out that way, depending on the applicable provincial law and the amount of money left, but in a great many cases the widow fares much worse. If there were children, the widow could get less than two-thirds of her husband's estate.

Once you've signed a will, you are giving the orders. You "speak from the grave," as the saying goes. And you'll be obeyed—unless your orders are obviously unjust or frivolous. In that case, a judge may have the last say.

Your will names a person, or financial institution—say, a trust company—to settle your affairs and to dispose of your assets. You can direct your executor to gather in and protect your assets; pay your bills, taxes and any death duties; make gifts; provide a home and maintain your spouse for life; distribute insurance money; hold and operate your business; sell your property at the best price; make a donation to your church or charity; hold money in trust and pay it out for the maintenance, education and benefit of your children.

In most provinces, the executor can appoint a guardian to look after your children if both parents are dead. That appointment must be confirmed by a court, but your clear wishes will usually be upheld. While you can legally write your will on a stationer's form, or even on a scrap of paper, it's best to have a lawyer or, in Quebec, a notary prepare it. He'll ensure that all the *t*'s are crossed, thus lessening the chances of your will being successfully contested.

SPELLING IT OUT

You resist going to a lawyer to draw up a will because you don't want anyone to know what you possess.

That's not a valid reason for putting off the duty. Your instructions to a lawyer can be such that he would know almost nothing about the extent of your assets. You may say, for example, that your spouse is to receive three-quarters of your estate and the rest is to be divided among your children; or your spouse is to have everything but, if he or she dies before you, the children are to share everything evenly.

So it's not necessary for you to specify an amount or identify an asset; every bequest can be expressed in terms of percentages of your total worth. Not necessary—but not smart, either. To assist you properly, your lawyer should know what your assets are, at least the major items. With this information, he can advise you on the best ways to organize your bequests, or to dispose of some assets while you're alive. It's called "estate planning," and it takes two to play.

What is "everything"? Whatever you tell your lawyer must be held in strict confidence. If that pledge is broken, the lawyer will be in serious trouble with the governing body of the profession. And he could be sued under common law. If you trust your lawyer but not his secretary, ask that all notes pertaining to your assets be put in a sealed envelope with your will. But, be realistic; you've got to trust *someone*.

If you direct in your will that "everything" is to go to your spouse, that's not much good if neither your spouse nor anyone else knows what "everything" is. The beneficiary has to know in order to collect. The court has to know, too, before the will can be probated—that is, officially approved. In Quebec, the government has to know so that estate taxes, if any, can be calculated. Playing it too close to the vest invites trouble. Many widows have no clear idea of what their husbands owned. Some don't know where the husband banked, what insurance he had, whether he owned stocks, bonds or term deposits. If he had a safety-deposit box, they don't know where it's located.

Buried treasure. Survivors can spend years collecting what's due them if, for example, they don't know the name of the life insurance company involved. A staggering amount of money lies uncollected because of assets that never come to light. The famous comedian W. C. Fields trusted few people and no governments. He is believed to have stashed a large fortune in banks, keeping the locations strictly to himself. Some of the money was located, but much of it wasn't and now can't be. His beneficiaries didn't see the joke.

Apart from sheer laziness, reasons for not "getting around to" making a will include the superstition that it is somehow tempting the Grim Reaper. But not making one is surely inviting trouble after death: family squabbles, dissension, bitterness. Make a will that spells everything out exactly the way you want it to be—else the law will dictate the way it *has* to be.

THE LAW DIVIDES

Your grandfather dies suddenly and leaves no will. The family is already squabbling about his property.

Everybody should relax. Quarreling is pointless because, in these circumstances, the established and inflexible law will finally decide who gets what. A person who dies without leaving a valid will is said to have died "intestate." The estate will be divided and distributed according to rigid rules, first favoring the surviving spouse and children, if any, then sliding down the family tree as far as is necessary to find proper heirs. The rules of "intestate succession" vary somewhat from province to province, but they are all basically the same in structure. The law makes a will for a person who dies without one.

The law also decides who may apply for the position of administrator, the person who winds up the estate. The grant of "letters of administration" is made by the Probate or Surrogate Court, in most provinces, usually in this priority: (1) husband or wife; (2) child or children; (3) grandchild or grandchildren; (4) great-grandchildren or other descendants; (5) father; (6) mother; (7) brothers, sisters. If no relative seeks the position, a trust company, the public trustee or even a creditor may be appointed. In Quebec, the beneficiary heir is charged with administering the property.

Heirs at odds. The administrator's duties are similar to those of an executor named in a will. He collects all money that may be due and pays all bills. After receiving formal notice that no government claims anything from the estate, the administrator seeks unanimous agreement among the heirs on the distribution of the assets. If such agreement can't be reached, he will sell all the property and distribute the proceeds as the law directs. The estate must pay the administrator's fee.

If the heirs are squabbling over the property, the law takes over and ends the matter once and for all. Usually, once debts and, in Quebec, any estate taxes are paid, the deceased's spouse and children get everything. If the deceased wasn't married, or if the spouse died earlier and there are no surviving children, the next of kin inherit. If there are no kin, the provincial government gets everything. The intestate succession laws of most provinces provide for a surviving spouse to get a "preferential share" of the estate, with the balance, if any, to be shared with the deceased's "issue"—his children, grandchildren and other lineal descendants. The amount of the preferential share varies widely across the country, as does the rest of the family split.

A surviving spouse is entitled to receive a preferential share of $20,000 in British Columbia, $40,000 in Alberta and Saskatchewan, and $50,000 in Nova Scotia, Prince Edward Island and Manitoba, out of the net value of the estate, or the net estate, as the case may be. ("Net value" and "net estate" are defined slightly differently in each province.) The surviving spouse gets this payment whether or not there are any surviving issue or next of kin. In New Brunswick, a surviving spouse is not entitled to a preferential share. In Newfoundland, she or he can get $30,000 only if no issue survive; if issue do survive, the widow is entitled only to a distributive share as provided in the law.

Where an estate is less than the preferential share, the surviving spouse gets the lot. If the estate is greater, the surviving spouse is entitled to his or her preferential share together with his or her distributive share. In Nova Scotia, the surviving spouse is entitled to claim the home—the "principal residence"—in lieu of the preferential share, if the value of the home exceeds $50,000; where the value of the home is less than $50,000, it can form part of the share.

$75,000 off the top. In Ontario, the intestacy law determines that the deceased's spouse receives at least the first $75,000 and, if there are no children, the whole estate. If there is one child, the spouse receives the first $75,000 and shares any remainder equally with the child. If there are two or more children, the spouse receives the first $75,000 and one-third of any remainder, the rest going to the children. If there is no surviving spouse or child, more distant relatives inherit. If the deceased has left a will that deals only with part of an Ontario estate, the surviving spouse takes whatever benefits the will provides him or her, plus an amount that brings the share up to $75,000. He or she also receives a share of the rest of the estate if it is not disposed of by the will.

Where the estate or its net value exceeds the prescribed amount of the surviving spouse's preferential share and there are surviving issue, the excess is distributed as follows in all provinces except Quebec:

If spouse and one child or issue of a predeceased child survive: one-half to that spouse and one-half to the child or issue of predeceased child in equal shares.

If spouse and more than one child or issue of a predeceased child survive: one-third to the spouse and two-thirds to the surviving issue of the deceased in equal shares.

The Quebec difference. Where the surviving spouse and a child or other lineal descendant are left by the intestate in Quebec, the spouse gets one-third of the estate regardless of its value. The issue take two-thirds. If there is more than one issue, they share equally in the two-thirds portion. If the surviving Quebec spouse is the wife, she must, in order to inherit, abandon all her rights in any community of property—the "partnership of acquests"—that may have existed between herself and the deceased, as well as all rights of survivorship accruing to her under her marriage contract or by law.

If the husband is the surviving Quebec spouse, he must renounce his rights in the "partnership of acquests," or pay into the estate his share in the community of property, if any. Alternatively, he must forfeit all the rights and advantages conferred on him by the marriage contract, if there was one.

CONFLICTING WILLS

Your father has become absent-minded in his last years and has apparently written several conflicting wills and codicils.

It's a common and confusing problem. The courts are often asked to decide which of two or more wills should be enforced. Essentially, the object is to determine which document is the testator's "last" will and testament—a task that can require the talents of Sherlock Holmes and the patience of Job. Even those with small estates often leave large legal omelets to be unscrambled by the courts. A testator might make five different wills and a court rule that only the first is valid. Expectant beneficiaries can be left in the lurch after a judge has picked his way through a maze of conflicting documents, especially when they're the handiwork of the "do-it-yourself" testator.

The "last" will and testament is not necessarily the last in point of time. One or more of the more recent wills may be void because the testator was "not of sound mind" or was subject to "undue influence" at the time of execution. An earlier will might also be invalid because it failed to meet the formal requirements as to signing and witnessing.

A testator might have intended to revoke a will by mutilating or destroying it, but the law may regard it as no more than an *attempt* to revoke, because he or she didn't go far enough; if so, the previous will stands.

Out in the cold. Law books teem with examples of testamentary mishaps that led to wills being challenged in court. The common denominator in these often bitter battles is the person who was taken care of in one will and left out in another. If he's remembered in the first will and forgotten in the second, he argues that the second is invalid, or vice versa.

The bigger the estate, the more likely it is that there will be a fight.

A will is, by its very nature, revocable, either in whole or in part, by the testator. He can revoke an earlier will simply by saying "I do"—because, except in Quebec, matrimony itself wipes out a will made before marriage, unless the will states that it's made "in contemplation of marriage" and names the person the testator plans to wed.

Apart from marriage, the two main methods of revoking a will are the due execution of

'Being of sound mind...'

The most notorious of Canadian wills was that penned, in legally watertight phrases, by Toronto lawyer Charles Millar, who died on Oct. 31, 1926. A wealthy bachelor without dependents or relatives, Millar left the bulk of his fortune to the Toronto mother who, within 10 years of his death, would have given birth to the greatest number of children as shown by registrations under the Vital Statistics Act. If there was a tie, the money, about $750,000, was to be divided equally.

Millar was an advocate of birth control. He apparently believed that his eccentric bequest would shame the government of the day into legalizing information on birth-control techniques. Instead, when the Supreme Court of Ontario refused to alter the will, it sparked a "baby derby."

Eventually, each of four mothers with nine children received $165,000. Two other claimants who had borne 10 children in the decade—most of them stillborn or unregistered—were awarded $12,500 each. Husbands of three of the big winners were civil servants, and one of them was a war amputee.

Quite a few of the wealthy and celebrated appear to share a penchant for writing curious or unexpected bequests into their wills. Since they can afford the best of legal advice, their last wishes are seldom vulnerable to upset in the courts.

Millionaire William H. Baxter left an allowance to his two sisters provided they did not entertain any male friends in their home.

Actor William Gillette ordered that "no blithering saphead" be permitted to buy his estate in Connecticut, which boasted three miles of narrow-gauge railway complete with bridges and tunnels. It eventually became a state park.

Joseph Valachi, one-time gangster and author of *The Valachi Papers*, gave his entire estate to a spinster in Niagara Falls whom he had never met.

Novelist Maurice Dekobra left all his books and paintings to Papeete, capital of Tahiti. He thought they'd be safe there, being convinced that "the release of atomic energy means the total destruction of Paris, London, Washington and New York."

A Cadillac in fine condition was offered for $50 in a classified ad in Boise, Idaho. No catch. It turned out that the late husband of the lady who advertised the bargain had willed the proceeds of the sale of the car to his girlfriend.

London banker Harold West was scared of being buried alive. He left instructions that at death a stake was to be driven through his heart and his coffin was not to be screwed shut. His wishes were duly carried out in 1972.

Playwright Eugene O'Neill wrote a 1,300-word will for his Dalmatian, Blemie. It bequeathed "my collar and leash and my overcoat, made to order at Hermes in Paris," to the new pet that would someday replace him on the living room rug.

The most vindictive will ever drawn up was surely that of the Munich businessman who ordered that a wake be held upstairs in his home. When all the relatives were gathered around the coffin, the floor collapsed. Several were killed, or injured. Later it was discovered that all the supporting beams had been sawn almost through.

a later will or codicil, and a proper act of physical destruction. Many wills are not duly executed—in other words, not correctly drawn up and witnessed—and so do not replace an earlier one, and many wills that were thought to be destroyed are still effective in the eyes of the law.

A new will does not automatically revoke prior wills; it does so only if it contains a clause expressly canceling former wills, or if the terms of the former will conflict with the later will. A person preparing his own will might forget to revoke expressly all earlier wills, and so create a legal mess for his survivors. Wills drawn up by lawyers always include the necessary revocation clause.

The vital intention. If a person dies leaving two wills, both of them are valid as long as there is no conflict in their terms. If the court finds an inconsistency, the terms of the more recent will are followed and the conflicting terms of the earlier will disregarded. The general rule is that if a gift is clearly given in a will, it won't be taken away unless the second will, or a codicil—which is an addition or supplement—clearly instructs otherwise. The intent of the deceased is the all-important factor.

The testator's intention is also of primary importance in the case of a will that's been destroyed. Did he mean to destroy it, or was it destroyed by accident? Did *he* destroy it, or did someone else? Was it so destroyed that it must legally be disregarded?

The wills legislation in all provinces states that a testator who wants to revoke his will physically must "burn, tear or otherwise destroy" it himself, or direct someone else to do so and be present when it is done. "Tearing" includes cutting; but "otherwise destroying" does not include mere cancellation. In an Ontario case, the testator wrote "canceled" across the face of the will and signed it. The court ruled that this didn't amount to revocation. Partial destruction won't suffice either, unless the part destroyed is so important as to lead to the conclusion that the rest of the will could not have been intended to stand.

If the physical act of destruction is done by another at the testator's request, but not in his presence, the act, no matter how complete, is not revocation. In such a case, a copy of the will or written evidence of its contents, or even oral testimony, may be accepted by the court.

If the testator's wife threw his will in the fire and he said "so be it," or words to that effect, it would not legally be canceled because the act of destruction wasn't done at the testator's direction. If a testator crumples his will and throws it in a wastebasket, he has not revoked it, because there is no completed act of destruction. If someone comes along later, empties the wastebasket and burns the will, it's still not revoked.

Sometimes it's only a case of partial revocation. In a Nova Scotia case, a will had been mutilated by scissors and certain clauses cut out, but it was admitted to probate because one of the clauses cut out was pinned back in another place. Whether the revocation is total or partial depends on the part excised. If the essence of the will is destroyed, there is total revocation, unless the act can be explained satisfactorily. In one case, the testator's signature was cut from the will and then pinned back on. The court ruled that the will had been totally revoked.

If the act of destruction is unintentional, it will have no legal effect, provided there is satisfactory evidence it wasn't intended. In an Alberta case, the testator tore his will into pieces, but then put all the pieces in an envelope which he kept until his death. The argument that he had intended to revoke his will didn't stand up because he had kept the pieces of the torn will and not made a new one.

Power of the postscript. A will can be revoked partially by a codicil—a separate document. It does not usually take the place of or totally eliminate the existing will. It has the effect, however, of making a new will that contains the same provisions as the old except for changes and new provisions. It's a legal postscript to the will. Even if a will has been revoked, it can be reinstated by a codicil stating that the former will is once again in force. A codicil can be revoked, too, but this must be done in a separate document. The revocation of a will doesn't automatically revoke a codicil to it.

When rival claimants fight for recognition

of competing wills, long and expensive lawsuits can chew up most of the estate. A well-known Toronto lawyer once quipped that it was a shame when things went smoothly because "the assets were frittered away among the beneficiaries."

UNDUE INFLUENCE

You are cut off without a cent in your father's will. He leaves everything to an obscure religious sect.

The courts are always loath to deny to anyone—dead or alive—the right to dispose of property as he or she alone sees fit. The will is "speaking from the grave" in your father's case. However, if you believe he was unduly influenced by others when he made his will, or lacked the mental capacity to understand the consequences of what he was doing, you can contest the validity of the will in court.

Look before you leap. Retain a lawyer to investigate all the circumstances. It's possible your father knew exactly what he was doing and meant just what he said, especially if your mother had died earlier and there are no legal dependents. Adult sons and daughters are not dependents unless they are totally supported by the parent for defined reasons.

When a will is successfully contested, the deceased is ruled to have died "intestate" and you, and other immediate family, might well inherit his estate. The judge, of course, knows that, and it may give him reason to suspect your motives. Remember, too, that you could be liable for heavy legal costs if your attack fails.

The state of mind. As a general rule, a person must be "of sound mind, memory and understanding" to make a valid will. A man who makes a will is called a testator—a woman, "testatrix"—and must possess what is called "testamentary capacity." The courts insist that a testator must meet the following conditions:
■ Understand what he is doing—that is, grasp clearly that he is giving his property by will to others;
■ Understand, comprehend and recollect the nature and extent of his property;
■ Understand the persons he might be expected to favor or benefit by his will;
■ Understand the claims of those persons he is excluding, and the extent of what he is giving to each beneficiary.

When you contest a properly executed will, common grounds for attack include circumstances where a testator is visited by delusions, or his mental powers are reduced due to advanced age, or where he suffers from alcoholism or some other disease affecting mental capacity. An insane delusion is a belief that has no basis in reason. In an Ontario case, a will was thrown out of court when it was established that the testator thought his daughter had wired his wheelchair to give him electric shocks. It must also be shown, however, that any delusion affected the exercise of testamentary capacity.

The slowing up of mental processes due to age is not, in itself, *senility*; that's a question of fact in each individual case. Goethe completed *Faust* in his 83rd year. Also, the fact that a person is not capable of managing his affairs is not conclusive proof.

Testamentary capacity. If the executor has established testamentary capacity of the testator and due execution of the will, it may still be set aside if fraud or deliberate influence is proved. That proof must be provided by the party making the allegations. Probate is refused if there is evidence of "undue" influence exerted by a third party. "The undue influence," one authority says, "must destroy the free agency of the testator." It must relate specifically to the making of the will, not to some other matter or transaction.

In a noted English judgment, followed in Canada, the court ruled: "Such influence must amount to a control over the testator's mind, subjecting his mental will to the desire of another, so that the document executed as his will is not in reality his will, but that of another."

If a will is prepared by, or on the instructions of, a person who is a beneficiary, this raises "suspicious circumstances." In British Columbia, a judge rejected a will prepared by a son for his 93-year-old mother. It bequeathed the entire estate to himself and his sister, excluding nephews and nieces who would have shared in an intestacy. The judge was not satisfied that the testatrix had proper knowledge of the contents of the will and that she had approved its contents.

Persuasion doesn't amount to undue influence. In the classic example of the pretty young thing marrying the septuagenarian and soon inheriting his fortune, the outraged family can do little but accept the situation philosophically. There must be an element of coercion to make influence undue. The degree must be such that "the testator has been put in a condition of mind that if he could speak his wishes to the last he would say, 'This is not my wish but I must do it.' "

SIMULTANEOUS DEATH

Your father and mother made identical wills leaving "all earthly possessions" to each other. They die together in a car crash.

When it's impossible to know which person died first, statutory "survivorship rules" come into play: the law simply presumes certain things to be so. In all provinces except Ontario and Quebec, if two or more persons die at the same time—or if it's uncertain which of them survived the other—the deaths are presumed to occur in the order of seniority. It means that if your mother was younger than your father, she inherits under his will, and what she inherited then passes on to the beneficiaries in her will. If your father was the younger, it works the other way around. In Quebec, the male is presumed to have survived the female.

Different statutory rules, often producing a different result, apply in the case of the proceeds of life insurance policies. In a "common disaster," the person named as beneficiary is deemed to have died before the person who took out the policy. Insurance law would rule that the proceeds of your father's policies be paid to his estate because your mother, the beneficiary, is deemed to have died first.

In Ontario, the law says that in the event of a common disaster, the property of each person involved is disposed of as if each had survived the other. Thus, if a husband and wife die together, each person's property will pass in accordance with the terms of that person's will; if there is no will, it will pass to that person's next of kin in accordance with the laws of "intestate succession."

Against the chance of "simultaneous death," and to make certain that their assets go where they really want them to go, husbands and wives should both have wills with a "survivorship clause." The clause states that nothing is to go to the other unless he or she survives for a stated period—perhaps 30 days.

PROMISED LEGACY

You have cared for a friendless old man for 10 years. He dies in your home, leaving no will—but half a million in securities.

Even though your motives were entirely unselfish, you have the right to ask for a reasonable amount from the estate. You should do so promptly, before everything is distributed to the next of kin under the laws of intestacy. If the person who is appointed administrator of the estate won't honor your claim, you could sue for it. On the face of it, your chances are good. One of the administrator's main duties is to see that the deceased's "just debts" are paid. The question is whether your claim can be regarded as a debt.

Where services have been rendered by one person to another and are of a kind that are "generally paid for," the law presumes a promise to pay for them. However, if "the conduct, situation and relation" of the parties are such that the services were performed for reasons other than money, the court won't award compensation. Services provided within the family—even tender loving care given at a financial sacrifice—are usually treated as having been performed "gratuitously."

Your claim as the Good Samaritan could be based on the existence of a contract, usually oral, between the deceased and yourself; maybe your elderly friend said you'd be "taken care of" for your kindness. Otherwise, you could argue that the deceased's estate would be "unjustly enriched" if you aren't now paid whatever the services were "reasonably worth."

Judges have ruled in the past that there can be no "unjust enrichment" if both parties believed that any services rendered were gratuitous. For example, claims by common-law wives have been struck down because the court felt that the woman did not expect remuneration, but was content to accept the lodging provided by the deceased and to live with him. It is incidental that she might have hoped he would marry her and leave her his property.

If your old house guest was not a relative, it can't be argued that you performed services out of "natural love and affection." Your claim is bolstered by the fact that the old gent said he'd look after you, implying that he'd leave you a bequest. Even if you cannot produce a witness to swear he actually said that, the courts have ruled that while corroboration is desirable, it's not essential. The obvious fact of your decade of care would probably be considered sufficient proof of the validity of your claim.

HEIRS AND WITNESSES

You are dismayed to learn that you cannot receive a legacy under your uncle's will because you are one of the witnesses.

When a beneficiary is also a witness to a conventional will, there is room for speculation that the testator may have been the subject of "undue influence." It can flatly rule out any chance of the person concerned receiving the legacy mentioned.

Your uncle had obviously made out a conventional or "English" form of will, and the laws of all provinces set out rigid rules regarding the witnessing of the document. The will must be in writing—not, for example, on a cassette—and must be signed at the close by the testator, or by some other person in his presence and by his direction. The testator must make, or acknowledge, his signature in the presence of two or more attesting witnesses. The witnesses must be over the age of majority and they must not be beneficiaries named in the will, or their spouses, or persons claiming through such beneficiaries.

In some provinces—British Columbia, New Brunswick and Saskatchewan, for example—a bequest to a beneficiary or spouse who witnessed the will is automatically washed out. The person eliminated is permitted, however, to swear that he or she saw the will signed; this helps to "prove the will" and preserve the legacies of those who didn't run afoul of the regulations.

In Alberta, Manitoba, Nova Scotia and Newfoundland, beneficiaries who would otherwise be cut out by this rule are saved if the will was also witnessed by two other persons whose signatures don't pose problems. This is limited protection, though, because most wills have only two witnesses. Ontario goes a large step farther. Any gift to a witness who is also a beneficiary won't be canceled if the court is satisfied that "no improper or undue influence" was exercised on the testator.

It's best to do things right the first time. In 1978, a Supreme Court judge in British Columbia ruled that a large bequest was void because the beneficiary's wife had witnessed the will. Incredibly, the lawyer who prepared the will had asked her to be a witness. The judge said that while he was convinced the wife had no ulterior motive, the law was the law. She got only one-fifth of the estate, instead of the third she would otherwise have received. Because of his negligence, the lawyer had to make good the difference—about $12,000—and also pay the legal costs.

HANDWRITTEN WILLS

Among your father's papers is a typewritten sheet entitled "My Last Will and Testament." It is signed, but not witnessed.

Whatever its contents, it has no legal standing at all. It looks as though there's been a terrible mix-up caused by Dad's misunderstanding of "holograph" wills. Derived from the Greek words, *holos* for whole and *graphe* for writing, a holograph will must be wholly handwritten by the testator and signed by him. No other formalities are required—not even witnesses. But, since the document we're discussing was typewritten, it cannot be regarded as a holograph will. Such wills are recognized for all purposes in Alberta, Saskatchewan, Manitoba, Ontario, Quebec, New Brunswick, Newfoundland and the Territories. The holograph must reveal the testator's *intent* that it form a will; in legalese, it must be "testamentary." The Supreme Court of Canada has ruled that a holograph isn't testamentary "unless it contains a deliberate or fixed and final expression of intention as to the disposal of property upon death."

The tractor that talked. Just because your province permits the making of a holograph will doesn't mean that's the kind *you*

should make. They're really intended for use in an emergency. If the danger of sudden death passes, you'll be well advised to have a new, conventional will drawn up by your lawyer. A Saskatchewan farmer, pinned under his tractor, scratched his last wishes with his penknife on the fender of the machine. He died and after proof of the validity of his words and signature was given, the fender was admitted to probate as a holograph will. The fender was removed from the tractor, the relevant part cut out and presented in court.

A whimsical Englishman wrote a holograph will on the shell of his breakfast egg. The court threw it out. The judge decided the testator was cracked. But the will of a shipwrecked naval officer scratched on a plank of wood was held to be valid.

Special consideration is given to the testamentary statements of armed services personnel on active duty, or sailors at sea. The

Calling all creditors

Before an estate can be distributed, all "just debts" of the deceased must be paid. Even if your provincial law does not insist that an advertisement be placed in the papers, it's a sound practice.

NOTICE TO CREDITORS AND OTHERS

IN THE ESTATE OF SALLY ROE, DECEASED

All persons having claims against the Estate of SALLY ROE, late of 432 Maple Lane, Anywhere, Manitoba, K2C 2P7, Teacher, who died on or about February 8, 1980, are hereby notified to send particulars of same to the undersigned on or before June 1, 1980, after which date the aforementioned estate will be distributed by the undersigned having regard only to the claims then filed.

Dated March 30, 1980.

> Prudent Trust Company,
> 123 Main Street,
> Anywhere, Manitoba,
> by Snow & Associates,
> its solicitors herein.

serviceman or sailor in such circumstances, even if underage, may dispose of personal property by an unwitnessed will.

One danger of the holograph will is that the signature of the testator must be proved. With the conventional will, that is achieved by the added signatures of the attesting witnesses. Another danger lies in the interpretation of such common terms as "my family," "my heirs," "my next of kin." The testator knows what they mean to him, but he's no longer around to explain them exactly to a judge.

An experienced lawyer won't allow fuzzy terms or definitions. He will also prod you to recheck your will every few years. Any change in your marital status, a birth or death in the family, or other major changes in your life or the lives of your loved ones, can make a change in your will both desirable and necessary. If you move to another province or country, have a lawyer check your will to see if anything should be changed to conform with the laws of that place.

In a few cases, courts have validated those parts of unwitnessed wills that were *handwritten* on the printed will forms available at the stationer's. But the clauses based on the *printed* part of the form were not admitted to probate. Thus the documents were riddled with holes, including such vital items as the appointment of an executor. Other courts have totally rejected such wills. If anyone insists on using the inexpensive printed form, he or she should make sure it is witnessed by two persons, in compliance with the rules governing conventional wills.

UNPAID DEBTS

A close friend, who owes you $1,000, dies suddenly while you are traveling abroad. Now his estate has been distributed.

You're probably out of luck unless you hold a promissory note from the deceased—that is, a written, signed promise to repay the debt either "on demand" or by a given date. A simple IOU would suffice, provided it is signed and bears the date of repayment.

Before any estate is wound up, the executor or administrator should publish an advertisement for creditors' claims. If that's not done, the responsible person has to assume liability for any debts of the deceased discovered after the assets have been distributed. Assuming the advertising requirement is fulfilled, the legislation protects the executor or administrator who distributed the assets, but does not usually cancel the right of an overlooked creditor—or someone who did not see the ad—from attempting to get satisfaction from those persons who shared in the distribution of the property.

If the public call for creditors is not made in strict compliance with the regulations—and the provincial requirements vary—the distribution of the estate can be delayed. In Ontario, for example, the administrator may not distribute assets until one year after the death of an intestate. If any legal debt should be discovered after distribution, the beneficiaries are liable to the administrator for their respective *pro rata* share of the payment.

Follow the form. Where publication is demanded by law, the form and frequency are usually set out in the relevant statute. For example, British Columbia requires publication of a notice to creditors in the provincial *Gazette* and in a newspaper circulated in the county in which the deceased resided, or in which the creditor resides. The ads must be published twice each week for two consecutive weeks, or once a week for four consecutive weeks. Distribution of the estate may be made 21 days after the last date of publication.

In some provinces, the nature and contents of the notice are not set out formally, but general principles have developed over the years and it would be wise to follow them closely. The advertising department of any newspaper will show you the form. (*See* "Calling all creditors," page 409.)

Publishing the correct notice does not exonerate an executor or administrator if he had actual notice of a claim before distribution, even though the creditor did not file a claim in response to the ad. It sometimes happens that an executor has properly advertised for creditors and then paid all the debts in full. Then another creditor appears with a valid claim but there's no money left. The executor is in the clear; the unpaid creditor's recourse is to compel the paid creditors to refund the amount they received in excess of the amount that would have been payable to them had all the claims been known.

The enforceable debt. The executor or administrator must pay all debts of the deceased that are enforceable. After paying the funeral expenses and any duties or taxes, he must pay the "just debts" and satisfy all proper claims against the estate. In all provinces except Alberta and Quebec, the law authorizes payments on evidence that the executor thinks is sufficient. This is a pretty wide discretion, but decisions must be "reasonable and prudent." Before paying a debt or satisfying a claim, he must be satisfied that it is, in fact, enforceable.

That probably rules out your verbal claim that your old buddy owed you a grand on a handshake loan.

UNJUST DIVISION

Your husband left little to you but a large amount to another woman. You are determined to "do something about it."

If you live in a province that offers dependents' relief, you should consult a lawyer promptly. Application must be made within six months of the date of the grant of the letters probate, unless an extension is granted by the court. It's not so long since your husband, or anyone else, had the ironclad right to dispose of his personal property in any way he saw fit, no matter what insult or hardship might have resulted. Nowadays, in all provinces except Newfoundland and Quebec, dependents are protected from being left destitute, or worse off than they "reasonably" should be.

These "dependents' relief" laws are invoked frequently to clear up the chaos left by testators who have ignored their responsibilities. Generally, the courts can make whatever orders they consider adequate for the proper maintenance and support of a testator's dependents. Some of the statutes—for example, those of Ontario and Nova Scotia—spell out in detail the factors to be considered by a judge hearing an application for maintenance. They include the financial circumstances of the dependent, any provision the testator made during his lifetime for the dependent, any service rendered by the dependent to the testator. In effect, the judge can look into just about anything in determining whether adequate provision has been made, and in redressing any injustice.

The milkman's reward. In 1979, Justice Roger Ouimet of the Quebec Superior Court threw out the appeal of a Roman Catholic priest that his sister's will be ruled invalid. The woman had left the larger part of her $1.3 million estate to her milkman and his wife, who had befriended her in her later years. The priest argued that his sister was senile and under "undue influence" when she drew up her 1973 will. The judge didn't agree.

The adult children and former wife of the late Charles Lachman, cofounder of the Revlon cosmetics empire, gave up their legal battle to upset his will which left half of his $30 million estate to his bride of one year. Lachman died at 81; the second Mrs. Lachman, a former French countess, was said to be "about half his age."

Only dependents have any chance of consideration, but the definition of "dependent" varies. Generally, it includes a spouse and a child of the deceased. But in some provinces—for example, Prince Edward Island and Ontario—the class of dependents has been extended to include a common-law spouse and a parent or grandparent of the deceased. Ontario also includes a brother or sister to whom the deceased was providing support immediately before death. A former spouse can apply if he or she had been receiving support from the deceased.

In British Columbia, Alberta, Saskatchewan, Manitoba and Prince Edward Island, illegitimate children may apply if they were dependent on the deceased. The same is true in Ontario, where the legal doctrine of illegitimacy has been abolished anyway. Ontario law now recognizes only "children," whether they are born in or out of wedlock. In British Columbia, only the illegitimate child of a deceased woman may apply.

In Alberta, Saskatchewan, Manitoba, Ontario and Prince Edward Island, dependent's relief applications will be heard if the deceased died without leaving a will. The applicant would have to prove that the share of the estate that would pass to him or her under the laws of "intestate succession" is not adequate. New Brunswick law permits an application to be brought in the case of a "partial intestacy."

The court first faces the difficult task of determining whether the testator made adequate provision for the dependent applicant. If the answer is "no," what *would* be adequate? In the words of a famous judgment, the court should "consider whether the testator has been guilty of a breach of that moral duty which a just, but not loving, husband or father owes toward his wife or toward his children. If the court finds that he is guilty of such a breach, it is its duty to make such an order as appears to be sufficient, but no more than sufficient, to repair it." Some judges balk at assessing "moral duty." They consider they must determine whether the testator made provision "within a range of reasonableness. Not how much *ought* to have been provided, but whether the bequest was adequate." One judge noted: "It does not mean that you can only give the dependent just enough to put a little jam on his bread and butter." Another ruled that a testator should leave enough "to enable the dependent to live neither luxuriously nor miserably, but decently and comfortably according to his or her station in life."

GIFT VERSUS TRICKERY

Shortly before she died, your mother gave your older brother power of attorney. He withdraws $50,000 from her account and claims it was a gift.

In the wrong hands, a power of attorney can be a lethal legal weapon. It made your brother a "fiduciary," a person in a position of special trust. But the law is careful to guard against such a person profiting from his trust, unless expressly authorized. He must ensure that his duty and his personal interests don't conflict. If you doubt that a gift was intended, you should see a lawyer immediately. When challenged, your brother must rebut the accusation that he obtained the money by duress or undue influence. He'd have to show convincing reason why it was a gift.

Except in Quebec, a gift *inter vivos*—between living persons—cannot be revoked once completed. An English judge stated three centuries ago: "If a man will improvidently bind himself up by a voluntary deed and not reserve a liberty to himself by a power of revocation, this court will not loose the fetters he hath put upon himself, but he must lie down under his own folly."

But a gift *inter vivos* must be a valid one. Sometimes, because of the relationship of the parties, the courts will infer that undue influence was probably exerted. Judges look searchingly at cases involving parent and child, guardian and ward, solicitor and client, spiritual adviser and pupil, doctor and patient.

When checking for undue influence, the judge need not restrict his examination to family or legal relationships. He can extend it to any transaction in which it can be shown that the person who benefited had influence, or was in a position to exercise influence, over the donor. But the courts don't upset every gift transaction where there's a special relationship. "The court," according to an oft-quoted ruling, "will not undo a trifling benefit conferred by one person to another, standing in a confidential relation to him, unless there be bad faith."

Every set of circumstances differs, and judges often face the most tangled situations. In an Ontario case, a wife was mentally and physically weak when she handed money over to her husband. When this *inter vivos* gift was challenged, the court decided she could not appreciate the nature and effect of the act, which would deprive *her* children by her first husband of the money, and enable her second husband to give it to *his* children by a former wife.

Tiger Dunlop's Testy Testament

Dr. William "Tiger" Dunlop is one of the legendary pioneers of Upper Canada. Born in Scotland in 1792, he served in Canada as surgeon to the 89th Regiment in the War of 1812. His book, *Statistical Sketches of Upper Canada*, published in England in 1832, is credited with attracting many settlers to his forested tract near Goderich, in southwestern Ontario. Before his death, at 56, the bachelor Dunlop drew up his will, revealing that his life as a backwoods laird had not diminished his sardonic sense of humor. Dunlop's signature was attested to by three witnesses. Appended to the document was the following statement by John Prince, Q.C., of Montreal:

"The will is eccentric, but it is not, on that score, illegal or informal. To a mind who knows the mind of the testator, it will remain a reflect of his perfect indifference (an indifference to be admired, in my opinion) of what is called 'Fashion' even in testamentary matters. I conceive it to be a just and a proper Will, and no person can question its legality in point of form or substance."

In the Name of God, Amen.

I, William Dunlop, of Garbraid, in the Township of Colborne, County and District of Huron, Western Canada, Esquire, being in sound health of body, and my mind just as usual (which my friends who flatter me say is no great shakes at the best of times) do make this my last Will and Testament as follows, revoking of course all former Wills.

I leave the property of Garbraid and all other landed property I may die possessed of to my sisters Helen Boyle Story and Elizabeth Boyle Dunlop, the former because she is married to a Minister whom (God help him) she henpecks— the latter because she is married to nobody nor is she like to be, for she is an old maid and not marketrife, and also I leave to them, and their heirs, my share of the stock and implements on the farm, PROVIDED ALWAYS that the en-

closure round my brother's grave be reserved, and if either should die without issue then the other to inherit the whole.

I leave to my sister-in-law Louisa Dunlop all my share of the household furniture and such traps with the exceptions hereinafter mentioned.

I leave my silver tankard to the eldest son of Old John as the representative of the family. I would have left it to Old John himself, but he would melt it down to make temperance medals and that would be sacrilege. However, I leave him my big horn snuffbox; he can only make temperance horn spoons of that.

I leave my sister Jenny my bible, the property formerly of my great-great-grandmother Bethia Hamilton of Wood Hall, and when she knows as much of the spirit of it, as she does of the letter, she will be a more guise Christian than she is.

I also leave my late brother's watch, to my brother Sandy, exhorting him at the same time to give up Whiggery, Radicalism, and all other sins that do most easily beset him.

I leave my brother Alan, my big silver snuffbox, as I am informed he is rather a decent Christian with a swag belly and a jolly face.

I leave Parson Chevasse (Maggy's Husband) the snuffbox I got from the Sarnia Militia, as a small token of my gratitude, for the services he has done the family in taking a sister that no man of taste would have taken.

I leave John Caddle a silver teapot, to the end that he may drink Tea therefrom to comfort him under the affliction of a slatternly wife.

I leave my books to my brother Andrew, because he has been so long a Jungley Wallah that he may learn to read with them.

I give my silver cup with a Sovereign in it, to my sister Janet Graham Dunlop because she is an old maid, and pious, and therefore will necessarily take to horning, and also my Granna's snuff mull, as it looks decent to see an old woman taking snuff.

To quote yet another judge in a similar case, your brother must "prove clearly not only that the gift was made, but that it was the voluntary, deliberate, well-understood act of the donor, and that the donor was capable of fully appreciating, and did fully appreciate, its effect, nature and consequence."

A DYING MAN'S GIFT

Your father hands you the keys to his safety-deposit box and limousine and says, "It's all yours." He dies of cancer a few days later.

No doubt your father's executor is trying to get these assets back into the estate for distribution under the will, but you probably have every right to keep them. If there's a legal challenge, a judge must decide if your father made a valid *donatio mortis causa*. This is the legal term for "a gift in anticipation of death." Lawyers call it a "d.m.c." and it is very close in effect to a will.

Before it can stand, a d.m.c. must pass three strict tests:

■ The gift must be of personal property and must have been made in contemplation of death;

■ There must have been delivery to the recipient of the subject matter of the gift;

■ The gift must be made in such a way as to make it clear that the property is to revert to the donor if he recovers.

As in the case of a will, the donor may revoke the gift at any time before death. And, similarly, the gift is canceled if the recipient dies before the donor. Unlike a will, a d.m.c. must be made in contemplation of death—not death generally, but from "an existing peril." When the donor fears death from a particular illness, the gift is automatically revoked if he recovers.

If the validity of this sort of gift is challenged, the onus is on the challenger to prove that there was undue influence or other impropriety. But your word alone won't satisfy a judge that the car and contents of the safety-deposit box comprised a valid gift; you'll need some other evidence that confirms your father's intention. You don't need an independent witness, though; the surrounding circumstances might provide enough confirmation.

A gift made in contemplation of suicide is invalid. The donor must die from the illness or peril from which death was feared. And it's not enough if the peril is "ordinary to human affairs." A Toronto man was terrified of air travel, and just before flying to Winnipeg on a business trip he gave his girlfriend the keys of his car and the vehicle permit endorsed in blank. He had done this twice before and had told her that if he died on the trip, the car was hers. The man arrived safely in Winnipeg but while there he died of a heart attack.

When the case reached the courts, the trial judge said there was an effective *donatio mortis causa*. The Ontario Court of Appeal thought otherwise and ordered the woman to give the car back or pay the value of it to the estate. "There is no evidence that the deceased contemplated his death from any physical disability," the appellate judges ruled. The risks in air travel were "no more than the ordinary risks that affect man in his ordinary and natural movements and pursuits."

Housekeeper loses. If the donor gives away physical possession of an asset but retains "dominion and control" over it, there cannot be a valid d.m.c. That's what happened in the case of an Ontario man who gave several promissory notes to his housekeeper. The notes were payable to him and, on the back of each, he wrote, "If anything happens causing my death, this note is to be paid to (the housekeeper)." He had a heart condition but he continued to do business in the normal way, collecting money owed on the notes, until his death two years later. The housekeeper was ruled to have "possession only," and she lost that, too, when she was ordered to give the notes to the executor.

Giving the keys to a car or to a safety-deposit box is generally considered to be the same thing as giving total possession. The Ontario Court of Appeal ruled that when a man gave his wife the keys to his box, "he transferred to her the only means he possessed of getting at the contents of the box. He parted with the control and dominion over the contents and with his facilities for dealing with them."

Handing over a bank passbook does not, however, transfer ownership of any funds on deposit; the book is not considered "a necessary link" in the obtaining of the money.

THE FORGETFUL GIVER

Your daughter was given an emerald ring by an elderly recluse whom she befriended. His heirs are now accusing her of theft.

Lonely elderly folk who arouse the sympathy of neighbors or community social workers often turn out to have numerous family connections who jump out of the woods when death occurs. When there is a legacy of property at stake, it's remarkable how quickly and vociferously blood ties are revealed. It's not uncommon for elderly people to make substantial gifts to those who befriend and help them in their declining years. Chauffeurs and housekeepers are occasionally bequeathed fortunes, to the chagrin of family heirs. Attempts are frequently made to upset such legacies by heirs who claim that the donors were incompetent, or under undue influence.

If the prosecution's case rests primarily on the fact that the ring was bequeathed in a will, that does not in any way prove theft. Memories fade with age. An elderly person may bestow a gift on a new friend and completely forget that the item has already been bequeathed to a niece in a will drawn up years earlier. But we are all permitted the luxury of changing our minds. It can pose a knotty problem for the judge. He would decide the issue on the facts of the case.

Whenever anyone is given something of substantial value, it is good insurance to obtain a signed letter from the donor describing the gift. This would normally serve as a "deed of gift."

7 YOUR RIGHTS ON THE ROAD

34 You, the driver

Cars are getting lighter and smaller, becoming more fuel-efficient and polluting less. Highway design is changing to reflect concerns for safety and the environment. But redesigning cars and highways is a matter of engineering. The enduring problem is the way we drive and the attitudes we have toward driving. Changes in our driving habits are not keeping pace with improvements in cars and roads.

Driver-education courses in our high schools have begun to make some impact. Private driving schools are taking a hard look at themselves and the drivers they are turning out; they see the need for more rigorous instruction and testing. The Canadian Professional Driver Education Association wants legislation to weed out the fly-by-nighters and incompetents in the driving-school business. Laws and courts are getting tougher on offenders who won't accept the responsibility that goes with the privilege of driving.

The basic responsibilities are obvious: to drive safely and courteously; to refrain from drinking or taking drugs when you're driving; to maintain your automobile in a safe, roadworthy condition and to know and follow the rules of the road. The alternative is chaos—and with more than 11 million vehicles (and 11 million drivers!) on Canadian roads, it sometimes appears we are not far from that state.

The federal Department of Transport maintains that we have one of the highest rates of road deaths in the world. In 1978 there were 5,419 persons killed in traffic accidents in Canada—1,776 in Quebec alone.

We have grown up with the automobile, often taking for granted the freedom of movement it provides. Future generations may not have as much freedom. During our generation, we have seen speed limits go down and our cars actually become slower than cars of a decade ago: society has felt the need to put the brakes on. Engineers and designers have been told not to develop faster cars. Superhighways designed for speeds of 120-130 km/h are restricted to 100 km/h.

The reasons? Our driving is a major factor—too many deaths and injuries on our highways. The cost in human suffering and in dollars is too high. Another reason is the waste of energy: the big gas-guzzlers are being legislated out of existence.

Historians will write that this was the generation that reversed the trend toward ever speedier personal locomotion which began when man invented the wheel. Safer cars, driven at lower speeds on safer highways—that's probably half the solution. But the single biggest factor in the safety equation remains the person behind the wheel.

GETTING A LICENSE

After passing an expensive driving course, you fail the road test for a license.

No driving school will guarantee you a pass on a driving test; there are too many variables. Some beginners learn more quickly than others and there's also a tendency for new drivers to want to try the test before they're ready.

Most students' first question is, "How soon can I get my license?" Few ask, "How good a driver will I be when I'm finished?" Experts suggest it takes a minimum of 20 to 30 hours under ideal conditions for the average beginner to learn to drive properly.

In Quebec, where the curriculums of driving schools are regulated, students are required to take 30 hours of classroom study and at least eight hours behind the wheel. All Canadian driving schools are licensed and instructors are required to pass a special examination, but even the schools themselves, for the most part, feel these controls are weak and inadequate. Tests are not tough enough to weed out poor instructors who pass on their own bad driving habits to students.

Driving authorities are unanimous, though, that beginners should take a driver training course rather than learn from a relative or friend. As well as reducing the risk of learning bad habits, an approved course will pay for itself in lower insurance rates. But you should discuss the school of your choice with an insurance agent before signing up. Some driving schools give the impression you'll get lower insurance rates if you complete their courses. And students may find out too late that their particular school isn't recognized by insurance companies.

Obtaining a license. It is necessary everywhere to apply for a learner's permit before beginning to take driving instruction. Minimum age is 16, except in the Yukon and the Northwest Territories, where it is 15, and in Newfoundland, where it is 17. Many provinces require parental approval before they will issue a learner's permit to anyone under 18, and most also require an eye examination and a written test on basic knowledge of the rules of the road.

In all cases, learners are not allowed to drive without a licensed driver in the front seat beside them. Learners' permits are valid from 90 days to a year, depending on provincial regulations. A learner must be 16 before attempting to obtain a regular driving license anywhere in the country. Tests vary from province to province, but most jurisdictions require written and road tests.

Some provinces allow any number of attempts to pass the tests. Others figure that three or four attempts should be enough for anyone with basic skills to pass what is, after all, a fairly easy driving examination. After the tests, some provinces grant "new driver" or provisional licenses which can be withdrawn for traffic violations, or, in the case of young drivers, for crimes unrelated to automobile driving. Demerit-points systems are often applied more stringently to new drivers than to experienced motorists.

Some provinces simply issue "operator's" or "chauffeur's" licenses, the latter being endorsed to show the holder is permitted to drive public vehicles carrying passengers or freight. Where a license classification system is used, drivers take the tests in the class of vehicle they intend to drive. The minimum age is 18 and the tests are tougher for licenses to drive such vehicles as tractor-trailers, heavy trucks, buses and ambulances. Classifications vary, although several provinces use a similar, numbered or lettered, seven-class system.

Motorcycle licensing. Motorcycles are a different case because the learner must ride alone. All provinces require that an applicant for a motorcycle learner's permit take tests on basic rules of the road and skills in handling a motorcycle. This presents a sort of Catch-22 for novice motorcycle drivers. They must learn how to handle a motorcycle *before* applying for a learner's permit, but without a learner's permit they are not allowed to ride a motorcycle on public roads in order to learn.

There are three solutions: learn the basics of motorcycle riding on an off-road motorcycle, which does not require an operator's license; learn on a road motorcycle on private property; or take one of the 75 courses in motorcycle driving offered across Canada by the Canada Safety Council. The third is by far the best answer and, in some provinces, passing the course automatically qualifies a rider for a motorcycle license.

MEDICAL CANCELLATION

You have been informed your driver's license is being canceled because you have a mild form of epilepsy.

Many diseases and conditions, including epilepsy, poor eyesight and the general effects of old age, can result in a loss of driving privileges. Generally, epileptics who have not had a seizure for a year, or who can effectively control seizures with medication, are permitted to drive passenger vehicles. Standards for epileptics are tougher if they drive commercial vehicles.

Doctors and optometrists are required by law to report to the provincial licensing authority any condition that may make it dangerous for a person to drive. This may result in the cancellation or restriction of your driving license. And doctors are protected against any legal action that ensues from supplying medical reports on drivers.

Conditions that may lead to cancellation of a driver's license include fainting spells, heart disease, mental disorders, chronic alcoholism, narcolepsy (sleeping sickness), muscle control

Points system—merit and demerit

All provinces have provisions for appealing at least some license suspensions, including appeals on humanitarian grounds. Where suspension could present undue hardship, a probationary license may be issued, allowing the person to drive at specified times or for specific purposes. Probationary licenses are often issued on condition that you complete successfully an approved driver-improvement course. If you are not satisfied with the appeal board's decision, you can make a final appeal to a county or district court judge, who has the power to confirm, modify or set aside the board's decision.

All provinces except Newfoundland use a points system, under which your license can be canceled when you accumulate the maximum number of points allowed in a specified period. Most traffic offenses—except parking violations—add demerit points to your record. Manitoba has a system by which points may be "forgiven" after they have been on your record for a certain length of time.

Newfoundland has no points system, but first conviction of a driving offense under the Criminal Code carries a license suspension of four to six months. A subsequent conviction within two years brings a nine-month suspension. Magistrates may, in addition, suspend licenses for serious violations of the provincial highways code.

Points systems across the country vary only slightly and penalties range from one to three months for the first demerit-points suspension. The number of points you lose for different offenses also varies. For instance, failing to remain at the scene of an accident costs you only seven points in Alberta (where 15 is the maximum), whereas in Prince Edward Island the offense brings an automatic license suspension. Some provinces allow new drivers fewer points in their first years of driving.

Drivers automatically come to the attention of the authorities when they accumulate the maximum number of infraction points allowed in their provinces. These were the maximum points and penalties in each province as of 1979.

British Columbia: 10 points. Suspension at the discretion of the superintendent of motor vehicles.

Alberta: 15 points. Suspension for one month.

Saskatchewan: no fixed limit. Drivers convicted of two or more infractions in a two-year period may have their licenses suspended or restricted.

Manitoba: indeterminate. Review of driving record, possible retest or order to take driver improvement counseling. The system allows drivers with accident-free years to erase infraction points and accumulate merit points.

Ontario: 15 points. Suspension for 30 days.

Quebec: 12 points. Suspension for three months.

New Brunswick: 10 points. Suspension for three months.

Nova Scotia: 10 points. Suspension for six months.

Prince Edward Island: 12 points (15 if you have taken a safe-driving course). Suspension for six months and no reinstatement before completion of driver-improvement course.

Newfoundland: no points system.

disorders and some forms of diabetes. There are others, and physicians normally judge patients' fitness to drive on a case-by-case basis. Some conditions—alcohol and drug abuse, for example—are curable: If you lost your license because of such abuse, and have since conquered your addiction, you can appeal to have your license reinstated.

Drivers who have lost their licenses for medical reasons often become angry with doctors or optometrists for "squealing" on them. They forget that doctors have a legal and moral responsibility to their patients and to the community. It is foolhardy and dangerous to drive with a condition that could cause an accident.

Licensing authorities will generally take into consideration the amount and type of driving done by drivers facing cancellation of their license. Mild disorders or the effects of aging, which might make it dangerous to drive in rush-hour traffic in large metropolitan areas, may be tolerable if the person is willing to drive only in more tranquil times and places. Some licensing authorities will restrict drivers with failing eyesight to daytime driving only, a restriction that is usually noted on a person's driving license, as, of course, is the need to wear eyeglasses.

Commercial licenses. Some medical conditions are more serious for drivers of commercial vehicles. The fatigue factor involved in driving heavy trucks or driving for long periods of time—as a cabbie does, for instance—can present serious problems with certain ailments or conditions. In some provinces, commercial drivers are required to have regular medical checkups as a condition of keeping their licenses. The licensing authority provides doctors with a list of medical criteria.

Many physically handicapped drivers are able to operate specially equipped motor vehicles quite safely. Cars with hand controls which enable a handicapped person to operate the foot pedals are fairly common. Your personal physician, organizations for the handicapped, or the Canadian Medical Association, 1867 Alta Vista Drive, Ottawa, Ont., K1G 0G8, can provide information about driving aids for handicapped persons.

SPEED LIMITS

You receive a speeding ticket for allegedly driving at 54 km/h in a 50 km/h zone.

Most police officers will ignore speeds of up to 5 or 10 km/h over the posted limit, except when road conditions—ice, snow, rain, fog—require a speed lower than the "normal" limit. Canadian courts almost always accept radar readings as incontrovertible evidence of speeding. Trying to fight a speeding ticket against radar evidence is generally a waste of time and money. About the best you can hope for is a sympathetic judge who may reduce the penalty if there are mitigating circumstances. Pleading a broken speedometer, or that you were hurrying to get to work on time, won't help your case, but a missing or obscured speed-limit sign might, especially if your claim is supported by a photograph.

In another province. If you receive a traffic ticket in another province or an American state, it is often impossible to return to fight the ticket. Many states provide for an immediate trial before a justice of the peace; others allow you to enter a plea of not guilty and present your case in a letter to the court. This is also possible in Ontario. If your defense by letter is accepted by the court as reasonable, you could be found not guilty or your penalty might be reduced.

Some provinces provide for on-the-spot payment of traffic fines for out-of-province drivers, often a flat fee that does not involve accumulation of any demerit points on your record. The penalty is usually lighter than the penalty you would face at home. Some states and provinces have reciprocal agreements to inform each other of convictions. The conviction is then entered on your driving record in your own province, just as if you had committed the infraction at home.

Harassment by police. Police working to the letter of the law can usually find a reason to ticket almost anyone. Motorists have been given tickets in Montreal for license plates partially obscured by snow—during snowstorms! But judges will often dismiss a charge when it seems the officer has been overzealous. In such cases, you have to decide if saving the cost of the fine is worth the time and trouble of a court appearance. But when demerit points are involved, it often is worthwhile to fight frivolous charges to protect your driving record and license.

TAXI PERMITS

Your son, who has a conviction for possession of marijuana, has been refused a permit to drive a taxi.

Taxi licenses are controlled and issued by the municipality in which you live, and the rules differ. In general, licensing is handled by the chief of police or by a commission regulating the operation of vehicles for hire. An applicant's driving record and criminal record are considered.

Usually, rejection of an application can be appealed to a special committee of the licensing commission; some municipalities even provide for a further appeal to an appeal board at city hall. Finally, any citizen has the right to apply to the courts if the grounds for refusal appear unjust—and simple possession of marijuana might well be deemed to fall into this category.

Municipal bylaws and insurance regulations usually require a taxi or tow-truck driver to be at least 18 and to hold a higher-class license than that issued for driving a private vehicle.

SPEED TRAPS

A policeman warns you that you may be charged with obstruction for flicking your headlights to warn oncoming drivers of a speed trap.

It is improbable that you would be charged with obstructing justice, an indictable offense under the Criminal Code. Authorities say it is unlikely a judge would regard "flicking lights" as proof of such a serious offense. But a police-

man might charge you with having defective headlights, especially if you denied that you were flicking your lights intentionally.

Speed traps are a contentious issue, because they are often set up on roads where the legal speed limit seems too slow for the actual conditions and thus they ensnare otherwise law-abiding citizens. The argument against speed traps is that, used this way, they are doing nothing to promote safe driving and are little more than revenue-producing schemes.

Permanent speed limits are seldom raised, even if road conditions are improved. And in some parts of the United States, speed traps are illegal on roads with obviously lower limits than conditions justify. But in Canada, the speed trap is regarded by authorities as a universally applicable deterrent against speeders and as a method of reducing traffic accidents.

Radar detectors. Devices used to detect police radar are banned in Quebec, Ontario, Manitoba and Alberta. These devices sound a signal, or light a lamp, inside your car when you enter the radar beam, allowing you to slow down before the car registers on the police radar. It is illegal in those provinces to use the devices or carry them in your car, although it is not illegal to sell or manufacture them. The detector can be confiscated and you can be fined up to $500.

CARE AND CONTROL

After leaving a bar, you decided to take a nap on the back seat of your car before driving home. You are awakened and charged with having care and control of a car while under the influence of liquor.

You may escape conviction. The evidence will have to show that you *intended* to drive the car. The fact that you were sleeping it off in the back seat indicates lack of such intent, especially if the keys were in your pocket or elsewhere in the back seat and not in the ignition. Your defense would be even stronger if you had left the keys with the bartender for safekeeping.

You need not be driving or even be behind the wheel of your car to be convicted on the "care and control" charge. One driver was convicted after he had been arrested as he was opening the door to get into his car. Another was convicted after police found him slumped over the wheel asleep, in his own driveway—with the keys in the ignition.

A fine line. Intent is the difference between being convicted or acquitted "of care and control," as the following two cases illustrate:

Case No. 1. An Ottawa man left a Christ-

CAA—a friend on the road

Joining a Canadian Automobile Association member club is one of the best motoring bargains around.

When you join the CAA, you become a member of one of the world's largest "clubs." There are more than 75 offices in Canada, 850 in North America and 2,500 club offices around the world—and all will serve you as an affiliate member.

Here is a brief explanation of the major benefits of CAA membership:

Emergency road service (ERS). Mechanical first aid, and towing where necessary, is provided to members whose automobiles break down. This service is available free of charge from trained staff personnel operating club-owned vehicles, or through ERS contract operators, whose stations provide this service to members. A directory is published listing all such stations in North America.

Travel service. This service is operated jointly by the CAA and its affiliate, the American Automobile Association. Trained field representatives inspect motels, hotels, and restaurants annually to ensure that members are aware of suitable accommodations whenever and wherever they travel. From reports of inspectors, *Tour Books* and *Camp Books*, which are distributed free to members, are published. These list "Approved Accommodations," providing guaranteed rates, together with regional and detailed maps covering North America by region and city.

Travel agency assistance. Members are provided with every conceivable type of travel service when they are planning an overseas holiday or business trip.

For example, trained counselors will issue tickets, obtain International Driving Permits, arrange for hotel reservations, provide auto insurance that is valid outside North America, help obtain passports, issue *Automobile and Camping Carnets*, take passport photos, and arrange for any excess medical and travel accident insurance that may be required. Substantial car-rental discounts are available to members. Purchase of travelers cheques in a wide variety of foreign currencies is also available from club offices.

Expanded vehicle services. One of the many consumer-protection services offered to members is the Approved Auto Repair Service. The AARS program ensures that members are provided with guaranteed repairs, backed by CAA as an arbitrator should there be any dispute over the cost or results of repair work.

Personal accident insurance. CAA members are automatically covered against death or dismemberment in travel accidents.

Arrest bond. Bail bond and arrest bond are provided for members held on traffic violations in the United States. Advice and legal assistance are also offered anywhere in the world through the CAA affiliated clubs, if a member is charged with a traffic violation.

Insurance agency. This service will provide members with wide insurance coverage to meet their needs.

Rewards. CAA clubs offer rewards for information leading to the arrest and conviction of persons found guilty of: stealing, or attempting to steal, a member's car or its contents; or hit-and-run incidents causing personal injury to a member or his vehicle.

mas party at his office and got into his car, but, before he could get the keys into the ignition, he passed out. Police found him there with the keys in his hand. He was convicted.

Case No. 2. A man in Barrie, Ont., was found asleep behind the wheel of his pickup truck at the side of the highway. The keys were on the floor of the truck on the passenger side. The man told the Ontario Court of Appeal that he had decided to have a nap, because he had had too much to drink. The location of the keys seemed to back up his statement and the court found him not guilty.

THE BREATHALYZER

You miss an important appointment because a constable insisted you take a Breathalyzer test—which shows zero alcohol in your blood.

This is one time when you probably can't fight city hall. In 1976, Criminal Code amendments gave police the right to demand that you take a Breathalyzer test if they have cause to "reasonably suspect" you of *drinking*.

In theory, you can sue if you can prove that missing the appointment actually cost you money. In practice, policemen usually have little trouble convincing judges that they had reasonable grounds to suspect motorists of drinking. Refusing to take a Breathalyzer test carries the same penalties as you would face if you had taken the test and the level of alcohol in your blood was over the legal limit.

You are considered impaired if your blood alcohol level is 0.08 or more—80 milligrams of alcohol per 100 millilitres of blood. And just because you don't register that much on the Breathalyzer doesn't mean you can't be charged with impaired driving. You could be considered impaired with as little as 0.05, although then the police officer's testimony about your erratic driving becomes more important as evidence. It is estimated that a person weighing 70 kilograms (150 lb.) who has had three normal cocktails, three beers or three glasses of wine will register about 0.09, which exceeds the legal limit. Alcohol disap-

pears from the bloodstream at the rate of about 0.015 an hour, so it will take about an hour after the last drink for the reading to fall below 0.08.

Penalty for first conviction of driving while impaired, or of having care and control of a vehicle while impaired, is a fine between $50 and $2,000, or six months in jail, or both. A second conviction carries a jail sentence of not less than 14 days or more than one year. Each subsequent conviction means jail for not less than three months or more than two years.

CARELESSNESS AND NEGLIGENCE

You are charged with dangerous driving after a minor accident.

If the police lay a charge following an accident, it is generally careless driving, dangerous driving, or criminal negligence. Dangerous driving and criminal negligence in the operation of a motor vehicle are indictable offenses under the Criminal Code. Careless driving is a summary offense under the Highways Act of your province.

To convict you of dangerous driving, the prosecution must prove that you drove in such a manner as to endanger the lives and safety of others. The maximum penalty is two years in jail. Conviction of criminal negligence can carry a sentence of up to five years' imprisonment. For a dangerous-driving conviction, the Crown does not have to prove you could foresee the possible results of your action. In criminal negligence, however, the prosecutor must show that although you might not have intended to create a hazard or dangerous situation, you recognized that this was a possibility and ran the risk of it happening.

Unless there are clear indications of a more serious offense, police and prosecutors tend to fall back on careless driving. The penalty for a conviction of careless driving varies, depending on the province. In Ontario, you could be fined $100 to $500, have your license suspended for up to two years and be imprisoned for up to six months. In Prince Edward Island, the maximum fine is $200, the maximum jail sentence 30 days.

In all provinces, legislation governing highway traffic describes "careless driving" in roughly the same manner: driving "without due care and attention, or without reasonable consideration for others using the highway." You will be convicted of careless driving if the facts of the case indicate that an accident would not have occurred but for your bad driving—driving that would not be expected of a reasonable man or woman in similar circumstances.

SEAT BELTS

You find wearing a seat belt is most uncomfortable, so you buckle it at maximum extension.

Apart from the fact that you are breaking the law if you live in a province with mandatory seat belt legislation, your chances of a serious injury or death are probably worse than if you

Seat belts increase longevity

The evidence that seat belts can prevent or lessen injuries and save lives is well documented, yet people dream up all kinds of excuses for not wearing them. One of the most common is that they are uncomfortable.

However, no less an authority than the Canadian Medical Association (CMA) has declared itself "unequivocally in favor of the use of restraint systems in motor vehicles by all passengers and drivers." Furthermore, the CMA advises all doctors *not* to grant medical exemptions from wearing seat belts, except in the most extreme cases of abnormal skeletal structure or cases where a patient must wear a medical appliance and the seat belt impinges on its use.

Dr. Reuben Devlin, a Toronto orthopedic specialist, says an unborn child stands a better chance of surviving a car accident if the mother is wearing a seat belt, since the most common cause of death for unborn children in accidents is the death of the mother. Death rates for pregnant women drop from 7.8 percent to 3.6 percent when seat belts are worn. Devlin says injuries or deaths of unborn children caused by the impact of a seat belt are usually a result of the seat belt being worn improperly. It should be worn, not around the stomach or waist, but lower, around the pelvis.

The National Highway Traffic Safety Administration of the United States will require passive-restraint systems—devices that do not require any action on the part of the driver or passengers—on all automobiles sold in that country by 1984. This means either seat belts that snap into place automatically when the doors are closed, or air bags that inflate on impact to form a cushion of air in front of drivers and passengers. Car manufacturers favor the automatic seat belts, both from a cost standpoint and because they worry that accidental triggering of air bags could actually cause accidents. And air bags have not been effective in protecting occupants from side-on collisions or rollovers.

Transport Canada is also studying passive systems, but this becomes an academic question if all provinces adopt compulsory seat belt laws. In the United States, where legislators have shied away from imposing seat belt laws, the passive-restraint laws seem more palatable politically. Canadians have voiced little opposition to compulsory seat belt laws, perhaps because the provinces that have them can all demonstrate dramatic drops in their rates of deaths and serious injuries since the laws have come into effect.

Two points worth remembering about seat belts:

Don't reserve their use for long highway trips only. Statistics show that more than 80 percent of injuries and deaths occur when cars are traveling below 60 km/h (37 m.p.h.), which implies short trips close to home.

Seat belts do nothing to *prevent* accidents. That's still largely up to you—the driver.

wore no belt at all. To be effective, a lap belt must be snug across the hips, holding you firmly in place. The shoulder belt should have a small amount of slack. Wearing it too loosely does not protect you from crashing into the steering wheel or windshield.

Quebec, Ontario, Saskatchewan and British Columbia make seat belts compulsory while you are driving or riding in an automobile, and the belts must be worn "in a properly adjusted and securely fastened manner."

Older seat belts—a lap belt and unattached shoulder strap—only need the lap belt buckled. Combined lap-and-shoulder safety systems have been installed in all cars sold in Canada since Jan. 1, 1974. They must meet Transport Canada specifications as to width, strength, method of attachment and retractability. In general, they are easy to put on and take off, and usually quite comfortable. Many people have their minds set against seat belts, remembering older designs that were uncomfortable. They refuse even to try the newer belts, a stubbornness that could, in a moment of bad luck, cost them dearly.

SPOT-CHECKS

You are stranded far from home because the license plates have been removed from your old car after a spot-check.

Chances are, there was something seriously wrong with your car for a policeman or inspector to take such measures. They can only remove the license plates and forbid you to drive the car if it is in a dangerous or unsafe condition. Normally, if an examination reveals a fault, the officer issues a ticket in writing—a notice of the fault—along with a demand requiring it to be repaired within 48 hours. If you feel that you have been detained without just cause, however, and that your car was not unsafe to drive, you can sue for damages, seeking compensation for the costs you sustained by being stranded far from home.

PARKING OFFENSES

On your third trip to put coins in the meter, you find an overtime parking ticket on your car.

The idea of metered parking is to allow motorists a place to park on a short-term basis, usually one or two hours at a maximum. Many drivers believe they can park all day as long as they keep putting coins in the meter. Not so. Although few municipalities bother ticketing overtime parkers at meters, you are obviously parked in one that does. It is likely that a policeman or Meter Maid chalked your tire and timed the length of your stay.

Another problem for the unwary motorist visiting away from home may be overnight parking. Some cities and towns ban overnight parking on streets the year round; others, during the winter months only. No matter what the weather forecast, your car could be towed away from any prohibited area, and you would be liable for towing and storage charges in addition to the parking fine. In a strange city, check with local police on parking regulations before leaving your car on the street overnight.

35 Buying and selling your car

The Canadian shift away from heavy, gas-guzzling automobiles reached a milestone in 1979, when some 52 percent of the cars sold were compact-size or smaller.

The trend really took hold in the mid-1970s when small, practical European and Japanese imports began cornering the increasingly energy-conscious North American market and native automobile manufacturers were forced to produce competitive models. Spiraling gas prices and heightened risks of gas shortages increased the demand for compact vehicles. This, plus safety and antipollution legislation, helped shape the newer, smaller designs on our roads today. But the business of buying and selling cars has also changed in recent years. Legislators have revised laws that protected only the seller, and courts have become more sympathetic toward victims of shady business practices and shoddy manufacturing that causes injury or economic loss.

Although consumer-protection laws, business-practice acts and special legislation governing auto sales have lessened the risks in acquiring a car, the buyer must still be wary. The biggest reason is cost. In 1979, the average Canadian family spent $2,400 in buying, owning and operating an automobile.

Your best chance of a fair deal when acquiring a car is to arm yourself with as much information as possible about the particular kind of automobile that interests you. Know what you can afford. Will the advantages of owning a new car rather than a used one justify your depreciation loss?

When you go to buy, remember that you are dealing with an expert who sells cars every day. You on the other hand, if you are a typical buyer, purchase a new model every four years. That doesn't give you much chance to practice the art of buying. So remember, don't allow yourself to be oversold. Salesmen will push what brings them the most profit—the biggest car with the most options. Never pay the full list price (manufacturer's suggested retail price) for any car. The markups allow plenty of room for dickering. On subcompacts they are 10 to 12 percent; on compacts, 15 to 17 percent; on intermediates, 18 to 20 percent; on full-size (standards), 22 to 24 percent, and on luxury cars, 25 to 27 percent.

Cutting dealer profit in half is probably fair to both parties. That is not to suggest you shouldn't attempt to get it for less. Options bring higher profits. The dress-up items and frills can be marked up 50 or 100 percent.

Even if a deal sounds good, shop around. You could stumble on a dealer with a large stock of the car you want. It costs money to carry those cars in inventory, so he will be eager to move them. If you have a good trade-in, you might find a dealer with a customer waiting for that kind of car. Seeing a fast profit in the trade-in, he will be generous.

In general, though, you will realize more from your old car by selling it privately. Dealers make a profit on every car they sell, even trade-ins. In fact, used-car departments are often more profitable than new-car showrooms.

Don't be misled when a dealer offers an unreasonably high price for your trade-in. He could be increasing the price of the new car in compensation. What should interest you is the price difference between your trade-in and the new car, which is the actual amount you are going to pay.

MISDATING

You bought a new car and now you discover that it is last year's model.

One of the basic laws governing any sale is that the article correspond with the seller's description of that article. If a car described as a current model turns out to be an earlier model, the seller is in breach of contract.

Canadian courts have ordered compensation for buyers duped in this manner. In most cases, though, the sums were small because the owners chose the simplest legal route, Small Claims Court (*see* Chapter 3, "You, the plaintiff") where actions are limited to modest sums. The limit might not cover a loss suffered when selling the car.

In the first year, a car depreciates by 25 to 30 percent of the original list price. Larger cars will generally depreciate more than compacts or subcompacts. Thus, on a $6,000 car, it would be realistic to seek damages of $1,500 to $2,000.

One Quebec Superior Court judge took the value of the car and the trouble and expense of a lawsuit into account. He awarded $10,000 to the buyer of a 1972 luxury car that was fraudulently sold as a 1973 model.

Determining the model year. There are two identification points for determining the model year of any car sold in Canada. A vehicle identification number (VIN) is inscribed on a metal tag affixed to the top of the dashboard on the driver's side. It can be seen from the outside, through the windshield.

The manufacturer's certification that the vehicle meets safety and emission requirements also bears the date of manufacture. This plate is found on the door or the door edge. If the inscription reads 7-79, you know that the car was built in July 1979, although 1979 is not necessarily the model year. Traditionally, assembly lines switch over to new-model production in July or August.

Notable exceptions to this practice are the General Motors front-wheel-drive compacts introduced in Canada in April 1979 as 1980 models. If you are considering buying a used one, take special note of the date of manufacture. You can be certain that used-car dealers or trade-in appraisers, with whom you may later trade, will view the early 1980 cars as 1979 models, no matter what GM calls them.

To determine the model year of a car built before the fall of 1980, you have to know the manufacturer's code. Each code is different. But your provincial registrar of motor vehicles can tell you the model year of an automobile if you provide the make and the VIN.

Motor vehicles built after September 1980 have a standardized, international 17-figure VIN. The 10th figure, a letter, indicates the model year—A stands for 1980, B for 1981, C for 1982, and so on.

Once you have established that the model year differs from the dealer's description at the time of purchase, assemble your evidence. If you were originally attracted by a newspaper notice, hunt up the particular issue at your local library or in the newspaper publisher's files and make copies of the advertisement. Do you have any witnesses—a friend or relative who was with you when you struck the deal?

Confront the dealer with your information. Suggest an amount of compensation. If he refuses and doesn't make an acceptable counteroffer, or if he denies your claim, write to the company whose dealership he has. It might also help to have your lawyer write to the dealer. If you still get no satisfaction, have your lawyer press charges.

LATE DELIVERY

Six months ago you paid a hefty deposit for an expensive foreign car but you're still waiting for delivery.

The standard sales contract used by most dealers provides for delivery within three months of signing. You may then either extend the contract or cancel it and get back your down payment or trade-in allowance. If you've waited six months for a current model, depreciation may have become a factor. The car may be almost a year old and worth less than the purchase price. Or, with inflation and currency fluctuations, the price of the car on delivery could have gone up substantially since you ordered it—a major factor if your contract specifies that you pay the current price. (Between February and September 1978, the price of a Porsche 928 went from $39,250 to $48,000.)

Canceling the contract. If your contract contains a three-month clause and that time

Victory after a 10-year fight

Background

Leo Kravitz had driven 11,200 kilometres (7,000 miles) in his new 1968 Oldsmobile Delta 88 before he called a bailiff, had the vehicle returned to the dealer, and demanded his $3,485 purchase money back. His act was the culmination of eight months of frustration with a host of problems, including rhythmic noises from the engine, vibration in the front end, tires that hit the fenders and oil leaks from the engine.

The Montreal lawyer had repeatedly asked the dealer to repair the problems. On one of at least 10 visits to the dealer, he urged that the car be kept as long as was necessary to correct the faults. His car was returned after three weeks but the problems remained.

Mr. Kravitz then tried to discuss the matter with the manufacturer, but a General Motors representative didn't keep the appointment. That's when Mr. Kravitz decided to take the matter to court. Ten years later he won a resounding victory—but he estimates it cost him $20,000.

Judgment

In January 1979, the Supreme Court of Canada ruled that GM was ultimately responsible for the defective automobile it produced. Even defects that surface after the warranty has expired are still the manufacturer's responsibility, the court said.

It ordered GM to pay Mr. Kravitz his $3,485 purchase price, plus costs of $1,785.

has expired, you can simply give the dealer written notice of cancellation. If you waived the original delivery date or your contract didn't specify one, you may give the dealer "reasonable notice" that you will accept the car only if delivery is made by a certain date. A month would probably be reasonable, but a lawyer should be consulted.

Canadian consumers and dealers have frequent delivery problems with some foreign vehicles. It is not the Canadian dealer's fault that his orders have been held up, but too much understanding of his problems can cost you a considerable amount of money and inconvenience.

THE LEMON

Your new car won't run properly and cannot be fixed. You want a refund or a replacement.

A few years ago, *caveat emptor* (let the buyer beware) was the rule of the marketplace. You would have been stuck with your lemon. Today, because of recent court decisions based on new consumer-protection laws, dissatisfied car buyers have some recourse.

Don't expect to just drive—or tow—your car to the dealer and get your money back, though. Prepare for a battle. Manufacturers have traditionally mustered their considerable financial and legal resources to fight demands for refunds or vehicle replacements. They don't want to set precedents, and would much rather replace every part on a car, one at a time, or replace one part several times. Said one auto executive: "Any manufacturer would rather jack up the radiator cap and build a new car under it than give the money back."

Your first problem is proving that the car really is a lemon. It is not enough that the horn doesn't work or even that the engine blew up. You have to convince a court that despite repeated and persistent repair attempts, the car has a basic flaw which can't be fixed and which renders it unusable and unsalable.

Laws vary greatly. Your chances of success depend largely on your provincial consumer-protection and business-practices laws. Saskatchewan and New Brunswick consumer-product warranty laws permit the buyer to reject an automobile if it is not of an "acceptable quality" which one could "reasonably expect," having regard to certain circumstances, such as price and manufacturer's warranty. Quebec's civil law states that every product is sold in the province with an implied warranty against "latent defects." To get a refund or a replacement in British Columbia, Alberta, Ontario, Nova Scotia or Newfoundland, you will have to prove that the seller employed unfair, deceptive or unconscionable practices, as prohibited by provincial business or trade-practices laws.

Most provinces limit the time you can keep the car before taking some action. Therefore, if you believe your car is a lemon, demand a refund or a replacement without delay.

Start worrying early. The time to start worrying about getting a lemon is when you start shopping for a new car. If the salesman promises performance above and beyond the terms of the manufacturer's warranty, get the promise in writing or included on the offer to purchase. Have it signed by an authorized company official.

Keep copies of any printed advertisements, especially ones that attracted you to the car in the first place. If the advertising is false or misleading and you can convince the court that the advertisement induced you to buy, you have a case.

Do not accept delivery until you are satisfied that the car has all the equipment you ordered and is exactly as specified in the sales contract. Be careful here. Some courts have ruled that telling the dealer you will come to pick up the car constitutes acceptance. Tell the dealer you want to inspect the car before accepting it and don't drive it until you have.

Keep meticulous records of maintenance and repairs. When you return the car for repairs covered by the warranty, give the dealer written instructions and keep a copy for your records. Keep all invoices, noting whether repairs have been completed. A complete diary of your contacts with the dealer will be valuable in the event of a lawsuit.

THE ONE-TIME TAXI

The dealer didn't tell you that the clean-looking secondhand car you bought was a retired taxi.

The law in most provinces requires dealers to inform you if the used car you are buying was once a taxi or a police car. Some provinces insist that dealers identify a former taxi or police car in all advertising and on sales contracts. If your dealer fails to do so, you can then have him charged—and probably get involved in a long court case. But if the car is performing well, it is unlikely you will receive any compensation.

Checking the car's history. The best defense against getting stuck with an old taxi or police car is to check the car's history. In most

Buying a used car

There it is, parked on the third row at Freddie's Friendly Used Cars, shining its little heart out. And it can be yours for only $1,595.

Play it cool. Don't let the circling salesman know you can't live without that car.

Buying a used automobile is a gamble: you could get stuck with someone else's recently unloaded problem. So here's what to do when you go shopping for the first time. For that matter, what to do the next time, too.

Get the money first. Decide how much you are going to spend. Include the sales tax in your calculation. Then make sure you have the money: it's amazing how many people go shopping with only a vague idea of how they will finance their purchase.

The car salesman may assure you that he will take care of financing. Right. He will steer you to a finance company where you will pay top interest rates.

Shop for the money as carefully as you shop for the car. Borrowing against an insurance policy or getting the money from a credit union are generally the best bets, with banks and trust companies in second place.

Check the car. You don't need a degree in mechanical engineering to know that worn tires aren't going to last long, or that variations in body color or finish indicate repairs—and possibly body damage from an accident. The clutch and brake pedals and the floor mats are clues to wear and tear. Are these more worn than you'd expect for the mileage?

Check for leak stains on the ground beneath the parked car. Is there any sagging, evidence of worn springs, when the vehicle is on level ground? Check the shock absorbers by leaning your hands on one corner of the car and pressing down hard. If the vehicle bounces back quickly, these may need to be replaced.

Check that the doors fit snugly, that the windows open smoothly and that all components—windshield washer and wipers, heaters, blowers, air conditioning, radio, dash and parking lights and headlights—work.

Road test the car. Start it up when the engine is cold—you can tell if it's warm by placing your hand on the hood. A tuneup or more is in order for an engine that splutters or cuts out. On a smooth stretch of road, take your hand off the wheel momentarily. If the vehicle pulls either to the left or the right, the alignment may need adjusting, or the tires need replacing. Note if the gears shift easily or jerkily and if the car responds easily or sluggishly to acceleration and braking.

Call in the experts. If you're now satisfied with the appearance and performance of the car, take it to a mechanic you trust. It takes a trained ear and eye to spot expensive trouble. (If the vendor won't permit an inspection, he's hiding something. Pack up your wallet and get out.) If the mechanic fails to turn up anything serious, make your offer. Remember that the salesman's first price is just that: the figure will be considerably higher than he expects to get. So be prepared to bargain.

provinces the dealer is required by law to keep records identifying the car's previous owner and showing the odometer reading at the time of purchase. If he won't show you the pertinent portion of the sales contract, or at least provide the previous owner's name and address, refuse to consider the car. The dealer is hiding something.

Your motor vehicle licensing branch can give you a history if you provide the license number of a vehicle. For a small fee you will receive a printout of all previous owners.

A visual inspection of a used car can be misleading. Worn pedals and floor mats are easily replaced. Holes in the roof, used for mounting signs, can be repaired. Indeed most taxi companies and police departments now use suction cups to attach their insignia.

Turning back the clock. Anyone with the right tools, a bit of know-how and larceny in his heart can reset the odometer of a car. His half-hour under the dashboard could cost you hundreds of dollars. A car dealer in Cambridge, Ont., was fined $4,000 for altering odometers on 10 cars. He had rolled off some 1.17 million kilometres.

Used-car prices vary greatly and one of the determining factors is the distance driven. A full-size, well-equipped, two-year-old car, which might be worth $5,300 at 60,000 kilometres would bring only $4,300 at 120,000 kilometres.

American Motors has a ratchet system on its Jeep vehicles which prevents rolling back odometers. General Motors cars strip paint off the odometer numbers if they are turned back. There is also a gearing device that prevents rolled-back numbers from lining up properly. The professional crook gets around such systems by rolling the odometer *forward*, past zero, to the figure he wants to show. To deter this, Chrysler and American Motors passenger cars both use an inking process that colors the numbers red or violet when the car reaches 160,000 kilometres (100,000 miles).

But there is no absolute protection against unscrupulous individuals. Nothing, that is, except common sense and the tenacity to check the car's history as thoroughly as possible. A former owner—unless he is the culprit who

reset the odometer or disconnected the cable—should have no qualms about telling you what distance he logged on a car. If the numbers don't check, call a policeman.

GETTING A CLEAR TITLE

You bought a secondhand car from a stranger and now his finance company is threatening to repossess it from you.

He looked like such a nice young man, the guy who sold you the car and swore he didn't owe any money on it. But the painful truth is that he did, and the finance company has every right to demand that you either pay the debt or relinquish the car. Legally, anyone with a registered lien or security interest (chattel mortgage or conditional sales contract) on a car owns it. Innocent purchasers caught in the middle have no recourse.

But before you give up the car, check the registry of liens and debts at your local courthouse to make sure that the finance company actually has a *registered* security interest. (There is no such registry in Quebec.) You can keep the car if the debt isn't registered. If it is registered, you can claim the excess value of the car above the sum owed.

Search the title. The best time to check the registry is before you buy a car. Then you can be fairly sure of getting clear title. Also, have the seller sign a statement saying there are no liens or encumbrances against the car (that he owes no money on it), and that he will pay any undisclosed security interest that might surface. (This is also a reasonable statement to request from a used-car dealer.)

Stolen cars. If you inadvertently buy a stolen car, you have no more claim to it than does the person who sold it to you. You can sue the seller for "total failure of consideration"—if you can find him.

As a safeguard against buying a stolen car, you can have your local police check the vehicle of your choice against their auto theft records. Also verify through your motor vehicle licensing bureau that the seller is the registered owner.

432

Bill of sale

Here is a sample bill of sale. Note that it refers to the need of repairs and that the price reflects this. Vendors in most provinces must now provide either a safety certificate or an unfit-vehicle permit. If the car were being sold with an unfit motor vehicle permit, the bill of sale would note that, too.

Bluefield, Alta., July 1, 1980, 3:30 p.m.

BILL OF SALE

This is to confirm the sale by Richard A. Roe of R.R.4, Bluefield, Alta., to Samuel Snow of 36-154th St., Calgary, Alta., of a 1973 Pontiac Parisienne 4-door sedan, serial number HJ3712293P, licence Alberta HOJ 546 for the sum of $600 (six hundred dollars), paid on this date by certified cheque.

This automobile is being sold with a safety standards certificate but with the express understanding of both parties that it is in need of mechanical repairs, which has been taken into consideration in the price charged for the automobile. Such repairs will be the responsibility of the buyer, Samuel Snow, who agrees that the seller will in no way be responsible for breakdowns or any repair costs from this date and time on.

Richard A. Roe
Richard A. Roe

Samuel Snow
Samuel Snow

IMPORTING A CAR

You plan to bring home the secondhand car you bought during your year-long assignment in the United States.

If you have owned and used the car for six months prior to your return, and if it is valued at not more than $7,500, you won't have to pay anything to import it. Cars valued at more than $7,500 are subject to regular duty and taxes over that sum. Canada Customs can get very sticky about value, insisting on its own assessment rather than relying on your bill of sale or receipt to determine duties and taxes.

Vehicles built in Britain or Australia, and imported from those countries, are duty-free. The duty on cars from all other countries is 15 percent. The federal tax on all imported cars is 9 percent of the value plus duty. If you have been out of the country for at least five years, the six-month ownership is not necessary. But you must have used the car. You can't just buy it and ship it home.

Canadian servicemen based out of Canada are subject to the same customs regulations as private citizens.

Away less than a year. If you have been away for less than a year, an entirely different set of rules applies. You may import a car of the current model year, or one that is at least 15 years old, by paying the regular duty and taxes. You may not import a vehicle that is more than one year, and less than 15 years old, unless it is a gift from a friend or relative (backed by a declaration that no money or "valuable consideration" was involved), or a replacement for a vehicle destroyed in an accident. Whether it is a gift or a replacement vehicle, duties and taxes must be paid.

A further $100 is levied if the car has air conditioning, and it will cost you another $100 if it weighs more than 1,814 kilograms.

Provincial sales taxes. When the vehicle is registered in your province, provincial sales taxes, where these apply, will be computed on the total import cost, that is, the purchase price plus duty, plus federal sales tax, plus excise tax.

If you are a resident of Ontario, where the provincial sales tax is 7 percent, here's what you will pay to import a $2,000 used car.

Duty (15 percent in most cases).........	$300.00
Federal sales tax (9 percent of $2,300)	207.00
Add excise tax of $100 for air conditioning and, say, $100 for weight in excess of 1,814 kilograms	200.00
Provincial sales tax (7 percent of $2,707)..	189.49
Total..	$896.49

Exceptions. Racing cars not for use on public highways and certain commercial vehicles (primarily those outfitted for construction, mining, exploration or well-drilling) are exempt from the ban on used cars less than 15 years old.

Antique cars (those 50 years old or more) are exempt from duty.

Safety and emission. All motor vehicles, except those built in 1970 or earlier, must meet federal safety and emission standards. Because standards in Canada and the United States are similar, there is usually no problem with cars from that country. But if you plan to import a car from anywhere else, make sure the cost of converting it to Canadian standards is not prohibitive. In fact, it may be impossible to bring some cars to our safety standards. Thus they could not be licensed.

Owning a car abroad. If you travel extensively or vacation regularly in a foreign country, you might find it advantageous to own a car, house trailer or motor home in that country. But if you attempt to bring the vehicle into Canada, even for a short period, Canada Customs will either demand payment of duties and taxes or seize the vehicle at the border.

RENTING

Your vacation was ruined when a wheel fell off your rented car, causing a serious accident.

While the fact your vacation was ruined probably won't enter the picture, you can sue for damages resulting from any injuries to you or

The time to sell

This graph shows the depreciation rate (green line) over 10 years, the average life of a car. The blue line indicates average maintenance and repair costs as a percentage of the vehicle's value. These expenses peak in the seventh year, when the cost of repairs becomes more than the value of the car.

Experts generally agree that the best time to sell your car is after the fourth year, when the gap between value and repair costs suddenly narrows. That way you can still get a reasonable price for a vehicle that has cost you little in repairs.

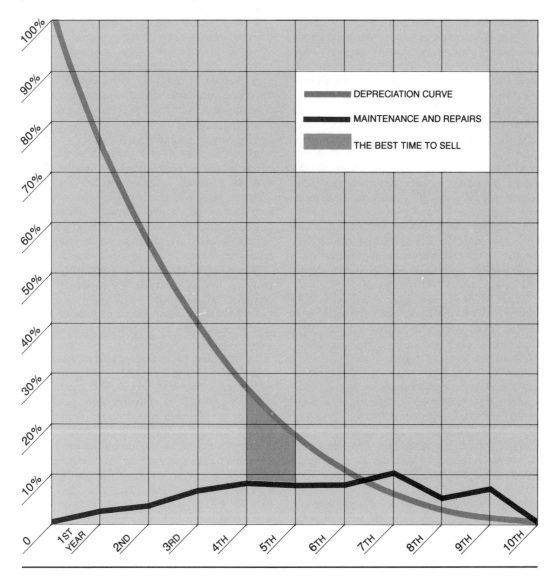

your family, and to recover any financial loss. Whether you would sue the rental company or the car manufacturer depends on what caused the wheel to fall off. If it was negligence on the part of the rental company (perhaps the wheel nuts were not properly tightened during servicing), you would sue it for breaching its "duty of care" to you. But your suit would be against the manufacturer if the accident resulted from a manufacturing defect.

You would possibly sue both the rental company and the car maker if both contributed to the accident or if a cause can't be ascertained. You can seek compensation for personal damages (injury, pain and suffering), property loss (clothing or personal effects damaged in the crash), costs (medical bills, advance payments for vacation reservations) and loss of income if you are unable to work.

Rental car insurance. The rental company's insurance may pay part of the damages caused in the accident. Major rental companies customarily carry $1 million public liability and property damage insurance on each vehicle. They also offer collision insurance with deductible amounts of $250 to $300. (This means that in the event of an accident you could be liable for the deductible amount.) Coverage with no deductible or lower deductible is usually available for about $3 a day, an extremely high premium.

Those who often rent a car should consider adding riders to their personal auto insurance policies to cover them no matter what car they are driving. They could then refuse the $3-a-day coverage without risk.

Rental fees. Costs vary considerably so you should compare companies carefully before renting a car. Some companies offer "unlimited mileage" without additional charges while others allow some free kilometres and charge for each kilometre over that. Be wary of low daily rates and high distance charges, unless you are certain you are not going far with the car.

Most weekend or full-week rates are considerably better than day rates. If the rental is part of a fly-drive vacation, check with your travel agent when booking your flight for special deals that airlines and rental companies sometimes offer. Cars rented in one city and left in another are often subject to drop-off charges, although some companies won't charge you when you are traveling between certain cities.

Car rental rates are computed on a 24-hour day but most companies allow an hour's grace if you are late returning the car. After that, charges are on the higher, hourly rate. In most cases, you can rent a car as cheaply for 24 hours as for three.

Reserving a rental car. To rent a car, you must be 21 years old and have a valid driver's license. You must guarantee not to drive the car in any races or speed events; to return it in the same condition in which you received it; to report any accident within 48 hours, and to advise the company of any claims, lawsuits or legal proceedings resulting from the accident.

The rental company will want to check your credit rating. If you pay cash, you'll have to complete a form in advance giving details as to your residence, employment and finances. The company will verify the information before renting you a car. You may also be required to put down a cash deposit. If you pay by credit card, the card serves as sufficient credit reference.

When you reserve a car, ask about the company's policy on substitutions. If you reserve a compact car, say, but the company is unable to deliver, some companies will provide a car of the next size up, an intermediate, at the lower compact price. Other companies will not guarantee to deliver a subcompact, to avoid having to provide a larger car at their subcompact rate.

Reliability. It is industry-wide policy to provide a replacement if your rented car breaks down. Competition between rental companies is stiff, so you are unlikely to be left stranded by the roadside for very long, but the company won't accept responsibility for any appointments you miss. Nor are the courts likely to award you compensation, even if the delay cost you a "million-dollar sale."

If the breakdown caused you to miss the last plane home, you might persuade the rental company to pay your hotel and meal expenses. If company negligence caused the breakdown—if, for instance, the engine seized because it hadn't been properly serviced—the company would be more generous in covering any costs you incurred.

LEASING

The dealer is willing to repair your new leased car, which has been troublesome from day one, but refuses to replace it.

Unlike a rental company, a leasing company hasn't a pool of cars from which to replace a balky vehicle. Basically, the leasing company buys a car and rents it to you. If the vehicle turns out to be a lemon, the company will have to buy another car in order to replace it. Naturally it is reluctant to do this. That's one of the risks in leasing a car. The contract runs for 24 to 36 months, and breaking it can be difficult.

First, suggest that the lessor take back the car and give you a new lease on another vehicle. If he refuses, complain by registered letter, listing all the service disruptions you have had. Tell him that you will consider the contract broken if you have any more trouble with the car, and that if you do, you will return the car and seek damages for any costs you incur. Keep a copy of the letter. Then, if

---

Driving costs

Gas hit $1 a gallon at most service stations in 1979, when every kilometre you drove cost you about 12 cents. The Canadian Automobile Association (CAA) found that it cost 12.2 cents a kilometre (19.6 cents a mile) to operate the "average" automobile that year. Tests were conducted with a 1979 Chevy Malibu, with 305-cubic-inch V-8 engine, power steering and power brakes. Fixed costs (insurance, licences, depreciation and financing) and variable costs (gas, oil, tires and maintenance) were taken into account.

Anyone driving 24,000 kilometres a year spent about $75 more for gas in 1979 than in the previous year. Greater increases are likely through the 1980s, when energy experts are predicting $1.50-a-gallon prices for gas.

(Most gas pumps are already calibrated in litres. There are about 4.55 litres to the gallon, so a price of $1.50 a gallon translates into approximately 33 cents a litre.)

The CAA comparisons between 1978-79 showed the costs of maintenance at 0.71 cent per kilometre (1.14 cents per mile) and tires 0.42 cent per kilometre (0.68 cent per mile) unchanged and insurance costs up $10 (to an average $366).

The distance driven each year must be considered in estimating the cost per mile or kilometre. This cost increases if you drive less than 24,000 kilometres (15,000 miles) and decreases if you drive more. But you must estimate another $35 in maintenance and depreciation for every additional 1,600 kilometres (1,000 miles), says the CAA.

In large cities, where motorists have higher-than-average insurance rates, and where stop-and-go driving adds to fuel costs, the cost per kilometre increases. In Toronto, for instance, the cost for the average car is 1.5 cents a kilometre (2.3 cents a mile) more than the national average.

Costs drop dramatically as the size of the car drops. Here is the CAA's comparison of costs in Toronto for a mid-size vehicle, a popular domestic compact with automatic transmission, and a subcompact with manual transmission:

Mid-size, 13.7 cents per kilometre (21.9 cents per mile);

Compact, 10.9 cents per kilometre (17.4 cents per mile);

Subcompact, 9.9 cents per kilometre (15.9 cents per mile).

the car gives you further trouble, consult a lawyer.

The lease agreement. Basically, this contract allows you the use of the lessor's automobile for the duration of the lease.

You are responsible for insuring and maintaining the vehicle unless the lessor contracts to provide these services. Either way, you pay. You are also responsible for replacing worn parts, including tires and batteries, and returning the car at the end of the lease in good condition, save for normal wear.

If you can pay cash for a car, or have a hefty down payment, it is uneconomic to lease. Because a large portion of your payments is for interest (you build up no equity or ownership in the car), leasing is always more expensive than buying.

The advantage in leasing is convenience. Negotiations are usually simpler and if the lease incorporates insurance and maintenance, you don't have to shop for them. The whole package can be handled with one monthly payment—albeit a substantial one.

You may have heard that leasing provides tax advantages that are not available to car buyers. Don't believe it. Attempting to deduct the full amount of a leased car, which is not used exclusively for business, will have the tax man knocking at your door.

Some contracts offer an option to purchase the car at the end of the lease, at the wholesale price as estimated by the lessor at the outset of the agreement. When used-car prices are high, lessors discourage "buy-back" clauses. But you should insist on this option. At the end of your lease, check used-car prices of that model. You will know the car and it might be a good buy. If it was a lemon, you can walk away.

Breaking a lease. One year into a three-year lease, your employer transfers you to New Zealand. Or your Uncle Bill dies and leaves you his new Rolls-Royce. Whatever the reason, you want out of the lease. Discuss the matter with the lessor. The company may cancel the lease if you pay the difference between the sum the company wants from that car and your payments to date plus the car's sale value.

Some leases will require you to pay a percentage of the monthly payments remaining on your lease. Others may even require full payment of the remaining monthly charges.

You can also sublease, much as you would an apartment or house, by turning the car over to someone who agrees to continue the lease payments. Or you can find someone willing to buy the car for the sum the leasing company needs to liquidate the lease.

Private leasing companies cannot offer the service car dealers with leasing divisions can, but their rates are generally slightly lower. Some private lessors have service facilities or arrangements with garages. Shop for leasing rates as you would for the best price on a new car. A difference of $10 or $20 a month adds up to a substantial amount over a 36-month lease.

Getting a "loaner." If your business depends on the uninterrupted use of a car, lease from a dealer who will provide a "loaner" or courtesy car in emergencies or while yours is being serviced. Listen to the lessor's advice about the type of car you should lease. In some cases, you can get a better-equipped, costlier car for a lower rate than you would expect because the lessor knows he can sell that model for a good price when the lease expires.

THE PRIVATE SALE

Your family sedan is starting to cough and sputter and the local dealer is urging you to trade it for a newer model.

Chances are that a minor tuneup will solve a cough and sputter. Should you decide to part with your automobile nonetheless, there is no justification, except convenience, to trade or sell to a dealer. You will fare better by selling the car privately. Dealers must make a profit on every car that goes through their hands. They buy at wholesale prices and sell at retail. The dealer's profit is your loss when you sell your car to him.

The current market value of your car can be found in "the red book" used by credit unions, banks and insurance companies. It lists up-to-date wholesale and retail values of all models of used cars and the price spread allowed for condition and mileage.

The most effective place to advertise your car is the want-ad section of your local newspaper. Make your advertisement informative: state the year, make, model and body style (two-door, four-door). Be honest about defects and general condition. You are wasting your time and that of the prospective buyer if you say the car is in excellent condition, when it obviously needs repairs. Conversely, many mechanically inclined buyers are looking for bargain-priced used cars that they can repair.

If your vehicle has been used only as a second car or has particularly low mileage, mention that, too. List optional or standard equipment. Power equipment (steering, brakes, windows), AM/FM stereo radios or tape decks, air conditioning and high-line interiors are strong selling points. State your asking price. Advertisements that include this information draw much more response than those that omit the figure. Set a realistic price, slightly higher than what you are willing to accept. This allows room to negotiate and most used-car shoppers expect to haggle.

List your telephone number and calling hours. Make it "call between 6 p.m. and 9 p.m.," not just "after 6 p.m.," or you may be bothered by midnight phone calls. Don't include your address. People dropping by to look at the car can disrupt your appointments with other prospects. Make appointments an hour apart, so that you don't turn off a hot prospect by hurrying a decision.

Getting it certified. In Prince Edward Island, Nova Scotia, New Brunswick, Ontario and most of British Columbia a certificate that the car meets minimum safety standards is required before ownership can be changed and the car driven on the road. Newfoundland requires safety certification only for vehicles two or more years old. The certificate is necessary in Quebec for vehicles purchased outside the province, or for those bought within the province but not registered the previous year.

If your province insists on certification but your car fails the safety check, you can still make a sale by providing an "unfit motor vehicle permit" and surrendering the license plates to your local motor vehicles branch. Obviously, the vehicle cannot be driven until the necessary repairs are made and the car is certified as roadworthy.

Take the car to a garage authorized to make safety checks a couple of days before you offer it for sale. Safety certificates are valid only for specific periods, usually 30 to 36 days.

Inspection fees range from $25 to $50. Any repairs required are extra.

Even if you have no plans to do any repairs, get a written estimate from the garage. A second estimate from another garage might also be worthwhile. A buyer will be more easily persuaded to buy an unfit vehicle if he knows the cost of making it roadworthy.

THE BEST OFFER

You advertise your car for sale at "$1,500 or best offer" and one prospect insists you accept his bid of $1,000, which was, in fact, the highest.

You are not obliged to take the $1,000 offer, regardless of whether or not it was the highest bid. But it could be argued in court that you are bound to accept an offer that *meets* the asking price. You are also entitled to change your mind about selling the car, even after advertising the sale.

On the other hand, if an offer is made and accepted, you have entered into a contract. Then, if the buyer abides by the terms of the agreement, you must deliver the car to him or her.

OUTSTANDING LIEN

You want to sell your three-year-old car, but you still owe $1,000 on it.

You must advise the lienholder that you plan to sell. If you don't, and sell the vehicle—which is still owned by the finance company—the sale is deemed to be a "theft."

After advising the lienholder, the procedure should be to sell the car, then immediately pay off the lien with the sale proceeds. If you plan to do otherwise, the lienholder should be consulted.

Some buyers will assume the debt owing on a car. In effect, the bank or loan company lends the buyer the $1,000 balance of the loan, after discussing the details with the buyer and checking his or her credit rating.

You cannot continue making payments on the $1,000 you owe and use the money from the sale for some other purpose. Your best course is to arrange a new loan and pay off the previous one.

CHANGE OF OWNERSHIP

The man who bought your car is involved in a serious accident before the change of ownership is registered and your insurance coverage canceled.

The moment the sale is completed, the car becomes the property of the new owner. It is no longer the concern of you or your insurers.

Canadian courts have ruled that an insurance company is under no obligation to the new owner of an automobile, even though the previous owner's policy has not been canceled.

The change of ownership occurs, not when the new owner registers the car in his or her name, but when the new owner takes possession. Bills of sale, therefore, should be marked with the time of sale as well as the date.

New owner's insurance. If the buyer has an insurance agent with whom he deals regularly, insurance is easily arranged by telephone. Otherwise, a short visit to an agent may be necessary. But don't delay making out a bill of sale or don't postdate the sale, while permitting the purchaser to drive the car with your insurance still in effect. Your rates could increase or your policy could be canceled if the buyer has an accident before possession is effected.

If your insurer discovers you were selling the car at the time of the accident, the company could refuse to pay the claim. Your only recourse would be to sue the company and you'd have little chance of winning.

All provinces now have compulsory insurance schemes. This means that no vehicle can be registered without proof of insurance.

36 Warranties and guarantees

Today's automobile buyers are demanding warranty protection that was unheard of a few years ago. And their demands are being backed up by court decisions and new legislation that is making manufacturers of all goods, including automobiles, accountable for the defects in their products. But the plain truth is that consumer-protection laws, sales acts, fair trade legislation and courts sympathetic to consumers cannot take the place of a careful buyer. When shopping for a new automobile, you should study carefully the warranties offered. Length of the warranty period and items covered vary from manufacturer to manufacturer. If this protection is a high-priority item in your selection of an automobile, compare the various warranties just as carefully as you do the prices and options on cars that interest you.

A warranty, in effect, is a contract by which the manufacturer agrees to repair defects if the product is properly used and maintained. Most buyers don't realize that they have to maintain the vehicle to the manufacturer's specifications to keep the warranty valid. Read the warranty carefully to inform yourself of the maintenance schedule for the vehicle you choose.

Most buyers also believe that warranty protection ends when the distance or time stipulations—usually 12 months or 20,000 kilometres—have been used up. But this is not necessarily so: courts have held that every product carries an "implied warranty," so that a product, having regard for its price and intended purpose, must be durable and suitable for that purpose. A court may well hold a manufacturer responsible if, say, the engine falls apart after 13 months or 21,000 kilometres.

Manufacturers can no longer get away with the old plaint of "There's nothing we can do." Aware of this, they sometimes extend the warranty on parts that turn out to be faulty. These are the so-called "extended" or "secret" warranties. The dealers are advised to replace or repair defective parts, even after the normal warranty period, if the customer complains. Customers are not advised of the defect however, and only those who complain get relief. Consumer advocates are critical of this practice, contending that all customers should be advised about potential defects and their right to repairs, or else that all such cars should be recalled. Manufacturers claim that a recall is not justified because all cars will not experience the problem. Yet most buyers, unaware both of the extended warranty and of the fact that their problem is a common defect in the car, will pay for the repairs. This is clearly unfair to owners who are too timid or too busy to kick up a fuss.

Most manufacturers provide warranties for five years or 80,000 kilometres on emission-control apparatus. Keep this in mind. Many owners forget and take their cars to private garages when they have problems, thus incurring unnecessary costs. Remember, too, that your car is guaranteed not to rust through for a period longer than the 12-month or 20,000-kilometre limitation provided for most parts, as long as you fulfill the periodic inspection requirements.

UNAUTHORIZED REPAIR

The dealer says the warranty on your new car is void because your mechanically inclined son tinkered with it.

A dealer can't void a warranty: the contract is between the car owner and the manufacturer who pays for warranty repairs done by the dealer. But he would seem to have good cause to refuse repairs to parts affected by your son's handiwork. Almost all warranties carry a clause absolving the manufacturer of any responsibility if repairs are necessary because of misuse or modification. This would certainly apply if your son tried to "soup up" the engine or took the carburetor apart to see how it worked.

But the manufacturer will probably honor the warranty if your son's tinkering had no bearing on the problem you are experiencing—if, say, he monkeyed with the engine and you are trying to get a leaky trunk fixed. And it would hardly constitute misuse if your son's repairs were done in order to get the car going when it stalled on a lonely highway in the middle of the night.

The Canadian Automobile Association advises you not only to read the terms of your warranty but also to read the owner's manual provided with your new car. Often, buyers of new automobiles waste time visiting a dealer to demand unnecessary repairs. They have simply misunderstood the operating instructions or they can't get something to work properly because they haven't figured out the dials or switches.

In general, a new-car warranty covers defects in workmanship and material on most parts of the car for 12 months or 20,000 kilometres. Items such as batteries and tires are usually covered separately. The warranty is good to the original expiry date even if the car is sold, so the new owner is justified in seeking repairs. Most automobiles and light trucks are also guaranteed against rust-through (holes caused by corrosion) for three years, some even for six years. Most emission-control components are covered for five years or 80,000 kilometres.

Some exceptions. Repairs arising from damage by fire, collision or any other accident are not included. If you race, rally or overload your car, the dealer will balk at fixing it—those things constitute abuse. And he won't touch parts added to the car that do not meet the manufacturer's standards.

The antiperforation portion of your warranty doesn't cover mufflers or exhaust systems, nor does it cover rust holes caused by bare metal being exposed through collision or acci-dent. Paint damage caused by stone chips, salt or sand is also excluded. Some warranties stipulate a one-time-only adjustment for parts such as windows, doors and trunk lids, so make sure the work is done properly the first time. Finally, heed the "normal-care" stipulations of your owner's manual. The use of improper oil, or failure to grease and wash the car, may provide the loophole for invalidating the warranty if there is a dispute about repairs.

EXPIRED WARRANTY

The busy dealer twice postponed your appointment for a 16,000-kilometre checkup and now he claims you have broken the conditions of the warranty.

Some dealers are reluctant to carry out warranty work, because it is less profitable than regular repairs. The manufacturer pays less than the garage charges for similar work to customers at large. If your dealings so far have been with the service manager, go to the owner of the dealership. Give him the details and politely, but firmly, demand action. If this doesn't work, get in touch with the manufacturer's zone office, explain the situation to the customer service manager there and ask that he either remind your dealer of his obligations or else authorize another dealer in your area to do the work. The manufacturer's warranty should be honored by any North American dealer franchised to sell your car line. Should this fail, send a registered letter to the president of the manufacturing company. You will find his name and address in the *Financial Post Directory of Directors* at your local library. Tell him you regard the warranty as a contract that his agent, the dealer, won't fulfill—and give a brief summary of your thwarted efforts.

It will help if you have documentary proof, such as a letter from the dealer canceling the appointments, or acknowledging your attempts to keep your service appointment. Ask for written assurance that the dealer will assume responsibility for any breach of the warranty conditions that the delay might cause. The wary consumer will document every aspect of maintenance and dealer contact.

Further recourse is available through your local consumer services bureau or the Better Business Bureau (BBB). In 1979, the BBB arbitrated several warranty disputes between dealers or manufacturers and customers when other avenues of appeal had failed. Another solution, of course, is to have the repairs completed at an independent garage and to sue in Small Claims Court for your costs, if the amount at stake is within this court's jurisdiction.

Additional warranties. Often tires, batteries and some options such as sun roofs or custom coachwork are not included in the new-car warranty from the manufacturer. They are guaranteed by whatever company made the battery, tires or accessory in ques-

tion. Generally, the manufacturer will replace the battery free in the first 12 months if it is defective. After that, and up to 36 months from the time you purchased your car, you will be charged on a *pro rata* basis for replacement of a defective battery. If, for instance, the battery is replaced in the 18th month, you will be charged half the price of a new battery.

Tire warranties are generally based on tread wear. If a tire proves defective when the tread is half gone, you are expected to pay half the price of a new tire.

Damages resulting from tire failure are not included in the warranty. If, for instance, you had a blowout, causing a collision, the warranty does not cover the cost of repairing the damage to the car. But you or your insurance company would have an excellent chance in court of recovering damages and costs from the tire company.

Your safety is their business

A number of private and government agencies in Canada and the United States constantly test new cars and automobile products. In general, Canada has followed the lead of the National Highway Traffic Safety Administration (NHTSA) of the United States. Before a vehicle can be certified for sale here the manufacturer and importer must submit to Transport Canada the results of crash tests—frontal and side impacts, as well as roll-overs. Doors must be strong enough to resist penetration in side impacts. Bumpers must be able to withstand an 8-kilometre-per-hour crash without damage. In 1979, Transport Canada opened its own $30-million examination site at Blainville, near Mirabel Airport, north of Montreal.

Consumers Union, a private American agency, created controversy in 1978 when the agency publication, *Consumer Reports*, claimed that the Dodge Omni and the Plymouth Horizon were "not acceptable" because of handling problems. The NHTSA and

Transport Canada then retested the automobiles and both gave the cars a clean bill of health, noting that the Consumers Union testing procedure was unrelated to real-world driving situations. In the test, the driver travels 80 km/h, turns the steering wheel 90 degrees, removes both hands from the wheel and waits for the car to right itself. Instead, Omnis and Horizons continued to oscillate.

Car magazines also test cars but their tests are aimed mostly at auto buffs. Nevertheless the findings of such reputable magazines as *Car and Driver, Road and Track* and *Motor Trend* will help the average consumer evaluate a car's braking and handling performance.

If you are concerned about the road worthiness of your tires or vehicle, get in touch with the Road Safety Branch of Transport Canada. It can tell you whether testing has revealed any defects and whether the vehicle—if you have bought a used car—or brand of tire has ever been recalled. Canadian Automobile Association clubs also publish test reports.

LOST WARRANTY

You want to sell your six-month-old pickup truck but you've lost your warranty.

No problem. Your dealer and the manufacturer both have records of the date the car went into service. Either will supply a duplicate of the warranty form containing that information. This is supposed to be a less cumbersome record-keeping system than the old practice of carrying a warranty plate or book. And, of course, the warranty will be as valid for the new owner as it would have been for you.

If a dispute should arise concerning the actual date the truck went into service, your sales contract will show the delivery date.

USED-CAR WARRANTIES

The used car that you bought "as is" a week ago has collapsed in your driveway.

Selling a car "as is" or "without warranty" just doesn't stand up these days, although most dealers use the disclaimer on sales contracts in the hope of convincing buyers there's no chance of getting anything fixed. You have the right to expect a used car to perform normally and no "as is" disclaimer absolves the dealer of that obligation. Demand that he either fix the car or take it back and return your money. If he does neither, get the car fixed at another garage, or have it towed to the dealer's lot, then sue him in Small Claims Court. (*See* Chapter 3, "You, the plaintiff.") The courts have enabled numerous buyers of broken-down or unsafe used cars to recover repair costs or purchase prices. And, if the car has a safety defect that caused an accident, the dealer could also be liable for damages resulting from the accident.

A word of caution. The laws apply only to dealers, who are presumed to know, or who should have known, about defects in their cars. There is little you can do to recover damages from an individual from whom you've bought a used car unless you can prove fraud or demonstrate that the individual knowingly sold you an unsafe car.

Safety certificates. Most provinces require used cars to be sold with a safety certificate unless the vehicle is sold without license plates, in which case it must be accompanied by an unfit-motor-vehicle permit. A safety certificate does not mean the vehicle is mechanically sound, however, so have the car checked by a trustworthy mechanic. (The Canadian Automobile Association keeps a list of reputable garages for members' use.) Don't buy from any dealer or individual who won't allow you to have the car examined in this manner.

Also, don't put too much stock in safety certificates unless you know and trust the garage or mechanic who performed the inspection. In Ontario, during a six-month period of 1978, 116 garages and 181 mechanics lost their right to issue safety certificates. Government inspectors found some mechanics issuing safety certificates without doing inspections and others doing unnecessary work on cars brought for certification.

You can purchase an "unfit" vehicle and use it unlicensed on private property such as a farm, fishing or hunting camp, but not on any public road. Even crossing a public road to another private property is illegal—and risky if the vehicle is not insured. If the vehicle is to be used to transport guests of a summer lodge or fishing-hunting camp, consult an insurance agent about liability.

Used-car warranties. Dealers sometimes offer warranties as sales incentives. Beware of the split-cost, 50-50 warranty, often worse than no warranty because it can be used as evidence of the dealer's good faith. A dishonest dealer can simply double the price of parts and labor, charging you half, which is really the full price.

If a dealer offers a 50-50 warranty for 60 days, suggest a compromise—a 100-percent warranty for only 30 days. If he strongly objects, you have a good idea what the 50-50 warranty is worth. Be wary, too, of dealers who offer you warranty on parts only. Remember that labor costs make up the bulk of most repair bills.

THE PUFFERY PROBLEM

The ads say your compact has all the best features of the luxury cars. After two months on country roads it is rattling like a bucket of bolts.

Consumers are expected to distinguish between puffery and fact and, no matter what the advertisement said, it is unreasonable to believe a $5,000 compact has the same features of a $15,000 luxury car. About the only similarity is that both cars have more or less the same warranty. You can return your three-month-old vehicle to the dealer and have the rattles fixed. Some people still misconstrue advertising puffery and warranty promises. For instance, an advertisement reads: "A Blotz Six is your best bet for trouble-free motoring." You buy one, have nothing but trouble and sue for damages, on the grounds that you bought the vehicle because it promised trouble-free motoring. The judge is unlikely to agree with your interpretation, because no car can be guaranteed trouble-free and no reasonably well-informed consumer would believe such claims.

Advertising guidelines. When a television commercial showed a car roaring down a dock and flying onto the deck of a boat, government officials ordered the advertisement off the air. They said it portrayed the car doing something that the average driver couldn't reasonably be expected to do without disastrous results. A Vancouver dealer was ordered to stop advertising the price of a car because he didn't include the freight and dealer preparation charges in the figure. Therefore, it was not the price the customer had to pay—the true "price" as defined by the Trade Practices Act of British Columbia.

In most provinces, an advertisement is considered misleading if it:

■ Advertises a price when the car is not available at that price.

■ Advertises credit terms without giving the cost of borrowing or the total price with interest added on.

■ Compares prices of cars that are not identical—for example, compares the price of a 1980 car with that of a 1981 car.

■ Advertises fuel economy without quoting Transport Canada test results along with a disclosure that actual mileage will vary depending on the owner's driving habits, and on the car's condition and optional equipment.

■ Advertises a specific car for sale, usually a base model, using a photograph or illustration of another car—one loaded with appearance options, for example.

FUEL CONSUMPTION

Your new car gets less than the kilometres-per-gallon promised by the manufacturer.

One of the unpleasant surprises of owning a new car is that you don't get the gas "mileage" the manufacturer says you should get. The only mileage estimates the manufacturer is allowed to use in his advertising are those based on Transport Canada tests. The testing procedures are modeled closely on those developed by the Environmental Protection Agency (EPA) in the United States. They're done under tightly controlled conditions so as to produce a reliable norm, against which mileage obtained under other conditions can be measured. By law, advertisements that refer to fuel consumption must note that "actual mileage will vary depending on driving habits, your car's condition and equipment," and such things as weather and road conditions. In addition, test cars are well broken-in; until a new car has been driven at least 5,000 kilometres (3,100 miles), moving parts are still getting used to their operation patterns and fuel economy is reduced.

Testing methods. The EPA tests cars on a dynamometer, which is a kind of treadmill. The dynamometer takes into account wind and rolling resistances. With a dynamometer, indoors testing at constant temperature and humidity—factors that affect mileage—is possible the year round. If cars were tested under all sorts of varying conditions, the ratings would be meaningless, even as a comparison guide.

EPA estimates are *not* a guarantee of minimum performance, but a guide to differences between cars. How and where you drive your car will determine your mileage. But a car ranked high in EPA testing will give you proportionately more mileage than one ranked lower.

Most new cars are equipped with catalytic converters and so require unleaded gasoline. Installed in the exhaust system, the "cat" uses chemicals to neutralize noxious gases. Lead would burn out the chemicals, rendering the "cat" useless.

Meantime, the octane content of all gasolines sold in Canada has been dropping as new gases are blended to suit new engines. As a result, many motorists whose cars run on regular-grade unleaded gasoline find that their engines "ping" and "knock." The condition usually clears up when they switch to premium-grade unleaded gas. Some experts claim that the pings and knocks are harmless; others say they are a symptom of unnecessary wear in the engine.

Cocktail mixes. Some older cars with high-compression engines were designed to run on leaded premium gasoline, which is no longer available in most Canadian filling stations. To get the required octane, it is necessary to use a premium unleaded fuel. If you own such a car and are concerned that it still needs the lubrication provided by leaded fuels, try a "cocktail mix" of leaded regular-grade fuel and unleaded premium about every third or fourth fill-up. There are octane boosters on the market, which can be added to gasoline to increase the octane rating. But these are very expensive and unnecessary in most cases.

Fighting rust is an endless battle

Several factors influence the speed at which your car rusts. The vehicle that remains wet and dirty over lengthy periods is inviting corrosion. So too is the automobile where dampness or moisture persists in one area, such as the floor section, while the rest of the car is dry. Atmospheric pollution from industries in your area or the use of salt as a de-icer on your city streets will also hasten the rusting process. Your automobile is especially likely to rust if you live in areas of high humidity or where winter temperatures regularly rise above freezing—regions such as the British Columbia coast, Southern Ontario, the St. Lawrence Valley, and the Atlantic provinces. Another major cause of corrosion is the removal of protective paints, either in accidents or as a result of driving on surfaces coated with gravel or loose stones.

While you may not be able to prevent corrosion altogether, there are some things you can do to delay the process. Wash your car once a week. Use a mild soap or detergent and use jets of water to rid the underside of dirt. Make sure that all caked mud is removed. Check that drain holes at doors and tailgates are not clogged with grit. Rinse with clear water, make sure that all soap is removed, and dry thoroughly. Hot water is not recommended at any time, particularly in cold weather when it may cause paint to crack. Special care should be taken to keep the car floor dry in winter. Remove loose mats often so that both mats and floor can dry out.

Mount mud shields on the body edge behind each wheel as protection against loose stones and salt. The shields should be as close to the road as possible and the fittings should be corrosion-resistant. Any damage from flying stones or any surfaces from which the paint has been chipped or scratched should be treated immediately at an auto body repair shop. If you do the work yourself, sandpaper the damaged area, apply an antirust primer and allow to dry before sanding the edges. This should be done lightly, so that the metal is not reexposed. Finally, apply the appropriate body paint.

RUST

Patches of rust have appeared on the new car that you had rust-proofed at the time of purchase.

Even with rustproofing, the metal in your car body and frame will eventually rust if you live in an area where the roads are salted and where near-freezing conditions are the norm in winter. The best you can hope for is delayed corrosion. Also, rustproofing, improperly applied or applied after the car has sat on a lot for several months, can actually hasten the rusting process. Rust on a new car, however, is a different matter. If the patches are on the outside surface, the problem lies with the paint and undercoating. Either the materials were defective or they were improperly applied. Whichever the case, the manufacturer should correct the situation without argument. Your new-car warranty covers defects in workmanship and material.

In addition, most manufacturers and importers provide warranties that match the Federal/Provincial Anti-Corrosion Code for Motor Vehicles. The code says: "Every new vehicle sold or offered for sale in Canada (1978 and later models) shall remain free from surface corrosion resulting from defects in design, materials or manufacture for a period of 12 months or 40,000 kilometres, whichever occurs first, from the date the vehicle is first put into service." In 1981, the code extends the corrosion-free period for both surface rust and perforation, but manufacturers are balking at adopting the new standards.

The code and warranties apply whether or not the car has been rustproofed after manufacture. The code and most warranties require that you maintain the car as suggested in the owner's manual and that you return the car to the rustproofer and dealer for periodic examinations, usually once a year. If the rusting is due to chipping by stones or occurs where metal was bared in a collision, you are expected to pay for the repairs.

Rusting from the inside. If your car is past warranty, and rust from the inside is starting to show on the outer body, complain to both the rustproofer and the manufacturer. Some major Canadian rustproofers belong to the Canadian Association of Automotive Rustprotectors (CAAR), which was formed in 1978. In an attempt to brighten a severely tarnished image of the industry, the association developed a fair warranty policy and an arbitration procedure. Customers' complaints are examined by a technical standards committee on which the public, the industry and government are represented. Under the association's standard warranty, damage arising from inferior workmanship or products will be repaired for up to five years of unlimited travel.

Rustproofing in Canada is a $100-million business with a high profit margin. It costs a dealer $30 to $40 to rustproof your car, but the cost to you is $150 to $250. With profits like this, the business attracts get-rich-quick artists and incompetents. Their "money-back guarantees" are of little value when your car requires body work costing many hundreds of dollars.

Choose a rustproofer or car dealer who will match the CAAR warranty or who is a member of the association and has been in business for some time. Some car owners have been stung by operators who performed shoddy work, then closed up shop and disappeared. If in doubt, check with the Better Business Bureau or your local consumer services bureau for advice.

Rust holes. Most new-car warranties protect you against perforation (rust holes) for three years or 120,000 kilometres. Anti-corrosion guidelines include structural damage to the vehicle for up to six years or 240,000 kilometres. But manufacturers' provisions vary. For instance, American Motors began rustproofing their 1980 cars on the assembly line and offering a five-year perforation warranty. Following several lawsuits involving rusted cars, manufacturers have also increased the use of galvanized metals, rust-inhibiting primers and paints, plastic fender liners and chip-retardant plastic coatings.

Whenever rustproofers, dealers and manufacturers have been sued, the courts have almost always found in favor of the consumer.

Small Claims Court actions have been especially successful. If you do sue, include the rustproofer, the dealer and the manufacturer in the action. This often results in one or more of them helping to place the blame on the other.

DAMAGE DURING REPAIRS

Your car is still under warranty but your local dealer will not replace the upholstery that was torn during a service check.

The fact that the car is under warranty has no bearing on the question of who is going to pay for the upholstery repairs. Clearly, the damage results from misuse, so it is not covered by warranty. If the dealer replaces the upholstery, the cost will come from his own pocket. Should he refuse, your best recourse is to sue him in Small Claims Court. You must then convince a judge that the damage occurred in the garage, caused, probably, by a mechanic with a screwdriver sticking out of his pocket. Pictures of the torn interior might help in court.

Ripped upholstery and oily stains on seats or carpets are common complaints after visits to any mechanical repair shop. Precautionary measures are worthwhile. Always advise the service supervisor that the upholstery is in perfect shape and ask the mechanics working on the car to cover the seats and carpet to prevent damage.

THE MAINTENANCE CONTRACT

You bought a maintenance contract when you purchased your car and it seems to cover everything except the things that have gone wrong.

Maintenance contracts, sometimes called continuous warranties or continuous protection plans, are sold just like any other new-car option. They are profitable for the dealer and the manufacturer. As one Canadian automobile executive puts it, it's a case of you betting the car company that some major repair is going to be necessary on your car in the first three years.

Typically, a maintenance contract costs $150 to $300 and runs for three years or 60,000 kilometres. In effect though, such contracts cover only the second and third years, since most of the first-year benefits are already included in the new-car warranty. In some cases the only bonus is an allowance for towing and car rental. If you do invest in a maintenance contract, bargain vigorously. A discount of 25 or even 35 percent would be fair. And make sure the contract doesn't require additional and more expensive "routine" maintenance.

The exceptions. Heading the list of exceptions to your maintenance contract will be any item costing less than the $25 or $50 deductible provision in your agreement. Hoses, filters, shocks, brake drums, discs and shoes, cables, springs and belts—the parts most likely to wear out in three years—are all excluded. If these were the source of your motoring troubles, the contract might appear to be a waste of money. On the other hand, if your car had three major breakdowns during the period covered, you would consider the contract a wise investment. Maintenance contracts are insurance against problems, not likely to occur but involving a great deal of expense when they do. Coverage will include the innards of engine, transmission and differential—the big-dollar items on your car.

RECALLS

The dealer refuses to fix your car under the terms of the manufacturer's recall because your deadline passed while you were out of the country.

The dealer is wrong; there is no deadline on recalls. Such a limitation would penalize second or third owners of vehicles whose original owners ignored the recall. Of course, a dealer may balk if you show up three years after the fact for replacement of a minor part that has never shown any sign of trouble. And he would probably be justified in not bothering with an outdated recall of owners' manuals for a change in wording. Only about 3 percent of owners return misprinted manuals.

Should the dealer, however, refuse repairs associated with a safety-related recall, get in touch with your car manufacturer's zone manager or your local branch of Transport Canada. The dealer will be advised of your entitlement to repairs or adjustments and of his liability for damages if the part fails and causes an accident.

Why a recall? Some recalls originate with the manufacturers and others are initiated by the Road Safety Branch of Transport Canada. More cars, about 1.5 million, were recalled in 1978 than were made in Canada that year.

The high figure was attributed to increased government testing in both Canada and the United States and to pressure from consumer groups that identify safety-related problems.

Canadian recalls cost the manufacturers about $10 million a year. The cost is 10 times greater in the United States, where automakers have had massive recalls to correct flawed antipollution equipment. In one case involving 2.4 million cars built by Ford, American Motors and Datsun, the cost was $48 million.

The owner's response to a recall depends on the nature of the ailment. The figure is as high as 85 percent when safety is a factor, but as low as 5 percent if the recall is merely to correct a fault in, say, a glove-compartment door.

The Firestone 500 case

There has been far more concern about tire safety since 1979, when Firestone Tires recalled almost the entire production of Firestone 500 radial tires. The recall came in the face of an American investigation of the tires and severe criticism of the product by consumer-protection groups. It cost Firestone $200 million in the United States and $20 million in Canada. Bad publicity associated with the Firestone 500 radial also cost the company uncalculated millions.

The rub is that no one, not the consumer groups that brought the matter to the attention of the U.S. National Highway Traffic Safety Administration (NHTSA), nor the NHTSA itself nor Transport Canada testers, ever found a single clear-cut defect in the Firestone 500s.

Publicity, not facts, prompted the recall, Firestone said. Day after day, the media reported the claims of the consumer champions who took the stand at the NHTSA investigation in Washington. And some witnesses painted grisly pictures of hundreds dead and maimed because of defective Firestone 500s. The company's sales went flat.

The NHTSA could find no safety-related defects in the tires when it tested them after the complaints began. Nor could Transport Canada when its Road Safety Branch took a harder look at Firestone 500s. In four years of testing, it found no failures in the 730 Firestone 500s tried. When Transport Canada laboratories examined 90 failed tires, the conclusion was that most of the failures were linked to severe under-inflation—which, of course, was the fault of the motorist.

Were Firestone 500 radials really defective or did media and consumer pressure force the recall? Maybe the tires were faulty. But many motorists who volunteered as witnesses, and unsolicited endorsements produced by Firestone, claimed that the 500s were the best tires they ever had.

Since that time, Transport Canada has taken a greater interest in tire safety, running tests on all makes and types available to the public. Meantime, if you have questions about the tires on your car, get in touch with Transport Canada, Road and Motor Vehicle Traffic Safety Branch, Tower "C," Place de Ville, Ottawa, Ont., K1A 0N5.

Hardly anyone returns to correct exhaust emission faults. American Motors of Canada (AMC) boasts of a 100-percent response to one recall. AMC spotted a problem with its 1979 jeeps early in the production run. Eighteen of the vehicles had already been sold and all 18 owners came back for repairs.

Checking on recalls. Manufacturers are required to advise owners-of-record by first-class mail in the event of a recall. But the letter will probably never reach you if you are the second or third owner of the car, unless you advise the manufacturer when you purchase a used car. Ask for copies of all previous recall notices pertaining to your year, make and model. It's also wise to check with your Canadian Automobile Association club or the Road Safety Branch of Transport Canada on recalls affecting your car and its equipment, such as tires and batteries.

Manufacturers do not compensate car owners for the inconvenience or indirect cost involved in recalls and Canada has no legislation compelling them to do so.

CONTINUAL REPAIRS

Your dealer has made three attempts to repair a faulty alternator on your new car but you're still having trouble.

Manufacturers pay dealers about 90 percent of the list price for parts such as alternators, starters and fuel pumps for warranty repairs. So there is no good reason why your dealer shouldn't replace the alternator instead of trying to fix it. Replacement is more costly for the dealer when large components such as engines, transmissions and differentials are involved.

If repairs to a major item haven't helped, and if your dealer refuses a replacement, take your car to another dealer carrying the same car line. If he agrees with the first dealer, but you are still not convinced that repairs alone will be satisfactory, take your car to an independent garage and get a written estimate of what is required to correct the problem. Then get in touch with the customer service representative at the manufacturer's zone office. If the service representative agrees with both dealers, ask for written assurance that repairs alone will solve the problem and request an acknowledgment that he is aware of the independent mechanic's analysis. Then press on with your demand, if necessary, right to the president of the company.

From the beginning, negotiate in writing as much as possible, keeping copies of both your letters and replies, plus estimates. Often, the mere knowledge that you are documenting the case will be enough to push the dealer or manufacturer to replace a part if it is truly necessary.

Rebuilt parts. In general, factory-rebuilt parts are manufactured to tolerances as good as or better than original equipment parts. Therefore, there is little to be concerned about if you find a dealer is installing such parts while the car is under warranty. Make sure, however, that the rebuilt parts have the same warranty as new parts and that any parts used on your car during the warranty period are 'authorized' replacement or remanufactured parts. Only in this way can you make sure that the manufacturer will not refuse to honor the warranty because of unauthorized parts.

37 Automobile insurance

The *theory* of insurance is simple: it is a pooling of risks, and a sharing of losses. The *practice* of insurance is not so simple—especially the insuring of automobiles. Owners, drivers, passengers, pedestrians—we all should know what the law requires and what common sense dictates in the way of coverage. Such knowledge is essential protection against losses we may cause others or others may cause us.

Public liability and property damage (PL&PD) coverage is "third-party" insurance—an agreement between you and your insurance company to cover damages you might cause to a third party. It is important to understand that the insurance company agrees to pay damages for liability imposed by law *only* if a judgment is awarded against you by a court—and only up to the limit of your policy. If you had $100,000 coverage under your PL&PD policy, for example, and a court awarded $200,000 in damages against you to someone injured in an accident, your insurance company would pay $100,000 only.

But while insurance companies are liable only if there is a judgment against you, they normally attempt to settle out of court with the injured third party. If the third party decides to sue you, your insurance company will probably have its own lawyer defend you. Your loss, after all, would be its loss. Even when you're entirely to blame for an accident, the company has a vested interest in making the least costly settlement possible.

As for protection against whatever losses you might cause to yourself, there are collision, comprehensive and special-peril provisions available in insurance policies. These are "no-fault" provisions, which means your insurance company pays for whatever damage you receive. It may later sue the other driver if your car was damaged in a collision, but it pays you immediately. Collision coverage usu-

ally includes a deductibility clause, the deductible amount ranging from zero to several hundred dollars. You pay the deductible and the company pays the balance of the cost of the claim. And the higher the deductible, the lower your insurance rate or premium.

Quebec, Manitoba, Saskatchewan and British Columbia have compulsory, government-operated car insurance schemes. Motorists *must* buy the compulsory package and may take additional coverage from private companies. And while insurance is not compulsory in other provinces, it is mandatory that a driver be able to produce an insurance card or certificate of financial responsibility.

Automobile insurance is a $4-billion-a-year industry in Canada. Yet some companies have had years when they lost money because claims paid exceeded premiums collected.

If there is a minimum of compulsory coverage required in your province, it is surely not enough to protect you against all costs that can arise from an auto accident. The size of damage awards and repair costs have been increasing sharply over the last 10 years.

The premium you pay for insurance depends on your age, sex, driving record, the type and amount of driving you do, where you do it, and the type of car you own. In the late 1970s, several provinces began to look for a way to eliminate age and sex from the calculation of insurance premiums, but an acceptable method of rating proved difficult to find.

Whatever your premium, it is worth remembering that increasing your insurance protection is relatively cheap. It doesn't cost much to increase your PL&PD coverage to $300,000 from $100,000, for example. And the few extra dollars of premium cost could save you from financial ruin in the event of a major accident.

You may be able to cut your insurance costs and still provide yourself with adequate protection by shopping carefully. A study by the Insurance Bureau of Canada indicates that premiums can vary as much as 20 percent from company to company. More surprising, a 1979 survey of insurance rates by Toronto's *Globe & Mail* showed that premiums varied as much as 300 percent within specific areas.

FINANCIAL RESPONSIBILITY

Auto insurance is not compulsory in your province. You wonder, then, why you must produce an insurance card on demand.

It's a matter of proving that you have the financial resources to pay for any damage or injury you may cause as a driver. The simplest way to do this is to buy an insurance policy. Some provinces make it compulsory for an owner to *buy insurance* before his vehicle can be licensed, or for a driver to buy insurance when he buys his driver's license—as proof of financial responsibility.

Other provinces simply make it mandatory for an owner to *prove financial responsibility* upon request of a police officer. Where this applies, some corporations and wealthy individuals prefer to be self-insurers—rather than buy insurance. They get certificates saying they have the financial resources to make good any injury or damage they, or their agents, may cause. Some corporations operating fleets of vehicles do this because it makes economic sense. Statistically, it costs them less to pay damages than to pay insurance premiums on all their vehicles.

Where individuals are concerned, only an eccentric millionaire would risk personal wealth against the payment of an insurance premium on his vehicle. This is the difference between compulsory and mandatory. If you live in a province where automobile insurance is not compulsory—and if you're sufficiently eccentric and well off—you can post a personal bond for the minimum financial liability required by your province.

Large corporations, public utilities and government departments or agencies—Bell Canada, the RCMP and the armed forces, for example—post bonds which guarantee that they can satisfy accident claims. If you have a claim against a party such as these, you or your insurance company must file it with the company or agency or utility in question in order to collect damages.

Unsatisfied judgment funds. In cases where the other driver is uninsured, or unknown (hit-and-run), you must collect damages from the unsatisfied judgment fund. Although the names vary, all provinces have some such fund. Even so, you are still 100 percent liable for any damages you or other drivers cause when driving your vehicle. If you or the other party in an accident are not insured, these are the choices:

■ You can negotiate a settlement with the injured parties and pay for property damage or personal injury that your actions have caused.

■ If you are unable to negotiate a settlement, or are unable to pay, the injured party will apply to the unsatisfied judgment fund, which will then advise you by registered letter that a claim has been filed. You have 30 days in which to deny or accept liability. If you deny liability, the other motorist must sue you and settle the matter in court. If you lose the case, you must pay the judgment, or the unsatisfied judgment fund will pay and then seek to recover the money from you. Your driver's license and motor vehicle permit will be suspended until you make arrangements to reimburse the fund and obtain regular liability insurance.

REPORTING ACCIDENTS

An uninsured driver damaged your car. He promises to pay for the repairs and pleads with you not to report the accident.

Failing to report an accident is a serious matter. It can result in criminal charges against you, or be grounds for your insurance company to refuse to pay claims arising from the accident.

In most cases, you must report an accident to your insurance company as well as to the police. Generally, insurance companies are not liable if policyholders don't report accidents within 90 days. Even if it appears that your insurance company will have no claims to pay, it is wise to report an accident.

Considerable time is allowed for instituting an action, regardless of whether the accident was reported to the police. In Newfoundland, it's two years for property damage and bodily injury, one year for death; Prince Edward Island, two years for personal injuries and six years for property damage; Quebec, two years for property damage, one year for bodily injury; Manitoba, two years for personal injuries and property damage; and Saskatchewan, one year for personal injuries and property damage. All other provinces allow two years. Time is counted from the date of the accident.

The law does not require you to report an accident to the police if there is no personal injury and property damage does not exceed a certain amount. This varies from province to province but ranges between $200 and $400.

Many motorists underestimate damage nowadays: a bumper alone can cost as much as $400 to repair or replace. The best way to protect your interests is to report an accident as fully as possible. Make detailed notes of the location, weather conditions, visibility, and names and addresses of witnesses. Cooperate fully with the officer investigating the accident, but be careful not to make any statements regarding fault or blame. Stick to the incontestable facts. Some insurance companies provide a checklist of procedures to follow in the event of an accident.

STOLEN CARS

Your car was stolen two months ago. You have given up hope of ever seeing it again.

About 100,000 cars are stolen every year: one of every 135 vehicles registered in Canada. Some 15,000 are never recovered. In Quebec,

---

No 'blockbuster' awards in Canada

You read about them all the time. Somebody in the United States is injured in an auto accident and sues the manufacturer. This results in headlines such as: *California youth, 19, gets $127 million in burning Ford case.* The young man suffered burns over 90 percent of his body when the Pinto he was riding in burst into flames after a rear-end collision. This award—later reduced to $6.3 million—is much higher than any Canadian judgments. The biggest accident settlements in Canada, according to Professor Reuben Hasson of Osgoode Hall law school in Toronto, have been for $1.5 million, $1.02 million and $875,000.

A major deterrent to Canadians seeking blockbuster awards is the high cost of legal proceedings. In Canada, if you lose, you pay the other guy's lawyer as well as your own. In the United States, lawyers use a contingency-fee system: you pay nothing if you lose, but the lawyer takes a quarter to a third of the settlement if you win. Some provinces permit a modified contingency fee, under which the lawyer quotes what you'll owe *if* you win.

Another deterrent—and a fundamental reason Canadians don't win blockbuster awards—is that cases in this country are usually heard by judges, who are less generous than U.S. juries in awarding settlements. The U.S. legal system allows for the awarding of *punitive* damages, which can be very high. Not so in Canada, where damages are *compensatory* and therefore lower.

If it becomes necessary to sue to collect damages, either from a third party in an accident or from a manufacturer whose defective auto caused the accident, your insurance company will provide legal fees to the extent that its own interest is served; you, however, will still have to finance your personal claim.

where auto theft is a major problem, police are constantly breaking up car-theft rings, but some 25 percent of the cars stolen disappear for good.

Canadian insurance companies usually pay claims on stolen cars within 30 to 60 days. Loss of your car through fire or theft can be covered by a "comprehensive," an "all perils" or a "special perils" insurance policy. "Comprehensive" means coverage in the event of fire or total theft, without having to pay any deductible. This type also covers you for damage caused by something other than a collision, and for theft of parts or for vandalism, less your specified deductible amount. All-perils insurance covers collision and all the areas normally covered in a comprehensive policy, although a deductibility clause applies in every claim except fire or total theft. Special-perils insurance covers you for damages or loss from certain causes only, as specified in your policy.

Replacement value. If your car is stolen, or lost in a fire, an adjuster will try to determine the general condition of the car and confirm the existence of special accessories that enhanced its value. Using current used-car price guides, he will arrive at a price. If you disagree with his evaluation, you can appeal to the insurance company for a reevaluation. A Montreal man once increased his settlement with a major insurer by $1,000 when he was able to produce evidence that his sports car had been equipped with an air conditioner and a tape deck. His car had been destroyed by fire and the destruction was so complete that the adjuster could find no trace of the equipment in the ashes. This is another reason for keeping records on your car.

Most Canadian insurance companies will also provide a loss-of-use clause in their policies to cover the cost of renting a vehicle if your car is burned or stolen.

Sometimes a stolen car is recovered long after you have been compensated for your loss and have purchased another car. The recovered car may then become the property of the insurance company, which will dispose of it and write off the selling price against the loss it incurred in settling your claim.

The best defense against theft is to wind up the car windows tightly, lock the car and take the keys with you. This is no guarantee that your car won't be stolen by a determined, well-equipped professional thief, but it lessens the chance of the car falling into the hands of youthful joy riders. Since the introduction of steering-column locks several years ago, "hot wiring"—bypassing the ignition lock by connecting the live or "hot" wire outside the lock—is gradually disappearing as a method of stealing cars.

About 15 percent of all cars stolen have had the key left in the ignition—an open invitation to theft. It is not uncommon for a car to disappear when it is left running outside a store while the owner is buying a pack of cigarettes. About 35 percent are driven away after the ignition-lock cylinder has been "pulled," with the help of a special tool. Other thieves use keys made from stolen key-code books, and a few stolen cars are simply towed away to a quiet garage where thieves can alter or strip them at leisure.

Stolen and wrecked. What if your car is stolen, and the thief gets away after wrecking it and damaging another in a head-on collision? Your insurance company may pay claims arising from an accident involving your car when it is stolen and it will pay for the loss of your car. If the thief is caught, you, your insurance company and the other driver can seek restitution. If the other driver's losses exceed your insurance limits, additional damages from the unsatisfied judgment fund can be claimed in some provinces.

DIFFERENT DRIVERS

A friend borrows your car and is involved in an accident. You didn't know that his driver's license had been suspended.

If your insurance company is satisfied that you were unaware that your friend's license was suspended, it will pay claims against you resulting from the accident, and then sue your friend to recover its costs. The insurance company would refuse to pay claims, however, if you were aware that his license was suspended, or if lending him the car was a regular occurrence and the insurer felt you should have been aware of your friend's status as a driver.

The same rule applies if a driver of your car is impaired or drunk while involved in an accident. If you were aware that your friend was in the habit of drinking and driving, or was borrowing the car to attend a party where drinks would be served, the insurance company will balk at your claim. It may, in fact, satisfy the claim, then sue *you* to recover its loss.

If your insurance company refuses to pay a claim, you do have the right to sue the company in the event you feel its refusal was unjustified under the terms of your policy. However, provided it's not a huge claim, insurers generally don't balk at negotiating a settlement—unless they're absolutely convinced they have no liability.

The borrowed car. Lending a car to anyone, even a member of your family, can result in legal entanglements for you. Generally, the owner of the vehicle is liable for damages resulting from any negligence on the part of the driver, unless theft can be established.

From the point of view of insurance coverage, the question of "consent" arises. This does not even mean that you have to give specific consent every time a member of your family or close friend borrows your car, in order to be considered liable. If someone is in the habit of using your car, it is assumed that there is an implied consent on your part whenever he does "borrow" it.

Be wary of lending your car to anyone not specifically covered in your policy, even if the person's own insurance covers whatever car he drives. You would certainly be named in a court action arising from the negligent operation of your car and, along with the driver, might be held liable for damages. It is even possible that the borrower himself could sue you if the mechanical condition of the vehicle contributed to an accident. If the borrower were injured and obtained a court judgment in excess of your insurance policy limit, you would have to pay.

TAKING THE BLAME

Your neighbor agreed that he was responsible for bumping into your car. But while his insurance company paid to have his car fixed immediately, you are still awaiting a settlement.

If there's no doubt about who was to blame, there is no reason why your claim should not be paid quickly. But you must file a claim with your neighbor's insurance company. It is not enough for him to file a report of the accident—his insurance company will not pay if *you* don't make a claim.

Although your neighbor may be willing to shoulder the responsibility for the collision, his insurance company may feel you should bear some of the blame.

Determining fault. Insurance companies warn policyholders not to admit blame in the event of an accident, even though blame is sometimes easily determined. In a rear-end collision, for example, the car following is presumed at fault. And when a car crashes into a legally parked automobile, or the driver falls asleep or loses control in a single-car accident, there is little doubt about who's to blame. Even though you may feel you are totally responsible for an accident, however, you should try to confine your reports and statements to the essential facts of the accident and let police investigators, appraisers and insurance companies determine fault. You have the right to protest any decision with which you don't agree, but you may weaken your case if you voluntarily accept any of the blame.

PREMIUM RATINGS

You were involved in two minor accidents for which you have been found partially responsible. Now your insurance company will not renew your coverage.

Perhaps your insurance company is one of those that can charge substantially lower rates because it accepts only low-risk policyholders, of whom you are no longer one. Too bad. It is more likely, however, that your insurer will offer to renew coverage but your premium will skyrocket after two accidents in one year—especially if you had had a clean record for the past five years, not having been responsible for a single accident. In such a case, your premiums could more than double.

The highest premium rate applies to drivers who have recently had several accidents for which they have been held partly or totally responsible. Each year that you are free from a "responsible" accident earns a discounted rate. Most companies operate under a merit system, where you pay less for insurance for each accident-free year up to five. For example, three years free of claims mean a reduction of 41 percent on the basic insurance premium and five years claim-free mean a reduction of 58 percent. If you have five years claim-free, many companies will allow you one claim before reducing your preferential rate to zero. Accidents for which you are not responsible don't affect your claim-free re-

It pays to shop around

You could be paying too much for your auto insurance—far too much. Premium rates vary considerably from company to company, so it pays to shop around.

Companies insure almost eight million vehicles annually and they are bound to make some mistakes. They use computers and number classifications and a simple mistake could result in a much higher premium for you than your proper rating provides. For example, the transposition of numbers, rating you 130 when you should be 013, would result in your insurance bill being four times more than it should. If in doubt, ask your agent to check and clarify your classification.

Here are some rates quoted by eight major automobile insurance companies in 1979. Some are high because the company didn't really want the business. In the first case, rates quoted for a 23-year-old male driver with one accident and one speeding ticket in the past year varied by more than $1,000. Case No. 2 shows the rates quoted for a woman of the same age with exactly the same driving record. In all quotations, the female driver's rates were substantially lower—in one instance by $542. Case No. 3 is for a family of four with two cars, one an Oldsmobile Cutlass driven exclusively by the 48-year-old father. He had a single accident four years ago, after 15 years of claim-free driving. The rest of the family—mother and a daughter, 19, and son, 17—share the driving of a Ford Pinto. The daughter, who has taken an approved driver-education course, is the principal driver of the Pinto, using it to get to school 11 kilometres away. In Case No. 3, rates varied by $354.

Here are the prices quoted, illustrating the saving you could realize by shopping around.

	Case No. 1	Case No. 2	Case No. 3
Allstate Insurance	$ 583	$419	$ 922
Commercial Union Assurance	964	664	696
The Co-Operators	1,092	794	930
Fireman's Fund Insurance	684	566	1,029
General Accident Assurance	424	339	941
Royal Insurance	448	368	870
State Farm Insurance	1,425	893	675
Zurich Insurance	487	361	924

cord, except for collision coverage when the company cannot recover from the other driver. Many companies also use surcharges for drivers with bad records, but these vary from company to company.

You'd also lose your preferred-rating classification if you were convicted of a driving charge under the Criminal Code—such as drunken, impaired, or careless driving—or had more than two traffic violations, other than parking, within a three-year period.

Terminating a policy. A condition of every insurance policy is that either party can terminate the policy at any time. You can cancel your policy and get a refund for the unused portion of the premium—and give no reason for the cancellation. In provinces where insurance is compulsory, the insurance company must inform the motor vehicle licensing branch of any cancellation. The company can legally cancel insurance with 15 days' notice by registered mail or five days' notice by personal delivery.

In practice, however, insurance companies do not cancel auto policies except for non-payment of premiums. It is accepted by the insurance industry that every Canadian driver has a right to be insured. High-risk drivers are not abandoned, but their premium rates reflect the risk.

Extremely high-risk drivers are shared by the entire insurance industry under what is popularly known as the assigned-risk plan. Since 1968, auto insurers have had a "facility association," which distributes the risk of bad drivers equally across the industry. If your driving record is so abysmal that you don't even fall into a regular category, you will be insured through the "facility," whether you are aware of it or not. The fact is, though, that high-risk premiums do not cover the losses that the insurance industry incurs through the facility. All insured motorists partially subsidize these high risks.

Your insurance premiums can be affected in a number of ways. A more expensive or exotic car will cost more to repair in the event of an accident, so your rates for collision, comprehensive, all-perils or specified-perils insurance will increase if you acquire such a car. Your rates will also be affected adversely if you acquire a high-performance car, because of the experience of insurance companies in frequency and severity of accidents with such cars.

Your PL&PD insurance will be less expensive if you move from a large city to a rural area. Your collision and comprehensive coverage, on the other hand, may become more expensive because it is more difficult to find expert repairmen in rural areas and some risks are greater, for example, the risk of stones breaking your windshield on a gravel secondary road.

Getting married moves you into a different insurance category. So does growing older. The effect in either case is usually to lower your premium. The premium also becomes less expensive as past accidents and driving convictions get farther behind you.

ADJUSTERS AND APPRAISERS

The "independent adjuster" sent by your insurance company has made a ridiculously low assessment of damages to your car.

No adjuster's word is final. You have the right to appeal if you feel the appraisal of your damages or loss is unjust. The appeal procedure is outlined very clearly in your insurance policy. It says that you and the company are both entitled to appoint an appraiser and that the person you choose need not be a professional claims adjuster.

If the two appraisers cannot settle on an award, they must select an impartial umpire. The umpire has the final word on what the company will pay. Each party pays its own appraiser and shares the expenses of the umpire. Thus, you have equal rights with the insurance company in obtaining expert advice and assistance.

Some see an insurance claim as an opportunity to gain something. However, you are entitled only to be put in the same position as you were before the accident, insofar as this is possible. Your insurer may agree to replace damaged auto parts with new ones. Strictly speaking, you are not entitled to new parts, which are naturally in better condition than the old ones that were damaged. In this sense, you may "make a profit."

Appraising the damage. The complicated business of determining losses in the event of an automobile mishap is gradually being taken over by staff adjusters employed by insurance companies. They are replacing the independent adjusters traditionally used by most insurance companies. The switch to highly trained company adjusters is most prevalent in large cities, where there are always more than enough claims to keep them busy. Independents still function in rural areas where one adjuster can serve the needs of several insurance companies.

Independent adjusters are licensed by the provinces, after completing written and oral examinations. Company adjusters do not have to be licensed, but an unqualified adjuster will either cost the company too much money in over-generous settlements or alienate policyholders by being too stingy.

The straightforward but time-consuming process of collision appraisal is best handled at an appraisal center approved by the Insurance Bureau of Canada. In 1979 there were 38 such centers across the nation. These centers quickly assess the damage to your car and make an estimate acceptable to most body shops.

If an appraisal center is not available, you may have to get three written estimates of the damage and submit them to the insurance company. If the company feels the estimates are out of line, it may not give the green light for repairs until an adjuster can look at the car, or it may suggest a repair shop known to it.

Some surprises in your auto policy

There is a good chance that you have been insured for years but are totally unfamiliar with what your insurance actually covers and what is required of you in an accident. The reason, simply, is that most people don't read their insurance policies. In fact, you may not even possess a copy of the actual policy. Many Canadian insurers provide a copy of the policy only if it is requested.

If you don't have a copy of your policy, ask your agent to send you one. You may be surprised to learn, for instance, that your insurance company can sue someone in your name. Your policy gives the insurer the right of subrogation—the substitution of one person for another—so that the same rights and duties attached to the original person are transferred to the substituted one. If the insurance company has paid you for damage caused by another person, it is quite likely it will sue to reclaim that money. It is legally entitled to sue in your name and to have your cooperation. If you refuse to cooperate, the company can sue *you* to get its money back.

If you have a claim against the insurance company for bodily injury, the company can demand medical reports "as often as it reasonably requires" while the claim is pending. If you die, the insurance company has the right to order an autopsy to determine the exact cause.

The insurance company doesn't have to pay if you rent or lease your car to someone else, if you use your car to carry explosives or radioactive material, or if you use the automobile as a taxi or sightseeing conveyance for pay.

If your policy carries an endorsement restricting occupant coverage in commercial automobiles and you carry more than three people in a pickup truck, you may not be covered.

Your liability and accident-benefits insurance are in effect if you borrow, rent or lease a substitute vehicle while your car is being repaired or serviced, or if the car is lost, destroyed or sold. But consult your insurance agent on this point if the substitute vehicle is to be used for some time.

YOUNG DRIVERS

Your teen-age son is a much more careful driver than his sister, yet his insurance premium is almost double hers.

Your son's premium is not based on his own record but on the statistical record of all teenage male drivers. Insurance rates are set on probabilities that are based on the experience insurance companies have had with defined groups of people. Single men under 25 are, statistically, the worst risks for an insurance company. Losses on these drivers are 48 percent higher than those on females under 25. Being single also counts against your son. Losses on young, single male drivers are 90 percent higher than those registered by young, married male drivers.

Insurance companies find insuring the young to be a costly business. Drivers under 25 had, in 1978, claims totalling 83 percent more than those against older motorists. A 1979 survey in Toronto indicated that insurance companies were charging as much as $1,250 more for an 18-year-old male with an accident on his record than for a couple in their mid-30s with a clean driving record. The survey also showed that a young woman could pay as much as $530 less than a young man with the same driving record.

Discrimination or common sense? The insurance industry claims that it would cost more to set the rates for young drivers on each driver's record and that this extra cost would have to be spread around; that other drivers would be dismayed to find their premiums climbing for no apparent reason; and that premiums for drivers with poor records would soar to the point where they simply could not afford insurance and, thus, they would not be able to drive! In effect, says the insurance industry, everyone will pay extra to subsidize the poor driving of young male drivers if age is eliminated as a criterion.

Youthful drivers can, however, reduce their insurance costs fairly quickly by avoiding accidents and traffic violations. And many insurance companies give substantial premium reductions to graduates of approved driver-education programs, which involve both classroom and on-the-road tutoring.

UNEASY RIDERS

You pick up a hitchhiker and he is injured seriously when your car spins off an icy highway.

Hitchhiking is risky for both driver and hitchhiker. The law says that when you pick up a hitchhiker, or agree to give anyone a ride in your car, you have assumed a "duty of care" to the rider. You have assumed some responsibility for the rider's well-being. By spinning off the highway, you may have breached that duty and may thus be liable for damages. You could be sued and forced to pay medical expenses, compensation for loss of income or potential future earnings, compensation for pain and suffering or loss of limbs and the cost of rehabilitation. In most provinces, if the hitchhiker dies, his survivors can sue.

You are protected in this event—as long as you are insured. In general, your coverage works thus: the accident-benefits portion of your auto insurance policy is payable to the victim (or his survivors) on a no-fault basis, but it is a minimum protection; the excess protection—the most important portion—comes under public liability coverage.

It is possible that your accident-benefits insurance is void if you are being paid for a ride, as you might well be if you participate in a car pool. Consult your insurance agent to see if your policy covers the passengers, and what steps must be taken if it does not.

LAPSED POLICIES

The company you've done business with for years neglected to send you a renewal notice. Now you are in a serious accident and you believe you are uninsured.

Auto insurance policies are automatically renewed each year unless you clearly indicate your intention to cancel. So although you may not be aware of it, you are still insured. If the company balks at paying your claim, you can sue, with an excellent chance of winning—although it is unlikely that this will be necessary.

Insurance policies are almost always written for a period of 12 months. And the insurance company automatically renews the policy at the end of this period and your agent or broker is responsible for collecting the pre-

The superintendents of insurance

The conduct of the general insurance business in Canada is closely supervised and regulated by federal and provincial governments. If you encounter a problem with the terms and conditions of an insurance contract—auto or otherwise—or have a complaint or question about the licensing of companies, agents and adjusters, write to the federal or provincial "Superintendent of insurance" at these addresses.

FEDERAL
Department of Insurance
L'Esplanade Laurier
140 O'Connor St.
15th Floor, East Tower
Ottawa, Ont. K1A 0H2

ALBERTA
Consumer and Corporate Affairs
9th Floor, Capitol Square
10065 Jasper Ave.
Edmonton, Alta. T5J 3B1

BRITISH COLUMBIA
Ministry of Consumer and Corporate Affairs
The Law Courts
850 Burdett Ave.
Victoria, B.C. V8W 1B4

MANITOBA
Department of Finance
1142–405 Broadway Ave.
Winnipeg, Man. R3C 3L6

NEW BRUNSWICK
Department of Justice
P.O. Box 6000
Fredericton, N.B. E3B 5H1

NEWFOUNDLAND
Department of Consumer Affairs
Elizabeth Ave.
St. John's, Nfld. A1C 5T7

NORTHWEST TERRITORIES
Government of the Northwest Territories
Yellowknife, N.W.T. X0E 1H0

NOVA SCOTIA
Department of the Provincial Secretary
Suite 201, Rothman Building
2745 Dutch Village Road
Halifax, N.S. B3J 2X3

ONTARIO
Superintendent of Insurance
555 Yonge St.
6th Floor
Toronto, Ont. M7A 2H6

PRINCE EDWARD ISLAND
Department of the Provincial Secretary
P.O. Box 2000
Charlottetown, P.E.I. C1A 7N8

QUEBEC
Surintendant des assurances
800 Place d'Youville
Quebec, Que. G1R 4Y5

SASKATCHEWAN
Department of the Provincial Secretary
Legislative Building
Regina, Sask. S4S 0B3

YUKON TERRITORY
Territorial Secretary
Government of the Yukon Territory
P.O. Box 2703
Whitehorse, Yukon Y1A 2C6

mium. If you have notified him of your intention to cancel the insurance, or if he is having a problem collecting the premium, he will advise the company. The company will then serve notice that your policy will be canceled. You will have 15 days' warning if you are notified by registered letter, but only five days if the information is delivered by messenger.

Insurance companies are aware, however, that Canadian courts almost always give the insured the benefit of any doubt in insurance disputes of this nature. In one case, the insurance company was ordered to pay even though the policyholder had advised the agent that he intended to cancel, and had been advised by regular mail by the agent that his insurance was terminated. The policyholder claimed he never received the agent's notice. The court agreed that this was a possibility.

PICKUP TRUCKS

You give some acquaintances a lift home in the back of your truck. One of them is badly hurt when he falls out as you go round a curve.

Unless you live in New Brunswick, your passenger will be able to receive all the accident benefits available to any passenger of a motor vehicle. If you are uninsured, he can sue you—and probably collect—if he proves you did not show sufficient care in operating the truck. In provinces (such as Quebec) where this type of court action is prohibited, the claim must be presented before a government *régie*, or board.

If you do live in New Brunswick, you are in the clear. New Brunswick is the only province that excludes liability to passengers in trucks.

Ontario and Prince Edward Island have also passed amendments to their provincial insurance acts to exclude liability for passengers riding in the rear of commercial vehicles. As of 1979, neither amendment had been proclaimed, however, and there was strong opposition from the superintendents of insurance. A similar amendment in Manitoba was dropped because of strong objections by the Manitoba Public Insurance Corporation.

This issue has become more contentious with the increased use of light trucks as personal transportation and recreational vehicles. Insurance companies want to have insurance acts changed so accident benefits don't cover passengers riding in the rear of trucks. They contend that protecting victims encourages this dangerous practice. Strangely, carrying passengers in the back of a pickup is not illegal, even in provinces where wearing seatbelts in autos is mandatory.

While agreeing that the practice is potentially dangerous and should probably be made illegal, insurance superintendents—the provincial watchdogs keeping an eye on the insurance industry—insist that every passenger in any vehicle is entitled to insurance protection.

38 Accidents

An accident is the screech of brakes, the tearing of metal and the anguished screams of the injured and dying. Not a pretty thought. More than 5,000 Canadians are killed in auto accidents every year and the annual toll has been mounting steadily. Almost a quarter of a million persons are injured in each 12-month period, some so seriously that they spend the rest of their days in hospital or in wheelchairs. The cost is staggering— more than $1.25 billion a year in property damage. And this doesn't include medical costs, lost production, loss of human resources, or the time and money involved in legal battles.

The conventional responses to what is becoming a national disaster—low speed limits, tougher traffic laws, demands that manufacturers build safer cars—are simply not working. Yet legislators tend, by and large, to be loath to tackle the major cause of accidents: drivers. You. Me. And the other guy.

Canadians are poor drivers. Often we can't even drive to the corner store without being involved in a crash. A large percentage of accidents happen within eight kilometres of home. We drive when we are drunk or drugged; fully 55 percent of drivers killed in car accidents have been drinking or taking drugs. The fact is, we've never really learned, to begin with, how to drive. Look at the shameful accident statistics of our young drivers: one in four will be in a crash in the next year. The young become slightly better drivers with experience . . . if they live long enough.

Stricter licensing is one answer to our accident problem. In most places, it takes only a few hours of instruction, a 15-minute written test and a couple of turns around the block to get a license to drive a powerful and potentially lethal machine.

Quebec is the only province in Canada to take a strong stand on driver licensing and a long-term view of the merits of strict testing. In June 1979, Quebec discarded its old system of a drive around the block with a bored examiner and a 20-minute multiple-choice examination, which featured such questions as "What does a yellow traffic light mean?" Now, license applicants face a 60-question test that can take 1½ hours to complete. The province has also introduced test areas where an examiner observes applicants driving alone for 30 minutes. And the Quebec government has proposed to introduce a plan for periodic testing of licensed drivers.

It is unlikely governments will start to take more drastic steps to cure our accident problem unless society as a whole indicates it is fed up with bad drivers and tired of paying the cost of accidents. Only then will things change. Until that day, drive defensively—as if every other driver on the road is irresponsible, inattentive, drunk or drugged. As the record demonstrates, many of them are one or the other.

THE GOOD SAMARITAN

You witness a head-on collision on a side road. It seems more sensible to speed to town and raise the alarm rather than to stop and try to help.

Our highway traffic legislation imposes no legal obligation to help or even to stop at the scene unless you were involved in the accident, nor do you even have any legal obligation to report it or to send help. There is a moral obligation, however, and in Quebec, for instance, there is also the Charter of Human Rights and Freedoms. It states: "Every person must come to the aid of anyone whose life is in peril, either personally or calling for aid, by giving him the necessary and immediate physical assistance, unless it involves danger to himself or a third person, or he has another valid reason."

This obligation involves a judgment call. A victim can bleed to death while you are summoning aid; just stopping the flow of blood could save a life. If the side road is remote or lightly traveled, you may be the only chance the injured person has for survival. On the other hand, it could well be more useful to fetch qualified help.

Assisting police. Police cannot compel you to assist at the scene of an accident if you were not involved. You can legally refuse to obey a policeman's demand for help. Of course, you must assist a police officer if he asks for help in making an arrest or if he is in danger, and you must obey his order or signal if he is directing traffic at an accident scene or elsewhere.

Unless there is an obvious and immediate need, to pull an injured person out of a burning car, for example, or to stem a flow of blood, the most sensible course of action is to make the victim comfortable, calm him as much as possible and wait for an ambulance or doctor. Most ambulance personnel are trained in stabilizing the condition of injured people and moving them without worsening their condition or causing further injury. Statistics indicate that many highway fatalities are the result of shock and loss of blood. The victim might well have survived with proper first-aid treatment. You should never move an injured person unnecessarily. So unless you are qualified in first aid, or the victim's needs are clear, it is wise not to attempt any treatment.

DUTY OF CARE

You thought you did your best to help a badly injured accident victim, but evidence from the autopsy indicates that you may have hastened her death.

This is one of those clouded areas of the law that is open to interpretation. But it is possible you have left yourself open for a lawsuit charging you with negligence. You assumed a "duty of care" to the injured woman by volunteering your services; in hastening her death, you may have breached that duty.

According to some legal authorities, you must *worsen* the condition of the injured person before you can be held liable. In your case, if the medical evidence suggests you actually caused her death when there was a chance she might have lived, you will be in a much more precarious position. If, on the other hand, the victim's death was inevitable, it is difficult to see how you could have worsened her condition. The term used in law when a well-meaning person does harm to an accident victim is "misfeasance." You volunteer, someone relies on your help, and then you make a mistake; your good intentions may not be taken into consideration.

Doctors and nurses. There is no legal obligation even for doctors and nurses to assist accident victims if they themselves are not involved in the accident. (The situation is slightly different in Quebec where the Charter of Human Rights and Freedoms obliges *everyone* to aid anyone whose life is in peril.) However, the legal risk should not prevent them from helping. The Canadian Medical Protective Association, a legal service for doctors, says that the risk of medical practitioners incurring a lawsuit because of a "Good Samaritan" act has been grossly overstated—that no action has ever been filed in Canada against a doctor or nurse for helping an auto-accident victim. There is no legislation to protect doctors from lawsuits for negligence in these cases, but the association points out that courts do not apply the same standards to treatment at an accident scene as they do in a hospital situation.

First-aid courses. But of course medical help at the scene of an accident is often many long minutes away. The life of a family member, friend or neighbor could depend on your ability to take quick, positive action in the event of an accident. A first-aid course can equip you to cope with emergency situations that arise on the highway or in the home. First-aid knowledge also minimizes the possibility of making a costly mistake if you find yourself at an accident scene.

The St. John Ambulance Brigade through its local brigades, offers first-aid courses in all provinces. The Canadian Red Cross Society and many YMCAs and service clubs also sponsor first-aid courses.

Some companies provide courses for employees and some trucking firms train and equip their drivers to give first aid at the scene of highway crashes.

WHEN YOU'RE INVOLVED

You don't stop when a car trying to pass you is forced into the ditch to avoid an oncoming truck.

You can be charged with the summary offense of failing to remain at the scene of an accident, or the indictable offense of leaving the scene of an accident. Your car does not have to come in contact with another vehicle, pedestrian or anything on the roadside; it is enough that you were a factor. And in this case, it is clear that you were "indirectly involved" in the accident, because the speeder was trying to pass your car.

All provincial highway codes require you to remain at the accident scene and to render all possible assistance. You are also required to give your name and address and, if the car isn't yours, the name and address of the owner of the car, and the vehicle permit, upon request of a police officer or anyone involved in, or witness to, the accident.

Maximum penalty on summary conviction for failing to remain at the scene is a fine of $500 and imprisonment for six months. Your driving license could be suspended for up to two years. However, if you are charged on indictment and convicted, this offense can bring a two-year jail sentence. Obviously, it is foolhardy to drive away from any accident in which you were even remotely involved.

Reporting an accident. All but the most insignificant accidents *must* be reported to the police, including any in which there is injury or in which property damage exceeds a certain amount (from $200 to $400 depending on the

The 50-50 chance

A bookmaker would give even odds that you will be killed or injured in an auto accident. Don't panic—there are things you can do to improve your chances. The most obvious is to drive carefully and defensively. Don't drive if you are tired, or have been drinking or taking drugs; even a cold tablet can make you drowsy and less alert.

Seat belts reduce the odds on you being injured or killed, and all cars sold in Canada are now equipped with lap-and-shoulder belts. Their effectiveness is proven: about half of all injuries could have been prevented if victims had been wearing seat belts. Your chances of avoiding accidental death are about four times as good as those of a driver who is in the same type of accident and is not using a belt.

In general, larger cars can absorb more damage and protect occupants better. Smaller cars, however, are usually more maneuverable and thus their drivers are better able to avoid accidents in the first place. So the driver, rather than the type of car, remains the major factor.

Multilane highways, where head-on crashes are a rarity, are safer than two-lane roads. If there's a choice, take the superhighway.

About 5 percent of accidents are caused by faulty automobiles and tires. Your odds are better if your car is properly maintained and your tires are in good shape and properly inflated.

Driving a car anywhere is a gamble. No one can predict for sure that he won't have an accident. A drunk or drugged driver could hit you, or you could simply be singled out by the fickle finger of misfortune. Good gamblers do everything they can to reduce their risk.

province). These days, even a small dent or scratch can exceed the limits; what appears to be minor damage can result in a major repair bill. Some provinces require repair shops to report accidents automatically unless a copy of a police report is attached to the vehicle being repaired.

You are required by law to make every effort to inform the owner or operator of any unattended vehicle that you have hit, or to leave a notice in writing on the unattended vehicle, giving your name, address and license number. This rule also applies if you damage property other than another vehicle—such as a sign, mailbox or fence.

SPEEDING

You are charged with speeding after an accident, even though you were driving below the posted speed limit.

You were driving below the limit but still faster than a police officer thought was safe under existing conditions—icy, wet, snow-covered, foggy, or whatever they were. The usual charge in this case is careless driving; speeding generally applies to exceeding the posted limit. If you believe that you were driving in a responsible manner, you should fight the charge vigorously; a conviction could cost you demerit points and there might be an attempt to use it against you if there is a subsequent civil action for damages. Your insurance company may provide legal help.

Speed limits. Unless posted signs indicate otherwise, the speed limit in towns and cities is 50 km/h (30 m.p.h.) and on highways outside towns and cities, 80 km/h (50 m.p.h.). Provinces, cities and towns have the right to alter the speed limit to suit particular roads. Superhighways and expressways commonly have higher limits—100 km/h (65 m.p.h.), for example. There is a blanket speed limit of 55 m.p.h. on all U.S. highways, but no common maximum speed in Canada, although the trend has been toward a 100 km/h maximum.

You can be charged with traveling too slowly on Canadian highways if a police officer feels you are holding up other traffic. In most cases, an officer will simply pull you over and caution you that you are driving too slowly. If you find you are holding up traffic, pull over to allow cars following you to pass. This could save you a fine and, more important, ensure that you don't contribute to an accident as impatient drivers try to pass the long line of traffic you have caused.

EMERGENCY VEHICLES

Your car is damaged when the driver of a speeding police car loses control trying to pass you.

You may be held responsible and charged under the section of your province's highway or motor vehicle code that deals with yielding the right of way to an emergency vehicle. The law in all provinces requires that you pull over as far as possible to the right of the roadway, clear of any intersection, and stop until any emergency vehicle using siren or flashing lights passes.

However, if the police car had no siren sounding or lights flashing, its driver will be held responsible for the accident. If traffic conditions made it impossible for you to get clear of an intersection, it might be found that the policeman was at fault even though he was using lights or siren. If the policeman was at fault, his liability is the same as if he were a private citizen. He and the municipal, provincial or federal government for which he works are liable for your damages. You can sue if compensation is not otherwise provided.

Rights of emergency vehicles. In most provinces, ambulances, police cars, fire engines and, in some cases, public-utility emergency vehicles are allowed to exceed the speed limit, go through red lights or stop signs, and disregard one-way and no-turn signs. But drivers of these vehicles must use caution in any of these maneuvers, and take into consideration the road conditions, the amount of traffic and the nature of the emergency. In some provinces, drivers of such vehicles must also pass special driving and medical examinations.

Motorists who attempt to take advantage of the path cleared by an emergency vehicle, or to follow too closely behind an ambulance or fire engine, may find themselves in serious trouble. It is usually illegal to follow closer than 150 metres (165 yards) behind an emergency vehicle.

High-speed chases are always a controversial issue, especially when innocent people are victims of crashes that result from them. Some jurisdictions in the United States have banned police pursuits on the grounds that the lives of innocent motorists or pedestrians are more important than the apprehension of lawbreakers. But high-speed chases continue in Canada. In October 1979, two Port Colborne, Ont., residents died when their car was struck broadside by another being chased by police. The driver of the pursued vehicle was a youth of 15.

Your rights to recover damages from police or pursued cars are clearly protected by law. As a practical matter, collecting from the police may be easier than collecting damages from a juvenile who has stolen a car, or from a bank robber who will likely go to prison if he's apprehended. You will probably then have to seek damages against the pursued from a provincial victims-of-crime compensation board, or from the Unsatisfied Judgment Fund.

ONE FOR THE ROAD

A guest who has had too much to drink is involved in an accident a few minutes after leaving your house. You wonder to what extent you are responsible.

A host's legal obligations have never been tested in Canadian courts in a case like this, and legal opinions differ. Some authorities believe that a 1973 case involving the patron of a bar would have some bearing; others argue that there is a great difference between your obligation to a guest and a bar's obligation to a customer who is paying for service.

The Supreme Court of Canada decided in the 1973 case that a hotel bar owed a "duty of care" to a customer of its beverage room.

Shortly after leaving the bar, where he had become intoxicated, the man was injured in a car accident. The court said the hotel had a duty to take reasonable care to safeguard the customer from the likely risk of personal injury after leaving the bar. The customer was well known to the hotel manager and his employees, putting them in a better position to assess his condition. The bar's negligence was found to have contributed to his injuries.

Your moral duty. While there may not be any similar legal obligation to worry about the condition of a friend visiting your home, your moral obligation to your friend and the community is clear. You should not allow guests who have had too much to drink to drive home. If you are persuasive and your guest is reasonable, he may welcome the suggestion that he accept a ride from you or another guest, or take a taxi.

If reason fails, you could conveniently "lose" his keys. The possibility of alienating a friend, who will probably have forgotten about it by morning anyway, is a more attractive alternative to seeing him kill or injure himself, or someone else, because you didn't try hard enough to prevent him from driving.

Laws governing the carrying of liquor in your car vary from province to province. Generally, it is illegal everywhere to carry open bottles of liquor or open cases of beer in your car. You can be charged under your province's liquor act, highways act or motor vehicle act. Carrying liquor in large quantities or transporting it to someplace other than your residence is also an offense in some jurisdictions.

SECOND-HAND LEMONS

Your son is seriously injured while driving home in a used car he has just bought. An expert mechanic tells you the vehicle was unfit to be on the road.

Your son can sue for damages if he bought the car from a dealer and the accident was caused by mechanical failure. Dealers are presumed to know of any latent defects in the cars they sell. In addition, the car was supposed to have been safety-checked and certified before it was sold—a requirement in all provinces. But there are some obvious dangers when you are buying a used car from a dealer whose own mechanics do the safety inspections.

Private sellers are *not* liable for defects in the automobile they sell unless there are unusual circumstances, such as a deliberate attempt to conceal a defect. In most provinces, they, too, must obtain a provincial safety certificate before selling a car.

Your lawyer would have to determine whether there were grounds to sue the mechanic who did the safety check and missed the defect.

If it can be determined that the defect was the fault of the car manufacturer, the fact that the car was secondhand or even thirdhand has no bearing on the manufacturer's liability.

Muscle cars. Every parent has cause to worry if a son or daughter becomes the owner of a high-performance "muscle car." Such vehicles are a disappearing breed, however, due to new safety legislation, the need for manufacturers to attain better fuel economy in their

Finding a needle in a haystack

Shortly before midnight on Nov. 27, 1978, Toronto dance instructor Judy Jordan was struck by a car in the driveway of her apartment building and dragged screaming to her death by a hit-and-run driver. Although witnesses heard the 29-year-old dancer's screams and saw the car, none could provide a license number or even the make or color. The only clues were a paint chip on the dead woman's clothes and two small bits of plastic recovered at the scene.

The bits of plastic were identified as parts of a fan shroud used on Chevrolets from 1971 to 1977. The Ontario Motor Vehicle Branch's computer provided police with a printout of all Chevrolets of those model years registered in Ontario. There were 100,000 of them! But the search was narrowed down to 20,000 cars when an engineer at the General Motors plant in Oshawa spotted a slight imperfection on one of the two pieces of plastic. It was caused by a damaged mold from which the shroud was produced; the mold was tracked down, and it was discovered that all 1977 and most 1976 Monte Carlos and Chevelles had the imperfect fan shroud.

The list was narrowed even further when the Ontario Centre for Forensic Sciences spotted a tiny paint chip, less than a quarter-inch across, embedded in Judy Jordan's purse. The search was now confined to blue 1976 and 1977 Chevelles and Monte Carlos.

Because the hit-and-run driver followed side streets when he fled, police figured he lived in the area. At 10:05 p.m. on Dec. 18, two constables were checking cars in an apartment parking lot two blocks from the scene of the crime. They found what they were looking for: a damaged fan shroud on a blue 1976 Chevelle Malibu Classic.

It was the 863rd car police had checked. Its owner was found guilty of criminal negligence and sentenced to three years in penitentiary.

Police in Ontario and other provinces frequently use computers in the hunt for criminals who have used cars in the commission of their crimes. The computer used by the Ontario Ministry of Transportation and Communications can scan its entire memory bank—6.2 million vehicles—in half an hour. It is used about once a week to track down hit-and-run drivers.

In the Judy Jordan case, the computer was used to refine the list several times as more information became available to Toronto police. Finally, it was called on to identify all owners of death-car models who lived in the area of the crime. Over a four-year period, the computer helped in the solution of all but one of 19 hit-and-run deaths in Toronto.

cars, and tremendously high insurance rates, particularly for young drivers.

There is nothing inherently wrong with a car that can travel 195 km/h (120 m.p.h.). In fact, they often handle better and brake better than the more sedate family sedans or economy cars. But they can be lethal in the hands of inexperienced drivers. Young people can often be steered away from acquiring these cars with the logical arguments that fuel costs and insurance premiums will be much higher than their limited budgets can stand.

NIGHT DRIVING

An oncoming driver fails to dim his lights and causes you to slide into a ditch.

If you could identify the oncoming driver, you could sue for negligence. Several cases have been tried in court on these grounds. If you cause some property damage and are charged as a result of running off the road, the interference with your vision, as created by the lights, could be accepted as an excuse for your accident.

But in some cases, the courts have also held that it is the duty of the driver dazzled by approaching headlights to slow down and be ready to stop. In Ontario and Quebec, the law requires you to dim your headlights when approaching within 150 metres (500 feet) of another vehicle and when following another vehicle at a distance of 60 metres (200 feet) or less.

In both provinces, legislation dealing with headlights requires you to have at least two, but not more than four, lamps of sufficient power to illuminate objects 150 metres away. You are also required to have red taillights—visible from 150 metres—on each side of the vehicle. Headlights cannot be colored or tinted, nor can they be covered with any material that restricts their beam. Since 1966, new vehicles have also had to have reflectors on the rear quarter panel. The intensity of lights on the front of the car is restricted, in some provinces. Some high-powered lights, sold especially for rally and racing cars, are illegal.

HORSE AND WAGON

Two passengers are injured and your car is damaged when you smash into a horse that has wandered onto the highway at night.

You could sue the owner, but you must prove that he was negligent in letting his horse run free. If it did escape through negligence—a gate left open, a poorly constructed fence, for example—then the owner or keeper is liable.

However, in most provinces, if the owner can show that the horse—or any other animal except a dog—escaped by means other than his negligence, he will not be liable for your damages. Following a snowstorm in Ontario in 1973, a horse escaped from a corral by climbing onto a snow drift. The owner was not held liable for the damage caused when a car hit the horse.

In fact, you may have to prove that *you* were not negligent if you strike an animal that is legally on the highway; that you were keeping a proper lookout and not traveling at excessive speed. In some parts of Canada where pastureland is adjacent to highways, a farm animal is usually considered to be lawfully on the highway.

A dog running at large is, in the eyes of the law, a different matter. If you hit the dog, causing an accident or damage, its owner is deemed to have been negligent in allowing the dog to run free on the highway.

As a motorist, you are required by law to drive with regard for the safety of any person driving, leading or riding a horse or other animal, or riding in a vehicle being drawn by a horse or other animal. Your driving must not frighten the horse, or other animal.

When you spot a horse and wagon on the highway, or any person in charge of an animal, you should give them as wide a berth as possible. If the animal appears frightened or skittish because of your approach, you should stop until the rider or handler can get it under complete control. In the case of wild animals on the highway, any damage you sustain by hitting them is a matter between you and your insurance company.

Repairs

If the auto-repair business in Canada is similar to that in the United States, half of the annual $3.5 billion Canadians spend on auto repairs and service may be going for unnecessary work. A 1979 government survey of seven American cities showed that 53 cents of every dollar spent on car repairs was unnecessary. Cases involving make-work charges, heard that same year by courts in this country, suggest Canadians, too, have cause to be wary. Indeed, car repairs top the list of consumer complaints. Among the factors responsible for this is the consumer's lack of knowledge about how a car works and where to go for honest, competent repair work. With the growing complexity of today's automobiles, the trend is toward replacing parts rather than trying to repair them. It has always been easier—if more expensive—to replace instead of repair; however, some of the complicated systems in the modern automobile are almost impossible to repair economically.

Another factor is the profit that dealers demand these days from their repair departments. Car sales once provided dealerships with their profits, and the service department was a customer convenience which helped sales. No more. Profit margins on new- and used-car sales have slipped to the point that most dealers look for overall profit to the back-shop—the parts and service departments. In many cases, managers of these departments are really salesmen, paid a commission to sell you as much repair work as possible—too often with little regard for whether it is needed or not.

Finally, the car-repair business has become increasingly competitive. With Canadians purchasing about one million new cars annually, franchise outlets and independent entrepreneurs, offering everything from jiffy tuneups to transmission repairs while you wait, are popping up everywhere. The industry has attracted more than its share of scoundrels and fly-by-night operators whose stock in trade is charging for work that never gets done; parts that are replaced unnecessarily; blatantly overcharging on written estimates; and frightening motorists into paying for unnecessary work to correct nonexistent "dangerous safety problems."

There are solutions to these problems, but most require tough, uncompromising consumer legislation and a willingness on the part of the repair industry to clean up its act. Quebec made a start with new laws introduced in 1979, which, when in force, will require garages to provide written estimates, get work authorization in writing, and guarantee repairs. But there's still a long way to go to clear up the national auto-repair headache. In the meantime, motorists should be constantly on guard, arming themselves with as much knowledge as possible. This doesn't mean that every car owner must become an automotive technician; everyone should, however, learn the *basics* of how a car works and what it takes to keep it working.

UNAUTHORIZED REPAIRS

The garage estimates repairs to your car will cost about $40, then presents you with a bill for $81.50.

Condolences. You have just joined the legions who have experienced the "five o'clock surprise": unauthorized or additional repair work and higher-than-expected bills. You probably won't have to pay if you fight, but the sad fact is that most people pay rather than go through the inconvenience and unpleasantness involved in asserting their rights.

You are not required to pay for work you did not expressly request or approve. If you asked the garage to change the spark plugs and the mechanic also installed new points, you don't have to pay for the points—even if defective points were the source of the miss in your engine. However, if you had asked the garage to fix a miss in the engine—without specifying what steps should be taken—then you must pay. Never leave a vehicle at a garage with a vague order to "do whatever is necessary": that could be a license to rob you.

Likewise, never request a "tuneup" without specifically authorizing parts and procedure. A tuneup can consist of relatively minor things such as cleaning and setting points and plugs and setting the timing, but could include such major—and expensive—jobs as replacing ignition parts and cleaning and adjusting carburetors or fuel-injection systems.

If you have been specific in authorizing repairs, the garage cannot charge more than the cost estimate without "sufficient justification." But this remains a rather nebulous term at law. Generally, you should not accept a bill that exceeds the estimate by more than 10 percent. And you should never pay for labor or parts that were not included in the estimate.

Always obtain a written estimate. When signed by you, this constitutes a legal contract between you and the garage. Make sure you get a copy. If you neglect to do so, you'll have little clout should there be a dispute; it's not unknown for signed work orders to be altered. The estimate should note that you must be consulted before any additional work is done—that you won't pay for anything not included on the estimate.

Mechanic's liens. The signed work order, explicitly authorizing repairs, provides the garage with a "perfected security interest" in your car, which means the garage has the right to keep the car in its possession until the bill is paid. In most provinces, if the bill remains unpaid for three months, the garage can sell the car to recover the amount of the bill and selling expenses. In some provinces, the garage is also entitled to charge for storage and maintenance of the vehicle. If the car is sold for more than the total due, the difference must be returned to the original owner; if for less, the garage can sue for the balance.

In most provinces, the garage must have the vehicle in its possession in order to place a lien against it. This is why garages are sometimes reluctant to release a vehicle until the bill is paid. In British Columbia, Alberta, Saskatchewan and Manitoba, a mechanic's lien may be placed after the car is released if the garage has the owner's acknowledgment of indebtedness.

If you refuse to pay for unauthorized repairs and the garage refuses to return your car, you can obtain a court order for its return pending settlement. You can also demand payment for costs of alternate transportation if the garage keeps your car without justification.

Labor charges. Some garages compute labor charges by the hour. Your bill will include the hourly pay of mechanic or body man for the actual time spent on your car, plus overhead, plus markup for profit. Other garages use the flat-rate method: the average time required to do a particular job has been worked out by car manufacturers and publishers of flat-rate manuals, and you will be charged for this amount of "labor," regardless of the actual time spent on your car. Again your bill will include a sum for overhead and profit.

Mechanics working on a flat-rate system are usually paid commission or have some kind of piecework incentive arrangement. This can lead to problems for the car owner. Under the flat-rate system, the customer generally pays more and is more likely to get lower-quality repairs.

The Canadian Automobile Association (CAA) advises against refusing to pay an inflated bill if it means the garage will not release your car. Keep in mind that it is illegal to refuse to pay for authorized work, even if the work doesn't appear to have cured the problem.

When you are charged for unauthorized work, point out that you are not legally required to pay. If the garage insists on keeping your car unless you pay, warn it that you'll send a bill for the cost of renting another car or for taxi fares. If the garage still won't release your car, you can pay the bill and sue to recover the unauthorized charges in Small

Making work orders work

The signed work order will be your protection if there is a dispute about the amount of the bill, or unauthorized work, or the quality of repairs. This mock work order is similar to those used by garages everywhere. Make sure the mileage is recorded accurately in case questions arise about a time-mileage guarantee. The space under the owner's name and address specifies work to be done, the time it will take to do each job, and the cost.

The letters *FC* mean failure code; *01* tells the mechanic the part is broken; *42* means it's leaking. The *operation* space is for the job number from the flat-rate manual, and the *time* space is the fraction of an hour the manual allots to do the job—1.5 means the labor charge will be for 1½ hours at the garage's rate. Maintenance operations—oil changes and lubrications—are listed, along with parts used to repair your vehicle. The *WI* box indicates repairs are covered by warranty.

Before signing, make sure prices and estimates meet with your approval. Draw a line through unused portions of the work order to prevent items from being added, and draw an arrow linking your signature to the "total customer charges" box.

Claims Court, if the amount falls within the jurisdiction of this court. (*See* Chapter 3, "You, the plaintiff.")

DIAGNOSING PROBLEMS

You take your balky car to four different garages and are offered four different diagnoses of its troubles.

Cars have become exceptionally complicated in the past decade and diagnosing their malfunctions has become something of a black art. The best way to protect yourself against incorrect diagnoses and unnecessary repairs is to take the car to an inspection center not connected with a repair shop, such as those operated by member clubs of the Canadian Automobile Association. The center will diagnose the ailment and then you choose a garage to do the work, advising it of the inspection center's recommendations.

Once you know exactly what is wrong and what repairs are needed, you can shop around. Price is important, but consider also the reputation of the garage for fair dealing and the guarantee it offers. Specialty shops—tuneup centers, transmission-repair shops, brake specialty shops—may have the expertise and the equipment to do a particular job more quickly and at less cost than a general repair shop.

ROAD SERVICE

A garage charges you $30 to tow your stalled car to its shop where the mechanic "fixes" it by charging the battery.

We all make foolish mistakes from time to time, and occasionally these mistakes are costly. Yours has cost you $30. You dealt with an incompetent—or unscrupulous—garage.

With a set of jumper cables in your car's emergency kit, and the foresight to check the battery as soon as you stalled, you might have saved yourself the cost and inconvenience of a service call altogether. But even if you failed to recognize the cause of your problem, any responsible road-service man would have checked, before towing, for such obvious things as a dead battery or an empty fuel tank. All tow trucks carry battery jumper cables and sufficient extra fuel to enable you to reach the next service station. A tow-truck operator may tell you it is necessary to tow your car quickly out of a potentially dangerous position, but this argument doesn't apply with a dead battery—it's faster to hook up jumper cables and start the car than to tow it.

Auto club services. One of the benefits of membership in the Canadian Automobile Association (CAA) is access to a service network that will dispatch a qualified service man. Emergency road service is provided to members, with participating firms billing the CAA directly for the service call. Your local CAA club can supply details of emergency road services offered in your area.

You should be wary of the "Good Samaritan" tow-truck operator who "just happens on the scene" of your breakdown or accident. He might have learned of your problem by monitoring police radio calls, or through the CB radio network, or he may be one of those operators who cruise a busy highway, looking for trouble.

Don't sign anything other than a towing authorization form which includes the charge—and get a copy of it. A common trick of unscrupulous operators is to have you sign a form that includes authorization for repairs, and when you go to collect the car you find work has been started. You must pay for whatever has been done if you want to take the car to your own garage for repairs.

Do-it-yourself procedures. Most motorists should be able to make minor emergency repairs and save a towing or service call. Your owner's manual will give you some hints about easily replaced parts, emergency repairs and tire changing. Learn how to use the jack and tire wrench and the location of the jacking points on your car. An emergency kit should be standard equipment in every vehicle and should include a flashlight; flares and matches; a roll of good-quality electrical tape; a roll of mechanic's wire; a hammer; several adjustable wrenches or an inexpensive wrench set;

an assortment of screw drivers; jumper cables; pliers, including cutting pliers and channel locks; an instant tire-repair aerosol can; and a small first-aid kit. Even if you're not able to make simple, emergency repairs, a friendly motorist who happens along may help you if you've got the tools for the job.

GARAGE'S NEGLIGENCE

The plug isn't replaced properly in the oil pan after an oil change, and the engine burns out.

A garage is responsible for negligence in any work it does on your car, so it is liable for the cost of the new engine you now need and alter-nate transportation while you are without the car. Make sure your just demands are met. The garage probably has insurance to protect it in the event of such an oversight. Your new-car warranty does not apply in this case be-cause of the clause excluding repairs resulting from negligence.

A garage is also liable for damages arising from an accident caused by faulty repairs. There are obvious problems of proof; usually you must find a qualified mechanic to testify as an expert witness. In the case of the missing oil plug, a court might find that you shared the blame for the burned-out motor if you ig-nored the red warning light on the dashboard, which tells you when you have lost oil pressure.

Care and repair

When your car needs service or repairs, there are alternatives to spending days shopping around for fair estimates and reliable work, or simply picking a garage at random—if you're a member of the Canadian Automobile Association (CAA). By providing an up-to-date list of ap-proved garages in your area, the CAA can help you get satisfactory auto servic-ing at a reasonable price. All approved garages have been investigated by quali-fied inspectors, and have agreed that the CAA or a member club will arbitrate any disputes with CAA members.

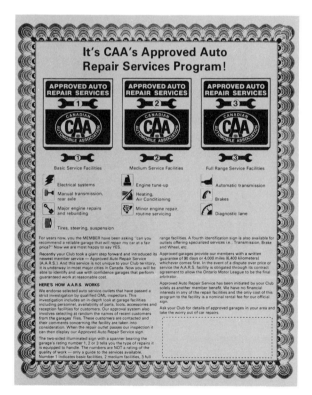

REBUILT COMPONENTS

Two months ago you had a rebuilt engine installed in your car. Now it is broken down beyond repair. You wonder if you're entitled to a replacement.

You should have no problem getting the engine replaced unless you dealt with a fly-by-night garage. Many rebuilt or "remanufactured" major components, such as engines, transmissions or differentials, are sold with warranties as good as or better than those covering the component in a new car. The latter are usually good for 12 months or 20,000 kilometres (12,500 miles). In addition to the warranty provided by the company, or the individual, that rebuilds a component, most reputable repair shops will guarantee their work, including parts. Usually this is for 90 days or 6,400 kilometres (4,000 miles). To settle for any less of a guarantee just because the price is lower may be asking for trouble.

When you are having a major component rebuilt, the guarantee should be printed on the bill or given to you in writing. The component is usually guaranteed by the rebuilder: ask to see the warranty before authorizing the work and be sure you get a copy of it before paying the bill. The warranty should cover 100 percent of parts and labor for a clearly specified time and distance. If a mechanic rebuilds the component himself, it is reasonable to ask him to sign his personal guarantee. The reputable individual will be proud to attest to his work.

Partial warranties are hardly worth the paper they are written on; a warranty should cover both parts and labor—one is not enough. A garage can inflate the price of the parts or labor, whichever is not covered, and effectively charge you full price for the repair. The same is true of "50-50 warranties," under which you pay half and the garage or dealer pretends to pay half.

Beware of vague warranty promises such as "good for the life of your car." This usually means that only the parts are covered; you will probably have to pay for various necessary auxiliary parts, as well as an inflated labor charge. Some muffler- and transmission-repair shops use this worthless type of guarantee. In the end, you pay for labor, clamps, a tailpipe and exhaust system—all of this amounting to almost the cost of replacing the muffler. This can mean that you actually pay for the warranty work.

This is not to suggest that all "lifetime guarantees" offered by specialty repair shops are worthless. Some, in fact, do cover all parts and labor. In general, though, "life of the car" means only as long as you personally own the car. The guarantee is predicated on the statistical certainty that most people will sell or trade the car before the part wears out.

REPAIR JOB 'SPECIALS'

You take your car in for a "brake job" that was advertised at $19.95. Later in the day the garage phones to tell you that more expensive work is required.

Thank the caller for his courtesy—and politely but firmly refuse any more repairs than are included in the $19.95 special. Be wary of the caller's warning of the danger to you and your family of driving with the vehicle in this condition, or of more costly damage that may result from neglected repairs. Your answer is still a polite, firm "no."

Some special offers for brake jobs, tuneups, transmission reconditioning and front-end checks are strictly come-ons. They get your car into the garage, which then "discovers" that more expensive repairs are needed. If you wish, take the car to an independent inspection center and ask for a check for sabotage. This is rare, but it does happen. Never agree to additional repairs over the telephone unless the garage is well known to you and its integrity is beyond question.

The fine print. Be sure you read the fine print of any special offer. The "brake job," for instance, is probably offered at the $19.95 price only on certain makes and models. If the ad says something like "slightly higher on other makes," you could be in for a surprise when you go to reclaim your car. It could also be

Clinics for cars

The modest cost of an expert inspection is a good investment, whether or not you are having trouble with your car. Since inspection centers don't do repairs, they have nothing to gain from overstating problems. Many Canadian Automobile Association (CAA) clubs provide vehicle inspection services and the following form illustrates the type of inspection provided to members in the Toronto area. (Not all centers are equipped to do as comprehensive an inspection as this.) For a small additional fee, these centers will also inspect the vehicle *after* your garage has completed the recommended repairs. In most areas, CAA inspection services are open to members only.

CAR INSPECTION CENTRE — CAA Car Inspection form (Customer's Copy), filled out for a 1977 Chevrolet Malibu, owner Richard A. Roe.

INSPECTORS COMMENTS:
1. Replace radiator cap (low pressure)
2. Replace upper radiator hose
3. Replace left front engine mount
4. Replace tailpipe hanger
5. Replace transmission oil seal
6. Replace (both) rear shock absorbers
7. Play in lower ball joints (but within specifications)

1. Replace air filter
2. Clean spark plug wires on left side
3. Adjust timing (advanced)
4. Replace (or clean) spark plugs

that the special "tuneup" or "brake job" covers only part of what is normally understood by those terms—only front-wheel brakes, for instance. And the tuneup special at $24.95 might include only new points and plugs on four-cylinder cars, a task you could complete yourself in about 20 minutes at less than half the cost.

Most problems can be diagnosed without taking apart the engine or transmission. Never let anyone dismantle either without a second opinion about the nature of the problem. And try to be there when they come apart, to prevent sabotage, or the switching of bad parts for the good ones that come out.

SERVICE STATION DISSERVICE

You are talked into fitting two new tires at an out-of-town gas station. Your old tires were only slightly worn.

You can complain to the office of the oil company that owns the gas station and demand a refund, using the old tires as evidence of the deception. Not all gas-station operators are honest, and there are all kinds of tricks they can pull on unwary motorists, especially those concerned about being stranded on the highway far from home.

A service station out to fleece you can easily punch holes in tires while checking air pressure—a practice known as "honking" tires. A radiator hose can be punctured with a sharp object, or shock absorbers can be sprayed with used oil to make them appear to be leaking. And there are other dirty tricks:

Short sticking. Inserting the oil dipstick down only partway to make you believe you need oil.

Shock treatments. Pouring oil on a hot engine or dropping a chemical—titanium tetrachloride, a meat curative sometimes used by the military to create smoke screens—on an alternator or generator to create a cloud of smoke that will convince you there is trouble.

Slashing. A fan belt can easily be cut partway through.

As you leave a faraway service station that

you suspect may have ripped you off, demand to be given any parts that were replaced. Keep all the receipts and make sure they are as detailed as possible, and try to get the attendant's name. If your own mechanic confirms your suspicions, consult your local consumer services bureau or the legal office of your automobile club for advice. Also, complain hard and long to the parent oil company, which doesn't court bad publicity and should be willing to investigate allegations of fraud against its lessees.

ESSENTIAL SERVICING

You fill up at a highway service station where the attendant on duty doesn't clean your dirty windshield.

Large highway stations don't have to count on repeat business. Therefore, attendants sometimes don't bother to check the oil, wipe the windshield, or check the water level in the battery. You should demand these services— you are still entitled to them.

Of course, you cannot get them at self-service stations. There, you may not pay as much for gasoline, but you may be paying in other ways. The few cents saved on each litre could be spent later on costly repairs. Motorists who regularly fill up at the pump-it-yourself spots are probably not getting those little maintenance checks that were almost a matter of course when every station had attendants.

Key checks. Regular oil changes are a case in point. Driving with too little oil in the engine means parts are not properly lubricated. Without oil, they wear out and you have an expensive engine job on your hands. There's one sure way to save that expense and still take advantage of the savings available at self-service stations: start performing those little checks yourself.

Sticking out of the engine block somewhere is an oil dipstick bent into a circle at the top. With the engine turned off, pull out the stick. It will have oil on it and a mark will show you the proper oil level. Wipe all the oil off, then reinsert the dipstick in the engine. When you pull it out this time, you will be able to see the oil level clearly. Use a funnel to add oil through the oil-filler cap which can be located by checking your owner's manual or asking a service-station attendant. Don't overfill: too much oil can also cause damage.

Most batteries have either two or six filler caps. Take them off and check to see if the battery fluid is up to a ring in each hole. If it isn't, top it up with water. Again, don't overfill and wipe up spilled water, which could short-circuit your battery.

Radiators have pressure caps, and you can check the level visually if your car is equipped with an overflow tank and special radiator cap. Never remove the cap when the radiator is hot: you could get a nasty burn. If the water level is low, fill it up—there's an overflow, so you can't overfill. Have the strength of the antifreeze tested at a service station. Check radiator hoses for wear and loose clamps. A soft, spongy hose should be replaced before it breaks.

Your fan belt should have some slack in it, but shouldn't be too loose. If in doubt, ask a reliable service-station attendant. Loose belts cause overheated engines, and will not properly charge the battery; check them for signs of wear. Fluid level in automatic transmissions is often neglected. This is checked in the same manner as oil, but with the engine up to operating temperature and the car running. (The transmission dipstick is farther back than the oil dipstick.) Add transmission fluid if necessary. Finally, check your tires often. Low pressure causes wear and affects your car's handling and can damage a tire, resulting in premature failure.

8 YOUR RIGHTS AT LEISURE

40 Sport and recreation

Leisure has become the major element in Canadian life. Nowadays, millions are at work less than 20 percent of their time, leaving a lot of hours for sport, recreation, hobbies or simply putting the feet up and doing nothing. The trend continues to a shorter work week, longer vacations and more statutory holidays, but the law in the field of leisure has been curiously slow to develop. Millions are spent on studies, investigations and prosecutions to ensure fair competition in industry and the marketplace, but virtually nothing on fair play and equal consideration for the consumer and participant in leisure activities.

Laws relating to commerce, property and the dignity of the individual are stretched, often awkwardly, to cover the new field. For example, traffic laws try to regulate the snowmobile, which can roam over territory far from any highway. Control of the trade in players between clubs in professional hockey and football is left mainly to private organizations, whose decisions are based on potential box-office receipts. Discrimination in sports on the grounds of sex, race, color or religion is difficult to stamp out because all the human rights codes relate to services or facilities "customarily available to the public." That seems to leave private clubs and organizations free to admit whom they choose.

The 1970s saw federal and provincial governments move more extensively into the realm of leisure activities. National pride and a concern with national flabbiness led Ottawa to establish, or subsidize, Recreation Canada, Sport Canada, Hockey Canada, the Canadian Coaching Association, the Academy of Sport Medicine, and the Canadian Olympic, Pan American and Commonwealth Games associations. The federal government also got involved in the creation and funding of national teams, "disparity" grants to have-not provinces, financial aid to aspiring athletes, support of wheelchair games for the handicapped, the Sports Caravan project—national tours by experienced athletes—and Participaction, the personal fitness program.

Consumer advocates have been instrumental in establishing standards for sports safety equipment—for example, the Canadian Standards Association (CSA) approved helmets and other headgear for football and hockey players, motorcyclists and amateur boxers. Protective brassieres are now available for women who want to play contact sports.

While accident insurance is not always compulsory, contributory plans at low premiums are readily available to strengthen the coverage under regular family package plans, which usually don't cover such things as dental injuries. But prevention is always better than cure—and mouth guards are cheaper than extra premiums.

SKI INJURIES

Your ski catches in a rut under the tow. You are dragged off and break your leg.

All sports involve some risk of injury and this is particularly true of skiing. Scores of enthusiasts break bones every winter and most go gamely back to the slopes next season. You're probably on a sticky slope in seeking compensation for your injury from the proprietor of the hill. A court is likely to decide that you freely chose to accept the inherent risks of skiing when you took up the sport.

The owner or operator does have the legal duty to ensure that his hill and equipment present no element of surprise that could reasonably be held to constitute a "trap" for his patrons. If he has prepared the runs properly and maintained the mechanical equipment, he can claim to have taken all reasonable steps to eliminate or reduce potential hazards. Your tow ticket probably includes a line of fine print in which the management warns you that it does not accept liability for accidents. While this kind of blanket exemption is of limited legal value, any claimant is usually faced with the task of proving *negligence* by the owner.

To protect themselves against claims, operators usually hold extensive public liability insurance policies and the skier is probably covered by his own personal accident insurance to some degree. Unless you are a professional jumper—or "hot dogger"—your premium rate won't be affected. Clubs and proprietors emphasize their sense of responsibility—but not their liability—by providing facilities for rescue and first aid.

The skier is expected to know that the tow won't pull him up the hill without his active participation and skill. As skiers advance in proficiency, some actually seek out risks, fully aware of the dangers involved. They scorn the gentle beginners' slopes and challenge the express-train runs. As with the long-distance swimmer setting out across Lake Ontario, the act itself announces acceptance of the inherent risk.

BOATS FOR HIRE

Your nephew drowns at a resort lake when a rented boat springs a leak and sinks.

It's the responsibility of anyone offering boats for hire to ensure compliance with the small-vessels regulations of the Canada Shipping Act. These include maximum-load notices, lifesaving equipment, fire extinguishers, provision of paddles and approved night lights. The skipper or operator of the craft assumes the same duty. Fines of up to $500 may be imposed for infraction. Every pleasure boat with an engine of 10 horsepower or more must have a license, which is free.

To prove at law *why* a given boat sprang a leak, and that the leak led to the sinking and to the tragedy, might well be impossible. The facts of the particular case would rule, not a general theory or even an act of Parliament.

The question of negligence would be paramount. When you rent a boat you are almost certainly taking it "as is." You owe it to yourself and your passengers to examine the craft to see if it is in good condition and able to accommodate, safely, the number of people intending to use it. If the renter assures you before a witness that it is in good condition and that it satisfies all the regulations, you would have grounds for suit if someone's foot went through a rotten hull. And the police might decide there's a case for criminal prosecution.

How far from shore? Water is the most powerful and dangerous natural resource. When you step off *terra firma* and launch yourself on the waters, you are accepting some part of that risk. It's wise to check into some things in advance: What are the winds like? How cold is the water at this time of year? Are there hazards, such as rocks or logs, shoals, or strong currents? Can all your passengers swim?

Whenever children are present, there's a special duty placed on the parent or supervising adult. (*See* Chapter 9, "You, the parent.") You must take extra precautions. Children cannot be expected to understand or perceive the potential dangers involved in many situations. Before you allow a child to step into a boat, be aware of the complications or dangers that could arise. Once any child gets into your boat, he or she is *your* responsibility.

COLLISION AFLOAT

You are tacking in a gusting wind when your sailboat is rammed by a speeding cruiser.

There's no essential difference between your responsibilities at law—or in your rights—when driving your car down the highways or sailing (or steering) your boat on the waterways. You and the other fellow have the right to expect each other to exercise due care and attention. Anything less than due care constitutes negligence; someone could be liable if there were an accident.

Nudging the nation

Alarmed by studies seeming to show
that old Swedes were fitter than young
Canadians, the federal Department of
Health and Welfare launched a nationwide fitness campaign. Coining the
title "Participaction," it attempts through
the media to get the sedentary out of
their armchairs and into the gyms or onto
the jogging tracks.

But, if *you* are of a certain age, and
not physically active, check with your
doctor before you buy those track shoes
or that cute sweat suit.

Is fitness Important?
Ask any body.

The Canadian movement for personal fitness.

If you think fitness is
a distant goal,
consider this:
you can walk
all the way.

The Canadian movement for personal fitness.

The small-vessels regulations dictate or advise all kinds of actions in all kinds of situations, but the possibilities are simply too numerous to be covered in any law—or book, for that matter. For a general outline in popular terms, get a copy of the *Boating Safety Guide* from the Department of Transport in Ottawa. Boat dealers and marinas usually have copies available.

There's a nautical tradition that "steam gives way to sail." (Steam these days means motorized.) But don't count on it. Even the most courteous cruiser skipper can't read your mind. Before you "go on a tack"—that is, change direction by altering the set of your sail—be sure that there's clear room to complete the maneuver, especially in crowded waters.

No license is required to operate a pleasure craft. Weekend sailors often take risks on the water that they would never dream of taking while driving the family sedan. The person at the wheel of that speeding cruiser may know very little about his boat and absolutely nothing of sailing rules and etiquette.

Life jackets always. Even a minor collision on the water can result in tragedy. People thrown overboard can panic and forget elementary lifesaving drills. Drowning comes terribly swiftly: only one or two minutes to complete unconsciousness. Death usually results within five minutes, although some lucky few have been revived by artificial respiration after much longer periods under water. You owe it to yourself and your passengers to be inflexible about the wearing of approved life jackets.

Adequate insurance is a must for all hobby yachtsmen and other boaters. Special policies are available to cover just about any risk, but the policies you already have may give you all the coverage you need.

Those who have a "floater" clause in their comprehensive personal liability insurance are usually protected against claims arising from accidents on pleasure craft. For example, no extra premiums are required for a yacht up to 8 metres (26 feet) long or a boat with an outboard motor of 16 horsepower or less.

The homeowner's comprehensive policy usually covers all his property at home or "temporarily distant." This would provide for the repair or replacement of your boat. But check for "exclusions."

FISHING FOULS

You're out fishing on your summer holidays and a game warden confiscates your tackle and boat.

Every year thousands of Canadians run afoul of provincial game laws. Depending on the seriousness of the violation, you may have not only your catch, tackle and boat confiscated, but your automobile or aircraft as well. And since the game warden has the full authority of a policeman in his field, he can arrest you.

Dangling a worm off the dock for pan fish—rock bass, perch and the like—you won't be bothered; but all across Canada, strict game-fish regulations are in force. They begin by requiring the purchase of fishing licenses.

Each province and Territory issues a free booklet every spring that explains current regulations. Special restrictions apply to the national parks. These publications are widely available, from government agencies by mail or from travel agents and campground, marina or resort owners. They describe the fish that can be caught legally and the number of fish allowed, the duration of the season, where to get licenses, restrictions on bait and tackle. For example, all torches and artificial lights are prohibited, you can use only one line at a time, and spear fishing is rigidly controlled. In designated areas, including many parks, you are required to hire a licensed guide before wetting your line.

No minnows allowed. British Columbia won't allow minnows to be used as bait, and Alberta forbids *all* live bait fish. All provinces have some restrictions, generally designed to prevent coarse fish from escaping into game-fish waters.

Canada is bounded by three oceans and the pleasure fisherman has the right to drop a line anywhere in the open sea at any time. Tidal waters, however, are governed under the federal Fisheries Act, mainly to protect spawning salmon.

The winter pastime of ice fishing doesn't escape the regulatory net, either. Tackle and bag limits apply, and huts placed on lake or river ice must be identified by name or number. Regional dates are set for the compulsory removal of fishing huts from the ice.

RESPONSIBLE HUNTING

There's a wolf scare in your northern district and a neighbor is organizing a mass hunt. But others are saying this is illegal.

The simple laws of survival existed long before any man-made statutes. Man has always presumed the right to protect himself and his property from all predators. Whether Canada's timber wolf attacks man without provocation remains a subject of controversy, but few working or living alone in the bush would be willing to take the chance. Children could certainly be in danger from this animal which can weigh up to 45 kilograms. Many municipal and township governments in remote areas still offer a bounty to wolf killers.

Before you join the wolf hunt, get in touch with your nearest game warden to ensure that you are aware of current hunting and camping regulations in the district. Remember that hunting is not permitted in any of Canada's 28 national parks.

Most timberlands are marked off into "fire districts" where strict regulations regarding camp fires are in force during certain seasons. When the danger of forest fire is high, the lighting of a cigarette can result in a criminal charge.

Don't take chances. Trigger-happy hunters in a mass drive can be more dangerous than any wolf. An experienced hunter, versed in animal lore and familiar with the terrain, should be elected to take charge. He may appoint deputies to control the gun line and make sure no individual hunter gets so far ahead that his movements attract shots from stragglers.

Gun-control laws generally set a minimum age of 16 for hunters. Newfoundland won't permit anyone younger than 16 even to carry a gun into the woods. Quebec will allow younger hunters if they are accompanied by a licensed hunter aged 21 or older. Alberta sets the minimum at 14. If the area is open for deer or moose hunting, there's probably a restriction on the caliber of shotguns and rifles. All pistols, revolvers and automatic weapons are prohibited.

And don't forget the cardinal safety rule for hunters: Never point your gun at anything you don't want to kill.

Conspicuous clothing should be worn; the traditional red cap may not show up against autumn foliage. Some provinces specify colors and clothing in their game regulations. For example, Saskatchewan insists on an outer garment of bright yellow, orange, scarlet or white, or a combination of these colors.

If the wolf is brought to bay, remember that it is a crime in Canada to inflict unnecessary pain or injury on any animal. Prosecution can bring a maximum of six months' imprisonment. No live game—including wolves—can be kept in captivity, outside of zoos, for more than 10 days; and while penned up, any animal must be treated humanely.

FIGHTING FOR FUN

Your young son suffers a broken jaw in an amateur boxing meet.

It's the kind of chance everyone takes when engaging in any active contact sport. And boxing is notably violent—in fact, that's the nature of it. Medical examination and insurance are compulsory for all contestants.

But if you're thinking of seeking compensation for injuries through the courts, you'd better forget it. No charge of assault will stand up where there's consent.

All amateur and professional boxing matches staged publicly in Canada are licensed and controlled by private athletic organizations under provincial authority. The ruling body for amateurs is the Canadian Amateur Boxing Association, Box 1980, Timmins, Ont., P4N 7E3. The size and construction of the roped ring, weight of gloves—for amateurs 10 ounces (283 grams), for professionals 8 ounces (227 grams)—number and duration of rounds, provision of a qualified referee and an impartial timekeeper, judges, medical supervision—all these and other matters are regulated.

Careful matching by weight and, to some extent, by experience is a safeguard against

'He brought English to the sports pages'

Andrew Ralph "Red" Allen (1913-1966), O.B.E., of Oxbow, Sask., is remembered by graying journalists as the revered redhead who, as editor of *Maclean's* in the 1950s, inspired a generation of Canadian writers. War correspondent, novelist and inveterate bridge player, "Red" Allen always remained a sportswriter at heart.

It was his passionate interest in prairie slough hockey that won him—at 16—a $15-a-week job on the sports staff of the Winnipeg *Tribune*. Jim Coleman, himself a legendary figure in Canadian sportswriting, described the Allen of those days as "a thin freckle-faced kid with a shock of red hair that looked like an unmade bed." Of the mature man, he wrote: "Before Ralph Allen, sportswriting in Canada was pretty pocky stuff. He brought English to the sports pages." At 20, Allen had his own sports column in the *Tribune*. In 1938, the bigger pay cheques of "the East" drew him to Toronto and he joined the sports department of the Toronto *Globe and Mail*.

Allen joined the army in World War II and in 1941 wrote reminiscently in the *Globe and Mail* about his civilian days: "A million hockey games, more or less . . . Some good, some bad, but none so bad that it wasn't better than no hockey game at all." From 1943 until the war ended, Allen filed sensitive stories from every front where Canadians were engaged.

Back in Canada, he joined *Maclean's* and within three years was managing editor. To the astonishment of many, he quit to return to his first love. His sports column in the Toronto *Telegram* (now defunct) immediately set a new standard. He didn't seem to be so much interested in any actual game as he was fascinated with the characters of the sporting

scene. A Winnipeg friend said, "I figure he could have been another Damon Runyon."

Allen did another stint as editor of *Maclean's* before returning once again to daily journalism—this time at *The Toronto Star*. On May 3, 1965, he wrote (of a Stanley Cup game at the Montreal Forum):

In spite of what they'll say in the commissions on culture and the proliferating expositions and festivals and grants-in-aid to anybody who knows anybody else, the only true Canadian invention is a game called hockey.

Hockey was, he added, "this most priceless ingredient of the Canadian tradition."

One of Allen's finest stories during his *Maclean's* years was a long series of articles entitled "Don't Call Me Baby Face," which he had written in collaboration with Vancouver's Jimmy McLarnin, one of the most successful boxers ever to emerge in Canada. McLarnin won the world welterweight title in New York in 1933, knocking out Young Corbett III in the first round. In 13 years in the ring, he defeated a total of 13 men who had held—or would hold—world titles. In 1965, reliving McLarnin's days of glory and comparing the 76-kilogram ex-newsboy with the heavyweight stars of the day—Sonny Liston, Cassius Clay (Muhammad Ali), Floyd Patterson, Canada's George Chuvalo—Allen told his readers that McLarnin could have beaten them all in one night, one at a time or all together.

Damon Runyon, whose fabulous short-story characters live on in the oft-revived musical *Guys and Dolls*, died of cancer at 62. In 1966, Ralph Allen, whose address book contained just as wacky and wonderful a set of characters, died of cancer at 53.

serious mismatches. Weight divisions in boxing are: flyweight, up to 112 pounds (52 kilograms); bantamweight, 118 pounds (53 kilograms); featherweight, 126 pounds (55 kilograms); lightweight, 135 pounds (59 kilograms); welterweight, 147 pounds (66 kilograms); middleweight, 160 pounds (72 kilograms); light-heavyweight, 175 pounds (79 kilograms); and heavyweight, over 175 pounds. The CABA designates no fewer than 36 competition categories by weight and age for juniors under age 16, and 11 categories for seniors.

If your son was injured in a publicly staged bout with a fighter far out of his weight class, you might consider a negligence suit against the organizer or the officials in charge. But it's a feature of the sport that the improving boxer seeks challenge by pitting himself against the next man up the ladder. No one is forced to fight. Sooner or later, every boxer meets a better or stronger man. Even Muhammad Ali had his jaw broken—during his 1973 bout with Ken Norton.

Once a boxing match begins, the referee is in control. It's his decision whether a bout should be continued or stopped. If the referee does not call a halt when, in the opinion of other experts, it should be stopped, he could possibly be liable. However, it's also true that, from the opening bell, the fighters have implicitly accepted his authority and judgment.

The private fight. Although the terms are often used synonymously, there's a great difference between boxing and prizefighting. The latter involves a fight with unprotected fists or hands between two persons for prize money and is illegal in Canada. Section 81 of the Criminal Code states: "Everyone who engages as a principal in a prizefight, advises, encourages or promotes a prizefight, or is present at a prizefight as an aid, second, surgeon, umpire, backer or reporter, is guilty of an offense." Contestants in a boxing match wear gloves. You cannot stage a boxing match in your barn between two local stalwarts for $100 (or $10,000), winner take all. It doesn't matter if you have a doctor present and follow all of the Marquis of Queensberry's rules. Without a license, you'll be charged and convicted. And

anyone who placed or accepted bets would almost certainly be charged under the gaming laws.

You can, however, arrange a private boxing contest between amateur sportsmen in your barn—or in your living room, for that matter. Gloves must not weigh less than 5 ounces (142 grams) each. The public cannot be invited; nor must any money or prizes change hands. Indeed, any amateur found fighting for profit would immediately lose his amateur status. (It would not be illegal, though, for two persons to make a private wager on the outcome.) It's not essential that a doctor be present. We still retain the right to fight, like gentlemen.

SEX DISCRIMINATION

Your daughter is the star catcher for the school baseball team, but she can't even get a tryout in the city leagues.

The problem of the woman athlete who wants to break the sex barrier in traditionally male sports is in limbo. Many courts have rejected attempts to force amateur athletic organizations to admit female players into certain men-only sports.

In 1976, complaints were lodged with the Human Rights Commission against the Ontario Rural Softball Association (ORSA) and the Ontario Minor Hockey Association (OMHA) on behalf of two young girls who wanted to play on boys-only teams. The hockey complaint went to a board of inquiry which ruled that discrimination on the grounds of sex had indeed occurred, and that the association's teams should be open to girls.

The hockey association appealed this decision and in 1978 the Supreme Court of Ontario overturned the inquiry board's ruling on the basis that the OMHA is not a person nor an entity against whom an action can be taken. To be successful, the complaint would have to be made against the association's officers rather than the association itself.

The inquiry board's ruling on the ORSA was also overruled by the Supreme Court of Ontario, which found that in view of the association's attempts to provide fairness of competition, some discrimination on sex grounds might be inevitable.

Beauty in the bull ring. In some cases, actions launched through provincial Human Rights Commissions on the grounds of sexual discrimination in sports have succeeded. For example, when a Manitoba teen-ager was refused permission to compete in a calf scramble at a winter fair, the commission found that she qualified in all respects, but one: regulations restricted the contest to "farm boys."

Fair officials argued that this was a rough sport but, under pressure from the commission, it agreed to revise the rules and in future consider applications from girls.

While the Canadian and American football leagues brighten the TV tube with cheerleader chorus lines, the day is probably still distant when we'll see women hunkering down among the male behemoths with "goal to go."

But maybe not all that distant. Says Abby Hoffman, five-time member of the Canadian Olympic track and field team, and 1977 Vanier Award recipient for her achievements in athletics: "There really isn't any reason why girls who want to play football or hockey, take part in wrestling, boxing, weightlifting, sky diving, or become jockeys, should not do so if they want to. It is merely a social convention that a woman should not be physically strong. . . . It is a North American cliché that a strong-looking woman is unattractive, a weak one appealing."

Abby herself first caught the public eye while playing defense for a "boys" hockey team in Toronto.

ROUGH STUFF

In the college football final, you are seriously injured by an illegal tackle.

Although every player who suits up for a football game is accepting the inherent risks of the sport, there can be grounds for legal action if the illegality is of such a vicious or deliberate nature as to place it outside the rough-and-

tumble acceptable in the "heat of the battle." From the kickoff, the game is under the sole control of the head referee, who has power to award a wide range of penalties for rules infractions, including suspension of any player on the spot.

However, no matter how gentlemanly the players, there's always a chance of being hurt, even in a "friendly" amateur game of hockey or football. For example, office employees of an Ontario supermarket chain took to the ice against a team of their warehouse co-workers. A player on the office team was badly hurt when hit in the face by a high stick. He was in hospital for six days with a broken jaw and 15 displaced teeth. He laid a charge of assault occasioning bodily harm against the player who hit him.

Provincial Court Judge S. R. Roebuck heard conflicting testimony about whether the blow had been struck deliberately or accidentally "in the heat of the game." The judge's decision, in November 1979, hinged on the statement of the referee that the accused had been attempting to make a hook check when his stick swung up and injured his opponent. The judge said that were it not for the evidence of the referee, "there is no doubt in my mind I would have convicted the accused.

"There is in sports, and particularly in this type of sport, the element of implied consent to such physical contact normally not permitted between ordinary individuals." Judge Roebuck added that "in the heat of the game, there is a tendency to be overzealous" and while "a limited overreaction" is permitted, he regretted that the hunger to win too often dominated the sporting aspect.

Dr. Robert G. Hindmarch of the University of British Columbia was commissioned by Sport Canada, a division of the federal Department of Health and Welfare, to study the incidence of injury in some of the most popular Canadian sports. He came up with the following report: in lacrosse, 24.49 percent; in hockey, 85.3 percent; in football, 121 percent.

This means that approximately one in four lacrosse players can expect an injury requiring treatment. The football player is likely to be hurt more than once.

JUDGING

Coaching at an important track meet, you see a flagrant case of unfair judging that costs one of your athletes a coveted trophy.

On such an occasion, there's sure to be a standing procedure for the hearing of a protest by the athlete or by his team officials. You have the right to demand review.

The record books—even at the Olympic Games—show many examples of disqualification, either on the initiative of judges and track stewards or in response to a sustained protest by a competitor.

Recent technological advances, such as electronic timing, high-speed photography, the measurement of wind advantage and the videotape replay, have sharply reduced the controversy that once swirled around athletic adjudication. But there's still the human fac-

---

'It's a game, not a war'

Hockey violence is as old as the sport itself. The first recorded fatality occurred in 1907, when Charles Masson was accused of clubbing Owen McCourt with his stick during an amateur game in Cornwall, Ont. McCourt died of head injuries, Masson was charged with murder, later reduced to manslaughter, but acquitted.

Traditionally, aggression in hockey has been regarded as a measure of a player's competitiveness. Yet despite its violent heritage, the National Hockey League, founded in 1917, has recorded only one fatality resulting *directly* from injuries sustained in a game: Bill Masterton of the Minnesota North Stars died in 1968 after his head struck the ice during a hard—but legal—check. Hockey's most publicized near-fatality occurred in 1933 when Boston's Eddie Shore slammed into Ace Bailey from behind, sending the Toronto player to hospital with a concussion. Bailey survived, but never played hockey again. Shore was suspended by the league for a month.

Until 1969, however, the courts seemed reluctant to prosecute and convict hockey players for offenses committed in the rink. That year, Boston Bruins defenseman Ted Green's skull was fractured in a violent stick-swinging duel during an exhibition game between Boston and the St. Louis Blues in Ottawa. As a result of the fracas, two NHL players were charged with assault and intent to injure. Both were acquitted in separate trials, but it was the first time players had been charged with assaulting each other. (Previous cases had involved players and fans.) And again, in the 1975-76 season, Detroit Red Wings Dan Maloney jumped Toronto's Brian Glennie from behind during a league game, pummeled him senseless, then slammed his head against the ice. Maloney was charged with assault. The jury acquitted him, but hockey had been notified that brutality between players—even with no resulting injuries—would not be tolerated in Ontario rinks.

The antiviolence campaign spearheaded by the Ontario government, and a series of international tournaments in which noncombative European teams frequently defeated Canadian squads, led officials and coaches to reevaluate Canada's amateur hockey program, including its imitation of the violent professional game. As a result, several leagues in Quebec and Ontario have banned body checking by players under the age of 12. The Kitchener-Waterloo, Ont., Minor Hockey Association outlawed body checking entirely from its house leagues. Some organizations have eliminated standings and playoffs at lower age groups to de-emphasize a "winning at all costs" philosophy. Perhaps they are heeding former Toronto Maple Leafs star Howie Meeker who said: "Let's put the fun back in hockey. It's a game, not a war."

tor. It's unrealistic to expect that emotion and favoritism can be eliminated altogether. The "hometown decision" can still occur, especially in events where points are awarded by a panel of judges.

Misguided nationalism plays a noticeable role in some international competitions. For example, Canadians have cynically come to expect some judges at world figure-skating championships to award "nines" to their own country's competitors while the rest of the panel think only "sevens" or "eights" were earned. Responsible organizers attempt to minimize these factors by juggling the appointments of judges so as to achieve the maximum of impartiality.

Athletes learn to accept the fact that the decision of the judge or referee is final. Only the most flagrant abuse is worth a protest. Sports events would degenerate into chaos if the on-the-spot rulings of the appointed officials were continually disputed.

PERILS OF JOGGING

You're jogging at the edge of town when a farmer sets his dog on you.

Joggers have the same rights as everybody else, but no extra privileges. If you jog outdoors, you must restrict your running to sidewalks, roads, parks—any public property. You must observe all the rules any other pedestrian is expected to follow. You must use pedestrian crosswalks (where provided) and obey stoplights and traffic signs.

When you venture into the countryside, no matter how "open" it appears, you are expected to observe the property laws. Private property means exactly what it says; it must not be intruded upon without permission.

However, the law does not grant the property owner the right to be judge and jury. He must use legal channels to punish those who trespass upon his land. Under no circumstances, short of self-defense, can a property owner encourage a dog to attack anyone. Even in threatening circumstances, he is permitted to use only such force as is necessary in the

mind of a reasonable person. The use of force of any kind is always the last resort, and must always be justified.

Joggers and other city-bred ramblers have been known to break down rural fences, leave farm gates open, run through crop fields and deposit litter indiscriminately. Some will blithely set off across the demesne of a country landowner when they wouldn't dream of cutting across a stranger's lawn in town.

Property-conscious individuals usually signpost their land "No Trespassing," but they are under no legal obligation to do so. Except for Crown lands, including designated public property and parks, all land in Canada is privately owned.

PARK RESPECT

A park ranger breaks up your beach party and orders the whole crowd to leave the park.

When you enter any national or provincial park, you should receive a brochure on the rules and regulations of that particular reserve. If you don't, ask for it.

The brochure explains exactly where you can camp and for how long, the number of persons per site, sanitary and power-supply facilities, restrictions on fires and noise, and applicable liquor laws.

The park warden normally has the powers of a police officer—including the power of arrest—in the park, sanctuary or conservation area. He can order anyone to leave the park who is breaking the regulations, or even threatening to do so. A refusal to obey will usually bring the municipal or provincial police to the scene as reinforcement.

Abuse of liquor and excessive noise are among the major problems that confront park rangers and wardens. Parks and conservation areas are provided and staffed through public funding and are intended for the "quiet enjoyment" of all the public; they're not to be regarded as a handy and cheap venue for a weekend bash.

Few campers will complain about happy or mildly boisterous parties—everybody is on holiday, after all. But the majority consists of young families or elderly couples, and the rangers will insist that they be left in the reasonable tranquillity they've come to seek.

Watching flora and fauna. Canada's 28 national and 494 provincial parks are protected areas in which wildlife is generally allowed to roam freely and all natural assets and resources are strictly guarded. Rocks and fossils must not be damaged or removed. Trees must not be cut or broken. You can't pick the wildflowers. There's no hunting whatsoever, unless a special permit is obtained.

In beach areas, picnics are always welcome, but rangers and wardens frown on the kind of beach party sometimes depicted in beer commercials. The consumption of any alcoholic beverage away from the confines of your tent or trailer—your "home" for the purposes of the law—is prohibited. The patrolling ranger has been known to "look the other way" when a glass of beer or wine is consumed at the park bench during a picnic lunch or evening cookout. But expect him to circle back in an hour to make sure that a drinking party isn't getting under way. Park wardens normally have the powers of any peace officer.

Those given to roaring around park roads on motorcycles, dune buggies or in cars may or may not get one warning before expulsion. Traffic signs demand a speed protective of young children and strolling couples.

TRAILER PARKING

You park your motor home on the shoulder of a remote country road. The police wake you up at 3 a.m. and give you a ticket.

Simple. You were illegally parked. No one in any kind of vehicle is permitted to park overnight on, or adjacent to, a highway or secondary road. You may get away with it a few times in the boondocks, but police cars check all roads periodically. They also investigate complaints from residents who regard parked motor homes as a nighttime road hazard, and a daytime litter or sanitation problem.

Even the long-distance truck driver, sometimes seen catnapping in his cab on the verge of a four-lane highway, is technically breaking the law. You can stop there only in emergencies.

Provincial and federal tourist offices, travel agents and some gas stations will provide free booklets listing the hundreds of campgrounds where motor homes are welcome. Sanitary facilities, power hookups and other conveniences are available there. If you're strapped for cash, a sympathetic landowner might permit you to pull into his field for the night. But drive up to the house and ask first.

Many cities and towns totally forbid overnight parking in the streets.

41 Entertainment

Food-service firms serve 1.5 billion meals a year, the equivalent of about 65 meals a year for every Canadian. It's expected that, before long, 50 cents of every food-and-drink dollar will be spent eating out. This represents a major change in the Canadian life style, at least in urban areas. A generation ago, only five cents out of every food-and-drink dollar went outside the home. In 1979, the eating-out industry employed 450,000 workers, full- or part-time, and an increase of 90,000 jobs was forecast over the next five years. The total value of all such food and beverages consumed annually exceeds $8 billion.

A major impulse behind this shift in the social gears is undoubtedly the entry of more married women into the labor force. When both partners work, who feels like fixing dinner? But there's more to it than that. Canadians seem to be moving away from the old idea of the home as the hub of the family; the crowded dinner table, heaped with plates of home-cooking, is becoming less and less the focus of family life. Certainly, the fast-food and takeout outlets are the swiftest growing segments of the industry.

Eating and drinking "out" is a response to the hunger for nonstop entertainment so noticeable in this restless "video era." It's aided by a general weakening of faith in the stability of our society and its values, leading to acceptance of the Biblical exhortation, "Eat, drink and be merry" (Luke, XII, 19).

The magnetism of television aside, live theater, concerts of every conceivable variety, theme parks of the Disneyland or African-safari type, disco dancing, and sex-oriented shows proliferate. And the movie theater—almost written off in the 1950s—is staging a comeback in multiscreen complexes.

Charting and enforcing the rights and responsibilities of patrons, performers and workers in this rush to the new hedonism has caught the law with its shoelaces undone. The ancient law of the innkeeper and the accepted morality of past times struggle to cope with the problem of bare-breasted girls serving cocktails in dimly lit lounges. Police and politicians, the judiciary and the clergy fumble to find standards to judge and control explicit performances on film, stage, or nightclub floor—performances that offend some and delight others.

In less sensational areas, consumer experts debate whether restaurant menus should be required to say that certain foods are prepared from frozen products, or that the stripes on a "charcoal broiled" steak may have been painted on with vegetable dye.

Should a separate set of values be applied to the world of entertainment? When a nightclub singer charged the band leader with assault because he "patted" her and kissed her ear, a jury gave her "peppercorn" damages—a derisory amount—and she was ordered to pay all the costs of the action: $2,000. Intoned the judge from the bench: "She was living in a world of artists where offstage it is not unusual to pass a young woman vocalist from one to another, hugging and kissing her."

And how does a rural Canadian township cope with the appearance in its midst of an African jungle, complete with roving lions? It happened in Beverley Township in southwestern Ontario, when Donald Dailey, a retired army officer, borrowed $250,000 and set up his African Lion Safari in 1969. The township council called a meeting and found that the main concern of the neighboring housewives was that snakes would escape. Dailey agreed to ban all reptiles and the enterprise was launched. Within 10 years this reverse-zoo, where the animals roam free and the patrons are locked in cars, covered some 300 hectares, contained 1,500 animals and was counting 650,000 paid admissions annually.

Trying to protect the careers of Canadian performers from foreign competition finds immigration officials lumping ballet stars with strippers, Frank Sinatra with an itinerant apple picker. When the immigration department questions the need to import a performer, officials consult Canadian Actors' Equity, the Association of Canadian Television and Radio Artists, or the musicians' union. Entry permits must be obtained before the performers arrive on Canadian soil. Complains Hamish Robertson, manager of the National Ballet of Canada: "What if I need a wigmaster who can make 18th-century beards? If I fill out an employment request, the bureaucrats will try to find me an unemployed hairdresser."

NEGLIGENCE IN THE RESTAURANT

At a pretheater dinner, your expensive gown is ruined by a clumsy waiter.

At the very least, the restaurant management will be liable for the cost of dry cleaning your gown. If, in the opinion of an impartial expert, it was ruined, you'll have little difficulty getting its replacement value.

It's unlikely that you'll even be forced to test the case in court. Management will hasten to apologize and rectify the damage as best it can. The dinner tab may be canceled and a bottle of wine may appear with the compliments of the house. The reputation of a restaurant for good food and service is usually its greatest asset.

There's no special legislative protection for patrons of a restaurant. Waiters, busboys, chefs and doormen are subject to the same legal duty as anyone else—that is, they must take reasonable care for the safety of others. The waiter, a practicing professional in the serving of food, could perhaps be expected to show a somewhat higher degree of care than, say, the average person placing a dish on the table in his own home.

General protection lies in the law of *negligence*, which is just a two-dollar word for carelessness. While there is nothing in law that demands that either waiter or diner must protect the other, there is in law a universal "duty of care" and a liability for any physical injury or material damage that results from the failure to carry out that duty. In short, whoever causes the damage is at fault. The law will usually insist that the victim be compensated.

Statistical spillage. There is no such thing as total safety for the person who moves in public places, nor is there any right to absolute care. Accidents will happen. If a waiter carries a thousand plates of soup, he is likely to spill a certain fraction. In every 160,000 kilometres (100,000 miles), the taxi driver statistically will have a certain number of fender benders—if not worse. That's why public liability insurance exists.

Your entitlement is to *reasonable* care. This is usually interpreted as the level of care that it is reasonable to expect under the given circumstances. It is certainly unreasonable for a waiter to tip cherries jubilee into your lap.

If you had to launch a civil suit for damages from such an incident—even in the Small Claims Court—it would be up to you as the plaintiff to prove the negligence of the defendant. (*See* Chapter 3, "You, the plaintiff.") This wouldn't be difficult if you could produce the stained clothing. It would be a case—as the lawyers say—of *res ipsa loquitur* ("it speaks for itself"). But perhaps you are also claiming damages for physical injury—a burn or shock—or compensation for other loss suffered because of the event.

If the case reaches the courts, it's probable that the waiter is claiming that the accident was not entirely his fault. Maybe a tipsy guest blundered into him as he was serving. This situation raises the doctrine of *contributory negligence*. If the evidence supports this argument, the court could assess the degree of responsibility of all the parties and make a split award. The third party could be found solely liable.

If an "accident" should arise out of the preparation of the food, say, a case of food poisoning, the proprietor not only faces the possibility of heavy claims for personal damages, but also prosecution under the strict regulations of the public health laws.

WHAT THE CUSTOMER ORDERED

You reserve a table at a seafood house famous for its lobster. When you are seated, the waiter announces that the lobsters are sold out.

You can exercise your right to walk out, paying nothing. Even if you had inquired about the lobster when you reserved, there was no guarantee that dish would still be available. Restaurant trade cannot be predicted with the accuracy that would be necessary to provide even an implied warranty. (*See* Chapter 19, "Furniture and clothing.") Before you got there, 50 members of a hockey fans' club may just have dropped in out of the blue for that famous lobster.

If the restaurant published an advertisement or displayed a sign that said "Lobster Always On," and then refused to supply that item to your party, you could consider complaining to your nearest consumer services bureau. It sometimes happens that a buffet restaurant will advertise "All the lobster you can eat, $7.95"—but when you arrive, it has run out. The consumer watchdogs may accumulate enough evidence to show that this has happened too frequently and that the advertising is misleading or deceptive. And that's a crime. (*See* Chapter 20, "Advertising.")

Make me an offer. The purchase of a meal in a restaurant involves a contract, but when is the contract struck? Generally, a contract is made when an offer by one person is accepted by another. Advertising is not an offer; it's an "invitation to treat." When the *maître d'* seats you and hands you the menu, he is simply inviting you to make him an offer. The contract is made when you offer to purchase rather than when he offers to sell. If your choice is no longer on the menu, you would not succeed in an action for breach of contract.

Let's say you switch to a steak and you instruct that you want it "well done." The restaurant is bound to deliver what you ordered; if it does not, you are not obliged to pay. Most restaurants work on the principle that "the customer is always right." They may not agree with you, but they'd prefer you—and everyone within earshot—to come back again as a satisfied customer.

If the steak arrives dripping red, you can decide to leave with no obligation, or you can ask for another. If there's an argument, the ruling criterion would be whether a reasonable person—not an international gourmet, but, say, your next-door neighbor—would consider the steak "well done" or "rare."

Tasting the wine. The trend to drinking wine with meals is the great dining phenomenon of the past decade. In a single recent year, the quantity of wines consumed in Canada jumped by more than nine million litres.

We tend to follow European table habits slavishly. Thus you'll see embarrassed diners solemnly attempting to judge the acceptability of a proffered bottle when, in honesty, they haven't the knowledge or taste experience to distinguish a Burgundy from a Bordeaux, a Barolo from a Barossa—or any of them from Niagara Nutty.

But the wine steward, or *sommelier*, is being more than courteous. "House" wines, usually served in the carafe or jug, are always young and bought in bulk by the restaurant. Tasting them with the traditional sip is akin to tasting a curry to see if it's too hot. With bottled wines—corks, not screw tops—it's an important ritual because wines aged and shipped in the bottle can improve or deteriorate. While famous labels can usually be trusted, the quality of an individual bottle is virtually impossible to judge with certainty until the cork is drawn and the wine tasted.

Fine wines are expensive and when the waiter offers you a small taste and waits for your verdict, he is shifting the purchasing contract onto your shoulders—or taste buds.

If for any reason you don't enjoy the taste, send the wine back. Simply say, "Sorry, I don't want that." That ends your obligation. You don't have to accept a different bottle. Don't be browbeaten into paying for something you don't like. The fact that the best champagnes cost an arm and a leg doesn't mean that everybody should like champagne. The truth is, many people don't.

How to 'read' a wine label

Strict laws govern the information given on the labels of wine bottles. This sample label is from an imported wine. The code shows you what to expect and what to look for when you choose a wine.

1. The country of origin—in this case, France.

2. The region in which the wine was produced—for example, Bordeaux, Burgundy, Champagne.

3. The appellation for which the wine qualifies, accompanied by A.O.C. (*Appellation d'Origine Contrôlée*—Controlled Appellation of Origin) or V.D.Q.S. (*Vins Délimités de Qualité Supérieure*—Superior Quality Wine of Limited Production), except in the case of champagne where the label need only read "champagne."

4. The name and address of the shipper, except in the case of champagne where, normally, the champagne house (brand) is also the shipper.

5. The name and address of the importer.

6. The alcoholic percentage by volume.

7. The net contents of the bottle.

The following optional information may also appear on the label:

8. Vintage.

9. Brand name or chateau name.

10. "Estate bottled," "Chateau bottled" or similar term.

REFUSAL AT THE DOOR

Your 25th anniversary party is spoiled when your T-shirted sons are refused admission to the restaurant.

It is the clear right of the owner of any restaurant or shop to restrict his clientele to those who meet his conditions for entry, subject always to the antidiscrimination provisions of the Human Rights Code. (*See* Chapter 1, "Civil rights.") Even in this egalitarian age, almost every city has establishments where jackets and ties are required for men, reasonably modest dress for women, and where the door is barred to those who prefer to live in jeans.

If this offends your democratic principles, there are always other eating places where dress codes don't exist. But even the largest fast-food chains will probably show you to the door if you stroll in wearing your bikini, or in dirty or disreputable attire that the average customer might find offensive. Should that happen, don't waste your breath arguing with the manager; his or her word is final.

Notice in advance. Most party reservations are made by telephone and it's a fine point as to whether the onus is on the restaurant to advise you at that time about any dress code that will be enforced. Some well-known restaurants mention their restrictions in their advertising, but most do not. They rely on common sense and public awareness. Everybody *knows* you don't dine at the Ritz in coveralls.

It's possible, theoretically, that if you were not advised—and if the boys in their T-shirts were barred at the door—you could succeed in an action for breach of contract. One party to a contract cannot unilaterally add terms to it after it is made. But the judge might well consider the action "frivolous" or a waste of the court's valuable time—and award you damages of $1. By the time you pay your legal costs, the anniversary outing will be expensive indeed.

If you arrive at a restaurant without reservations and are refused admission, there is little you can do. We are not speaking here about illegal discrimination in the human rights sense. If others are being admitted without reservations, don't stage a brawl at the door, but provide your Human Rights Commission with all the details.

A restaurant is private property and the owner can refuse to admit whomever he chooses. There are many areas of discrimination that are entirely legal. Consider the photographs in the gossip magazines showing eager patrons lined up to get into the jet-set discos. The doorman or manager gives the nod to the chosen few.

In public places. Many people who hear restaurants, theaters, taverns and similar establishments referred to as "public places" conclude that, as members of the public, they can't be excluded. This is a misconception.

There are two definitions of "public place." The first refers to those "places" that the public has the right to use: the sidewalk, highway and park, for example. The second applies to "places," such as commercial shops and eating places, that, although privately owned, are commonly frequented by the public. In this latter broad group, there exists a general invitation to the public to enter. But it is an invitation that can be withdrawn.

TIPS AND SERVICE CHARGES

A 15-percent service charge is added to your lunch bill but you don't want to pay it because the service was terrible.

Tips or service charges? The question swings like a pendulum in the catering business. The service charge, which may run to 20 percent of the bill, is routine in Europe, and well-heeled and well-satisfied clients still tip on top of that. There's an unwritten law that when a service charge is mandatory, that portion of the payment goes into a staff fund, generally shared *pro rata* to supplement the traditionally low wages in the industry. The chef sweating in the kitchen gets part of the folding money slipped to the suave *maitre d'*.

In Canada, there's no law, written or unwritten, about either tips or service charges.

The customer can't be sure what happens to that "little extra." Unions representing workers in the industry claim flatly that tips are the sole property of the staff and that they should be left to share them as they see fit. They argue that wage levels should be set regardless of any gratuities. The employers point out the obvious fact that a waiter or waitress *does* get tips from a majority of patrons, whereas a bricklayer, say, does not. They think this social truth should be reflected in hourly rates. Most provincial governments agree, setting the hourly minimums lower in the service trades. It's the simple truth that doormen at some first-class hotels actually pay to hold their jobs.

Pay up and smile. If the service charge was brought to your attention before you began lunch, you are bound to pay it even if the service was below par. The charge is for "service," not necessarily "superior service" or even "good service."

This doesn't mean you can't complain later—to the management, to the nearest consumer services bureau, to the Canadian Restaurant and Food Service Association, 94 Cumberland Street, Toronto, Ont., M5R 1A3, to the Consumers' Association of Canada, 251 Laurier Avenue West, Suite 801, Ottawa, Ont., K1P 5Z7, or by letter to your local newspaper. All restaurants and hotels fear bad publicity.

If a restaurant wishes to include a service charge in the price of your meal, it must declare this policy before you order. Normally, this is done through a notation on the menu in small type. Small print on the back of a menu may not amount to "reasonable notice," but clearly legible print on the front may do. If in doubt, ask.

Rights and wrongs. Tipping is, socially, a pleasant custom: you reward the servant for extra thoughtfulness or diligence. Those subtle attentions can make or break the occasion. Almost everyone responds to a little deference when "out on the town." It's hardly the time to be trumpeting about "rights."

But there's a dark side. Self-conscious people often feel that they *must* tip, or be castigated as cheapskates. Some waiters and bar attendants are notably adept at plying the noisy big tipper with service and attention while giving humbler clients short shrift. Don't expect the law to ensure fair play in this kind of social situation. Like the denizens of George Orwell's *Animal Farm*, all animals are equal, but some are more equal than others.

LIQUOR AND LEGISLATION

There is a half bottle of wine left but the restaurant manager refuses to let you take it home.

And he is obeying the law; you're trying to break it. It's just one of dozens of liquor laws handed down from the days when Demon Rum was a popular bogeyman. But because the sale of liquor is everywhere a state monopoly—and the source of a torrent of money—incumbent politicians move like molasses in reforming any liquor legislation. Our federal and provincial governments derived revenue of $1,942 million from the sale and taxation of alcoholic beverages in 1978.

A restaurant or bar licensed to sell liquor can provide drinks only for consumption on the premises; you can't tote it with you when you go. A 31-year-old Ontario school trustee who refused to accept this ruling from the management of a Toronto restaurant in 1979 was fined $250 and put on probation for two years. There was a half bottle of white wine left when his party had finished dinner and he attempted to carry it away. After an argument, a fight ensued.

The trustee faced five charges. He argued that he wanted to take the unfinished wine to the beach the next day and since he had paid for it, he felt he had a right to take it with him. He pleaded guilty to doing bodily harm to the restaurant manager with the broken bottle, assaulting the policemen who came to arrest him, assaulting another patron of the restaurant who intervened, causing mischief, and damaging the restaurant. He was ordered to make good all damage. He was also defeated in the next school board election.

No time to tipple. The serving of liquor on all licensed premises is restricted to stated times of opening and closing. Ontario restau-

Blacks to the Balcony

Background

For decades after the abolition of slavery throughout the British Empire in 1833, black citizens in Nova Scotia barely noticed any change in their lot. They lived in impoverished ghettos, went to segregated schools, prayed in segregated churches. Theaters and taverns had separate facilities, and second-rate service, for blacks.

Members of Nova Scotia's black community served overseas in a segregated unit—No. 2 Construction Battalion of the Canadian Expeditionary Force—in World War I, but in World War II they served and were commissioned in all branches of the armed forces. This desegregation wasn't matched in civilian life, however. Even after the war, theaters in New Glasgow still confined black audiences to the balcony, reserving the orchestra section for whites. Before the era of provincial human rights legislation, such segregation was legal across Canada.

On Nov. 8, 1946, Mrs. Viola Irene Desmond approached the cashier at a New Glasgow theater and asked for an orchestra seat. The cashier gave her a 30-cent balcony admission. Mrs. Desmond presented the ticket to an attendant, who directed her to the balcony. She then returned to the cashier, repeated her request for an orchestra seat and offered to pay the 10-cent difference in price. The cashier refused and called the manager, who made it clear that Mrs. Desmond was welcome in the theater—but in the balcony section only.

Mrs. Desmond then marched into the orchestra section, sat down and refused to leave. She was forcibly removed by the police, arrested and jailed overnight. Next day she appeared before a magistrate, charged by the police with unlawfully entering a theater without paying the tax imposed by the provincial Theatres, Cinematographs and Amusements Act.

The prosecution pointed out that although Mrs. Desmond's 30-cent ticket included two cents in tax, she had sat briefly in a 40-cent seat for which the tax was three cents. Said Mrs. Desmond, who was not represented by a lawyer:

"I offered to pay the difference in price between the tickets. They would not accept it."

Judgment

The magistrate found Mrs. Desmond guilty and imposed a $20 fine or a month in jail. The black woman paid the fine and later hired a lawyer to appeal the sentence. But by then the 10-day limit for lodging an appeal had expired.

Nevertheless, her lawyer asked the Supreme Court of Nova Scotia to have the decision struck down on the grounds that it was against natural justice. But the court ruled that in following correct procedures, the lower court *had* served natural justice. Mrs. Desmond's remedy, said the Supreme Court justices, had lain in the appeal process. And although the issue of racial discrimination had not been raised, Mr. Justice William Lorimer Hall said:

"One wonders if the manager of the theater who laid the complaint was so zealous because of a *bona fide* belief that there had been an attempt to defraud the Province of Nova Scotia of the sum of one cent, or was it a surreptitious endeavour to enforce a Jim Crow rule by misuse of a public statute."

It was 1963 before human rights legislation forced an end to segregation of blacks in theaters and other public buildings in Nova Scotia.

rants and taverns, for example, cannot sell or serve liquor between 1 a.m. and noon. Some provinces set a time when all drinking must cease—usually 30 minutes after the bar closes—even when the restaurant itself remains open. There are two reported cases, one in Nova Scotia and the other in British Columbia, where a patron was not permitted to *finish* his wine and where legal action ensued. The patrons refused to pay and police were summoned. The patrons were arrested and jailed overnight.

Not having committed any criminal offense, each man sued the restaurant for damages, and won. Police have no right to arrest a person merely because he refuses to pay for goods or services he alleges he did not receive.

Anyone who sells or serves liquor has the right to refuse to supply a customer who appears to be intoxicated. In fact, he can face stiff fines or a jail term if this law is not observed. More than that, the individual and the management will be open to a suit for damages if a drunk reels or drives away and is involved in an accident.

QUALITY AND QUANTITY

You have ordered a top-quality rye by brand name, but you suspect you've been given the cheap bar whiskey.

You have the right to get what you order or there's no obligation to pay. It's a sales contract, in a small way.

All provincial liquor-control boards demand that alcoholic beverages be kept in the bottles in which they came, and these must be displayed to the patrons. All drinks must be poured in a place that can be viewed by the purchaser and in measures defined in the regulations.

This is one reason why you see that tempting array of bottles behind the bar, and why your favorite bartender mixes your highball on the counter before your very eyes. If a "house" wine is served to you in a carafe, you have the right to be informed truthfully about its origin.

Veteran barmen say that only one patron in 10 orders spirits by brand name. If a brand is not specified, they'll use either popular brands by rotation or whatever the manager has previously indicated as "house" liquors. Some of these brands are virtually unknown to the retail customer—but it won't be the 12-year-old stuff. If you order a top-quality brand, expect to pay a premium.

The same general rules hold for beers. Obviously, bottled brands are identifiable by label but when draft is served from an unmarked spigot, the tavern must display a sign naming the brewer. When you order drinks from your dining table, it's obvious you won't be following the waiter out to the dispensing bar to check on either the measure or the brand name. There's an element of good faith involved.

If you believe you were duped or short-changed in your drink, your recourse is to complain to the liquor board. The board's inspectors usually investigate all complaints and their inquiries are taken very seriously indeed by all liquor vendors. After all, the board has the power to suspend or revoke licenses.

RESERVATIONS

Claiming a booking error, the theater manager won't honor your reserved orchestra seats. He offers balcony seats instead.

When you do not receive the seats that the theater agreed to sell, you can demand the return of your money. You can, of course, accept the balcony seats and a price adjustment, although you are not obliged to do so. But, from the practical point of view, you want to see the show and it's futile to try to force the manager to give you the exact seats you purchased. The people already occupying the disputed seats will have *their* ticket stubs and will no doubt maintain they're in their rightful places. By the time it's all sorted out, the first act may be over.

It is a curious fact that trivial mishaps, usually arising from simple human error, often enrage some people when they are out trying to enjoy themselves.

If you are given a table behind the potted palms at the restaurant, there's not much you can do except demand a better table or leave the place. Even if there is an empty table you'd prefer to have, you have no right to insist that it be made available to you. Yes, it's quite likely the *maitre d'* is holding that empty table for his own selfish reasons, but you're on private property and he's king of that little castle. Try a sawbuck.

Plain mad at Mirabel. A case was decided in Ontario in 1979 in which an innocent mistake by a travel agency caused a middle-aged married couple considerable frustration and inconvenience. They had saved up for a long time for their first winter vacation in the south. They were told their flight would depart from Mirabel Airport, at Ste. Scholastique, Que. They traveled from Perth, Ont., to Mirabel only to discover the flight departed from Dorval Airport, which is closer to Montreal.

They missed their flight and all their onward bookings. They had to stay over in a Montreal hotel, then return disconsolately to Perth the next day. A local lawyer helped them to launch a suit for damages. Quite apart from the cost of the tickets and the hotel charges, they were awarded substantial damages for inconvenience, frustration, mental distress and loss of enjoyment.

Maybe the judge had been the victim of a booking foul-up, too.

ACTS OF GOD

A power failure blacks out the final reel of a suspense movie. The manager offers a rain check but no refund.

You had the right to see all of the film for which you had paid. However, since it was no fault of the proprietor that the show could not be completed, his offer of a rain check was reasonable. The law will not ask him to bear all of the loss for something that was beyond his control.

It's a compromise and you'll lose if you insist on a full refund. The law tries to deal with human situations; things are the way they are,

not the way we'd like them to be. You'd be in the same fix if the projectionist fell ill suddenly or went on a wildcat strike. Or if the theater caught fire—the possibilities are endless.

The law also recognizes "acts of God" which can prevent the fulfillment of contracts without liability. God is blamed for earthquakes, lightning, gales, floods—anything that is unforeseen and cannot be prevented by mere humans.

The governing law is the ordinary law of contract, which includes the "doctrine of frustration." This seldom heard doctrine is part of common law, but most provinces have spelled it out in a statute usually called the Frustrated Contracts Act. Simply put, when some event occurs that is outside the control of the parties to a contract and the event is such as to prevent the performance of the contract in the way the parties intended, each party is discharged from its obligation.

If one party has paid money under the contract, that party is entitled to the return of that money, but the other party is entitled to compensation for partial performance. Now whether our movie-theater proprietor is entitled to partial compensation because of the blackout is a question that could involve 1,000 pages of argument.

The "doctrine of frustration" owes a great deal to the development of entertainment cases. Even accepting the parallel "doctrine of reasonableness," who can say whether, for example, a movie that promised "nerve-tingling excitement" really delivered? Whose nerves? Did they tingle reasonably?

If we were all held strictly accountable for all of our promises the law courts would never get to hear any other cases.

THE BUTT OF THE JOKES

The nightclub comedian makes a disparaging remark about your guest as part of the "participatory entertainment."

This is a fairly recent trend in club entertainment, and the law makes little attempt to keep up with trends. If the disparagement escalated into insult or substantially harmful comment, the ancient law of slander could be invoked. Deliberate slander lies within the *tort* (civil wrong) of defamation. Your good name is part of your property and it can't be harmed with impunity. If the defamation is spoken before witnesses, it's slander; when written and published, it's libel. (*See* Chapter 1, "Civil rights.") But there is also something called *privilege*. This can be both absolute and qualified.

As illustration, on the floor of the House of Commons a Member of Parliament is free to say anything he chooses. Even an unsupported accusation of treason would bring no legal penalties. The newspaper editor also is permitted a very wide—but not absolute—right of statement under the doctrine of "fair comment." Some of that right spills over to protect the entertainer. If there's no provable malice in his pointed comments, he can get away with mild insults that would earn him a black eye out in the alley.

Into the lion's den. When you enter a nightclub where a name entertainer is performing, it's reasonable to assume you know

---

Feeding the party of the first part

Don't send the busboy for your lawyer, but that menu you're handed in your favorite restaurant is a contract. In flowery script or in gravy-stained type, it is a written instrument offering you a deal.

An *à la carte* menu, such as the one reproduced here, promises to provide you with any of the dishes named at the individual price stated. A *table d'hôte* menu offers you a complete meal for the one price listed.

When you make your choice and order, you are essentially promising to pay the price asked. The proprietor, in accepting, warrants that the food will be produced as advertised.

The food must meet all standards set by the public health authorities, and it must be prepared and served to standards that would be acceptable to any reasonable person. If you want your steak rare, for example, you must specifically order it cooked that way.

For English-speaking diners, the restaurateur's love of French for his menu can make the contract as baffling as most legal documents. What is *potée limousine*—something you eat while driving? Is *pétoncle* your uncle's favorite? The best solution is to ask your waiter.

Harrop Restaurant

Lunch

Soup of the day	$.95	Baked French Onion	$1.50
		Homemade Clam Chowder	$1.65
Side Salad	$1.05	Seafood Salad	$3.45

Harrop Beef Pie, chunks of beef, potato, onion in a flaky pie crust_____ $4.25

Mixed Grill, lamb chop, sausage, bacon, potato, poached egg and broiled tomato _____ $5.25

Steak and Kidney Pie, chunks of beef and kidney in a rich gravy, topped with a pastry crust____ $4.75

Filet Mignon, 4 oz. filet with onion rings_____ $4.95

Eggs Argenteuil, poached eggs, ham, asparagus in a tartlet with hollandaise _____ $3.00

Quiche Lorraine, bacon, ham, onion in a savoury custard____ $3.00

Sandwich of the Day, with french fries_____ $2.95

Crab Legs, thick and juicy, served with garlic butter_____ $5.95

Fish of the Day, with lemon butter_____ $3.75

Light Lunch

Herring with Sour Cream $2.95
Eggs with Caviar $1.95
Mushrooms Maison $1.75

Braised Artichoke Hearts $1.65
Garlic Shrimp $2.95
Escargot $3.25

Choice of Desserts

Apple Pie   Cherry Pie   Apple Crisp $1.05

English Trifle   Desert of the Day

Coffee and Tea $.45

what you're paying for. If that performer's specialty is trading barbed quips with the patrons, well, you are sticking your head into the lion's den.

The law really assumes that each of us has a thick skin. Unless the defamatory remarks about your guest caused economic loss, he will not get very far in an action for damages.

A complaint about entertainment to the liquor board might bring action, depending upon the province in which you reside. In Ontario, a license holder must not permit any "drunkenness or any riotous, *quarrelsome,* violent or disorderly conduct."

OFFENSIVE ENTERTAINMENT

You take your middle-aged parents to a nightclub for their anniversary. They are offended by the nude dancers.

At a time when moral standards rest on shifting sands, it's extraordinarily difficult to define the right of the innocent bystander to be protected from moral offense. The law is reasonably clear about prohibiting nudity and indecent conduct in public places—and, in this context, a nightclub is a "public place." (*See* Chapter 5, "The question of morals.") But libertarians claim with much success that "community standards," against which such behavior must be measured, have changed dramatically since the relevant law was written. They can produce hard evidence. Acts of heterosexual gratification are openly depicted in widely shown films, and magazines in which explicit nudity is a routine feature are sold by the thousands. Prosecution or confiscation is rare.

Topless waitresses in licensed restaurants are no longer uncommon. Even in small towns, many taverns provide nonstop striptease shows for their clientele.

Faced with such "community standards," you could be told that you were careless in not investigating the premises chosen for your parents' anniversary celebration. Most establishments featuring nude or seminude entertainment advertise in such a way—"red-hot

exotic dancers"—that the average person is impossibly naive if he doesn't anticipate pretty gamy fare. Alternatively, their entertainment policy could easily be proved to be well known locally.

Was Bridget bare? If nudity in public is tolerated, what about the more serious charge of public indecency? This question, too, appears to be slipping into the legal mists.

Ontario Assistant Crown Attorney Peter DeJulio, after losing cases brought in 1979 against Toronto strippers for public nudity, threatened to take members of the public into court in an attempt to define public decency, even if they had not witnessed the actual performances. His frustration was easy to understand. He had prosecuted a girl called Bridget who danced at a tavern wearing only a G-string. During the performance, he alleged, she had several times exposed herself completely. Judge Carl Waisberg acquitted Bridget because, he ruled, the Crown had not proved that public decency had been offended.

Those whose concept of "community standards" differs from that currently accepted by the Bench should continue to complain to the police about entertainment that is offensive to them. When you "lay an information," police can't shrug it off. Be prepared to appear as a witness and try to get others of similar mind who witnessed the performance to back you up. Don't be rattled by clever lawyers who imply that you are an old fuddy-duddy.

SKILL OR LUCK

You lose $25 at games on the midway at an exhibition. You feel sure they're rigged.

Games of skill, but not of chance, are permitted on midways, at fairs and at similar public functions. Midway operators are all licensed and should be strictly supervised. Cheating a player is a crime. If you are convinced the games at the exhibition are rigged in favor of the house, lay a complaint with the police. In 1972, an operator of one of the most traditional of all fairground games—knocking down the pyramid of milk bottles with a ball—was convicted of cheating. He had weighted the bottoms of the "bottles" so that they would be much harder to dislodge.

Bingo is purely a game of chance but it is permitted when operated under provincial license. On the midway, the prizes must be goods, not cash. When bingo is operated by a *bona fide* social club for charitable or other approved purposes, only a small sum per card may be charged the players. Games such as roulette, slot machines, *chemin de fer*, blackjack, poker and other card games are generally forbidden for public play under the Criminal Code. There are no casinos in Canada of the Las Vegas-Atlantic City type.

Gaming and betting. "Gaming" is the legal term for the playing or operating of any game of chance—or of mixed skill and chance, such as cards. Anyone who tries to make a business out of it is risking the charge of keeping a "common gaming house," which can earn a sentence of two years' imprisonment. Anyone found on the premises can get six months.

The Criminal Code provides that an "incorporated *bona fide* social club" can operate a gaming or betting house if it obtains a license from the provincial government, as long as none of the profit finds its way into the pockets of the operators.

This provision leads to some abuses. The slick operator who wants to run a gaming house can buy suitable premises, then incorporate a charitable society—say, "The Society for the Care of Retired Chimney Sweeps." The society gets a gaming license and rents the hall from the owner. He takes his profit in the form of a stiff rent, "maintenance charges" and other fees. His scheme is not without risk, however, as the Crown prosecutor may still be able to make a case against him.

All raffles and lotteries, from Super Loto with its million-dollar prizes down to the Royal Canadian Legion branch's flutter on a trip for two to Barbados, are games of chance. While they are, by definition, prohibited, wide exemptions are allowed. Churches, charities, art galleries, social clubs and sports groups all operate them under provincial license. When you send in that box top in the hope of winning a new home or a trip around the world, you are "gaming."

Betting is also "gaming" in the eyes of the law. But you have the right to bet any amount of money with anyone on anything as long as it's a private matter. No one in Canada is permitted to make a business out of betting.

Horse racing clubs are exempted, provided all wagers are placed through an approved parimutuel machine, from which the government gets a tidy rake-off.

SECURITY GUARDS

Your son and his friends say they were hassled by police and security guards at a rock concert.

The police can search anyone when they have reasonable grounds to suspect that person of illegal possession of drugs or liquor. (*See* Chapter 5, "The question of morals.") No doubt this occurs more often at rock concerts than at performances of the symphony orchestra, for the simple reason that violence and lawlessness—and sometimes tragedy—seem to follow the amplified guitar like the legendary Ancient Mariner's albatross.

In December 1979, 11 young persons died in Cincinnati, Ohio, when an unruly mob rushed the entrance doors of Riverfront Coliseum to catch a show by the British rock group, The Who. Performances by the Rolling Stones and other bands have been marked by violence and open use of narcotics. The lead guitarist of the Stones was convicted in Toronto on a charge of possession of heroin. Several pop idols have died from drug overdoses during the last decade.

Security guards have no more authority to conduct searches than any other person, for they are not peace officers. It may, however, be a condition of admission to a rock concert that you submit to a search. A security guard can, of course, make a citizen's arrest, turning his captive over to the police as soon as possible. (*See* Chapter 2, "You and the police.")

Sometimes, people believe they are being "hassled" when, in fact, they are breaking the law themselves.

42 Traveling

The average Canadian travels an estimated 16,000 kilometres (10,100 miles) a year, commuting to work and in pursuit of recreation and vacations. This is the equivalent of four transatlantic trips. Perhaps because of the great distances over which we are scattered, we spend more time and money per capita in traveling than any other people. And while bus and train are certain to maintain, or even increase, their importance in short-haul and medium-haul passenger traffic, Canadians continue to take to the air in large numbers. In 1979, approximately 45 million passengers disembarked at Canada's 50 airports from business and vacation flights.

It remains something of a puzzle why so many Canadians, in pioneer fashion, try to absorb and understand the bewildering choices and prices of the travel scene and make their own arrangements for their transportation by common carrier. For more than 50 years, the travel-agency business has been begging for custom, and its expert services are free to the traveler. An experienced travel agent knows his business as well as a lawyer knows the law.

Whether you want to go by bus, train, plane, or ship, he will not only handle all the details, but provide you with a buffer and a complaints channel against the problems that so often arise in unfamiliar activities and places. Do you need a visa for Venezuela? Can you take a stopover in Tahiti or Timbuktu? What's the weather like in Wellington? Can you go topless in Bali? Must you wear a tie to dinner? Can you enjoy a cigarette on your four-hour flight or must you sit there biting your nails? Can you pack a bottle of rye for your train trip? Will they take your harp on the bus? Ask your travel agent. The rights and obligations of the traveler and the common carrier are the subject of an ever-changing body of law and regulation.

There's hardly any such thing anymore as a fixed fare to anywhere by any kind of carrier. Apart from the advance-payment discount air charters, there are excursions and round trips, youth and senior citizen, nighthawk and off-season, standby and all-inclusive fares. It can pay you to know about them.

FLIGHT DELAYS

Because of flight delays, you waste two days of your European vacation in an airport waiting room.

Big airports are fascinating places to visit, but boring and uncomfortable when you're just killing time—especially holiday time. No matter what it says on your ticket or on the airline's printed schedule, there's no guarantee you'll take off or arrive at the advertised times. All of the 100 or so airlines that are members of IATA (International Air Transport Association, 1000 Sherbrooke St. West, Montreal, H3A 2R4) strive to operate on schedule in all weather, but they are not bound to do so by law.

There are just too many variables that can cause delay or cancellation of a flight. Safety of the passenger is the first consideration—and that is primarily in the hands of government agencies. An airport can be shut down because of weather and all planes diverted to other airports. If the plane you're waiting for to continue on your vacation is one of them, you're just out of luck.

"Stacking" of incoming planes over a busy airport due to local conditions can cause long delays for those waiting to make connections. When a defect—or even a suspected defect—develops in an aircraft (or in a whole family of them), the plane will be grounded immediately for checkup.

"Mechanical difficulties" is frequently given as the reason for flight delays, and airlines are seldom eager to be more specific. Air Canada once informed one argumentative passenger: "It is not our policy to start detailing what the term means. It would only scare people if we did. A mechanical difficulty may mean nothing more than a wobbly pilot's chair."

While you have the right to insist that the company that contracted to carry you make every reasonable effort to fulfill all the terms of the contract, it cannot be held liable in any way for delays arising from circumstances outside its control.

It's very difficult to sue an airline successfully for damages resulting from delays because of equipment failures or weather conditions. All common carriers have an overriding responsibility for public safety and the regulatory agencies will applaud rather than criticize any actions that lessen the chance of accident. You'd probably have to prove that "mechanical difficulty" was just a cover-up for negligence or service failure—and you'd need your own team of independent engineers to prove that.

Some more punctual. The best way to avoid hanging around airports is to make your bookings on a direct flight. Whenever a plane stops off at intermediate points, the chances are greater that something will go wrong. If a stopover is inevitable on your trip, try to choose an itinerary that avoids airports known for delays because of weather conditions or poor administration. And some airlines are simply more punctual than others. Independent travel guides contain this sort of information. Airports are less busy early in the morning or in the evening. There's less pressure on the ticket clerks, the air-traffic controllers and the baggage people. The chances of delay are minimized if you fly during these hours.

When a delay is announced, you have the choice of making alternative arrangements personally or waiting as patiently as you can. If the delay occurs around meal time, request a meal or snack voucher. If you are stranded for more than four hours, you are entitled to a meal if one would have been served to you on the scheduled flight. You can also claim a free long-distance phone call to explain your delay to anyone waiting for you at your destination. On "deep discount" tickets, however, you may get none of these allowances or privileges.

If the delay will result in your missing an important connection, speak to the passenger agent immediately—and be flexible. There are often several ways of reaching your destination, especially in Europe where distances between cities are relatively short. European trains are numerous, fast and reliable; it could be that you can make your onward connection by rail, getting a refund for your unused plane ticket. If the delay results in an overnight stay (10 p.m. to 6 a.m.) the airline will usually pay a set maximum for meal and hotel charges. If the delay occurs in your own city, you are expected to return home for the evening.

OVERBOOKING

The plane is overbooked and the airline refuses to honor your confirmed reservation.

In trade jargon, you are getting bumped. By the time you checked in, the airline desk had already issued enough boarding passes to fill the plane.

But how can this happen, you ask. You booked weeks ago for the flight, you picked up your ticket, your reservation was confirmed, and you're at the airport desk well within the stipulated reporting time. Well, it happens simply because all airlines follow the practice of selling more confirmed reservations for each flight than the aircraft can accommodate. They do this in self-defense against the "no show."

And they can produce all the statistical evidence necessary to prove that an average of about 20 percent of the people holding reservations will not show up before boarding time. Businessmen not sure of their personal schedules get their secretaries to book them on several flights, then take the one most convenient for them. They know that they can only be charged for the flight they actually take.

Other passengers misjudge the time needed to get to the airport through heavy traffic. Still others get sick and don't bother to cancel.

If only the exact number of seats were sold in advance, the airlines estimate, many planes would be flying at only 80 percent capacity. This would result in unprofitable operation and ticket prices would have to be hiked for everybody. The airline has no recourse against the "no show" passenger.

Right to compensation. In essence, your confirmed reservation merely gives you the right to a seat in that particular plane—provided the plane and the seat are available.

There is no law in Canada that will enforce your right to fly in that particular aircraft at that time. However, all Canadian airlines do accept a liability to the holder of the confirmed reservation, and the bumped passenger's right to compensation has been upheld in court.

In 1976, CP Air was ordered to pay $500 damages to a family that had been bumped from a Hawaii-bound Christmas flight because the plane had been oversold. Mrs. Dutchie Mathison of Maple Ridge, B.C., and her family of four were rebooked on a flight three days later. Upon their return from Hawaii,

Reservations about reservations

A confirmed reservation for a scheduled flight gives you a right of priority over other passengers, but it doesn't give you an ironclad guarantee that you'll get a seat on the plane you want. It's not all that different from a table reservation in a restaurant.

You'll be seated before "wait-listed" passengers or "standbys," those without any reservation, but you can still be bumped for any one of several reasons. To increase your chances of a trouble-free trip, follow this advice from Gerald Heifetz of Toronto, a legal consultant experienced in the travel business:

Make sure that you have a confirmed reservation. Request the file number that identifies your reservation.

If reconfirmation is required, be sure to do it. It's usually not required for flights within Canada and the United States, but is a must on flights between Canada and other countries, including Mexico.

Arrive at the airport early—at least 30 minutes before domestic departures, one or two hours before an international flight. Allow time for checking in and reaching the gate. The heaviest traffic times at airports are usually between 7 a.m. and 9 a.m., and 4:30 p.m. to 7 p.m. on weekdays. The morning hours are always busy on Monday and Saturday.

Canadian airlines have instituted a system of compensation payments to bumped passengers. The payment is generally equal to a percentage of the first flight coupon, subject to ceiling amounts. But compensation may not be available for all international flights on Canadian carriers.

If you are denied the right to board the plane, register your complaint immediately at the checking desk. Don't make your own alternate arrangements but request airline personnel to find you another flight. Compensation will *not* be forthcoming:

■ If you are a "standby";
■ If a flight is delayed or canceled altogether;
■ If the lack of space is due to government requisition of part or all of the aircraft;
■ If a smaller aircraft is substituted because of operational or safety conditions;
■ If you are given a seat on the scheduled flight but in a different class from the one shown on your ticket;
■ If, on domestic flights, the airline arranges transportation that is scheduled to arrive at your destination within two hours of the originally planned arrival time. (And should the flight on which you are rerouted encounter delay, the originating carrier is not liable.)

Mrs. Mathison successfully sued the airline in Small Claims Court for the inconvenience caused.

If you are bumped when flying in the United States, the airline must pay you the face value of your first flight coupon—minimum $37.50, maximum $200. If the airline can't get you to your destination within four hours of the original arrival time, the compensation is doubled. You *retain* your ticket; the payment is to compensate you for inconvenience and extra expenses incurred.

Call for volunteers. When a flight is oversold in Canada, the major airlines usually ask for volunteers to take a later flight, offering a cash payment of from $50 to $100. If there are not enough volunteers and you're left behind, they'll pay an amount equivalent to 100 percent of the cost of your flight to your next stopover point and put you on the next available aircraft. Some carriers do not advise passengers in advance that they don't conform to either the U.S. or Canadian rules. So before you book a flight, ask if the airline complies with the over-booking regulations. On flights between foreign points, don't expect protection if the plane is overbooked. British airlines will, however, pay compensation at half the amount of the ticket—minimum $20, maximum $200—plus reasonable expenses.

Although it's usually first come, first served with boarding passes, "gamesmanship" can play a part in deciding who gets bumped. If you get turned down when time is of the essence, insist firmly on your contractual right to travel; your ticket is the contract. Then the airline clerk will likely try to bump someone else. In this, as in many other human situations, it's the squeaky wheel that gets the grease.

STRIKEBOUND

A strike delays your return from a one-week package holiday in the Caribbean.

When unions strike to force employers to meet various demands, the immediate sufferer is usually the consumer. When you are on holi-day far from home, there may be little you can do—except fume. The airline cannot be held liable for any loss or inconvenience you suffer because its workers leave the job, either on a wildcat walkout or on a strike sanctioned by law. Your baggage may even be trapped behind an aggressive picket line.

If it is a legal strike, there would have been advance notice of the action and your carrier or travel agent would make whatever alternative arrangements were possible to get you home. This might involve the individual passenger in extra expense. If your airline is struck, or a strike is looming, don't wait for official action. Investigate quickly whatever space may be available from other carriers. Most North American companies will accept tickets issued by other airlines. A problem will arise if you are on a special or discounted fare, however. You may be required to pay a supplement.

To keep your goodwill, some airlines will reimburse stranded passengers in situations like this. The degree of compensation voluntarily offered to cover out-of-pocket expenses will depend on various factors: mainly the type of expense incurred (no champagne) and the time involved. When Air Canada was on strike in 1978 on its Florida run at peak season, it reimbursed passengers for all of their reasonable expenses within the first 24 hours of delay. Later, management quietly decided that additional sums would be paid to persistent claimants.

If the airline refuses to compensate you, you'll have to see your lawyer. If the delay was due to any negligence by the airline, you have a legal remedy. It's also possible to receive general damages for embarrassment, inconvenience and aggravation, or even loss of business if your customers, clients or patients were affected by your delay.

Your plane ticket may include a disclaimer of liability due to labor problems. The airline can fairly argue that a wildcat strike was an act beyond its control, and beyond the contemplation of the airline or the passenger. Although "blanket exclusion clauses" are falling out of favor, these exemption clauses have been upheld by the courts.

TRAVEL AGENCIES

At the airport you find that your travel agent had booked you on a flight canceled weeks ago.

There are 3,500 travel agencies in Canada and some 15,000 scheduled flights a week. Timetables, routes and fares change constantly. No one person can keep track of them all and human error is bound to occur. If the airline can't accommodate you on another suitable flight, telephone the agency and demand that the situation be corrected with as little inconvenience to you as possible.

If your trip is postponed or canceled because of an incorrect booking by your travel agent, you have legal recourse. You can sue him for negligence and almost certainly be awarded all out-of-pocket expenses and probably general damages for inconvenience and loss of enjoyment. The usual criterion is that you must have incurred financial loss, whether specific or general.

In these circumstances, you would probably also have grounds for suing the airline for negligence and breach of contract. The contract action would be open because the airline has obviously accepted a reservation for a nonexistent flight. Claiming clerical error will not save its skin. Legal precedents exist for the granting of compensation to business and professional men for loss of profits due to negligence by agents or airlines in booking or bumping.

Agent's role. The majority of Canadian travel agents are expert and honest, but in some provinces there's no bar to anyone off the street setting himself up in the business. Those who have passed a qualifying exam set by the Canadian Institute of Travel Counselors are designated as Certified Travel Counselors (CTC). Provincial regulations provide for varying levels of supervision. Be skeptical of any agent who offers travel deals at prices noticeably below the going rates.

The agent gets his income from commissions paid by the travel supplier. The commission is not an added cost to the traveler. By providing you with expert independent advice and handling all the technical details, the good agent can save you time and possibly money as well. For example, if there's a cheaper weekend fare to your destination that you don't know about, you could save enough extra dollars to add an interesting side trip.

You're on safe ground if your agent is a member of the Alliance of Canadian Travel Associations. The 1,500 members of ACTA include both the largest chain operations and many of the single-location agencies. As the acknowledged voice of the Canadian travel and tourist industry, it is vitally interested in protecting the public from unethical practices.

In Quebec, Ontario and British Columbia, check that your chosen agent is registered under the provincial travel laws. All ACTA members are so registered. In the other provinces, travel agents may show credentials from the International Air Transport Association (IATA), the Air Transport Association of America (ATAA), or the Air Transport Association of Canada (ATAC). These bodies have financial and professional standards for the appointment of agents.

Travel agents not appointed by any of these associations deal mostly in package tours, hotel and car-hire reservations, or arrange their own packages. They are not supervised under provincial regulation except in Quebec, Ontario and British Columbia. If your travel agent goes bankrupt or simply disappears, you could lose any funds you have paid. Worse, you can be stranded far from home with invalidated tickets and hotel reservations. Some jurisdictions have established a fund that will reimburse clients unable to recover legitimate financial losses from travel agencies. The wise consumer looks—and checks—before he leaps.

LOST BAGGAGE

The airline loses your bag, which contains important documents, expensive clothing and jewelry.

Did the airline lose it, or was it stolen at the baggage carousel? This type of jet-age theft is more prevalent than many travelers realize.

507

Although every passenger who checks his baggage gets a numbered claim stub—which is usually stapled to the ticket folder and should be matched with the stub attached to the baggage—very few airlines or airport managements go to the trouble of checking the stubs before the passenger in possession leaves the building.

The airlines have taught the humble, obedient passengers—old and young alike—to scramble around the carousel and collect their own bags. A sharp-eyed thief can quite easily lift a promising bag and walk briskly out in the crowd. It can happen even on international flights when the thief is willing to risk a customs delay or search.

The thief may have noted that particular bag being checked at departure by a prosperous-looking fellow passenger. He apologizes profusely if he should be detected by the owner, claiming that "all the luggage looks alike these days." Which is true enough. This is good reason for you to buy distinctive bags, or to mark them quite blatantly with color stripes or other devices. Be sure you attach strong tags bearing your name and address. And watch that baggage carousel like a worried parent at a merry-go-round.

For YUL or YMX? Many travelers are strangely trusting about their valuable baggage. They seem to feel that once they plunk it on the scales at the check-in desk, all will be well. But baggage loss is the number one headache of the airlines, the greatest cause of consumer complaint by far.

Take these precautions: when you check your bag, the clerk will affix part of the claim stub to the bag and give you the other half. If

Lost, strayed or stolen

Airlines handle hundreds of millions of pieces of baggage each year, and—aggravating as it is when you're the victim—it's inevitable that some will go astray, at least temporarily. Long-suffering travelers often suspect a conspiracy among baggage-handlers, as acidly suggested here by Ottawa cartoonist Jim Unger, creator of the internationally syndicated "Herman."

"We've lost your stuff, but you get first choice of any bag off Flight 601 from Athens."

the ticket is torn in your presence, you can be sure the numbers will match. But the busy clerk may have torn several in advance of the check-in rush, and a mix-up is possible right there.

Every major destination has a shorthand letter designation, which is printed on both parts of the stub. Frequent travelers get to know the code and watch to see that the correct letters are used. For example, just about all Canadian destinations begin with "Y." Thus, Toronto is YYZ, and Montreal (Dorval) is YUL. Be careful, though—Mirabel Airport, also a Montreal stop, is YMX.

The carrier must produce your checked baggage at your destination or pay you compensation. If the baggage is stolen, it's up to the airline to catch the thieves. That baggage claim stub is part of your contract. The first thing to do is report the loss immediately. Most lost baggage does turn up within 24 hours and the airline will deliver it to you when it is found, no matter how far you've traveled since.

Before you leave the airport, ask the airline to provide you at least with toilet articles. Some airlines perform this service with ready-made packs. If your luggage has not arrived within 24 hours, ask the carrier for money to purchase other necessities—perhaps a new shirt and underwear. The airlines will normally come up with an allowance to replace necessities in your bag, depending on how far you are from home and how long it takes to find your luggage.

If your bags can't be located, lodge a claim. Here's the rub: do you carry an inventory of the contents in your pocket? Expect your credibility to be questioned. The airline's liability is limited to $500 per passenger on domestic flights and $20 per kilogram on international flights. These are maximums; and they'll insist that you prove your loss, item by item above a voluntary minimum for simple necessities. It's not easy to put cash value on all items that you need or cherish. Cheap baggage insurance is available on simple forms at most large airports.

The carrier can take a long time responding. Some airlines, shipping companies, rail-ways and other carriers are easier to deal with than others. Keep after them. If you show little interest in pursuing your claim, then the carrier may conclude that your claim is fraudulent or unimportant.

Don't forget that you can also be compensated for damaged luggage. Fill out an official damage report at the airport where you discover the damage.

Under lock and key. You have the right to demand that your bags be treated with care but you are expected to realize that they won't necessarily be handled with kid gloves. In fact, they'll be piled up and thrown about. Buy luggage for strength rather than beauty. Always lock your bags, and don't overpack them. Overstuffed bags frequently pop open during handling. Write your name, address and phone number on the outside and inside of your bags. Remove all outdated name labels and old destination tags.

Use your carry-on bag for such essentials as medicines, glasses, toilet articles and valuable documents. Many experienced travelers, tired of baggage problems, have thinned down their flying luggage to a single "one suiter" that they can slip under the seat. A garment bag can almost always be hung up on the plane's cloak racks.

CANCELING A CHARTER

You paid for your charter flight many weeks ago. Now another company offers the same deal for much less.

You won't be able to switch your booking without a cancellation fee that would wipe out the advantage of the new deal. Further, the stipulations for advance booking and payment probably rule out the switch anyway.

Since 1978, when the U.S. Civil Aeronautics Board decided to open the air lanes under its jurisdiction to freer competition, there's been a genteel price war raging over fares. The Canadian Transport Commission, though more conservative in its policies, also relaxed its rules; the results were nationally advertised "seat sales," the introduction of CP Air's no-frills skybus, and "nighthawk"—or "red-eye"—specials.

The public is now thoroughly confused about plane fares. In the summer of 1979, for example, one travel expert estimated that there were 140 different fares for transatlantic flights! The consumer looking for the best deal faces a lot of homework. A basic step is to send away for a copy of *Scheduled Air Travel And The Canadian Consumer*, available from the Canadian Transport Commission, Information Services, Ottawa, Ontario, K1A 0N9. It gives detailed information about travel documents, customs, delays and cancellations, baggage carrier liability and complaint procedures.

Jet-age wheeler-dealers. The charter flight is, at its simplest, merely a contract between the tour operator and a passenger group by which the operator agrees to hire a plane to fly you both ways between given points for a stated fare on stipulated dates. Some charters include ground accommodation, all meals, side trips and gratuities. The prices depend largely on the deals the package company is able to make with the carriers, hotels and others involved. They are, in turn, influenced by the popularity of that route, the normal demand on hotel space, the season of the year, and so on.

There are four general types of charters available in Canada for international and domestic travel:

1. The *advance booking charter* has a minimum length of stay, advance booking and pre-payment date requirements. Cash penalties for cancellation are usually strict, but modestly priced insurance—$6 for domestic flights and up to $12 for internationals—can be bought to protect you in case of illness, say, or death in the family.

2. The *inclusive tour charter* is a package that offers ground facilities as well as air transportation. The price paid must include air and surface transportation costs, accommodation and, where applicable, tour features. "Accommodation" includes not only hotels but also any sleeping facility provided on a commercial basis to the public. The tour price could also include meals, car rentals and

sightseeing. Other options are usually available at extra cost. These charters always have a minimum tour price, fixed length of stay and fixed destinations.

3. The *common purpose charter* provides that passengers must travel as a group with the cost of the total round trip shared equally on a *pro rata* basis. Full payment of the round-trip fare is required before the charter begins and no alternate transportation or refund is permitted should you miss the return flight. This kind of charter is usually arranged for special events or educational programs, not for tourist travel.

4. The *entity charter* is used by specific organizations; for example, by sports clubs. The organization pays the full cost of the trip for members. A company may arrange an entity charter for a group of customers, or employees. These used to be known formally as "affinity" groups.

Charter conditions. Before you buy a charter, check all the conditions, however fine the print. Tickets must be purchased in advance, anywhere from 30 to 45 days. There are minimum and maximum staying periods, from 7 to 45 days. It's the rare charter that permits you to change your mind at the last minute, or even earlier, and receive a full refund. You can lose up to 100 percent of the value of your ticket. Charter tickets are seldom transferable.

Charter travel is the most inexpensive way to travel by air. The major problems are advance booking, cancellations, and takeoff delays. When everything goes smoothly—and it usually does—it's a great bargain. If things go wrong, remember that you were bargain-hunting.

CRUISES

To celebrate your retirement, you are taking an all-inclusive cruise. The ship is dirty, cramped and noisy.

Assuming that you booked and paid for the cruise in Canada, the agent for the tour operator or steamship company will be held responsible under the law for the full execution of your contract. In other words, you must get what you were clearly promised and what you paid for. Of course, it's easy to make such comforting generalizations, but extremely difficult to prove misrepresentation, negligence or omission in the individual case.

Every other person has a different concept of reasonable comfort and enjoyment. The cruise packagers naturally want to make money and they won't stand a chance in the long run unless the majority of their patrons have a good time, and tell their friends about it. A busy, noisy ship is perhaps exactly what the majority seeks.

Did you read the cruise brochure and the ticket conditions carefully before you signed up? Did you check the size of the ship, its passenger load, the location and dimensions of your cabin, meal sittings, entertainment, and dress regulations? What languages are spoken on board? What type of cuisine is featured?

ACTA will act

The voice and conscience of the Canadian travel industry is the Alliance of Canadian Travel Associations (ACTA), federally incorporated, and very conscious of good customer relations. ACTA will go to bat for you if your travel or vacation booked through any of its 1,500 retail member agencies fails to deliver the promised quality or enjoyment. It also represents about 100 of Canada's largest travel wholesalers, the "packagers" who put together those attractive deals for "14 worry-free days in the sun." A third category accommodates "travel-service suppliers." That label takes in airlines, hotels, tourist boards and other businesses and agencies who cater to travelers.

ACTA realizes there's no pot of gold at the end of the rainbow unless it safeguards the public from the shady operator. It has been mainly responsible for the establishment of funds that reimburse any traveler stranded or otherwise victimized by the bankruptcy of a registered travel agent.

If you have any travel query or complaint, write to ACTA at Suite 1207, 130 Albert Street, Ottawa, Ont., K1P 5G4, or any of the following regional affiliates:

Atlantic Travel Industry Conference
c/o Blenus Travel Service
Micmac Mall
Halifax, N.S. B3A 4K6
(902) 469-7396

Quebec Association of Travel Agents
410 Henri-Bourassa Boulevard East
Montreal, Que. H3L 1C4
(514) 381-8541

Ontario Travel Industry Conference
Suite 1208
67 Yonge Street
Toronto, Ont. M5E 1J8
(416) 366-1909

Manitoba Travel Industry Association
St. Boniface Postal Station - Box 54
Winnipeg, Man. R2H 3B4
(204) 786-5411

Saskatchewan Association of Travel Agents
c/o 230 - 22nd Street East
Saskatoon, Sask. S7K 0E9
(306) 652-0161

Association of Travel Agents of Alberta
Hotel MacDonald
Edmonton, Alta. T5J 0N6
(403) 426-4115

Association of Travel Agents of
   British Columbia
409 Granville Street
Suite 251
Vancouver, B.C. V6C 1T2
(604) 688-0516

Study before you sail. Novice sailors should immerse themselves in relevant guide and travel books before deciding on a cruise. Your public library will suggest titles. Learn about currencies and rates of exchange, religious observances, eating and drinking customs, climatic conditions, medical facilities on board or ashore at your points of call.

In any of our larger cities you'll find a travel agency that specializes in cruises. Tell the consultant exactly what you are looking for and what you want to pay. He's not likely to put a waltz couple on a disco ship.

A dirty ship is a serious matter. The majority of cruising Canadians board their ships in American ports. (At this writing, there's not a single cruise ship of Canadian registry.) The U.S. Public Health Service reported in 1979 that about 20 percent of cruise ships sailing regularly from ports under its jurisdiction failed to meet basic standards of sanitation and cleanliness. However, while its inspectors can board and inspect any ship, they have regulatory power over only those vessels of U.S. registration. Most cruise ships are registered in countries outside North America and Europe.

When shopping for a cruise, ask your travel agent to find out whether the ship of your choice meets the standards of the World Health Organization as stated in its *Guide to Ship Sanitation*. Or tell him that the U.S. Public Health Service, Room 107, 1015 North America Way, Miami, Florida, 33132, will supply a copy of its current inspection report of any ship plying American waters.

Tips and slips. Concealed or unmentioned charges for gratuities, cabin service, deck chairs, saunas, games facilities, or shore trips sour many a cruise patron who took too literally the "all-in" price tag. Ask the travel agent to spell out exactly what's included in the "inclusive" tariff. It's quite possible for some customers to enjoy a cruise without requiring any of the above-mentioned services or facilities. But even the most spartan usually succumb as they begin to merge with social groups aboard.

There's still a lingering mystique about sailing the seven seas. The new voyager often worries unnecessarily about making social gaffes in the unfamiliar shipboard milieu. Unless you are traveling in one of the few first-class ships still afloat, the best course is to relax and be yourself. A jacket and tie for men in the evening is usually indicated, but even that level of formality has been discarded on the fun ships. Don't tip until the last day out. Keeps the stewards on their toes.

CROSS-COUNTRY BY TRAIN

Your first-class cross-country train trip is marred by long delays and noisy parties.

Crossing Canada by train was not so very long ago considered by travel connoisseurs to be one of the world's most spectacular trips. Since the last spike in the Canadian Pacific Railway was driven at Craigellachie, B.C., in 1885, the rails that bound the country together have provided a unique experience across 65 degrees of longitude, through forest, prairie and majestic mountain. Now operated by Via Rail Canada Inc., the Crown corporation that has handled all passenger traffic since 1977, the trains still snake across the land but punctuality, equipment and service en route all give rise to frequent complaint.

You can't say you weren't warned. The first item of information brought to the attention of passengers in Via Rail's *System Timetable* warns that changes may be made to the timetable without advance notice; the third item states that while delays sometimes occur, the management will accept no responsibility for them, nor for any inconvenience they may cause.

If noisy beer parties are spoiling your trip, complain to the conductor. The regulations state that no liquor can be consumed in the coaches. Most trains include either a licensed car or bar lounge where beverages are available during the licensing hours of the province in which you happen to be traveling. But all alcoholic drinks must be consumed on the "premises" where they are sold. In other words, a passenger can't go to the bar and buy beer to take back to his seat. Nor can he consume any private liquor he has brought on board. Via Rail states that its employees are required to enforce these regulations. The continual blare of rock music from transistor radios can frustrate any effort to read or converse quietly. The passenger who tries to insist on "quiet enjoyment" may be either ignored or scorned.

If appeals to the train officials get you nowhere, write your complaint in detail to the Vice-President, Operations, Via Rail Canada Inc., P.O. Box 8116, Montreal, Que.,

An ounce of prevention

APPLICATION

This Will Be Your Identification Number. Please Quote This Number On All Correspondence...

H 00000000

Please Print Clearly And Return Entire Application

I have read and understand the terms and conditions relating to the Ontario Blue Cross "Health Plan While Outside Canada", and want to apply for this coverage as follows:

OR
- Single coverage for _____ days at $0.50 per day (minimum 7 days/$3.50)
- Family coverage for _70_ days at $1.00 per day (minimum 7 days/$7.00)

A maximum of 240 days is permitted. "Family" means the subscribers, spouse, and unmarried, unemployed children under age 21 years of age.

My cheque or money order payable to "Ontario Blue Cross" is attached in amount of $ _10.00_. I understand that coverage will not be effective unless payment is received with my application.

My date of departure is ____19____ ____06____ ____80____
                         DAY   MONTH   YEAR

Refunds – must be requested in writing before coverage expires; and will not be made if a claim is pending. Refunds of less than 7 days will not be considered.

I understand that if this application is received and accepted by Ontario Blue Cross prior to departure date, benefits commence at the time of crossing the border into another country (or if travelling by air, at the time the airplane takes off). Otherwise, benefits commence as per Terms of Agreement (reverse side). Further, I understand that no person will be covered under this Agreement who is in hospital on the day the Agreement becomes effective.

I certify that no one covered under the Agreement applied for is travelling for the purpose of obtaining hospital or medical treatment. Also, that as of the date of signing this application I am not aware that I or an

TELEPHONE NUMBER ___(514)___ ___123-4567___
                  AREA CODE   NUMBER

Medical or hospital expenses while you're out of the country can be ruinous. You can guard against the cost of an unexpected illness by taking out the kind of low-cost protection offered by Blue Cross in all provinces, *before* you leave the country.

Terms of the Agreement

a) This health agreement shall be available only to Canadian residents covered by a provincial government health plan and travelling outside the boundaries of Canada. This health agreement shall become effective at the time of crossing the border into another country provided application and payment are received prior to departure date. Otherwise benefits commence at 12:01 A.M. on the day following receipt of application and payment in this office, and shall terminate at the border on the return home or 12 midnight on the expiry date of the agreement, whichever comes first. If travelling by air, the agreement shall become effective at the time the aeroplane takes off in Canada (if application is received prior to departure date) and shall terminate when the aeroplane lands in Canada on the return home, or at 12:00 midnight on the expiry date of the agreement, whichever comes first.

b) The benefits described in this Agreement are available to the applicant, or if enrolled under a family Agreement to the applicant, spouse, and the unmarried, unemployed children under age 21.

c) All benefits listed herein shall be payable only on the submission of certification by the attending physician that services included in the benefits have been required.

d) It is understood and agreed between the participants in this agreement that no benefits for hospital or medical care shall be paid until after accounts have been appraised by the provincial government health plan and benefits if any have been paid by that plan.

e) Payment will be made by Ontario Blue Cross by cheque, directly to the subscriber, upon receipt and appraisal of the necessary accounts and information concerning the accounts as detailed. **Payment will be made in Canadian currency, based on the rate of exchange in effect at the conclusion of the service rendered, as determined by any Canadian Chartered Bank.**

f) The Agreement may be renewed (requiring additional payment) for one additional period only, provided that benefits under the subscriber's provincial health plan remain in effect, and request for renewal is received with payment by Ontario Blue Cross prior to expiry to the first period of coverage.

H3C 3N3. There are also Via Rail regional offices in Moncton, Toronto, and Winnipeg.

In the private car. Depending on how much you wish to spend above the basic fare, passenger trains on major routes offer varying levels of private accommodation.

This begins with what Via Rail calls the "Dayniter." It is a deluxe coach, with 36 seats as compared with the 78 seats in the regular coach. The seats recline into a reasonably comfortable sleeping or napping position and both bar and meal service is provided at the seat. It's similar to the familiar "club car" of old.

Upper and lower berths are available in the sleeping cars. A couple can combine them into what's known as a "section." Privacy is afforded only by heavy curtains.

The roomette is a separate unit equipped with private toilet and hand basin.

The bedroom, three times larger than the roomette, provides upper and lower berths, the latter convertible to a sofa for day use.

Top of the line is the drawing room, with three berths and private washroom.

Room service is provided to all private compartments, by bell-call. There's a premium on the cost of all meals brought to your private quarters.

Seeing the country. Via Rail still runs cross-country trains, even if passengers to and from the Atlantic provinces must change at Montreal. Every day *The Canadian* leaves Montreal in the forenoon, scheduled to arrive in Vancouver some four days and four hours later. *The Super Continental* leaves Toronto each afternoon. The routes diverge at Winnipeg, with *The Super Continental* swinging on a northerly arc through Edmonton and Jasper while *The Canadian* strikes west via Calgary and Banff. Sleeping-car passengers on *The Super Continental* enjoy through service, but all others taking the northerly route must change trains at Winnipeg. Matching trains leave Vancouver daily for the East.

When you're in a rush to catch a train, remember that you can buy a ticket—to the nearest major city—from the conductor on board. Cash only. If you think you have been charged too much, pay up anyway, get a receipt and forward it later with a letter of explanation to the nearest Via Rail office. You won't win any arguments with the conductor. He has the right to order you to leave the train at the first scheduled stop.

NONSMOKING TRAVEL

Heavy smokers are spoiling your long-distance bus trip. The driver won't do anything about it.

Almost all public transportation now provides segregated seating for smokers and nonsmokers. On long-distance buses, the first five rows of seats are usually marked off clearly as a nonsmoking section.

When a ticket is bought, sealing a contract between the carrier and the passenger, the passenger is accepting the conditions imposed by the operating company whether they are firmly based on the law or not. Smoking regulations are brought to the passengers' attention either by a statement on the ticket itself, or by notices in the bus terminal or in the vehicle. Anyone breaking the regulations by lighting up in a nonsmoking section or area should immediately cease if you request him to do so.

If you meet defiance, there's no point in ruining your trip with an argument or altercation. Notify the driver and insist that he, as agent for the carrier, rectify the situation. The driver has the power to order the offender to disembark at the next stop. He can also call on police assistance if he's not obeyed.

All long-distance buses are air-conditioned but when there's a full load, passengers are still packed into a relatively confined space.

Some tobacco haters have become deadly serious about their rights to smoke-free air. In December 1979, the captain of an American Boeing 727 carrying 177 passengers from Washington to New York made an unscheduled landing when he failed to quell a violent argument aboard between nonsmokers and smokers. The U.S. Civil Aeronautics Board had ruled earlier in the year that a nonsmoker had an absolute right not to sit next to a smoker. A carrier faces a $1,000 fine for noncompliance.

# 43 Accommodations

Whether you're taking afternoon tea in Victoria's elegant Empress Hotel, grilled char in the Explorer at Yellowknife or cocktails *cinq à sept* in the Chateau Frontenac in Quebec, you are under an umbrella of laws that protect a guest's rights. This legislation includes provincial innkeepers acts, the laws of contract and negligence, and the Human Rights Code of the host province.

Since Jacques Boisdon opened Canada's first tavern, in Quebec in 1648, a spreading web of proclamation, legislation, regulation and accepted custom has attempted to ensure the paying guest a cool drink, a hot meal, a clean bed and safety for his baggage. It guarantees the innkeeper's right to prompt settlement of the bill and protection of his private property.

Beyond these basics, the rights and obligations of both guest and hotelkeeper have mushroomed in bewildering volume and variety. Just about every problem and dispute that can crop up in the home happens in Canada's 10,000 hotels and motels, often several times a day. The modern hotelier can find himself refereeing a marital spat or smoothing out an international incident. At one Grey Cup whoop-up in Toronto, the manager of the huge Royal York Hotel had to cope with mounted cowboys prancing through the lobby.

In pioneer days, mine host had simpler problems. In the Macleod Hotel, pride of Fort Macleod, the first town in southern Alberta, the house rules stated:

■ Boots and spurs to be removed at night.
■ Every known fluid (water excepted) for sale at the bar.
■ Assaults on the cook strictly prohibited.
■ To call the waiter or bellboy, shoot hole through the door (three shots for a deck of cards).
■ Payment must be in cash or gold or blue chips.

Many hotels still guard jealously their right to run things as they see fit. The deluxe Keltic Lodge at Ingonish on Cape Breton Island decrees, for example, that ladies will wear skirts or dresses at dinner—no pantsuits, thank you. And gentlemen must dress like gentlemen, naturally.

In a free-choice society, the prospective hotel guest can choose to stay in a Mom-and-Pop motel or the poshest place in town. Common sense dictates that the more you pay, the more you should get, but the ancient innkeeper laws, constantly under revision, apply to all equally.

In choosing your hostelry, you can enlist the help of a travel agent or your provincial Department of Tourism. The services of both are free to the user and they provide a channel of complaint if you're not satisfied with the deal. There are literally hundreds of commercial guide books that list or rate hotels, motels, tourist resorts and camping grounds. Many of them are aimed at suiting selective tastes and needs.

The Canadian Automobile Association (CAA) and its American counterpart, the AAA, provide their members, through their affiliate clubs and leagues, with tour books for every province and state. Included with these are graded lists of every kind of available accommodation, all systematically and independently investigated.

Where the CAA or AAA symbol is displayed, you are guaranteed that rigid specifications are either met or exceeded. Room rates as published in the annual tour books are guaranteed to members. If you are charged more, the CAA will go to bat to get you a refund. And the establishment concerned runs the risk of being dropped from the next edition.

Only about one hostelry in seven makes the grade in the first place.

RESERVATIONS

You have a reservation, confirmed weeks in advance, but the hotel is full when you arrive to check in.

The guest with a written confirmation—*including a commitment to provide alternate accommodation*—who arrives at the selected hotel before the stipulated deadline, usually 6 p.m., has the right to demand accommodation, but not necessarily at *that* hotel. If reasonable effort to house you adequately is not made, you will almost certainly succeed in a court action for compensation against either the hotel or the travel agent or other company that confirmed the booking.

The Bucholtz precedent of 1973 is often quoted. Mr. and Mrs. Bucholtz of New York bought a three-day package tour to Las Vegas from a travel agent. Everything went wrong: their plane was delayed, their baggage mislaid and the hotel wouldn't honor their reservation. Although their tour wholesaler held the primary liability, they sued their travel agent and were awarded one-third of their ticket price: $106. A judge ruled—for the first time anywhere—that travel agents had a duty to verify or confirm reservations.

Firmly stating your intention to sue may galvanize the hotel management into extra effort to find you a room, but it's not much consolation if you're still left standing in the lobby, tired and hungry, with no place to lay your head that night. Overbooking at hotels at popular destinations is an even greater problem than it is with airlines on busy routes. That same culprit, the "no show," gets most of the blame from the hoteliers. Some chains report a steady 10 to 15 percent of customers with reservations who fail to reach the hotel desk by 6 p.m., or neglect to cancel or call ahead to advise of late arrival. The percentage of package-tour "no shows" is even higher. A tour group may be held up in a distant airport by "mechanical difficulties," bad weather, or any of dozens of other causes outside the control of either tour operator, travel agent or hotel manager.

Another complication can arise when a hotel is stuck with an unusual number of overstaying guests whom it is loath to turn out.

Where the buck stops. One thing is certain: even a confirmed prepaid hotel or motel reservation is no absolute guarantee of a room. So the experienced traveler takes certain simple precautions.

If possible, obtain written confirmation of your reservation. Hotels differ in the methods they use to guarantee reservations. It's becoming standard throughout North America for the guest to pay in advance the basic room charge for one night for any stay of less than three nights; or the equivalent of three nights for longer stays in high season. Reservations are sometimes "guaranteed" when the guest supplies the number of his credit card to the booking agent; in that case, the cardholder may be charged for one night whether he turns up or not.

A certain number of old-line "quality" hotels still believe, once they have confirmed a reservation, that their word is their bond; they'd rather leave a room empty for the night than cause distress to a client.

No matter what the procedure, try for a written, guaranteed reservation signed by the person making the confirmation. Even with that, unless you arrive before 6 p.m., your reservation may be lost. Early-afternoon arrivals run the least risk of being told that their reservation can't be honored. When you think you may not make it by 6 p.m., telephone the desk clerk.

Let's say you booked a double room at regular rates but the desk clerk apologetically tells you the hotel can't honor your reservation. Request another room immediately—even the penthouse—at the same price. Many large hotels will comply with such a request to maintain good will.

If the hotel is full, the clerk will usually offer to locate an equivalent room at another hotel at the same cost, at least for one night. The hotel will pay for the taxi to get you there and for one telephone call to your home.

If a hotel refuses either to honor your reservation or to relocate you, then, of course, unless you want to sleep in the park, you've got to get moving and find something yourself. When this happens abroad, and you can't speak the local language, you are plumbing one of the depths of tourism. In Canada and the United States, you can try to enlist the help of the local hotel association, the government tourist agency or the police. Remember, however, that the prevailing law is that of the province or state where you are staying—and that can be quite different from the regulations or customs you take for granted at home.

If your bookings were made through a travel agent, call him long-distance if you're stranded. The agent may send a lot of business to that hotel and could apply pressure. In any case, when you get home, complain to the agent, who should be willing to act as negotiator in seeking compensation.

You can launch legal proceedings, claiming everything from breach of contract to negligence, fraud or breach of innkeeper's duty. Of course, when you simmer down, you may well decide that the time, effort and possible cost of legal action simply isn't worth it. It's an imperfect world.

EXTENDED STAY

You are having a great time in Calgary but your hotel refuses to let you keep your room for a few days more.

There's a widespread but mistaken belief that once you are ensconced in a hotel room, it's yours to hold for as long as you pay the bill. This idea is grounded in earlier centuries when the English courts ruled that once the "innkeeper" had accepted a guest, he could not evict him without cause. Provided the guest was reasonably clean, sober, orderly and solvent, he could presumably stay forever. While this common-law precedent is still followed hazily in Canada today, there is actually no such guest's right granted by any legislature. So don't count on it in your case. The Alberta Innkeepers Act leaves the decision at the discretion of the hotelkeeper.

Every popular hotel would soon be in an impossible situation if an unusual proportion of its guests decided to stay over. Incomers with confirmed reservations, including perhaps whole charter-tour groups, would have to be directed elsewhere. Resort hotels often rely on package-tour guests for between 40 and 60 percent of their business.

No doubt the manager in Calgary will do his best to accommodate you; he's shooting for 100-percent occupancy and doesn't want to turn out a paying guest. But if his commitments to new arrivals force his hand, you're likely to get marching orders, and you'll have no alternative but to obey. If you decide to stay in town, ask him to try to relocate you elsewhere.

The important question. If a dispute over these rights arose in Canada today, the issue would probably be resolved under the law of contract. When you reserved, either by mail or phone, you probably stated the number of nights for which you required the room. Or, when you checked in, you were almost certainly asked that question at the desk. Possibly, you filled in the dates yourself on the registration card, along with other data. Your acceptance as a guest—actually, your "offer to buy"—makes the contract, based on the information given.

If you said you wanted the room for three nights, and the clerk gave you the key, then you are entitled to accommodation for that period. Not continuously in that particular room, however: the management can shift you into another room, though it cannot raise the room charge.

When you are not sure how long you will wish to stay, your best protection lies in making an indefinite booking if you can. Give your arrival date and time and describe the period as "for a few days" or "a week or so." All the better if it's in writing—keep a copy. Not all hotels will accept that kind of reservation, however. Some chains insist on a fixed date of departure in all circumstances; this gives them the right to allow an extension only if it suits them.

If your indefinite booking is accepted, your position is virtually unassailable, as long as you can prove ability to pay and have broken none of the general regulations. These can be summed up as the requirement that your conduct as a guest conforms to the standards commonly accepted by any reasonable person.

DEPOSITS

You have had to cancel your confirmed hotel reservation. But now you're having trouble getting a refund of your deposit.

Hotel policies vary widely on this question. Some grant an automatic refund of that first night's deposit while others never do so. Some require notification of the cancellation before 6 p.m. on the day prior to the reservation taking effect. Others will return a deposit only if the reserved room is actually sold to another guest so that the hotel incurs no loss. Still others demand 7 to 10 days' notice. Many popular resort hotels require 30 days' notice of cancellation in high season, and 14 days' in low season.

If you are dissatisfied with the response of the hotel where you have paid a deposit, complain to the local hotel association or to the Department of Tourism. If you booked through a major travel agent, your chances of getting your money back are considerably stronger.

Hans Sternik, president of Inter-Continental Hotels, revealed in 1978 that 60 percent of the chain's business stemmed from travel agents. Through a telex link (average time lapse 20 minutes), the chain guarantees rooms to agency clients when a credit-card number is provided. Conversely, it permits cancellations if made before 6 p.m. on the day preceding the scheduled arrival.

Sternik also divulged one of the more un-

Diamonds not necessarily forever

Everybody on wheels—members or not—can benefit from the independent accommodation ratings issued by the Canadian Automobile Association (CAA) and the American Automobile Association (AAA), working in conjunction.

Wherever you may roam on the North American continent, the CAA/AAA field representative has most likely been there ahead of you. When lodgings display the symbol denoting either association's approval, it's a finger beckoning to the 18 million members of the motor leagues—and to all tired travelers looking for a square deal.

The CAA uses clusters of diamonds to tip you off to the best and most suitable buys in rooms. Because the field representatives systematically recheck the listings, a motel or hotel with slipping standards can lose a diamond or two, or be dropped altogether.

◆ Meets CAA/AAA basic requirements for recommendation.

◆◆ Exceeds CAA/AAA minimum requirements in *some* physical and/or operational categories.

◆◆◆ Significantly exceeds CAA/AAA requirements in *many* physical and operational categories.

◆◆◆◆ Exceptional; significantly exceeds CAA/AAA requirements in *most* physical and operational categories. Offers luxurious accommodations, as well as extra amenities. The establishment's management and staff, the housekeeping and maintenance rank well above the average.

◆◆◆◆◆ Renowned; awarded only to those exceptional properties that are widely recognized for marked superiority of guest facilities, services and overall atmosphere.

The rating assigned to each establishment reflects its overall *quality* compared to others of the same classification; for example, a motel cannot be compared to a hotel. One or more diamonds indicate that the establishment meets or exceeds basic CAA/AAA requirements for that classification.

usual hazards of guaranteeing reservations in hotels abroad. "In some countries," he said, "if the government demands 20 rooms that night for visiting firemen, you provide the rooms, because if you don't, they'll take them by force."

On individual guaranteed reservations, Canadian Pacific Resort Hotels require 72 hours' notice of cancellation, unless you reserve using an American Express or Diners Club credit card, in which case you can cancel up to 6 p.m. the day previous.

GREAT EXPECTATIONS

After you check in, you discover that facilities advertised in the brochure are not available.

Perhaps the simplest and soundest action is to check out immediately, demanding a refund of any deposit you have paid. Of course, this assumes there is other suitable accommodation available locally. Otherwise, keep the room after lodging your complaint, but ask for a reduced charge commensurate with the shortfall of advertised facilities.

Short of deliberate misrepresentation, which would be the crime of *fraud* in Canada, the situation could turn on a somewhat innocent acceptance by the guest of the "puffery" in the advertising brochure. (*See* Chapter 20, "Advertising.") The skilled copywriter knows how to sail close to deception without hitting the rocks. Consider the following definitions prepared by a legal expert in the field:

Oceanfront location. This term is applied to all rooms from which the ocean—or bay, or gulf—may be seen without actually facing the ocean front. A room could be described as "ocean view" when located in a hotel wing at right angles to the beach, or where the hotel faces the ocean but at some distance from the water—maybe a kilometre or more away. The view may be partially obscured by trees or other buildings.

Beachfront location. Similar to "oceanfront," but indicates the presence of a beach.

Island or mountain view. Similar to "ocean view." The island interior, mountains, or a mountain range can actually be seen from the room. The mountains could be 20 kilometres distant from the hotel.

Poolside rooms. Rooms at the same level as one of the hotel's swimming pools, facing the pool area and usually giving direct access.

Rooms overlooking pool. From the room windows you can see the pool—or part of it—but maybe from the 20th floor. You'd need binoculars to watch the beauty parade. No direct access to the pool.

Hotel swimming pools. Most hotels in warmer climates boast one or more swimming pools, but no standard specification exists. Pools vary from Olympic size with diving facilities to paddling pools of little use to adults. They may be filled with fresh or salt water, heated or unheated. There may or may not be a lifeguard, depending on municipal, provincial or state regulations.

Sauna and massage. It may be a very small sauna room, open only a few hours on weekdays, and never on Sunday. The masseur, or masseuse, may be available by appointment only, at a stiff fee.

Television in all rooms. Could be non-cable black-and-white, and "under repair."

Dinner dance every night. Yes, but on a pocket handkerchief floor, from 7 p.m. to 9 p.m., to a semi-amateur group or amplified phonograph.

Room service. There is no legal definition of this term. If the room is swept daily, and the bed made—that's service in the room. As for room-served drinks and meals, or errands, as long as they are available at certain restricted hours per day, the brochure is technically accurate. Nobody ever promises "swift" service.

In a materialistic world, your best guide to the facilities you'll find at a new hotel is the basic room charge. Expect a descending level as you go down the ladder from *deluxe* hotels to family hostelries, to motels, inns, taverns and pubs. By rule of thumb, cut-rate prices indicate cut-rate services. Read what the guide books say about your chosen hotel. Check the quality listings of the Canadian Automobile Association. If you're in any doubt about facilities and services, inquire in concrete terms before you reserve, or before you check in.

IDENTIFICATION

You are embarrassed when the room clerk asks you and your wife to produce identification. You feel that this is an unreasonable demand.

The law everywhere requires innkeepers to maintain a register of guests. The extent of the information demanded depends upon local regulations. In many European countries, passports must be surrendered temporarily—for overnight check by the police.

Certain information is needed so that the hotel can do its job efficiently. Of course, it wants to be able to trace you if you skip without paying your bill, but the same information can be used to contact you if mail or other important messages arrive after you've checked out, or if you've left your watch behind. If you want your car brought to the front door, the porter will need your license number.

Refusing a room. Ancient common law holds that an innkeeper cannot select his guests. If accommodation is available, he must admit anyone who can pay for a bed. Now comes the big "but." He can, however, legitimately reject any applicant whose presence would harm his business or place himself, his family and other guests at hazard. All these grounds are, of course, arguable but the manager has the "say" at the time. A Canadian hotel cannot refuse accommodation on the basis of race, religion, color, nationality or social origin.

Exclusion on the basis of dress is highly discretionary—and also highly controversial. Some hotels will admit anyone who is decently covered, however unconventionally; others will exclude you if you are "immorally" dressed, wearing pit boots or backpacks, or other gear that, within the sole discretion of the management, is not appropriate.

Certain hotels just won't take those who are traveling with children or pets. Almost all *deluxe* hotels refuse service in the hotel restaurant to those who don't conform to their dress code. (*See* Chapter 41, "Entertainment.")

PRIVACY

The maid barges into your hotel room without knocking and finds you undressed.

As a guest, you have a right to privacy in a hotel or motel room. It's your home for the duration of your stay. But this right is limited to some extent by the exigencies of operational efficiency.

Most rooms are equipped with a "Do Not Disturb" sign that can be hung on the outside doorknob. And there are locks or door chains to guard your privacy. But the staff must still clean up and make beds and, sooner or later, they'll pound on your door or, more often, use the passkey. Management always retains the right to open any door, if only for safety and health reasons.

The $10,000 glimpse. A busy New York City bellboy once entered a room without knocking. The guest, an attractive young woman, was naked. She screamed and the bellboy fled. But that wasn't the end of the matter. She sued the hotel for damages on the grounds of her embarrassment and eventually collected $10,000. Don't accept that as a strong precedent these days. It's doubtful any Canadian judge would rate the embarrassment of one glimpse at 10 grand. Keep a bathrobe handy.

LOSS OR DAMAGE

A thief ransacks your hotel room and steals some of your personal belongings.

Every guest has the right to expect that the hotel management will exercise reasonable care of goods left in its possession. But, unless property is deposited at the desk for safekeeping under receipt in the hotel safe, the hotel's liability for loss or damage is strictly limited under provincial statutes.

Only if you are able to prove that the hotel was negligent in its duty do you stand any chance of full recovery on valuables. For example: if a member of the hotel staff was found guilty of the theft. And even then, your case would rest upon your ability to prove every item of financial loss.

If the judge should decide the guest contributed toward his loss through his own negligence, the loss would probably be apportioned between the hotel and the guest.

Lock all doors and windows, and never leave valuables "lying about" in the room. As the law terms it, don't be the author of your own misfortune.

Many hotels post signs in conspicuous places stating that they will not be liable for any damaged or stolen goods. These "total exclusion" signs do not automatically shield the hotel from liability, however. The law never grants anyone, hotel or individual, immunity from damage or injury caused through their willful negligence.

Car care. The hotel's responsibility extends to the guest's car when it is parked on the premises. There is a duty of care to ensure that vehicles are not damaged or stolen while on the parking lot or in the underground garage. It's not a total liability, but you'd have to prove that the hotel staff took less than reasonable care to safeguard your property while you were a registered guest.

The American Plan—and others

Hotels frequently offer business discounts, family rates, weekend and monthly rates, and various plans that include certain meals in the room tariff. Most inclusive charter tours incorporate these services. When you make your own reservations, however, the onus is on you to inquire about the room rate and all other charges. Don't expect automatically to be charged the lowest rate to which you might be entitled. The key is to know what questions to ask.

Here's a list of the most commonly used "plans" and travel terms.

American Plan. Your daily charge includes hotel room and three full meals per day—breakfast, lunch and dinner.

Modified American Plan. Room, a full breakfast and dinner daily.

Bermuda Plan. Includes room and full breakfast only.

Continental or Jamaica Plan. Includes room and continental breakfast only—usually toast or rolls, butter, jam, tea or coffee.

European Plan. Room only.

Set dinner. Relatively new, this plan offers room and daily *table d'hôte* dinner.

Full pension. Accommodation at a European-style guesthouse, including three meals per day, one of them a continental breakfast.

Demipension. Guesthouse with a continental breakfast, and lunch *or* dinner included.

Full breakfast. A three-course meal including juice or cereal, bacon or sausage and eggs, toast, coffee or tea. In some countries, there'll be variations in the breakfast menu. In Europe, the beverage is not always included.

Meal credit. Package-tour companies may offer a credit toward the cost of breakfast in European-Plan hotels. Check your hotel bill before departure to ensure that this adjustment has been made.

Meal voucher. If the tour operator supplies meal vouchers for the hotel, they may not cover the full cost of the meal chosen. Unused vouchers cannot be redeemed for cash.

Checkout time. If you check in during the late afternoon, you'll find that the hotel "day" doesn't have 24 hours. Usually, checkout time is at noon, but some hotels want you out as early as 11 a.m.; others allow you to remain until 2 p.m.

If you want to hold your room later than the advertised checkout time but not actually stay another night, you can probably arrange a late checkout with the management at a nominal fee, or sometimes at no fee at all. It all depends on the policy of the individual hotel, or group, and the state of business that day.

There is also the question of comparative or contributory negligence on the part of the guest. You should never leave your keys in the ignition unless that's the stated policy made known to you by the parking attendant. Wind the car windows up and lock all doors and the trunk when you leave your car. Don't leave valuables in the car or in the trunk. All baggage should be brought with you into your hotel room. Periodically, you should check your car to ensure that all's well.

The guest, or *his* guests, who suffer any personal injuries or harm in the hotel or its environs due to any negligence on the part of the hotel will be compensated. The same holds true for any casual patrons of the restaurant, bars or swimming pool.

Many travelers and their families are covered against injury or loss anywhere by "floater" clauses in their personal insurance policies. It's usually easier, and certainly faster, to recover from your insurer and let him settle with the hotel, unless deductible amounts in your policy make this inapplicable.

HOST'S RESPONSIBILITY

You can't get to sleep because of the noise from the party held in the next room.

A collision of rights. The partymakers through the wall have the right to entertain their guests and to enjoy themselves. You have the right to a night's sleep. The saw-off is: what's reasonable? And the hotel manager is the referee.

If the noise is more than a reasonably tolerant person could be expected to endure, or if it goes on too long—say, past 11 p.m.—the manager changes his role to that of enforcer. Primarily, people hire hotel bedrooms to sleep in; the innkeeper's obligation is to provide the proper environment.

Not everybody enjoys playing the "party pooper" when others are having a celebration, but if sleep or rest is impossible, you should first call next door—personally or via the house phone—and suggest politely that the merrymakers hold it down a bit. If this doesn't produce favorable results, you should complain to the management.

It may be news to some travelers, but hotel managers have a good idea of what is happening in "the house" at all times. However unobtrusive they may seem, bellboys and maids have eyes and ears. Security guards patrol the passageways. Room Service knows what's going down—and how much of it. And doormen do more than open doors.

By checking his guest list, the manager learns the name of the offender and probably his company or official affiliation. Even the location and grade of the room can be revealing; most big hotels maintain party suites and steer known *bons vivants* into them.

The manager is trained as a diplomat. The last thing he wants to do is have the police tramping through the lobby or to throw paying guests out into the night. If the party has got out of control, he'll try to use the iron hand in the velvet glove. He'll intervene, but he'll probably accept a promise from the party to quieten down. When it doesn't, the ball is back in your court. You have several choices, depending upon your determination to stick up for your rights:

■ Inform the manager that you intend to sue the hotel for breach of contract;

■ Demand another room, in a quieter location, immediately;

■ Check out and refuse to pay your bill: suggest they sue you for it. As long as they have your correct name and address on the register, it's perfectly legal. You can't be arrested for debt in Canada, but remember that in some provinces the innkeeper has the right, in these circumstances, to seize your luggage.

Although damages for "loss of enjoyment" have been awarded in a few clear-cut cases where package-tour holidaymakers have been treated badly by hotels and tour operators, about the best you can expect in a court action for loss of sleep, or inconvenience, is a partial refund of the room charge. If you did check out and refuse to pay your bill, and if the hotel went to the courts to seek a judgment against you, you could raise "breach of contract" as a defense and counterclaim for damages. An out-of-court settlement would probably be forthcoming.

If the action in the next room becomes so rowdy that you are insulted, intimidated or even assaulted by the revelers, then call the hotel management *and* the police—immediately. The hotel will no doubt order the obstreperous guests to leave, and offer you a partial refund of your bill as a placating gesture. And, of course, you may also have a legal recourse personally against the offenders.

MEDICAL ATTENTION

Your husband is taken ill suddenly at a resort hotel.

Help is as near as your room telephone, or the hotel desk. Everyone in Canada has the right to medical attention in an emergency—and this can take in ambulance or even aircraft transportation. (*See* Chapter 46, "Doctors and dentists," and Chapter 47, "Hospitals and nursing homes.")

A large resort complex may have a resident doctor. Certainly, the desk clerk will have a list of emergency telephone numbers. The ill person should remain in the room, preferably in bed, if the attack appears to be in any way serious. In other situations, the best course is probably to ask the clerk to call a cab and rush the patient to the nearest hospital outpatient department.

If a physician is called to your room anywhere in Canada, provide him with your provincial health-insurance registration number. Any physician who has withdrawn from Medicare will require cash payment but, on your return home, you can file his receipt and be reimbursed in whole or in part. You'll probably have to pay at least a percentage of any ambulance charges. At the public hospital, your provincial health plan should cover all your medical and accommodation costs.

If the illness occurs in the United States, or anywhere else abroad, your plan will still pay off at the rates current for the same treatment in your home province. Obtain a detailed diagnostic report from the doctor, or an official hospital bill, for later reimbursement.

If you wish to be covered completely for medical care while away from home, there are several private insurance plans that will meet just about any expenses beyond those paid under your Medicare plan.

COTTAGE WOES

You rent a lakefront cottage for the season and now the owner presents a bill for "damage."

Although you have hired "accommodation" similar to a chalet or self-contained apartment at a resort hotel, any disputes arising from a private rental contract will be settled under the Landlord and Tenant Act of your province, not under the Innkeepers Act.

Even if the renting agreement was quite informal, the law is similar everywhere in requiring the landlord to provide and maintain the premises in a good state of repair, in compliance with safety and sanitation standards. The tenant is responsible for normal housekeeping and for the repair of any damage caused willfully or negligently by himself or by his guests.

If you got the cottage through an agency, you were probably required to lodge a deposit against damage. In that case, you should have been presented with an inventory of the contents when you moved in and that list should be checked in your presence when you move out. Unless damage can be proved, the deposit should be returned to you intact.

It is also possible to purchase policies offered by many insurance companies for accidental damage to someone else's property. So if that villa burns down accidentally, you will be covered.

If you believe that the landlord is trying to penalize you unfairly for damage to his cottage, complain to the rent-control office in the province concerned. Some provinces have appointed an official whose sole task is to adjudicate landlord-tenant disputes. Should the owner ask the Small Claims Court to force you to meet his demands, you'll get every opportunity to tell the judge your side of the story.

44 Trouble abroad

The real and imagined problems of traveling abroad—outside Canada and the United States—are sometimes magnified to the point where it seems much safer to stay at home. It probably is, but why shut the door on opportunities to see how others live, to examine cultures and structures much older than our own, and to dodge the severities of our climatic seasons? It's well worth the usually small risk.

From 1970 to 1978, applications for passports, valid for five years, rose by 10 percent annually. About 1.5 million passports are used for overseas trips each year. In the first six months of 1979, however, applications fell by 4 percent compared with the same period in 1978. This probably reflected the steeply rising price of foreign travel, due mainly to inflation and energy costs—and the success of "See Canada First" promotions. Compared with almost all western European destinations, for example, Canada has emerged as a travel bargain.

The prospective foreign traveler has two choices: take a package tour with all the pluses and minuses of shepherded group travel, or strike out independently. The first is by far the simpler and cheaper. Bulk buying of transportation and accommodation, for fixed dates, allows large savings. The organizers will steer you through all the problems related to passports and visas, health, customs, currencies and clothing, and pull you out of bed at 6 a.m. in Brussels to make the next connection. The independent traveler may have to battle the bureaucracies single-handed, but within the limits imposed by national laws and customs, is free to roam the globe as long as the travelers cheques last.

If either type of tourist does run into serious trouble abroad, the extensive web of Canadian embassies and consulates will come to the rescue, with helpful advice if nothing else. Their addresses and telephone numbers can be found in the booklet, *Canadian Representatives Abroad*, available at your public library or from bookshops stocking government publications. In those few areas where Canada is not represented, approach the nearest British consulate.

Don't imagine that a Canadian diplomat can get you out of trouble merely by waving the flag, however. And there are many problems that mere money won't solve. In every foreign land, the tourist is subject to the laws of that land. The rules may be bent here and there for the naive but innocent traveler, but don't count on it. Canada's foreign representatives have been called upon for assistance on a yearly average of 250,000 times. These calls range from the furious Canadian welfare recipient who pounded consular desks in Mexico because his cheque was late, to a search for a traveler missing in the south of France—found on a beach stabbed to death.

Apart from official agencies, help abroad can usually be expected from the international travel agencies, motoring or professional associations, trade unions, churches and the police.

Ignorance of foreign customs—or careless disrespect—is the source of more problems than actual law violations. Most Canadians observe the Sabbath on Sunday, but in the Moslem world it falls on Friday and in Israel, it's from sunset Friday to sunset Saturday. Forget this and you can unwittingly cause offense. You don't play in shorts and T-shirts at the better golf clubs in Europe, and it's strictly traditional white attire on the tennis courts. At the ballet, opera, symphony concert, and at the premieres of plays you'll see an elite sprinkling of black ties and sometimes tail coats.

There's no call, of course, for the tourist to emulate the locals. As a bird of passage, you are probably as interesting to the natives as they may be to you. Yet, for a rewarding and trouble-free trip, it's a good idea to write, on the back of your ticket, that old adage: "When in Rome, do as the Romans do."

STRANDED OVERSEAS

Your daughter phones from Italy in a panic: a purse-snatcher has taken all her papers and money.

It's not the end of the world, nor necessarily the end of her vacation. Tell her to inform the police, and then cable her money to the nearest bank or American Express office. Her insurance, or yours, may cover the loss. The chances of catching the culprit and recovering the property are about the same as in Canada—not good. The street thief everywhere usually rifles a purse or wallet around the next corner and disposes of the container within minutes. Cash money recognizes no owner.

If it's difficult to send money quickly, advise her to report to the nearest Canadian embassy or consulate. After hometown references are checked, Canadian officials will usually make short-term loans while a traveler is waiting for money or needs to purchase a return ticket.

The most dangerous way to carry money anywhere is in a highly visible purse or wallet. Young travelers today often carry small purses tucked under shirt or blouse. It's a version of the old Victorian moneybelt, but more comfortable to wear. It can take a minute or two to get at it but the security is worth the inconvenience.

Getting money from home. When you're in a foreign country and you need money urgently from your bank account at home, find a bank in the nearest city that has "correspondence status" with your bank. All the Canadian chartered banks have "correspondents" abroad; they'll happily supply you with a list for your destination country. You'll have to pay to cable your hometown bank and then wait for the funds to be sent. It shouldn't take more than a day or two, however.

Investigate the currency regulations of your host country; you may inadvertently commit an offense if you try to leave it with more money than you entered.

And, on this subject anyway, believe the TV commercials. The safest way to carry your money *is* in travelers cheques. Keep most of it in the smaller denominations. Travelers cheques issued by all the big banks and agencies, such as American Express and Thomas Cook, are replaceable if you keep a careful record of the serial numbers. Always leave one copy of the numbers at home and use the cheques in sequence. When you cash each cheque, score the number off your list. That way, you'll be able to supply the issuer with the number of the uncashed cheques if they're stolen. Don't keep your cheque record in your wallet with the cheques.

Most thefts occur in hotels, restaurants or crowded streets, or while you're napping on a train. Don't leave valuables in your hotel room. If you're sleeping in dormitory accommodations, put your camera inside your sleeping bag.

Foiling passport thieves. If you lose your passport, notify both the local police and your nearest Canadian diplomatic office. Any Canadian embassy or consulate can issue you a temporary replacement, provided you have proper identification with you. But this can take time; and it may not be possible to leave the country or to enter another one without a passport. Most countries require tourists to carry their passports at all times. In the wrong hands, this item can be more valuable than money and passport theft is a highly specialized trade in many countries.

Many travelers leave all their valuables—including their passports—in the hotel safe. Obtain a receipt from the desk clerk enumerating the articles or documents you leave for safekeeping. If you should be asked by police to show your passport on the street, you'll be given the chance to retrieve it from the hotel safe and bring it to a police station or other government office.

Abroad, it's often necessary to produce your passport to check into a hotel. You may have to surrender it overnight, but always insist upon getting it back again. Passports placed by clerks in the drawer behind the counter sometimes get "lost." Never use your passport as collateral for a debt or as security for any unpaid bill.

The wise traveler carries a facsimile birth certificate whenever he is abroad. It takes up no more space than a credit card and, if your passport is lost or stolen, it can solve many problems. Do *not* pack it with your passport.

VISAS AND VACCINATIONS

You are stopped at a border in central Europe. You had assumed your passport would give you entry to all countries with which Canada has diplomatic relations.

Wrong. It's better to assume that you *will* need a visa, a special permit to enter stamped into your passport. Canada maintains diplomatic relations with 140 countries, but not all of them are friendly next-door neighbors. Some require both entry and exit visas.

This visa problem does not apply to Western European and most Commonwealth countries, but your best approach is to inquire from the Ottawa embassy of the country you wish to visit. Also, travel agents usually have lists of countries that require visas for Canadians.

To obtain a visa, get an application form from the embassy. When you have filled it out, submit it together with your passport, three photographs and the required fee. Within two or three weeks, your passport, stamped with the visa, will be returned.

Some countries demand to know when you wish to arrive and leave. The visa fee may vary depending on the length of stay. If you want to enter more than once, a multiple-entry visa will be necessary. That costs more, too.

You may be required to change a certain amount of money into local currency for each day you intend to stay. The embassy usually provides a voucher which can be cashed at a bank upon arrival. When you enter certain countries by train, there may be an official aboard who will cash your voucher. Apart from a desire to be sure you'll spend a minimum number of dollars, this is a defense against black market currency dealings. The Canadian dollar is still prized in many countries, and you can expect to be approached furtively by street dealers offering much higher conversion rates than those posted in the banks or listed in the financial columns of your newspaper.

If you want to extend your visa once you are in the host country, go to the nearest police or immigration office. Extensions are not normally hard to get for the ordinary tourist, but permission can take a day or more to come through. And there'll be another fee.

Sometimes a visa won't be granted—and entry thus refused—unless proof of certain vaccinations can be shown. Make inquiries well ahead of time. The embassy of the destination country, your travel agent, or the Medical Services Branch of the federal Department of Health and Welfare can advise you.

Many a long trip has been ruined because travelers forget about their stopovers or side-trips. You must meet the domestic health requirements of every country along the way, or else risk spending a lot of time in the quarantine rooms of airports. For example, you may not need a vaccination to fly from Canada to your final destination country but, if you make a stopover en route, you may need shots when proceeding from *that* country to your journey's end. The record of your vaccinations should be kept in the little booklet, *International Certificate of Vaccination*. Certain shots can only be obtained at an office of the Department of Health and Welfare; others will be given at your municipal public-health clinic. Most can be obtained from your doctor.

Make sure that each of your shots is correctly recorded: type of inoculation, date received, name and qualification of the person who administered it, and the official stamp. Each vaccination holds good for only a certain period.

If you plan travel to a troubled area of the world, telephone the Consular Affairs Office at the Department of External Affairs for advice. Even though a foreign country may permit you to visit, Consular Affairs may suggest that it's unwise to go there for the time being. Some countries, although ostensibly at peace, simply don't admit foreign visitors. North Korea, Vietnam and Albania were cases in point in 1979.

LIQUOR OFFENSES

Your son runs into serious trouble in the Middle East when a customs officer finds two bottles of rye in his luggage.

The possession and consumption of alcoholic liquors are forbidden by the Koran, the Holy Writ of Islam—and increasingly the basic legal text as well. Orthodox Moslems believe the Koran is the literal word of God as revealed to Mohammed by the angel Gabriel. In some Moslem countries, violations that we would consider minor can result in public floggings. Theft can cost a hand, surgically removed.

Some partly Moslem countries, such as Lebanon, permit visitors to bring in some liquor for their own use only. But Saudi Arabia strictly forbids the importation of liquor or *any* narcotics. In Iraq, you are allowed to take in one litre of liquor or wine, plus 200 cigarettes. The same goes for Syria. Turkey permits two quarts of liquor, but the bottles must

Where malaria can strike

In malarial areas (*see* map), the visiting Canadian is vulnerable even during the shortest stay. Prophylactic drugs are effective only if taken before your departure, without fail during your visit, and for six weeks after your return home. After sunset, the whole body should be protected from mosquito bites and any exposed areas treated with a good brand-name repellent.

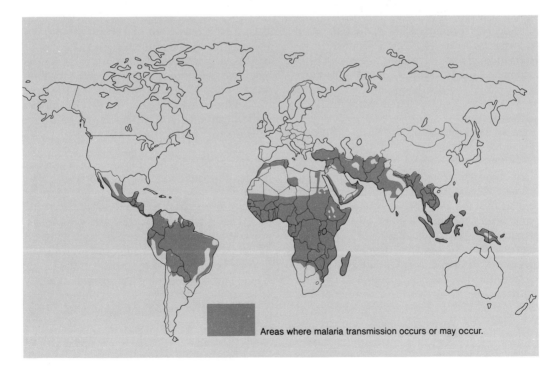

Areas where malaria transmission occurs or may occur.

be opened. Oman, largest of the Persian Gulf states, will not let you through Seeb airport, even with a briefcase full of documentation, if you have any liquor, pets, toy guns or naughty books.

The nearest Canadian embassy will try to help your son. Don't expect our diplomats to do the impossible, though, when local law or custom is violated or breached. Nevertheless, they will do their best to have his offense regarded in the light of Canadian law. Your son has the right under international law to get in touch with a Canadian consul. Even if this official can't intervene directly, he will keep you informed about your son's case, provide the names of local lawyers, assist in obtaining funds, and attempt to improve the conditions of detention. The official will also try to get your son medical or other professional assistance.

The innocent abroad can be shocked to learn at first hand that, in many countries, police can detain nationals or foreigners for several days for interrogation without preferring charges. It's during this period that third-degree techniques are sometimes used on suspects, to develop leads for further investigation. Prompt consular access is therefore important to ascertain that no brutality is being used; or if it has been, that a strong protest is quickly registered with the local government.

Down Mexico way. The easy airline access to Mexico, the relaxed life style there and the common cultivation of marijuana, all lead many unsophisticated young Canadians to mistake Mexico for a narcotics haven. It can be a big mistake. Any foreigner in Mexico carrying even a minimal amount of narcotics is presumed to be "trafficking" and can be hit with a seven-year sentence. Compared to the prisons of Canada, the United States and Western Europe, the penal conditions in Latin America, the Arab world, Communist Europe, Africa and the Far East range from poor to primitive. Any Canadian unfortunate enough to be jailed can expect sparse food, scant medical attention and primitive sanitation.

Foreigners involved in minor infractions in the Soviet Union are frequently held in an austere hotel across the street from Sheremetevo Airport, outside Moscow. The rooms are Spartan, with two beds, one table and little else. Two elderly beldames are in attendance and they profess to speak no English. There are telephones but no phone books, thus no easy way of obtaining a useful number.

Local legal help can actually backfire. In some countries, prisoners or their friends and relatives have been bilked by lawyers who extort extravagant fees or retainers with florid promises backed by scant results. The Canadian embassy will furnish a list of local lawyers whom it has screened for competence and honesty.

CUSTOMS DECLARATIONS

You are bringing home a sealed package from Turkey as a favor for a fellow Canadian you met in a hotel. What about the customs inspection?

Perhaps it is only a box of Turkish delight, but you are taking one of the biggest risks of your life. A cardinal rule of international travel is: never carry anything across a border for anyone you don't know very well. Even the little old lady who asks for your help at the railway station can stick you with a kilo of hash in a brown paper parcel.

Under the Canadian Criminal Code, the maximum penalty for trafficking in narcotics is life imprisonment. (*See* Chapter 5, "The question of morals.") This law may seldom be applied, but it is there. Even if you have no idea what is in that package under your shirts, you can be convicted of either "trafficking"—which includes transporting or delivering—or of possession "for the purpose of trafficking." Even "simple possession" of a small quantity of controlled narcotics—a few joints of marijuana—rates a maximum penalty of seven years' imprisonment.

Lulled into a sense of false security by the many lenient sentences handed down in homeland courts for "simple possession," scores of Canadians traveling abroad have found themselves either severely fined or thrown into jail for relatively minor drug offenses. Some countries draw no distinction between trafficking and possession.

In its booklet, *Information for Canadians Traveling Abroad*, which you get when you apply for a passport, the External Affairs Department bluntly warns:

"Many countries impose severe penalties on persons convicted of possessing, smuggling or trafficking in drugs: heavy fines, property confiscation, prison sentences—or all three. Persons apprehended under suspicion may be held in jail for long periods awaiting trial.

"Canadian government representatives have little authority to intercede on behalf of citizens who are arrested as possible offenders, except to inform relatives and ensure that legal defense is available before trial. If convicted, an individual will be assisted in transmitting personal funds to pay fines and in transmitting periodic reports of the prisoner's welfare to his relatives.

"Representatives are not authorized to provide you with legal advice and they cannot intervene in the regular local course of justice."

Despite such warnings, about half of all Canadians in foreign jails—not including the United States—are serving time for narcotics offenses. One week's tally in 1979 in Paris alone was 15. Mexico, Spain, Morocco and India are rated highly as potential danger areas.

The perilous pickup. Trouble can strike long before you reach any customs barrier. Two young Canadians touring Morocco in a rental car picked up a hitchhiker. At a police checkpoint soon afterward, police found three kilograms of hashish in the hiker's backpack. The tourists pleaded their innocence but still got a month in jail and an $800 fine. Foreign police sometimes use undercover agents who first sell narcotics to tourists, or enlist them as gullible carriers, then turn them in to the authorities.

When you reenter Canada, you must declare to Customs everything you have acquired abroad, whether as purchases or as gifts. This includes anything you bought at a duty-free store. The RCMP enforces the Customs Act. Anything that is not declared is liable to seizure. So keep all receipts for anything purchased, or repaired, abroad, and your hotel bills, and be prepared to produce them. Repairs and new parts may be subject to duty and taxes. However, if they were essential to your safe return to Canada, a remission of duty and taxes may be granted.

Personal exemption. Any resident of Canada returning from a trip abroad may qualify for a personal exemption and therefore bring into Canada goods up to a certain value free of duty and taxes. Even a babe in arms qualifies; in which case, the parent makes a customs declaration on behalf of the infant. The only proviso is that the goods purchased in the child's name must obviously be for his or her use. In general, goods brought in under a personal exemption must be for personal or household use, as souvenirs of your trip, or as gifts for friends or relatives. Exemptions cannot be pooled or transferred.

After 48 hours' absence or more, any number of times per year, you may bring in goods to the value of $10. Only an oral declaration is needed. Once every calendar quarter, you can bring in goods to the value of $50. In this case, a written declaration may be required. Once every calendar year, you may bring in goods to the value of $150 after seven days' absence or more. A written declaration is required. You can claim both a ($150) yearly and a ($50) quarterly exemption in one calendar quarter, provided these are claimed for separate trips.

If your travels take you far afield, things you have bought may follow you by mail or other means of transport. List them on your declaration form when you go through Customs. You will have 30 days in which to clear them, by presenting your copy of the declaration form.

If any of the goods you bought abroad have to be repaired or replaced, you have 60 days from the date of your return to Canada in which to inform Customs and arrange documentation.

When you are bringing in a number of items, Customs should advise you which goods to charge to your personal exemption, so that minimum duty and tax penalties will apply.

Penalties for goods not declared or falsely declared—and, in plain language, that's smuggling—are subject to seizure, forfeiture and probably fines. Let us say, for example, you are caught smuggling an item worth $400. The item could be seized and forfeited outright, or you might have to pay much more than its actual value to have it released. In addition, your car, boat, or aircraft that transported the item could be seized and forfeited, or it might cost you or the owner more than

Don't bring them back

Whether they are herbs from your grandmother's herb garden in the Old Country or rare birds from your uncle's aviary in the subtropics, the best rule of thumb, says Agriculture Canada, is: Don't bring them back. The Information Services of the Department of Agriculture explain why.

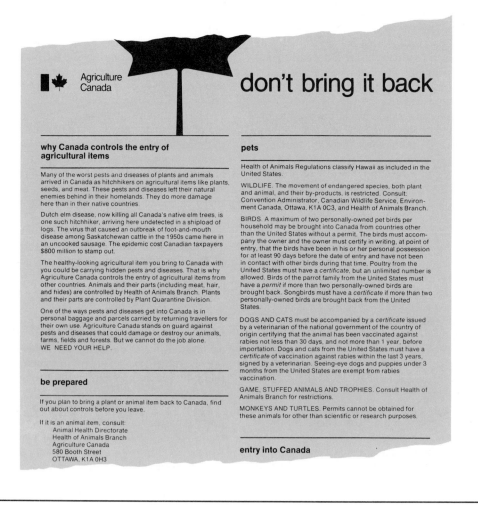

Agriculture Canada

don't bring it back

why Canada controls the entry of agricultural items

Many of the worst pests and diseases of plants and animals arrived in Canada as hitchhikers on agricultural items like plants, seeds, and meat. These pests and diseases left their natural enemies behind in their homelands. They do more damage here than in their native countries.

Dutch elm disease, now killing all Canada's native elm trees, is one such hitchhiker, arriving here undetected in a shipload of logs. The virus that caused an outbreak of foot-and-mouth disease among Saskatchewan cattle in the 1950s came here in an uncooked sausage. The epidemic cost Canadian taxpayers $800 million to stamp out.

The healthy-looking agricultural item you bring to Canada with you could be carrying hidden pests and diseases. That is why Agriculture Canada controls the entry of agricultural items from other countries. Animals and their parts (including meat, hair, and hides) are controlled by Health of Animals Branch. Plants and their parts are controlled by Plant Quarantine Division.

One of the ways pests and diseases get into Canada is in personal baggage and parcels carried by returning travellers for their own use. Agriculture Canada stands on guard against pests and diseases that could damage or destroy our animals, farms, fields and forests. But we cannot do the job alone. WE NEED YOUR HELP.

be prepared

If you plan to bring a plant or animal item back to Canada, find out about controls before you leave.

If it is an animal item, consult:
Animal Health Directorate
Health of Animals Branch
Agriculture Canada
580 Booth Street
OTTAWA, K1A 0H3

pets

Health of Animals Regulations classify Hawaii as included in the United States.

WILDLIFE. The movement of endangered species, both plant and animal, and their by-products, is restricted. Consult: Convention Administrator, Canadian Wildlife Service, Environment Canada, Ottawa, K1A 0C3, and Health of Animals Branch.

BIRDS. A maximum of two personally-owned pet birds per household may be brought into Canada from countries other than the United States without a permit. The birds must accompany the owner and the owner must certify in writing, at point of entry, that the birds have been in his or her personal possession for at least 90 days before the date of entry and have not been in contact with other birds during that time. Poultry from the United States must have a *certificate*, but an unlimited number is allowed. Birds of the parrot family from the United States must have a *permit* if more than two personally-owned birds are brought back. Songbirds must have a *certificate* if more than two personally-owned birds are brought back from the United States.

DOGS AND CATS must be accompanied by a *certificate* issued by a veterinarian of the national government of the country of origin certifying that the animal has been vaccinated against rabies not less than 30 days, and not more than 1 year, before importation. Dogs and cats from the United States must have a *certificate* of vaccination against rabies within the last 3 years, signed by a veterinarian. Seeing-eye dogs and puppies under 3 months from the United States are exempt from rabies vaccination.

GAME, STUFFED ANIMALS AND TROPHIES. Consult Health of Animals Branch for restrictions.

MONKEYS AND TURTLES. Permits cannot be obtained for these animals for other than scientific or research purposes.

entry into Canada

$100 to get it back. In addition, you might face prosecution for smuggling and a fine of up to $1,000, or imprisonment from one to four years, or both.

To avoid reentry problems, declare all valuable items—cameras, jewelry, furs—to Canada Customs before you leave the country. And if you are traveling with large amounts of medication, a doctor's letter could save you unnecessary or embarrassing difficulties.

DRIVING PERMITS

Your globe-trotting daughter discovers that her Canadian driver's license is not accepted overseas.

The fact that you have the privilege of driving in Canada doesn't necessarily mean you can drive abroad as well. You may need, apart from your current operator's license, an international driving permit, a *carnet de passage*, and special accident insurance protection. Before you fly or sail away—or even drive to the United States—it is a good idea to check with the Canadian Automobile Association (CAA) through any of its member clubs: the British Columbia Automobile Association, Alberta Motor Association, Saskatchewan Motor Club, Manitoba Motor League, Ontario Motor League, Touring Club Montreal, Quebec Automobile Club, or the Maritime Automobile Association.

Most European countries will accept a North American driver's license. But others such as Italy and the Federal Republic of West Germany demand an international driving permit which you can obtain easily if you have a valid Canadian driver's license and pay the required fee. The *carnet* is often demanded if you want to take a vehicle through a country. Its real purpose is to ensure the host country that you won't sell your car without paying local duties and taxes. The permits are sold by the CAA, the only Canadian organization authorized to do so. The service is available to all travelers, not just CAA members.

Renting your wheels. When you rent a car in a foreign country, be sure it's a popular make that can easily be serviced. You should also pack an automobile phrase book. Car parts have very technical names. While a mechanic may know a few words of English, it's unlikely you'll be able to explain that curious knock in the transmission. Obtain a booklet or guide illustrating the international road signs, and obey them religiously. Driving on the left, for example, in Britain, Ireland, Finland, Japan, New Zealand and Malaysia can be extremely confusing for Canadians, particularly when making turns.

As for insurance, don't rely on your Canadian policy. Check very carefully at embassies and with your motor league. For example, no Canadian automobile insurance is valid in Mexico. You will be approached at border points by agents selling coverage by the day.

For Europe, you need an international insurance certificate, known as the Green Card. It verifies that your insurance company will pay off if you are the guilty party in any accident—and sometimes even if you're not. In Eastern Europe, beyond the Iron Curtain, you'll probably need supplementary insurance on top of that.

If you're involved in a car accident in a foreign country, show the police your passport, your automobile registration, or rental contract form, and say as little as possible. Seek legal advice from the nearest Canadian embassy or consulate. The tourist in a comparatively expensive car can face an uphill task in a foreign court against a local plaintiff pleading economic hardship.

NATIONAL CUSTOMS

You are humiliated in Spain when you are ordered back to the hotel to change out of your shorts and halter.

Respecting national customs—even when they appear restrictive or eccentric—is not only simple courtesy to your host country, but it can keep you out of embarrassing trouble. For example, the wearing of any style of bathing suit away from the beach is discouraged in Spain, except on such international strips as the Costa Brava and the Costa del Sol. In inland and northern areas, the thoughtless female tourist with bare legs and midriff can expect to be told to cover up. Indeed, you may be escorted back to the hotel by a frowning policeman. And in just about all countries, the Canadian woman should, generally speaking, exercise great tact and care.

In many countries, the role and conduct of the respectable woman, while not sociologically inferior to that of the man, can be quite different from the Canadian or American norm. The sight of a woman driving a car may draw crowds. In South Africa, women are not normally served in street bars. In Zambia, they'll be served liquor only if accompanied by a man. In Australia and New Zealand, women are not welcome in public bars and in some establishments are excluded by posted notice. In Turkey, neither women nor men should wear shorts, even when the temperature in Istanbul hits 30°C.

Conversely, in many countries, hotel staff of either sex may enter your bedroom after the briefest knock, or perhaps with no warning at all. No offense is intended. In some Asian countries, young girls assist in male bathhouses without any embarrassment or lack of modesty.

Always be aware, too, that you are subject to the laws of your host country. It's up to you to be prudent. Many countries have substantially different local customs, legal systems and judicial processes. Don't expect that, because you are a foreigner, you will automatically enjoy preferential treatment or be exempt from any law or regulation.

Your behavior, dress and general appearance, even the taking of harmless photographs, may be considered an affront to local custom, or be against local regulations. Many tourists have run into serious trouble for snapping shots around airports, factories, bridges and railway stations: Such places are considered to be of military significance and photographing them may be regarded as an act of espionage. Picture-taking from planes can cause a crisis over much of Africa, Latin America, Asia and Eastern Europe. When in doubt about any matter of local law or custom, it is just as well to seek the advice of those in the know. Get in touch with the Canadian embassy or consulate before you act.

BLACK MARKETS

In India, you are approached by a well-dressed stranger who offers to exchange your dollars for more than the official rate.

It's inevitable that in every country where there are foreign exchange controls, there'll be a black market in cash money. The hard currencies of the world can be worth double or triple the going rate set by the government, and individual free enterprisers move in to clean up. It's a tempting situation for the budget-conscious tourist trying to make his travel dollars stretch, but changing money on the black market is always risky.

In the first place, it's probably against the law and you could be arrested; in the second, the expert changer may slip you phony bills. By the time you discover this, it will be too late—and you won't be able to complain to the police!

You can count on getting the most favorable official rate of exchange at banks, where the conversion rates are usually posted daily or provided on request. City newspapers invariably publish the rates for major currencies at the closing of business the previous day. However, in lands where the banks are state controlled you may be offered quite a bit less than published world-market levels. In the Soviet Union, the rates of foreign exchange are revised only on the first day of each month.

The international travel agencies usually provide money-changing facilities, at rates close to bank levels. Hotels will often oblige you, but will certainly charge you for the service. Many of the larger restaurants and shops abroad will accept travelers cheques, returning change in local currency. But it can be difficult for the convivial diner to figure out whether he's getting a fair deal for his money.

Some countries demand that you declare how much money you are bringing in, and how much you are taking out. That way, they can keep tabs on your expenditure. If it doesn't add up, you could miss your departing plane. For example, the import or export of rubles is forbidden in the Soviet Union. You can take in as much foreign money as you like, declaring it on a customs form; when you depart, your unused rubles will be reconverted to your own currency based on the recorded figure. The same holds good in general terms for the Australian dollar, the Thailand baht, the Kenyan shilling and many other national currencies.

Colombia will permit the traveler to take out a maximum of 500 pesos. Tunisia forbids the import or export of dinars and will reconvert to other currencies only 30 percent of the amount originally exchanged into dinars. You cannot leave the Republic of Ireland legally

You're the foreigner now

Nowadays, Canadians of British stock may get an immediate culture shock at their airport entry into Great Britain when they find themselves queuing up in the "foreigners" line to have their passports examined. What happened to the Empire or Commonwealth upon which the sun never set? Well, as far as "British preference" is concerned, it died without a whimper when Britain entered the European Economic Community (EEC) in 1973. Today, the French, Germans, Danes and Dutch—all EEC members—walk through the airport lineups while Canadians, Australians and New Zealanders shuffle slowly through immigration checkpoints.

While most English-speaking Canadians still feel very much "at home" in Britain, their official status is no more privileged than that of a Solomon Islander. However, because most Canadian law—in all provinces except Quebec—is based on English common law, and our statutory law often follows British initiatives, the Canadian is unlikely to run afoul of strange laws in major situations. Just don't try to drive on the right-hand side of the road!

Until 1978, any Canadian who could produce a British parent, or grandparent, could deplane in Britain and take a job without seeking official permission. This is no longer the case. You now require a work permit—the same as any foreigner in Canada—and they're not all that easy to come by. You need a sponsor who will swear that the job can't or won't be done by a Briton.

To work in almost any other country, you have to obtain a work permit before you leave Canada. And you'll probably have to convince the local immigration officials that you have sufficient funds to support you for the term of your intended stay, that you possess a ticket for a return home, and that you are in good health.

Every working day, up to 100 serious problems of Canadians in trouble abroad reach the Department of External Affairs in Ottawa's Lester B. Pearson Building. The run-of-the-mill items will have already been filtered out by the 500 consular officials abroad. Among the trickiest are those of traveling Canadians caught in dual-nationality situations.

Your Canadian citizenship protects you in those countries that will totally honor your valid passport or visa. But the citizenship law of the host country is paramount.

Many naturalized Canadians are still regarded as nationals in the land of their birth. If you married an alien, you may have acquired his or her nationality. Even the Canadian-born son of foreign-born parents may be regarded as a citizen in their homeland. Unless you have formally renounced the original nationality—and some countries, Uruguay and Panama for instance, don't permit even this—you may be, in effect, a citizen of two countries. And in those countries such as France and Israel that maintain universal military service, Canadians with dual nationality can be seized by the draft board.

with more than 25 Irish pounds. Sweden will allow you to bring in or take out up to 6,000 kroner.

The shirt off your back. Many items available cheaply in Canada are in very short supply in some countries overseas. Don't be surprised if you are approached by someone who wants to buy your camera, film, jewelry, jeans, or even the shirt off your back. You may be offered double what you paid.

Unless you intend to travel with an officially approved guided group, learn as much as you can about the currency and customs laws of your destination country before you leave home. Foreign embassies and tourist offices will usually provide information by mail. *TIM*, the travel information manual revised yearly by a group of 15 international airlines—including Canada's CP Air—is a gold mine of concise data. It covers every country from Abu Dhabi to Zambia. Single copies can be purchased from Box 7627, 1118 sj Schiphol Airport, the Netherlands.

ILLNESS

While in the Orient on a business trip, you suddenly feel deathly sick.

Get in touch with the nearest Canadian embassy or consulate. They usually have a list of local doctors who have treated Canadians at one time or another. These doctors will probably be able to speak some French or English, and may have trained in North America or Europe. If you have a history of recent illness, you'd be wise to carry an explanatory letter from your doctor.

When hospital care is necessary, you'll probably feel more secure and comfortable in a private clinic that specializes in international medicine. While this almost certainly means you'll be facing a steep bill, it's no time to be budget-minded. Most private clinics will accept travelers cheques; some will take international credit cards. They won't accept your provincial health-insurance card, so be sure to keep receipts for all medical expenses and submit them to the Medicare office upon your return. You will be reimbursed, but probably not to the full amount. For about 50 cents a day, several health-insurance companies or co-ops offer you virtually full coverage while you travel abroad.

The worldwide Intermedic agency (head office: 777 Third Avenue, New York, N.Y. 10017) supplies subscribers with an up-to-date directory of 400 English-speaking doctors in 92 countries. If you need to take any medicine, pack enough to last the trip. And carry your prescription, written in generic terms.

The water problem. The oldest cliche in international travel still rings true: Don't drink the water. Most tourist health upsets are sudden and agonizing stomach troubles linked to a change in drinking water and diet. You're seldom in one place long enough for your system to become accustomed to the local conditions in which everybody else obviously thrives.

In an unfamiliar country, you ought to drink mineral water, internationally known soft drinks, or bottled light beers and ales, or boil the tap water before cooling it in the refrigerator. Give up milk whenever you are not sure it is pasteurized. Ice cream may be hazardous in some countries, and the same applies to ice in drinks. If you're heading for the tropics, get a copy of the Department of Health and Welfare's booklet, *Staying Healthy in Warm Climates*. Apart from information on immunization (*see* Chapter 42, "Traveling"), it advises Canadians on body acclimatization, heat exhaustion, prickly rash, sunburn and sunstroke.

Careful eating and drinking habits will lessen your chance of suffering traveler's diarrhea in hotter climates. For example, don't brush your teeth in tap water unless it's almost too hot to touch. Raw fruit should be washed and then peeled. Choose well-cooked foods, preferably boiled or baked, and quell that urge for oysters or clams on the half-shell.

Bare feet or sandals may be trendy, but the urban Canadian will be safer in shoes or slippers. Newcomers to the tropics are very susceptible to fungus infections such as "athlete's foot." Sea beaches away from all sewer outlets are usually okay.

EATING ADVENTURES

There is a rowdy scene in a small restaurant near Budapest. You couldn't understand the menu and apparently have ordered too much.

After a quarter-century of mass jet travel, English-speaking natives, including most Canadians, still cling stubbornly to what they conceive as the right to be understood in their own language no matter where in the world they alight. At almost every tourist destination abroad, it's a commonplace to hear desperate Anglophones trying to solve language difficulties by the hilarious process of speaking very slowly and very loudly, emphasizing their points with kindergarten sign talk. The strange thing is, it often works. No doubt, if the average Chinese had the money and freedom to travel, he'd do exactly the same thing in Winnipeg or Toronto.

While you'll probably find workaday English spoken in the main hotels and restaurants in large foreign cities, don't count on any English word being understood in the smaller restaurant, tavern or shop. But menus are set up in much the same way everywhere and the prices should guide your ordering. In many places, the day's menu is posted outside the restaurant so that you can consult your budget before entering. The "blue plate special" is an international custom, probably three or four items bracketed at a single price. You cannot go far wrong if you order that.

Sampling unusual dishes in a different ambiance is one of the major pleasures of foreign travel. Try the local specialties. The waiter will probably help you understand what's available by means of sign language or by pointing to what others are eating. You'll probably enjoy a few laughs together.

One Canadian traveling independently in Poland in 1979 entered a clean and busy restaurant. He could not understand a single word on the menu he was handed. With smiling gestures, he indicated to the waiter that he was pretty hungry. He was served a delicious four-course meal. The bill: $3.50.

That's entertainment! Any trip abroad can be ruined by the prejudice that the foreigner is out to bilk the virtuous Canadian. Off the well-beaten tourist tracks—"where the people eat"—the traveler with no knowledge of local language, culture or customs can be more of a pain in the neck than anything else. The patience of the waiter can be severely strained.

If a dispute does arise over your bill, examine your copy carefully and check off each of the *à la carte* items you were served. Consider whether a service charge has been included. You'll find that many places abroad—especially where there's music or any other entertainment—apply a table minimum or add an entertainment surcharge. A bemused Canadian traveler in Yugoslavia once noted an entertainment surcharge on his dinner bill at a country inn. There had been no entertainment whatever. When he demurred, it was laboriously explained to him that there was always entertainment at dinner but the musicians and the management were having a quarrel. The surcharge stayed on, and the diner paid.

If you are not as amenable—or cowardly—you can always call for the manager, or for the police. But it would be better to pay the bill, keep your receipt bearing the name of the restaurant and the date, and take your complaint to the nearest government tourist bureau. Only a handful of countries scorn tourist dollars, and they are all aware of the penalties of bad "word of mouth" publicity.

If you were booked through a big travel agency, or if the establishment is linked to any of the international credit-card companies, automobile associations, or guide-book organizations, you have allies who should investigate and act upon your complaint.

9 YOUR RIGHTS TO SOCIAL SECURITY

45  When in need

There's nothing new about welfare. Civilized societies have always paid at least lip service to the needs of the poor, the helpless and the disabled. When the world Depression of the 1930s threw hundreds of thousands of able-bodied Canadians into poverty, a public outcry demanded that the patchwork of relief schemes be strengthened and coordinated into a national system. The term "social assistance" was born in an attempt to avoid distasteful labels.

Over the next 40 years, the modern system of "cradle to grave" social security developed, and now, health and welfare programs consume 25 cents of every tax dollar. But the national self-interest, along with social conscience, has caused the system to be evaluated in more than monetary terms: Poverty breeds social problems that are difficult and costly to treat.

Everybody now has the right to seek assistance on the basis of need alone. Checks and tests have been devised to reduce abuses, but if the need exists it will be met, though the response is sometimes at minimum levels.

Whatever need you may have—a problem you can't solve from your own resources—there is probably a program designed to meet it. Many communities have a community services referral office (the names vary) that can direct you to the most likely source of help.

As well as government agencies, there are dozens of private voluntary organizations helping those besieged by hardship and misfortune. "Needs" are not "wants"—they are goods or services urgently required for the maintenance of a basically decent standard of living by people who, for whatever reason, can't provide for themselves. That situation may be temporary, or permanent.

Is Canada a rich country? In 1979, it was estimated that one in every 10 Canadians was receiving welfare in some form.

A MATTER OF RIGHT

You are out of work and broke. And your unemployment insurance benefits have run out.

No matter how black your personal picture may seem, help is at hand as a matter of right. No one in genuine need, either citizen, recent immigrant or visitor, is refused practical assistance. Financial aid, advice and guidance, and even personal encouragement, are as close as the nearest telephone, post office, police station or city hall.

Your first refuge is the welfare office. Since most welfare plans are administered at the municipal level, you'll probably find the office at your city or county hall. Here, you will be required to answer a lot of questions, giving the welfare officer an account of your worldly goods. You must sign forms describing all your circumstances and family assets, plus other relevant data. Some of the queries may appear to invade your personal privacy but, human nature being what it is, the welfare department is wary of abuse and insists on all manner of checks and tests in an effort to protect the public funds from which welfare payments are drawn. Officials must weed out the few who try to make welfare a way of life.

You may be required to sign a form known as the "Consent to Inspect Assets." This gives the administrator access to an applicant's bank account and any safety-deposit boxes, and authority to consult insurance companies. The administrator can also request information from the Canada (or Quebec) Pension Plan office and the Canada Employment and Immigration Commission.

Cutting the red tape. But don't let the red tape deter you. A case worker will explain the procedures and assist you in filling out the forms. Where extreme necessity is evident, immediate cash payments can be made at the discretion of the district welfare administrator, usually to cover a two-week period. If you are a resident, or intend to be a resident, of a municipality, you have the right to claim welfare when in need. Transients can receive benefits from any municipality in the country as long as they are staying there and have a fixed address.

You'll be requested to swear that you will not fail to advise the welfare administrator of any changes in your circumstances, such as the acquisition of additional assets or income, and of any substantial change in your living arrangements. Within two weeks of getting a grant, a case worker will visit your address to check on your living conditions and financial affairs. If, by any chance, you are overpaid by welfare, you are required to pay back the surplus. The administrator has the power to withhold or reduce payments to retrieve any amount paid to you illegally. It's a serious offense to claim welfare by providing false or misleading information; the penalty may be a fine or imprisonment.

The people who are most commonly found on the welfare rolls are elderly persons in need, whether or not they are working; adults who are sick and unable to work; and divorced, separated, widowed or unwed women with dependent children.

The destitute person who cannot obtain public assistance, for whatever reason, can turn to other agencies, mainly of a volunteer nature. The Salvation Army, the Red Cross, your local community services bureau—any of these will offer help or advice. The Canada Manpower Centre, located in most towns, will discuss work opportunities or retraining with you. Support payments can be made to sustain your family during the retraining period.

EXTRA ASSISTANCE

You are a welfare recipient, but the amount you get won't keep your family together.

There are probably not two homes in Canada where all problems, needs and commitments are identical. When you explain your predica-

ment at the welfare office, you can expect both a sympathetic hearing and a searching inquiry into your individual circumstances. You may qualify for extra assistance such as family benefits or a spouse's allowance, as well as the guaranteed income supplement. Remember that, under the Canada Assistance Plan which effectively governs all welfare, it is the *need* that is important, regardless of its cause.

You can apply for family benefits as an individual or as head of a family, a "family" being defined as a group of individuals sharing a common dwelling unit and related by blood, marriage or adoption. A family is also seen as a "spending unit," that is to say, a group of persons dependent on a common or pooled income for the major items of expense and living in the same dwelling. Eligible family groups could include the elderly, blind or disabled, permanently unemployable, foster parents, a dependent father with a dependent child, or a mother raising her children alone.

The long-term need. The family-benefits program runs parallel to the general welfare assistance program; the main difference is that family benefits are issued on a long-term basis, while general welfare is intended mainly to help over a difficult temporary period. Family benefits are usually higher than the general welfare rates and they are administered by the provincial governments; general welfare payments are usually made through the municipality.

The family-benefits program covers the cost of everyday expenses and helps maintain a reasonable standard of living for the unit. Children's needs are assessed according to age: the older the children, the more money they can get. The rates are subject to periodic change based on the cost-of-living index.

If you qualify for family benefits, other services become available, such as free medical and hospital insurance. Anyone 65 or over in receipt of an old-age pension is automatically eligible for drug benefits. Funds may be available for repairs to your home, provided you own it and live in it. You'd have to submit two estimates of the proposed cost of materials and labor.

You may be entitled to free spectacles or

Being poor in Ontario in 1871

Poor houses weren't restricted to England in Charles Dickens's time. This old poster makes the Poor House of Ontario's Norfolk County sound as cheery as a dungeon. Rule IV isn't much different from that in force at today's minimum-security prisons; the others are probably a bit harsher.

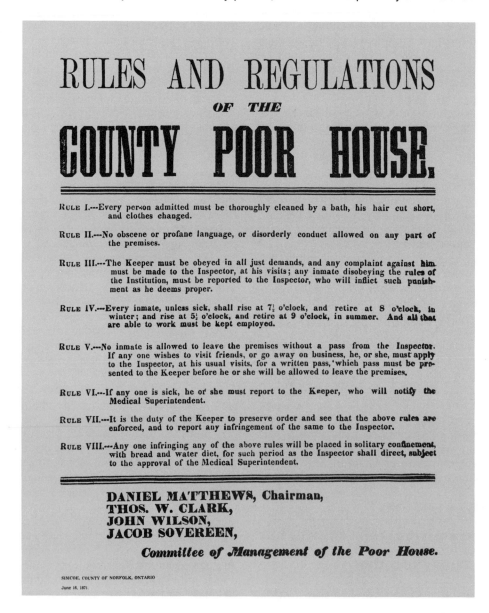

RULES AND REGULATIONS
OF THE
COUNTY POOR HOUSE.

RULE I.---Every person admitted must be thoroughly cleaned by a bath, his hair cut short, and clothes changed.

RULE II.---No obscene or profane language, or disorderly conduct allowed on any part of the premises.

RULE III.---The Keeper must be obeyed in all just demands, and any complaint against him must be made to the Inspector, at his visits; any inmate disobeying the rules of the Institution, must be reported to the Inspector, who will inflict such punishment as he deems proper.

RULE IV.---Every inmate, unless sick, shall rise at 7½ o'clock, and retire at 8 o'clock, in winter; and rise at 5½ o'clock, and retire at 9 o'clock, in summer. And all that are able to work must be kept employed.

RULE V.---No inmate is allowed to leave the premises without a pass from the Inspector. If any one wishes to visit friends, or go away on business, he, or she, must apply to the Inspector, at his usual visits, for a written pass, which pass must be presented to the Keeper before he or she will be allowed to leave the premises.

RULE VI.---If any one is sick, he or she must report to the Keeper, who will notify the Medical Superintendent.

RULE VII.---It is the duty of the Keeper to preserve order and see that the above rules are enforced, and to report any infringement of the same to the Inspector.

RULE VIII.---Any one infringing any of the above rules will be placed in solitary confinement, with bread and water diet, for such period as the Inspector shall direct, subject to the approval of the Medical Superintendent.

DANIEL MATTHEWS, Chairman,
THOS. W. CLARK,
JOHN WILSON,
JACOB SOVEREEN,

Committee of Management of the Poor House.

SIMCOE, COUNTY OF NORFOLK, ONTARIO
June 16, 1871.

hearing aids, for yourself and your dependents. Extra necessities can include surgical supplies and dressings, moving allowances, funeral expenses or virtually any special item or service approved by the administration.

Supplementary aid is payable to people who are already receiving other benefits such as old-age security, family benefits, a blind person's or disabled person's allowance, or a training allowance through rehabilitation services. It can meet the cost of fuel, extra furniture and other special needs of people who are financially unable to provide such services for themselves and their dependents.

WELFARE AND WORK

You are on welfare but are willing to work. The trouble is, the jobs Canada Manpower offers to you are not suitable.

When you are drawing welfare, you are expected to accept any kind of work that is offered: full-time, part-time or casual. Jobs offered to you by Manpower may not be your cup of tea on a permanent basis, but welfare payments are made on the assumption that you'll soon be able to rectify your own personal situation. General welfare is not intended as a permanent income. If you are physically capable of working, you will be expected to accept any kind of job. If you insist on being choosy, or if you think you're "above" manual labor, you could be in trouble. You could lose your conditional right to welfare.

Another important condition of welfare payments is that you must be making reasonable efforts to find work on your own. If you have to stay home to look after small children, you may be exempted from this rule, but generally for not more than a six-month period.

If you are 21, single, employable, and still supported at home, you will not be able to collect welfare. The same applies if you are a resident of an institution other than a nursing home. You will be disqualified if you are enrolled as a day student at any educational institution, unless you are also the head of a family.

All government departments are bound by rules and regulations that cannot always be bent, no matter how eager the average civil servant may be to help. There are times when they are simply unable to oblige you. When applicants are denied certain benefits because they are ineligible under the rules, complaints can arise about the attitudes of the department's clerks or executives. Claimants are apt to vent their ire upon an information clerk who is simply doing his job. Not infrequently, a claimant loses his temper and uses profanity. The clerk—no less human than the inquirer—is apt to retaliate. The complaint, then, is that the civil servant has been rude; the provocation is seldom brought to light.

Play it cool. A polite approach works wonders; at least, it may bear more fruit than the aggressive or offensive approach. If there is a reason why you cannot collect welfare, or any other social security benefit, it will be explained to you. In a cooperative and pleasant atmosphere, all other choices will then be pointed out.

NONRESIDENTS

Hitchhiking his way west, your son wound up flat broke in a small town. He has applied for welfare, but is told to move on.

A welfare applicant must be living in the municipality where he is applying, not just passing through. Itinerant claimants for welfare will be refused unless they can give an address, which will be verified.

During the summer months, thousands of young Canadians take to the road. It's not so long since federally employed youth leaders were encouraging them to do just that. But many of these travelers are still of school age and they are frequently ill prepared and underfinanced. When they throw themselves on the mercy of the chain of welfare administrators, they're very likely to be told to go home, or keep moving.

For one thing, the able-bodied welfare applicant has to be willing to work, and, more than that, has to be trying actively to find work. This rule alone will baulk those who are seeking a fancy free tour of the country at the taxpayer's expense.

Probably nothing annoys the small-town welfare officer more than to be faced with a grinning gaggle of jeans-clad youngsters who give a nearby hostel as their address and who profess to be willing to take a job. In these times, the town no doubt already has its own list of unemployed residents. Even if the administrator is certain it's a rip-off, the applicants "know their rights" and he may have no legal choice except to give them a cash handout.

ALCOHOLISM

You have an alcohol problem and are willing to take treatment at a rehabilitation center, but you can't afford to take the time away from your work.

Alcoholism is generally regarded as a sickness today, and many enlightened employers are anxious to help employees willing to try to overcome their problem. You should discuss the matter frankly with your boss or foreman; it's unlikely your trouble is a secret, anyway. The befuddled, or hung-over, worker is a danger to himself and to his buddies on the production line. And his work is usually substandard.

The sympathetic employer often arranges confidentially for the staffer to have treatment in a rehabilitation center or in an approved home or farm facility, without loss of job. Where sick-leave provisions are in force, there may not be loss of pay.

Government departments on all levels now make it possible for public servants to be absent for sufficient time to attempt a cure for alcoholism. They hope this lead will be followed by private business.

Your doctor—or the staff at any outpatient clinic—will advise you on the therapy available under the provincial Medicare plans. It isn't always necessary to take inpatient treatment.

Facing up to the fact. Alcoholism has been a major cause of family breakdown since time immemorial and the cost to society in

---

Dignity and indignation

Hard-pressed taxpayers are sometimes filled with indignation by stories of "welfare bums" taking outrageous advantage of the nation's tax-supported system of social assistance.

But the fact is that families forced to live on welfare payments exist on the hard edge of poverty. The public tends to generalize from the occasional spectacular welfare fraud.

For example:

A Toronto woman deliberately squandered an accident settlement of $28,000 so she could requalify for welfare. The authorities learned of her windfall, but the Social Assistance Review Board reinstated her to the welfare rolls anyway.

A Los Angeles woman became known as the "Queen of Welfare" by collecting $239,500 on behalf of a fictitious family of 70 children. She used eight false names before her deceit was discovered. Charged, she arrived at the courthouse for her trial in a Cadillac—when she didn't arrive in her Porsche or Mustang.

An Oshawa, Ont., woman was jailed for collecting more than $16,000 in mother's allowance for her children while living with a common-law husband who was supporting them all.

The real welfare story, however, is anything but exciting. While recipients may occasionally be better off than the "working poor," today's welfare family still has to struggle to maintain the semblance of a reasonable standard of living.

broken lives is immeasurable. In one typical year, 11,626 admissions to psychiatric institutions were alcohol related. And the problem is growing: the per capita annual intake of pure alcohol in Canada increased in a recent decade to 11.55, from 8.55 litres, a jump of 35 percent.

The first important step is to recognize and admit the problem, and be willing to correct it. In most cases, the person concerned is perfectly aware that he needs help, but is reluctant to admit it to himself or to anyone else. This is where the counselors at Alcoholics Anonymous are invaluable, because they have all trodden the alcoholic route before you. They'll help you make the right decision about your condition.

It's a common fallacy to think that alcoholism is mostly restricted to the poor or poorly educated. The pathetic "wino" tumbling off the park bench just happens to be highly visible. Abuse of liquor, and then addiction to it, is rife at all socio-economic levels, white-collar and blue-collar alike.

With all the strains and stresses of our competitive society, it's not at all uncommon for a person who has always lived a sensible, responsible existence to find himself, quite unexpectedly, dependent upon artificial stimulants. In the older age brackets, alcohol is the tempter. Even among the younger set, where misuse of drugs seemed a major menace in the Sixties, the ubiquitous bottle claims more addicts than it did in the past. What begins as a social habit can become a crutch and then lead to mental and physical breakdown. Evasion of responsibility, loss of employment and integrity—the downward path is well charted. Inevitably, it becomes a family trauma.

WIDOWS

Your common-law husband dies and you are unable to find a job. You wonder if you qualify for a "widow's pension."

You have full marital rights as far as social security is concerned, provided you lived as husband and wife and represented yourself as such for at least one year. (If either partner was still legally married to someone else, the qualifying term is three years.) You will have to make a sworn statement to this effect.

Your spouse was almost certainly a contributor to the Canada Pension Plan (CPP) which began paying out benefits in January 1967. As long as he contributed for at least one-third of the calendar years for which he was eligible, the full "survivor's" pension will be paid to a disabled spouse, a spouse with dependent children and a spouse aged 45 or over. A partial pension is paid to the spouse between 35 and 45.

When you reach 65 and qualify for the old-age pension, the CPP survivor's payment increases to 60 percent of the deceased contributor's retirement pension.

FAMILY ALLOWANCE

You want to adopt two young nephews orphaned in a family tragedy, but your take-home pay won't stretch to cover the extra expense.

You will earn not only the applause of the community but the right to claim an orphan's allowance.

These payments are administered by the Canada Pension Plan. If either of the deceased parents had made contributions (as is very likely), there will be a death benefit due, as well as survivors' benefits.

Since 1974, monthly allowances have been provided on behalf of a dependent child under 18 who is maintained in Canada by either a Canadian citizen or a landed immigrant. Payment is normally made to the mother. Adopted children become in every legal sense the dependents of the new parents.

Payments are revised upward each year in relation to the Consumer Price Index. Prince Edward Island, Quebec and Alberta set their own rates, but the end result is roughly the same. The provinces can't alter any special allowance granted by Ottawa.

There is no minimum period of residency required for benefits but claimants must be living in the province in which they apply.

Godsend or ghetto?

Government-owned housing is an attempt at making decent accommodation available to low-income families. Rent is tied to the tenant's income. The Winnipeg Regional Housing Authority's application form is typical of that used in many places.

The size of the family, its income and the quality of its current accommodation are major criteria with most housing authorities. Some, fearing that public housing projects might become "welfare ghettos," try for a mix of working families and families on welfare.

THE MANITOBA HOUSING AND RENEWAL CORPORATION

APPLICATION FORM FOR FAMILY DWELLING

1. Name of Family Head Roe (LAST NAME (Print)) Richard A. (FIRST NAME)
2. Address 100 Walnut St. Phone 200-1234
3. State in order of preference, the area of your choice:
   i .... ii ....
   iii .... iv ....
4. Do you require parking space? Yes ☐ No ☐
5. **Information concerning yourself and your family.**
   (a) (Write below your own name and income, and also the name(s) and income(s) of all persons who will be living with you. Do not include Family Allowance.)

	NAME	AGE	SEX M	SEX F	RELATIONSHIP	MONTHLY INCOME AMOUNT(S)
1.	Roe Richard	50	✓		HEAD	$550
2.	Roe Sally	47		✓	wife	—
3.	Roe Robert	20	✓		son	$480
4.	Roe Lesley	16		✓	daughter	—
5.	Roe Alice	12		✓	"	—
6.						
7.						
8.						
9.						

Is a baby expected? Yes ☐ No ☑ If Yes, when approximately? ....

Please read carefully: Details of income received by you and any member of the family living with you MUST be reported. Income from salaries, wages (per hour or per week), pensions, unemployment insurance, sick benefits, compensation, commissions, fees, agreements, part time work, etc., must be reported in full. DO NOT INCLUDE FAMILY ALLOWANCE.

(b) Monthly rental of your present premises is $ 300.00

(c) This rental fee includes HEAT: Yes ☑ No ☐ WATER: Yes ☑ No ☐
FRIDGE: Yes ☐ No ☑ RANGE: Yes ☐ No ☑ FURNITURE: Yes ☐ No ☑

6. **ASSETS**
   Cash on Hand and in Bank $ 500.00 Stocks — $ —
   Real Estate — $ — Other Assets — $ —
7. Name and Branch of your Bank Plant Credit Union
8. **CREDIT RATING**
   (a) PREVIOUS ADDRESS (Please begin with last) Name and Phone of Landlord
   i 100 Walnut St. from 1976 to 1979 Mr. Smith 100-1000
   ii 500 Pine Blvd from 1971 to 1976 Mrs. Jones 200-2000
   iii 200 Cedar Ave from 1960 to 1971 Mr. Black 300-3000
   (b) PRESENT FINANCIAL OBLIGATIONS (other than rent). To Whom (If to a Bank, please state branch)
   i/ Loan, Plant Credit Union $ 1,400.00
   ii/ .... $ ....
   iii/ .... $ ....
   (c) EMPLOYMENT (Present and Past)

NAME & ADDRESS OF EMPLOYER	EMPLOYED FROM	EMPLOYED TO	POSITION HELD	FOR REFERENCE CONTACT MR. OR MRS.	AT
XYZ Novelties Co. Ltd.	1960	1979	Driver	Mr. Snow	400-4000

FORM T-2

OFFICE USE ONLY

SIZE: 1 2 3 4 5

Applicant's No. ....

SA ☐ SS ☐ Mixed ☐
1 Parent ☐ 2 parent ☐

Income:	Month	Year
Head:		
Spouse		
Others under 25		
Others over 25		
Total M.I. Rental Calculation		

☐ Reg. mthly. ☐ Avge. mthly.

	Max. Points	Score
	30	
— 250	30	
— 300	25	
— 350	20	
— 400	15	
— 450	10	
— 500	5	
Rent: Shelter M. / Heat M. / Water M. / Hot Water M. / Total Per M.		
Ratio Inc. to Rent:	20	
+		
— 40%	20	
— 35	16	
— 30	16	
— 25	8	
— 20	4	
— 19	0	
Dependents:	15	
+ 5	15	
4	12	
3	9	
2	6	
1	3	
Dwelling:	25	
OR Quality of: Overcrowding	5	
Disrepair	4	
Inadequate kitchen	3	
Lack of private toilet	3	
Lack of shower or tub	3	
Lack of running water	3	
Inadequate heating	2	
Inadequate light	2	
OR Lack of: a/ Eviction	25	
or b/ Separated Locations	25	

9. **PRESENT LIVING ACCOMMODATIONS:**
   (a) Do you occupy a self contained unit, complete with kitchenette and bathroom? Yes ☑ No ☐
   (b) If you share living quarters with others, which of the following are shared?
   Bathroom ☐ — by how many people? ....
   Kitchen ☐ — by how many people? ....
   Fridge ☐ — by how many people? ....
   Living room ☐ — by how many people? ....
   (c) Is the building you are now occupying slated for demolition? Yes ☑ No ☐
   (d) What is the condition of your present living quarters? Very good ☐ Fair ☐ Poor ☑ Very Poor ☐
10. Give additional information, if necessary, which might help consideration of your application.
    Present accommodation has been allowed to deteriorate badly. We have not been able to find an alternative home in that price range.

OFFICE

Health Factors: ....
Broken Home
Physical or m
handicap
Residence in Ma
of less than six
TOTAL ....
Suitability: (A - E
State of Furnitu
Management of
Temperance ....
Home Atmosphe
Waiting Period: (1 Pt. a M. after on file) ....
Investigation Date
Per ....

APPLICATION FOR ACCOMMODATION

(Confidential)

I DECLARE THE ABOVE INFORMATION TO BE CORRECT

I understand that this application does not constitute an agreement on the part of the MANITOBA HOUSING AND RENEWAL CORPORATION or its agent to provide me with rental accommodation.

I acknowledge that this application becomes the property of the MANITOBA HOUSING AND RENEWAL CORPORATION upon delivery by me to it or its agent.

I further acknowledge the right of THE MANITOBA HOUSING AND RENEWAL CORPORATION or its agent at any time prior to the execution and delivery to me of a lease hereby applied for, to withdraw, revoke or cancel, without penalty or liability for damages or otherwise, any acceptance or approval of this application previously made or given.

I HEREBY AUTHORIZE YOU TO CONDUCT A PERSONAL INVESTIGATION.

I declare the information contained herein to be correct.

DATED at Winnipeg, Man., this 7th day of September 1979.

Richard A. Roe
APPLICANT'S SIGNATURE

Please return to:
THE WINNIPEG REGIONAL HOUSING AUTHORITY
410 - 352 DONALD STREET,
WINNIPEG, MANITOBA, R3B 2H8
PHONE 943-0861

DESERTED MOTHERS

Your mother was supporting you and your two small children, but she died recently and you don't know where to turn. Your husband cannot be located.

As a single parent caring for children, you probably qualify for the mother's allowance.

Those eligible are: a woman who is widowed, divorced or has been deserted by her husband for at least three months; a mother (16 or older) who is unwed and whose child is at least three months old; a woman whose husband has at least six months of a prison term to serve, or to spend in a psychiatric ward, or who is in a nursing home or home for the aged.

A mother is said to be deserted when she is no longer living with her husband because he has physically or mentally abused her and refused to provide enough money to buy food and necessaries when he was able to do so.

A woman who leaves her husband for those same reasons will be considered for family benefits, provided she has begun legal action to obtain financial support from her spouse.

If your mother was receiving payments under the Canada (or Quebec) Pension Plan, there may be grounds for an application for help under the plan.

You should also apply for provincial social assistance. Temporary welfare is normally handled at the municipal level, but yours is a long-term need. However, emergency interim assistance might be arranged with municipal officials if you need immediate help.

DAY-CARE CENTERS

Your married sister cares for your child so that you can work. Now she is moving and you can't afford a housekeeper.

There are day-care centers available in most districts, some of them supported by public funds for mothers who can't afford to pay the fee. Where a fee is charged, it's usually low enough so that the average working person can afford it. In a day-care home, the children of up to three families are given care during the day in a private house or apartment, usually by a mother with small children of her own. The parent is responsible for transporting the child to and from the home.

The licensing and supervision of day-care facilities vary widely across the country. Your community services bureau or the provincial departments of health and welfare will provide addresses and guidance. If centers are not licensed, the responsibility for selecting a suitable place rests on your own shoulders.

A mother's absence from the home because of illness, or in other emergency, can create a crisis when there is no one readily available to care for young children. In these cases, the social service agencies may provide a visiting homemaker or nurse right in your own home. An elderly, disabled or handicapped person may also obtain this kind of help at home.

Those who are able to pay for this service are naturally expected to do so, but for those on the poverty line, all or part of the cost may be met by the municipal government. A person considered to be "in need" is one whose income is less than the amount the municipality deems to be necessary to meet the everyday needs of that person. There's no hard-and-fast rule. The municipality may employ its own nurses or homemakers, or purchase such services from individuals, private non-profit groups or other organizations.

GUARANTEED SUPPLEMENT

You admire your elderly neighbor who insists on taking care of himself. But you know he's only got the old-age pension—and a bad heart.

The Good Samaritan could quietly discuss the circumstances with the nearest social services agency, if the gentleman is too proud to ask for help. One of the most important of the federally administered benefit programs is the Guaranteed Income Supplement (GIS). It's an addition to the Old Age Security pension

(OAS) of a person who has no other income, or only a very limited one.

Entitlement depends upon the income received in the preceding calendar year, and a fresh application for the supplement must be made each year. If it's learned, after submitting the application, that income for the previous year was different from that reported, the OAS office must be informed without delay. It should also be told of any change in marital status, or address. A special postcard is available for this purpose at any post office, and it can be mailed free.

If a single person had no income the previous year other than the OAS pension, the application for the supplement should indicate "nil" income. For a married couple in the same circumstances, the form should state that both had "nil" income. These points can all have a bearing on the amount of supplement that will be forthcoming.

For GIS entitlement, an applicant will be treated as a single person if he or she has been separated for at least one year from the spouse. The same applies if, through circumstances beyond their control, spouses are unable to live in the same dwelling and that arrangement will continue for some time, or indefinitely. This situation can arise when one or the other is in a nursing home.

Proof of marriage may be required. Send in the marriage certificate; if it's been mislaid over the years, a copy can be obtained from the Registrar of Vital Statistics in the capital city of the province where the ceremony took place. Those married outside Canada will be given an address to contact by the provincial OAS office.

DISABILITIES

Your father's vision is almost totally gone, but the medical authorities say he is a borderline case. He is refused a disability pension.

A person's need is the criterion for a pension, not his vision difficulty. No blind millionaires need apply.

If your father is in need, he will receive the pension if he is certified as legally blind by the pension board's medical advisers, or is registered with the Canadian National Institute for the Blind.

A person is legally blind when sight in either eye cannot be so corrected that he is able to see at least as much at six metres as a person with normal vision can see at 60. Severely restricted peripheral vision also constitutes legal blindness.

Anyone who suffers a permanent mental or physical handicap that prevents or severely impedes normal daily functioning is eligible for a disability pension.

Blindness and disability pensions are covered under separate federal laws, but the provinces administer both programs under the Canada Assistance Plan. Ottawa pays 75 percent of the pension for the blind and 50 percent of that for the disabled.

Appeal procedures from welfare decisions vary widely. The Department of Health in your provincial capital (or in Ottawa) will put you on the right track. If the appeal goes against you and you're still not content, remember that ombudsmen exist to examine complaints against the bureaucrats. (*See* Chapter 1, "Civil rights.")

Helping the handicapped. The Canadian National Institute for the Blind (CNIB) is a world leader in care and training for the blind. The organization has 46 offices and is financed by municipal grants and through private donations and legacies. It provides instruction in Braille reading and writing and rehabilitation training to enable the blind to become wholly or partly self-supporting. Selections from its large libraries of Braille and "talking" (recorded) books are carried free in the mails.

The Canadian Council of the Blind (CCB) complements the work of the CNIB by forming clubs of 10 or more blind persons. It cooperates with the CNIB in recreation programs, employment services, research and White Cane Week. The CCB was founded in 1944. Its national office is in London, Ont.

There are also many public and private programs designed to assist physically or mentally handicapped individuals become employable. Governments will pay costs of education or training and there are on-the-job training schemes where governments subsidize wages.

Early retirement. If you become unable to work, you'll be eligible for a disability pension under the Canada Pension Plan, provided you have made contributions for five of the last 10 years. Dependent children also receive benefits, at the same rate as orphans. You may also qualify for family benefits under the Canada Assistance Plan.

In professions and businesses that provide a contributory pension scheme, there's usually the choice of early retirement on medical grounds. You will probably have to accept the penalty of a lower pension; these schemes are usually based on life-insurance principles. Depending on the employer, you may be able to work out a solution under which you could work part-time, if long hours or standing aggravate your condition.

Seek a medical certificate from your doctor. If he states that you are not capable of carrying out your present duties and recommends early retirement, it will be up to your employer and the pension company to decide the best course of action.

VETERANS

Your uncle, who was wounded in World War II, is almost an invalid at age 59. He is unable to support his dependents or pay for the specialized care he needs.

He is entitled to the full support of the federal Department of Veterans' Affairs, including specialized hospitals and medical treatment, augmented pension and special housing assistance.

Four agencies—the Canada Pensions Commission, the Pension Review Board, the War Veterans' Allowance Board and the Bureau of Pensions Advocates—are responsible for the men and women who served in Canada's wartime armed forces.

Pensions can be paid for disability or death resulting from injury attributable to service with the armed forces in war or peace, to the eligible dependents of service personnel and to surviving dependents of a deceased pensioner. They are indexed to the cost of living.

Compensation for POWs. A veteran who was a prisoner of the Japanese for one year or more is entitled to a pension at the 50 percent disability rate. For imprisonment of 3 to 12 months, the pension is at the 20 percent disability level. Those taken prisoner by other enemy states are eligible for pensions from the 10 to 20 percent disability level, depending on the length of time they were in captivity behind the wire.

The total range of social, medical and financial assistance available to veterans—apart from disability pensions—is too long to list here. Under the War Veterans' Allowance Act, payments can be made for just about any proven need.

About 91,000 Canadians—veterans, their widows and orphans—were receiving veterans' allowances in 1979. So, too, were some 4,500 civilians who served in close support of the armed forces. Eligibility is reviewed by 19 regional offices. Extra payments are made from a special fund when the total income of a recipient is lower than the permitted maximum.

46 Doctors and dentists

The concept of "the doctor" as a kindly healer-sage, fashioned from a superior mold, still lingers. The sharp edge of consumer criticism that carves up politician and lawyer, tycoon and tradesman hesitates to stab the man or woman in spotless white who stands between us and eternity when we are ill.

In esteem polls, the doctor is sure to come out on top. One reason is the mystery that enshrouds his profession. The doctor works within a discipline that remains closed to the average person. Often he speaks and writes in a language that, to many patients, might as well be Kurdish or Xhosa: to the doctor, baldness is alopecia, hay fever is rhinitis, and a birthmark is a hemangioma. The obscurity of the prescribing physician's handwriting is legendary.

Since its misty origins under Hippocrates in ancient Greece, the medical profession has remained largely self-regulatory in virtually every society. The Royal College of Physicians was chartered in England by Henry VIII in 1518. In Canada, in 1788, Drs. Charles Blake and James Fisher of Montreal established regulations to safeguard the community from "inexperienced and illiterate men practicing the art of physic and surgery." And in 1867 the Canadian Medical Association (CMA) was founded from earlier associations of doctors in Montreal and Toronto. Its first president, Sir Charles Tupper, M.D., a Father of Confederation from Nova Scotia, said its primary purpose was "to protect the health and the lives of the people from the unskilled treatment of incompetent men, and to provide for the qualification of the members of a profession so important as our own." Without shucking that assessment of self-importance, the CMA still does that job well today. Through its provincial affiliates, it speaks with one voice for all doctors.

Similarly, the Royal College of Physicians and Surgeons of Canada and the Royal College of Dentists of Canada control the licensing of all practitioners through affiliates in each province.

By their own code of ethics doctors are cast as dedicated servants of the public. They are also the delivery personnel in the nationwide health service that guarantees all Canadians whatever medical care they require—need being the only criterion for treatment.

There's clear evidence, however, that many doctors are chafing in their chains. Feeling pressed by red tape and inflation, some have withdrawn from the provincial health-insurance plans. Another sign of a rift in the love affair between the Canadian people and their doctors is the rising number of lawsuits by patients. "There is a trend to question the judgment of all professionals," says Dr. Norman Brown of the Canadian Medical Protective Association. This nonprofit organization, which insures more than 32,000 doctors against claims, reported 323 malpractice suits in 1978, a jump of nearly 100 percent over a five-year period. The box score in these battles has not, however, changed for many years. It is, roughly, doctors, 60; patients, 40.

HOUSE CALLS

Your frail, elderly father is ill in midwinter but the doctor refuses to make a house call.

Although Medicare plans provide treatment for all Canadians on the basis of need alone, there's no law requiring a doctor to make house calls. Today's doctor is probably as principled and idealistic as his predecessors—and no doubt more skilled—but the notion of the family physician turning out at all hours and in all weathers is fast slipping into folklore.

Some general practitioners (G.P.'s) still make selected house calls, but the decision will depend on several factors—the urgency of the problem; how recently he saw the patient; where the doctor is when he receives the call. He may be doing hospital rounds, or in obstetrics preparing to deliver a baby. His waiting room may be filled with patients, all of whom claim his time and attention. His car may be snowed in. Or, if he risks driving on icy roads, he may be immobilized for hours, unable to help others needing his services.

Getting to the hospital. Obviously very few doctors can, or will, drop everything else and rush to your father's bedside. Often this is simply not the most beneficial action for the patient.

Heart attacks are a frequent cause of emergency calls to the doctor. Time can be vital, and the sensible course is to get the patient to the nearest hospital by private car, taxi or ambulance. The outpatient department is open 24 hours a day and there are qualified personnel to handle emergencies.

In any medical emergency, ambulance service is available—even by air in some instances. There's an ambulance telephone number on the inside cover of some telephone directories. Usually, it's a free call (Zenith exchange). Where the number isn't listed on the "HELP" page of the phone book, subscribers are advised to write the ambulance number in an allotted space. Ambulance personnel have first-aid training and some of them have become, by experience, very skilled in life-and-death situations.

Provincial health plans vary when it comes to payment of ambulance charges. You may have to pay part of the service charge, with your plan picking up the larger part.

It is thoughtless and selfish to call an ambulance except in serious situations. The vehicle and its staff could be drawn away from a real emergency—say, a traffic accident—where minutes count. You can expect to pay a sizable charge if you demand ambulance service in trivial cases. If you haven't your own car, a neighbor will almost certainly be willing to make a run to the hospital.

APPOINTMENT GRIEVANCES

You had a 10 a.m. appointment at the doctor's office. Apparently, so had a dozen others. At noon, you're still waiting.

Cooling one's heels in the waiting room is the most common complaint received by the Canadian Medical Association. This grievance far outnumbers complaints of unsatisfactory treatment, poor facilities, and callous or discourteous staff.

Delays usually occur because of "block booking." Doctors soon learn how many patients they can normally see during office hours. Appointments are scheduled to allow perhaps 10 minutes of the doctor's time per patient, for a flow of six patients an hour. But should the first two patients occupy the doctor for 20 minutes each, or longer, the whole day's bookings go haywire.

Most of us feel slighted if hustled through a consultation, and just as offended if forced to wait while the doctor takes his own good time with the patients ahead. But sometimes, there's more than slight involved: there can be monetary loss to the patient—and the patient's employer—when hours that should be spent in productive work are wasted in a doctor's waiting room.

Mother comes first. Many things can throw a doctor's appointment schedule out of kilter. En route to their offices, doctors get caught in the traffic or suffer flats like the rest of us. A doctor with a large obstetrical practice will frequently be detained by a patient in labor. The mother-to-be gets top priority but the new citizen is often unpunctual. When delay appears inevitable, conscientious doctors notify their offices. Patients who can't wait are given other appointments; those who have not yet arrived are advised of the delay.

When you wait too long too often, you may be right in suspecting that your doctor overbooks and that he's fattening his bank account at the expense of your convenience and of the health plan, which pays on a per-patient basis. If you are right, you can take your business elsewhere or complain to the head office of

549

your provincial health-insurance plan—as well as to the secretary of your provincial medical association. The provincial officials keep watch on the number of payments to individual doctors and, if the tally veers greatly from the norm, they investigate.

THE RIGHT TO KNOW

The doctor tells your mother she has a terminal illness. You think he is callous.

Much is said these days about "the right to know." But when the news is bad, some people still think that ignorance is bliss.

A generation ago, many doctors sincerely believed that they should, in terminal cases, withhold their diagnosis from the patient. The sad news was usually broken to a near relative.

Today, the attitude is that most patients should be told the truth, so that they can plan accordingly. If the prognosis is poor, a patient may want to make or update a will, or to make specific plans for his final days.

In spite of this contemporary attitude, there are still more complaints about doctors' secretiveness than about their frankness. On hospital rounds, residents and interns sometimes discuss a patient's condition as though he were merely a numbered exhibit. They use terms baffling to the patient—who often frets that things are worse than they really are. Should this happen to you, ask your doctor politely but firmly to explain everything in everyday language.

The unexpected recovery. The more experience a doctor has, the less likely he is to deliver Olympian judgments. Every doctor knows that the worst of cases can inexplicably recover. The veteran quickly admits that the will to live works wonders where all the science of modern medicine fails. This is one reason why the doctor is sometimes unwilling to make a black-and-white prognostication.

In your mother's case, she may have demanded that she be told her true condition—then collapsed or became hysterical when she learned she had a terminal illness.

Some patients, having received the bad news, ask the doctor not to tell the family. Yet, if kept in the dark, most family members will be incensed.

The right to die peacefully. Every doctor is bound to save life and ease suffering. But in terminal cases, a moment may come when treatment only adds to the patient's burden. (*See* Chapter 47, "Hospitals and nursing homes.") This has given rise in recent times to the "living will"—written instructions that no artificial life-support systems should be used if you fall victim to a severe stroke or similar condition, or suffer a terminal illness. The "living will" is prepared while one has full possession of one's faculties. Copies of the will should be given to the doctor and family members.

A SECOND OPINION

Your doctor objects when you request a second opinion before undergoing radical treatment.

The code of the Canadian Medical Association states that if a patient insists upon a second opinion, it must not be denied. And, except in a crisis, surgery cannot be performed without the signed consent of the patient—or, in cases of incapacity, by the next of kin or legal guardian. There can be several reasons, however, why your doctor feels that further consultation is pointless. He will most likely have discussed your case with colleagues, including a specialist, before proposing radical therapy. There could be a time factor. Delay might add to your risk.

Furthermore, doctors are taxpayers, too, and are keenly aware of the zooming expense of patient care. Prodded by the hospital bureaucracy, they are unlikely to encourage longer occupation of high-cost "active" beds than is strictly necessary. Under present financing, administrators are struggling to maintain a ratio of 3.5 active-treatment beds per 1,000 population. (Tough on the patient who gets that half bed!)

Normally, when a patient facing surgery or other radical treatment requests a second opinion, the attending doctor will react sym-

Cause not reasonable

Background

Before 1976, the College of Physicians and Surgeons of British Columbia refused permanent licenses to non-Canadian citizens until such doctors had spent at least three years practicing medicine in remote areas of the province.

No such restrictions applied to Canadian citizens.

As a result, a non-Canadian doctor who wished to practice in British Columbia, and who had qualifications and experience identical to those of a Canadian, was treated differently in two respects:

■ The Canadian could receive permanent registration from the college; the non-Canadian could not.

■ The Canadian could practice anywhere in the province; the non-Canadian was restricted to certain areas.

The College of Physicians and Surgeons had implemented the policy, however, to meet the acute need for qualified doctors in the interior of the province and felt that this situation constituted "reasonable cause." (The B.C. Human Rights Code prohibits discrimination "without reasonable cause.") The matter was referred to the Human Rights Commission and in 1976 the Minister of Labour appointed a board of inquiry.

Judgment

Although it acted with a "high public purpose" and administered the policy with "tact and sensitivity," the college was still guilty of discrimination, inquiry chairman Leon Getz ruled on May 27, 1976.

Neither noble intentions, nor even the provision of medical services for British Columbians who might not otherwise receive them, justified discrimination on the basis of citizenship or nationality, said Getz.

pathetically. The second opinion can be valuable to him, too. Not only is it another expert opinion that will assist his judgment, but also it gives him extra protection against the bogey of the medical profession—a malpractice suit.

THE 'OPTED-OUT' DOCTOR

Your doctor informs you he has withdrawn from Medicare. He's the only general practitioner in town.

If you want his professional services, they're still available to you. Your provincial health plan will pay the same fee on your behalf as if the doctor had remained with the provincial plan. (Quebec is an exception: some of that province's doctors have withdrawn totally from Medicare. These must tell you in advance that you cannot be reimbursed by the provincial plan.) There are, however, two important differences when dealing with doctors who have partially "opted out" of Medicare. First, the doctor will charge or bill you directly and provide you with a receipt which you must then send to the Medicare office for a refund. Second, his fee will be about 30 percent more than the sum allowed under the plan. You will not be reimbursed for this portion of the bill. The doctor doesn't *have* to inform you that he has "opted out." It's up to you to ask. But you have the right to know in advance if the fee will be above the health-plan rate.

Many physicians and surgeons withdrew from the government-supported health plans in the 1970s. To many, this was the beginning of the end of equal care for all.

The doctors' Bill of Rights. In 1979, the Canadian Medical Association (CMA) appointed a committee to study the Canadian Bill of Rights and to recommend how doctors could be protected against "arbitrary government actions affecting their civil and professional rights." Dr. Peter Banks of Victoria, B.C., who headed the committee, stated: "The more governments legislate rights, the more they confiscate freedoms." Said Banks: "Doctors' rights should include the right to practice where they wish, to decide how they practice

and how they are paid, and the right to be free from 'bureaucratic harassment.' "

The opposite case is that since the education and training of doctors costs the Canadian public a substantial sum, doctors may be greedy in demanding a larger slice of the pie. Arguments that doctors should be grateful for the opportunity to serve their fellowman cut no more ice with doctors, however, than with schoolteachers, policemen or auto workers.

The Medicare plans vary in what they require of doctors. In Ontario, a participating doctor must offer the provincially insured services to all his patients. In Nova Scotia and Saskatchewan, doctors can bill the plan for services to some patients while demanding direct fees from others. The latter will be partially reimbursed by Medicare—the portion being equal to the health plan's fee schedule for the services provided.

Do doctors make too much? A 1978 study of 600 Ontario doctors by researchers from the University of Toronto indicated that general practitioners (G.P.'s) who had withdrawn from the plan had less take-home pay than those who elected to remain in it. The average "opted-out" G.P. was earning $47,000 (a net of $23,000 after expenses) while those still billing the plan directly averaged a $62,000 gross (net $39,000). The researchers also found that the average Ontario doctor, in or out of the provincial plan, specialist and G.P. alike, worked 47.8 hours a week, grossing $67,937 for a net income (before taxes) of $46,066.

In Manitoba, the Health Services Commission reported in 1978 that the gross average income of doctors in that province was $60,440, up nearly 8 percent from the previous year. At the top of the money pile were nine thoracic and vascular surgeons who averaged $105,230.

Administrators of the government health plans keep close tabs on the high rollers and lay charges against the few doctors who mulct the fund. An Ottawa doctor got 90 days in jail and a $25,000 fine for defrauding the Ontario Health Insurance Plan (OHIP). He gave acupuncture treatments for obesity and smoking addiction and billed OHIP. The Chinese needle therapy was not an accepted treatment under the provincial plan.

During a seven-year period, OHIP investigated 600 doctors involved in billing disputes, and recovered money from 200.

PROFESSIONAL MISCONDUCT

Your young daughter says that she was sexually assaulted during an examination at the doctor's office.

This is a serious charge at any time, but particularly in the confines of a doctor's office. Even when a patient must submit to intimate examination, she has the right to privacy and protection. If your daughter's allegation is borne out by early independent medical examination and other supporting evidence, it can mean the end of the doctor's career.

But if you or your adult (18 or over) daughter decide to lay information with the police under the Criminal Code (*see* Chapter 4, "You, the defendant"), see a lawyer before proceeding. There could also be avenues to sue for damages in the civil courts.

The Canadian Medical Association (CMA) advises its members never to examine a female patient without a nurse being present. Many patients, however, object to this precaution. They don't want to appear undressed or to discuss certain problems before a third party. In such cases, the CMA recommends that the nurse stay in an adjoining room and that the examination room door be kept ajar.

Sexual arousal. One walks on eggs in discussing the relationship between female patients and male doctors. There have been instances where young girls and sexually repressed or prudish women thought "something funny" was going on while they were undergoing quite routine pelvic examinations. Such misinterpretations are not uncommon.

Dentists are also vulnerable to such charges. Patients who are given nitrous oxide ("laughing gas") may have erotic dreams as the anesthetic wears off. The female patient may be quite convinced she was assaulted while helpless.

No laughing matter. When a syndicated medical columnist wrote somewhat lightheartedly about sex in the doctor's office ("It takes two to tango," he quipped), his mailbag bulged with letters from angry readers. A Quebec mother, who said her daughter had been raped by a physician, accused the medical bureaucracy of sweeping her charges under the rug. A Winnipeg woman wrote: "Maybe you meant it as a joke, but it wasn't funny. M.D.'s can be crazy fools and they should be exposed." Several readers complained of being kept undressed during long conversations, of kisses on the cheek and "pats on the fanny."

Short of actual intercourse, however, it can be difficult for a woman to prove sexual assault or harassment in the doctor's office. But if you've got the facts straight, the law and the rules of the medical profession are on your side. In 1978, an Ontario doctor who engaged in "acts of sexual impropriety" with a woman patient was suspended from practice for eight months.

MIRACLE CASES

You read in a newspaper about a new treatment for your illness. Your physician says it is unproven and he won't try it.

It won't be the first time your doctor has run into this problem. A well-publicized example is the controversy over laetrile, a cyanide treatment for cancer which is not acceptable to Canadian medical authorities. (*See* "Laetrile" in Chapter 18.)

But there's no law preventing you from seeking any treatment, however dangerous and bizarre. And if you're still adamant about trying some treatment after the doctor explains the possible dangers, he'll likely suggest you see another physician. If he has your welfare at heart, however, he is unlikely to refer you to a doctor who uses an unproven treatment.

The Quebec Professions Tribunal recently decertified for life a doctor who treated a breast-cancer patient with honey, beet juice and clay.

New faces for old. Medicine has made astonishing progress since the days when just about all sick persons were bled to release evil "humors" from the bloodstream. When George Washington was on his deathbed in 1799 at the age of 67, suffering from what we know today as streptococcic laryngitis, his doctors bled him, gave him a potion of molasses, vinegar and butter, applied "a blister of Spanish flies" to his throat, gave him both an emetic and a laxative and applied hot wheat bran to his feet.

Cosmetic surgery is among areas of medicine where tremendous advances have occurred in the last 40 years. It's as easy to get a new nose today as it is to have your appendix removed. But you'll have to stand in line for an appointment with one of the dozen or so Canadians who specialize in plastic surgery.

And you'll need your cheque-book. None of our provincial health plans pay for cosmetic surgery unless it is ruled essential for the full recovery of a patient, as in the case of someone disfigured in an accident or fire.

SPECIALIST REFERRALS

Your family doctor says the Pap test you request must be done by a specialist. You think this is a blatant kickback deal.

Any trafficking in patients for financial gain is forbidden by the ruling bodies of the medical profession.

Most general practitioners (G.P.'s) will do a Papanicolaou ("Pap" for short) test but a few will not. If yours is one of the few, and you are so concerned about the cost to your provincial health plan that you feel like complaining, ask him to arrange for another G.P.—rather than a specialist—to do the test.

Health authorities recommend that every woman have a Pap test as part of her routine medical checkup. This simple procedure can detect cancer cells in the cervix (the entry to the uterus, or womb) before symptoms develop. It's only one of several simple tests developed by cancer research.

The referral system. Each of some 40,000 working physicians in Canada is qualified to diagnose and treat most adult illnesses and to perform certain surgery. Many deliver babies, set broken bones and treat infants and small children. The conscientious family doctor will frequently recommend that a patient see an expert more qualified than he in the diagnosis and treatment of the problem at hand.

Some doctors specialize in operations of incredible delicacy: in 1979, Siamese twins joined at the top of the skull were successfully separated. Doctors qualified in other major specialties include:

Anesthesiologist, who administers anesthetics in surgery.

Gynecologist, who treats special problems of women.

Pediatrician, for children to about age 12.

Gastroenterologist, for disorders of stomach and intestines.

Obstetrician, for care of the pregnant woman and delivery of babies. Many obstetricians are also gynecologists.

Orthopedist, for diseases and injuries of the bones and joints.

Allergist, for asthma, hay fever and other allergies.

Ophthalmologist, for surgery and other treatments of the eye. (Optometrists and opticians are not medical doctors.)

Urologist, for the kidneys and male genital organs.

Radiologist, for taking and interpreting X-rays.

Psychiatrist, for emotional disturbances and mental illness. The psychiatrist is sometimes also a *neurologist*, or nerve specialist.

The services of all of these, and other specialists, are available to you by right through your provincial health-insurance plan. Under the federal Medical Care Act, there can be no dollar limit or exclusion unless the service is not medically required.

Specialists usually accept patients only on referral from another doctor and most specialists are so busy that kickback allegations are generally foolish. When you seek an appointment, you'll discover the truth of this.

But, if you have good cause to suspect a

Guidelines for doctors

Medicine, like most professions, is basically self-regulated. Canadian doctors practice within these detailed guidelines issued by their national organization, the Canadian Medical Association, founded in Confederation year, 1867.

RESPONSIBILITIES TO THE PATIENT

An Ethical Physician:

Standard of care

1 will practise the art and science of medicine to the best of his ability;

2 will continue his education to improve his standard of medical care;

Respect for patient

3 will ensure that his conduct in the practise of his profession is above reproach, and that he will take neither physical, emotional nor financial advantage of his patient;

Patient's rights

4 will recognize his limitations and, when indicated, recommend to the patient that additional opinions and services be obtained;

5 will recognize that the patient has the right to accept or reject any physician and any medical care recommended to him. The patient, having chosen his physician, has the right to request of that physician opinions from other physicians of the patient's choice;

6 will keep in confidence information derived from his patient, or from a colleague, regarding a patient and divulge it only with the permission of the patient except when the law requires him to do so;

7 when acting on behalf of a third party will assure himself that the patient understands the physician's legal responsibility to the third party before proceeding with the examination;

8 will recommend only those diagnostic procedures which he believes necessary to assist him in the care of the patient, and therapy which he believes necessary for the well-being of the patient. He will recognize his responsibility in advising the patient of his findings and recommendations;

9 will on the patient's request, assist him by supplying the information required to enable the patient to receive any benefits to which the patient may be entitled;

10 will be considerate of the anxiety of the patient's next-of-kin and co-operate with him in the patient's interest;

Choice of patient

11 will recognize that he has a responsibility to render medical service to any person regardless of colour, religion or political belief;

12 shall, except in an emergency, have the right to refuse to accept a patient;

13 will render all assistance in his power to any patient, where an urgent need for medical care exists;

14 will, when the patient is unable, and an agent unavailable, to give consent, render such therapy as he believes to be in the patient's interest;

Continuity of care

15 will, when he has accepted professional responsibility for an acutely ill patient, continue to provide his services until they are no longer required, or until he has arranged for the services of another suitable physician. In any other situation, he may withdraw from his responsibility for the care of any patient provided that he gives the patient adequate notice of his intention;

Personal morality

16 when his morality or religious conscience alone prevents him from recommending some form of therapy will so acquaint the patient.

Clinical research

17 will, before initiating any clinical research involving human beings, ensure that such clinical research is appraised scientifically and ethically, and approved by a responsible committee, and is sufficiently planned and supervised that the individuals are unlikely to suffer any harm. He will ascertain that the previous research and the purpose of the experiment justify this additional method of investigation. Before proceeding he will obtain the consent of those individuals or their agents, and will do so only after explaining the purpose of the clinical research and any possible health hazard which he can foresee;

The dying patient

18 will allow death to occur with dignity and comfort when death of the body appears to be inevitable;

19 may support the body when clinical death of the brain has occurred, but need not prolong life by unusual or heroic means;

Transplantation

20 may, when death of the brain has occurred, support cellular life in the body when some parts of the body might be used to prolong or improve the health of others;

21 will recognize his responsibility to a donor of organs to be transplanted and will give to the donor or his relatives full disclosure of his intent and the purpose of the procedure; in the case of a living donor, he will also explain the risks of the procedure;

22 will refrain from determining the time of death of the donor patient when he will be a participant in the performance of the transplant procedure or when his association with any proposed recipient might influence his judgement;

23 who determined the time of death of the donor may, subsequent to the transplant procedure, treat the recipient;

Fees to patients

24 In determining his fee to the patient, will consider his personal service and the patient's ability to pay and will be prepared to discuss his fee with his patient.

kickback, complain in writing to your provincial College of Physicians and Surgeons or get in touch with your provincial or federal ministries of health and welfare. Any solid evidence of fee-splitting will cause an immediate investigation.

COMMITTAL

Your husband has been behaving strangely for years and your doctor wants him committed to a mental institution.

Human rights campaigns on behalf of the mentally ill have sparked many revolutionary changes. In some provinces, change is already in effect; other provinces are still moving cautiously. These rights are increasingly held to prevail—even if the person in question has no coherent idea of what they are—and are placed above the concerns, feelings, convenience or troubles of all others involved in the situation.

The changes are basic. Except under the ruling of a judge, the "committing" of a person to a mental institution is a dead letter. No doctor can "commit" anyone, no matter how disturbed the person may be.

The concept of the competency, or mental judgment, of the sick person is also changing. Landmark laws restrict assessments of competency to the areas of financial judgment alone. For someone to be "ruled incompetent" is now a complex procedure; it can only be achieved within strict guidelines.

But because of such legislation, the position of the anguished wife in our example is an unenviable one. She's faced with the task of gaining her husband's agreement by signature to seek psychiatric treatment voluntarily, or standing by while the law takes its course. In many cases, the problem is being left squarely in her lap.

The question of danger. The doctor faces equally unpalatable alternatives. In the first instance, no independent action can be taken simply because of the patient's strange or uncooperative attitude. No matter how convinced the doctor may be that a patient is mentally ill or senile, he cannot put any forcible procedures in motion unless there is the element of present and immediate physical danger.

The danger must exist in relation to the patient himself or to another person or persons. Distressing actions such as incontinency, throwing of food, refusal to dress, or breaking of crockery, are not thought to contain the requisite element of danger. It could, however, be present in a refusal to eat, or move, or talk. Family physicians, psychologists and psychiatrists across the country are currently in a polite uproar as these situations are argued and tested.

The doctor must also face his duty to act for the welfare of the patient, regardless of other factors, if convinced that the element of immediate danger is present. This obligation exists even if the next of kin are aghast at the idea. The sequence of events in such cases is usually as follows:

The general practitioner would almost certainly refer the patient to a psychiatrist. What happens if he refuses to go? The next move would be to check the availability of a bed in the psychiatric unit of a chosen hospital. (Canada has 148 of these units and they're often filled to capacity.) After this, an ambulance is dispatched for the patient. In the worst situation, if anyone at the address offers violence, the police are called in. Great care and much thought precede these events, for the doctor is always open to the possibility of a malpractice suit and he will only act when the evidence is almost overwhelming.

At the hospital, the patient can be held for a fixed period only—about 120 hours. His condition would be assessed by a psychiatrist. The specialist can either discharge the patient, or fill in another form under which the patient can be held for 14 days. At the end of that time, his condition is reviewed and, perhaps, another certificate issued that would be valid for a further period.

A perpetual review. In Ontario, the Mental Health Act goes no further toward "committal." The patient may appear to be almost hopelessly insane, and can be transferred to one of the province's 42 public mental hospitals, but, by law, the case must be reviewed continually. The patient must be released as quickly as possible.

Things are different when the judiciary steps in. When a crime is committed, and prosecution ensues, the presiding judge can order psychiatric treatment or imprisonment (and care) in one of the several hospitals for the criminally insane. A person so imprisoned remains confined until considered cured, or at least fit to face the court. Judges usually take this step only after hearing extensive medical opinion.

Most patients in our mental institutions are voluntary inmates. Many who are compelled to enter later switch to voluntary, or "informal," status. The attending psychiatrist has the power to issue a certificate validating that change. Unless rated dangerous by psychiatric evaluation, the inmate can insist on being released, even though the hospital staff may not think he is ready.

Treatment in a psychiatric facility today can be very effective. A high percentage of patients are discharged after a relatively short time.

Before you 'open wide'

Before your dentist begins to treat you, he wants to acquaint himself with your medical history.

The use of anesthetics for extractions or other dental surgery can depend on your general state of health, and on any drugs you may be taking for other problems. And your dentist likes to know the name of your physician, in case a consultation is indicated at some point.

Dentists are aware of radiation dangers. That's why they ask when your mouth was last X-rayed. Many use a questionnaire similar to this one.

THE MALPRACTICE SUIT

Your hyperactive son was put on tranquilizers and now he doesn't seem able to get along without them. You are determined to sue the doctor for letting him get hooked.

Civil action for damages against a doctor or other professional is usually termed a malpractice suit. Your case would rest on whether you could prove that the doctor, who purports to have special knowledge, failed to utilize that knowledge in a reasonable and responsible manner.

Malpractice suits are common in the United States, where legal procedure and tradition differ from Canada. Such suits in this country, however, are on the increase. (*See* the introduction to this chapter, and Chapter 3, "You, the plaintiff.")

The condition called hyperactivity can have many facets. It can have its origin in a dietary problem, for instance. It ranges from the child who can't sit still in school, and so disturbs the rest of the class, to the uncontrollable child. Most doctors are loath to prescribe tranquilizers (barbiturates) for children and are likely to do so only in serious cases. They are well aware of the danger of addiction to such a drug. Usually, after a course of this medication, they prescribe other drugs that desensitize the patient through a controlled procedure.

A doctor who prescribes mood-altering drugs for a child should advise the parents, and record his action. He should never supply the drug longer than is absolutely necessary.

VENEREAL DISEASE

Your doctor treats you for a venereal disease, and shortly afterward you are laid off your grocery store job. You suspect there's a connection.

Canadian physicians are required by law to report all cases of venereal disease (VD) to a public-health officer. These officials will try to track down any sexual contacts named by the patient and suggest that those persons submit to a medical test and accept treatment if necessary. The delicate task of dealing with sexual contacts is undertaken by specially trained health workers and there is little chance of an information leak. If there *were* a leak, and you were fired because of it, you could sue for wrongful dismissal. The fact that you are a food-handler is immaterial because VD is transmitted by sexual contact only.

The hidden scourge. Although both gonorrhea and syphilis—the major venereal diseases—can now usually be cured or controlled by antibiotics, the number of reported cases has not decreased significantly in Canada. In a recent year, the total was 56,344—but health authorities estimate that the true incidence is three or four times greater.

The recorded figures for gonorrhea alone indicate that, at a very minimum, three of every 100 Canadians are, or have been, recently infected. And the percentage is rising in the face of all efforts to educate the public to the dangers. Federal health authorities ascribe this to an increase in sexual permissiveness, promiscuity and homosexuality, the contraceptive pill, increased population mobility, changes in social values, and more frequent case reporting. Ignorance also remains a factor, along with feelings of shame or embarrassment.

All provinces provide free VD clinics, and free drugs to physicians treating cases privately. Educational programs are carried out in schools and in the media.

DENTAL X-RAYS

It appears that every time your child goes for a checkup, the dentist X-rays her mouth.

The dental profession does not recommend the routine use of X-rays, but it says that their judicious use is a valuable diagnostic tool. Dentists point out that their X-ray machines are monitored by provincial authorities and that the type and speed of film used guarantees minimum exposure of the patient.

Dental patients are unlikely to be X-rayed

more than twice a year. Dentists claim such exposure is the equivalent in radiation of a sunny day.

Don't hesitate to ask pointed questions about any treatment, however. Doubts and unfounded fears can best be removed by discussing them with your dentist. If you still want him to limit your child's X-rays, ask him politely but firmly to do so. When you go to a new dentist, tell him when your mouth was last X-rayed.

DENTAL TECHNICIANS

Your dentist says that dentures will cost you $1,500. He advises against going to the dental technician who advertises in the local newspaper.

The medically unqualified technicians are usually called "denture therapists" and most are perfectly capable of providing you with a

To honor, to protect, to teach . . .

Much of the confidence that society bestows upon its doctors is founded in the knowledge that these highly skilled practitioners adhere to a strict moral code. The seven principles listed here are at the heart of the Canadian Medical Association's Code of Ethics—and are a standard for the physician's conduct in the community.

CODE OF ETHICS

Principles of Ethical Behaviour for all physicians, including those who may not be engaged directly in clinical practice.

I

Consider first the well-being of the patient.

II

Honour your profession and its traditions.

III

Recognize your limitations and the special skills of others in the prevention and treatment of disease.

IV

Protect the patient's secrets.

V

Teach and be taught.

VI

Remember that integrity and professional ability should be your only advertisement.

VII

Be responsible in setting a value on your services.

properly fitting full set of dentures. They charge less. It's your mouth, and the decision is yours.

In most provinces, denture therapists are licensed to carry out certain procedures—and only those procedures. All do dental repairs, sometimes in a few hours. They are not licensed to perform what is called "an irreversible act." They may not extract teeth, cut any tissue or set a partial plate. They are not permitted to fit anything tooth-borne—such as a bridge that depends on the support of tooth structure. They are permitted to build you a full set of uppers against a natural lower set of teeth.

The "denticare" tortoise. Revenue Canada statistics show that the average dentist is fast catching up to the doctor in the income stakes and, in some areas, forging ahead.

Ontario has 40 percent of Canada's 10,500 dentists and the Ontario Dental Association reported in 1978 that the average gross income of its members was $100,000. Overheads soaked up about $54,000, leaving a net income some $10,000 greater than that of the average family doctor. Public authorities have approached "free" dental-care plans very cautiously. Most provinces support schemes only for the young and old. But oral surgery performed in a hospital is covered by the provincial health-insurance plans.

About 6.4 million Canadians are covered by private dental plans, either contributory or paid for by the employer. We are not a tooth-conscious society, however. Canadians spend only 4.4 percent of their health dollars on dental work and only 44 percent of all adult Canadians go for that annual checkup. In Quebec, the visitation rate is a mere 29 percent.

DEATH AT THE DENTIST'S

A child dies under anesthetic in the dentist's chair. The dentist maintains that he and his staff are not responsible.

Determining the cause of death in these circumstances is the duty of the coroner, who is appointed by the provincial cabinet. If there is any doubt, or if the case is of high public interest, he will convene a Coroner's Court, which, in all provinces except Quebec, includes a five-member jury. Death in a dentist's chair is an extremely rare occurrence and the dentist will be cross-examined rigorously by experts.

If the coroner found, or his verdict implied, that there was professional negligence, the way would be open to a civil suit for malpractice. The police could lay a charge of manslaughter or criminal negligence.

The Royal College of Dental Surgeons, the licensing body, will monitor the case closely. Independently, it will check all the circumstances, the medical-dental data, the type and dosage of the anesthetic used. The dentist is legally bound to examine the medical history of a patient before administering any anesthetic, and to keep precise and detailed records. The disciplinary committee of the college can reprimand, fine and suspend offenders.

A suit for damages based on negligence may be difficult to prove in court. The dentist, as the doctor, will seldom be found liable for a simple error of judgment. He must, of course, work to a high standard, but it is not demanded that he be infallible. He is expected to exercise the degree of skill and care that is reasonably demanded of the prudent medical practitioner of the same experience.

Professional discipline. Consumer complaints against dentists will be investigated by the profession's ruling body; there is a "college" of dental surgeons in every province. This institution reports to the Minister of Health on the outcome of disciplinary hearings, naming suspended dentists.

By the time a complaint reaches the College of Dental Surgeons, it has usually been screened by one of the several mediation committees of the provincial dental association. In 1978, the Ontario Dental Association investigated 521 complaints, and found some 37 percent were justified. A total of 193 complaints went forward to the provincial college in that year and 12 of them resulted in license suspensions of varying periods. One dentist was found guilty on no fewer than 121 charges involving 11 patients. He was suspended and fined $2,500.

Hospitals and nursing homes

With the advent of Medicare, we have come to consider "free," high-quality treatment in hospitals a right as basic as education. Some provinces demand a direct contribution to the hospital-insurance plan. In others, residents may not always be aware of the fact that they are paying for this service. But in either case, most contributors are content knowing that they and their families are "covered" for accident or illness that could otherwise spell bankruptcy.

Some may argue that accessibility is not equal to all, or that the standard of care is not high enough. On the other hand, more and more doctors and hospital administrators are protesting that these publicly financed health plans are abused, and that government bureaucrats sometimes hamper their professional work.

With rising expectations all around, all governments are caught in the squeeze between mounting costs and the sure knowledge that cutting back in hospital services is political suicide. But after a decade-long spending splurge on health care, which saw government expenditure almost triple from $165 a person annually in 1969 to $483 in 1978, governments are now trying to cut costs. In 1979 these costs were running from more than $100 a day per patient in convalescent-rehabilitation institutions to $140 a day in general hospitals and up to $300 in pediatric units.

While this controversy swirls, the total range of hospital services remains available as a right to virtually everyone in Canada. When medical treatment is required, there is no means test or other barrier. This applies to the most complicated and expensive surgical procedures as much as it does to a simple fracture.

In an emergency, even the tourist will be treated first and billed later.

Services that are not covered by the public-health plans—such as semiprivate or private rooms—are offered by commercial or non-profit organizations on an insurance basis.

HOSPITAL BACKLOGS

You are in pain with a prostate condition, but your doctor claims he can't get you into a hospital until next month.

It's a matter of priorities. There are only 201,413 beds in Canada's 1,389 hospitals—about six for every 100,000 persons—and only a certain number are vacant on any given date. Very few, in fact. Although you have the right to treatment in any hospital to which your physician has admitting privileges, the regulations don't say *when*.

Public hospitals everywhere grade their admitting priorities as follows:

Emergency. When life hangs by a thread. Accident victims, poisonings, and cases such as acute appendicitis, cardiac arrest and premature birth will qualify.

Urgent. When acute pain or prolongation of life are involved—for example, cancer operation or gallbladder removal.

Elective. The run-of-the-mill case. The operation is necessary but time is not a pressing factor.

If your doctor is convinced you need immediate attention, a bed will be found for you. But a prostate problem is usually a long-term affair and rarely "urgent." Your pain can probably be controlled by drugs.

When beds are scarce, long-term (chronic) cases may be treated in the outpatient department. If the overall circumstances—both medical and social—rule out this method, the patient may be admitted to an extended-care hospital or to one of the many "special-care facilities" financed jointly by the federal and provincial governments. These include nursing and convalescent homes, sunset lodges and homes for the incurable and disabled.

It may not be much consolation, but under the National Health Service in Britain, sufferers in the "elective" group sometimes wait three years for surgery.

SIGNED CONSENTS

You had authorized the hospital to conduct an exploratory operation, but your doctor performs a hysterectomy.

Your signature gives wide powers to the hospital but there is good reason to be confident they won't be abused. Quite apart from medical ethics, there's a backup of legal recourses all the way to the Supreme Court.

An exploratory examination often reveals that a further surgical procedure is needed immediately. The surgeon has the choice of sewing you up and scheduling the operation later after receiving your detailed consent, but it's more likely that he will perform the operation on the spot. In such cases, the doctor will usually consult with one or more colleagues.

If you are unconscious and no close relatives can be reached, the doctor can perform whatever operation is considered necessary.

If the consensus is that your disease has gone too far and the operation has no chance of restoring you to reasonable health, the surgeon may decide to close the incision and let nature take its course.

Only if the surgeon botches the job through negligence—and you have to prove this—is it sensible to take the case to court. In one instance, a woman sued because a complete hysterectomy was performed even though she had signed a release only for an exploratory examination. The surgeon's diagnosis was backed by the disciplinary committee at the hospital and by other doctors and the woman lost the case.

In California a girl was partially paralyzed when an excessive dose of radiation for a thyroid cancer destroyed her spinal cord. In the ensuing legal action a jury awarded her the highest personal damages on record: $7.6 million. The girl was not covered by any hospital-insurance plan and most of the money will go to meet lifelong medical expenses.

Much care is taken to ensure that the patient's rights are not forgotten on the operating table. When a woman died in an Ottawa hospital after a tumor was removed from her breast, a coroner's jury found that death was caused by brain damage from lack of oxygen, the result of a defective anesthetic machine. This case triggered a federal investigation of medical devices. Consequently the health protection branch of the Department of Health and Welfare recalled or banned 12 defective machines in the period between December 1977 and April 1979.

BEDSIDE TV

In your ward, everybody else has a television set. You cannot afford the rental charge.

The flicker and murmur of bedside television has become an inescapable feature of Canadian hospitals, often to the distraction of those patients not addicted to soap operas or game shows. But for the majority, television relieves the boredom of long and uncomfortable days in bed.

Sets are supplied by outside contractors and rentals are not paid for by the health-insurance plans. If you cannot afford the cost, put the problem to the hospital chaplain or ask for the resident social worker to call on you. In many places, service clubs such as the Lions, Kiwanis and Rotary are happy to help in situations such as this, or the hospital itself may have some funds in its social-amenities budget.

Almost all public hospitals provide bedside telephone service today. You can assume that local calls will be free, and that long-distance calls will be charged to your account. At a certain hour, usually 9 or 10 p.m., incoming calls to patients will be intercepted by the switchboard to maintain quiet for those patients settling down for the night.

A much appreciated free luxury is the

library-on-wheels brought to the bedside by volunteers. These kindly "pushers" will try to find paperbacks to your taste if their current stock lacks your preference.

SIGNING YOURSELF OUT

You think you'd be better off at home, but the hospital won't discharge you unless you sign a complicated legal form.

If you insist upon rejecting medical advice, you can sign yourself out of hospital. But the form you sign exonerates the hospital from any blame or liability resulting from your premature discharge.

Doctors can often be persuaded to allow a patient in fairly stable condition to go home, even if considerable care and therapy are still required. They will probably arrange for a nurse to visit you. If the discharge is arranged on these terms, your health plan will still pick up the costs.

If you discharge yourself, then you're on your own—financially and otherwise.

'ROOM SERVICE'

You sometimes wait half an hour before a nurse answers your bell. What if a real crisis occurs?

No hospital is overstaffed. Although you are guaranteed all necessary care and attention while in hospital, there's no rule about snappy room service.

To the busy staff at the nurses' station, the switchboard appears to blink almost constantly. Familiar with all the cases in the ward, the nurses respond to simultaneous calls on the basis of medical priority. If you have to wait, it usually means someone else has a greater need than you.

In a job that can easily breed hard-shelled cynics, most nurses remain polite, sympathetic and cheerful. But amid so much genuine suffering, they quickly develop an aversion to the "whiner." As soon as your medical condition permits, especially if you are able to walk, do everything possible to ease the nurses' labors. Your stay in hospital will be more pleasant for the effort.

Serious or critical?

Hospital administrators admit that their terminology can be confusing, or even misleading, to patients and their relatives. On being told that a patient is in "serious" condition, frightened families are apt to drop everything and rush to the bedside.

Actually, things may be proceeding quite normally under the circumstances. "Serious" often means "as well as can be expected," especially when the patient has just undergone a major operation.

To reduce ambiguity, the Toronto Western Hospital recently issued a pamphlet defining its terms:

Good means that the vital signs, such as pulse and breathing, are stable and within normal limits; the patient is conscious and comfortable, and future improvement can reasonably be expected.

Fair implies that the vital signs are stable, giving no cause for alarm; the patient is conscious and the outlook satisfactory. He is something less than comfortable and minor complications may develop.

Serious means that the patient is seriously ill with a questionable prognosis; his or her immediate future is in some doubt. The vital signs are unstable but there is a good chance of improvement.

Critical indicates there's cause for real and immediate concern. Not only is the prognosis questionable, but the vital signs are very unstable and there are major complications. Death may be imminent.

DADS IN THE LABOR WARD

You want to be present at the birth of your child, but hospital rules don't permit this.

Some hospitals encourage fathers to be present at births, even organizing classes to prepare you for the experience. Others will permit your presence, but a few still slam the delivery-room door. Make inquiries in advance about your hospital's policy or ask your family doctor or obstetrician. If all else fails, you can always change doctors. These days, some doctors even permit fathers to be present at Caesarean deliveries.

The argument against the father being present is usually that if he is unprepared, he may become emotional and disrupt proceedings. But if the partners have taken a prenatal course, for example in the Lamaze method, the birth can be the culmination of a wonderfully satisfying experience. The mother remains conscious throughout the birth and both parents share immediately in the joy of the new arrival.

Home births. Routine hospitalization under a doctor's care for childbirth is still a relatively modern phenomenon around the world. In Britain there has been a swing back to the traditional way. There, midwives (trained obstetrical nurses) now attend about 80 percent of all births. Home births virtually vanished, in Canada, with the advent of hospital-insurance plans. Because of the danger of complications, few doctors now will agree to deliver a baby in the home, even if prenatal examinations indicate that everything is normal. But if a home birth is what you want, shop around. You may find an obliging doctor.

VISITING HOURS

Your wife is distressed because the children are not permitted to visit her in the hospital.

Almost all hospitals forbid children under the age of 14 from visiting patients—even their parents.

This ban is based on the hospital's concern and responsibility for the patient. Children can become very emotional when they see a loved one in pain, in traction, or receiving blood or other fluids intravenously. This reaction usually rebounds on the patient, creating a setback.

The experience can also create in the immature mind a deep-seated aversion to hospitals and doctors. This psychological scar may one day hinder that person from seeking needed treatment.

Even in the corridors and elevators of hospitals there are often sights and sounds not suitable for children. A burn victim doesn't enjoy a curious child piping up, "Look at the man with the funny face!" or, "That lady's only got one leg!" And children *do* say things just like that.

MEDICAL RECORDS

You do not trust the hospital to keep your medical records confidential, but the administration refuses to hand them over.

Hospital records *are* confidential. No outsiders can have access to them without your written consent or a court order. But they are the property of the hospital.

While you may have good reasons for not wanting your medical records to remain in the hospital, society holds that there's a greater good involved. If you should again become ill or have an accident, time can be saved and tests avoided by a swift check of your records. This remains true even if you are admitted to a different hospital. Quick access to those recorded medical facts may save your life in an emergency.

Also, the hospital needs all the details of your treatment to recover its expenses from the provincial health-insurance plan.

When medical records are necessary for the prosecution of a crime, they can be obtained by police on production of a court order, or by your lawyer if he has a signed consent form from you.

In general it is extremely difficult for anybody to gain access to your records without a court order, and that simply will not be issued unless a judge believes there is a valid reason.

A case in point. Two workers in the records library at a Toronto hospital testified that they had been threatened with arrest if they refused to give confidential medical information to police officers not in possession of a court order. The librarians stuck to their guns and no charges were ever laid.

One major exception to the rule of non-disclosure is that cases of venereal disease must be reported to the public health authorities.

ABORTION COMMITTEES

You and your husband feel you cannot support another child, and you want an abortion. But the hospital abortion committee rejects your request.

It must do so, on those grounds alone. Most general hospitals have a therapeutic abortion committee which considers these requests according to stringent guidelines. If the majority of the hospital committee believes that you are in good health, and that you have no medical reason to be apprehensive, it is required to refuse you an abortion. (*See* "Abortion" in Chapter 5.)

In 1978, there were 54,478 therapeutic abortions reported to Statistics Canada. This constitutes an increase of 5,167 over the previous year. In national percentage terms, this amounts to 14.9 legal abortions for every 100 live births.

When abortions are approved on medical grounds, all costs are absorbed by the provincial health plan.

Financial aid. The pregnant mother should consider that although another child may add to the financial burden, the government provides many benefits. (*See* Chapter 45, "When in need.") For example, in Quebec in 1978 family allowance benefits for a third child were $47.45 per month, and for each additional child beyond the third, benefits were $59.13. An additional $6.42 monthly was paid for every child age 12 and over.

SEDATIVES AND THE ELDERLY

Your elderly father has gone downhill since he entered a private nursing home. He always seems to be sedated, and your questions get evasive answers from the staff.

All nursing homes, private or public, are subject to strict scrutiny and licensing by your provincial Department of Health. If you can't get reasonable answers from the director of the institution, take your complaint to the department.

If your father is being heavily sedated, there must be a medical reason for the treatment but you have the right to an explanation. A discussion with your family physician may resolve the matter.

Private nursing homes, which have many different labels, offer an alternative to public institutions. Costs and facilities range from the moderate to the very expensive—up to $1,000 a week.

The accommodation and treatment of a patient in an approved private home is paid for by the provincial health plan at the same rates as those set for public institutions. The excess sum is charged to the patient or his family.

An aging society. The average Canadian can expect today to live twice as long as he might have 100 years ago. Canada's current annual death rate is one of the world's lowest at 7.3 per 1,000 population.

With the national annual birthrate at an all-time low of 15 live births per 1,000 population (compared to 30 per 1,000 at the turn of the century), Canada is a rapidly aging society. In fact, if present trends continue, natural increase will not be sufficient to replace the present population.

These figures all point to the need for more special-care facilities, more personnel trained to work with the elderly and infirm, and more intensive study of geriatrics (the science of aging).

Working with the aged. Complaints about ill treatment of elderly patients in special-care facilities are always investigated by the licensing authority. From time to time a few are substantiated. Suspensions of staff, more intensive control procedures, and even withdrawal of licenses follow.

But it is everywhere agreed that nursing of the elderly infirm is the most wearing and perhaps the most difficult of all hospital services. Staff are often unable to cope with the sometimes bizarre or unresponsive attitudes of patients who are either senile or verging on that condition.

LIFE-OR-DEATH DECISIONS

Your sister was critically injured and will never recover. You think the hospital should discontinue maintaining her life by artificial means.

However strongly you feel, this decision is not up to you. The law does not grant any lay person the right to make life-or-death decisions. A few minutes' reflection should convince you of the justice of this.

It is the sworn responsibility of the doctor to maintain life wherever possible. It is also within the bounds of his discretion, after consultation with qualified colleagues, to omit to take steps that would prolong life. But in the majority of these tragic cases, the hospital staff will continue life-preservation procedures as long as possible.

There will be no extra financial burden on the family, no matter how long treatment is continued. All provincial hospital-insurance plans cover all treatment and all drugs as long as medical care is considered necessary.

Distress of the death watch. Each year, thousands of families endure lengthy anguish watching a loved one die slowly and painfully from cancer or some other incurable disease. Although cancer research has scored some heartening victories, this baffling disease remains the highest cause of death in Canada after heart disease. Cancer accounts for about one in every five deaths, usually in the middle or later years.

Often families come sorrowfully to believe the sufferer would be "better off dead." Some cancer patients think likewise; others cling tenaciously to life, even in the terminal stages.

Pain and the law. In North America terminally ill patients do not have the right to treatment with heroin, one of the strongest known painkillers. The prescription of this drug remains illegal even though addiction doesn't have much relevance to the doomed cancer sufferer. Defenders of the current law in Canada maintain that morphine (like heroin a derivative of the opium poppy) alleviates pain just as effectively.

SUSPECTED NEGLIGENCE

Your grandfather died while undergoing minor surgery. You are not satisfied with the hospital's explanation, but you don't know how to carry the matter further.

Any operation on an elderly person is relatively serious. The cause of your grandfather's death will be stated on the death certificate issued by the attending doctor. If the circumstances are unusual, or mysterious, the coroner will be called in.

If you are not content with the explanation, or believe that negligence played some part in the death, make a written complaint to the executive medical director of the hospital. Send it by registered mail or deliver it by hand. Send copies to the provincial medical association and the College of Physicians and Surgeons. You can be certain the complaint will be investigated—and not solely by other doctors. If you are still unsatisfied, get in touch with the provincial Ombudsman. (*See* Chapter 1, "Civil rights.")

CARE OF THE MENTALLY ILL

You visit your old aunt in the provincial mental hospital. You are appalled by the conditions you witness there.

A generation ago that reaction may not have been uncommon, but it is rare today. Millions of dollars have been spent on new facilities for the mentally ill and retarded, and every effort has been made to get away from the prisonlike atmosphere of the old "asylums."

A new breed of psychiatrist is committed to progressive treatment—based largely on drugs, and the avoidance of restraint and drastic surgery. The idea is that the patient should maintain as much contact as possible with normal life. The mentally ill person is seen as no different from any other patient needing medical help. (The new approach to "committal" is explained in Chapter 46.)

But a first visit to a close relative who is legally confined to a hospital, or in residence on a voluntary basis, can still be traumatic.

Almost always there are unsettling or distressing scenes.

Talk it over first. Perhaps you'd be wise to withhold comment until you have made several visits and have a reasonable grasp of the workings of such places. Approach the hospital staff or ask for an appointment with the psychiatrist who attends your aunt. Do not hesitate to express any dissatisfaction or fears for her welfare. State the conditions that shocked you. There may be quite simple and logical explanations.

If you aren't reassured, your best recourse is to write in detail to the responsible provincial department. It is probably the Department of

Green light for surgery

If you are undergoing medical therapy or surgery and are of age (18 or over), you will be asked to sign a form similar to the one shown.

If you are unconscious or incapable after an accident or collapse, and you have no relative present, the hospital has the authority to take whatever action it deems best to save your life.

While the consent form will specify a certain operation or procedure, your signature gives the surgeon, or any other member of the hospital staff he calls in, "discretion" (permission) to perform *any* additional or alternative procedures considered "immediately necessary."

If you want to restrict this blanket permission—say, to the removal of your appendix only—then you should delete the supplementary paragraphs, and initial the deletions. But are you really equipped to be your own doctor?

BELLEVILLE GENERAL HOSPITAL

CONSENT TO OPERATION
AND ANAESTHETIC

This authorization to be signed by patient or by the nearest relative in the case of a minor or when the patient is physically or mentally incompetent. In maternity cases, a separate authorization will be required if any procedure is to be performed on the newborn.

I, _Richard A. Roe_, hereby consent to undergo the treatment or operation of _appendectomy_

ordered by or to be performed by Dr. _Samuel Snow_;

the anticipated effect and nature of such treatment or operation has been explained to me by Dr. _Snow_.

I also consent to such additional or alternative treatment or operative procedures as in the opinion of Dr. _Snow_ are immediately necessary.

and to the administration of a local or other anaesthetic for the purpose of the same.

I further agree that in his discretion, Dr. _Snow_ may make use of the assistance of other surgeons, physicians, and hospital medical staff, and may permit them to order or perform all or part of the treatment or operative procedure and they shall have the same discretion in my treatment and in the execution of any surgical procedure as Dr. _Snow_.

Dated this _5th_ day of _October_, 19_79_.

_____
Witness

Revised Aug/76
BGH 194

Richard A. Roe
Signature of Patient, Parent or Guardian

100 Maple Road, Belleville, Ont.
Address

_200-3214_
Telephone

Health, but (as in Ontario, for example) it may be the Department of Social Services.

Perhaps you will decide to pay the extra costs involved in having your aunt transferred to a private hospital. The surroundings may be more congenial, but it's doubtful the quality of the medical treatment will be superior. The provincial health-insurance plan will make the same payment on your aunt's behalf regardless of which approved Canadian or foreign institution she's in. Any extra charge is your responsibility.

Mental health consumes a large portion of the Canadian health dollar. In 1977 the national bill for the provincially operated services was $681.9 million, an increase of nearly 20 percent over the previous year. Staff numbered 51,582, compared with a patient total of 48,238. But there has been a gradual decrease in the number of inpatients over the past few years as several provinces now arrange for some stable patients to live in the community in boardinghouses. Other patients are supervised in special day-care centers, returning to their family homes at night.

'PORTABLE' HEALTH CARE

Your husband will be transferred to another province, and you are worried that the family's Medicare coverage won't apply there.

Stop worrying. All provincial hospital-insurance plans are "portable." They travel with you to keep you and your family covered until you qualify for membership under the plan in your new province. Most plans require a qualifying period of three months after a permanent move.

You should check with your present medical insurance plan before you move, and find out just what services are covered and to what extent, as well as how long after your move you will be covered. Provincial plans vary widely in coverage, and in the method of collecting contributions.

In Manitoba and some other provinces, for example, residents pay no direct contribution: all approved charges are met from general provincial revenue. (Manitoba also has a Pharmacare plan under which the Health Services Commission reimburses residents for 80 percent of the cost of most prescription drugs after the first $50.)

Canada's health-care plans will pay for your medical care *anywhere* in the world, as long as you are insured. Bear in mind, however, that medical practitioners and hospitals in other provinces and other countries are not bound to accept the fees laid down in your home-province plan. You could face a substantial extra bill.

In fact, Canadian medical charges used to be so favorable as compared to those in many other countries that ailing "visitors" would come here for treatment. Attracted by the high standard of Canadian medical care, some still do—but they no longer enjoy cut rates. Recently the largest Toronto hospitals raised their prices to non-Canadians by up to 100 percent.

48 Retirement

Some of us can hardly wait for the day when we stop punching a clock or pounding a typewriter; others dread the thought. Some enjoy years of contented retirement; others cannot make the transition and soon fade away. Social, psychological and economic factors make the difference.

The controversy over retirement (usually at age 65) revolves around the social and psychological issues—whether people should be compelled to retire. The question of whether they can afford to retire is generally not given as much attention.

Some people are in a position to enjoy a reasonable standard of living when regular paycheques stop. Children are grown, mortgages are paid off and the need for major investments in goods and services has slackened.

Others, however, face serious money problems because their pensions will not meet their high fixed overheads. Perhaps they married late in life and still have children in school or college, or there may be some years remaining on the house mortgage. They may even have lived up to their incomes and acquired debts and a life style which pension benefits won't support.

Since retirement is inevitable for almost everybody—the Arthur Fiedlers and Pablo Picassos are exceptions—advance planning is essential if those years are not to be a time of poverty and hardship.

Judges and senators excepted, there's no national law that says when you have to stop working for your living. The idea of fixing an arbitrary retirement age originated in Germany in the 19th century, when Bismarck was pioneering various social-security measures. In 1889, he introduced legislation that provided a pension for workers at 70, earlier if disabled. Since then, 65 has become the Western World's gateway to retirement, cemented into our way of life, widely supported by in-

dustry and unions, and written into numerous statutes.

Thus, despite the fact that people are living longer and remaining healthier, unwilling thousands are still being put out to pasture at 65. That will change perhaps, but it won't happen tomorrow. Although society is gradually acknowledging the fact that physical and mental health have more to do with the ability to work than chronological age, we have all been conditioned to believe that a person is over the hill at 65.

Consider these statistics: a male born in the 1950s had a life expectancy of slightly more than 66 years; in the 1970s it was more than 69 years. Females improved their longevity even more in the same period, going from just under 71 years to more than 76 years. A man who reaches 65 today can expect to live until age 78; a woman will probably reach 80. The 80-year-old male can look forward to another six years. If he makes it to 90, he should live another three years or more.

But, like it or not, society continues to regard the 65-year-old as a "senior citizen." You may have to give up your job but you will gain a whole new set of rights and privileges. Your well-being will be protected without further effort or cost to you, and other "perks" will come your way as compensation for being shunted to the sidelines.

PENSION PLANNING

There is no pension plan where you work and now that you're in your fifties, you worry about how you and your spouse will manage after retirement.

Take some comfort from the fact that Canada grants an income to just about everyone at the age of 65—not a fortune by any means, but

569

something to help you make ends meet. Monthly Old Age Security (OAS) payments are due to all residents who have lived in Canada for at least 10 years since age 18. These payments are in addition to benefits from the Canada (or Quebec) Pension Plan to which all employed persons must contribute. At 65, you will no longer be required to pay Medicare contributions. Prescribed drugs, and some appliances, are provided without charge to those who are 65 and over.

If you have no significant income apart from these pensions, there are several other federal plans for which you and your spouse may qualify. These include the Guaranteed Income Supplement (GIS) and the spouse's allowance—in 1979, payable if she was between 60 and 65 years of age and your combined incomes, excluding OAS payments, did not exceed $8,784 annually. There are also several supplemental allowances paid for by the provinces. (*See* Chapter 45, "When in need.")

About half of all Canadians 65 and over receive financial aid above the basic pension. The income of anyone who receives OAS or the supplements is reviewed annually.

Then there are special pensions paid to the disabled and to war veterans. Numerous service clubs and volunteer agencies stand ready to help the elderly, sometimes with cash grants, but more often with services such as meals and transportation assistance. You may even qualify for housing geared to income.

Information on government benefits is available from provincial or federal departments of health, welfare or social services.

Looking after No. 1. About 70 percent of Canadians employed by private companies are not covered by staff pension plans. These millions—and even many who belong to company plans—should get the facts about the Registered Retirement Savings Plan (RRSP).

The RRSP allows you to make tax-free contributions now while you are earning and to withdraw the money, plus accumulated interest or dividends, after retirement, when your tax rate will be lower. (*See* Chapter 29, "Your income tax.")

Even if you borrow to invest in an RRSP, it's still a good deal. The interest you pay for such a loan is tax-deductible. You can reduce the tax bite further by putting some or all of your contributions into an RRSP owned by your spouse.

And you're still not too old to invest in one of the many insurance policies that will pay you a lump sum on a given date or an annuity from retirement age to death. Any policy you hold now can almost certainly be rearranged to produce an annuity. (*See* Chapter 32, "Life insurance.")

65 AND OUT

Your company's rules state that retirement is compulsory at age 65. You are in robust health and want to keep on working.

The way things stand in Canada, you are not likely to succeed. Governments, collectively our largest employer, and trade unions not only favor the "65-and-out" rule, but resist any effort to change it. In fact, they are seeking to lower the compulsory retirement age— maybe to 60.

At present, federal civil servants, age 55, who have 30 years' service can retire with full pension. And their pensions are "indexed," so they automatically keep pace with the cost of living.

The Canadian Labour Congress, which represents about 2.4 million union members, claims that mandatory retirement at 65 opens the door to promotions for younger workers and leads to reduction of unemployment.

If, however, you are determined to fight for your job after 65, complain to your Human Rights Commission. Most of the human rights codes forbid discrimination on the grounds of age—but they seem primarily concerned with workers between 40 and 65. (*See* Chapter 6, "Discrimination.") A few complaints have succeeded, but courts and labor relations boards have generally upheld policies that require workers to accept retirement at 65.

Federally appointed judges can continue until age 75 in the Supreme Court and until 70 in the lower courts. Senators are obliged to retire at 75. Even Roman Catholic bishops, once ensconced for life, are now obliged by the Holy See to vacate their dioceses at 75.

Soldiering on. Private corporations often waive compulsory retirement for executives and also for some key workers, with the tacit agreement of the union.

If you can convince your boss that he should keep you on, you'll begin drawing your noncontributory Old Age Security (OAS) at 65. You can continue your contributions to the Canada (or Quebec) Pension Plan (CPP or QPP) until age 70, however, thus increasing your monthly income when you finally decide to call it quits.

As an alternative, you could begin drawing CPP (or QPP) benefits along with OAS, and putting the money into a Registered Retirement Savings Plan (RRSP). You can deduct your RRSP contributions from your taxable income until, say, age 75, when your RRSP matures and starts to pay you an annuity income. If you don't have an RRSP in operation already, consider opening one for this purpose. But seek expert advice before you make a final decision; there are advantages and disadvantages, depending on individual circumstances.

Your unemployment insurance coverage ends at 65, but you're entitled to a one-time special benefit even if you keep on working. The benefit is equal to three times the weekly payment you would get under a regular unemployment insurance claim. Not a large sum, but still worthwhile.

Savings and self-respect. When a special Senate committee under Senator David Croll studied the problems associated with the rising number of Canadians of retirement age, it learned that the majority of workers wanted to retire at 65 or earlier. Job satisfaction— "the joy of working"—had disappeared. Too many jobs were routine; the challenge was gone. Only 20 to 25 percent preferred to stay on the job.

On the other hand, the Canadian Pension Conference, a national organization which acts as a watchdog on all forms of income security, told the Senate committee that a nonmandatory retirement policy would use the country's resources more effectively, foster self-respect in the elderly, and lower social-benefit costs for the taxpayer. It urged that people be allowed to work as long as they can remain productive.

The Ontario Council of Health has warned of an impending health and housing crisis, because 13 percent of the province's population (1.3 million persons) will be over 65 by the year 2001. Oldsters will be consuming about 30 percent of all services paid for by the provincial health insurance plan.

EARLY RETIREMENT

You won't reach pensionable age for another five years, but your health is so poor you don't think you'll be able to hang on.

All pension plans are based on averages, in the knowledge that a certain percentage of participants will not be able to carry on until retirement age. Each plan, therefore, has provisions for early retirement—in your case, on health grounds.

If you are contributing to a company pension plan, you may have to accept a reduction of the monthly benefit, although many plans pay the full amount if there is satisfactory medical evidence. When your health is poor, the entire range of Medicare benefits is open to you by right.

The CPP parachute. The Canada Pension Plan (CPP) and the Quebec Pension Plan (QPP), which are interchangeable and virtually identical, have special provisions for the worker struck down by ill health or disability. These compulsory, contributory plans are considered among the world's most comprehensive and generous.

Launched in 1965, the CPP began making partial payments to the first pensioners in 1967. By 1977 the plan was fully operational and paying benefits (at age 65) equal to 25 percent of the participant's earnings averaged over a set span of years.

The noncontributory Old Age Security pension and the CPP are the basic platform for the financial independence of the elderly. Even if you contributed for only a single calendar year to the CPP in your working life, you'll still receive a partial retirement pension.

There are a few exceptions in the coverage. For example, a wife employed by her husband does not qualify.

If your health breaks down before 65, or you are disabled by accident, you will receive a pension for yourself and your dependents. Payment to qualified contributors will begin in the fourth month and will continue until you recover. To be classed as a disability, your physical or mental ailment must be "severe and prolonged." "Severe" means that you are incapable of *regularly* pursuing any *substantially* gainful occupation. "Prolonged" means of indefinite duration.

Should you die at any time after completing the qualifying period, a lump-sum benefit will be paid to your estate. It equals six times the monthly retirement pension. If death occurs after you have contributed for at least one-third of the years for which you could have contributed, your spouse will get a pension and your children will receive payments until the age of 18—to 25, if they are at school or college full time.

$100 million a month. CPP and QPP payments are adjusted annually to cover increases in the cost of living. In 1979, more than 1.3 million Canadians were receiving benefits totaling almost $1.2 billion.

If you served in the armed forces in any of Canada's wars and are now in poor health, you may be entitled to a veteran's pension on top of any other public or private pension. (*See* Chapter 45, "When in need.")

The CPP or QPP benefits are paid, however, *only if written applications are made.* The federal Department of Health and Welfare has offices across the country. (The person responsible for the welfare of a disabled CPP contributor can make the application.)

PENSION SUPPLEMENT

You admire your elderly neighbor who insists on taking care of himself, but you know he's only got the old-age pension and has trouble making ends meet.

One of the most important benefit programs is the Guaranteed Income Supplement (GIS). It's an addition to the old-age pension of a person who has little or no other income.

"Income" does not include possessions, sav-

Don't be a sitting duck

Some criminals regard senior citizens as sitting ducks—easy targets on whom the season is always open.

Beware of the unctuous stranger who claims to have found a large sum of money which he'll share with you, if you'll put up some money as evidence of your good faith. If you do, you'll probably never see him or your money again.

Beware of the suave "bank examiner" who asks for help in catching a dishonest employee. He will ask you to withdraw a large sum from your account so that he can check the serial numbers of the bills. If you do, you'll never see him again, either.

Beware of the easy contest that requires you to put up a sum of money to win. You won't.

Beware of those tempting home-improvement deals offered by a convincing character who just happened to notice that your chimney was leaning. He wants payment in advance and he promises to be back in two hours with his crew. Good-bye!

Beware of the seductive "retirement estates" on sunlit lakes, offered at ridiculously low prices to selected individuals like you.

It's the same old world that you used to know in your 9-to-5 days. Anyone who thinks he's going to get something for nothing gets . . . nothing.

ings, investments, property or the old-age pension itself. It means such things as other pensions, earnings, interest, dividends and rents.

If your elderly friend is married, his and his wife's combined income would be taken into account. Entitlement depends upon the income received in the preceding calendar year and a fresh application for the supplement must be made annually.

An applicant is treated as a single person if he or she has been separated for at least one year. This also applies if spouses are not able to live in the same dwelling, as, for example, in a nursing home.

SENIOR CITIZEN HOUSING

Your parents are close to retirement and they don't own their own home. Their pensions won't cover their present rent.

Some 40 percent of retired Canadians do not own their own homes and about half of all retirees have little or no income aside from their Old Age Security (OAS) and Canada Pension Plan (or Quebec Pension Plan) benefits.

Society's major response has been senior citizens' rental projects in which rents are usually geared to income. Federal, provincial and municipal governments share construction costs and rent subsidies. Some religious and charitable organizations—and some major corporations—maintain their own "sunset lodges."

Everywhere demand outstrips supply, although construction of senior-citizen units has been speeded up. Supplementary benefits include assistance for those having difficulty paying commercial rents. British Columbia began a program in 1977 of making direct cash payments to senior citizens for this purpose. Anyone over 65 who has lived in the province for the previous two years may apply. An applicant paying more than 30 percent of income for rent will receive 75 percent of the excess, within certain limits.

The Manitoba government will pay a quarterly cash supplement to needy pensioners and their spouses, in addition to all other supplements and the spouse's allowance.

Similar provincial plans are in force across the country. The basic qualification is that you must be in receipt of OAS and provide evidence of further financial need.

PENSION PORTABILITY

You have contributed to your company's compulsory pension plan for 20 years. You are leaving for another job and you learn that your coverage has ceased.

A serious flaw in private pension plans has been their lack of portability: they couldn't be retained by an employee when he left a company.

In 1979 a group of insurance companies agreed to permit a pension participant to retain his coverage if the pension plan at his new place of employment was operated by one of the other insurance companies in the group. In effect, pension plans became portable for employees of the firms serviced by this group.

If you've been paying an average of 5.5 percent of your wages or salary for two decades—and your plan isn't portable—you'll have a sizable sum to collect if you leave the company. Your pension membership ends but your employer's contributions, which are at least equal to your own, may also go to you.

In some plans, however, if you do not remain a participant for a stated time (often 10 years), you will not receive the company's contribution when you leave. You may be granted a fraction, based on years of service. This is known as "vesting" and it is regulated by law in Nova Scotia, Quebec, Ontario, Saskatchewan and Alberta. The main point of the legislation is that the vesting of pension rights in the employee is compulsory when he reaches 45 and has been on the staff continuously for 10 years.

Government employees' pensions are portable from one department to another. You can also transfer from the federal to a provincial civil service without losing pension rights.

Pension and tax shelters

Registered Retirement Savings Plans have become popular as a way of reducing income tax now and providing a pension later on. Participants can invest up to 20 percent of their earnings to an annual maximum of $5,500. (The annual limit is $3,500 for anyone already covered by a company pension plan.) Contributions are deductible for income tax purposes, including interest charges if you have to borrow the money to invest. It's also possible to make the contributions (and claim the tax exemption) in your own name and to name your spouse as the person to receive the benefits when the plan matures. Participants' contributions are held in trust by the company operating the plan, in this case Guaranty Trust Company of Canada.

DECLARATION OF TRUST

Guaranty Trust Company of Canada, a trust company incorporated under the laws of Canada having its head office at the City of Toronto, in the Province of Ontario (hereinafter referred to as the 'Trustee') hereby declares that it accepts the office of Trustee for the applicant (hereinafter referred to as the 'Member') named on the face hereof under the Guaranty Trust Self-Administered Retirement Savings Plan (hereinafter referred to as the 'Special' Plan) upon the following terms:

1. REGISTRATION. The Trustee will apply for registration of the 'Special' Plan with the Minister of National Revenue pursuant to the provisions of Section 146 of the Income Tax Act Canada and amendments and regulations thereto, and such Provincial Acts having jurisdiction, as determined by the Province stated in the application therefore.

2. MEMBER'S ACCOUNT. The Trustee will maintain an account for the Member and will record the deposits made by the Member and all investments selected by the Member as described hereunder.

3.(a) DEPOSITS. Deposits received by the Trustee from the Member and the income derived therefrom shall be held by the Trustee in accordance with the provisions of Section 146 of the Income Tax Act Canada and amendments and regulations thereto, and such Provincial Acts having jurisdiction. These monies shall be invested as hereinafter provided for the purpose of providing to the Member a Retirement Income as provided for in Clause 12 hereof. Deposits shall be in amounts of not less than $100 at any one time.

3.(b) REFUND OF CONTRIBUTIONS. The Trustee shall, upon written application by the Member or the Member's spouse, refund to that applicant all or part of the amount established to be an excess amount for the year, as defined in Clause 146(2) (a) (i) (B) of the Income Tax Act and, if any, the corresponding provisions of the applicable provincial tax legislation in respect of such applicant but not exceeding the amount contributed to or under this plan in the year.

3.(c) REFUND OF PREMIUMS. On or after the death of the Member in the event of death before the Plan's maturity, the refund of assets in the Plan shall be paid out in a single payment only, less any applicable taxes.

4. INVESTMENTS. The Trustee shall invest monies from time to time contributed by the Member together with any interest or dividends received from such investments in accordance with the instructions of the Member or his duly appointed agent. Provided, however, that the Trustee shall not be obliged to act upon the instructions of the Member hereunder to make any particular investment, unless the proposed investment and related documentation complies with the Trustee's reasonable requirements from time to time. The Member hereby expressly acknowledges that the Income Tax Act Canada and regulations thereunder and applicable Provincial laws provide that only certain investments are "qualified investments" for Retirement Savings Plans and hereby assumes sole responsibility for ensuring that all investments made under the 'Special' Plan are "qualified investments" as aforesaid.

5. MANAGEMENT AND OWNERSHIP. The Trustee may hold any investment for the Member in its own name, or in the name of nominees for it, or in bearer form. Where monies have been invested, at the request of the Member, in any mortgage, the Trustee may, upon receipt of written instructions from the Member, renew, extend, modify the terms of, or waive any default in such mortgage. Upon the written request of the Member, the Trustee will authorize the Member in the name of the Trustee, to institute collection procedures with respect to any mortgage arrears; provided, however, that should the Member decide to proceed to institute legal action for foreclosure or sale, the Member shall take all necessary action, at his own expense, to acquire the mortgage from the plan and to proceed with such legal action on his own behalf without further reference to the fund and the Trustee may generally exercise the power of an owner with respect to all stocks, bonds or securities held by it for the 'Special' plan, including the right to vote or give proxies to vote in respect thereof and to pay any assessment, taxes or charges in connection therewith or the income or gains derived therefrom.

6. MEMBER'S STATEMENTS. The Trustee shall forward to the Member an annual statement of the Member's 'Special' Plan showing all deposits, investments, investment transactions, investment income and expenses incurred during the preceding period.

7.(a) TRUSTEE'S FEES.

(i) A charge of $25.00 will be made by the Trustee upon application by the member.

(ii) The Trustee shall be entitled to an annual administration fee of ¾ of 1% of the book value at the end of November of each year of the Member's 'Special' Plan subject to a minimum fee of $100.

(iii) For each $10 of annual fees determined in the foregoing manner the Member shall be entitled to one transaction (purchase or sale) of a particular investment. For each transaction in excess of the number of transactions so determined, the Trustee shall be entitled to a fee of $10.

(iv) Where mortgages are included in the 'Special' Plan the Trustee shall be entitled to a fee of ¼ of 1% of the principle balance outstanding at the end of November of each year subject to a minimum fee of $100. per mortgage in addition to any other charges which apply to the member's plan.

7.(b) Annual Trustee's fees shall either be charged to the member's account or billed to the Member directly if the Member has so instructed the Trustee in writing. Notwithstanding anything herein contained the Trustee is empowered to realize, in its discretion, sufficient assets of the 'Special' Plan for payment of the Trustee's fees and out-of-pocket expenses. Any such sale shall be made at such price or prices as the Trustee may in its sole discretion determine and the Trustee shall not be responsible for any loss occasioned by any such sale.

8. GUARANTEED INVESTMENT CERTIFICATES. Where the sole investments of a 'Special' Plan are Guaranty Trust Company of Canada Guaranteed Investment Certificates the Trustee's fee shall be ⅜ of 1% of the book value of the Member's 'Special' Plan at the close of the accounting period, with a minimum annual fee of $25.00.

9. OUT-OF-POCKET EXPENSES. Out-of-pocket expenses incurred by the Trustee in the administration of the Member's 'Special' Plan such as certificate fees, postage, delivery charges, taxes, etc., shall be charged to the Member's 'Special' Plan and reported in the 'Special' Plan's annual statement.

10. INCOME TAX RECEIPTS. On or before the 31st day of January of each year, the Trustee shall forward to the Member a receipt to be filed with the Member's personal income tax return with respect to the deposits made under the 'Special' Plan during the preceding taxation year. On or before the 31st day of March of each year, the Trustee shall forward to the Member a receipt to be filed with the Member's personal income tax return with respect to the deposits made under the 'Special' Plan during January and February.

11. MEMBER'S BIRTH DATE. The statement of the Member's age on the face hereof shall be deemed to be a certification by the Member of such age and an undertaking by the Member to provide any further evidence or proof of age that may be required when an annuity is purchased.

12. RETIREMENT INCOME. At the date chosen by the Member for the provision of a retirement income, which date shall not be earlier than the Member's sixtieth birthdate nor later than 60 days prior to the calendar year in which the Member attains seventy-two years of age, the deposits held by the Trustee for the Member's Plan shall be used, on the written instructions of the Member, for the provision of a retirement income.
A retirement income means any one or a combination of the following:

(i) an annuity commencing at maturity, with or without a guaranteed term commencing at maturity, not exceeding the term referred to in (ii) below, or, in the case of a plan entered into before March 14, 1957, not exceeding 20 years, payable to
(A) the Member for life, or
(B) the Member for the lives, jointly, of the Member and the Member's spouse and to the survivor of them for his or her life, or

(ii) an annuity commencing at maturity, payable to the Member, or to the Member for life and to the spouse after death of the Member, for a term of years equal to 90 minus either (A) the age in whole years of the Member at the maturity of the plan, or
(B) where the Member's spouse is younger than the Member and the Member so selects, the age in whole years of the spouse at the maturity of the plan.

The annuity payable shall be in equal annual or more frequent periodic payments and shall not be capable, except on the death of the Member, either in whole or in part of surrender, commutation, or assignment. The Plan provides for the commutation of an annuity payable to a person other than the Member's spouse on or after the death of the Member.

Where a Member fails to instruct the Trustee within sixty days prior to the calendar year in which the Member attains seventy-two years of age, the Trustee shall purchase for the Member an annuity of such type, subject to the requirements of the Plan, as the Trustee may in its absolute discretion determine.

13. IN THE EVENT OF DEATH of the Member prior to the purchase of the annuity referred to in the Clause entitled "Retirement Income" immediately above, the Trustee, upon receipt of satisfactory evidence of the death of the Member and upon receipt of such Government or other releases and such other documents as may be required by the Trustee or as counsel for the Trustee may direct, may realize in its discretion the investments held by it for the Plan and after failing realization of investments by the Trustee, upon receipt by the Trustee of sufficient funds to cover any and all taxes payable on the then realizable value, its fees and other charges applicable, pay the net proceeds or deliver the investments held by the Trustee in negotiable form, whichever is applicable, to the personal representatives of the Member. Provided, however the Member may by testamentary instrument or other instrument authorized by the Trustee for such purpose designate any person or persons to receive all benefits payable under the Plan on the death of the Member and may alter or revoke any designation so made whether by subsequent testamentary instrument or by other instrument authorized by the Trustee for such purpose irrespective of the manner of original designation provided that no such designation or alteration or revocation thereof shall take effect until the Trustee shall have received notice thereof. On the death of the Member, the Trustee is hereby authorized to pay the net proceeds then held for the Member under the Plan or deliver all investments in negotiable form then held for the member under the Plan to the person or persons so designated by the Member.

14. GENERAL. A 'Special' Plan may not incur a liability nor is it assignable.

15. AMENDMENTS TO THE PLAN. The Trustee may from time to time upon at least 60 days' written notice to the Member amend this Declaration of Trust with the concurrence of the Minister of National Revenue and, if applicable, the concurrence of provincial tax authorities; provided, however, that any such amendments shall not have the effect of disqualifying the 'Special' Plan as a registered retirement savings plan within the meaning of Section 146 of the Income Tax Act Canada and amendments and regulations thereto, and such Provincial Acts having jurisdiction.

16. MAILED NOTICES. Any notice given to the Trustee hereunder shall be sufficiently given if mailed, postage prepaid, addressed to the Trustee at the office stated on the face hereof and shall be deemed to have been given on the day that such notice is received by the Trustee. Any notice, statement or receipt given by the Trustee to the Member shall be sufficiently given if mailed, postage prepaid, addressed to such Member at the address of the Member set out in the application for the 'Special' Plan unless the Member has notified the Trustee of a new address, in which case notice shall be addressed to the Member at the last address or such purposes so notified and shall be deemed to have been given on the day of mailing.

17. TRUSTEE'S LIABILITY. The Trustee shall not be liable to ascertain whether any investment made in accordance with the instructions of the Member or his duly appointed agent is a "qualified investment" as aforesaid and the Member assumes all liability for any consequences resulting from the 'Special' Plan making or holding an investment which is not such a "qualified investment". The Trustee shall not otherwise be liable for the making, retention or sale of any investment or reinvestment made by it as herein provided nor for any loss or diminution of the Member's investments, except due to the negligence, wilful misconduct or lack of good faith of the Trustee.

18. INTERPRETATION. This agreement shall be construed, administered and enforced according to the laws of the Province of Ontario.

APPLICATION
Complete in Duplicate. Please Print Clearly.

Guaranty Trust
COMPANY OF CANADA

Special Retirement Savings Plan

I hereby request Guaranty Trust Company of Canada to act as Trustee of my registered retirement savings plan (herein referred to as the "Plan") on the terms and conditions set out in the Declaration of Trust, set forth on the reverse side hereof, and to cause such Plan to be registered under the provisions of the Income Tax Act (Canada) and amendments and regulations thereto, and Provincial Acts having jurisdiction, as determined by the Province in my address below. I understand that income tax may be payable on any benefit derived under this Plan, in accordance with the Income Tax Act or Acts mentioned above.

FOR COMPANY USE ONLY

Section	Trust No.		Account No.	Branch No.	Start Date D M Y	Withholding Tax Rate
4 4	R					

Prov., Country Code | Lock-in Code | Lock-in Date D M Y | | | Br. Code | Deposit

PLANHOLDER INFORMATION

NAME (One given name initials & surname)
25 1 R I C H A R D   A L B E R T   R O E

ADDRESS (include apt. no. city or town & province)
26 1 1 0 0   M A I N   A V E N U E
27 1 A N Y W H E R E   N O V A   S C O T I A
28 1
29 1

Postal Code	Business Phone No. Area Code	Social Insurance No.	Date of Birth D M Y
30 1 A 1 8 2 C 3	10 5 6 7 2 0 0 1 2 3 4	0 0 0 0 0 0 0 0 0	1 9 0 6 3 3

CONTRIBUTION

72

☐ I have enclosed a cheque for $ 5 5 0 0 0 0 * As my initial deposit (minimum initial deposit $100.00)

☐ My securities have a total market value of $ _____
Please supply detailed list of securities

* It is the member's responsibility to ensure deposit does not exceed the maximum amount permitted under the Income Tax Act (Canada)

Transfer   I am transferring $ _____

☐ TRANSFER UNDER 60(J)
☐ TRANSFER UNDER 60(L)   Tax free under the Income Tax Act (Canada) from my former plan.
☐ TRANSFER UNDER 146(16)   NAME OF FORMER PLAN _____

SPOUSAL CONTRIBUTION
If spousal contribution please print the letter X here ☐
Complete form GT 392

BENEFICIARY DESIGNATION — NOT APPLICABLE IN P.E.I. AND QUEBEC

Complete this Section if you wish to designate someone as Beneficiary under the Plan in the event of your death. NOTE: IN CERTAIN PROVINCES, A DESIGNATION OF BENEFICIARY CAN ONLY BE MADE BY INCLUDING A SPECIFIC CLAUSE IN YOUR WILL.

I HEREBY DESIGNATE MY _(WIFE)_ _SALLY ROE_
Relationship   Full name of beneficiary

OF _100 MAIN AVENUE, ANYWHERE, N.S._ as the person entitled to receive payment of the Plan in the event
Address
of my death, prior to maturity of this plan, reserving the right to revoke this designation.

Nov. 5, 1979   _John Doe_   _Richard A. Roe_
Date   Witness   Applicants Signature

AGREEMENT ACCEPTANCE

I acknowledge that I have read the Declaration of Trust set forth on the reverse side hereof which governs the "SPECIAL RETIREMENT SAVINGS PLAN" and I understand that my membership in the 'Plan' is subject to the provisions therein contained.

LANGUAGE PREFERENCE ☑ English ☐ French

Nov. 5, 1979   _Richard A. Roe_
Date   Applicants Signature

This Application is accepted by the Trustee on _____ 19 ____ as a Guaranty Trust SPECIAL Retirement Savings Plan in accordance with the Declaration of Trust.

Samuel Sams   _M A Hasley_
Authorized Signature   Authorized Signature

REGISTERED REPRESENTATIVE OF CANADIAN INVESTMENT DEALER, STOCKBROKER OR OTHER AGENT

GT 1053E (11/78)

Please make cheque payable to Guaranty Trust Company of Canada and forward BOTH copies of this Application to your nearest Branch as listed on the back of the brochure. One copy will be returned to you for your records.

Portability arrangements are included in some municipal, university and other pension plans as well.

Look before you leap. You may be protected if there's an industry-wide pension plan, such as exists in the Quebec construction industry. Under these circumstances, your pension plan stays intact when you move from one employer to another. But the national odds definitely run against the worker who switches jobs. Women frequently fall victim when they take time off to bear and raise children.

When a private plan is terminated and its assets distributed to the members, or when a member takes out a lump sum on changing jobs, different courses of action may be followed. The plan at the new company may permit an incoming member to "buy in," thus providing roughly the same protection given to existing members of the same age. The older worker might use the cash available to buy an annuity that will begin paying at 65 (or any selected age). Or the money could be invested in a Registered Retirement Savings Plan.

RESIDENCE REQUIREMENTS

You would like to move to California when you retire, but you worry about losing your pension if you leave Canada.

Both the Old Age Security (OAS) and payments from the contributory Canada (or Quebec) Pension Plan (CPP or QPP) are paid to qualified persons no matter where they reside.

The basic requirement in the case of OAS is that you must have resided in Canada for at least 20 years after age 18. If you don't qualify under this rule, you'll get the pension for the month of departure and for the next six months only.

The relatively new (1975) spouse's allowance, payable in some circumstances to a pensioner's spouse who is between 60 and 65, ceases after a six-month absence from Canada. There is no residence qualification for CPP payments.

The Guaranteed Income Supplement (GIS), paid on top of OAS to those with little or no other income, is available to a recipient outside Canada for six months only. It can be reinstated upon return to Canada.

All war veterans' pensions are paid to any address in the world.

If you currently receive—or expect to receive—any other social security payments or pensions, check on their residence requirements individually.

Change of "residence." Before you take the decision to move permanently to the American South—or to any other country—you'd be wise to investigate lots of things besides the climate, the crime rate and the cost of groceries.

In the United States, for example, you will be required to pay state and local taxes. You may well be leaving some assets in Canada and expecting to live partly off rents, interest or dividends. Many types of income from Canadian sources are subject to a withholding tax. Visit your District Taxation Office and ask for details.

If you spend winters in the South and summers in Canada, you can retain Canadian status as long as your northern sojourn exceeds six months—even by one day. Your American hosts will then consider you a visitor, even if you buy a home down there.

Because of your age, you should be particularly careful about looking into your Medicare coverage when you move. If you leave the country permanently, your coverage under your provincial health plan will cease after three or four months—and the place where you are going may offer no similar tax-supported protection. One serious illness could make a big hole in your retirement nest egg. Ask in advance about private plans you can join.

Any Canadian visitor to another country remains covered by his hospital insurance plan as long as the contributions are paid up. And remember that after age 65, no contributions are required. Needed hospital care and physicians' services will be paid for at the rate that applies in your home province. Keep in mind, however, that charges outside Canada can be considerably higher and you'll have to pay the extra yourself.

Many hospitals in Florida, and in some U.S. border states, will accept your Canadian hospital insurance card and send bills to the plan. Elsewhere, you will have to pay for services and apply for reimbursement at home yourself. All claims must be submitted within six months.

If you find yourself in financial difficulties because of a medical emergency outside Canada, ask the hospital involved to phone or write to your health plan office, quoting the number of your insurance card. Your card will be honored anywhere in Canada, although benefits may differ.

Visitors to Canada do not qualify under our Medicare plans unless (a) they hold an employment visa, and (b) they apply and are accepted for coverage.

SENIOR CITIZEN DISCOUNTS

Public transit in your provincial capital offers half-price fares to senior citizens. Your town's bus company refuses to follow suit.

There's no legal requirement for any company or organization to allow discounts based on age. Get the support of other pensioners in your town and make a forceful public presentation to the bus company. Unions, service clubs, church groups, Royal Canadian Legion branches and other service groups will support your crusade.

Ironically, you'll get a break if you travel outside your hometown, for Via Rail, Air Canada and CP Air offer discounts to passengers 65 or over.

Businesses in many communities offer reduced theater prices, free or cheaper entry to museums and tourist attractions, reduced taxi fares and special property tax allowances. Bell Canada offers directory assistance free of charge to its subscribers over 65, as well as to the handicapped.

All provinces give old-age pensioners prescription medicines free or at reduced prices. Legal Aid plans will probably be available to you without cost, including guidance in making your will. The same is true for credit and nutritional counseling.

The National Film Board of Canada offers free loans of hundreds of films on travel, the arts and sciences.

Some universities waive tuition charges for senior citizens. In Ontario, there's no age bar on student loans (or grants) for full-time study. Correspondence courses in just about every primary-, secondary- or university-level subject are available in every province, at little or no charge. Your local school board can supply exact information, or you can write to the provincial Department of Education.

Old-age pensioners automatically receive a numbered Old Age Security Identification Card. Most provinces also issue similar plastic cards. Carry this proof of age at all times in case the bus driver or ticket taker insists that you look too young to be "on the pension."

CAPITALIZING ON EXPERIENCE

You are a retired executive who would like to continue contributing to society.

Half a hundred worthy volunteer organizations are looking for you! Your executive skills didn't vanish on your 65th birthday and you've every reason to look forward to a long span of good health.

As a person with no pressing money worries, you might get a highly satisfying assignment from either Canadian Executive Service Overseas (CESO) or Canadian University Services Overseas (CUSO), two of Canada's most interesting volunteer organizations, which work to raise living standards in developing countries.

CESO is a nonprofit corporation run with federal government support by a group of Canadian business leaders. It accepts short-term (average, four months) requests from developing countries for expert consultation on everything from agriculture to transportation. No salaries are offered but plane tickets (for two) are supplied. The host country also provides accommodation, meals, expenses and medical services. Consultants are also supplied to native projects in Canada and some 200 persons were thus employed in 1979. For information write: CESO, Suite 350, 1130 Sherbrooke St. West, Montreal, Que., H3A 2M8.

CUSO operates under the wing of the Canadian International Development Agency and is financed by the federal Department of External Affairs. The organization seeks qualified people in the fields of agriculture, business, education, health and technology who are willing to take up two-year assignments abroad.

It's a businesslike arrangement. The volunteer goes on contract to the host country at its prevailing salary rate and lives there under local conditions. Age is no barrier: in 1979, one spry 84-year-old was happily on contract abroad. And there's demand for both white-collar and blue-collar experts: a retired welder was hired to teach African students. Write to CUSO at 151 Slater St., Ottawa, Ont., K1P 5H5.

The Federal Business Development Bank (FBDB), a Crown corporation, makes use of the business skills of retirees in its Counselling Assistance to Small Enterprises Service Program. The head office of the FBDB is located at 901 Victoria Square, Montreal, Que., H2Z 1R1, and there are regional and branch offices across the country.

The Canada Manpower office should not be overlooked by the retired person who still wants to work. Don't be put off by the published unemployment statistics. There are often suitable jobs available that youngsters won't take because there is no chance of advancement or the pay is less than princely.

New Horizons. Since 1972, the federal New Horizons program has offered grants to encourage over-65s to start up new community projects. The idea is to make use of skills and experience that might otherwise be left to wither and die. You need a group of at least 10 retirees who are willing to become directors of your approved project.

The grant runs for an initial 18 months and may be extended for a similar term. The money can't be used for salaries and any profits must be plowed back into the project. Seed money has founded such projects as an orchestra, a bus service for the aged and a "nearly new" shop. If you have an idea for a worthwhile project, write to the head office of New Horizons, Brooke Claxton Building, Tunney's Pasture, Ottawa, Ont., K1A 1B5.

A retirement home quiz

Sunset Hill may seem like heaven in the sales brochure, but will it suit *you*? Get answers to these practical questions:

Is the home close to doctors, dentists, libraries, and inexpensive restaurants? Where's the nearest bus stop or train station? Is there free parking for you and your friends?

Is it in a high crime area? How about night noise from the freeway or rail line? Is the home on an airport flight path?

Is the place specially designed for the elderly? Do all doors allow clearance for wheelchairs? Are there ramps instead of stairs?

Are kitchen and dining areas planned for the convenience of the handicapped? Can a person in a wheelchair reach the taps and stove controls? Where are the phones?

Is the bathroom equipped with safety rails and handgrips? Can a wheelchair be maneuvered under the washbasin? Are all light switches low?

Is the unit planned for easy cleaning? Can the windows all be cleaned from the inside? Are the floors safe for anyone using a cane?

Is the place equipped with alarm bells (to summon assistance in an emergency)? How about smoke detectors?

If your unit is small, is there a pleasant communal lounge where you can greet or entertain visitors?

DRIVER'S LICENSE

You're feeling fit as a fiddle at 80, but the motor vehicle bureau won't renew your license.

There's no law that says you can't drive your car at age 80, 90 or even 100. But all provinces require the aging driver to undergo retesting. The key birthday is usually the 75th.

Licenses are normally renewed for two or three years at a time. When the computer notes that your key birthday is coming up, you'll receive a request to present yourself for a driving test. You can be sure the examiner will be interested in your eyesight, hearing, reaction time and your general health record.

It is always a condition of any operator's license that the holder notify the authority of any previously unreported disability.

The fact that you need glasses or use a hearing aid won't prevent you from getting your license renewed. The license will be marked on the face with a code letter or number to indicate a disability.

EDUCATION TAX

Now that you're retired, you don't think it's fair that you must still pay education taxes.

There's no escape from this obligation. You'd best try to think of it as your contribution toward the education of Canada's future taxpayers.

Although a declining birthrate is shutting down schools all over the country, and our 81 degree-granting universities and colleges are beating the bushes for students, the cost of education is nevertheless zooming past $15 billion a year.

Education costs can claim as much as 75 percent of the total of local taxes. And this tax bite is only the tip of the iceberg. By national average, municipalities or local school boards collect less than 20 percent of the costs of elementary and secondary education. Provincial governments pick up most of the balance with money that they collect from you in other ways.

49 Death and burial

It isn't easy to anticipate death calmly or to plan objectively for the disposal of your body. It is harder still to cast yourself as the thoughtful consumer, making the last purchase of all. Yet the funeral business is one of the very few of which you are certain to be a customer. So, unless you really don't care how you go, it is wise to give some thought to your own rights, wishes and obligations in the matter—and to your means.

While living, you have the right to dispose of your body, just like any other "property," through your will. If you want an inconspicuous exit, and your family knows this, it won't feel any social pressure to do what others may consider "the right thing."

The average cost of a funeral today is $1,400, but for those with deep purses or a solemn sense of occasion, the sky's the limit.

In 1979, an Ottawa undertaker was offering his finest bronze coffin at $6,780. These days, with cosmetic effects, flower wreaths, hired limousines, choirs, professional pallbearers, ushers, memory books, photography, carved headstones, statuary and special catering, the total cost of a lavish funeral is anyone's guess.

It's unfair, though, to regard the nation's licensed funeral directors as ghouls luring the grieving family into extravagant and unnecessary expenditures. They perform an indispensable function and most perform it compassionately and well.

It seems reasonable to face the inevitable, rather than leave the necessary decisions to survivors who will be coping with one of life's most upsetting experiences.

You can make advance decisions, in consultation with your family, on such practical questions as burial or cremation, choice of coffin or urn, the desired range of funeral-home services (or none at all). Discussions with a clergyman or other counselor, and your lawyer, will be helpful.

You're making an expensive purchase, so examine the undertaker's wares and services carefully. Compare prices, the personalities of the funeral directors and their staffs and the "atmosphere" of their premises; these factors will be important for your family during those two or three trying days.

While the law won't bind your survivors to follow your plans to the letter, you'll have the satisfaction of knowing you've done your best to ease their burden. You can even pay for it in advance.

If the traditional funeral seems distasteful or wasteful to you, consider joining a memorial society. There are societies in all provinces. Their purpose is to help members preplan low-cost burials or cremations.

If you'd like to be buried under your favorite oak tree, you will require special permission. Permits for burials on private property are rarely granted nowadays.

THE FINAL REQUEST

You want your body to be buried with minimum ceremony at the lowest cost.

You have the right to demand that you be given a no-frills burial, but the final decision will lie with your executor or your family or with the state, in the event that there are no friends or relatives (or they can't afford to bury you). A dead person owns nothing—not even his body.

You have the right, of course, through your will, to dispose of your property after death. The law will generally insist that your wishes be carried out, unless your will is successfully contested. (*See* Chapter 33, "Wills and gifts.") But it's doubtful if any judge would order next of kin to follow your precise instructions about things such as the type of coffin or flowers, or a eulogy. Funeral ceremonies are really for the living, not the dead. Most families, of course, follow the wishes of the deceased. And *you* can do a lot to shape things the way you want. Visit your undertaker and choose a coffin. This can run from about $100 for a cloth-covered plywood model to $900 and up for hardwood. Metal coffins start at about $1,500 and run to $6,000 and more for bronze.

Cutting out the frills. Outer receptacles to protect coffins underground are expensive and unnecessary, unless there's a prospect of reburial elsewhere at a later date. They range in price from $80 for pine to $450 for steel.

In British Columbia and Manitoba, fiberboard coffins costing about $5 are widely accepted. The city of Edmonton permits burial in a cloth shroud. You can arrange to dispense with the funeral home's limousine service, if you wish, and shorten the visiting period at the chapel from, say, two days to one—or even dispense with the "viewing" entirely. Then there's "direct disposal": the body is taken straight from home or hospital to the cemetery or crematorium.

When you purchase a burial plot, it's basically no different from buying any other piece of land. Prices vary from place to place, single plots generally starting around $125 in cases where the funeral is at public expense. You will pay from $600 to $1,200 for interment in a privately operated (commercial) cemetery, including the cost of the plot, opening and closing of the grave, maintenance, and vault or grave liner; about $1,600 for a crypt in a mausoleum. Burial in municipal and church cemeteries is cheaper, but the latter is probably restricted to members of the church or faith. Cremation is cheaper, but the pomp and ceremony can be just as elaborate.

A DECENT BURIAL

You want to give your husband a decent burial but you haven't any money.

What most Canadians think of as a "decent burial" is a basic, traditional funeral—not elaborate and ostentatious, but not "cheap"

either. Even though attitudes have been slowly changing, the minimum remains a funeral procession, service at the graveside and a simple grave marker.

The state—that is, the taxpayer—will foot the bill if you can't. But in most cases where there is need, private or public pension plans, government programs, life insurance policies, or organizations with which the deceased was associated, pay for burial.

Canadians are the world's biggest buyers of life insurance. Payment on a policy normally follows probating of the will. (*See* Chapter 33, "Wills and gifts.") But the insuring company will usually allow an advance for funeral expenses. It will require a "proof of death" document, generally provided by the funeral director, based on the death certificate issued by the attending doctor. Most funeral homes will provide the "proof of death" free of charge; others impose a small fee (about $2).

The Canada and Quebec Pension Plans provide lump-sum death benefits if your husband had been a contributor—and since 1965 all working Canadians *are* contributors. (*See* Chapter 48, "Retirement.") The person responsible for administration of the estate (the executor) should ensure that application is made. Forms are available at the nearest pension office, listed in the telephone book under "Government of Canada (or Quebec)."

If your husband had been paying in for 10 years, the maximum current benefit is $1,040; five years' payments would mean a benefit to you of $520. The minimum qualifying period is three years. The pension office will calculate the amount.

Most municipalities provide funeral benefits for welfare recipients. This is usually a fixed amount and the family may not add to it. The municipality negotiates costs with local funeral directors.

The Workmen's Compensation Board in each province makes a grant toward the cost of a funeral if the death was related to a work injury. The size of the grant will vary, depending on regional costs, but it's likely to be about $500 to $600.

The warrior's end. Did your husband serve in any of Canada's wars? In some cases the Department of Veterans' Affairs (DVA) will pay in whole or in part the funeral expenses of any war veteran who dies while receiving treatment, or who is the recipient of a veteran's allowance. (*See* Chapter 45, "When in need.") Subject to a means test, the DVA can also provide the funeral allowance in cases where the deceased would have qualified for veterans' allowance had one spouse not been receiving the old-age security pension. There may be other financial help available from the Canadian Pension Commission. Any pension or balance of pension due a deceased disability pensioner may be applied toward the expenses of burial. If there's not enough money in the estate to pay the final expenses, the commission may grant an award to cover all or part of them. Applications for grants can be made at the nearest DVA or Pension Commission office, or to the Ottawa head office of either.

The private *Last Post Fund* will, under certain circumstances, pay a fixed amount for funeral expenses and a grave marker. This benefit comes into the picture when the veteran dies indigent or friendless, whether in Canada or abroad. Local representatives of the fund can be found in most urban centers; they are easily reached through veterans' organizations, undertakers and DVA officers. The secretary-general's address is 685 Cathcart St., Montreal, H3B 1M7.

EMBALMING

The undertaker claims that embalming is the accepted thing but you don't see why the procedure is necessary.

Embalming is not required by law except when a body is to be transported across provincial boundaries for burial, or is being carried by public transport, such as airlines and trains, in other than a hermetically sealed container.

The average charge for embalming is about $100 and many undertakers automatically embalm unless told not to. Most funeral homes will not keep a body on their premises for more than 24 or 30 hours without embalm-

ing. They say they don't want an "untreated" body exposed to their staff or the public, because of the problems associated with decomposition.

If you reject embalming, the undertaker will require that the funeral be held within 30 hours of the time of death. You may find this does not allow time for the customary notification of relatives and friends, or for traditional funeral arrangements.

Members of the Jewish and Moslem faiths generally bury their dead within 24 hours, without embalming.

Modern embalming merely postpones the start of natural decomposition, primarily to make the body more acceptable for viewing before burial or cremation. It does not permanently preserve the body.

Dermasurgery, or post-mortem plastic surgery, is sometimes used when a corpse has been disfigured by disease or accident, although in most of these cases the coffin is not opened for viewing. Cosmetics are employed to create an impression of serenity in death; this is undoubtedly consoling to the mourners.

FOREIGN WAR GRAVES

Your father was killed in action and buried overseas during World War II. You want to bring his remains home.

If you are willing to go through formidable paper work and expense, you can probably have your wish.

There are 82,000 Canadians buried in military cemeteries overseas. The Commonwealth War Graves Commission says there have been only two disinterments for reburial at home. The practice is not popular in Canada, although widespread in the United States.

First, you must obtain permission from the Ottawa office of the War Graves Commission, which is responsible for the marking and maintenance of the graves of Commonwealth troops who lost their lives on foreign soil.

Next, you have to get the approval of the authorities in the country of burial and follow its directions regarding disinterment. You'll almost certainly have to hire a funeral director in that country.

A sealed container of prescribed construction is required for the shipment of bodies to Canada, and special customs procedures must be followed. Before reburial, the regulations in your home province must be satisfied. A funeral director will probably be required to handle the details.

FINAL RESTING PLACE

You bought a burial plot in the local cemetery years ago and now you've decided to move away.

Your cemetery plot is like any other piece of real estate: if you have clear title to that little piece of land, you can sell it. The exception would be where the original sales agreement specified that you could sell only to the cemetery company or administrators, not on the open market.

Your plot could be worth considerably more today than the price you paid. Many urban cemeteries are sold out and you should have no trouble finding a buyer. Some cemeteries allow two burials in the same grave.

Prepaid funeral and burial costs must be refunded. Funeral directors are required by law to place such funds in trust accounts and return them with agreed interest, on request.

Don't be too hasty in giving up your old hometown plot if you decide to retire to some distant location. Nostalgia usually increases with age and you may come to derive comfort from the idea of a final resting place amid the scenes of your active life.

Even if you object on principle to the idea of elaborate burial rites, you shouldn't attempt to deny them to others who think differently. When your time comes, you will be under no obligation to make use of the family plot. If you prefer, you can instruct that your body be cremated and the ashes scattered—even from the top of the Yukon's Mount Logan if you know any climber willing to lug your remains 5,951 metres to our highest peak.

Death on the Nile

About 1200 B.C., a boy named Nakht died a painful death in his village near Deir el-Medina in Egypt. His poor parents didn't know what illness carried him off, but they spent what probably amounted to a tenth of their annual income on his funeral.

Thirty-two hundred years later, a team of doctors at Toronto's St. Margaret Hospital began an autopsy which showed that Nakht died of schistosomiasis, a parasitic disease carried by snails in stagnant waters. Nakht probably picked up the tiny parasite while wading or bathing. The disease has never been totally eradicated. It still occurs but it can be cured nowadays.

In 1904, Toronto archaeologist Charles Trick Currelly discovered Nakht's body lying undisturbed in the carefully decorated mummy case his loving parents had scrimped to provide for him. But, Nakht hadn't been mummified—his parents couldn't afford that. The body, wound in cloth and wearing a long blue-striped wig, had simply been placed in the mummy case and the hot, dry air of Thebes had preserved it.

Examination of the lungs showed mild pulmonary anthracosis, caused by smoke from heating and cooking; a tapeworm infestation probably contributed to malnutrition; the fatal illness led to damage of the liver and finally rupture of the spleen and death.

The autopsy, begun in 1974, was completed in 1976.

Modern embalming is not like that practiced by the ancient Egyptians. Their methods of embalming to preserve the body would change the color and appearance of the corpse so that it would not be suitable for viewing.

EXPROPRIATION

You object when the city hall announces it's cutting a street through the churchyard in which your ancestors are buried.

Progress can often seem insensitive, but the simple fact is that, in large urban areas, hundreds of old cemeteries have been obliterated after Canada's population more than doubled in the three decades following World War II.

When burial grounds are expropriated, authorities must take scrupulous pains to reinter remains at a properly hallowed location. When the St. Lawrence Seaway was built, cemeteries were moved to new, landscaped sites, which, aesthetically, were generally regarded as great improvements over the old.

Ye olde churchyard. Pioneer graveyards were patches of cleared bush near small settlements. The rough wooden markers were obscured by time and fell to the plow when new immigrant waves arrived.

When permanent churches were established, part of the adjacent clergy reserve lands became cemeteries for use by the parish flock. Sometimes, when sons and daughters of the pioneers moved on to break new land, the old cemeteries fell into disrepair, or were simply abandoned to weeds and second-growth timber.

Today old churchyards are regarded as historic sites. Their tombstones tell the story of earlier and more spacious days. Burial in the parish churchyard is still common, except in densely populated areas where there is no room for expansion.

CREMATION

You and your wife agreed years ago to be cremated, but when she dies some of the family object to carrying out her wishes in this regard.

The application for cremation usually includes the question of whether "any relative of the deceased, or any other person" objects.

A strong objection could lead crematorium officials to refuse to approve the application. Under the Cemeteries Act of Ontario, for example, a crematorium can refuse to cremate "without assigning reasons." In Quebec, the wishes of the deceased's spouse overrule objections by other family members.

In any event, the law demands a 48-hour waiting period after death before any body can be cremated. There must also be an authorization from the coroner or medical examiner. Crematoriums are controlled by provincial law and regulations may vary from province to province. A local funeral director or the coroner's office will advise you.

Pros and cons. Cremation was practiced by the ancient Greeks, but fell into disuse with the spread of Christianity. However, it has again become common. In Quebec and British Columbia about 30 percent of all funerals involve cremation.

A cremated body ends as a couple of kilograms of ashes, and private disposal is generally permitted. Proponents argue that cremation saves money as well as useful land since a burial plot isn't needed. Basic cremation fees range from $90 to $150.

MEMORIAL SOCIETIES

You would like to set up a memorial society to handle burials but local funeral directors refuse to cooperate.

Some funeral directors criticize memorial societies as consumer groups which concern themselves solely with the cost of funerals and ignore the value of the traditional funeral ceremony in coping with grief. But, while most funeral directors prefer to deal with the bereaved family directly, they will supply services under the direction of a memorial society and within its costs scale. In fact, most memorial societies do not conduct funerals or burials at all, but act as a third-party adviser or agent. The funeral director will almost always be involved.

He cooperates by accepting the memorial society document which states what the member family wants in the way of funeral arrangements. When death occurs, the funeral director registers the death and issues the "proof of death" needed to release advance insurance payment and other death benefits.

There are at least 22 memorial societies across Canada. Membership costs about $12. These associated societies are grouped within the nonprofit Memorial Society Association of Canada (MSAC), P.O. Box 96, Station A, Weston, Ont., M9N 3M6. This association will provide information brochures to any group seeking to establish a society.

The basic purpose is to provide practical, up-to-date information and recommendations on economical burials and cremations so that thoughtful preplanning can be done in unemotional circumstances.

The individual society arranges "package deals" with selected local undertakers who keep a copy of the member's instructions on file. This makes it unnecessary, when death occurs, for next of kin to make any decisions about the many details that arise during the time of grief. Total cost averages out at about half that of the traditional funeral.

Should death occur away from home—say, in the United States—one of the many societies associated with the MSAC will supply services on the agreed basis.

SUICIDE

There was a suicide in the family and you fear your parish priest will refuse permission for burial in consecrated ground.

This would be most unusual in Canada today. It's true that at one time a Roman Catholic who committed suicide would have been buried outside the consecrated section of the graveyard. But nowadays the church holds that the person who took his own life was disturbed and no longer acting responsibly.

Suicides are buried or cremated today with no distinction, although the religious service and prayers may vary to some degree. A frank discussion will help your clergyman avoid any anguish or misunderstanding.

STYLE VERSUS ECONOMICS

Your father left detailed instructions and money for an elaborate funeral and a marble memorial statue. It will be very expensive and your mother needs the money for living expenses.

When you die your body becomes part of your estate, to be administered by your appointed executor, or by the Public Trustee (in Quebec, the Public Curator). If it should be apparent that your father's estate could be better allocated to provide for his widow or other dependents (or heirs, under his will), the executor is legally justified in not carrying out certain of the instructions. For example, he can authorize a less expensive funeral and a more modest headstone.

However, when the deceased has willed his body, or parts thereof, to medical science, the executor is bound to see that this wish is carried out. It should be added, though, that even when a gift of human tissue has been properly documented, the recipient organizations are unlikely to invoke the law to get their "pound of flesh."

The provincial Public Trustee assumes responsibility for the affairs of the deceased, under certain conditions. The most common situation occurs when a person dies intestate (that is, without having made a will) and when there are no known relatives. (*See* Chapter 33, "Wills and gifts.") The Public Trustee will also act if neither the executor nor the beneficiaries can or will take action.

Dying in style. Postwar generations have a less reverent attitude to the final rite—the "obsequies." Conflict can occur within families when the elders announce their intention of investing in burial space in one of the fashionable perpetual-care cemeteries. Large monuments are rare today; "lawn" cemeteries forbid them. But it's still possible to lavish a lot of money in "honoring" the dead. If your parents can afford it, it gives them peace of mind and the perpetual-care provisions of the contract will relieve the survivors of responsibility for caring for the gravesite.

DEATH AWAY FROM HOME

Your husband died from injuries in a car accident while on a business trip. You have not yet received a death certificate.

A death certificate must be issued by a doctor—either the attending physician or the coroner. It may seem to be just a formality, but it is a very important piece of paper. It attests legally to the death and gives the cause, time, date and place.

The death certificate allows the death to be registered and the "proof of death" document to be issued, which permits subsequent action, including settling of the estate.

A death from accident, with no unusual or suspicious circumstances, or from natural causes (illness or old age), will be routinely

---

When there's a death in the family

In many ways, leaving this life causes more complications than entering it. There's the question of the legal disposition of your worldly goods and the tasks you leave behind for your next of kin or executor.

Probate. It's a legal word meaning "proof." Your executor must prove in Probate (or Surrogate) Court that he has your last will and testament before proceeding to administer your estate. Notarial wills do not have to be probated in Quebec. Other wills are probated before the Superior Court.

Administration. If you haven't left a will, your spouse has the prior right to apply to the court for permission to handle your affairs and seek "letters of administration." These steps are not required in Quebec. Should no one apply, the public trustee or a local trust company will probably be appointed. Usually, after debts and taxes are paid, the spouse and children get the balance. When an estate is small (say, under $1,000), permission may be granted for administration and disposition without formal application and approval.

Funeral. The executor is responsible for funeral arrangements. Otherwise, next of kin assume the task. Funeral costs have precedence over all other debts.

Bank accounts. The survivor can withdraw money from a joint account. In Quebec, withdrawals are limited to $1,500 by specific persons. Funds in your personal accounts will remain there until probate or letters of administration have been granted. The bank manager will want a copy of the relevant document before releasing the money to the executor or administrator.

If the bank manager knows the family well he'll probably release a reasonable amount of the frozen funds to the surviving spouse. He would ask for a form of indemnity covering the bank in the event that something went amiss in the settlement of the estate.

Safety-deposit box. If the box is held jointly, the survivor is entitled to the contents; otherwise, "certificates of dispersal" must be obtained before the contents are released. If you were the sole holder, the bank must have evidence of the granting of probate of the will or the issuance of letters of administration.

The bank is authorized to open the box in the presence of the executor, for the purpose of listing the contents. It can immediately release the will of the deceased (presuming it was stored there) and any birth certificate, marriage license, title deed, lease, mortgage, sales contract, or document dealing with the funeral or burial.

Life insurance. When the surviving spouse (or anyone else, really) is named as beneficiary in your policy, the insured sum will be paid to that person upon completion of the insurer's "proof of claim" forms. Documents required include a copy of the death certificate and the "proof of death" form routinely issued by the funeral director.

certified by the attending doctor. The law requires the coroner (or medical examiner) to decide the cause of death if there is the possibility of foul play (murder, manslaughter or suicide). An autopsy may be ordered, and an inquest held at which evidence will be presented in an effort to determine cause of death.

If the police were able to reach you quickly after the fatal accident, you will be asked to make funeral or transport arrangements. The body will probably be in the morgue. Get in touch with a local funeral home (or your memorial society) and explain the circumstances. Your funeral director will notify a counterpart in the area where the accident happened and coordinate the arrangements. He has seen it all before. By the way, there is no legal requirement for you to bring the body home; it can be buried or cremated where the accident occurred.

ORGAN DONATIONS

Your son was killed in a motorcycle accident. You would like to cancel his agreement to donate his eyes for transplant.

The relevant provincial laws do not allow your son's agreement (provided he was 18 or older at signing) to be canceled, except by himself. No agency, however, is likely to enforce the contract against vociferous objections. Many still have qualms at what they perceive as interference or violation of the body, but all provincial legislatures have been convinced that the individual's right to donate all or part of his body to medical science should have official sanction. In fact, it would be difficult to think of a more meaningful and thoughtful bequest than, say, the gift of sight. The Canadian National Institute for the Blind maintains an Eye Bank to receive gifts of eye tissues either for transplanting or research.

The CNIB head office is at 1929 Bayview Ave., Toronto, M4G 3E8. Divisional headquarters are located in the provincial capitals.

Provincial legislation usually grants the next of kin the right to donate the body of a deceased—or parts of it—unless this runs counter to the expressed wishes of the deceased.

A gift to science. There is a continuing need for donations of human organs. The entire body may be accepted for research or teaching purposes by your nearest medical school; Canada has 15 of them, attached to universities in all provinces. (Medical education in the Maritime provinces is centralized at Dalhousie University in Halifax.)

Many thousands of successful kidney transplant operations have been performed since the 1950s. More lives could be saved if organ donations were increased. The Kidney Foundation of Canada, 5780 Decelles Ave., Montreal, H3S 2C7, will provide information and donor cards. There are regional offices across the country.

Research is proceeding with transportation and other problems that, when solved, could heighten the success rate of transplant operations involving the liver, pancreas, heart and bones.

Holders of driver's licenses in Quebec, Ontario, Manitoba, Saskatchewan and British Columbia can agree to donate organs at death by filling out a section of the license. Anyone who changes his mind can simply destroy this section. Organs for transplant must be removed within an hour of death; removal costs nothing and does not hold up or change funeral arrangements in any way.

If a donated body is accepted by a medical school, the funeral home will arrange for transportation and the family is not involved any further. A suitable burial will follow later in a cemetery which has set aside a special area.

10 | EFFECTIVE COMPLAINING